made

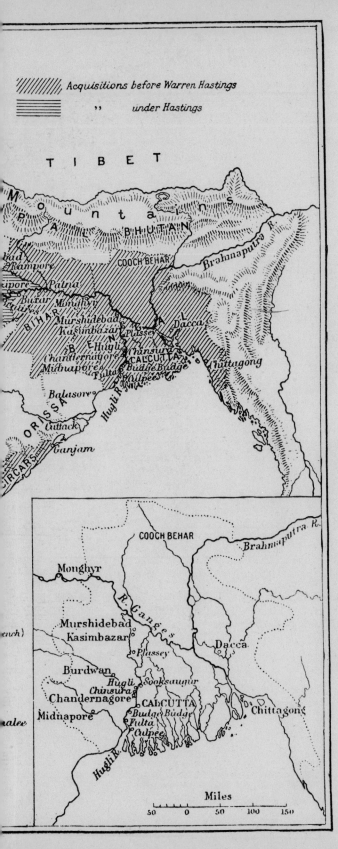

Acquisitions before Warren Hastings

,, under Hastings

TIBET

Mountains

BHUTAN

Brahmaputra R.

COOCH BEHAR

Rampore

Patna

Bihar

Monghyr

Bihar

Murshidebad

Kasimbazar

Plassey

Dacca

Hugli

Chinsura

Chandernagore

CALCUTTA

Midnapore

Fulta

Budge Budge

Culpee

Chittagong

Balasore

Hugli R.

ORISSA

Cuttack

CIRCARS

Ganjam

COOCH BEHAR

Brahmaputra R.

Monghyr

R. Ganges

Murshidebad

Kasimbazar

Plassey

Dacca

Burdwan

Hugli

Chinsura

sooksaugur

Chandernagore

CALCUTTA

Midnapore

Budge Budge

Fulta

Culpee

Chittagong

Hugli R.

Miles

50   0   50   100   150

Strange Destiny
A BIOGRAPHY OF
WARREN HASTINGS

WARREN HASTINGS, 1796
(From an original portrait by Lemuel Abbott; reproduced by kind permission
of Captain D. M. Anderson)

Strange Destiny

J. F. McCarthy

A BIOGRAPHY OF
WARREN HASTINGS

Oconomowoc

∧∧∧

Wisconsin

BY A. MERVYN DAVIES

*"That tower of strength
Which stood four-square to all the winds that blew"*

G · P · PUTNAM'S SONS
NEW YORK

Copyright 1935 by A. Mervyn Davies

MANUFACTURED
IN THE UNITED STATES OF AMERICA
AT THE VAN REES PRESS

TO MONICA,
MY WIFE,
With Infinite Gratitude

PREFACE

I NEED offer no apology for presenting a biography of Warren Hastings. Much new material has been unearthed since the last "life" appeared in 1894; various phases of his career have been subjected during recent years to detailed special study which has thrown important fresh light on many obscure points; mistakes of earlier biographers have received correction; and for that reason it is possible to hope that a new detailed study of the man and his achievements will not be unwelcome.

I lay no claim to overturning hitherto accepted views, though here and there I have tried to modify some, commonly held, which seemed to me in need of correction. Nor do I make any pretense of having produced a work of original research, with important discoveries of fact. The essential facts about Warren Hastings have long been known, but —and herein lies the origin of this book—a certain deficiency has always seemed to me to mark the manner in which those facts have been presented. For the space of fifteen years the subject has held me under a spell of extraordinary fascination, producing in me a kind of inner compulsion to embark upon a new biography that would attempt, despite all that had been written about Hastings, to do him more complete justice than had yet been done. An excessive amount of attention has always been paid to certain of his actions—those which caused his impeachment—and this has resulted in a distorted view of his career as a whole by throwing it out of focus. One of the things I have attempted to do is to place him in a better perspective and to present a well rounded view of his life in its entirety. There is an epic grandeur about his life that demands a certain spaciousness of treatment, and for that reason I have purposely not confined myself within any narrow limits. One has to remain with Warren Hastings for some time in order to appreciate properly the rare genius and spirit of the man.

How gigantic was the task I set myself, the reader will speedily discover for himself. Suffice it to say, that for twenty-five years Warren Hastings was the central figure in a stupendous drama, when the destinies of the great subcontinent of India were being decided—a drama that had not unity of time, place or action, that spanned two continents and the intervening sea, involved two rival European nations and innumerable Indian races and rulers, embraced a labyrinth of plots and sub-plots, and employed a multitude of actors. Doubtless any author who undertakes to tell such a story is rash, but if I have had the temerity to do so, I can only express the hope that I have succeeded in moving the story a little nearer to the place that it ought to occupy in the historical memory of the English speaking peoples and of our Indian friends. In conclusion, I think I do well to warn my readers that present day controversies have in no way been my concern. I have sought only for the facts and not to provide material for the disputants on either side of the Indian constitutional question.

I am indebted to a number of kind friends. For the inspiration of this book I owe all to the late Sir George W. Forrest who, when I was an undergraduate at Oxford, first aroused my interest in this subject on which he was himself so great an authority. It was a very great privilege for me to have had him as a friend, mentor and tutor; his kindness was inexhaustible and I take this opportunity to pay an affectionate and grateful tribute to his memory. I wish to thank two good friends, Mr. Alan Dudley and Mr. R. J. Cruikshank, for reading the book in manuscript; Mr. Alan Green for his painstaking criticisms and helpful suggestions; and Sir Arthur Knapp for having given me invaluable assistance with the illustrations as well as for his special contribution printed in the Appendix. For the translation of the testimonial appended to Chapter XXVIII I am indebted to Mr. C. A. Storey, librarian at the India Office, where the originals lie. I am also under grateful obligation to the Librarians of the British Museum, the Guild Hall, and the British Library in New York, and to Mr. Ottewill of the India Office. Finally, I welcome this opportunity to acknowledge the debt I owe my father—a debt that has now mounted so high as to render any kind of a statement of it impossible.

A. MERVYN DAVIES

Silvermine, Norwalk, Connecticut,
January, 1935.

CONTENTS

ILLUSTRATIONS

The numbers placed within square brackets in the text refer to the authorities cited. To avoid defacing the narrative page with footnotes that have little interest for the ordinary reader, these authorities are grouped together at the end of the volume.

Strange Destiny
A BIOGRAPHY OF
WARREN HASTINGS

"All these circumstances are not, I confess, very favorable to the idea of our attempting to govern India at all. But there we are: there we are placed by the Sovereign Dispenser, and we must do the best we can in our situation. The situation of man is the preceptor of his duty."

EDMUND BURKE

THE thirteenth day of February of the year 1788 was a memorable day in the lives of those people of England who had the advantage of living in London or whose good fortune had taken them to the capital on that date. For on that day they were treated by a kind Parliament to one of those dramatic spectacles that so delight the heart of a great metropolis ever eager for some new sensation. It cannot be said that life for the Londoner had been at all dull in the preceding twenty-eight years of King George the Third's reign. He had enjoyed to the full all the entertainment provided by the irrepressible John Wilkes, the city's darling. If he belonged to the law-abiding element of the population he had not enjoyed so much the wild and unchecked confusion of the Lord George Gordon Papist riots when the infuriated mob had the city at its mercy for seven whole days. But since Mr. Pitt had laid his firm hand on the helm of government the Londoner had had to content himself with such quieter excitements as the successful fight of Charles James Fox to force his way back into Parliament as member for the Westminster constituency, despite the decree of exclusion that Mr. Pitt had sent forth against him.

This February morning provided something new, something entirely unique in the experience of Englishmen of that day and generation. Not for seventy-one years had the awful majesty of the Law in the supreme exercise of its power been invoked to bring to justice a man charged with heinous crimes and misdemeanors. Nothing less than the dire process of impeachment had been considered proper and adequate by the Commons of England that Justice should be served. The setting appointed was the historic Hall of Westminster and the judges to try the case were the whole body of the Peers of the Realm, lords spiritual as well as lords temporal.

The occasion was one that took the mind of every historically minded Englishman back into the pages of history, calling to remembrance that to this same Hall were brought by the same sovereign Commons of England no less persons than the great Earl of Strafford and King Charles I. That each had lost his head as a result of the judgement there passed upon him must have added not a little to the interest and piquancy of this occasion.

But whereas the crimes of which Strafford and Charles were accused had been the intimate concern of Englishmen of every rank and class, and matters of common knowledge, those charged against the man now to be tried were to the last degree bizarre and foreign. Their scene had been laid, not in England, but in a distant and mysterious continent, and the victims had been a people of different race, color and religion. They were known by such outlandish titles as Zemindar, Rajah, Begum, Vizier, Mogul, Nawab, and they were connected with such incomprehensible things as lakhs of rupees and ryots. Yet it soon became clear that these were superficial differences, for when the real nature of the charges was exposed to the common view and stated in simple terms they were of an order that excited public curiosity to no less a degree. They involved the ruin of provinces, the despoiling of princesses, the overthrow of sovereign princes, the acceptance of bribes, and the committal of deeds of injustice, cruelty, extortion and oppression almost too horrible to describe. India might be a remote country, but none the less its woes and distresses were become the burning topic of the day in Parliament, in clubs and coffee-houses, at the Court and the drawing-rooms of great ladies, even no doubt along the busy streets of the great city. It was novel. It was unique. It was an amazing phenomenon.

So it was for a new and sensational spectacle that all London congregated on this February day—for something much more interesting and important than the ordinary show in which the Londoner takes delight, such as a Lord Mayor's procession or a state opening of Parliament. Nor were the usual appurtenances of pageantry lacking. Uniforms, robes, scarlet-clad troops on parade, tossing plumes and manes, the glitter and flash of steel accouterments, color, dignity, pomp, crowds, cheers. The scene was indeed worthy of the extraordinary occasion, as the Peers of the Realm in their robes of crimson and ermine marched in stately procession to Westminster Hall. Demos had to be content with this, but inside the Hall a still more magnificent scene was laid before the gaze of privileged Society. Every inch of the great edifice was occupied by the *élite* of a proud and powerful nation. Tremendous had been the competition for places. Ladies and gentlemen rose at six in the morning so as to be outside the hall by nine, where they waited shivering in the cold till eleven. Tickets for admission had sold at a great premium. The Queen and her ladies-in-waiting were there in one box; the Prince of Wales and other princes of the blood royal in another. Up in the gallery were ambassadors, peeresses, leaders of every profession and art, Mrs. Siddons the actress, Gibbon the historian, Reynolds the painter. On the Woolsack sat the Lord Chancellor to preside over the proceedings. Before him His Majesty's Judges and on each side the Peers, spiritual and temporal. Before very long at the other end filed in the Commons, the accusers to face the judges. In the forefront of their ranks were the greatest orators of that or any other age, Edmund Burke, Charles James Fox, Richard Brinsley Sheridan, each prepared to deliver, as soon as his moment arrived, the supreme oratorical display of his career to an audience that would come in happy anticipation of hearing nothing less. Was there ever a more perfect setting for a great act of justice? Was there one element lacking to ensure the complete success of the forthcoming proceedings? Their stupendous novelty, a nation's curiosity at fever-pitch, accusations that gripped the imagination and stirred the emotions, appetites that had for years been whetted by stories of dark and terrible deeds wrought by Englishmen in India. Every ingredient of great drama was present. For there in the midst of the mighty throng was the accused, a small but dignified figure, clad in a simple and sober suit, the lonely object of all this pomp and circumstance, the Governor-General of India, Warren Hastings.

Chapter I

EARLY YEARS

THE name of Hastings is an old and honored name in English history. Tradition has it that it is derived from a Danish sea-king who was defeated by Alfred the Great. But recorded history points to the Norman Conquest as the more probable date of origin. Down the centuries from that time onward men of the name of Hastings played a prominent part in the history of England. Two great branches of the family soon sprang into prominence, to one of which belonged the warlike Earls of Pembroke of the fourteenth century, who fought with the Black Prince in Spain; the other claimed the Lord Hastings who was chamberlain to Edward IV and lost his head in Richard III's reign, and whose descendants became Earls of Huntingdon in Tudor times. During the turbulence of the Middle Ages the direct Pembroke line became extinct; it is said that for five successive generations the father never laid eyes on his son and heir. But there was an old and humbler branch of the Pembroke family that maintained its continuity through the centuries. As early as the reign of Henry II in the twelfth century we find a certain Myles de Hastings in possession of the manor of Daylesford in the County of Worcestershire, and we recognize in him the ancestor of Warren Hastings.

At the beginning of the seventeenth century the Hastings of Daylesford held large estates in Worcestershire and Oxfordshire and were living in considerable affluence. Then came the Civil War which proved to be the graveyard of so many ancient families and fortunes. John Hastings, the lord of the manor, was a gallant gentleman and a die-hard loyalist. He not only fought for the King: he beggared himself for the King. To maintain the royalist cause he sold his Oxfordshire property, mortgaged his Worcestershire property, and melted down his plate; but all to no avail. When the cause was lost he had to ransom himself to the victors by giving up most of what little remained of his possessions to Mr. Lenthall, the Speaker of the House of Commons. Nor did the restoration of the monarchy result in the restoration of the fortunes of the Hastings family. The Lordship of Daylesford remained, but all wealth and power were gone. And it was not long before Daylesford itself, the family seat for centuries, had to go too. The manor house decayed, fell into disrepair, and it seemed that the glory of the line of Hastings had departed forever.

Three generations of Hastings with the Christian name of Penniston (or Penyston) formed Warren Hastings's immediate ancestry. This name was introduced into the family through intermarriage with the Pennistons of the neighboring manor of Cornwell in Oxfordshire. Warren's grandfather, the Rev. Penniston Hastings, was born in 1678. After four years at Balliol College, Oxford, he graduated in 1699 and, after his ordination, two years later, he was presented to the living of Daylesford by his father, Penniston the first, the lord of the manor. Practically nothing is known about the personality of the Rector of Daylesford except that he was keenly interested in antiquarian and genealogical research, being bold enough to put forward a claim that his family was descended from Hastings the Danish sea-king.

Warren's father, Penniston the third, was the Rector's eldest son. When he was ten years old, that is to say in the year 1715, the sad event occurred which separated the family from the old ancestral home. The squire was compelled to sell the estate to a Mr. Jacob Knight, a Bristol merchant, who promptly pulled the ancient house down and built a new one in its place. The Rector retained his benefice, and some time later took up his abode at Churchill, Oxfordshire, a neighboring village.

When Penniston, Junior, was nineteen, he went up to Balliol as his father had done before him, but he did not take a degree. And in 1730 at the age of twenty-five, shortly after being ordained, he married, his wife being Hester Warren of Twyning in the county of Gloucester. Four months later he obtained the benefice of Bledington, a little parish immediately adjoining Churchill and two miles from Daylesford, [1] but he seems to have continued to live with his father, the Rector, at Churchill, because it was there that both his children were born and that his wife died. The first child was a girl, Anne; the second was Warren; and the mother died a few days after Warren was born.

Seven months after his wife's death the young widower remarried, and shortly afterwards he deserted his family and went off to Barbados, leaving the two orphans to the care of their grandfather. Little more is known about Warren Hastings's father. Within two years of leaving England he became Rector of Christ Church, Barbados, took unto himself a third wife, Jemima Mascoll, on Christmas Day, 1737, and died six years later. [2]

Thus it was that Warren Hastings grew up without knowing either his father or his mother and, what is also important, with scarcely a penny to his name. And this in an age when family, wealth and established position meant so much in a young man's career.

Such an origin, while humble enough at first sight for a man destined for so much greatness, was obviously not lacking in potentiality. For the soil from which Warren Hastings sprang was the good clean loam of rural England that has produced many a fine crop of noble men and women. As he was the last of his line, it might almost seem as though in producing him nature had intended that the name of Hastings—the Hastings of Daylesford—after an existence of centuries, should at last be crowned with special honor and glory, and that having exhausted itself by the prodigious effort, the stem from which he sprang should die. Fanciful as the idea may be, it is nevertheless remarkable how the distinctive traits and qualities of his ancestors were all brought together and represented in the formation of his character—as though Providence had chosen to bestow on the last of the line all the gifts that his forbears had shared between them, each possessing only a small portion of the whole. The spirit of the fighter, the love of the land, loyalty, self-sacrificing devotion to a cause, courage and tenacity—these may be traced to his earlier forefathers, and particularly to that one who had given all that he had to his King. The gentle nature of the scholar, the love of books, the spirit of reverence and the eager curiosity—surely these were his inheritance from his grandfather. So little is known of his father that it is impossible to say whether he received anything of value from him, but at least the father possessed sufficient of the spirit of adventure to make him, like his son, seek his fortune on distant shores. All too little is known of Warren Hastings's paternal forbears, and of his forbears on his mother's side nothing, but what is known is sufficient at least for us to see that he was not the product of haphazard forces.

The date of his birth was December 6, 1732. He was baptized on December 15 in Churchill Church, the same day as his mother was buried in Daylesford Church, two miles and a half away. His birthplace still stands, a modest but solid and fair-sized stone house, a typical residence for a country parson. Here he spent the first eight years of his life, attending the village school, which has long since been pulled down, and having the village boys as his playmates.

Scarcely anything is known about these early years. Hastings himself was always extremely reticent about them. He left behind him a fragmentary scrap of autobiography, but it contains only the barest mention of a few outstanding events, such as, "at five I had the smallpox. At eight I was carried to town and after a short stay with my uncle was sent to a school at Newington Butts." [3] Perhaps this reticence was due to the uneventfulness of these humble beginnings rather than to any marked unhappiness. Until he was eight he no doubt lived the simple, pleasant, unspoiled life of the country among the green fields and wooded slopes of the Cotswold Hills, and the grown man may have felt such a life had no special interest for anybody.

The one fact we can deduce with tolerable certainty is that he early showed intense interest in the history of his family and pondered sadly over its departed greatness. Many a romantic story must have been told him by his grandfather of the wealth and importance of his ancestors, of their broad acres and hospitable halls, their heroic deeds, and their noble services to their country and king. We can see the lad on Sunday mornings accompanying the Rector to church at Daylesford, and seeing his ancestors' graves in the churchyard and the big new square house that Mr. Knight had built.

Family pride was a strong feature in the mature man's character, enabling him to face a world in which birth largely determined a man's station of life, with a calm and easy dignity and an assurance that must have seemed to some arrogant presumption. Horace Walpole tells an anecdote that illustrates this aspect of his nature. Hastings one day in 1765 met the Earl of Huntingdon: "Lord Huntingdon, by way of acknowledging him, told him he believed they were related. 'No, my Lord,' said Hastings, 'I am descended from Hastings, Earl of Pembroke,' meaning that he was of the elder branch." [4]

New wealth made in England's expanding trade had given a Bristol merchant the Hastings estate, and only the same new wealth could ever give it back to its former possessors. Yet even as a child Warren Hastings made up his mind that some day he would buy it back. We have the story of his resolve from his own lips. Flowing by the little village of Churchill is a small stream, the Kingham Brook, which flows into the Evenlode. To its banks, rich in associations with his family, the boy used to come to think over the stories his grandfather had told him of the glorious past, of the days when Hastings were lords of the surrounding fields, passing on their lands and power and wealth from father to son. In his old age he tells us how,

"to lie beside the margin of that stream and muse was one of my favorite recreations. And there, one bright summer's day, when I was scarcely seven years old, I well remember that I first formed the determination to purchase Daylesford. I was then literally dependent upon those whose condition scarcely raised them above the pressure of absolute want; yet somehow or other, the child's dream, as it did not appear unreasonable at the moment, so in after years it never faded away." [5]

This gives us one key to explain the extraordinary career of triumph and defeat that followed. If he cared to remember nothing else about his childhood, he remembered this.

Hastings spent two years at the school at Newington Butts, near London, where he was placed at the age of eight, and good schooling but bad feeding were all that he could recall about them in after life. He attributed largely to them his stunted growth and delicate frame. At the age of ten he was removed to Westminster, the famous public school in London. Here he received all the benefits of the best education obtainable in the England of his day. The school numbered among its *alumni* such noted men as the Marquis of Rockingham, John Dryden, William Poulteney and Sir Christopher Wren. Among his own schoolfellows were William Cowper, the poet; Elijah Impey, the future Chief

THE BIRTHPLACE OF WARREN HASTINGS AT CHURCHILL, OXFORDSHIRE

Justice of India; and Lord Shelburne, the future Prime Minister. Impey and he were to be close friends for life. Almost of the same age— Impey was his senior by six months—they were boon companions, so we are told by Impey's son, swimming in the Thames together, and enjoying in common both rowing and cricket. [6]

Hastings was an apt scholar. He had early given promise of unusual intellectual ability, and these hopes were abundantly realized during the six years he spent at Westminster under the tactful and sympathetic guidance of Dr. Nichols, the headmaster. His inclinations led him towards the classics, and he became adept at the writing of Latin verses and the imitation of Horatian odes in English, the favorite intellectual exercises of those days. At the age of fourteen he won first place in the examination for a King's Scholarship (Impey was fourth in the list), and his prospects for a successful career in England must have been assured. He might, if he had wished, have followed the path of his father and grandfather and entered the Church. No course would have been more obvious, none better suited to one of his gentle, studious and refined nature. He would have been an ornament to the Church and might have ended life as a bishop. But fate, and he himself, willed it otherwise.

During his years at school in London, Hastings had been dependent on his uncle, Howard Hastings, at whose house he spent his holidays. The uncle now died, leaving the lad in the care of a distant kinsman named Joseph Creswicke. Mr. Creswicke was the executor of the uncle's will, under which £40 a year were set aside for the maintenance and education of his nephew, who received, in addition, a small legacy in South Sea Annuities. It was at this time, 1748, that Warren Hastings received another legacy, that of the property of the Plough Inn in Cheltenham, which had belonged to his mother. A Chancery suit instituted by his uncle John Warren had been necessary to establish his right to it, as his father in his will had bequeathed the property to his widow. After obtaining possession Hastings turned it over to his sister. [7]

The death of his uncle, whose kindness he always gratefully remembered, changed the course of Warren Hastings's life. His new guardian, for reasons not entirely clear, abruptly terminated his schooling. Soon after his uncle's death, Hastings tells us in his fragment of autobiography:

"I was taken from school. I hazard the imputation of vanity in yielding to the sense of gratitude and justice which are due to the memory of my ever revered master, Dr. Nichols, to relate, that when I waited upon him to inform him of that purpose of my guardian, he in the most delicate manner remonstrated against it, adding that if the necessity of my circumstances was the only cause requiring my removal, and I should still continue at school, he would undertake that it should be no expense to me. I have been told that many similar instances of his bounty were carried into effect. I could not profit by it." [8]

Hastings never expressed any resentment against his guardian; in fact, he was always sensible of an obligation to him for his generosity, and especially to Mrs. Creswicke, who had shown him much kindness.

He made his own choice of a career. Realizing how grave a handicap poverty was for any kind of a career at home and remembering, no doubt, his boyish resolve to restore the fallen fortunes of his house, he decided to seek what he wanted abroad. His youthful spirit craved adventure and enterprise and spurned the impecunious life of rural seclusion in a country vicarage that might have been his if he had accepted Dr. Nichols's kindly offer. And the advice commonly given to young Englishmen of his day, circumstanced as he, was to go East. It so happened that his guardian was an official in the Customs House and influential with the great chartered Company of "Merchants of England trading into the East Indies," and thus the way was made easy for him.[1] By the interest of Mr. Creswicke he was appointed a writer in the East India Company's service. "My uncle," he wrote in later life, "never had the most distant intention of such a destination." [10]

So it was that, towards the end of 1749, he left Westminster and his classical studies, parted also with his chum Impey—for whom a brilliant career at Trinity College, Cambridge, was in prospect—in order to take a course in book-keeping and commercial accounts under a private tutor. And on January 27, 1750, at the age of seventeen, he set sail for Bengal on board the East Indiaman *London*. "On the 8th of October 1750 I arrived in Bengal, being the last of eight young men who composed the same list of that establishment."

With these words Hastings concluded all that he ever wrote in the nature of autobiography:

"This is all that I shall retain in writing of my private history; though the particulars of it, if known, might afford much subject of curious speculation; both from their influence on the temper and disposition of mind which constituted my public character; and from one circumstance of peculiar uniformity attending the whole course of my existence to its present moment, and probably to its ultimate and now not remote period; that of a solitary, insulated wanderer through life; placed by His will, who governs all things, in a situation to give birth to events, which were connected with the interests of nations; which were invariably prosperous to those of his own; but productive to himself of years of depression and persecution, and of the chances of want only relieved by occasional, and surely, providential means; though never affecting the durable state of his mental tranquillity."

[1] Hastings in his autobiographical note stated that his guardian was a director of the Company, but in this his memory erred, as Mr. Creswicke did not become a director until 1765. [9]

Chapter II

INDIAN ADVENTURE

I

SIXTY years before Warren Hastings came to India, on August 24, 1690, a small English vessel cast anchor off a mud-flat on the eastern bank of the River Hugli at a point seventy miles from where the muddy waters of the wide river poured into the Bay of Bengal. It carried a party of some thirty merchant adventurers of the English East India Company, whose leader was the Company's indomitable agent, Job Charnock, the Daniel Boone of English enterprise in the East. For forty years and in the face of every kind of obstacle, Job Charnock had traded and fought on behalf of his masters in this distant part of the world, but hitherto he had failed to obtain for them a firm foothold in the country. Here now on the bank opposite his anchorage was where he wished to establish a new and secure headquarters for the Company's trading operations. Twice in the previous five years had the Mogul Emperor's officers driven him away from the spot, but with characteristic pertinacity he had refused to admit defeat. At length peace with the Emperor had given him his opportunity. So now in his old age Job Charnock had come again, and this time success was to crown his efforts.

There was little discernible to make Charnock's goal appear a desirable site for a European settlement. Two little villages clung precariously to the mud-bank. One was, as its name Sutanuti indicated, a cotton mart. The other, Kalikata, had grown up around a shrine of the bloodthirsty goddess Kali, from which steps (ghat) led to the river. Nothing else disputed nature's powerful sway over the spot to rid it of its aspect of deathly desolation. So far as the eye could see beyond a small stretch of slightly rising ground were mud-flats, swamps and jungle, a vast beguiling expanse of green that concealed the white man's deadliest enemy, malaria. Nevertheless, it fulfilled Job Charnock's main requirements. It was defensible—which could not be said of the populous town of Hugli farther up the river where the Company's agents had previously maintained for fifty years a precarious existence.

At high tide it was accessible to the largest ocean-going ships of the Company; and no native town was there to prevent the Englishmen's exclusive possession.

The monsoon season was at its height and rain was falling day and night. All trace of Charnock's previous occupation had been erased, and he and his men had at first to betake themselves to their ship. But they persevered. They lived first in tents and then built for themselves mud-huts with thatched roofs. Man after man was carried off by the deadly fever, but sturdy old Job remained, and for three years, after which he himself at last succumbed, he "smoked and drank and did his huckstering with the natives, and lived with his native wife, the unconscious forerunner and father of dominion." [1]

In this humble unpretentious way was the great city of Calcutta founded, a city that today boasts a population of one and a half million people and the proud title of "the London of the East"; of western rather than eastern origin, and more famous for its department stores, wide thoroughfares, factories and shipping, than for its mosques, temples and bazaars. A proud and affluent city, the rendezvous of wealthy society, the resort of pleasure-seekers, a center of culture, commerce and power.

When young Warren Hastings sailed up the turbid waters of the Hugli, only sixty years had elapsed since Charnock had pitched his tent on a mud-bank, but already a great and impressive change had come over the scene. In 1716 the English merchants had obtained their charter of freedom from their imperial sovereign, the Mogul Emperor at Delhi, in the form of a royal decree or firman, granting them complete liberty of trade throughout the whole of India free of custom duties; and they had not failed to take advantage of their opportunity. In a few years they had increased greatly in wealth, strength and numbers, so much so that many native and foreign traders came seeking the protection of the British flag. In place of a few mud-huts, a prosperous town had sprung up, thriving on its ready contact with land and sea. Little by little jungle and swamp had retreated. The mud alone remained: and to this day Calcutta is a city built on silt. Sailing-craft of every size and description, from flimsy native boats to East India merchantmen and ships of war, spoke life and activity and a seaport of no small importance. Yet only a beginning had been made in the building of the modern city.

One edifice, confronting the river, dominated the low-lying horizon, the citadel built by Charnock's successors to defend the infant settlement. There the Union Flag proudly waved from a lofty flagstaff, proclaiming the rule of English law. The long outer wall of Fort William was comparatively low, but inside, rising well above the houses that clustered about it on the flat bank were the main buildings of the seat of government of the settlement, the Governor's House and the Factory offices, well-designed buildings and worthy of their dignified function. Landing at the steps below the Fort, one passed by the watergate through the main entrance into the Factory, and thence into the heart of the settlement.

Behind the Fort was a wide promenade and to the southeast a large square open space known as the Park, in the middle of which a reservoir, known as the Tank, provided the settlement with its main water supply. The Park was the center of the little community. To the west, on the river bank, lay what was known as the Company's House, a large three-storied mansion which the Governor had adopted as his residence in preference to the Fort. Next to it, abutting on the Fort, were the export and import warehouses. To the north, facing the Park, was the community church, and next to it the Writers' Building, which would be young Hastings's home for the next few years. Eastwards lay the Court-house and the Play-house, southwards the Hospital and the Cemetery, whilst on all sides scattered about within easy reach of the Fort were the dwelling-houses of the principal members of the settlement, most of them three-storied buildings, and built in the typical English Georgian style of the period. The whole area was less than one square mile. Immediately beyond, principally to the north, lay the native town, already grown to a considerable size and increasing rapidly.

Few places in the world could have held less attraction than eighteenth-century Calcutta for the refined and cultured Englishman fresh from home. Though Bengal has sometimes been called a Garden of Eden—for reason of its rich fertility—Calcutta was emphatically no paradise. As late as 1780, after it had been largely rebuilt by Clive and his successors, it was described by a visiting traveler as

"that scattered and confused chaos of houses, huts, sheds, streets, lanes, alleys, windings, gutters, sinks and tanks, which, jumbled into an undistinguished mass of filth and corruption, equally offensive to human sense and health, compose the capital of the English Company's Government in India." [2]

The surrounding swamp was poorly drained, the jungle was malarious, the innumerable ditches were cesspools, putrifying bodies of men and animals lay on the banks of the river and in the streets and watercourses, the only drains were open canals, the scavenging was done by jackals at night and by vultures, kites and crows by day, sanitation even of the most primitive kind was nonexistent, and even in the great tank, which provided the settlement with drinking-water, pariah dogs with mange were known at times to bathe and drink. [3]

The results of these conditions hardly need stating—an everlasting and appalling stench, myriads of flies and mosquitoes, fever, disease and death. Only when we read that within the Fort were "good gardens and a fish pond," and that the gentlemen of the settlement were building themselves what were called "garden houses," do we feel that these Englishmen had not left behind them all that made life naturally agreeable in their own country. And added to it all was the climate—hot, sultry, humid, almost unbearable for six months of the year, deadly for several of these when the rainy season was on, and pleasant only during the winter. No wonder that when the cool weather arrived the survivors would meet and celebrate their survival with large banquets. [4] Apparently, there is nothing that men will not face for the sake of gain. It was, as Kipling expressed it of Calcutta in his "Song of the Cities," "Death in my hands, but Gold!"

The settlement was as small in population as in size. Fewer than fifteen hundred Europeans sheltered here under the shadow of the Fort, but even these numbers, small as they are, were a great increase over the thirty reckless spirits that accompanied Job Charnock on his adventurous quest. The Company's garrison accounted for about a thousand of these fifteen hundred, and their indentured servants for another sixty. And of these sixty a number were always away at the up-country "factories" and depots that the Company had established in several of the great cities of Bengal like Patna, Dacca and Kasimbazar. Clearly, no elaborate system of government was needed for a community whose sole business and occupation was trade. The members of the Company's service were graded according to seniority. The staff of each subordinate factory consisted of a senior merchant as chief, a warehouse-keeper, an accountant and several writers or clerks. Exercising direct supervision and control over all was the Governor, or President, of Fort William, assisted by a council of sixteen, composed of the senior merchants. Their most important function was to preserve friendly relations with the native government, maintain the Company's valuable trading privileges, and settle disputes with the natives. Justice was administered by means of a Mayor's court with jurisdiction over the whole European community.

Life was circumscribed and confined. Travel was dangerous and difficult. For lack of roads and for greater security most of it was done by river. The country was infested with dacoits (armed robber bands) up to within a mile of the settlement. Highway robbery and murder were prevalent and every traveler needed to be well armed and well escorted. But within their square mile of territory the Europeans were able to live their lives in their own way, and for the English that way was very similar to the way of their countrymen at home.

With pathetic fidelity they adopted the same fashions of dress, the same manners, the same habits and customs, disregarding the fact that for the most part they were entirely unsuited to their new condition of life. What could be more unsuited to the appalling heat and humidity of Calcutta than the wigs, laces, hoops and stays of fashionable London? Or the rich and heavy meals and the excessive drinking? Yet there was little relaxation of the strict conventions of English life. The King's Birthday had to be observed with a formal banquet and ball at the Governor's house, though it might occur—and did occur when George the Third came to the throne—in the middle of the hot season. (Hastings when Governor showed greater sense and courage than his predecessors by risking the charge of disloyalty and changing the celebration to a more seasonable date, namely, December 7 [5].) If the little burial-ground on the southern edge of the town filled up rapidly the English had themselves partly to blame. A typical menu for dinner —which was eaten at 2 P.M. in the hottest part of the day—is given to us by Mrs. Fay, that amusing but most unfortunate English lady who visited Calcutta in 1780: "A soup, a roast fowl, curry and rice, a mutton pie, a forequarter of lamb, a rice pudding, tarts, very good cheese, fresh churned butter, fine bread, excellent Madeira." Mrs. Fay adds: "People here are mighty fond of grills and stews, which they season themselves and generally make very hot." [6]

Tedium was the worst evil that these exiles had to contend with. They suffered severely from lack of intellectual outlets and of healthy outdoor sports, and indulged in heavy gambling and drinking to relieve their ennui. The work of the settlement was light; as the day began at 6 A.M., most of it was finished by dinner-time. The afternoons following the hearty eating and drinking were spent in sleep. Around four o'clock the community awoke to spend the rest of the day until well into the night in various forms of social activity. First tea was served, then came the evening's promenade around the Park and along the Esplanade by the Fort, and social calls, followed by supper, entertainments, concerts, gambling and dancing. They flirted, intrigued, quarreled and gossiped more freely, perhaps, than their countrymen did at home living a freer, more natural life. Some of them maintained zenanas and, owing to the chronic shortage of white women, unions with native women were common. But being strangers in a strange land they felt a greater sense of dependence upon each other, which led to greater openness of heart and hand and a more hospitable and sociable spirit. For exile intensified both virtues and vices. Less content, they were more extravagant. Less comfortable, they had more servants. Life in India was, indeed, "only an exaggerated and vulgarized edition of contemporary fashionable life in England." It was not their fault that they suffered from a lack of the background and traditions of English society. But the monotony of their life was soul-destroying for all but the strongest characters. Yet the time was fast drawing nigh when these men with their narrow interests and self-centered lives would have to assume the responsibilities of Empire.

The trade that accounted for their long exile from home was chiefly export; they exchanged the gold and silver and some of the manufactured products of England for the valuable and much sought after products of the Orient: silk and cotton cloths, calicoes, muslins, Kashmere shawls, embroideries, spices, gems and precious stones, ivory, saltpeter and gum. Most of the buying was done up country at the subordinate factories and by native agents traveling through the country. The goods were then brought down the river to Calcutta to be stored in the warehouses to await the arrival of the Company's ships. Both the arrival and departure of sea-going ships were intermittent, owing to the action of the trade winds and the monsoon in these waters. Entire months would pass when no ship could make the passage between Calcutta and Madras—or took months instead of the normal fourteen days to do it. The winter was the season for departure, the summer and autumn for arrival, and at these times the settlement awoke to activity. Frequently departures had to be hastened to catch the season before its close.

II

WARREN HASTINGS was a merchant's clerk. His duties were those of any junior employee in a London merchant's office—keeping the ledgers, copying invoices, appraising silks and muslins, receiving and storing goods, supervising their transfer to the East India merchantmen. He was poor, and he was miserably paid. Not for him as yet, nor in the ordinary course of events for a number of years to come, were the far-famed opportunities for self-enrichment. The rungs of the Company's ladder were carefully spaced at regular intervals of years, and none could ascend more than one at a time. For the first year of his service young Hastings's emoluments amounted to not more than £36. Three years later he was receiving £60.

All salaries, those of the junior clerks and those of the senior merchants alike, were small, but little more indeed than retaining fees. What made the Company's service attractive was the opportunity to trade on their own account. The managers of the Company were shrewd business men: they knew that the privilege to trade privately under the Company's protection was so valuable that there would be no lack of applicants for their service, who in return for this privilege would act as the Company's agents for a mere pittance of a salary, even possibly for no salary at all. One restriction only did they place on this private trading—it could not compete with the Company's own jealously guarded monopoly. That is to say, there could be no trading done with Europe.

Hastings, no less than Robert Clive, must have found the humdrum life of the warehouse extremely tedious after having tasted the delights of classical literature. But whereas Clive chafed against the indoor life and the harsh discipline because he had a rebellious and adventurous spirit and a restless and melancholy nature, Hastings had quite a different temperament, one that was more philosophic, tractable and serene. Discipline for him was a necessary part of life, both the discipline imposed by self and that imposed by authority. A certain amount of drudgery, too, was part and parcel of his chosen career. The way to the golden future he was seeking lay on top of a high stool in the warehouses of Calcutta. Clive, with the help of fortunate circumstances, might break loose from the set course and take a short cut to fame, but this was not within Hastings's power.

Having been a good pupil at school, a favorite with his master, he was now to be a good apprentice. He had the virtues that an employer appreciates and rewards: diligent in his work, quiet and serious in his demeanor, respectful to his superiors, always cheerful, conscientious and eager to learn. No anecdotes of youthful scrapes and impulsive acts of insubordination are told of him as they are of Clive. If he was adventurous, it was in ways that would increase rather than lessen his efficiency as an employee of the East India Company. Only through exceptional competence could he hope for high promotion. Other young men had family influence or a personal connection of some sort with a Director to help them forward. He had only his own merit. In order to get on he had to be better qualified for any post waiting to be filled than his fellows.

Happily for him he did not confine his attention to purely commercial detail. Being of a curious and inquiring turn of mind he regarded all as grist that came to his mill. Even a writer's routine existence in the factory was not devoid of opportunities for useful observation. Though he could gain no faintest conception of what lay outside the European settlement, though India would for a time remain a closed book to him, a fabulous land, even as it was to his stay-at-home countrymen, he could still learn much about the nature of one type of Indian native, almost the only one with which the English merchants came into intimate contact. That was the banyan, the Hindu middleman, shopkeeper, money-lender and general business agent. And such knowledge was worth much because so long as the English remained primarily merchants they could not escape having close relations with this class.

To know the Indian people only through the banyans was somewhat like knowing the citizens of New York only through the Tammany politicians, for there was no more unpleasing type of native. Most of them were arrant scoundrels, excelling in every kind of chicanery and low cunning that could possibly help them in the business of making money. Hastings learned their true nature and called them devils, and his opinion differed in no way from that of countless other observers.

The banyan owed his special importance in the affairs of the English merchants to the fact that few of them took the trouble to learn the language of the people. The consequence was they could not transact business with the native merchants and cultivators without the assistance of the banyan. Countless evils were to spring from this dependence, when the English merchants became the actual rulers of the land.

The Englishman is not famed for his curiosity about other peoples. It is not the characteristic mark of an Englishman that no sooner does he set foot on an alien shore than he sets himself to learn its tongue, to inquire into its history and institutions, and to acquaint himself with its peculiar customs and modes of thought. He may make himself quite at home, but it is a peculiar and very exclusive kind of home, constructed with the ever-present sense that it is the home of an exile. He tries to make himself as comfortable as he can until the day of his happy return to his true home, and by comfort he means chiefly the exclusion of all that is alien to himself, to his inherited ideas and to his racial traditions. Hence his comparative lack of interest in what lies outside his four walls.

One thing only had brought these Englishmen to India, one thing only held them there. Money. Their object was to make enough money so that they could return to England, there to live in ease and comfort for the rest of their days. And they wished to make it quickly. Not only because they found no pleasure in their exile, but because for most of them life in India was a race against death, the climate being such that for a white man to live there for long at a time when the laws of health were little understood and still less observed was not a little hazardous. And since it was not necessary to understand the language—more, that is, than the merest smattering—in order to trade and make money, it is scarcely surprising to read that, though the Company encouraged its young men to learn and maintained masters to teach them and gave an annuity to those who became proficient, "few attempted and fewer attained" such perfection. Perhaps, as one observer suggested, such ignorance was safer than to hazard being poisoned for prying too deeply into the affairs of the banyans. [7]

If Hastings from the first day of his arrival obtained an insight into human nature not at its best, it did not deter him from pursuing his search for knowledge further. In everything that he did he proved that he was different from the average Englishman, and in nothing so much as his desire to be really at home with the people of India, to know something about them and, above all, to know their language. There were two languages to be learnt, Hindustani, the most widely spoken of the country, and Persian, the official language of the Mogul Empire and the one used in all diplomatic matters. Even though some of the Company's servants learned Hindustani, as being useful in communicating with their servants, there were but one or two who troubled about Persian, for even though the Governor and Members of Council had to correspond in Persian with the Moslem rulers of the country, they had their Persian secretary to translate all letters exchanged. But Hastings learned both, and learned them so well that before he had been seven years in the country, he was being employed on a diplomatic mission to the native court. Thereby did he give concrete proof that he was a man of unusual vision and ability. It is true that he did not claim to be a good Persian scholar, and some critics have seized upon this to insinuate that his Persian was poor, but this is a dangerous conclusion.

It is scarcely to be expected that many would recognize the value and merit of this accomplishment. By most of his contemporaries it passed unnoticed. There was one among them, however, who knew. That was John Shore, later known as Lord Teignmouth. Having served under Hastings in Bengal as one of his chief lieutenants and gained intimate acquaintance with him, and subsequently having been Governor-General himself for a term, Lord Teignmouth was well qualified to judge. Writing some years after both men had retired into private life, he stated:

"The common dialects of Bengal, after his (Hastings's) arrival in the country, soon became familiar to him; and at a period when the use and importance of the Persian language were scarcely suspected, and when the want of that grammatical and philological assistance, which has facilitated the labors of succeeding students, rendered the attainment of it a task of peculiar difficulty, he acquired a proficiency in it. His success not only contributed to make known the advantages of the acquisition, but proved an inducement to others to follow his example, and the general knowledge of the Persian language, which has been since attained by the servants of the East India Company, has conspired to produce political effects of the greatest national import, by promoting and accelerating the improvements, which have taken place in the system of internal administration in Bengal." [8]

Hastings had shown intellectual powers of the first order while at Westminster, and he was to show them again in India. He was essentially the man of letters rather than the man of action. When the time for action came he was to reveal unexpected powers of decision, but it was circumstances, his own perception of the need of action, not any innate love of action for its own sake, that compelled him. It was in the realm of the intellect that his nature roamed most freely. If he had not devoted the best years of his life to affairs of state, and those of a nature too arduous to leave him leisure for other pursuits, he could without question have gained high distinction in the spheres of science and philosophy. Even so, he was not to leave India without having placed his mark on these branches of knowledge. For his acquisition of two Oriental languages only whetted his desire for knowledge of the culture of India, and the boy who had been a King's Scholar at Westminster soon became interested in Moslem law, Hindu philosophy and the Natural History of Asia. Not for him was the soul-destroying immersion in the sordid and pettifogging routine of the warehouse or in the empty round of social entertainment in the Calcutta of that day. He really wanted to know and understand the land in which he had chosen to make his career. He was really interested in its people, really keen to probe into the accumulated wisdom of its centuries of civilization, really anxious to study its forms of governments, its laws and institutions. He was also, therefore, to have his adventures, and they were to prove very satisfying to the mind, and very refreshing to the spirit, of the mature man. And very valuable, also, to him in his work, because everything that he was to do was to be illumined by a rare knowledge, sympathy and understanding. Thus it may truly be said of him that a mind that had given great promise in England of brilliant achievement in the classical field of western civilization ripened to maturity under an Eastern sun to make its possessor the first of a noble line of English Oriental scholars.

III

HASTINGS arrived in India at a fateful and opportune moment. In 1750 events were moving rapidly towards precisely that kind of situation in which a man could rise to his full potential stature of greatness. He needed a few years in which to mature and gain experience, and it so happened that when he was ready the crisis of opportunity came.

India was in a state of turmoil similar to that in China in recent years. The future of the entire great sub-continent was in suspense. The Empire of the Moguls that had maintained a semblance of political unity for two hundred and fifty years had collapsed. The pieces of which that Empire had been composed had split apart, so that the map of India had come to resemble that of Europe. Former provinces of the Empire became independent kingdoms, some ruled by descendants of men who had been imperial governors, others by adventurers who had carved their way to power. All were in a state of constant war with their neighbors, and there were few which were not also torn by the strife of rival claimants. The miserable descendants of the great Akbar still reigned at Delhi, but it was a capital bereft of power and glory, a capital that had undergone the supreme degradation of sack at the hands of a foreign invader.

India was a prize waiting to be won, and already the chief contenders were on the scene. At this very moment events were in train or impending that were to decide the future destiny of the land. And it must have been a fascinating and exciting experience for the young apprentice fresh from England to watch them unroll and to know that his future career was bound up with all that was happening.

The first contender to enter the lists of empire was a race of fanatical Hindu freebooters, the dreaded Marathas from the hill-villages of the Western Ghats. They had descended from the hills to the plains, and on the plains they had become horsemen, and it was as mounted raiders that they made themselves the scourge of all Central India. Wider and wider grew the area of their depredations, and larger and larger the number of states that submitted to their power and paid them tribute. Southwards their bands swept through the Carnatic and the English merchants at Madras trembled at their advance. Northwards they made themselves masters of Gujarat, Malwa and Bundelkhand. They even threatened Delhi. Eastwards they had advanced their territory to the borders of Bengal. And once, eight years before Warren Hastings's arrival, they had overrun Bengal itself, and so unable was Aliverdi Khan, brave and able ruler that he was, to resist them, that he had submitted to their demand for *chauth,* or blackmail, rather than run the risk of annihilation. In Calcutta itself there was mute evidence of the terror that their name inspired. One of the first things that Hastings must have seen was a fosse surrounding the town known generally as the Maratha Ditch, which the panic-stricken settlers had dug when they heard of the raiders' advance.

At this time, then, there was a very real possibility that the Marathas, with their pronounced military superiority over all their native rivals, might extend their power over the whole of India and by changing their methods to those of settled government build up a stable dominion, might substitute, in other words, a Hindu Raj for the centuries old rule of Moslem invaders from the North.

The second contender for empire was the French East India Company. Four years before Hastings's arrival the great duel between Great Britain and France for naval and colonial supremacy had spread to Indian waters, and Dupleix, the new governor of Pondicherry, the chief French settlement, had conceived the great design of expelling the English from their neighboring settlements on the Coromandel coast and of acquiring for himself and for France a position of dominating political power in this part of India. Startling success had marked all of his efforts hitherto, and in 1750 the two chief native rulers of the Deccan, the Nizam of Hyderabad and the Nawab of Arcot, both owed their thrones to French arms. Madras itself had for a time, until a treaty of peace between the two countries had compelled its restoration, been in French hands. Now Dupleix with his grandiose schemes and restless ambition was once more steadily driving the English into the sea. Only a miracle, it would seem, could save them from the loss of their settlements. And should Dupleix succeed in this enterprise it was scarcely likely that he would rest content until he had captured Calcutta also and expelled the English from Bengal, the richest by far of all the prizes at stake.

The English at Calcutta had every reason to be fearful with these various dangers threatening them. It would have needed no unusual powers of perception for them to realize that the peaceful existence they had enjoyed for so many years under the protection of the Mogul Emperors was in dire jeopardy. Yet they gave little outward sign of anxiety. They had allowed the Maratha Ditch to fall into disrepair and to become half filled with refuse and the decomposing carcasses of animals. Only from the sea did they seem to think that immediate danger threatened and only on its seaward side was Fort William at all defensible. India itself might not have existed for all the concern it appeared to excite in the breasts of these complacent and dull-witted gentlemen.

While Hastings was still serving his apprenticeship, a decision was reached in the struggle in the South. The miracle that was needed to save the English was actually performed when young Robert Clive, Hastings's senior by seven years, emerged from the gloom and obscurity of the counting-house and exchanged his pen for a sword. The result was amazing. Every ship from the south now brought tidings of thrilling events. The fortunes of the English had reached their lowest ebb when Dupleix needed only to capture the fortress of Trichinopoly to make his candidate for the throne of the Carnatic master of the whole country. Then, suddenly, when all seemed lost, there came the news of Clive's first great exploit, how with a handful of men he had seized Arcot the capital, and how he had held it for fifty days against every effort of the French and the Nawab to dislodge him.

The tide of defeat had turned. Success after success for the English arms followed. Clive was a veritable child of victory. Trichinopoly was relieved and the French besieging force taken prisoner. One more effort and the brilliant campaign was over. Dupleix was beaten and all his ambitious schemes were brought to naught. At last, towards the end of the year 1754, there arrived the news of his downfall; of how his successor had arrived from France with orders for his arrest and of how he was sent home, a broken, discredited, ruined man. It was a tragic and shameful end to a great career, but the English at Calcutta would not have been human if they had not murmured a "God be praised" and breathed more freely now that they knew their most formidable enemy had gone. France as a serious contender for the prize of India had been eliminated—at least, for the time being.

IV

HASTINGS was no longer in Calcutta. After three years there he had been sent a hundred miles up the river to join the staff of the factory at Kasimbazar as assistant. It was a valuable change for him. It took him away from the stultifying and demoralizing atmosphere of Calcutta, with its feeble, tragicomic Englishness, and plunged him into India—India with its teeming millions, its wealth, its squalor, its many races, religions and castes, its glory and its tragedy. At Kasimbazar he found a great and rich city of some 200,000 inhabitants, next to which lay Murshidebad, the capital city of Bengal, the seat of the Nawab's government, with its gleaming Moorish palaces, its fabulously rich bazaars, its winding streets and overhanging balconies, a city which, according to Clive, was as "extensive, populous and rich as the city of London, with this difference, that there are individuals in the first, possessing infinitely greater property than any in the last city." [9] And in his journey up the Hugli he saw with his own eyes the fertility of the land, its rich alluvial soil, green rice fields, many villages and industrious peasantry. Before he had been many days away from Calcutta, he must have gained an entirely new outlook on India.

Kasimbazar's proximity to the Court made the chiefship of the English factory there a post of peculiar importance, involving delicate diplomatic relations with the Nawab's government. For that reason it was always given to an able man. Hastings's chief, Mr. William Watts, was one of the best in the Company's service, and under his tutelage the young man made rapid progress. Here he learnt another side of the work, the collecting, sorting and pricing of the goods that were sent down to the export warehouses at Calcutta. And here, too, he obtained, what was equally valuable, a close-up view of the state of affairs at the Nawab's Court and an excellent opportunity to extend his study of the native mind and character and the peculiar customs of the country.

What he observed at the Court could not have increased his confidence in the security of the English position. Aliverdi Khan, the Nawab, was a seventy-six-year-old dotard. For thirteen years he had firmly held the throne that he had won with the sword, and Bengal in that time had been well governed. The only serious difficulty he had encountered had been in repelling the incursions of the Marathas. In every respect his dominions were more prosperous and better administered than the rest of India. But in his senility he was lavishing doting affection on a miserable young grandson whom he had adopted as his heir. This was the infamous Siraj-ud-Daula, a vicious, cruel, cowardly, weak and utterly incompetent youth. Any day the old man might die, and as the deaths of princes were all too frequently followed, especially at this time, by violent upheavals in the state—plots, rebellions, wars of succession, palace revolutions—as well as invasion by predatory neighbors, especially if the chosen heir was unfit to govern, the outlook was dark and foreboding.

Mr. Watts was impressed by the ability of his new assistant. At the end of two years, Hastings was promoted to a place on the factory council and then to the posts of secretary and storekeeper. His emoluments at this period amounted to 487 rupees a year, or about £61. A month after this promotion he was sent out on a tour of inspection through the surrounding country, visiting the villages where the cocoons were grown and the silk cloths woven. He was given the sum of Rs. 10,000 with which to make purchases as he moved from place to place, and told to obtain information about the prospects for the next crop and the trend of prices. We can follow in the Kasimbazar records his movements until January 12, 1756, when they come to a sudden break.

In April the old Nawab died, Siraj-ud-Daula ascended the throne, and at once there came trouble, grievous trouble, for the English merchants. Warren Hastings's apprenticeship was finished, and at the age of twenty-three, amidst the crash of war and revolution, his real career began.

Chapter III

A NEW EMPIRE IN THE MAKING

I

THE blow fell suddenly and with devastating force. Almost before the English realized that their days of peaceful, undisturbed trading were over, they were either prisoners in the hands of the Nawab or fleeing for their lives. Two months after his accession Siraj-ud-Daula made up his mind to expel them from his dominions. The reports of what had occurred in the Carnatic filled him with alarm lest Bengal suffer the same fate at the hands of these insolent strangers. He was afraid, and not entirely without grievances against them. Being a miserable coward at heart it was a natural impulse that led him into the rash decision to attack them while they were still weak and unprepared. He had visions, too, of an enormous hoard of treasure within the walls of Fort William, and he itched to lay his hands upon it. So it was that while the English merchants at Calcutta were still speculating about the possible effects of the change of rulers, Siraj-ud-Daula collected together a great army and marched upon their city.

First to fall into his hands were the Englishmen at Kasimbazar within a few miles of his capital, and among them was Warren Hastings. He was at once taken to Murshidebad and imprisoned. And not more than three weeks had passed before he was joined in captivity by four of the scant two dozen survivors from the garrison that had bravely defended Calcutta to the last. The rest—one hundred and twenty of them—had perished during the one fearful hot night of confinement in "the Black Hole" while the Nawab slept and could not be disturbed.

It was a sickening story that these survivors told Hastings. The fact that the settlement was entirely unprepared for resistance, the fortifications in deplorable disrepair, the ammunition defective, the cannon antiquated, the powder damp, the garrison untrained, explained the feebleness of the defense but not the disgraceful cowardice and incompetence of Governor Drake and his chief officers. They had main-

tained a spirited fight for two days and then panic had seized them
and they had rushed for the boats and made their escape with the
women and children, leaving the remnants of the garrison to their fate.
After one day more of gallant fighting Holwell and his betrayed comrades were forced to surrender. The tragedy of the Black Hole followed.
Holwell and three of his companions were brought to Murshidebad
and paraded in chains through the city. The rest of the survivors
were liberated and allowed to make their way towards safety. Nawab
Siraj-ud-Daula returned in triumph to his capital. It had taken him
only three weeks to wipe out the frail foothold of the English in
Bengal.

Hastings was treated with special indulgence and respect. After
a short period of confinement he was allowed to go free, and took up
his residence at the local Dutch settlement. Undoubtedly he owed this
favor to his own tact and diplomacy. Even at this early period of his
life he was able to make himself *persona grata* to the ruling classes of
India. And now, especially, did his command of Persian stand him in
good stead.

Unlike too many of his countrymen, familiarity with the natives
of India did not breed in him contempt, nor in his intercourse with
them was he ever guilty of a loud and overbearing manner. When it
was a common opinion among the English that the natives of Bengal
were untrustworthy, he was conspicuous in maintaining a contrary view.
Six years later, when referring to this time when his countrymen were
subject to "the most slavish dependence" on the Nawab's government,
he acknowledged that he had met with the greatest indulgence and even
respect from the native officials and declared with the greatest confidence that there was no ground for the belief that power could not
be safely entrusted to them. [1] The Indians are quick to sense a
foreigner's opinion of them and to appreciate his quality. Hastings
with his insight and sympathy had learned to understand their nature
and the way into their confidence. Naturally considerate, affable, kindly
disposed and straightforward in all his dealings, he was among the first
of his race whom the Indians could regard as a real friend. There is
nothing really surprising, therefore, in the fact that at a time when,
as he himself said, "the English were never mentioned but with pity
or contempt," [2] he should have been treated more as an honored
guest than as a prisoner of war. Not only that, but it soon became
clear that he could exercise a very real influence on the Nawab's counsels. First he interceded successfully in behalf of Holwell and his three
companions and obtained them better treatment. Next he took up the
urgent appeal for help that the Dutch had received from Governor
Drake. The cowardly flight of the Governor and those who accompanied him had availed them little. They had taken refuge at Fulta,
a small fishing village forty miles below Calcutta, where they were
cut off from supplies and suffering greatly from exposure and priva-
tion. Hastings managed to gain the ear of the Nawab and prevailed

upon him to allow the refugees to purchase food and to issue an order for the restoration to them of the personal belongings they had left behind in their flight.

Hastings remained at the capital until October, and during that time acted as the unofficial diplomatic representative of his country. Then, the weak, petulant boy-Nawab, as feeble in intellect as he was unstable in action, flew into another ungovernable fit of rage against the English, and Hastings was compelled to flee. There was only one place for him to flee to. Somehow—we wish we knew exactly how— he made his way through the many miles of hostile country that separated him from his friends. He arrived safely at Fulta, where he joined them in their wretched existence. Their plight was pitiful in the extreme. Living in tents and mud-huts, nearly destitute of food and water, and ravaged by fever and disease. Over half of them died before relief came.

It was while at Fulta, not knowing what miserable fate might be in store for him, clinging to life with all his hopes and fortunes wrecked, merely one of a sorry mob of ragged, demoralized, destitute refugees, that Hastings took to himself a wife. It may have been love that made him do it. Or maybe it was only pity, a desperate longing to comfort another poor soul in dire distress and to be comforted by her. Their plight would account for any such impulsive step. For the girl he married had just lost her husband. Captain John Buchanan had been one of the officers who had behaved with conspicuous gallantry throughout the siege, and he had perished in the Black Hole.

It was not the end of tragedy for Mary Buchanan. Her marriage with Hastings seems, judging from the very scanty evidence, to have been happy, but it lasted for all too brief a space of time. A son was born to them. Then a daughter. But the daughter died in less than a month, the son was never to grow into manhood, and the mother herself was dead within three years of her marriage. A sad and painful experience for a young man still in his twenties, it may well have left a permanent mark on his nature and disposed him to fits of acute loneliness and depression.

Relief came at last. A few days before Christmas, after five months of waiting, the sails of the relieving expedition from Madras, led by Clive and Admiral Watson, with twenty-four hundred men aboard, hove in sight. The apathy of despair was changed instantly into the delirium of joy. But they had arrived too late to save more than a score of the several hundred men, women and children who had taken refuge at Fulta. And among the survivors there were still fewer who had the strength to enlist in Clive's army.

Hastings was among the more fortunate. He hastened to meet Clive and to place himself under his command. For the only time in his life he became a soldier, enrolling in a volunteer company of Bengal civil servants. The advance to recover Calcutta began, and Hastings accompanied it. Through malarious swamp and dense jungle they marched, crossing marshy streams, meeting and overcoming stupendous obstacles, swiftly and victoriously. Disaster threatened once when three thousand of the enemy eluded the outposts and fell upon the weary sleeping men, and only Clive's invincible calmness and fortitude saved the situation. The enemy fled, the fort of Budge Budge was carried by assault, and on January 2, 1757, the British flag was once more hoisted above the ramparts of Fort William, which the surprised and demoralized enemy made no attempt to defend.

Hastings's soldiering days were soon over. He marched with the army to the capture and sack of Hugli, returned with it to Calcutta when the Nawab approached with his host, was present when Clive, sallying forth from the city, thoroughly discomfited Siraj-ud-Daula by the vigor of his attack and compelled him to make a hasty retreat. The Nawab, thoroughly cowed by these reverses, was now ready to make peace, and terms were arranged on the basis of the restoration to the Company of its former settlements, rights and privileges, and restitution of all the property belonging to it and its servants that had been seized.

It must have been a dismal experience for Hastings and his Bengal comrades when they reassembled in Calcutta and beheld the havoc that had been wrought in their once proud and prosperous city. The settlement lay in nearly utter ruin, and while many of the houses were still standing, none of them had escaped the attentions of pillagers. But at least it was now more securely British territory than it had ever been before. What they had previously held on sufferance and by right of treaty they now held by right of conquest. The Nawab had used the sword against them and now they would use the sword, if need be, against him, and with Robert Clive in command, what had they to fear? So they could begin rebuilding their city, confident that the work would be permanent.

II

CLIVE had the good sense not only to appreciate Hastings's abilities but to recognize the particular field in which his talents lay—political affairs and diplomacy. On February 14 he reappointed him to Kasimbazar as second in command to William Watts. The greater the power that the English acquired in Bengal, the more important did the Kasimbazar post become owing to its nearness to the seat of government. Whoever held it was virtually the eyes and ears, sometimes too the voice, of the Calcutta Council in all that appertained to the Nawab's affairs.

The recapture of Calcutta was merely one link in a chain of momentous events that, following rapidly one upon another, ended by transforming the entire status of the English in the country. Clive had already changed the course of history in the Carnatic, and he had begun to change it again in Bengal. War had broken out afresh with

France, and in March the land and sea forces of the Company under Clive and Watson captured the French settlement at Chandernagore. Three months later the Nawab himself was overthrown. The peace that he had made with Clive had been no more than a truce, which Siraj-ud-Daula was glad of an excuse to break. In the events culminating in the decisive battle of Plassey, the treachery of Siraj-ud-Daula's officers, and the revolution in the government, Hastings played no part. It was the consequences of those events that vitally affected his career. For when the smoke of battle and revolution cleared away it was seen that Bengal had a new set of masters. Not the treacherous Mir Jafar who had taken Siraj-ud-Daula's life and set himself up in his place. Mir Jafar was a mere puppet of these new masters, who had put him on his throne and could keep him there or pull him down as they pleased. The real power lay in the hands of Clive and the army that he led. And Clive took from Mir Jafar ample reparation for all the loss and damage the English had suffered from his predecessor's rash and violent action. Mir Jafar had to pay a very heavy price for the doubtful benefit of his benefactors' continued support: he had to bind himself hand and foot to them, enslave himself to their interests, give them whatever they asked for; more land, for example, and the exclusion of the French from his dominions. Over three million pounds sterling left the Nawab's coffers before Clive was satisfied that sufficient reparation was made and the services of his colleagues and himself adequately rewarded. No wonder that there was great rejoicing at Calcutta, that "a world of guns" were fired off and the ladies all got footsore with dancing and tipsy from drinking bumpers to Clive's health, and that there was no less jubilation in London. Instead of having lost their chief trading settlement, as the directors and shareholders of the East India Company were fearing, they suddenly found themselves in possession of a veritable empire of trade.

During the months and years that followed the battle of Plassey, Hastings's advance to a position of influence and importance was steady, if not spectacularly rapid. His appointment to Kasimbazar made him the acting chief of the factory, as Watts was now on the Council Board and his connection with the up-country station was nominal. At the beginning of October even that connection ended and Hastings was given formal charge. Less than a year later, on August 12, 1758, he was appointed Resident at Mir Jafar's Court. This meant, in common parlance, that he was British Minister to the Court of Bengal. At the age of twenty-five he held a position second only in point of responsibility to membership of the governing Council itself.

There was nobody better fitted for this delicate post, and there was no post that better fitted Warren Hastings for still higher rank in the Company's service. To be in daily contact with the man who ruled the country, to meet the varied society of the Court, the high officials of state, the leading nobles, priests, bankers, merchants, both Hindu and Moslem, to watch the functioning of the administrative system, the play of character, the clash of rival personalities, the hatreds, jealousies and intrigues, the virtues and the vices, the vivid life of a complex Oriental kingdom, to probe the processes of the subtle Indian mind, the modes of thought, the hidden motives and the secret desires—in other words, to have the opportunity to discover the real nature of the people over whom his countrymen now exercised supreme power, what was this but to be given the most valuable post of all? To any man with foresight, ambition, and high aspirations, it was infinitely preferable to any kind of post at Calcutta, where power too often went hand in hand with ignorance. Yet nothing could be more anomalous than the part that Hastings now had to play. He was the agent of a government which was legally subject to the Court to which he was deputed, but actually its master. He had to give advice to it when what he was really giving was an order or a threat. And all the time he had to thread his way through a baffling maze of intrigue, conspiracy and duplicity, amidst constant alarms of war and invasion. It was a hard school in which to learn the art and science of statecraft.

The revolution that made Bengal a puppet state of the East India Company, as Manchukuo is today of Japan, bore no promise of increased political stability. Rather the reverse. Mir Jafar was helpless without English support. His personal character was very similar to that of his predecessor, and there was no loyalty to him among his nobles. Conspiracies were constantly being hatched to displace him. The Mogul's heir was invited to lead an invasion, which only Clive's speed of action prevented. When the Dutch threatened to make trouble and a powerful armament was being sent from Batavia, no one knew the state of Mir Jafar's mind. He was suspected of intriguing with the Dutch, of trying to rid himself of the English yoke, which had already become extremely irksome, by raising up a rival European power. It was Hastings's task to uncover the facts, and he duly reported to Clive that the suspicions were correct. Duplicity was second nature to a man like Mir Jafar.

Clive dealt vigorously with the Dutch menace. When the Dutch transports arrived in the Hugli and attempted to pass up the river, Clive stopped them. And when they tried to force their way, he allowed them to commit what appeared like an overt act of war and then fell upon them by land and sea, despite the fact that England and Holland were at peace, and completely defeated them. Thus Mir Jafar's hopes of gaining his independence were completely dashed, as Bengal was now held more firmly than before in the English grip.

The character and example of Clive must have exercised a profound influence on Warren Hastings during these formative and impressionable years. Though there was a difference of only seven years between them, the older man was much more mature. His character was the relatively simple one of a blunt soldier who saw the plain line of his duty and followed it unswervingly, unworried by doubts and fears, or by scruples and divided loyalties, whether he was battling the French in the Carnatic, making and unmaking kings in Bengal, repelling the Dutch, or wrestling with the insubordination and licentiousness of the Company's servants. His qualities were the kind that have an irresistible appeal to youth: resolute will-power, inflexible strength of purpose, superb self-confidence, calm, sagacious audacity, and unlimited resourcefulness; and these qualities were combined with an eager readiness to assume responsibility and to act in an emergency in whatever way seemed to him best, regardless of possible consequences to himself. In a word, he personified courage, both physical and moral. There were innumerable ways in which the much more complex character of Warren Hastings, as seen in the mature man, was to differ from that of Clive, but in the possession of these qualities, albeit in a more subtle and subdued degree, Hastings was not to fall far short. If he tried to model himself on Clive the result did credit to his artistry. When Clive tersely remarked, regarding the possible repercussions at home of his conduct in the Dutch affair, "a public man may occasionally be called upon to act with a halter round his neck," he was stating a fact to the truth of which Hastings several times in the course of his career was able to bear witness.

It took time to develop these qualities in Hastings, and during the three years he served under Clive they were not conspicuous. What especially commended him to his superiors were his industry, enthusiasm and integrity. He was as devoted to his work as Clive himself, and whatever he did, he did with his whole heart and with a thoroughness that had no bounds. What he as yet lacked was self-confidence. Clive for his part discerned three weaknesses in his character, and at a later stage of his career wrote to tell him what they were. One was diffidence in his own judgement; another was "too great an easiness of disposition, which may insensibly subject you to be *led* where you ought to *guide*"; and the third, an inclination to look upon things in the worst instead of the best light.

Hastings was not yet sure of himself, nor of the ground upon which he stood—that is certain. Self-confidence in Clive was a gift of nature; he was born with it. The younger man had to acquire it gradually; it came with the growth of knowledge and experience. He had to feel his way because his path was not to be as clearly marked as Clive the soldier's. Yet Clive may not have fully understood the mind and nature of his subordinate. He thought he was too apt to see things in their worst light. It is more likely that what he took for unjustified pessimism was evidence only of Hastings's greater caution and profounder judgement, compelling him to look deeper beneath the surface of affairs and enabling him to perceive dangers and difficulties to which Clive was blind. This was no time for easy optimism. The man of action may have thought he had solved his masters' difficulties in Bengal by cutting the Gordian knot with his sword and substituting Mir Jafar for Siraj-ud-Daula; whereas the Bengal civilian, young and inexperienced as he was, early sensed that knot-cutting would be no solution, that it would only result in the tying of fresh knots that might have to be painfully untied because they could not be cut. Disquieting thoughts such as these inevitably lessen confidence and operate against a serene optimism. Hastings must have done a great deal of hard thinking while he watched the swift and dizzy rush of events carrying the Company into deeper and ever deeper water. He was a man who would study every new situation carefully before coming to a decision, who would keep an open mind and not jump hastily to conclusions and from conclusions to action. No doubt, at first, he was diffident about his own abilities, as Clive thought, but such a diffidence is that born of intelligence and reason, a perception of hidden dangers and immense difficulties to be overcome, a wise apprehensiveness, sensible misgivings, rather than an inherent weakness of disposition. Only fools and heaven-born geniuses like Clive are unconscious of such self-distrust.

On two occasions in the course of his correspondence with his subordinate, Clive made striking comments, which throw additional light on Hastings's character. Once when Hastings reported a conspiracy against the life of the Nawab that had turned out upon investigation to be a deep-laid scheme of the Nawab himself to ruin the supposed conspirator, one of his own ministers, whom the English had taken under their protection, Clive warned him that he had not been long enough at the Durbar to make himself acquainted with the "dark designs of the Mussulmans." If it is also true, as Clive thought, that he was apt to pay too much attention to the reports of the natives, the explanation is pretty clear. His relations with the people were altogether different from those of Clive and the Councilors at Calcutta; his real liking for them was in marked contrast to their attitude of racial antipathy, and it may have blinded him sometimes to the Indians' less desirable qualities. His estimate of them was indeed as high as Clive's was low, for Clive believed them devoid of sentiments of honor and conscience. "The Moors in general are villains enough," he wrote to Hastings, "to undertake anything which may benefit themselves at another's expense." [3] It was a trait of Hastings's character that he liked to think the best of his fellow-men, whether light skinned or dark skinned, and as a result his judgement was sometimes at fault. He was apt to give his trust unwisely, and not infrequently was he to have it abused.

The other occasion is still more significant as evidence of Hastings's Indian sympathies. The first duty assigned to him as Resident was to see that the revenues of the lands that Mir Jafar had assigned to the Company in payment of the bill of reparations—these were the districts of Burdwan, Midnapore and Chittagong—were collected in full and paid over to the Treasury at Calcutta. Hastings either did not realize that ordinary gentle methods of tax collection would not suffice in India, or he was reluctant to employ the necessary stern methods; because Clive had to tell him to be "a little severe." "It is the nature of these people," he wrote, "to do nothing through inclination. Ten sepoys, now and then, will greatly expedite the payment of the money." He laid it down as a maxim that the Indians would never be influenced by kind treatment to do the English justice: "their own apprehensions only can and will induce them to fulfill their agreements." [4] And when he penned these words he was pressing the Directors for more sepoys to aid in the collections.

It is interesting to note, in passing, that later these districts, through Hastings's initiative, were ceded to the Company as a *Zemindari*,[1] and it was in them that the Company's agents first came up against the hard and stubborn problems of direct administration of an Indian estate. They have well been called for that reason "the nursery of English administrators for Bengal."

The differences between Clive and Hastings made it inevitable that they would have different views and different methods. Clive was essentially the soldier, stern, inflexible, brusque and imperious. Hastings just as essentially was the diplomat, tactful, patient, affable and persuasive, with a natural gentleness and a much greater command of temper. Nothing reveals this difference better than their subsequent attitudes towards the misconduct of the Company's servants. They both sought the same end—the curbing of abuses and excesses—but how different were to be their methods and motives! To Clive it was a matter of discipline and stern duty; for, as a good soldier would, he detested the gross insubordination and corruption he found when he returned to Bengal for a second term of office, and he crushed it as he would have crushed—and did crush on occasions—a mutiny in his army. But to Hastings it was to be less a matter of discipline and much more one of justice, of regard for the rights of the Indians and for fair play. He did not hold the Company's servants wholly to blame, or to try to enforce discipline on them; but he sought by his influence and example to lead them gradually to adopt higher standards of conduct. Both men were loyal servants to the Company, but Hastings tried to reconcile his duty to the Company with the moral duty that he felt that he, the Company and all its servants owed to India—and this dual loyalty is the key-note of his career.

III

THE departure of Clive in February 1760 precipitated a crisis in the affairs of Bengal. Hastings was distinctly apprehensive about what would happen. His study of the situation at the capital had convinced

[1] No precise definition of a Zemindar is possible. "The position is not easily defined by reference to European analogies or brought under English categories. Sometimes Zemindars appear with the characteristics of landowners, sometimes their position suggests a faint analogy with feudal lords; they act now as revenue collectors, again as local magistrates or chiefs of police. The Zemindars' position, in fact, seems to have hovered between these conceptions and partaken of their various attributes. Zemindars have been more or less independent, according to the strength or weakness of the superior Government." [5]

him that only Clive's presence could preserve the delicate relationship between the English and the native government. He feared that with Clive away the weak and irresolute Mir Jafar would be thrown into the arms of those of his counselors who hated the English, and that military action would then be needed to preserve the Company's position.

There was another danger of which both Clive and Hastings were well aware. That was lest the possession of power so suddenly placed in its hands might corrupt the Company's service and lead it into the kind of conduct that has too often disgraced the record of the white race in its dealings with subject peoples of another color. Already signs were not lacking that this was about to happen. Clive had managed to preserve discipline. When he left, as Mir Jafar put it, "the soul departed from the body," for the situation that Clive had created required his genius to maintain. No man of merely ordinary ability could hope to cope with it. A show of force might continue to overawe the decadent Moslem Court, but it needed power of another kind to hold in check the lust for wealth that threatened to gain control of the English themselves.

Only the possession of superior military strength could, indeed, have saved the natives of Bengal at this time from the rapacity of these agents of a trading company. For no sooner was Clive's back turned than these men began to give free play to their acquisitive instincts. The temptation was more than many of them could withstand: it was more than most men could withstand. Some of them lost all sense of justice and decency. Allowed by their employers to indulge in private trading, nay, forced to do so in order to make even a bare living, they were quick to perceive their opportunity under the new dispensation. As the virtual overlords of the land they had privileges which could easily and very profitably be abused. They were exempt from the jurisdiction of the Courts, all but their own Court in Calcutta, and they could pass their goods through the country under cover of a permit (known as a *dustuk*) exempting them from payments of any tolls or customs to the native government or its agents. Nothing could be easier than for them to use this permit illegally to cover all and sundry kinds of goods, even those of native merchants, and the only loser would be the Nawab and his agents.

The refined sense of fairness that governed some of these Europeans did not permit them to stop at this mild form of cheating. The export trade was profitable, but it was not nearly so profitable as the internal trade in which they had no right to participate. The latter was a very humble kind of trade, it is true, not at all what a European merchant would normally care to lower himself to touch, consisting as it did only of a simple commerce in such common necessities of the Indian peasant's life as salt, grain, betel-nut and tobacco, and the native merchants needed no outside assistance in conducting it. There was money in it, however, and that was all that the worst of these Englishmen were thinking about at present. There was money in it—but only if they applied the same methods as they were already applying to the export trade. That is to say, if they did not compete on equal terms with the native traders; if, in short, they paid no duties. For then it would be easy for them to squeeze out their competitors and obtain a monopoly for themselves. Then they could apply western business methods one step further and charge the consumer famine prices for these necessary articles of life. Then, indeed, it would be worth their while to lower their dignity, as the resulting profits would be quite considerable. Nor were the English the only ones indulging in these practices. Their success in opening up Bengal for easy exploitation had attracted a swarm of free merchants from Europe, who were not under even the degree of restraint that the chartered companies of England, France and Holland imposed upon their servants. And as it is scarcely to be expected that the natives of Bengal would make nice distinctions between their several sets of robbers, the East India Company had to bear the entire odium.

The English merchants were chiefly to blame, but no account would be fair that did not mention the real root of a great part of the mischief they were causing. That highly pernicious species of the human race, the banyan, had come triumphantly into his own with the new order of things. There was something diabolical in the way that he turned events and circumstances to his own advantage. How he gained his nefarious power was described by Clive to the House of Commons. [6]

When a young writer arrived in Bengal, "not worth a groat," as Clive put it, a banyan worth, perhaps, £100,000 would call upon him and ask if he could serve him for four shillings and sixpence a month. It was a tempting offer to the impecunious youth, and the wily native knew well how to make it still more tempting. The Company had provided lodgings for him, but not very good ones, and the banyan would find him better. The young man would then take a walk around the town, and soon he would observe that other writers, who had arrived only a year before him, lived in splendid apartments or had houses of their own, rode upon fine prancing Arabian horses and in palankeens and chaises, kept seraglios, gave large entertainments and treated their guests to champagne and claret. He would upon his return tell the banyan what he had observed, and the banyan in return would assure him that he also might hope to share the same good fortune. The banyan would then furnish him with money, and from that moment the writer was at the banyan's mercy. The banyan would entice him into trade, the details of which he would attend to himself. It would not be long before he had prevailed upon him to give him his *dustuk*, and then, before the young writer knew anything of what was being done, the banyan would be using his name as a shield for all manner of iniquitous practices. Ignorant of everything, the writer would soon be a helpless tool in the hands of his unscrupulous agent, who thought nothing of pillaging and torturing the manufacturers and weavers of his own race. Soon other native ruffians appeared on the scene, disguising themselves as the agents of the English merchants and their armed rabble as English sepoys. And before long the whole land was being devoured by these scoundrels trading under the English name.

Everything went rapidly from bad to worse after Clive's departure. While the tide of robbery and violence rose and the Europeans flouted the Nawab's authority with ever-increasing insolence, Mir Jafar's difficulties with his own people became more acute. His army was mutinous, his treasury empty, his finances disorganized, his nobles rebellious. Even the English had tired of him and his utter incompetence and, not liking his incessant complaints about their conduct, were looking around for some one more to their taste whom they could put in his place.

The time had now come for Hastings to assert himself. His ten years of service and his position as Resident gave him the right to do so. And it had clearly become the duty of any right-minded man to take a stand. His views were positive and he had the command of English to give them forceful expression. The needs of the situation called for plain speech, and it was not his way to cloak his meaning in ambiguous phrase or attempt to conceal the facts in a mass of polite verbiage.

If the members of the Council Board were serious about desiring to depose Mir Jafar, the sooner the better they made up their minds and decided on a substitute. For his part he did not at once see the need. "Let the Nawab be ever so bad, we are bound if not in justice, in honor and policy to support him through these troubles, now we are so far engaged. I do not suppose he is grown a worse man since the commencement of this war." With his knack of blunt, incisive statement of the truth stripped of all pretence and evasion he added, "that he is a usurper is certain, and one of our making." [7]

A new governor arrived at Calcutta. Henry Vansittart, formerly of the Madras service, was selected for the post by Clive himself, but he proved to be an unfortunate choice. Ordinary honesty and diligence did not qualify a man for it. Vansittart was weak, irresolute and wanting in judgement, and in the circumstances of 1760 these were defects that outweighed his very evident virtues. Before the year 1756 he would have made an excellent Governor. As things were, good intentions could not undo the evil caused by his failure to control the more turbulent spirits among his colleagues.

When the hesitations of the Council over the proposed change of rulers ended, Mir Jafar lost his throne. His abdication was obtained without difficulty, and his son-in-law Mir Kasim, to whose claims Hastings had given strong support, was elevated to his place.

Hastings had good grounds for preferring Mir Kasim. If the intention of the change of government was to improve the quality of rulership and to stop the growing disorder in the country, then Mir Kasim was the right choice, as he was an able and determined man, the very opposite to Mir Jafar. Hastings testified to the fact that he was pacifically inclined, well disposed towards the English, intelligent, thrifty, and possessed of an uncommon aptitude for business. [8] It might seem from this description that he was ideal for the position. There would no longer be any need for the English merchants to interfere in affairs of state, as they could rely entirely upon Mir Kasim for protection of their rights. There would, in fact, be nothing to prevent them resuming their former status of quiet, law-abiding traders. Strange to say, however, this reasoning did not impress the Council Board. They even ignored the implications of Hastings's report: was it possible that they did not want to change the situation created by Siraj-ud-Daula's mad escapade? Could it be that they had developed rather a liking for their new position as the power behind the throne? Hastings had not reckoned on this possibility when he pressed the superior claims of Mir Kasim; for otherwise he would never have done so. Whatever kind of man Mir Kasim was he was certainly *not* the kind that would be content to be a docile puppet of the English.

Nevertheless, Mir Kasim became Nawab, and even while he was still adjusting the princely robes to his person, he found himself under the necessity of being just as obnoxious to his benefactors as his predecessor. For it was one thing to accept a throne from them and quite another to permit them to rob him as they pleased. He was at first orientally courteous about pointing out the inconsistency, but when politeness brought no result he became more explicit, and when still his complaints were ignored he lodged a really strong protest, and when that went by unheeded he ordered his officers to stop all boats illegally engaged in the inland trade and bring the offenders before his courts.

In February 1761 Hastings was promoted to a seat on the Council Board at Calcutta and he left Murshidebad to take up his new duties. Normally it would have been every man's ambition to attain this rank, but it may be doubted whether Hastings relished the promotion at this time. It put him in a very unenviable position. As Resident he had merely to obey orders, whether he liked them or not. As Member of Council he had to decide on policy and take a definite stand on all issues; he had to choose between supporting or opposing the views of his colleagues. It is not a happy lot for a junior member of a large Board to be in a constant minority of two, but that was the prospect that faced Hastings when he left Murshidebad.

He was joining a Board that was solidly opposed to its presiding officer, Governor Vansittart, on the one all-important question of the day—what policy to pursue towards the Nawab and his insistence on his rights. He was to come face to face with a set of men who were deaf to all considerations of justice and fair play, who were thinking only of their own gain and who were so arrogant that they were prepared to go to any length to prevent the Nawab from collecting what rightfully belonged to him. Their rank and seniority in the service had given them the choicest posts—by which is meant the biggest opportunities for profitable trading—and they were not disposed to use their votes on the governing council against their own interests. There was Amyatt, the senior member, bitterly disappointed because the transfer of Vansittart from Madras had robbed him of the Governorship; Ellis, Collector of Rents and Revenues; Hay, Provincial Chief at Patna; Batson, Chief at Kasimbazar; Johnstone, Resident at Midnapore. All these men had a vested interest in the helplessness of the native government, because they were the chief offenders in the matter of the internal trading without payment of dues.

There was no room for compromise. Whoever was not with this faction was against it. Hastings had to choose, and choosing to stand by the Governor meant exposing himself to certain obloquy. These men were powerful and influential, and it was not impossible that they could wreck his whole career. It seemed about the worst thing that could befall him to get involved in bitter factional strife in which he would make a host of enemies and no friends—or, at best, one only—and having no influence of his own at home, making enemies was likely to be a costly business.

This was the crucial test of his life. If he had failed now, history would never have heard of him, though he might well have grown rich. So far his reputation had been spotless and his hands clean. Among the names of those known to have taken money from Mir Jafar or Mir Kasim his does not appear. He had made considerable money through trading, but not so much as to lay him under suspicion of having acquired any of it illicitly. In other words, he had shown himself a wholly honest and upright man, and, such was the nature of the times, the same could not be said of more than a few of his colleagues in Bengal. The test was crucial because the time would come when his employers would be looking everywhere for such a man, and it would indeed have been a pity if they had not thought of him.

Hastings as the experienced diplomat of the Board was employed on repeated missions to the Durbar. In November 1761 the majority faction of the Board gave him the odious task of demanding payment from the Nawab of £200,000 as their reward for having raised him to the *Musnud*.[1] Mir Kasim had offered the sum to Vansittart at the time of his accession and Vansittart had declined it. The attempt of the Council to reverse their chief's decision met at first with a spirited refusal, but subsequently Mir Kasim paid the money, over a quarter of which went into Vansittart's pocket, the rest being shared by the other gentlemen concerned.

In the following April Hastings went up-country again, this time to study conditions. On his journey up the Ganges he saw plenty of evidence of how flagrantly and universally the Company's privileges were being abused. The English flag flew on every trading boat and storehouse without warrant. Parties of sepoys were ravaging the country at will, and so great was the people's fear of the English uniform that

---

[1] Cushion which takes the place of a throne in the East.

at the approach of his sepoy escort they closed their shops, barred their houses and deserted their villages. How great must have been his feeling of shame to know that had his countrymen been Marathas or Afghans their appearance could scarcely have aroused greater terror!

In the brief time that Mir Kasim had been on the throne he had more than justified Hastings's hopes. Though cruel and ruthless in his methods he had proved himself an able ruler, and it was still Hastings's wish to reconcile him to the English connection. To make this possible an immediate stop had to be put to the abuses, and all the negotiations of Hastings and Vansittart were directed to this end. A third visit that Hastings, in company with his chief, paid to Murshidebad, resulted in a treaty which, if carried out, would have removed every grievance and held out a fair prospect of peace. It was agreed that every time a merchant produced the *dustuk* it had to bear the Company's seal upon it and that the Nawab should have the right to suppress the illicit traffic. No European was to be allowed to go up-country without permission from the Governor-in-Council, after first giving security for his good behavior. As for the banyans, the sternest measures were to be taken to deal with them. No longer were the English factories to be allowed to send parties of sepoys to punish the Nawab's officers every time they dared to interfere with the banyans' villainous conduct. Instead, the banyans were to be made subject to the Nawab's authority.

Hastings returned to Calcutta well satisfied with the fruits of his mission. But he at once found that it had all been wasted effort. His colleagues on the Council would not hear of such a treaty. The very idea of subjecting either them or their servants to any kind of native control was anathema. What they wanted was complete license to do as they pleased. And apparently this was the common feeling among the English in Bengal as indignant protests flowed in from all quarters and preparations were everywhere made to resist the Nawab. In vain did Governor Vansittart and Hastings make proposals for a fair settlement. The councilors would not listen to them, but cried out the more for their rights as Englishmen. It was useless to remind them that the honor and dignity of the British nation would be better maintained by scrupulous use of the *dustuk* than by extending it beyond its usual bounds. [9] And it only infuriated them the more to know that Vansittart and Hastings would sooner see the whole trade forbidden than to have it carried on by armed force with the banyans exercising that force over the inhabitants at their own discretion.

Hastings recorded his protest at the repudiation of his treaty in the following terms:

"It is now proposed absolving every person in our service from the jurisdiction of the Government. This, it is true, will prevent their suffering any oppression; but it gives them a full license of oppressing others, since, whatever crimes they may commit, the magistrate must patiently look on, nor dare even defend the lives and properties of the subjects committed to his care, without a violation of our rights and privileges. Such a system of government cannot fail to create in the minds of the wretched inhabitants an abhorrence of the English name and authority, and how would it be possible for the Nawab, whilst he hears the cries of his people which he cannot redress, not to wish to free himself from an alliance which subjects him to such indignities?" [10]

Kasim, his patience exhausted, tried a last, desperate expedient to free himself from the toils of the English monopolists. He declared all dues abolished, both for his own people and for the foreigners. Since the English would not make right use of their privilege, the Nawab cut the ground from under them by abandoning his entire revenue from tolls. Only in this way could he obtain conditions of fair and equal competition for his people and save them from ruin. Surely, if ever a ruler deserved credit for showing courage and fortitude at a moment of extreme difficulty, it was Mir Kasim. Like all Oriental despots he was a man of strong passions and unstable disposition, capable of dark and terrible deeds, and even with the utmost of goodwill it would not have been an easy thing for the English to maintain good relations with him. Without any goodwill at all it was impossible. The more Kasim saw of them, the more intent he became to throw off their yoke and establish his independence. With this object in view he reorganized his army, getting rid of the old rabble and introducing recruits from the warlike races of the north and drilling them in European manner. As a precaution against being taken by surprise he moved his capital to Monghyr, a strong rock fortress more than three hundred miles from Calcutta.

It was a wise move because the war spirit had already seized some of his enemies. To his defiant abolition of customs the Council replied by demanding, with truly colossal effrontery, that he reimpose them, a demand against which Hastings protested with vehemence and indignation: "The Nawab has granted a boon to his subjects, and there are no grounds for demanding that a sovereign prince should withdraw such a boon, or for threatening him with war in the event of his refusal." [11]

War was what the patriotic party at Calcutta wanted, and they were not without a Dr. Jameson to precipitate matters. Ellis, the chief of the Patna agency, was a man of violent temper and a rabid hater of the natives. In October 1763 he attempted by a sudden stroke to seize the city of Patna and hold it against its sovereign. He failed dismally, but the consequences of his act were to be swift and terrible. For Kasim, driven mad with fury at this outrage, lost all control over his passions. He took Ellis and his men prisoners, and then seized every European within his reach, including the British mission of Amyatt and Hay as it was on its way back to Calcutta with a safe conduct, holding them all as hostages, threatening them with death if the English did not cease making war against him. And when he found that his threat went unheeded and the English army from Calcutta continued its advance, he murdered them all, two hundred in number, in cold blood with fearful barbarity. Thus did Ellis pay with his life for his mad folly.

The ferocious barbarity of this act sealed Mir Kasim's doom. Even Hastings found it impossible any longer to espouse his cause. For months now he had been steadfastly opposing his colleagues, trying desperately, vainly, to save the Company's name, the English name, from shame and dishonor. Tempers had become heated and relations strained to the breaking point. His colleagues had grown to hate him. Bitter taunts were hurled at him. He was accused of disloyalty and cowardice and denounced for espousing the Nawab's cause and, "as a hired solicitor, defending all his actions, however dishonorable and detrimental to the Company and the nation." [12] Stanlake Batson called him a liar and struck him on the face in a Council meeting.

At length his sensitive pride and strong sense of public duty drove him to the bitter conclusion that it would be better for all concerned if he ended the chronic discord by withdrawing from the scene:

"being unwilling on the one hand to give authority to past measures of which I disapproved and a new establishment which I judged detrimental to the honor and interest of the Company, and apprehensive on the other that my continuance at the Board might serve only to prejudice rather than advance the good of the service, in keeping alive by my presence the disputes which have so long disturbed our councils." [13]

The news of the massacre made him postpone his departure. War was inevitable, and he felt it was his duty to stay and see it through. When the danger was past he would go.

He did not have very long to wait. The English army advanced remorselessly in pursuit of Mir Kasim. He had already been deposed, and Mir Jafar, now an infirm old man of seventy, brought out of his seclusion in Calcutta and compelled to reassume the title that had been stripped of all power and glory. Mir Kasim fled to the frontier. On October 23, 1764, his last flickering hope was snuffed out when the great host that his allies, the Emperor Shah Alam and the Nawab-Vizier of Oude,[1] had assembled was utterly defeated at Buxar by the British general Hector Munro.

If Plassey delivered Bengal into the hands of the English, Buxar in like manner settled the fate of Oude; in fact, it demonstrated that the British military power was superior to any that could be brought against it by the native princes in the North of India, with the one important exception of the Marathas, and for the moment the Marathas themselves were not serious rivals. In January 1761 the flower of their chivalry had been destroyed on the fatal field of Paniput by an Afghan invader Ahmed Shah, and they were to need ten years and more to

---

[1] For convenience, and to distinguish the Nawab of Oude from other Nawabs, he is called by his imperial title "the Vizier" (Prime Minister) throughout the book.

recover from that disaster to the point where they could again threaten the peace and security of their neighbors.

Two months later, on December 20, Hastings bade farewell to his colleagues and, in company with his chief Vansittart, sailed for home. He was leaving more behind him than a scene of incessant wrangling and bitterness, of bloody violence and shameful greed. He was leaving behind him his career, his means of livelihood, his future. Returning to England in those days meant resigning from the Company's service, relinquishing all claim on the Company for further employment; it meant a prospect of permanent retirement without pension. Hastings was taking with him ruined hopes, wrecked ambitions, the consciousness that, while he may have deserved well of his employers for his fearless stand for Right and Justice and the Company's best interests, he had made many enemies, aroused bitter animosities, gained for himself the reputation of a trouble-maker, with no certain hope that his employers would approve his conduct. So, at the age of thirty-two, he was returning, a far richer man, it is true, than when he left home fifteen years before, but not nearly rich enough to realize his dreams of happiness as the owner of Daylesford manor, not nearly rich enough to be financially independent for the rest of his life, and until he succeeded in obtaining fresh employment from the Company or entering some other field of activity, doomed to lifelong obscurity. There is no ready-made alternative avenue of public service through which an Indian civil servant can usefully employ his talents; nor was there in Hastings's day.

This period of Hastings's life—his resignation, his return home, and the years immediately following—was dead low tide in the ebb and flow of his fortunes, the lowest point they ever reached. Never again was his life to be so barren of result, so empty of all that gives value and interest to existence. Full of grief and disappointment, he must for a time have thought it a complete failure. The news that greeted him on arrival—the death of his seven-year-old son, a very promising lad—ended a pathetic chapter in his private life and made of his ill-fated marriage with Mary Buchanan nothing but a tragic memory which died with him. His supposed fortune, estimated by a friend at £30,000, did not remain in existence long enough for him to enjoy it. He had brought £5000 with him, which he lived on until it was spent, but the rest, which he had invested in India, soon met with the common fate attending Indian fortunes left behind by their owners. (It was a matter of frequent note at this time how quickly they vanished into thin air!) Thus within the space of two years he was *sans* career, *sans* family and *sans* money. What he did, how or where he lived, what were his thoughts and emotions, none of these things are known, for he left no record of them. Whatever he suffered was suffered in silence. They were years of defeat, bereavement and misfortune, but out of their weakness was to come forth amazing strength.

Chapter IV

MERCHANTS, NABOBS AND POLITICIANS

ONE of the first things that a returning "Indian" did upon reaching London was to pay his respects to his august employers at East India House. The house, the headquarters of the East India Company was situated in Leadenhall-street in the heart of "the City." And thither on some unknown day in the year 1765 Warren Hastings must have gone, if only to see his former guardian, Mr. Creswicke, who was now a Director. The most remarkable thing about the building was its inconspicuousness. A stranger passing down the street would never have guessed that the plain, narrow-fronted, four-story stone building housed the government of the sensational new empire springing up in the East. But no thoughts of empire were in the minds of the men who erected it. Sober men of business they were, caring neither for the æsthetic nor the ostentatious, but only for serviceability, solidity and economy.

As London buildings went it was quite modern, having been built in 1729, and its narrow frontage suggested that it was a *parvenu* on the street, which had had to squeeze its way to the front between its older neighbors. The real extent of the house lay concealed from view. A narrow passage, so typical of the City, led to a spacious hall where the General Court met, then on to a large Sale Room where periodical auction sales of Indian produce were held, also to numerous committee rooms, dingy offices, several courtyards and a garden, until at the back were reached the warehouses opening on to Lime-street. But even this more extended view still left an impression of inadequacy, not at all in keeping with the Company's importance. Charles Lamb described the house as "a dreary pile with its labyrinthine passages and light-excluding, pent-up offices, where candles for one half the year supplied the place of the sun's light."

If Hastings had arrived at the house before ten o'clock he would have found the clerks busily engaged in drinking tea from the Company's kitchen. For the work was not heavy, even though the lines that

44

EAST INDIA HOUSE, LEADENHALL STREET, LONDON
(From an engraving in the Guildhall Library)

a wit once composed to describe it may have been nothing more than a monstrous libel:

> From ten to eleven, ate a breakfast for seven;
> From eleven to noon, to begin 'twas too soon;
> From twelve to one asked: "What's to be done?"
> From one to two found nothing to do;
> From two to three began to foresee
> That from three to four would be a damned bore.

Admission to the Company's service, both foreign and home, was secured by favor and not by competition, and the favored ones were not required to show any undue amount of knowledge. Lamb, who entered the house as a clerk in 1792, confessed to knowing no geography and less mathematics. Profound ignorance about India was general, nor was it confined to the Directors and shareholders but extended through the whole house, though it was compensated for by a good working knowledge of commercial law and merchants' accounts.

The Directors were men of substance and great self-importance. They liked to surround themselves with ceremony and to exact ample respect from the Company's servants. When the officers of the Company's ships appeared before the Court they had to wear full dress. The Directors lunched and dined at the Company's expense and always in great style, their banquets at the London Tavern in Bishopsgate-street on state occasions being famous for their lavishness and magnificence, sometimes costing as much as £300. But despite the airs that they gave themselves they were seldom men of any personal distinction or importance. What made their office highly sought after were the prestige and the patronage; particularly the patronage, which was extensive and extremely lucrative. Occasionally a man of real weight was elected to the chairmanship and became a powerful figure. Laurence Sulivan was such a man. Domineering and dictatorial, he was one of the few men in East India House who had first-hand knowledge of India, and he used that knowledge to make his influence supreme. First elected Chairman in 1758, he became for many years a great power in the Company, hated by some, courted by more, feared by all.

The most celebrated man in the house at the time of Hastings's return was Mr. Auditor Hoole, who was its literary light. Perhaps his light would not have shone very brightly if it had not been for the generous patronage of Dr. Samuel Johnson, as Charles Lamb described his coruscations as "more vapid than smallest small beer sun-vinegared." He translated Tasso and Ariosto with much popular success; and some years later Johnson besought Hastings's support for him: "It is a new thing for a clerk of the India House to translate poets; it is new for a Governor of Bengal to patronize learning." [1] More recent critics are inclined to agree with Lamb rather than with the Doctor in their estimates of John Hoole's work.

The inhabitants of East India House were merchants whose main interest was the price of their Indian cargoes. Outside their walls and appearing occasionally within them for a General Court were share-holders interested mainly in the annual dividend rate. And so it had been ever since the East India Company was founded on the last day of the last month of the last year of the sixteenth century. Not that the course of the Company had always flowed smoothly. For many years its affairs did not prosper, and once for a short time its dearly prized monopoly of the Indian trade had been seriously endangered by the formation of a rival company; and it had always had to contend with "interlopers" and foreign competitors. (Thomas Pitt, the founder of the Pitt fortune and the grandfather of the Earl of Chatham, had been an "interloper," and the Company had wisely put an end to his interloping by making him Governor of Madras.) But ever since the time of Charles the Second the Company had waxed rich and pros-perous, and by the year 1750 the value of its imports was £1,000,000, its capital £3,200,000, it was paying a dividend of eight per cent, and dispatching to the East an average of twenty ships a year. Occasionally, and quite spasmodically, the State had interfered in its affairs, not with the purpose of exercising any control but in order to obtain money. The opportunity to do so had only occurred when the Company's charter expired. "Loans" could then be demanded as the price of renewal. The last previous occasion had been in 1744, when in return for the pay-ment of £1,000,000 at three per cent interest the charter was extended for thirty-nine years.

The interlopers were annoying enough, but they were as nothing compared to the new kind of pest which the recent happenings in India had produced. A new age began in England with the battle of Plassey—the age of the Nabobs.

The Nabobs were men who had acquired great wealth in India and who were trying hard to find ways of spending it in England. Their numbers were not large—Clive, Drake, Holwell and Vansittart were the most noteworthy—because only the senior members of the Company's service had the opportunities to acquire great wealth, but in proportion to their numbers they produced a phenomenal effect on English society. In the history of the country no group of men had ever stirred up so much ill-feeling and bitterness. Not because they were too radical in their political views or atheistical or heretical or anarchical or dis-loyal to the House of Hanover, but because their manner of living clashed with the accepted standards of English life at that time. They were breaking down the old social order, and the old social order resented the process intensely.

Birth was the only proper passport to the seats of the mighty. Every man had his station in life and he was expected to remain in it unless invited to move up by those above him. Wealth was the privi-lege of the upper classes—wealth derived from a long line of ancestors and the possession of good English acres. Wealth made by trade was vulgar but tolerable, so long as it was not made in too great quantities and did not flaunt itself unduly. To make it a man had to be a prudent, diligent, sober man of business and was not likely to behave in a manner distasteful to his betters. But these "Nabobs"—what right had these sons of London merchants and army officers, these products of country parsonages and the homes of impoverished gentry, these middle-class Englishmen, to so much wealth? It was intolerable to see them as millionaires giving themselves extravagant airs, flaunting their superior wealth before every one, disregarding the refinements and conventions of polite society, and introducing the barbaric ways of the East. Their wealth was not even commercial. If it had been acquired in the course of honest trading it might have been forgiven, but it had been made corruptly, covertly, scandalously, by robbing the princes and nobles of India. The manner in which they had made their money, the manner in which they spent it, and the fact that they possessed it at all—each was equally outrageous, and caused the Nabobs to be socially ostracized and everywhere greeted with jeers and insults. Unhappy men, they found very little contentment when they returned home to enjoy their fortunes.

The Nabobs were not the only offenders. West Indian sugar planters, African slave traders, Government war contractors—they were all destroyers of the social order. "Africans," "Americans," Nabobs, Scotsmen, the old squirearchy hated them equally because they were all equally barbarians in their eyes.

The merchants of East India House, too, held no love for the Nabobs. They brought the whole body of "Indians" and the Company's service into disrepute, besides introducing a new and distracting influence into the Company's Courts. Stockholders lamented "that old commercial dividend...which we enjoyed for a series of years, long before we had to do with Nabobs." [2]

English thought of that day on public questions was marked by credulity and cynicism. No one expected to find disinterestedness in public office, and they were seldom disappointed by finding it. On the subject of India the general credulity and cynicism were further nourished and fostered by abysmal ignorance. For the next twenty-five years the people of England, from the King and his ministers downwards, were to show a startling, and almost limitless, readiness to believe anything in regard to India and the conduct of the East India Company, and what they believed was usually the worst. It was at about the time of Hastings's return to England that showers of abuse first began to descend upon the Company's officers and agents. Epithets of varied hue were bestowed upon them freely in the daily press: "That horrible Society," "The Plunderers of the East," "The Robbers and Murderers," "Perpetrators of every species of crime that could disgrace the human character." The English conscience was awakening from its long sleep and expressing itself in no uncertain terms. There were even Englishmen who rejoiced when they heard of English disaster. Horace Walpole hoped that Haidar Ali would extirpate the English bandits entirely.

England was indeed as full of Little Englanders grieving over the wrongs of the natives as ever it was to be in the following century.

An anonymous pamphlet of the time gives the average stay-at-home Englishman's picture of the Indian scene: "Lakhs and crores of rupees, sacks of diamonds, Indians tortured to disclose their treasure; cities, towns and villages ransacked and destroyed; jaghirs and provinces purloined; Nabobs dethroned and murdered." [3] That was written in 1771, but one has only to turn the pages of this book forward to the description of the trial of Warren Hastings to see that Burke and his fellow-accusers used precisely the same language. Here, indeed, is the source of the impeachment, the little trickling spring from which flowed that mighty torrent of accusation. During these years the English public and their leaders were to be fed on stories of this sort, and it is scarcely any wonder that they—both the leaders and the led—came to believe them.

The popular ferment was reflected in Parliament. Clive by his conquest of Bengal had done more than gain for his employers a new source of wealth; he had introduced a highly controversial question into British politics. For it was not to be expected that Parliament would permit a great empire to be created and ruled by Englishmen entirely outside the control of the State. From 1707 onwards the East India Company, as Burke was to declare, "did not seem to be merely a Company formed for the extension of the British commerce, but in reality a delegation of the whole power and sovereignty of this kingdom sent into the East." [4] What was matter of controversy was the amount of State control that was desirable and the precise form it should take. The advocates of State sovereignty came into collision with the upholders of property rights, of the rights of the Company, which had been solemnly granted to it by charter until the year 1783. And when the champions of private property had been defeated, it still remained a question how to divide the control between the State and the Company. The result was that India became a political question of the first magnitude and was soon entangled in party politics. Not for many years was it to be treated as an essentially national problem requiring the most careful non-partisan handling. Consequently the affairs of the Company, the welfare of its servants, and the interests of India, all suffered.

The primary motive behind the interference of Parliament in the Company's affairs was financial. The land-owning class considered itself over-taxed. Yet the country had just emerged from a long war with seriously embarrassed finances. The principal tax was upon land, and with that already at four shillings in the pound on an assessment nearly a hundred years old any proposal to increase it would have met overwhelming opposition. Ministers had to look elsewhere for revenue, and they looked towards India and America. They first tried to find it in America, and passed the Stamp Act. When that was repealed they turned their gaze towards the East.

It was excusable for them to think that India was going to prove a source of immense wealth. All kinds of tales were spreading of the fabulous resources that were waiting to be tapped. The Company itself was under the same pleasant delusion. No longer were its shareholders content with a moderate dividend; the year after Hastings's return they demanded an increase, and though the Directors reminded them that the Company was still heavily in debt and that the condition of its affairs did not warrant any increase, they carried their point and compelled the Directors to declare a dividend of ten per cent. Promptly the stock soared until it reached two hundred and sixty-three. The attention of the whole nation was riveted on the Company's affairs, for in an age of small business it was the one great joint-stock corporation, towering up in solitary splendor.

The Nabobs, too, contributed to the general misconception, and so helped towards the downfall of the Company from its Olympian position. The sight of these men bringing back princely fortunes was enough to convince anybody that India was a land of inexhaustible wealth. And the eyes of the country squires, groaning under taxation, turned green with envy and covetousness.

The politicians had another grievance against the Nabobs, which did not sweeten their attitude towards "Indians" in general. The Nabobs were treading on their preserves, having the audacity to buy their way into Parliament. Again it was their wealth that caused the trouble; they were using their longer purses to outbid England's aristocracy, and not only were they getting into Parliament, but what was even worse, they were forcing up the price of seats. Lord Chesterfield tried to buy a seat for his son at £2500, only to be told that there were none to be had, as the East and West Indians had been paying as much as three, four and even five thousand pounds. It was certainly high time for the politicians to begin crying out that the Constitution was in danger, and their cries were to be heard for many years to come.

In one of his speeches in the House of Lords, the Earl of Chatham described the situation confronting the nation's ruling class succinctly and with refreshing candor:

"For some years past there has been an influx of wealth into this country which has been attended with many fatal consequences, because it has not been the regular, natural produce of labor and industry. The riches of Asia have been poured in upon us, and have brought with them not only Asiatic luxury but, I fear, Asiatic principles of government. Without connections, without any natural interest in the soil, the importers of foreign gold have forced their way into Parliament by such a torrent of private corruption as no private hereditary fortune could resist."

A number of motives, therefore, were operating on the minds of Members of Parliament to help form their views on the Indian question. Prejudice, snobbishness, envy, covetousness and self-interest. Ministers were divided in their views and pulling in opposite directions; Chatham wanted flatly to deny the right of the Company to the revenue of its new conquests [5]; others having East Indian connections of their own, wanted to drive a bargain with the Company; none had any wider views of imperial policy.[1] And as Chatham, the head of the Government, was sick, the task of initiating a policy fell into the hands of his Chancellor of the Exchequer, Charles Townshend, a brilliant but unprincipled politician, who proceeded to distinguish himself, first by making a foray for revenue on the East India Company, and then by resuming George Grenville's policy of taxing America.

The question came before Parliament in the spring of 1767. On March 6 a number of gentlemen who had been in the Company's service were summoned to give evidence at the Bar of the House of Commons. Among them were Vansittart and Hastings. Unfortunately no record was kept of their testimony and we only know by hearsay that Hastings attracted attention by his "prompt, masterly and intelligent expositions." [7] It is not difficult to imagine the tenor of his remarks.

In June Townshend introduced and carried a bill compelling the Company to make an annual payment to the Exchequer of £400,000 in return for the privilege of retaining its territorial acquisitions. The Company acquiesced with an ill grace, fearing that worse might befall if it objected too strenuously. When the Court of Directors heard the Government's decision the Chairman exclaimed: "It is the ultimatum of the Treasury. There, gentlemen, take it or go into Parliament, and God knows the consequences!" Townshend preferred what looked suspiciously like political blackmail to statesmanship.

---

[1] "It is difficult to attribute any sense of the responsibilities of an empire to Chatham and his government....They were out first and foremost to obtain, and, if possible, to justify a division of the spoils." [6]

Chapter V

GOVERNOR OF BENGAL

I

FOUR years had passed for Warren Hastings—four years of a silence that concealed—who knows how much unhappiness and despondency? And now on a March day with his star again in the ascendant he was once more to say "good-by" to his native land and resume his interrupted quest for fame and fortune.

When Hastings allied himself with Henry Vansittart he had done so for reasons of public duty affecting Bengal and the vital interests of the Company. He could scarcely have known then, or even imagined, that such an alliance would result in his being involved in a bitter struggle between rival factions in the Company at home. Vansittart in India had seemed to be on the side of the angels. Unfortunately in England after his return he preferred the side of the politicians. Despite his good intentions, he had been an incompetent governor and had paid for his incompetence by being doubly humiliated, first at the hands of his intractable colleagues on the Council Board, and then when he learnt that Clive had been sent out to undo the mischief caused by his ineffectualness. Clive had been six months on the way when Vansittart and Hastings sailed for home, but a more than usually protracted voyage had delayed his arrival so that they did not meet. Clive's return, however, implied a censure upon Vansittart which he bitterly resented, and when he reached England he joined the ranks of Clive's enemies, led by the powerful Laurence Sulivan, the former Chairman of the Company. Whether Hastings allowed his friendship with Vansittart to drag him into this political arena and to take sides with him against Clive or whether he merely incurred suspicion owing to their close connection is not clear. What is known is that he lost some of his former favor with Clive and paid the penalty by being refused employment for nearly four years. For Clive, before accepting from the shareholders the commission to save Bengal, had dictated his terms, and, among other things, he had insisted upon Sulivan's ejection from the Chairmanship, and it was not until five years later that Sulivan regained his place in the Court. In the interval Clive's supporters controlled the management of affairs, and they were not disposed to accede to Hastings's application.

Hastings was hard pressed financially while he was vainly knocking at the door of the Company. If he had husbanded his resources he would still not have had much margin. But it was not his nature to be sparing with his money. Frugal he was in his own style of living, but he was the soul of generosity where it concerned other people, and particularly needy relatives and friends. It was characteristic of him to present his sister Anne with £1000 and his aunt Mrs. Elizabeth Hastings with an annuity of £200, and to continue the latter even after he learned of the loss of his own fortune. He also arranged to have the expenses of a nephew's education charged to his account. [1] Such lavishness can hardly help but involve a man of moderate and uncertain means in financial difficulties, and Hastings was deep in debt before the eagerly sought opportunity to recoup himself came his way.

These had not been entirely wasted years nor had they been passed in complete obscurity. His appearance before the House of Commons brought him to the notice of prominent men of the time, including Lord Mansfield, the eminent jurist, and Lord North. These years, too, had brought him the friendship of Dr. Johnson, founded on their mutual interest in the Persian language, an interest which had given Hastings the idea of establishing a chair for Persian at the University of Oxford in order to promote its study in England, [2] and had also led him to propound to the Company a scheme for the instruction of its servants in Persian before sending them out to India.

Reëmployment, however, was his vital need, nor was he without friends anxious for his welfare. One of them, Francis Sykes, who had gone out to India a year after Hastings and been Resident at Murshidebad during Clive's second administration, happened to be an intimate friend of both Hastings and Clive. While still in India he remarked on the fact that Hastings had "managed his cards very ill.... I never saw such confused accounts as he left behind him." And returning home in 1768 he was distressed to find the straits to which he was reduced. Writing to Clive he said that Hastings was "almost literally worth nothing and must return to India or want bread," and he begged Clive to be generous: "if he could not consistently promote his reappointment, at least, not to oppose it." And Lord Clive was generous. "Mr. Hastings's connection with Vansittart," he replied, "subjects him to many inconveniences. The opposition given to directors this year prevented my obtaining his return to Bengal in Council. Indeed, he is so great a dupe to Vansittart's policies, that I think it would be improper that he should go to Bengal in any station, and I am endeavoring to get him out to Madras, high in Council there, in which I believe I shall succeed." [3]

A word from the great Lord Clive was enough to remove the obstacles from Hastings's path, and a new and much brighter day dawned for him when Clive penned these words. Before long he received word that the Directors had been pleased to appoint him second member of

Council at Madras with a title to the succession to the Governorship, and Mr. Josias Dupré, the Governor of Madras, received from them a letter recommending Warren Hastings to him as a man of "great ability and unblemished character." [4] Thus it was that on March 23, 1769, he embarked at Dover on board the *Duke of Grafton* bound for the East Indies. Over sixteen years were to pass before he was to see his native land again. A heavy load of worry had been lifted off his shoulders and he was in high spirits as the moment of departure arrived. He wrote to his sister and her husband that the omens were favorable for a pleasant and prosperous voyage—"a good apartment, less confusion and difficulty than I expected, a fair wind and most pleasant weather." [5] A month later an election to the Court of Directors brought the party headed by Laurence Sulivan back into power, and this was another stroke of good fortune, for he was sure of Sulivan's support and friendship and, therefore, the bitter warfare that Sulivan and Clive were waging against each other, both in the Courts of the Company and in Parliament, would not affect him. For once in his life he was not to be made the victim of political faction and personal spite. With both parties to a greater or less extent well disposed towards him he was assured of being given a fair chance and being treated with favor and consideration. It was indeed a fair and propitious wind that was wafting him eastwards.

The voyage realized Hastings's hopes, but hardly in a way that he could have anticipated. The usual traveler's prayer for pleasant company was answered for him by the presence among his fellow-passengers of the woman whom he was to love with adoration for the rest of his life.

The circumstances were conducive to the formation of intimate friendships. A voyage to India lasted at least four months, and in a ship of six hundred tons there was little privacy, little choice of companionship and still less variety of diversion. The entertainment in large measure had perforce to be human. If there were any germs of congeniality between two people, they were bound to be soon discovered and, once discovered, cultivated to the fullest extent in the desperate hope that through them might be found an escape from the fearful boredom of such a voyage. Such a situation holds all kinds of possibilities. Place on board such a ship an eligible bachelor—or widower—with fine prospects and unusual personal charm, and with him an equally attractive young woman, and one must not be surprised if more than a passing acquaintance develops between them.

Warren Hastings was such a man and Maria Imhoff was such a woman, and the fact that she was accompanied by a husband and a child, while it complicated matters, did not change the essentials of the situation. For Mrs. Imhoff was an extraordinarily charming woman. German both by birth and marriage, though of French extraction, she was very striking in appearance and, more important than her physical attractiveness, she had a cultivated mind, a lively wit, a keen intelligence, and a gay and vivacious disposition. She was thus the happy possessor of a combination of qualities that, to a man of Hastings's type, might well prove irresistible. He was a lonely man, much in need of cheerful companionship, and he had a warmly affectionate nature that craved an outlet. She was a young woman of twenty-two—fifteen years younger than he—and the fascination that she held for him never lessened during the passage of years, remaining with him until he died.

Her husband was a gentleman from Franconia of noble birth but very slender means. He laid claim to the title of Baron but wisely dropped it when he reached India. In an ineffectual sort of way he was trying to combine the profession of arms with the painting of portraits. With a wife who undoubtedly aspired to a different kind of life he had become a penurious wanderer in search of fortune. Together they had crossed from Germany to England, where he had applied for and received a cadetship in the East India Company's military service. Now, sword in one hand and paint brush in the other, he was on his way to Madras, hoping that with this choice of weapons he might be able to carve some kind of livelihood, sufficient at least to support a wife and two children, one of whom, the elder boy, he was taking with him.

The story of the relations between the three is veiled in obscurity, which is a pity, as it was a situation full of interesting possibilities. At what point affection blossomed into love, whether the love was mutual or felt at first only by Hastings, whether the realization that he loved another man's wife caused him more anguish than happiness, whether he openly avowed his love, or not expecting that the day would ever come that would set her free, kept it tightly locked away in his own breast, and what was Imhoff's attitude, there seems no way of knowing. All we know is that Fate took a hand in developing their relationship, for when in the course of the voyage Hastings fell sick it was Mrs. Imhoff who nursed him back to health and strength, which alone must have created a strong bond of friendship between them. When they arrived at Madras Hastings took the Imhoffs as guests into his house, and there is no doubt that Imhoff had a share of his friendship.

II

HASTINGS's stay at Madras completed his preparation for highest office. His whole career was to be one of facing new situations and solving new problems arising out of the gradual transition of the East India Company from trade to administration, from commerce to empire. In Bengal he had already stepped into the breach when the need arose for men with political and diplomatic ability to manage the new relationship with the native government. Yet in order to win real favor from the Directors and shareholders of the Company a man had still to show himself capable of taking care of their business interests. This was something that Hastings had scarcely yet had the opportunity of doing. But it came to him at Madras, where his special charge was the provision

THE SHIP "PITT" (755 TONS) OF THE EAST INDIA COMPANY'S FLEET, 1787
(From an aquatint in the Guildhall Library)

of "the Investment"—the goods bought with the Company's money for export to Europe. The Governor's post was full of dignity, but the man in charge of the investment was the one upon whom the Company depended for its dividends, and he was therefore chosen with especial care and his work given the closest inspection.

Hastings was lucky in that he found the commercial department at Madras so grossly mismanaged that it was a comparatively simple matter to devise improvements which would yield his employers many thousands of pounds. He did it by striking at the root of the trouble: private interest. He saw at once that the Company could not expect loyal and efficient service from its agents so long as it paid them such small salaries; the agents naturally devoted themselves to private trading and neglected the Company's affairs. So he urged upon the Directors the need of "making the rewards of the service generally more adequate to the duties of it," and at the same time, in order to get quick results, he introduced a system of commission purchase. He appointed one man to do all the buying and paid him a commission on the value of his purchases, thus insuring his personal interest in the quantity and quality of the goods and making it unlikely that the Company would be cheated. Hitherto the silk and cotton cloths had been supplied by middlemen under contract, and it had been no one's concern to see that the cloth came up to standard. Big frauds had been practiced on the Company by the native contractors supplying inferior goods. And the contractors in turn were exploiting the weavers. Hastings, in the face of bitter opposition from these vested interests, abolished the system and substituted one of direct purchase by the Company's purchasing agent; an arrangement that benefited both the Company and the weavers by eliminating the middleman's profits. [6] The result was in every way most gratifying to his employers and supplied the final proof of his fitness for the Governorship of Bengal, the most important of the three Presidencies.

Humanitarian considerations were always present in Hastings's schemes for the improvement of trade and business management. It would have been strange, indeed, if with his gentle upbringing and religious background he had been untouched by the vast amount of human suffering observable everywhere in India or unconcerned by the numerous oppressions inflicted upon the toiling masses. Even while he was loyally serving a corporation that was by no means free from the taint of oppressiveness, his mind was busy with the problem of how best to alleviate the lot of the unfortunate weavers in the villages around Madras who were earning a precarious livelihood by supplying the English trade. And he saw with his practical common sense what it has taken most of his fellow-men a hundred and fifty years to see—and even now some of them do not see it—namely, that it is good business to pay good wages, that the prosperity of an industry depends upon the welfare of its workers, and that sweated labor is uneconomic. The way in which he expressed this truth to his employers was, "The weavers are, or ought to be, the strength of the *Jagir*," [1] and his report was full of solicitude for their welfare. He tried to visualize a time when the inhabitants of the Carnatic would be free from tyranny and exploitation, adequate means of defense against marauding neighbors provided, industry, trade and irrigation promoted, stores of grain laid up against future scarcity, and a numerous and contented people settled on the land. But what he witnessed during his two years' stay at Madras inclined him to the view that this change could never be accomplished without a transfer of the government from the hands that then held it into those of his countrymen. [7] The victories of Clive had here, as in Bengal, made the English supreme, but the Company had shied nervously away from the responsibility that should normally go with such power, being satisfied to let the native prince whom it had set up in opposition to the French carry on the actual work of government and administration. Mohamed Ali's rule was unspeakably vile, and history was to show the correctness of Hastings's belief that no improvement in conditions could be brought about without a complete change of régime. When that day came his hopes for a happy, peaceful, and prosperous country were realized.

Hastings's stay at Madras was uneventful, but it was far from being uneducational. If he became a great statesman, if he evidenced a strong desire for peace and an aversion to war, if he was intolerant of blundering incompetence, it must have been to a marked extent due to the lessons he learnt at this time. Because never in the whole history of the Company had there been, or was there to be, a worse scene of general fatuity than had been displayed by the Company's agents at Madras at the time that Hastings joined them. In every possible way affairs had been grossly mismanaged. Not content with mere negligence in providing the Company's investment the Madras service had become thoroughly corrupt, and not content with being merely corrupt it had involved its employers in a needless and ruinous war which was the principal cause of the virtual bankruptcy of the Company. For two years Haidar Ali, the new upstart ruler of the neighboring kingdom of Mysore and the most formidable of all the foes that the English had to meet in the South of India, had laid waste the Carnatic and destroyed the sources of the Company's wealth, and whatever chance there had been of repelling him through the brilliant generalship of the British commander had been consistently ruined by the blundering interference of the civil authorities. Peace had at length been dictated to the thoroughly cowed and terror-stricken councilors at the very gates of their city only a few weeks before Hastings's arrival. He had, therefore, come to a land that had just been desolated by the worst horrors of barbaric war, and as long as he lived he could never erase from his mind the fearful memory of what he saw and the terrible waste of everything that had value in terms of human life and happiness. Terror, starvation

---

[1] A *jagir* was a tract of land the public revenues of which belonged to the tenant together with the power to administer general government.

and disease stalked the land. When later he himself fought a long and desperate war against the same enemy, he did so to prevent a recurrence of the disaster on a wider and more calamitous scale.[1]

As the year 1771 closed, Hastings received word of his promotion. No one in the Company's service had a higher reputation for ability and reliability than he, and now to his other services he had added that of very materially reducing the losses that the Company incurred from the Madras agency. There was accordingly no dissenting voice to his appointment as Governor of Bengal. Clive was for him—had, indeed, proposed his name [9]—so were Sir George Colebrooke, the new Chairman of the Company, and Laurence Sulivan. Clive was so anxious for the success of his former subordinate, remembering their close association, that he wrote him a friendly letter full of wise counsel, such as a father might write to his son:

"The situation of affairs requires that you should be very circumspect and active. You are appointed Governor at a critical time, when things are suspected to be almost at the worst, and when a general apprehension prevails of the mismanagement of the Company's affairs. . . . In this situation you see the necessity of exerting yourself in time, provided the Directors give you proper powers, without which, I confess, you can do nothing, for self-interest or ignorance will obstruct every plan you can form for the public good. You are upon the spot, and will learn my conduct from disinterested persons. I wish your government to be attended as mine was, with success to the Company, and with the consciousness of having discharged every duty with firmness and fidelity.

"Be impartial and just to the public, regardless of the interest of individuals, where the honor of the nation and the real advantage of the Company are at stake, and resolute in carrying into execution your determination, which I hope will at all times be rather founded upon your own opinion than that of others. With regard to political measures, they are to be taken according to the occasion. When danger arises every precaution must be made use of, but at the same time you must be prepared to meet and encounter it. This you must do with cheerfulness and confidence, never entertaining a thought of miscarrying till the misfortune actually happens, and even then you are not to despair, but be constantly contriving and carrying into execution schemes for retrieving affairs, always flattering yourself with an opinion that time and perseverance will get the better of everything.

"From the little knowledge I have of you, I am convinced that you

---

[1] Needless to say, I utterly disagree with the view expressed recently by Messrs. Thompson and Garrett, "that he was not very sensitive to the suffering caused by warfare (as he showed consistently)." [8] I can see no warrant whatever for such a statement; in fact, such evidence as there is seems to me to point in the opposite direction. Perhaps, on a careful rereading of Hastings's *Memoirs Relative to the State of India,* the authors of *The Rise and Fulfilment of British Rule in India* will feel that they have been hasty in their judgement. They go on to state: "He accepted it as a necessity; you could not make omelettes without breaking eggs." I would like to ask them to name the statesmen who have not "accepted war as a necessity." Even such undoubted peace-lovers as Abraham Lincoln, Herbert Asquith and Woodrow Wilson "accepted the necessity."

have not only abilities and personal resolution but integrity and moderation with regard to riches; but I thought I discovered in you a diffidence in your own judgement and too great an easiness of disposition, which may subject you insensibly to be *led* where you ought to *guide*. Another evil which may arise from it is, that you may pay too great an attention to the reports of the natives, and be inclined to look upon things in the worst instead of the best light. A proper confidence in yourself and never-failing hope of success will be a bar to this and every other ill that your situation is liable to; and, as I am sure that you are not wanting in abilities for the great office of governor, I must add that an opportunity is now given you of making yourself one of the most distinguished characters of this country." [10]

Clive was still thinking of the young man of twenty-six that he had known twelve years before and had not allowed for the changes in his character that those years had produced. A hardening process had taken place that had left little sign of any diffidence, while his easiness of disposition was more apparent than real.[1] He now knew his own mind and what he wanted to do, and it was not long before Clive awoke to the unpleasant realization that their ideas were very far from being the same; he then began to regret that he had helped Hastings into his high office, and before he died he was to be reckoned among his severest critics.

III

HASTINGS had now become a person of real importance, and the change in his fortunes is reflected in the fact that his relatives and friends now thought it worth while to preserve his letters. Through them we can obtain a more intimate glimpse of the man than has hitherto been possible. We can at last see something of the human being behind the bare record of his life. Gradually as the years pass the curtain is drawn away from the portrait.

"FORT ST. GEORGE,
"30 *January,* 1771.

"MY DEAR BROTHER AND SISTER,
"I am at this time busied in preparations for leaving this settlement, and repairing to my new residence; may it prove as easy, as comfortable, as this has been, but more profitable, I hope. I have only time to inform you that I have cased a pipe of old Madeira, and ordered it to be sent to England in the first ship, directed to you. I beg you will divide it with Mrs. Hancock; it will last you both, I hope, till I can send another, for your families are but small and consume but little wine in the year. You will be informed by my attorneys in what ship it goes.
"I shall make another remittance of money, sufficient to discharge

---

[1] Sir George Forrest, in his *Life of Clive,* says: "Clive, the soldier, stern and imperious, blunt and outspoken, did not perceive that the calm judgement and courtly manner of the young diplomat cloaked an inflexible will. Hastings possessed more patience, equanimity, and command of temper than Clive. Clive had the qualities for laying the broad foundation, Hastings the genius for erecting the Imperial fabric." [11]

the remainder of my debts; but I am not yet sure of the amount; that, too, Mr. Woodman will learn from my attorneys.

"I cannot answer your letters, for I am at a distance from them. I remember they told me you were all well; that Tommy was become a great scholar and my niece a most thriving and fine child; indeed, I have letters that speak wonders of her accomplishments. May every year bring me the same glad tidings; I wish not for better, and would compound for many a misfortune to be sure of such an annual present. I leave this place in health and in spirits, except what I feel in parting from it. Accept the repeated assurance of my affection, of my warmest wishes for long, long continued happiness, my dearest brother and sister, aunt, Tommy, Bessy; may God bless and protect you is the prayer of your most affectionate,

"WARREN HASTINGS." [12]

The style of his letter is a pleasant contrast to the stiff and formal mode of address characteristic of the period. To Francis Sykes he wrote:

"I have not the time, as you may well imagine, for a long letter, but hope for more leisure in my passage to Bengal, and more composed thoughts. I am now taking leave of this place, and shall embark the 2nd, in the morning. Yet I would not lose the first occasion to tell you how much joy it has given me to learn that I am much indebted to you for my late appointment. How sensibly I feel the obligation I cannot tell you; but you are the friend you have always professed yourself, and you shall always find me your most warm and hearty friend. I leave this place in actual peace, and likely to continue so for a couple of years to come; what will afterwards follow God knows. It will depend more on the measures from home than on what can be done here. I am happy in leaving Mr. Dupré still in the chair. I hope the Directors will encourage him to continue in it. His abilities are very great, and if equaled by any quality it is by his unwonted assiduity and application.

"I have sent you one pipe of Madeira; I forget by what ship. You will receive another by one of the two next. Old wine and the pipe cased. My attorney will inform you by what ship it goes. Adieu." [13]

To another friend, Mrs. Hancock, he expressed his regret at leaving Madras. "I am flattered with the assurance that I shall leave more who are sorry than who are glad that they lose me." He had the kindest remembrance of his colleagues, the most agreeable he had ever been associated with. "I doubt whether I shall really profit by the change, but either my pride or partial attachment to Bengal makes me much pleased with it." His fortune was not worse than when he came to Madras, but he doubted whether it was much better. What there was of it he had sent to Bengal for investment. "My health has held out amazingly, though I seldom stir from town. I attribute much to the dry air of Madras, but more to temperance, which necessity has now rendered almost habitual to me. Kiss my dear Bessy for me, and assure her of my tenderest affection. May the God of goodness bless you both.

... Remember me, and make my Bessy remember and love her godfather and her mother's sincere and faithful friend." [14]

It may seem a little strange that Hastings was able to think so highly of his associates at Madras, considering the mess that they had made of their affairs, but he was always generous in his estimates of his fellow-men, and whatever their particular shortcomings had been, he had enjoyed his stay among them. When he left he declared, "I cannot wish myself a better fortune than to be seconded by men equally disposed to support and coöperate with me, and equally satisfied with the rectitude and propriety of my conduct." Regarding the situation generally at Madras he was not optimistic. He told the Company frankly that they had nothing to hope for from Madras but "a conduct guarded against legal censure and a procrastination of the dangers with which it is surrounded." [15]

To Sir George Colebrooke and Laurence Sulivan he wrote long and able letters, stating clearly and explicitly, but with the respect due to his employers, his views on a variety of matters relating to the Company's affairs and his own share in them, and expressing his sense of gratitude and appreciation for the new appointment. These letters reveal a brilliant and acute mind, able to grasp with equal facility and thoroughness every aspect of the Company's complex affairs and to reach clear-cut and intelligent conclusions, keenly alive to every danger and difficulty, fertile in suggestion and wise advice, and not altogether deficient in the rare gift of accurate prophecy. His style is direct, concise, assured and convincing; without ambiguities, evasions, ponderous platitudes, or reflections on other men, and the impression it leaves on the mind is highly agreeable.

It is possible now to see him clearly, as a man of keen perception and sound judgement who was not afraid to state his views candidly and forcefully, who took much pride in his achievements, claiming without false modesty due credit for them, who was ambitious, eager for praise and appreciation, fervently anxious to succeed, conscious of dangers and difficulties but not deterred by them, too frank to be altogether discreet, rather inclined to give his confidence imprudently, who knew his own worth, set a high valuation upon it, and sought from his employers not so much advice and guidance as confidence and support.

There was one fear only that he could not easily dispel from his mind. It was not concerned with any troubles he might encounter in Bengal or his own possible inability to cope with them, but with the uncertain and highly prejudiced state of public opinion at home and the baneful hold that politics had on the proceedings of the Company's directors and shareholders. He knew from his own observation how dependent he would be on favor and interest. In order to hold his new post and safeguard his reputation he had to have friends at Court, effectual friends with power and influence. Otherwise the constant intrigues of cliques in the Company would assuredly before long bring about his recall. Therefore, he appealed to Colebrooke and Sulivan to stand by him. On the eve of sailing he wrote:

"I feel too sensibly the weak ground on which my interest stands, unless supported by the most wary conduct in the administration of the very weighty affairs entrusted to my charge; and I know too well both the proneness which people in general have to misrepresent the actions of those in authority, and the too great readiness with people at home to credit implicitly such misrepresentations." [16]

These words have a melancholy interest in the light of what was to follow. He had no delusions regarding the many difficulties and pitfalls that lay ahead of him in his new post. In his fortieth year he had reached the top of the tree, but it was here that the danger of a fall became greatest.

IV

HASTINGS sailed from Madras the 2nd of February 1772, and reached Calcutta before the end of the month. Not until April did he take over the reins of government from the retiring governor, Cartier, and he therefore had two months in which to take stock of things. Much had happened in Bengal during his seven years' absence.

The general condition of the country was every bit as bad as in the Carnatic. Here not war but famine had been the deadly agent of desolation. The failure of the rains of 1769 throughout the greater part of the province had deprived the people of their supply of food for the following year. No famine relief system existed, even in a rudimentary form: it had never been included among the obligations of government by native rulers and the British were not yet responsible for the administration of the country. The result was one of the most appalling disasters in the recorded history of India. Nearly the whole of the two provinces of Bengal and Bihar was devastated. We read in the official reports of the Resident at Murshidebad that the living were feeding on the dead and the streets were choked with corpses. Scenes of like horror were witnessed in every town and village. No less than one-third of the population, according to the best estimates, perished; according to others, it was a half. Whole districts were left entirely depopulated and returned to jungle. And so lasting were the effects that even thirty years later the Governor-General of India, Lord Cornwallis, described one-third of Bengal as "a jungle inhabited only by wild beasts," and this was the most fertile and normally the most thickly populated province of India! The garden had withered and become a desert.

If this had been the only misfortune to overtake Bengal in these seven years the story would have been tragic enough, but, as though an avenging deity had determined to ruin the country almost beyond hope of redemption, it had been accompanied by a complete collapse of government. The Company was not responsible for the famine, but it and its agents were largely to blame for the second disaster. The heavy hand of Clive had fallen for the space of two years on the English officials, and he had striven manfully to curb the abuses and reintroduce a sense of decency and discipline. But though the reforms that he made in the service were valuable, he had not touched the real root of the trouble; so far from improving the state of the province and the lot of the hapless peasants, he had in a measure made them worse. This was because he had knocked the last nail into the coffin of the native government without at the same time setting up any proper substitute. He had obtained from the Mogul Emperor, whom the crowning victory of Buxar had made a pensioner of the Company, the grant of the *Diwani* of Bengal, which, in plain terms, meant the charge of the finances and the right to receive its revenues. He had then allotted a pension to the Nawab, who, following the death of Mir Jafar, was a minor and a mere puppet prince, and turned over the whole work of administration to a powerful Moslem nobleman, Mohamed Reza Khan. After paying the stipulated tribute to the Mogul (twenty-six lakhs, £260,000),[1] the pension to the Nawab, and the expenses of government, the Company was enabled by Clive's arrangements, theoretically at least, to pocket whatever was left over of the revenue. This should have been a substantial sum of money if the excessively heavy costs of the military and civil establishments at Calcutta and the war in the Carnatic had not more than absorbed the surplus. The rather natural belief of people in England that the Company was about to receive a vast annual revenue by the acquisition of the *Diwani* completed the irony of the position.

Yet, if the Company did not derive much benefit from Clive's "Dual System," Bengal certainly derived none at all. The Company accepted no responsibility for the administration of the country, not even for the collection of the revenues; at the same time it completely undermined the authority of the native executive by ordering the disbanding of the Nawab's army on account of its being a useless rabble and an unnecessary item of expense, disregarding the fact that a military force was necessary for the maintenance of law and order and the collection of the revenues. When Clive tried to overcome this difficulty by substituting the Company's sepoys, the effect was to lower their morale and weaken their discipline, as the service was considered degrading.

The chief result of the Dual System was to let loose a horde of minor officials to prey on the peasants. The minister was helpless as he could not enforce his authority, and the English were largely indifferent. The few who were sympathetic had not the necessary knowledge, experience or power to intervene effectively. There inevitably followed a rapid increase in internal disorder. Crime, dacoity, vagabondage grew by leaps and bounds. The oppression of the peasants led to decrease in cultivation, and that to a loss of revenue as peasants left their land in despair. Thus the famine was not the only cause of the return of the jungle. Incursions of bands of roving robbers and beggars and of neighboring

---

[1] A *lakh* of rupees at this time approximately equaled £10,000 and a *crore* £1,000,000.

wild tribes grew yearly more serious. And in a very short time Bengal was reduced to a pitiable state.

Gradually realization began to dawn on the English that, whether they wished to or not, they would have to intervene decisively, if only to protect their investment. For there could be no hope of revenue from a ruined land. Prior to Hastings's appointment the Company had made one move in that direction by appointing a number of its servants to supervise the revenue collections and control the native officials. But owing to the ignorance and lack of experience of the men selected the experiment failed. Matters had only been made worse when the supervisors' functions had been extended to include drawing up of the assessments and presiding over the collections, for then their powers became excessive and liable to grave abuse. There were as yet few Englishmen in Bengal fit to exercise unlimited rule over an Indian District. The habit of greed had become so ingrained that it could only be eradicated slowly. When the senior members of the service had found out how profitable these posts were, they had promptly forsaken Calcutta, with its hum-drum duties of government and lesser opportunities for money-making, and hurried up-country to take their own share of the spoil and, needless to say, this did nothing to strengthen the influence and authority of the Calcutta Government, which was left in the hands of the Governor and any juniors he could find to make up a quorum. [17]

Such was the state of Bengal as Hastings found it.

Chapter VI

THE TASK

I

THE Directors' dissatisfaction with the way things were being conducted at Calcutta had grown more acute as each year had passed and brought no improvement. Their dispatches to the Governor and Council expressed ever greater vexation and concern. Why, they asked, has so little attention been paid to our repeated orders for economy and retrenchment? Why were the military and civil establishments increasing all the time and to such an extent that there was no surplus from the revenues to provide the investment? Why had their government failed to apply means to correct the disorders? At last their tone became desperate, as full realization of the shame and humiliation of the Company's position came upon them:

"We wish we could refute the observation that almost every attempt made by us and our administration at your presidency for the reforming of abuses has rather increased them and added to the miseries of the country we are so anxious to protect and cherish.

"Are not the tenants more than ever oppressed and wretched? Are our investments improved? Has not the raw silk of the cocoons been raised upon us fifty per cent in price?" [1]

The note of despondency is remarkable. It would be hard for any government to make a more positive and damning admission of failure.

The desperation of the Directors was increased by the fierce attacks that were being made upon them. They were under intensive fire from two directions: on the one hand the shareholders demanding dividends, and on the other Parliament fulminating more vehemently than ever against the mismanagement of the national interests and the misconduct of the Company's servants. It was plain that something had to be done, and in the autumn of 1769 the Directors appointed a Commission of three, one of whom was Vansittart, to carry out a thorough policy of reform, with overriding powers over the governing council. The three Commissioners sailed, but never reached India. Their ship was lost with all hands, and none on board was ever heard of again.

The discomfiture of the Directors was complete when the news of the famine disaster reached England. Howls of rage and indignation went up to heaven against the iniquity of these Englishmen in India. No one seemed to doubt that they were to blame. "We have outdone the Spaniard in Peru," wrote Horace Walpole, whose letters chronicle the opinions and emotions of the age. "They were at least butchers on a religious principle, however diabolical their zeal. We have murdered, deposed, plundered, usurped—nay, what think you of the famine in Bengal, in which three millions perished, being caused by a monopoly of the provisions by the servants of the East India Company?"

After waiting for months in the vain hope of news of the Commissioners the Directors had appointed Hastings as Governor, intending that he should fill their places. One man to do the work for which three men had been designated. On this one man's shoulders had been laid the task of rescuing an empire from imminent dissolution and bankruptcy. "The evils which have been so destructive to us," declared the Directors, "lie too deep for any partial plans to reach or correct": they had to be torn up by the roots. [2] Therefore they told him, "We now arm you with our full powers to make a complete reformation," and they made him heir to the sweeping instructions they had given to the Commission.

II

So shocked was Hastings at the state of affairs he found at Calcutta that in a letter to Dupré he stated:

"The portrait of Bengal falls short of the life. Will you believe that the boys of the service are the sovereigns of the country, under the unmeaning title of supervisors, collectors of the revenue, administrators of justice, and rulers, heavy rulers, of the people? They are *said* to be under the control of the Boards of Revenue at Murshidebad and Patna, who are lords of those capitals and of the districts annexed to them, and dispose of the first offices of the state; subject (as it is said also) to the Governor and Council, who, you may take my word for it, if the conclusion be not self-evident, have neither honor nor emolument, but are honored only with responsibility." [3]

Nor did he mince his words in writing to the Directors. The existing system of government, he told the Chairman of the Company, was one in which "all trust, power and profit are in the hands of its deputies, and the degree of each proportionate to their want of rank in the service." "I solemnly declare," he added, "that I speak my real judgement when I say that the lowest of the supervisors is a man of more trust, dignity and consequence than the Governor of Bengal." With the result, "the Governor and Council are literally devoid of all power and authority beyond the narrow limits of the town of Calcutta." [4]

With biting irony, yet with evident good humor, he described the kind of duties in which he found the Council Board engaged. He had been with them six weeks and during all that time they had done no more than inspect raw silk and piece-goods, dispatch a ship to England, negotiate the terms of an abortive contract with some merchants, censure a captain of a ship for dismissing his chief mate, settle a violent contest about a dismissed alderman of the Mayor's Court ("in which I had happily no share"), and receive from the army commander "the report of orders which *he* had given for the disposition and movement of troops and of the political measures which *he* had thought proper to pursue.... Do not take my word for this abstract of the acts of this government, but be pleased to peruse our records of the intervals which I speak of— *ex pede Herculem*—I am much mistaken if you find the rest more important."

To crown it all, Hastings related how a member of this puissant government had declared to him that he could not send an agent into the country for the purchase of a single article without applying to the supervisor of the district for his permission! "And if it was granted it was looked upon as an encroachment." [5]

If Hastings's predecessors had tolerated this eclipse of their authority, so much the worse for them and the Company. He at once decided that if he could not be master in his own house, Governor in fact as well as in name, he would not be Governor at all. "This is the system," he told Dupré, "which my predecessor was turned out for exposing, and I will be turned out too rather than suffer it to continue as it is." [6] Englishmen in Bengal were now to learn for the first time since Clive had left them that there was a man at the helm of affairs who was determined to make his authority felt in no uncertain way.

Hastings was the chosen agent of reform to save Bengal and the Company from ruin, but the difficulties with which he was faced in attempting to carry out this mission were great enough to daunt even the most courageous.

He lacked power, the autocratic kind of power that is needed to enforce a scheme of radical reform against the opposition of vested interests. When his employers wrote to him, "we now arm you with our full powers to make a complete reformation," they used meaningless words; his actual position made a mockery of them. He was one in a council of nine, and the sole additional constitutional prerogative that he possessed in virtue of his office as Governor was a casting-vote. In other words, notwithstanding their high-sounding declaration, the Directors armed him with no increase of authority: the same powers that had proved inadequate to his predecessors were still to be his.

With powers as he said "more ostensible than real" he was ordered to remove abuses, introduce sweeping reforms, conduct investigations, prosecute misconduct, and destroy the settled sources of wealth of most of the Company's servants in Bengal. When the arming process about which the Directors boasted was completed, he emerged with but one weapon in his hand, a wand presumably magical called Moral Suasion. With one wave of it Circe was to be vanquished and the men that she had transformed into swine were to resume their god-like forms. But the amazing thing is, not that the miraculous transformation was not at once complete, but that it was actually begun and carried half-way to completion during Hastings's tenure of office.

Hastings was eager to begin his great constructive work. Yet instead of being allowed to do so he first had to satisfy his employers' demand for punitive measures. Instead of being content to wipe the slate clean, forget the unhappy past and make a fresh start, the Directors not only enjoined on him all manner of criminal investigations— including among those to be tried Mohamed Reza Khan, the Diwan of Bengal, and Mohamed Shitab Roy, who filled the same position in Bihar —but they insisted that these inquiries take precedence over the thousand and one other tasks of much greater importance which they imposed upon the new government. And not content with this, they gave Hastings secret orders respecting these inquiries, which were not to be divulged even to his colleagues; thus making his position doubly invidious at the very outset. Had they forgotten what had happened to Vansittart when, like Hastings, he was brought from Madras to supersede the gentlemen at Calcutta? If *they* had forgotten, certainly Hastings had not. "I shall be sorry," he wrote to Dupré, "to begin my new office with retrospections. These measures are arming my hand against every man, and every man's of course against me." [7]

Characteristically, he did not blame the men whose misconduct he had to prove and punish. He blamed the system which permitted, nay encouraged, such misconduct. At the close of his scathing exposure of the evils of the supervisor system, he made the statement that the supervisors themselves "are in general composed of the best of the Company's servants and such as I am acquainted with amongst them I know to be men of worth and ability." [8] In a letter to the Court of Directors, written eighteen months after his assumption of the government, he expounded his theory in words that reveal exceptional sagacity and discernment:

"May I be permitted, in all deference and submission to your commands, to offer it as my opinion, that whatever may have been the conduct of individuals, or even of the collective members of your former administrations, the blame is not so much imputable to them as to the want of a principle of government adequate to its substance, and a coercive power to enforce it. The extent of Bengal, and its possible resources, are equal to those of most states in Europe. Its difficulties are greater than those of any, because it wants both an established form and powers of government, deriving its actual support from the unremitted labor and personal exertion of individuals in power instead of the vital influence which flows through the channels of a regular constitution, and imperceptibly animates every part of it. Our constitution is nowhere to be traced but in ancient charters which were formed for the jurisdiction of your trading settlements, the sales of your exports, and the provision of your annual investment. I need not observe how incompetent these must prove for the government of a great kingdom, and for the preservation of its riches from private violence and

embezzlement. Among your servants, who for a course of years have
been left at large in possession of so tempting a deposit, it is not to be
wondered at that many have applied it to the advancement of their own
fortunes, or that those who were possessed of abilities to introduce a
system of better order, should have been drawn along by the general
current, since few men are inspired with so large a share of public
virtue as to sacrifice their interests, peace and social feelings to it, and
to begin the work of reformation on themselves." Accordingly, he predicted that when Bengal had been furnished with an adequate system
of government, "from the knowledge which I have of the general habits
and manners of your servants, that you will hear of as few instances
of licentiousness amongst them as among the members of any community in the British Empire." [9]

The wisdom of these words is profound, especially written as they
were at a time when the general opinion in England was that no good
could come out of the Company's service: as though the Englishmen
who went to India were a set of men quite distinct in character and
moral standards from the rest of their fellow-countrymen and distinguished by a special and peculiar depravity—a judgement as undeserved
as it was sweeping. There may have been others besides Hastings who
could look beyond the deceptive appearances and discern the day when
English rule in India was no longer to be a byword for extortion and
greed. But it was Hastings who first caught the vision splendid of the
Indian Civil Service as it was to be—a service without a peer in the
world for integrity, honesty and just dealing, and it was he who laid
the foundations for its creation.

He never ceased to plead the vital importance of sane, sympathetic
and generous treatment of the Service. Young and able-bodied Englishmen did not go to India for their health, nor to earn the miserable pittance of a salary that was all the Company had hitherto allowed them.
Nor was it reasonable to expect them to leave their families and friends,
endanger their lives, undergo hardships and discomforts unknown in
England, assume weighty responsibilities and arduous labors, all for
the same salary as was considered suitable for the equivalent rank and
office at home. It was monstrously unfair, as Hastings pointed out, to
base their salaries on the rate of exchange between the rupee and the
pound sterling, and then to compel them to sign covenants binding them
not to accept presents from Indian rulers and officials and threatening
them with severe pains and penalties if they transgressed the prohibition. It was not only unfair; it was stupid.

"Here," said Hastings, "the administration of a rich and extensive
kingdom is in the hands of a few, and the whole wealth of it at their
disposal. The distance of the supreme power on which it depends, the
servile habits and characters of the people, and the nature of landed
property, which by the constitution is solely vested in the government,
throw so vast a trust into the hands of the members of the Council as
requires adequate profits and incitements for the just discharge of it,

or, in default of such a provision, they will act as men ever do in such cases, and carve for themselves." He insisted, therefore, as he had insisted at Madras, that what was needed was "some advantageous concessions" that would engage these men to the faithful observance of their covenants by the principles of honor and gratitude.

There was yet another difficulty that made the work of reform exceptionally hazardous. If, as Hastings maintained, the chief source of trouble was the supervisor system, then the obvious remedy was to abolish it, recall "the rulers of the land" and substitute a better system. But most of these men had powerful connections either in the Council or at home in the Government and the Courts of the Company. They were the sons, brothers, cousins, friends, élèves and protégés of this Director or that wealthy shareholder. It was impossible to effect reforms without treading on some toes, but their toes were the biggest and the most sensitive. Regardless of the plain necessity of changing the system, it behoved any governor to beware of laying too heavy a hand on their jobs if he did not wish to raise up a host of enemies. Hastings had to walk warily if he was to be permitted to walk at all.

Thus, when Hastings wrote to the Chairman of the Company shortly after his arrival at Calcutta, "whether I have really benefited by my removal from Fort St. George to a station of more éclat, but of more trouble and difficulty, and I fear of more danger, from its being an object of more competition, I must doubt," [10] he must have been conscious of some understatement of the facts.

III

For a year after Hastings assumed the government he was deluged with fresh orders on every conceivable matter, great and small. But there was one order in particular that exceeded in importance all the others put together, by changing the whole character of the Company's position in Bengal. In a dispatch received at Calcutta on August 6, 1772, the Directors declared their determination "to stand forth as Dewan and by the agency of the Company's servants to take upon ourselves the entire care and management of the revenues." [11]

This was an epoch-making decision. It meant the scrapping of Clive's Dual System and the assumption by the Company of the undivided responsibility for the administration of the provinces that it had for so long refused. For it was but a short and immediate step from management of the revenues to management of the whole machinery of government, a step that Hastings was forthwith to take. Thus at one stroke a company of merchants transformed itself into a company of imperial administrators, and from it dates the establishment of British rule in India.

The added burden that the new policy threw on Hastings and his colleagues was tremendous. Ample as had been the Directors' orders and instructions, too ample to be always wise, they indicated as a rule merely the general lines along which the Governor-in-Council was to proceed. It was left to him to devise the practical measures to give effect to them. Not only were the Directors as a body too ignorant of the actual conditions in India, but they were too deeply immersed in their own affairs at home to give helpful suggestions. As soon as Hastings came to grips with his task he saw that there were all manner of problems involved that were scarcely, if at all, realized at the Company's offices in Leadenhall-street.

What, for instance, were to be the Company's relations with the Mogul Emperor? At the moment the Company was at one and the same time his nominal vassal and actual tributary and his protector and benefactor. How long could such an anomalous situation last? Likewise, what was to be the future status of the Nawab of Bengal? At the moment he was a minor and therefore, conveniently for the Company, could exercise none of the powers that were his by hereditary right, though the Company paid him a generous share of the revenues. How was he to be regarded when he came of age? How much power was he to be given? Or was he to be regarded merely as an unduly expensive ornament whose pension must be reduced? The Company had decided to assume the administration of Bengal. What manner of government was to be established—one based on English law and institutions, or one based on Indian? How was it to be constructed? And who was to operate it? The solution to all these, and many other equally complex problems, was left to Hastings's discretion, subject, of course, to the subsequent approval or condemnation of his employers.

The Directors described the work that was to be taken in hand as "reforms." This was a misnomer. One cannot reform what virtually does not exist. In the Bengal of 1772 there was no organized government, functioning regularly and properly through all its branches; there was no systematic administration of law and order, no security for person or property, no police force, no system of taxation. There was only anarchy, universal and unlimited. Carrying out the Directors' orders involved reconstructing the edifice of government from the bottom up. The magnitude of this task has never been properly appreciated. It is only recently that this phase of Hastings's work has received the attention and praise that it so richly merits.[1] For the most part biographers and historians have concentrated their attention on the more dramatic events that followed.

It might have been easier if Hastings had had a complete *tabula rasa* on which to build. But, though Moslem authority had disappeared, the country was strewn with its vestiges. Here was no people newly arrived at nationhood calling for the services of an organizer and lawmaker, but a population of mixed race, conflicting religions and complex caste distinctions, which bore the marks of centuries of civilization

---

[1] Miss Monckton-Jones, in her valuable contribution to the subject, has redeemed this neglect and supplied ample evidence of the true greatness of Hastings's work.

deeply engraved upon it. The ground could not be swept clear of the débris, for the débris was embedded in it. Hastings had to take the débris as his foundation and build his new structure upon it. He had to penetrate the bewildering maze of Hindu and Moslem law, institutions, customs, ideas and prejudices, and master their baffling complexities and inconsistencies. Only when he had done this could he proceed to the work of reconstruction with any confidence of being able to make it acceptable to the mass of the people and, therefore, successful and lasting.

If he decided to return to the best usages of Mogul rule—which was actually what he sought to do—he had to find out what those usages were. In the fifty years since the death of Aurangzeb the system had crumbled and become so debased as to be worthless. Its state of perfection was during the time of Akbar who died in 1605, and he had to read and study the records of that time. As it happens the name of one of the books he studied is known to us. It is the *Ain-i-Akbari* by Abu-l Fazl, recognized to be the best contemporary authority. When Lord Moira became Governor-General (1812) Hastings recommended the work to him as containing all useful information regarding "that magnificent machine." [12] But more was required of him than to apply the historical knowledge so acquired. Essential as he believed it to be to preserve all possible continuity with the past, he could not merely copy an old design and produce an exact replica of the Mogul system. He had to modify and adapt the old to fit English ideas and standards. He had to produce a piece of machinery that English officials could operate and English opinion tolerate. The second part of his task, therefore, was to graft Western notions and methods on to the main stem of Eastern institutions. And here he had to break new ground. As there was no model for him to follow, he had to improvise.

The man to whom this double task was entrusted had had no formal training in the sciences of politics and jurisprudence. In fact, he had had no formal training at all except as a merchant. The only assistance, too, that he had was from men with the same fundamental handicap. He lacked, indeed, both the material and the immaterial aids to wise statesmanship—the expert counsel and assistance of jurists, financiers, scholars, and a trained and experienced civil service, and the guidance of law, tradition and precedent. As a result he was compelled to return to first principles and depend on common sense and natural reason instead of the accumulated wisdom of past experience. But there were advantages as well as disadvantages in this. For India it was probably a very real blessing. Hastings approached the task of giving Bengal a new administrative system and a new set of institutions, with a singularly open mind, a mind free of prejudice, bigotry and dogmatism, uncolored by long and intimate contact with English law and the fabric of English government and society. He was thereby saved from the besetting weakness of so many of the men who followed him, who saw India through English spectacles, interpreted Indian institutions in terms of English, and legislated accordingly. India, Hastings knew well, was another world with a set of values, ideas and institutions entirely different from those of his own country, and he never made the mistake of confusing the two. In large measure he succeeded in ruling India as an Indian and not as an alien.

His method was that of an experimental scientist, not a theorist. Experiment was the key-note of all his early measures. "The new government," he wrote in his usual graphic way, "consists of a confused heap of undigested materials, as wild as the chaos itself. The powers of government are undefined; the collection of the revenues, the provision of the investment, the administration of justice (if it exists at all), the care of the police, are all huddled together. We have them all to separate and bring into order at once. We must work as an arithmetician does, with his Rule of False, adopt a plan upon conjecture, try, execute, add and deduct from it till it is brought into a perfect shape...." [13]

Having thus surveyed the situation, weighed the difficulties, read and digested the voluminous orders from home and formed his conclusions, Hastings was ready to begin his momentous work. He summarized the primary aims of his policy under seven heads:

"1. To implant the authority of the Company and the sovereignty of Great Britain in the Constitution of this country.

"2. To abolish all secret influence, and make the Government itself responsible for all measures, by making them all pass by its avowed authority.

"3. To remove all impediments which prevented the complaints of the people from reaching the ears of the supreme administration, or established an independent despotism in its agents.

"4. To relieve the ryots from oppressive taxes.

"5. To introduce a regular system of justice and protection into the country.

"6. To relieve the distresses of the Company and pay off their heavy debts here by a uniform and regular mode of collecting their rents, by savings in expenses and by foreign acquisitions of wealth.

"7. To enlarge the political influence of the Company without enlarging its territory or dividing their military strength." [14]

Chapter VII

THE RECONSTRUCTION OF AN EMPIRE

I

HASTINGS'S first duty was to depose Mohamed Reza Khan and Shitab Roy from their posts of Diwans of the provinces of Bengal and Bihar respectively. He had received secret orders from the Directors to have the former arrested and brought down from Murshidebad to Calcutta to stand his trial on charges of embezzlement and peculation and of cornering grain during the famine.

The deposition of this powerful minister was entirely consonant with the Governor's ideas, as it was an essential preparatory step to the reorganization of the government. But his arrest and prosecution were a different matter. Hastings was keenly conscious of the ignominy and injustice of the Company's attempt to pin the chief responsibility for the recent calamities and evils on this one man, and the fact that Mohamed Reza Khan was one of the greatest Moslem nobles of Bengal made the injustice seem still more glaring. But as his employers gave him no option in the matter, he lost no time in obeying their orders. Both the Diwans were seized and hurried down to Calcutta, where they were placed in easy confinement pending the result of investigations into their conduct.

From the day that Hastings took over the reins of office from Cartier the conduct of affairs underwent an amazing transformation. Slackness, indifference, quiescence vanished before the dynamic energy and drive of the new Governor. Every department of government was galvanized into furious activity. Orders, codes and regulations began to pour from the committees of Council, all of them directly inspired, and most of them actually drafted, by Hastings himself.

The speed with which he worked is clearly proved by the fact that the first of his great administrative measures was issued within six weeks of his inauguration. This was the Land Settlement, which was passed by the Council and published on May 14.

When Sir Walter Lawrence tells us in his reminiscences of his Indian service that the Land Revenue is "the key to India, for the land

and agriculture count more than the problems of the great cities, of Frontier defense, of commerce and finance," [1] he states an axiom that was first postulated and acted upon by Warren Hastings. For no sooner had Hastings received word of his appointment, and while still at Madras, than he began to give anxious thought to the matter, and when he reached Calcutta, he made it the principal object of study and investigation. Hence the swiftness with which he was able to act.

There was no more urgent need than some kind of Land Settlement. One might almost say, indeed, that *any* kind of settlement was better than none at all, so long as the rents demanded were not exorbitant. An end had somehow to be put to the existing state of chaos, which had destroyed the old Mogul land system, deprived the cultivators of all protection against extortion and oppression, and greatly reduced the revenue. Yet there was no branch of government in which the English were more woefully ignorant, and none which was more difficult to understand. They knew no more to whom the rightful ownership of Bengal lands belonged, confessed one of their number, than they did of the landed property of the moon.

The complexity of the subject was, indeed, tremendous. All preconceived ideas based on English notions of the nature of landed property had to be thrown into the discard, for there was no such thing as ownership of land as the term is understood in England and America. What was owned was not the land itself but a right to a share in its produce, and this right was divided between three parties—the State, which came nearest to being absolute proprietor; the zemindar, that is to say, the collector or farmer of the rents for the State; and the cultivator of the soil. The crux of the problem that confronted every government, the Mogul Emperors as well as the English Company, was how to secure to each party its just share of the produce and protection against encroachments on its rights by either of the others. It could not be done without, first, a thorough understanding of the problem involved; secondly, an exact knowledge of the value of every estate and holding; thirdly, a system of collection that would be efficient; and lastly, a system of law and law-courts.

Not one of these four essential requisites existed when Hastings assumed the government. He himself, indeed, confessed an ignorance as great as that of his colleagues, though before the year was out he was able to claim that he had mastered the intricacies of the subject. All he could do at the outset was to contrive a makeshift settlement that would serve until it could be improved upon. Time was the essential need—time to accumulate the facts of land tenure, time to survey the whole province in the same careful and methodical way that William the Conqueror had done in England, time to solve the problem of collection, and time to get the machinery of government working smoothly. In order to obtain this breathing space the lands were leased for five years to their existing holders on the most advantageous terms obtainable.

The problem of revenue collection came next. How was it possible to insure honesty and just dealing in this important branch of government? The existing system was unsatisfactory. It placed excessive power in the hands of the English officials—the so-called supervisors—which most of them were unfit to exercise. "They are most of them the agents of their own banyans, and they are devils," was Hastings's terse verdict. [2] Nor did he hope for any improvement under the existing conditions. Eighteen years of experience, watching the results of close contact between the dominant West and the subject East, had convinced him that the Indian would not obtain fair treatment from the European, so long as the Government was without means to subject the European to the rigid control of the law.

"There is a fierceness in the European manners, especially among the lower sort, which is incompatible with the gentle temper of the Bengalee and gives the former such an ascendent as is scarce supportable even without the additional weight of authority. By the principle of justice the inhabitants of every country are entitled to share of its emoluments, and happily the dictates of reason and sound policy concur in giving this privilege to people, whom as our subjects we are bound to protect, and whose subjection is the best pledge for the faithful execution of the trust reposed in them."

Hastings could see but one satisfactory solution: that of withdrawing all Europeans from the country districts, leaving the work of local administration in the hands of native officials, and centralizing the Government at Calcutta.

He would have liked to have adopted this plan immediately, but dared not attempt it. Officials resent being deprived of their posts, and he feared that the measure would "provoke an army of opponents against every act of Administration." He showed his resourcefulness by ostensibly letting them remain, but changing their title to that of "collector," reducing their power and quietly paving the way for their removal. He was satisfied to move slowly and cautiously towards his ultimate object, which was that of bringing government into direct touch with the landed property owners and abolishing intermediate agencies.

By the end of May Hastings was ready to undertake the next part of his program, which was the establishment of the Company's authority in every part of the government of Bengal. Accordingly, he left Calcutta on June 3 and went up to Murshidebad, where he remained for the next two and a half months.

It is not a little ironical that the man who only eight years before had been the champion of the native government against his own countrymen should now have to deliver the *coup de grâce* to it. But the change in his own attitude showed only how completely the situation as a whole had changed, for he was now whole-heartedly in favor of what he would before have equally strongly opposed. The step was indeed unavoidable. Since there was no longer room for two rival and incompatible governments, the old had to give way to the new, if there was to be any hope of restored order and good government. "You must establish your own power or hold it dependent on a superior, which I deem to be impossible"—so wrote Hastings to his employers. [3] Such action meant a revolution in the government—and revolutions, however peaceful and tenderly carried out, always involve some hardship to individuals. Yet, if it was to be done at all, it had to be done thoroughly and completely. There had to be nothing left of the former régime that might conflict with British supremacy. That meant destroying every thread of the extensive network of power and influence that Mohamed Reza Khan had built up for himself during his seven years in office. Hastings may have known some regrets at having to destroy the last relics of Mogul rule, but his mind was now concentrated on the splendid new State that he was planning to build in its stead.

He set about the disagreeable task with tact, caution and delicacy, and was able to effect everything without provoking violence or resentment. The chief change was, of course, in the Nawab's position. Deprived of the powers of government, he was henceforth to be nothing more than a pensioner of the Company and, as such, he needed only a stipend sufficient to support his dignity and provide for his numerous family. The Directors had ordered his stipend to be reduced from thirty-two lakhs to sixteen, and this was accordingly done. His pension list and other expenses were then carefully examined with a view to a similar reduction. As the prince was a minor, new arrangements had to be made for the management of his affairs, which had hitherto been part of Mohamed Reza Khan's duties. As his guardian until he came of age Hastings selected the widow of Mir Jafar, Munny Begum, in preference to the Nawab's mother who, by right, had the better claim. It was an excellent appointment, for Munny Begum at once revealed a firm grasp of administrative affairs. Hastings wanted a person who would look only to his government for authority, and by appointing Munny Begum he gained his object. The relations between them were always most cordial. To the post of Diwan, or Master, of the Household he appointed Rajah Goordass, but to this selection hangs a tale. It introduces us to the dark and ominous figure of Nuncomar,[1] whose son Rajah Goordass was.

It is a curious and significant commentary on the way in which Indian history has been presented to British readers that the three Indian celebrities whose names are best known to them, are indeed as "familiar as household words," should be "villains." If they can recall little else of their school-days' reading of Macaulay and the traditional stories of the Indian Mutiny, they can at least recall the names of Siraj-ud-Daula, Nuncomar and Nana Sahib and the lurid details of

[1] The correct spelling of his name is Nanda-kumar, but long usage makes the old form more familiar and therefore, perhaps, preferable.

their misdeeds—and with the name of Nuncomar they no doubt couple that of Warren Hastings!

That Nuncomar was an arrant and accomplished scoundrel is indisputable. In his picturesque way he personified the conventional novelist's idea of an Oriental villain. The subtle, underground plots and conspiracies were all abundantly present in his life. Perjury, bribery, intrigue, forgery, theft, fabrication of evidence, subornation of witnesses—these were his stock-in-trade and in his handling of them he was a past master. When he enters our story his criminal record was already of a remarkable length.

He and Mohamed Reza Khan were the two most prominent and wealthy noblemen of Bengal of their day, one a Brahmin, the other a Moslem, and they were bitter enemies and rivals. It was Nuncomar's dearest ambition to ruin Mohamed and supplant him as Diwan, and when the Moslem was deposed and held for trial he thought his chance had come. The Directors had privately suggested to Hastings that the Brahmin's abilities and disposition might be put to good use by employing him in the investigation of his rival's conduct, and that if his services proved useful he might be rewarded in such manner as Hastings saw fit; always providing that he was not given any place of trust or authority, since the Directors were well acquainted with the man's character.

These secret instructions—they were not to be divulged even to the Council—put Hastings in a false and very difficult position. For more reasons than one he had no wish to appear to be Nuncomar's patron. Not only was Nuncomar's reputation notorious throughout the length and breadth of Bengal but the Governor had private grounds of his own for hating the man: Nuncomar had crossed his path when he was in Bengal before. "From the year 1759 to the time when I left Bengal in 1764," he told his employers, "I was engaged in a continued opposition to the interests and designs of that man, and in the course of this contention I received sufficient indications of his ill-will to have made me an irreconcilable enemy, if I could suffer my passions to supersede the duty which I owe to the Company." [4] But at this time Hastings had no other thought than to obey both the spirit and the letter of his instructions, and accordingly he did exactly what he was told to do and employed Nuncomar in the unpleasant task of uncovering incriminating evidence against Mohamed Reza Khan. The Brahmin's reward was the appointment of his son as the Begum's Diwan, which served the additional purpose of furthering Hastings's plans to uproot the late minister's influence.

The appointment naturally provoked much adverse criticism in Bengal, notwithstanding the fact that Rajah Goordass had not inherited his father's evil character but was an inoffensive person; and Hastings, unable to divulge the Company's instructions, was hard put to it to give a plausible explanation to his indignant Council. Only with the utmost difficulty was he able to get them to confirm the appointment.

Nor was Nuncomar satisfied. He had confidently reckoned on receiving his hated rival's post. Instead, he found the post abolished and himself left out in the cold. As a result he turned his anger against Hastings. He lusted for power but he knew that power would be denied him so long as this man was Governor. As it was never his way to forget a grudge, he bided his time waiting for an opportunity to revenge himself. And before very long it came. . . .

Hastings's next step was to remove the principal offices of government from Murshidebad to Calcutta. These included the Chief Court of Revenue and the Superior Courts of Justice, which he then reorganized to fit in with the new system and placed under the immediate control of the Council. These measures made Calcutta the seat of government of the provinces of Bengal and Bihar, destining it to become (until 1912 when it was moved to Delhi) the capital of all India, as the Empire expanded and consolidated. With a prophetic eye Hastings looked forward to the time when the settlement that Job Charnock founded would be "the first city in Asia." However, he was far from thinking that Calcutta was the ideal capital. Indeed, ten years later he expressed the decided opinion that "the permanency of the British dominion in India can never be insured while Calcutta continues to be the capital of it." He condemned it heartily, because of its inaccessibility (except, of course, by water), its situation on the periphery, instead of at the center, of Bengal, its insalubrity, and the depressing effect it exercised on those who resided there. In a minute to the Council, dated June 4, 1782, he suggested removal of the seat of government to Colgong, which was situated in the center of the province and in a much more healthy locality. [5]

II

THE plan for the Administration of Justice, the second of Hastings's great legislative measures, was issued on August 15. In no sphere of the government had the collapse of native rule been more complete. In fact, Hastings's first impression was that the province was without any courts of law at all. Certainly in the districts the old Mogul courts had largely vanished, having been displaced by those maintained irregularly by zemindars and other local officials, who dispensed in them their own individual brands of "justice," capricious, arbitrary and usually oppressive. Under the new plan these irregular jurisdictions were abolished and properly constituted courts for civil and criminal suits were set up in each district, to which the *ryot* could have ready and easy access. In default of any better qualified legal body to act as a Court of Review and Appeal Hastings had to add this fresh responsibility to the many that these far-reaching changes were laying upon the Council. And it was a heavy responsibility indeed, because as Hastings admitted, there was not a lawyer among them. He arranged that they should have the assistance of native lawyers to expound the law. Finally, in order to increase the efficiency of the system, he issued a number of regulations designed to simplify legal procedure, all of which possessed no little merit, especially in view of the fact that they emanated from the mind of a man who had no pretensions to legal knowledge.

The governing principle of his policy appears nowhere clearer than in these judicial reforms. It was Preservation, not Innovation. The net result of them, he said, was "little more than a renewal of the laws and forms established of old in the country, with no other variation than such as are necessary to give them their due effect, and such as the people understand and were likely to be pleased with." [6] Years of lawlessness had corrupted and distorted the original institutions, and all such vicious growth he sought to cut away. But he was adamantly opposed to the idea of superseding the indigenous system with new-fangled courts, codes, and juridical principles imported from abroad, much superior though they might seem to most Western minds. "Who was it," asked Hastings of Dupré, "that said that he had given such laws to his people as they were capable of receiving, not the best that could be framed? On a similar principle we have suffered one capital defect to remain in our constitution—I mean the collectors." [7] And it was on the same principle that he fashioned his law-courts.

Already reports were reaching him from England of a grand new judicial system that a beneficent Parliament was preparing to give to the poor, benighted and downtrodden people of Bengal, as the sure cure for all their ills. "We have been very unfortunate in the time which we have chosen for our judicial improvements," wrote Hastings to Dupré, to whom he was able to speak his mind freely; "for we cannot undo what we have done; and if the Lord Chief Justice and his judges should come amongst us with their institutes, the Lord have mercy upon us! We shall be in a complete state of confusion here, and we shall be cruelly mauled at home, for we have not a lawyer among us. Necessity compelled us to form some establishment of justice; we chose the best we could; and if this shall not be found so perfect as more time and more knowledge might have made it, it is yet capable of receiving improvement, and is a good foundation for a more complete system of judicature." "Is it not," he added, "a contradiction of the common notions of equity and policy that the English gentlemen of Cumberland and Argyleshire should regulate the polity of a nation, which they know only by the lacs which it has sent to Great Britain, and by the reduction which it has occasioned in their land-tax?" [8]

In the hope of forestalling this measure he wrote to his friend Lord Mansfield, the Lord Chief Justice of England, pointing out to him that the prevailing notions in England about Hindu law were entirely mistaken. It was being asserted that written laws were unknown among them. "Nothing can be more foreign from truth," he asserted. "They have been in possession of laws, which have continued unchanged from the remotest antiquity, and the members of their legal profession were held in the greatest respect and consequence." [9]

To prove the truth of this assertion, as well as to assist the new courts in their work, he caused a compilation of the laws to be made. "For that purpose," he told Lord Mansfield, "ten of the most learned pundits were invited to Calcutta from different parts of the province, who cheerfully undertook this work, having incessantly labored in the prosecution of it, and have already, as they assure me, completed it, all but the revisal and correction of it. This code they have written in their own language, the Sanskrit. A translation of it is begun under the inspection of one of their body into the Persian language, and from that into English. The first two chapters I have now the honor to present to your Lordship with this, as a proof that the inhabitants of this land are not in the savage state in which they have been unfairly represented, and as a specimen of the principles which constitute the rights of property among them."

At first sight it might seem that Hastings's instant hostility to the very idea of an English court of law for Bengal was unwarranted and a sign of wounded pride. To some extent this is probably true. He was consumed by one great ambition surpassing for the time being all others; that was to carry through to completion the work that he had begun. He was founding a new state on the ruins of the old. That new state was his. He had laid out the ground plan, he was building the structure, stone by stone, and he was maturing his plans for the future stages. No one else could carry out those plans so well as he the architect, and he was jealous of what he regarded as his right to be allowed to carry them to completion. He prayed fervently to be left alone. Saint-Simon reminds us that "in order to do something great, one must be passionate." Hastings was doing something great—and he was passionate. The barest hint that Parliament might interfere with his schemes was received by him with the deepest misgivings, not unmixed with resentment. Knowing what a jaundiced view it took of Indian affairs and how ignorant people at home were on the subject, he felt no confidence at all in their ability to legislate wisely. Indeed, his worst fears seemed about to be realized and the success of his plans endangered.

But, it may be asked, was it not unreasonable and paradoxical for him to oppose the introduction into Bengal of the strong arm of English law clothed in all the majesty of a Supreme Court by Act of the Imperial Parliament? Was not such a court and its terrors exactly what was needed to impose discipline and regard for the law upon the licentious Europeans? Was it not exactly what Hastings needed for the full realization of his plans and hopes? No answer to these questions can be given without considering all that was involved in the proposal. It is particularly necessary to consider the state of English law at this time, something that Hastings knew but we have to remind ourselves of.

The age in which Hastings lived saw a conflict between two broad streams of English thought upon the established order of government

and law. One was predominant, and because of this predominance, the
age has been termed "the age of Blackstone," Sir William Blackstone
being its most typical representative. The key-note of his writings was
a supreme and aggressive optimism. England was the most blessed of
countries because of its glorious constitution, "the best birthright and
the noblest inheritance of mankind." His *Commentaries* are a panegyric on the Laws and Liberties of England and, pervaded as they are
with a feeling of complacent satisfaction and patriotic pride, "they express the sentiment not of an individual, but of an era." [10] They did
not, however, express the sentiments of all the individuals in that era.
A new spirit was moving the waters of English thought even during the
years (1760 to 1790) when Blackstone ruled: the spirit of humani-
tarianism. And it was far removed from the comfortable feeling of
vainglorious contentment that intoxicated Blackstone and his disciples.

The essence of the humanitarian movement has been defined as "a
deep-rooted aversion from physical pain or moral suffering, together
with the consequent desire to put an end to all manifest forms of
cruelty, oppression, injustice." The cruelty and callousness of the age
was what gave rise to the movement and invested it with a compelling
power over the minds and emotions of sensitive people, arousing in its
adherents an intense ardor to do battle for the cause. There was, for
instance, the Curé Meslier in France who on his death-bed asked the
pardon of God for having been a member of a church that had inflicted
such miseries on the poor in the name of Christ. There was Voltaire,
the greatest intellectual force in Europe for half a century, the scathing
enemy of cruelty, oppression and cynical indifference, using his vast
influence to destroy the established order. There was, also, Rousseau,
the child of nature. The movement had many manifestations and enrolled men of vastly different temperaments and ideas—Edmund Burke,
for example, who feared and detested the doctrines of Rousseau. A
mighty river, it poured like the Ganges through many channels.
Some, solicitous for the interests of the depressed peasants, sought to
encourage agriculture. Others, economists, sought to free enterprise by
breaking down trade restrictions and the artificial restraints of the old
order. In the religious field in England it led to that increased emphasis
on the Humanity as opposed to the Divinity of Jesus which produced
Unitarianism. A matter of feeling not of dogma, it inspired atheists
and skeptics in France equally with High Churchmen and Evangelicals
in England. Turgot striving to save the *ancien régime* of France by
financial reform, and Wilberforce striving to abolish the Slave Trade,
were both proofs of how widely and diversely the leaven was at work.

On the Continent the attention of the reformers was largely centered on social and political reform. In England, where there was less
need for such reform, the movement took a somewhat different course.
There the tyrant to be overthrown was not the monarchy, the church,
or the nobility, but the law. The sixteenth century had destroyed the
authority of the Church, the seventeenth the Divine Right of Kings, but

the eighteenth groaned under the new tyranny set up in their place. In the constitutional field it resisted parliamentary reform; in the religious it resisted Catholic Emancipation and the claims of Nonconformity. But most oppressive of all was the manner in which the law treated the least fortunate members of society—criminals, slaves, lunatics, and the poor. The barbarous punishments, the vile prisons, the hideous slave-trade, the atrocious lunatic asylums, the inefficient courts, the gross miscarriages of justice—these were the objects that chiefly absorbed the reforming zeal of the English humanitarians—William Wilber-force, John Howard, and, in the next century, Jeremy Bentham and Samuel Romilly, to name but four of a noble army.

These were the two main streams of social and political thought in England during the years of Hastings's maturity, and the two books that exercised the widest influence on each were both published during the period after his first return home. It is not extravagant to suppose that he read them both. The one was Blackstone's *Commentaries,* which appeared between 1765 and 1769. The other was the work of a young Italian named Beccaria and was called *Dei Delitti.* Published in Italy in 1764, it appeared in an English translation four years later and quickly ran through several editions. By asking a number of those fundamental questions about Law which Blackstone ignored—what is the object of Law and of punishment, for instance—it drew men's attention to the appalling condition of English criminal law and in-spired the work of reform. It made them conscious of the fact that the laws were unbelievably obsolete and rested on custom and tradition instead of on reason and justice, that they were chaotic, appallingly technical, and for the most part entirely concealed from common view by masses of verbiage, and that the punishments they imposed seldom fitted the crimes committed. It made them wonder whether after all it was rational or just to impose the death penalty on innumerable petty offenses, and made them realize that there could be no justice for the poor so long as the processes of law were expensive, slow, uncertain and vexatious. Finally, it was to prepare the way for Bentham, who was to declare that judges were more maleficent than the worst criminals they sent to the gallows and that the laws of England were "made by judges for the benefit of judges."

Among the many manifestations of the humanitarian spirit there was no area of human activity where it had a profounder or more beneficial influence than in the treatment of the subject peoples of India. Edmund Burke was to be the prophet of the new age, the pro-claimer of the doctrine of trusteeship—that "all political power which is set over men ought to be in some way exercised ultimately for their benefit"—and the man who applied the doctrine with special force to India, as he applied it also to Ireland and America. But if Burke was the inspired prophet, Warren Hastings was the man who first applied the new principle in the practical work of administration. He believed as firmly, if not as eloquently, as Burke that the Indian people had rights and that it was the duty of their rulers to maintain them, that their rulers had one fundamental obligation, which was to secure the happiness and prosperity of the people. Burke's noble efforts were made in speech and writing. Hastings spoke and wrote but little, but if actions do speak louder than words, his humanitarian voice should echo down the ages quite as loudly as Edmund Burke's.

The two men did not, however, speak with exactly the same voice. To Burke the Hindus were a backward race for whom the British as the forward race had to act as trustee. [11] A governor was faithless to the trust if he did not govern according to the superior code of Western morality. It was natural that Burke should hold this view as he stood with one foot planted in the camp of the Humanitarians and the other no less firmly planted in the camp of the Blackstonians. The great superiority of the British Constitution, laws, liberties and institutions over those of other lands and races was a basic element in his *credo*. England was to him God's most favored country and he adhered to that conviction all the time that he was championing the cause of the oppressed and downtrodden, whether at home or abroad.

We do not find the same idea expressed in Hastings's writings. His words never imply a belief that the British owed a special duty to the Indians because they were "a backward race." In fact there is a singular freedom of any assumption of moral superiority and higher civilization. When the question arose of framing a system of government and law for Bengal, he was not concerned with abstract speculations regarding the comparative worth, according to some absolute scale of values, of Eastern and Western institutions, but with one question only: which system would conduce most to the happiness and contentment of the people? And he decided emphatically in favor of the Indian. Did not the Moslem rulers, he asked, leave their Hindu subjects in possession of their own laws and customs? The least, therefore, a Christian government could do was to show the same degree of tolerance. "It would be a grievance to deprive the people of the protection of their own laws, but it would be a wanton tyranny to require their obedience to others of which they are wholly ignorant, and of which they have no possible means of acquiring a knowledge."

The fact that Hindu law and custom sanctioned practices repellent to Western minds did not in his opinion invalidate his argument.

"Even the most injudicious or most fanciful customs which ignorance or superstition may have introduced among them, are perhaps preferable to any which could be substituted in their room. They are interwoven with their religion, and are therefore revered as of the highest authority. They are the conditions on which they hold their place in society, they think them equitable, and therefore it is no hardship to exact their obedience to them. I am persuaded they would consider the attempt to free them from the effects of such a power as a severe hardship." [12]

It is plain, therefore, that Hastings's objection to the extension to Bengal of English law to be administered by a body of judges chosen

from Westminster Hall was based on more than personal pique or
vainglory. He may not have held any pronounced views about the merits
or demerits of the English penal code as applied to English conditions,
yet it was a true instinct that caused him to shudder at the thought that
the code might be transplanted to India. Bad enough in all conscience in
England, in India it would be an abomination.

Forty years later, when nearing the close of his long life, Hastings
was to make still clearer what he thought of the idea that the people of
India were a backward race waiting with grateful mien to receive all
the benefits of the superior civilization of their conquerors. The occasion was his friend Lord Moira's (afterwards the Marquess of Hastings) appointment to the Governor-Generalship. Hastings at his request
sent him a memorial of advice in which the following passages occur. [13] They refer particularly to two related trends of British policy
in India at that time (1812); namely, the exclusion of native Indians
from government, accompanied by their relegation to an inferior place
in British-Indian society, and the admission of Christian missionaries.

"Among the natives of India there are men of as strong intellect,
as sound integrity, and as honorable feelings, as any of this Kingdom.
I regret that they are not sufficiently noticed, sufficiently employed nor
respected, so much as they deserve to be. Be it your Lordship's care
(forgive, my good Lord, this imperative style) to lessen this distance:
be their especial Patron, friend and protector, and by your own example
make it the fashion among our countrymen to treat them with courtesy
and as participators in the same equal rights of society with themselves,
in all cases not excepted by the institutions of legal authority. . . .

"I cannot dismiss them [these suggestions] without warning your
Lordship to keep a jealous eye on any attempts of self-authorized or
self-ordained preachers, to introduce their gross superstitions into the
provinces of your jurisdiction, under the name of Christianity. If for
the holy purpose of implanting the faith and doctrine of our blessed
Redeemer on the rational faculties of the people, ministers qualified by
education shall be sent out, and I am sure no other will be, by the
authority of the British state, or of the East India Company, yet even
in that case too much care cannot be taken to obviate the suspicion,
that the hand of Government will be employed to enforce their proceedings, or its influence afforded to them, beyond mere sufferance and
protection. I feel that I tread on dangerous ground; but there is one
argument which has been too vehemently urged, and too popularly
credited, for enforcing the conversion of our Indian subjects to the
Christian religion, which is so contrary to truth and the spirit of Christian charity that I cannot pass it unnoticed. They have been represented
as sunk in the grossest brutality, and defiled with every abomination
that can debase humanity; and it is therefore said, that as we possess
the power, so it is our duty to reform them, nay to 'coerce' them into
goodness by introducing our faith amongst them. If the debasement of
their moral character is the only plea for the positive intervention of
our government to bring about their reformation, indeed, my Lord, it
will be better to leave them as they are, especially that race of them, the

Hindoos, against which these aspersions are particularly fulminated. These I dare to pronounce, and your Lordship will have ample means of knowing, with what truth, are as exempt from the worst propensities of human nature as any people upon the face of the earth, ourselves not excepted. They are gentle, benevolent, more susceptible of gratitude for kindness shewn them than prompt to vengeance for wrongs sustained, abhorrent of bloodshed, faithful and affectionate in service and submission to legal authority. They are superstitious; but they do not think ill of us for not behaving as they do. Coarse as the modes of their worship are; the precepts of their religion are admirably fitted to promote the peace and good order of society; and even from their theology arguments, which no other can afford, may be drawn to support the most refined mysteries of our own. The persecuting and intolerable spirit of Mohammedanism has spared them through a course of three centuries, and bound them into union with its own professors: the least therefore that can be expected from the most liberal and enlightened of all nations, that which providence has appointed the guardian of their civil rights, is to protect their persons from wrong, and to leave their religious creed to the Being who has so long endured it, and who will in his own time reform it."

III

"LOADED with all these materials I returned to Calcutta. Here I now am, with arrears of business of months, and some of years to bring up; with the courts of justice and offices of revenue to set agoing; with the official reformation to resume and complete; with the trials of Mohammed Reza Khan and Raja Shitab Roy to bring on, without materials and without much hope of assistance (*on ne pend pas des gens qui ont un million dans leur poche*), and with the current trifles of the day, notes, letters, personal applications, every man's business of more consequence than any other, complainants from every quarter of the province hallooing me by hundreds for justice as often as I put my head out of window, or venture abroad, and, what is worse than all, a mind discomposed, and a temper almost fermented to vinegar by the weight of affairs to which the former is unequal, and by everlasting teazing. We go on, however, though slowly; and in the hopes of support at home, and of an easier time here when proper channels are cut for the affairs of the province to flow in, I persevere. Neither my health nor spirits, thank God, have yet forsaken me. I should have added to the list of things to be done, an inquiry into the trade in salt, betel nut, tobacco, and rice, carried on by the principal persons of this Government, which their commands have directed me to prosecute, a mark of distinction on which my friends in England congratulate me. Such partial powers tend to destroy every other that I am possessed of."

So he wrote to Dupré on October 8, 1772. [14]

The burden of work that his government had to sustain was indeed staggering. It was humanly impossible for them to give proper care and consideration to every matter. The Company required them to make detailed reports of all their consultations, so that every opinion that a member wished to express had to be carefully written out in full. The labor that this alone involved was immense. Four meetings of Council, and often six, were held each week.

New problems arose to increase the strenuousness of Hastings's life. Every year during the cold season a human plague descended upon Bengal. Bands of wandering beggars—*sunnyasis* and *fakirs,* both Hindu and Moslem—came down from the hills and ravaged the country far and wide, moving in bands of anything from one thousand to ten thousand, bold, fierce and fully armed. Being largely naked and free from the encumbrances of civilized life they moved about with great rapidity, and wherever they appeared they plundered, kidnaped children, and terrorized the countryside. Their incursions had been going on for centuries and the Moslem rulers had troubled as little about them as they had about other classes of pious criminals like the thugs and the dacoits, even at times enlisting them as mercenaries in their State army.

This was an evil that Hastings naturally was not inclined to tolerate, and he was especially concerned about it, not only because of the actual damage done, considerable as this was, but because the incursions of these bandits afforded the people an excellent excuse for withholding the land revenue. Accordingly, when they made their annual appearance early in 1773, he employed every means in his power to drive them out and to keep them out. But he soon found that it was extraordinarily difficult to do either. Their guise of religious zeal made them objects of fearful veneration to the simple and superstitious peasantry, who would not even give information about their movements, despite the most stringent orders of government, so that they would often, Hastings said, "appear in the heart of the province as if they dropped from heaven!" He sent flying columns of sepoys after them to whatever point they were last heard of, and twice—such was the fighting quality of these vagrants—small parties of sepoys were cut up and their commanding officers killed. By March Hastings had no less than five battalions rushing up and down the country in pursuit of the elusive bands. They finally departed, but, notwithstanding the precautions that Hastings took along the frontier to prevent a recurrence, they were frequently heard of in the northern districts right up to the end of the century. To remedy the threatened loss of revenue the Council, on Hastings's suggestion, resolved to admit no pleas for reduction of rent that were not accompanied by concrete proof of property loss.

The *dacoits* were another heritage of evil from the lax days of the Nawabs, which could only be extirpated by measures of the utmost severity. They were a caste of hereditary criminals who also operated in bands of several hundreds, but, unlike the *sunnyasis,* lived in communities and maintained families with the spoil they took from their neighbors. They were the declared enemies of all government and beyond the pale of the law. To exterminate them Hastings decreed the most ruthless punishments: death for the convicted dacoit, slavery for his family and a heavy fine for every inhabitant of his village. Death alone meant little to them, but death dealt to them in the midst of their neighbors and relations, and combined with the ruin of their families, acted as a very strong deterrent. Hastings confessed he knew of no other means that would rid the country of these abandoned wretches.

Equally indicative of the disturbed state of the country, and another consequence of the years of anarchy, was the fact that the Bhutanese, the fierce and warlike tribesmen from the mountains, had descended into the plains and taken possession of the rich and fertile district of Cooch Behar. A whole battalion of troops had to be sent to expel them, and success was not gained without some hard fighting. There were also other semi-savage tribes near the frontier which had to be reduced to subjection and taught the ways of civilized living if Bengal was to enjoy peace and prosperity, but the work went rapidly forward under the powerful impetus that Hastings with his great enthusiasm and energy had imparted to not a few members of the service, both civil and military.

March came, the settlement of the land was completed, and at length Hastings was ready to open the trials of Mohamed Reza Khan and Shitab Roy. But here his ardor left him. The lack of relish he had felt from the time of their arrest had deepened as the futility of the proceedings became clearer. Whether Mohamed Reza Khan was guilty or not he did not pretend to know; nor did he much care, as from the outset he foresaw the impossibility of proving the charges, even with the very active coöperation of Nuncomar. The Moslem had been all-powerful for seven years and had many, too many, friends. There was a mountain of accusation, but scarcely a mole-hill of reliable evidence, and the English officials were too inexperienced and too unversed in the legal ways of the East to penetrate the intricacies of the case, the details of which were largely unintelligible to them.

On one point only was Hastings against the former Diwan: "I will never suffer him, if I can help it, to regain his power. The Directors are mad if they do; for the government of the provinces is now entirely at their disposal, without a competitor for the smallest share of their authority." [15] He cursed every one of the investigations as being utterly baneful; "they are death to my views, as I have not an hour to spare from the business of the day, even if they did not interfere with it." Only fear of his employers' displeasure made him persevere with them at all. As for the trial of Shitab Roy, it was obvious from the beginning that it would end in his acquittal, and he was at a loss to know why he was ever called to account. Shitab Roy had in the past proved himself a brave and loyal supporter of the Company, having fought gallantly on its side in the war with Mir Kasim, and Hastings grieved to see him treated so ungratefully.

Both men were acquitted. Hastings suggested to the Directors that some reparation was due to Shitab Roy, but before anything could be done for him, the unfortunate man died, his heart broken by the humiliation and disgrace he had undergone. The English, Hastings sadly declared, could not expect to be served so loyally again by native noblemen. The inquisitions into the conduct of the Company's servants mostly came to the same abortive end. Only exceptional zeal on the Governor's part could have surmounted the difficulties in the way, and even that might not have sufficed.

On March 23 Hastings issued his third great constructive measure of reform, dealing with the customs duties and trade policy. And here the humanitarian spirit of the age again found expression in his aims and policy. He recognized the principle put forward a few years later by Adam Smith in his *Wealth of Nations,* that the first interest of a sovereign is that the wealth of his people should increase as much as possible.

The trade of the country had been brought by the long-continued misgovernment nearly to a standstill. Nothing had contributed more to stifle it than the innumerable tolls and impositions that had been irregularly levied upon it by every zemindar and petty local official, with the result that the whole commerce of Bengal with the rest of Asia, which at one time had flourished, amounted in 1770 to no more than £100,000. [16] The internal trade was in the same miserable state. The monopoly established by the English and other European merchants had ruined the native trader. The system hitherto in use for the purchase of the silk and cotton cloths had reduced thousands of weavers to a state of virtual slavery; they had not been permitted to work for anybody but their particular master, and consequently they had been systematically defrauded, receiving for their piece-goods much less than the market value. It had been a common practice to keep them constantly in debt and, consequently, at the mercy of their employers.

Under the new regulations the *dustuk,* that fruitful cause of evil, was abolished, according to the instructions of the Directors, and the trade of the province was thrown open to all on an equal basis. The number of customs houses was reduced to five and all irregular customs and tolls were entirely suppressed. A fixed and uniform duty of two and a half per cent was placed on all goods to be paid by everybody alike: the Company, its servants, European merchants and native traders. Furthermore, Hastings sought by every means in his power to increase the foreign trade of the province. He tried especially to break down the barriers which had been raised against commercial intercourse with Bengal by the Vizier of Oude in his fear of quarreling with the English merchants. And he was successful in negotiating commercial treaties both with the Vizier and his feudatory the Rajah of Benares on the basis of equal duties, thus opening up once more to Bengal its great natural highway of trade with the interior of India, the river Ganges. He even looked still further afield, to Tibet, China and Egypt.[1]

In place of the vicious system of buying the cloths for export he

---

[1] See Chapter Twenty-five.

established one of ready-money purchases and declared the weavers free to work for whom they pleased. He knew that the result would be a rise in prices to a more normal level. But he had the wisdom to see that a more prosperous country, capable of returning increased revenue in land rents and customs duties, would more than compensate the Company for a dearer investment. He realized, what as yet his employers did not, that revenue was now more important to the Company than profits from trade, and declared that the Investment was no more than a secondary object of their attention. He tried to elevate their minds above regard merely for their mercantile interests and to make them realize that they were no longer a body of traders but a body of imperial administrators, with very definite duties not only to their shareholders but to their subjects. Yet he had to proceed warily. Any imprudent move or undue frankness on his part, causing the shareholders to think that he was not wholeheartedly caring for their interests, would inevitably have led to his recall. He had of necessity to compromise; always seeking the welfare of the province, whenever possible, without at the same time appearing to sacrifice any essential interest of his employers.

A further big improvement was effected by turning over the entire charge of the Investment to a single official, thus divesting the Governor-in-Council of all but supervisory concern in commercial matters and enabling him to give his whole attention to political and administrative affairs, an object that Hastings had very much at heart.

Only two essentials were now lacking to set the economic life of Bengal once more on a sound basis. One was a sound and stable currency, the other a banking system. And both of them Hastings sought to provide. For the first time Bengal was to know the advantages of being able to do business with a single standard rupee of good quality, issued only from the government mint at Calcutta, in place of rupees of many different values, issued at different places and subject to rapid depreciation.

IV

WARREN HASTINGS's true place was the place that he filled at the beginning of his administration. Great as were his subsequent triumphs in war and diplomacy, magnificent as was the way in which he met and overcame the assault of a great coalition of foreign enemies, superb as was his conduct in the face of adversity, the task for which he was best fitted was that of evolving order out of chaos. This was his pride and his joy, the work that was nearest to his heart and expressed his deepest aspirations. He had no desire for military glory, for the glory that accompanies the conquest and annexation of new provinces. He sought only the more lasting triumphs of peace, the satisfaction of having saved a country from ruin, the credit of having reconstructed its political, social and economic life. The work that he accomplished in this first year of his administration forms one of the most remarkable achievements of modern times. His constructive measures effected a practical revolution in the state of Bengal and laid the foundation of the mighty structure of empire that was to spread from Bengal over the whole of India during the succeeding hundred years. They are his real and most solid monument of fame.

The qualities of mind and character that enabled him to achieve these great results in so brief a time and in the face of tremendous difficulties can now be more clearly discerned. He possessed the finest of all virtues, the mark of true greatness, wholehearted devotion to a great purpose. It sustained him in his hours of physical weakness and mental depression, lent him energy that never flagged, and ruled out all trivial thoughts of self. His mind and intellect were exceptionally powerful and gave him equal facility in grasping the work of every department of government from the highest principles of policy down to the smallest details of application. His industry was prodigious. There was not an official who did not feel the quickening touch of his hand and the consciousness of there being a mind guiding and directing all that he did.

An equally important factor in his success was his ability to handle men. That he possessed such ability is beyond question. As we follow the smooth, swift flow of codes and regulations, we could well believe that the man from whose brain they sprang had dictatorial powers, whereas we know that his constitutional authority was that of *primus inter pares*—but slightly greater than that of the other members of the Governing Council. Indeed, his position was not nearly so strong as that of the Prime Minister in his Cabinet, because the latter is the chosen leader of his party, can both select his own colleagues and demand their resignations, and can dissolve the body to whom he owes his office; whereas Hastings possessed no more tangible supports than the confidence of his distant employers and the strict orders they had given to his colleagues to support him. Whatever else was needed to save him from Vansittart's fate he had to supply himself. In order to establish a moral ascendancy strong enough to give his word the force of a command he required abundant tact and exceptional powers of leadership. That he did establish such an ascendancy from the very beginning is clearly shown by his success in carrying even such an obnoxious proposal as that for the appointment of Rajah Goordass.

Hastings had no love of controversy or strife. His desire was to live in peace with all men, and "it shall never be my fault if I fail in my aim." So it pleased him greatly when, in quite a brief space of time, he and his colleagues were working together in perfect harmony and confidence, having smoothed out their early differences without any bitterness. When once he was assured of their support he was happy. [17]

There were only two men who did not entirely fit into this picture. One was Richard Barwell, and the other was the Commanding Officer of the Bengal Army, Sir Robert Barker. Both of them displayed jealousy of the exceptional authority assumed by Hastings and the use that he made of it. Barwell, the son of a former governor of the province, was a man of more than ordinary ability. His business sense enabled him to amass one of the largest Indian fortunes of his day, while as a member of Council he was distinguished for his proficiency in revenue matters. His letters home are full of complaints of the way in which the Governor tried to make ciphers out of his colleagues, to profit by their labors and monopolize all the credit, while condemning every proposal not emanating from himself. Barwell disclaimed all responsibility for their differences, attributing them wholly to the jealousy of Hastings's temper, "which cannot yield to another the least share of reputation that might be derived in the conduct of his Government." [18] Hastings had his own opinion of Barwell. He considered him contentious, with marked talents for opposition, and he suspected that his fondness for drawing up great schemes of his own, which, when he could not get them accepted by the Council, he sent to England, sprang from a wish to maintain his prestige at home, rather than from a sincere desire to assist the work of the Council; in fact he suspected him of trying to advance his own reputation at the expense of his colleagues. [19] However, Barwell soon moderated his behavior when he began to receive insistent warnings from home, telling him how advisable it was for him to give his whole support to the Governor; and before very long he was to win far greater glory by acting the part of Hastings's faithful ally than he could ever have gained by nursing wounded feelings.

The cause of Sir Robert Barker's discontent was the eternal jealousy of the military for the civil department. Barker believed strongly in the general superiority of the former and tried to claim exclusive control over everything pertaining to it—and much that lay outside it. He believed, for instance, that the conduct of diplomatic relations with the Vizier came within his province, and was mortally offended when Hastings withdrew his agent from the Vizier's Court and substituted one of his own selecting. He was still more mortified when the Governor excluded him from his conference with the Vizier in the summer of 1773. Other grounds of offense were given to him when the Council for reasons of economy disbanded three squadrons of his worthless cavalry without his leave, and again when it countermanded his orders for the movement of the army. Clive had, of course, given a preponderance of power in the government of Bengal to the military department: a soldier himself, the purpose of his expedition in 1756 had been to save the helpless, incompetent civilians from complete obliteration; and ever since the army had had the controlling voice in determining policy. It was Hastings's firm purpose to correct the balance and restore the civil power to its proper place of supremacy, and he succeeded, General Barker not being in a position to wage such a fight as Kitchener waged against Curzon in 1904.

Hastings conducted these disputes with perfect good temper and admirable forbearance. He met Barker's displays of peevishness, his accusations of want of attention and respect, and his bitter reproaches, with nothing more than a mild and dignified remonstrance. Abhorring controversy, he practiced all the arts of bending men to his way of thinking, humoring them, flattering them, reproving them when necessary, though very gently, conciliating them with concessions that meant more to them than to him, but never threatening or upbraiding them, and, above all, never impugning their motives. If want of attention was imputed to him, he was profuse with apologies, and, whatever the occasion, he never failed to be liberal in his expressions of cordial regard and good feeling. The great object that he sought was to obtain compliance with his wishes; unable to dictate, he had to be pliant and, at times, to make sacrifices and compromises which his judgement disapproved. In his controversies with Barwell and Barker he took great pains always to state his case in that lucid, persuasive and vigorous prose of which he was a master, but, having done so, he adhered rigidly to his own views, whether or not he had succeeded in winning over his opponent. For beneath the velvet glove was the hand of a man who was determined, if possible, to have his own way.

V

AT the beginning of November 1773, Hastings received the first intimation of how his employers regarded what he was doing. They had received his reports to September 1 of the previous year, and the letter was dated April 16, showing that over twelve months were required for an exchange of views.

The Directors not only testified their entire approbation of his conduct but assured him "of our firmest support in accomplishing the work you have so successfully commenced." [20] Though there never has been a promise that was worse fulfilled than this, it naturally rejoiced Hastings's heart when he read it. He had been nervous about what they would think of his conduct. He had done his best, but was his best enough? He had left undone things that he was supposed to have done. Even the receipt of this encouraging letter did little to diminish his anxiety lest his omissions might since have turned their smiles to frowns. He had repeatedly promised that he would prosecute the inquiries into the conduct of their servants, but now, replying to their letter, he found himself under the disagreeable necessity of avowing his inability; for reasons, he asserted, outside his control. And though his government had accomplished much, much had necessarily remained neglected. In March he had written to his friend Sykes that while, when he looked back upon what he had done, he sometimes exulted in the thought of having merited the applause of his employers, he oftener dreaded censure arising from the misrepresentations of enemies that he may have made, the disappointment of the Directors' expectations, and their inability to understand exactly what he had done and why he had done it. [21]

The Directors' friendly letter encouraged him to unburden himself to them of his hopes and ambitions. First, he pointed out two major defects in the constitution of his government as experience had taught him. One was the rapid succession of Governors; the other, the undefined powers of members of Council, including the Governor. Both had produced the same bad effects, a want of vigor and consistency in the measures of government and a spirit of diffidence, distrust and intrigue, and a general lack of confidence. The first defect was especially serious because it prevented the growth of a good understanding with the native rulers of India; for no sooner had they come to know a Governor, and confidence was established between him and them, than he was recalled, and they had to begin all over again with his successor. He also pointed out that short terms were conducive to misconduct on the Governor's part as, denied the chance of gaining fame and reputation, he would be tempted to spend his time exploiting the opportunities that the post offered for money-making instead of attending to his duties.

The second defect was even more vital. The Company was still trying to govern India by a committee, and in his opinion it could not be done. Somewhere there must reside a power that could act with vigor and decision. The supreme authority of the Company was too distant and too slow to interpose in times of crisis; its power could not be more than supervisory. The Council was too large and variable and too subject to divisions. He proposed, therefore, a division of power between the Council as a whole, the Select Committee, and the Governor, along lines analogous to the division devised a few years later for the Constitution of the United States of America.

The crucial suggestion related to the Governor's powers. He proposed that he should have the right of acting by his own separate authority and on his own responsibility on such urgent and extraordinary occasions as should in his judgement require it, notwithstanding any contrary decision of Committee or Council. The entire wisdom of this proposal is incontrovertible. "Of this I am certain," he wrote to Laurence Sulivan, "that at some period not far distant, the powers which I have solicited, or greater, will be given, whether it be my lot or that of another to possess them." He was right: this discretionary power was granted, precisely as he suggested, not to him but to his successor, Lord Cornwallis, in 1787.

He did not ask for these enlarged powers with any improper motives of self-interest but on the highest grounds of the public interest. Yet he was quite candid in admitting to the Chairman of the Company "an honest ambition that stimulates me to aspire at the possession of my present station for years to come."

"Those who know my natural turn of mind will not ascribe this to sordid views, a very few years possession of the government would undoubtedly enable me to retire with a fortune amply fitted to the measure of my desires, were I to consult only my own ease; but in my present situation I feel my mind expand to something greater. I have catched the desire of applause in public life. The important transactions in which I have been engaged, and my wish to see them take complete effect, the public approbation which you have been pleased to stamp on them, and the estimation which that cannot fail to give me in the general opinion of mankind, lead me to aim at deserving more; and I wish to dedicate all my time, health and labor to a service which has been so flattering in its commencement." [22]

In the same strain he wrote to Sulivan:

"I must beg leave to add a very bold word in my own behalf, which is, that I do not know a man who may be more safely intrusted with extraordinary powers than myself, or who would be more likely to make a moderate use of them, as I am neither vehement in the pursuit of gain, nor apt to convert the authority which I possess to an instrument of partial favor or enmity to others. I wish to merit reputation, and as I am happily placed in a scene in which, with the aid that I have required, I know myself capable of attaining it, I would sacrifice every consideration to so tempting an object. God forbid that the government of this fine country should continue to be a mere chair for a triennial succession of indigent adventurers to sit and hatch private fortunes in."

His words have the ring of passionate sincerity, and there is nothing in the whole course of his career to make us doubt their utter honesty. Warren Hastings here reveals to us the motive forces of his life. Shakespeare tells us that "Greatness knows itself." Hastings's egotism was the egotism of greatness. He knew his purposes to be high and honorable; he knew, too, that he was the kind of man that was needed for his post. When a man so identifies himself with the public interests as Hastings did now, and continued to do to the end of his Indian service, it is impossible to lay a dividing line between personal ambition and altruism. Hastings wanted glory and fame, as did Nelson, but, like the great admiral, he sought them only in the direct path of duty. It was his consciousness of integrity that made him fearlessly candid and nobly proud. The self-praise was too intensely objective in its cause to be dismissed as mere arrogant conceit and vainglory. It sprang from passion, not from complacency, and was designed to further his aspirations, not to minister to his vanity.

A sad and tragic irony surrounds this petition. His fate, though he knew it not, had already been decreed before he wrote. Five months earlier he had been appointed by Act of Parliament Governor-General of Bengal for a term of five years. Two of his demands had thus apparently been granted without the need of his asking—the dignity, and presumably the authority, of higher rank and the security of a fixed term of reasonable length. Yet in reality the grant was to be nothing but a ghastly mockery of his hopes and ambitions. He had asked for power, but what he had been given was to prove little better than a worthless bauble, a high-sounding but empty title. He had asked for increased authority, and had been given a cabal to deprive him even of what little authority he already possessed. He wanted to win reputation and applause, but instead he was to win a criminal's reward.

Chapter VIII

THE PROBLEM OF SECURITY

WHEN the Directors of the East India Company found themselves possessed of an empire when all that they really wanted was a profitable investment, there was no problem that worried them more than that of defense. Robert Clive and Eyre Coote had between them disposed of the French menace, but they could not treat the native occupants of India quite so summarily. The emergence of the Company as one of the powers of India of necessity involved it in the complicated politics of a continent that was in a constant state of war. There had been no diminution of insecurity. Peace was naturally the object of men who were not empire-builders but merchants. Sir Thomas Roe, King James the First's Ambassador to the Court of the Emperor Jahangir, had put their point of view succinctly when he said, in condemning the idea of basing trading operations on military force, "War and traffic are incompatible." The expense as well as the danger made them put the avoidance of war in the forefront of their policy.

The problem was: How was peace to be obtained in a continent that knew no peace? The Directors said, by pursuing a policy of isolation and eschewing all entangling alliances with native states, by keeping their troops within the borders of their dominions and interfering in no way with the affairs of their neighbors. Yet even with such a pacific policy their hopes were largely chimerical. Statesmen who, like Fox, indulged in similar hopes when Napoleon was at the height of his power were guilty of no more vain a delusion. As in Europe so in India, peace was "a goddess only when she comes with sword girt on thigh."

Hastings wanted peace no less than his employers: and for a very definite and personal reason. If his employers were concerned about their profits, he was concerned about his own handiwork—the reconstruction of Bengal. Any threat to the success of that work caused him pain and anxiety, and what threat was to be more feared than the threat of war and invasion? "A tempest or an earthquake could not be more fatal to a builder whose walls were uncovered and his unfinished columns trembling in the breeze, than the ravages or terrors of war would have been to me and to all my hopes." [1] But he was too practical a statesman to nurse any illusions. There were hard facts that could not be ignored, and it was these facts that made him write to the Chairman of the Company a month after reaching Calcutta, "Yet if the Marathas proceed with the same rapid success which they have hitherto met with, I fear nothing but a war prosecuted against them with vigor at a distance from our borders can insure peace and quiet to Bengal." [2]

The Marathas had again begun to invade Northern India with their strength apparently but little diminished. Each year brought the terror of their arms nearer and nearer to Oude and Bengal, and as their armies triumphed so did their confidence and insolence renew themselves. In 1771 they occupied Delhi, and in the same year they renewed their demand on Bengal for *chauth* (blackmail). May of that year saw the defection of the Mogul Emperor from the side of the English. Forsaking their protection and alliance, he chose to throw himself into the arms of the Marathas, and on Christmas Day he was escorted by them back to his old capital.

The next year the Marathas advanced as far as Rohilkhand under the very shadow of the Himalayas. Invading it, they drove the inhabitants to take refuge in the forests and marshes, spread fire and sword through the land, then openly boasted that Oude and Bengal would be the next to suffer the same fate. The greatest alarm prevailed in both countries and was shared by their respective governments.

It was at this critical moment that Hastings arrived from Madras. The danger was at its height during the weeks immediately before he assumed the government. And he had every reason, therefore, to be apprehensive of an unavoidable war. While assuring the Directors that he had the firmest intention of adhering to the strictly defensive policy they had laid down, he did not guarantee that he would be able to do so. The Directors allowed for the possibility of absolute necessity demanding more vigorous action, and Hastings foresaw that this necessity was "likely to be brought to a nearer period than we could wish," and he warned them, too, that he would "sedulously promote every undertaking which can complete the line of our own possessions or add to its security." [3]

One thing was clear to him. Oude had to be defended at all costs. Bengal and Oude together were a geographical unit, forming part of a continuous plain inclosed by the Himalayas to the north and the Ganges to the west and south, with no natural frontier dividing them. Should Oude fall into hostile hands Bengal would lie exposed to invasion. The Ganges was, therefore, the natural military frontier of Bengal; and along the greater part of its length it was an excellent barrier owing to its unfordability. But there was one point where it was weak. This was where the river breaks through the Himalaya wall and flows on to the central Indian plain. Not yet fed by its numerous tributaries it is at this point still a small stream and during the dry spring months before the melting of the snows on the mountains it is easily fordable. The crux of the strategic problem of defense lay in the fact that the country immediately to the east of this weak spot, known as Rohilkhand, was not part of the Vizier's dominions and, therefore, was outside the limits imposed by the Company for the employment of their troops.

Some forty years before, during the general disruption of the Mogul Empire, this fertile district with its six millions of Hindu inhabitants had been seized by a numerous band of Pathan soldiers of fortune from Afghanistan called Rohillas, who had settled upon the land with their families and mercenaries and proceeded to live upon the wealth produced by the Hindu cultivators in a manner familiar in Indian history. "They sowed not, neither did they reap." Their rule was no worse than that of most of the Moslem conquerors from the north, but they were a constant thorn in the side of their neighbors. Being Pathans, they were naturally turbulent, treacherous, cruel, and warlike.

Under different circumstances Hastings would undoubtedly have wanted to leave them alone, but it was clear to him from the beginning that Rohilkhand held the key to the security of Bengal and that it would be well to have that key in safe keeping. It was to Bengal what the Khyber Pass was to India—the gateway of invasion. As early as March 1772 he had recognized the desirability of joining the country to Oude. [4] At that moment the Marathas were in possession and threatening to carry their ravages into Oude and Bengal. The Rohillas, riven by internal feuds, had proved unable to defend their territory.

Hastings was keenly conscious of the insecurity of the British position. As he saw it, they were still clinging precariously to a weak foothold and in imminent danger of being swept away by the Maratha flood. He may have exaggerated the peril and underestimated the ability of the Bengal army to meet and repel invasion, but terror of the Marathas was intense and universal. The fact that the British troops had not yet had to meet a Maratha army in battle added an element of the unknown to the well-grounded fear that their name inspired. And there was still the Maratha Ditch at Calcutta to bear silent witness to their military prowess.

Nor was the Company's government doing much to improve the situation. Instead of deciding on a definite course of action and pursuing it, it was afraid to commit itself, and as a consequence its policy was weak and vacillating. Sir Robert Barker exercised the chief political influence and, while he may have been a thoroughly competent soldier, his ideas on policy were distinctly limited. Oude was the Company's only ally and the only barrier against the Maratha menace, yet the military mind was unable to regard it in any other light than as a danger to Bengal. It failed to realize how entirely the position had changed since the Vizier had united his forces with Mir Kasim against the Company; instead of looking upon him as a valuable ally and buttress and doing everything possible to strengthen him, it continued to regard him with the deepest suspicion and jealousy.

Hastings at once changed the whole spirit and direction of British policy. The alliance with Oude, as it stood, was thoroughly unsatisfactory to both parties. To the Vizier, because he did not derive from it the whole-hearted support of the Company to which he was entitled. To the Company, because it was a source of much expense. The misguided policy of "taking every occasion to reduce the Vizier's strength and peck at his authority" had so weakened him that now on every little alarm the Company's army had to run to his assistance, and the subsidy that he paid for such aid by no means covered the cost involved. [5] A special brigade had had to be formed in order to carry out the terms of the alliance, the greater part of the expense of which was borne by the Company, an arrangement which seemed to Hastings manifestly bad. Furthermore, he ridiculed the idea that Bengal had anything to fear from Oude, and made up his mind to strengthen the Vizier in every possible way, so that his alliance should be an asset instead of a liability. He wanted to win his confidence and make him feel that the Company had no other object in their mutual alliance than mutual security. Above all, he wanted him to be left the uncontrolled master of his own dominions, an independent ruler and not a second Nawab of Bengal.

The immediate state of affairs that confronted him in April did not greatly perturb him. He felt sure that the season was too far advanced for the Marathas to attempt the invasion of Oude that year. He attributed the failure of the Vizier to attack them when they invaded Rohilkhand to the hesitation of the British to promise armed support, the result being that both the Vizier and the Rohillas, left to their own resources, had been secretly negotiating with the Marathas and threatening to join them in alliance. This had to be prevented at any cost. So when the Vizier appealed to Hastings for help, he sent it, notwithstanding his belief that it was at the moment unnecessary. He ordered Barker to occupy the line of the Ganges. And in June the Marathas withdrew before the flood season rendered the river impassable to their horsemen. This gave Hastings a breathing-space to initiate his new policy.

There was another angle to the problem that equally called for attention. A crisis had arisen in the relations of the Company with the Mogul Emperor, or King of Delhi, as he was usually called at this time. Clive had contracted to pay him an annual tribute of twenty-six lakhs in return for the Diwani rights of Bengal, and had in addition given him the provinces of Cora and Allahabad, formerly part of the Vizier's dominions, "for the support of his dignity and expenses"—which was, perhaps, an unnecessarily generous concession considering the respective positions of the Emperor and the Company and the fact that it made the latter the only one of the Indian states to pay him any tribute at all, let alone over a quarter of a million pounds. In view, however, of the Emperor's action in placing himself under the protection of the Marathas, the question had at once arisen: should the Company go on paying him tribute, the strain of which on their reduced and embarrassed finances was nearly breaking the Bengal government, when every rupee of the money was going straight into the Maratha war-chest?

Hastings did not hesitate over the answer. On March 26, 1772, he wrote to the Chairman, Sir George Colebrooke:

"In the King we have another idol of our own creation to whom we have bound ourselves to pay an annual tribute, and most punctually have we paid it even when he was in arms against us, for such I consider the cause he is now engaged in. His title, dignity, state, and the territory which he possesses, he holds by our bounty; and what has he given us in return? a piece of paper which acknowledges our right to the dewannee (Diwani) of Bengal, a right which we can have no pretense to hold from him, because we denied his right to possess a single acre in either of the provinces. We hold the sovereignty of them by the best of all titles, power. He could not transfer what he never had to give; and twenty-six lakhs of rupees are rather too much to give away annually for the purchase of a flimsy argument, not intrinsically worth three halfpence. You have been deceived, if you were told that the Powers of India set any value on the King's grants. They laugh at them. Not a state of India ever paid him a rupee, not one of his natural subjects offered any kind of submission to his authority, when we first fell down and worshiped it. Yet for this idle pageant we have drained the country, which has a right to our protection, of its current specie, which is its blood; for him we continued to exhaust it of its wealth, while we wanted means to furnish the necessary expenses of the Company, while we draw on them for crores and run them crores in debt, and to this wretched King of shreds and patches are we almost to this day sending supplies of treasure to enable the only enemies we have in India to prosecute their designs of universal conquest, which if successful must end in our destruction; for the Marathas are not his protectors on the principles which we observe. We have been his tools, the instruments of his grandeur. He is theirs and his name, authority, wealth, and all he possesses is theirs with his person." [6]

Holding such views it was natural that as soon as Hastings became Governor he should withhold all further payments until compelled to resume them by the orders of his employers, and such orders never came.

Early in the next year the situation again became acute. The Marathas compelled the Emperor to cede to them his two provinces and announced their intention of taking immediate possession. If they had been allowed to carry out this intention there would then have been a second gap in the defensive line of the Ganges through which they could have sent their armies, taking Oude between two fires. Hastings replied by repudiating the Emperor's right to alienate the provinces and ordering Barker to hold them against the Marathas.

An attempt had been made in the previous year to close the other gap. Through the mediation of Sir Robert Barker a treaty had been signed between the Vizier and the Rohilla chiefs under the terms of which the Vizier undertook, in return for a promised payment of forty lakhs of rupees, to defend the territory of the Rohillas from Maratha attack, "either by peace or war." The General stood as guarantor on behalf of the Company for its performance. Yet, even at the time of its negotiation, the Rohillas were suspected of having secretly gone over to the side of the Marathas, and the Vizier himself was not dependable. If the line of the Ganges was to be held, the Bengal army would have to hold it. And so when with the arrival of spring a Maratha army of fifty thousand horsemen once more crossed the Ganges and entered Rohilkhand, Barker, acting under Hastings's orders, advanced to meet them, accompanied by the Vizier and his army. The approach of the allied forces caused the Marathas to retreat in haste, and the danger passed when dissensions at Poona led to the recall of their armies from Northern India.

The Vizier had in this way carried out the terms of his treaty with the Rohillas, but he received from them not one of the stipulated rupees, and their whole attitude had been doubtful and wavering. As Barker aptly put it, their game was to "treat with both parties and adhere to neither." This duplicity and bad faith on their part gave the Vizier his opportunity. He had long coveted possession of Rohilkhand but had not felt strong enough to attack its warlike rulers single-handed. So he suggested that the Bengal Government lend the assistance of its troops for the purpose. Hastings now decided that the time had come for a general settlement of all these questions. He arranged a meeting with the Vizier at Benares and left Calcutta on June 24, 1773, armed with plenipotentiary powers from the Council. He reached Benares on August 19 and found the Vizier awaiting him.

In the negotiations that now took place, the treaty that resulted from them, and the expedition against the Rohillas to which it led, a new aspect of Hastings's character as a statesman appears. In his handling of the problems of internal administration he was governed by liberal and enlightened ideas, far in advance of his time. He was the idealist striving for perfection in the new State he was constructing. In his handling of problems of politics and foreign affairs, he was a realist, a man of his time, content to adhere to the standards of political morality of that age and to employ the methods of political action sanctioned by it. In fact, he came very close at times to putting into practice the maxim, "the end justifies the means." He was essentially the opportunist, grasping with both hands his chances as they occurred, without being over-fastidious about the details. He was extremely resourceful and, like many men so gifted, occasionally lacking in scruple. Less speed of decision and more hesitation might have lessened his success as a statesman but not his standing in the eyes of posterity. True, he never allowed considerations of any narrow, self-regarding prudence to dictate his course of action. He was courageous often to the point of rashness in making decisions on his own responsibility, and he was seldom deterred from following his own judgement by any fear of censure. He felt that the man on the spot should be allowed to use his own judgement, especially in dealing with a complex and constantly shifting situation, without being subjected afterwards to ill-informed criticism by the people at home, and even the knowledge, gained from long and bitter experience, that the people at home would not grant him that right did not prevent him on future critical occasions from doing what he, thinking always alone, deemed necessary or advisable for the good of the State and of the Company.

It must be admitted, too, that Hastings held views about political action that were incompatible with the theory of popular responsible government. "It is impossible to avoid errors," he declared shortly before he became Governor; "and there are cases in government in which it may be necessary to adopt expedients which are not justified on such principles as the public can be the judges of." [7] Dangerous doctrine, indeed! Would he also, one wonders, have subscribed to the dogma that the necessity of the State is the supreme law?

The two great ends that Hastings had in mind when he met the Vizier were, first, to make Bengal safe from invasion along its western boundary, and, second, but equally important, to relieve the financial distress of his government. The thought that must have been uppermost in his mind as he sailed up the Ganges was the imminent danger of bankruptcy. These grim facts could never be forgotten: the country was so ruined by famine and anarchy that its revenues had enormously diminished, the balance-sheet showed a large deficit, the public debt amounted to £1,500,000, the credit of the government was exhausted, the treasury contained only 50,000 rupees, the financial remedies that Hastings had applied could only take effect slowly, and the Company was urgently demanding remittances to relieve its own embarrassed finances at home. If ever there was a situation demanding exceptional action, it was surely this; and its pressing urgency goes a long way towards justifying Hastings for the means that he took to extricate his employers from their desperate straits.

The first matter of importance to be settled at the conference was the disposal of the Emperor's alienated provinces. As the Governor flatly refused to recognize his right to cede them to the Company's most powerful enemies, there were only two possible alternatives: they must either be annexed by the Company or be handed back to their former possessor. Hastings rejected the first because of the distance of the provinces from Bengal, their exposed position, and his pronounced aversion to enlarging the Company's dominions and increasing its political and administrative responsibilities. He chose the second alternative and at the same time drove a good bargain with the Vizier by selling the provinces to him for the sum of fifty lakhs, twenty of which were to be paid in ready cash. This, he was frank enough to admit, was "a very advantageous compensation for a territory which perhaps ought in policy to have been given to him, even though no return had been made for it."

To a peremptory demand of the Emperor not only for the restitution of the provinces but for the tribute of Bengal with full arrears, Hastings replied with an equally peremptory declaration that not a rupee should pass from the provinces till they had recovered from the distresses to which the lavish payments made to him had principally contributed. He saw no use in excuses and evasions and was quite convinced of the justice of his stand, though there were many persons, both in Bengal and at home, who thought differently.

The second matter was the subsidy paid by Oude for the Company's military aid. The Vizier agreed to pay all the expenses of one brigade of the Bengal army for such periods as he required its services, these being placed constantly at his disposal for the defense of his dominions; and he accepted the computation of the British commander, which fixed them at 210,000 rupees a month. The obvious effect of this arrangement was to make it highly advantageous to the Company for the Vizier to employ the brigade as often and for as long as he wished, as the Company would then be relieved of its expense and at the same time the security of its own provinces would be increased.

At the back of, and to some extent conditioning, both these arrangements lay the Vizier's proposal for the annexation of Rohilkhand. He laid a tempting offer before Hastings: payment to the Company of forty lakhs of rupees, and all the expenses of its troops for the duration of the campaign.

Consideration of the Vizier's offer brought Hastings face to face with a perplexing problem. Acceptance would lead to some very solid advantages for his government: completion of the natural line of defense for Oude and Bengal, termination of a constant source of trouble on the Vizier's exposed northern flank, acquisition of a large sum of money for his empty treasury, and the profitable employment of the Company's troops for a considerable period. And he could see no corresponding disadvantages to offset these tangible gains. At the same time he knew that he stood on dangerous ground. The Directors had given him strict orders not to employ their troops beyond the limits of the Vizier's territory, though they had foreseen the possibility that urgent necessity might compel departure from the rule and their words seemed to imply that they gave their Governor a limited discretionary power. Also, they had promised him further orders to cover all possible eventualities. These orders had not come, and Hastings had to decide for himself whether he should break the letter of his instructions while adhering to their spirit.

Another thought gave him pause. There was a crisis in the affairs of the Company at home. His employers were struggling under a load of embarrassments. He wanted neither to add to them nor to aggravate the fierce popular odium that had lately fallen upon the Company and its servants. With the eyes of the whole nation concentrated on the affairs of the Company and the passions and prejudices of almost every man in the country inflamed against it, he realized that it was not a propitious moment to embark on a new and unauthorized enterprise.

What was he to do? Considerations of statesmanship seemed to him to demand that he accept the Vizier's offer. The operation fitted perfectly into his rapidly maturing scheme for a comprehensive political system for the defense and consolidation of British India; therefore in his eyes it was wise and expedient. On the other hand, the safest course for him personally was to decline. He had little to gain and everything to lose. He knew that it would be extremely easy for his enemies to misrepresent the aims and methods of his policy and for arm-chair critics to exercise their time-honored privilege at his expense. Common prudence pointed one way, uncommon initiative pointed another. Was he to further the national interest and possibly jeopardize his own position, or was he to play safe and let the opportunity slip?

Hastings was not the man to hesitate long over a choice of this sort. He accepted—provisionally at least—the Vizier's proposal, and his acceptance enabled him to win the Vizier's ready consent to his own proposals for the sale of Cora and Allahabad and the increased subsidy. While they were still in conference the Vizier asked leave to suspend the expedition as he doubted his ability to fulfill the conditions. Hastings readily agreed, and no mention was made of the undertaking in the treaty of Benares, which was signed in September.

His mission done, Hastings immediately set out on his return journey, reaching Calcutta inside of a month. Within a week he was able to report to the Directors that his conduct had been approved by the Board, Barker being the sole dissentient. "I am not apt," he said, "to attribute a large share of merit to my own actions, but I own that this is one of the few to which I can with confidence affix my own approbation." [8]

He had, however, made a serious mistake. In making his report to the Council he had said nothing about the Rohilla understanding. Proud as he was of the treaty, he could not help but be uneasy about this part of it. He declared afterwards that he saw no reason to disclose to them something that was merely tentative and not binding as yet on either party (though he did, indeed, tell his employers). In this he was wrong: the expedition had been set aside, but the agreement stood nevertheless. For, at the same time as the Vizier had asked for its suspension he had also asked for a promise of Hastings's coöperation on the terms agreed upon, should he wish to renew the matter at a later date, and Hastings had given it to him. What he had done was to sign and hand over a check without filling in the date of payment. As he had received value for the check, clearly, if the Vizier should ask him to supply that deficiency, he was honor-bound to do so. Consequently, he should have taken the Council into his confidence.

The more he thought about the undertaking the more he seems to have regretted it. Afterwards he even went so far as to say that he had always felt a strong repugnance for it. He nursed the hope that he would not be called upon to make his promise good.

Vain hope! If his consent had all been a piece of bluff, if he thought that he could come away from a business deal with an Oriental prince with all his objects attained and not be called upon later to fulfill his part of the bargain, it must have been because he was not yet fully versed in the difficult art of diplomacy. The Vizier, as it happened, had only delayed the day of reckoning in order to utilize the absence of the Marathas to appropriate territory on the other side of the Ganges. There was little likelihood that he would put it off altogether, for he had long yearned to add the country of the Rohillas to his own.

Early in the next year the Vizier asked that the agreement be renewed and carried out. Hastings was now forced to confess to his Council how it had come about that he was "embarrassed in a peculiar matter." [9] The only way out of the dilemma that he could suggest was to attach such conditions to their consent that the Vizier would forthwith drop the whole matter; to withhold consent entirely he rightly saw was no longer possible. The Council concurred heartily in wishing to avoid the obligation for the same reasons that had weighed on Hastings's mind, but they could suggest no better way out of the difficulty. Hoping and trusting that his solution would have the desired result, they authorized him to lay his terms before the Vizier.

For the moment all was well. The Vizier cried off, and the Governor and his colleagues congratulated themselves on their *finesse* and informed their employers that the affair was now happily terminated in the manner they wished. They could continue as before to be "mere watchful spectators of the distant scene." They spoke too soon. Within a month the Vizier, emboldened by his success in the Doab, definitely renewed his demand and accepted the Council's terms, and the Bengal Government could return no other reply than a consent. For good or ill the expedition had to be undertaken.

A small English force was set in motion at the end of March 1774, under the command of Colonel Champion, who had succeeded Sir Robert Barker as Commanding Officer. In the third week of April it entered Rohilkhand accompanied by the Vizier's army, and within three weeks the country was conquered. One brief but hard-fought battle, in which the Bengal troops did all the fighting, sufficed to overthrow the Rohilla chiefs. Two thousand of their warriors fell, out of forty thousand, and among them was their brave and able leader, Hafiz Rahmat Khan. All that then remained to be done was to occupy the country and reduce to submission the remaining chiefs, who had taken no part in the battle owing to their bitter feuds. But no sooner had the victory been gained than there began all the trouble that was to recoil so heavily on Hastings's head.

It seems certain that Hastings did not foresee all that might, and probably would, happen when he dispatched an English force to act as the subsidized ally of an Indian ruler. He must have realized that

Shuja-ud-Daula's methods of conducting war might prove different from those approved, if not always practiced, by his countrymen. But his attitude was that it was no business of the Bengal Government or the commander of its troops to regulate the Vizier's conduct. Colonel Champion's orders left to the Vizier the power of directing the services to be performed and to the Colonel only the power of directing the military operations necessary for performing them: his sole duty was to fight. But the arrangement of necessity meant the creation of an intimate and, by its nature, extremely delicate relationship between the Colonel and the Vizier, which demanded the exercise of the utmost tact and good sense by the former—and this was something that was woefully lacking from the first.

Hastings's experiences with Barker might have prepared him for trouble with Champion, an officer of the same type, utterly unsuited by temperament and disposition for the rôle he had been called upon to play. Barwell described him as "a character long known among Indians to want every happy distinction." [10] He had all the military distrust of the Vizier, together with an insolent contempt for native ways and susceptibilities. He treated the Vizier without the respect due to his rank and without conforming to the rules of etiquette, intruding upon him whenever he pleased and allowing inferior officers to take part in the interviews. The Vizier naturally resented his conduct and complained to Hastings. Champion retorted by accusing him of committing foul atrocities in the conquered country and ill-treating his prisoners-of-war. He further showed what kind of officer he was by encouraging the demands of his army for prize-money and claiming for it a right to share in the plunder of captured towns and villages, entirely contrary both to the accepted rules of war (since none of these places had been taken by storm) and to his government's agreement with the Vizier. He also abused his discretionary powers and interfered in political matters outside his sphere by conducting negotiations with the defeated Rohilla chiefs. The result was a bitter quarrel between him and the Vizier, which very soon involved Hastings too.

The Governor at once showed that he was not prepared to tolerate such conduct. To Champion's suggestion of prize-money he replied that the very idea was to be avoided like poison. The result of this was that the troops, their appetites whetted by the prospect held out to them by their commanding officer, became mutinous and Champion upheld their cause, waxing eloquent in denouncing the gross injustice to his brave men, who had done all the fighting while the Vizier's rabble had done all the plundering. He ended by condemning the whole policy of the war as a blot on the reputation of the British nation for fair and honorable dealing, and by becoming one of Hastings's bitterest enemies. Fortunately for Hastings's reputation his damning testimony regarding the manner in which the war had been conducted was not supported by any of the other officers who later gave evidence.

As soon as Champion's lurid reports of the Vizier's atrocities and cruelties began to reach him, Hastings wrote to Nathaniel Middleton, his political agent at the Vizier's Court, instructing him to make strong remonstrances against every act of wanton violence. He was to remind the Vizier that the land and its people were now his and had a claim to his protection, that the family of Hafiz Rahmat Khan, which he had taken captive, had done him no injury, and that England abhorred every kind of inhumanity and oppression and enjoined the gentlest treatment of a vanquished enemy. If these arguments did not prevail, then Middleton was to insist, as the honor of the English nation was involved in every act of barbarism committed under cover of the alliance, and Hastings would publicly exculpate his government from the imputation of assenting to such conduct and hold it against the Vizier in the future. [11]

These remonstrances proved effective. Indeed, it soon appeared that Champion had grossly and maliciously exaggerated the outrages. Hastings repeatedly asked him for specific details, but could obtain none. He was most anxious to obtain the fullest information and asked Middleton to make every effort to get it and to support his accounts with the strongest proofs obtainable. "I wish the truth to appear, neither glossed by favor nor blackened by prejudice." But neither Middleton nor any one else was able to discover any evidence that corroborated Champion's story. In fact, no one who has studied the testimony of numerous officers of the expeditionary force given at the inquiry held later by the Bengal Government can be left in much doubt that Colonel Champion either deliberately lied or too willingly accepted as true stories that he heard second-hand.

The truth of the matter is that the expedition was notable, not for its inhumanity, but rather for its freedom from the kind of excesses usually associated with Indian warfare. The cultivators, who formed the vastly greater part of the population, were hardly affected at all. At the beginning of the campaign the Vizier undoubtedly burned a few villages, submitted his prisoners for a time to harsh treatment, and laid his hands on all the wealth he could find, though it would seem that the English army also did its full share of plundering. There is no good reason for believing that the Vizier did anything worse. [12] The war ended with a treaty of peace with the last remaining Rohilla chief Faizulla Khan, who was left in peaceful possession of a considerable part of Rohilkhand under the suzerainty of the Vizier. The majority of the chiefs were driven out to rejoin their countrymen on the other side of the Ganges, together with all their feudal retainers. Some eighteen thousand to twenty thousand persons in all were evicted, many of whom subsequently returned in peace and accepted service under the Vizier. Some three thousand had been killed in battle, being the only ones to lose their lives as a result of the invasion. Those who migrated were allowed to go unmolested, but many remained behind with Faizulla Khan. The land soon took on its wonted aspect with no diminution in its prosperity—at least not until Shuja-ud-Daula died and was succeeded by a worthless and incompetent son, and even then it is difficult to prove that its worse condition was due only and entirely to its change of masters. Oude and Bengal were secured from invasion and never again were they to be so much as threatened by the Marathas at this point in the line of the Ganges.

The whole Rohilla episode would have little importance but for the monstrous and fantastic myth of the destruction of a whole nation that grew out of it, originating in the reports of Colonel Champion, elaborated by Philip Francis, perfected by Edmund Burke, converted into history by James Mill and Macaulay, and still occasionally given currency by careless writers. Hastings has been condemned on the ground that he hired out British troops as mercenaries of an Indian ruler. Against this must be set the fact that it had hitherto been the rule for the European nations to fight their Indian wars as allies of native rulers rather than as principals. The practice had little to recommend it, and happily this was the last instance of the kind. He has also been condemned on the ground that the Rohillas had given the English no provocation. This also is largely true, though it should not be forgotten that the treaty between them and the Vizier had been guaranteed by General Barker on behalf of the Company. The provocation was slight but Hastings thought it sufficient: "We made war on them on just grounds surely, unless any other process than that of the sword can be devised for recovering the rights of nations." [13] It is no justification of him to affirm that many wars have been fought for less cause, but it at least exonerates him from the charge of having committed a "crime."

Again, he has been condemned because he made the war profitable to the Company. This was nothing more than a piece of sheer cant and hypocrisy on the part of his enemies. If he put financial considerations first in his reports, it was because he knew what came first in the calculations of his employers. They were ready to pardon much if financial profit could be shown attaching to it. What would his critics or his employers have said if the war had been *unprofitable?* He did not fight the war for profit, but he had enough common sense not to miss the opportunity to obtain some financial benefit for his impecunious employers from an operation that primarily benefited the Vizier. He himself put the case very sanely and candidly when he told his judges, "I never in any period of my life, though long engaged in public affairs, gave my consent for taking up arms in an unjust cause, and I never shall, but in cases of very notorious enormity, give my consent to take up arms in an *unprofitable* one"—which, until war became sheer insanity, was the policy of most statesmen worthy of the name. In fact, it would be hard to name a statesman of the eighteenth, or even of the nineteenth, century who, given the same set of circumstances, would have acted in any very different way from Hastings.

In March, just a month before completing his second year of office, an extremely interesting item of news had caught Hastings's eye as he glanced over the latest issue of the *Brussels Gazette* just received by the overland route to India, via Bussora and Aleppo. It informed him that the Parliament of Great Britain had appointed him Governor-General of Bengal under a new instrument of government for the British Dominions in India. But the details given in this, his first, intimation of his new position were too few and vague for him to tell whether he should be pleased or sorry for the change. Within six months he was to know very definitely....

It must have been evident to him when he left England in 1769 that a crisis in the affairs of the East India Company was approaching. Already the editor of *Cobbett's Parliamentary History* had noted that they had become as much an object of annual consideration by Parliament as the raising of the supplies. Townshend's taxing measure had merely been a preliminary and had not touched the real heart of the matter. It had established a precedent for the interference of Parliament and hastened the time when that interference would be applied in a radical way. The rights and privileges of the Company had ceased to be indefeasible and were to become such as Parliament willed them to be.

Chapter IX

PARLIAMENT INTERVENES

I

AN Oriental Empire was still an incredible novelty to the rulers of England, for which none of them as yet was properly prepared. It involved a multitude of hitherto undreamed of problems, and the past experience of the nation disclosed few reliable signposts to wise statesmanship. Here was a state greater in size and population than Great Britain itself, which was more or less the private domain of a body of private citizens whose rights and privileges were still those that had been granted to it a hundred years before for the purpose of secure and profitable trading. They were entitled to fortify and colonize their settlements, to have power and command over them, to appoint their governors and officers, to administer justice, coin money, make peace and war with native states, and send troops, warships and munitions of war for purposes of defense. Wide and liberal powers, indeed, but how inadequate to form the constitution of an empire!

Events had moved so fast that there were few men in England able to keep pace with them. The need for legislation became clearer every day, but not the form that it should take. Before there could be any clear-cut decision some baffling questions would have to be answered. To whom did these territories by right belong? To the East India Company? or to the Crown and people of England? Or did they in truth belong to neither, but to the Mogul Emperor? Did not the Company acknowledge his sovereignty and pay him tribute?

For the time being the sovereignty of the Emperor was tacitly and, by most, explicitly acknowledged. Clive, indeed, had other views and conveyed them to Chatham, but though the idea of formal annexation by the Crown appealed strongly to him, Chatham realized that it was not as yet practical politics. Leaving on one side the abstruse question of legal sovereignty, England's political leaders leaned increasingly to the view that some way must be found to reconcile the quasi-sovereignty of the Company in India with a proper subordination to the Crown and to Parliament. It was wholly alien to the traditional

British way of thinking that Parliament, the custodian of rights, liberties and powers, should have so little say or concern in the proceedings
of this great corporate body of His Majesty's subjects. The position
was too anomalous even for these lovers of anomaly to tolerate. Yet it
was equally alien to British ways to destroy rights and privileges that
had been solemnly granted by royal charter. The situation clearly indicated that a typical British compromise would be the chosen solution.

So long as the Whigs were in power the East India Company was
tolerably safe; for the Whigs were the champions of the rights of property as well as of the Hanoverian succession and the Constitution. The
little band in the House of Commons, led by Beckford, Barré, and General Burgoyne, who favored extreme measures, were in a seemingly
hopeless minority. Parliament had interfered in 1767, and the financial
bargain then reached in the teeth of the bitterest opposition had seemed
to be the furthest it was likely to go. If in the meantime the Company
had set its house in order, all might still have been well for it.

In the spring of the year 1772, just when Hastings was beginning
his administration, the crisis came. Two years before, the Whig administration of the Duke of Grafton had given place to the resurrected
Tories led by Lord North. If the Whigs were the champions of vested
rights, the Tories were the champions of any principle that would
quickly restore them to power; they had been too long excluded from
office to care very much what they upheld. In 1770 they were the champions of the royal prerogative, the willing tools of George the Third
in his attempt to regain some of the lost personal power of the Crown.
Then, as now, political power was in large measure derived from patronage, and to extend the area of royal patronage was consequently a
prime object of the new government. As India was as yet virgin ground,
and very rich, it was natural that the eyes of the King and his new
ministers should have been cast longingly toward it.

It was an ill-chosen moment for the East India Company to go
bankrupt, especially since it had so few friends; for it was hated by
"the City" as well as by the country gentry. Yet that is what it con-
trived to do. A blind folly had for some time possessed its Directors
and shareholders. In 1769, when the Company was in debt over £6,000,-
000, a dividend of twelve and a half per cent was declared, though the
Directors had to conceal facts and falsify accounts. When news reached
England of the famine in Bengal and Haidar Ali's successful onslaught
into the Carnatic, the stock began a spectacular decline, and before long
rumors got abroad of the Company's true financial position. The Directors, in desperation, applied to the Bank of England for a loan of
£600,000. It was refused. Panic-stricken and foreseeing ruin, they and
their friends began frantically to unload their stock. Then, when it was
announced that the Company was unable to meet its obligation to the
State, the crash came. Wails and curses went up from the stricken in-
vestors. Many members of Parliament and their friends lost heavily.
Execration was poured upon the Company, and cries for vengeance

were heard on every hand. All ranks in the State would benefit by the downfall of the Company. The King would have the patronage of a great empire. The courtiers would have lucrative jobs for themselves and their friends. The country gentlemen would have the land tax lowered through possession of the revenues of India. The public at large would have the National Debt paid off and the cost of living reduced. Every taxpayer in England thought that his burdens could have been relieved if the shameful rapacity of the Company's servants had not absorbed the wealth of India.

The fat was really in the fire when the Directors of the bankrupt Company applied to the Government for relief; for in doing so they signed the death warrant of their Company's independence. The opportunity to turn its distress to the advantage of the State, and especially of its royal Head, was too good for ministers to miss. Lord North, with secure majorities in both Houses, prudently referred the application to Parliament. The Directors, at last thoroughly aroused to the danger, vainly tried to forestall the drastic house-cleaning that threatened to be forced upon them, by asking leave to introduce a bill of their own for the regulation of their affairs. The request met with a flat refusal, and General Burgoyne carried a motion to appoint a Select Committee to inquire into the Company's affairs. The Committee was to serve a double purpose: to provide ammunition for an attack, not only on the Company, but on its most distinguished servant, Lord Clive. Certainly, the conduct of the Directors supplied abundant food for speculation. In March of that year they had declared another dividend of twelve and a half per cent; in August they asked the Government for a loan of £1,000,000. The discrepancy was so glaring that it caused the House of Commons to appoint a Secret Committee to investigate the reasons for it. Why should a company go bankrupt, members pertinently asked, when its servants were returning home with their pockets bulging with gold? It was an interesting question.

There now ensued an unedifying spectacle. Politicians and Directors vied with each other in pouring indiscriminate abuse on the Company's servants in India. What the Directors wanted was a scapegoat. Nothing could be easier than to shift the blame for the collapse of the Company from their own scandalous mismanagement to the misconduct of their servants. The public was prepared to believe anything it was told about them. To produce evidence the Directors appointed a special official charged with the duty of digging it up. The proprietors of the Company, for their part, laid the blame squarely on the heads of the Directors, indignantly accusing them of mismanagement, fraud and stock-jobbing, and they wanted to carry their charges to the Bar of the House of Commons. The tactics of the Directors aroused intense disgust among the more intelligent and fair-minded of them. "Such stabbing and dirty work has been used," wrote Francis Sykes to his friend Hastings, "that I assure you the body of Indians"—which was what the members of the Company's service in India were at this time commonly called—"have through the means of the Directors not suffered a little"; adding, "I am, my dear Hastings, heartily tired of them, there are so many tricks and such a scene of villainy amongst them from the highest to the lowest that the very worst Indian is a mere child in iniquity to these in Leadenhall Street." [1]

If the Directors had hoped to evade all responsibility in this manner, they were disappointed. The temper of the House of Commons rose to such a pitch of indignation that it was said they would gladly have hanged both the "Indians" *and* the Directors. The rumors of iniquitous deeds in India only served to increase the clamor against the Company generally. The obvious retort was made to the Directors that if they could not control their servants better they were clearly not fit to exercise any power of control at all.

In the spring of the next year the Committees of Inquiry issued their reports. As expected, they were highly condemnatory. The tongues of orators in Parliament were at once unloosed and from their mouths poured a torrent of bitter denunciation. Thus spoke Burgoyne: "The most atrocious abuses that ever stained the name of civil government call for redress.... If by some means sovereignty and law are not separated from trade, India and Great Britain will be sunk and overwhelmed never to rise again." [2] Lord Chatham, also: "India teems with iniquities so rank as to smell to earth and heaven." [3] Horace Walpole recorded his impression: "Such a scene of tyranny and plunder has been opened up as makes one shudder.... We are Spaniards in our lust for gold, and Dutch in our delicacy of obtaining it." [4] And the public echoed these outcries. There was no doubt in the minds of ninety-nine Englishmen out of every hundred that the misdeeds of their countrymen in India had equaled the Spanish atrocities in Mexico.

Oratory had found its mark. Why ask whether there were not other marks of the same kind equally worth shooting at? We read of a subject country, its commerce regulated in the interest of its masters, the mass of its people excluded from all share in the government and public life, its land owned by absentee landlords, its peasants crushed by exorbitant rents and unjust dealing; we read of taxes being levied only on the poor and farmed out to men who used their contracts as a means of extortion from the peasants, of the depopulation of villages, of starving cultivators leaving their lands, of an alien caste of rulers different in race and religion from their wretched subjects, of violence, cruelty, rapacity and injustice. A true picture of Bengal in 1772, one may say. No doubt it is, but it is also a true picture of Ireland in 1772. In our history books we read of these facts, as we read also of the horrors of the slave-trade, which made the fortunes of so many English merchants and shipowners, of the hundred and sixty crimes which were capital felonies, of the barbarities of the pillory, of the burning of women, of the horrors of imprisonment. But we do not read of them in the debates of Parliament at this time. The guardians of England's reputation for justice and humanity were for the moment more interested in other things. However, deaf though they were to the cries for mercy and justice that came to them from near at hand, they nevertheless, such was their extraordinary altruism, heard those that came from far away oppressed India, and hearing they gave vent to their anguish, though the evil was not one in which they had any personal interest.

In this way began the growth of tradition that for long was to be accepted as history. According to this tradition British rule in India remained unspeakably vile until a beneficent Parliament displaced the East India Company as the controlling authority and appointed its own men to the highest offices, instead of servants of the Company like Warren Hastings, and that from that happy day (1784) onwards, night having changed into day, the British Raj became a model government and the source of untold benefit to the ill-treated and unhappy people. It was a pleasant tradition for those who believed in the infallibility of Parliament, and it suited the beliefs of our Victorian ancestors, but it was scarcely more true than a similar myth that collected around the figures of Charles the First, Strafford and the parliamentary leaders in the Civil War. For a long time we allowed Parliament to write our history and we believed implicitly all that it wanted us to believe, taking no heed of the fact that in the two great issues, Parliament versus the Crown and Parliament versus the Company, Parliament was no more than a party to a cause. We deluded ourselves into believing that Hansard and his forerunners were the repository of truth. Who dared to challenge the case presented by John Pym in the one instance or by Edmund Burke—the Burke of the later phase—in the other?

Happily we no longer allow our respect for parliamentary institutions to distort our historical sense. We are now able to see that the object of the men who dominated the deliberations of Parliament between the years 1769 and 1785 was to discredit the Company preparatory to stripping it of its power and that the voluminous reports on Indian affairs issued by successive committees of the House of Commons during these years, while valuable as sources of information, are no more to be relied upon than a prosecuting attorney's brief. We are also able to see that it was perfectly natural for Parliament to change its tone and its whole manner as soon as it itself became responsible for the government of India. Lord Shelburne, who was Prime Minister for a short time during the period of conflict, perceived the truth when he reluctantly admitted that there could not then be found anywhere in the House of Commons "that firm, even, judicial spirit, capable of administering, much less originating, that justice which the case requires." [5]

The Earl of Strafford was the chief victim in the one instance and Warren Hastings the chief victim in the other. Both men can now be seen in proper perspective and without having recourse to parliamentary spectacles.

II

THE Directors had appealed unto Cæsar—and Cæsar was determined that they should abide by that appeal. Becoming alarmed at their rashness, they tried to wriggle out of their perilous position by appointing another plenary Commission similar to the ill-fated Commission of Three of 1769. But Parliament at once passed a restraining bill. As Lord Clive aptly put it, the Directors should not quarrel "with the mouth that is to feed them." [6]

No one was more vehement in supporting the Company and denouncing the restraining bill than a certain Irishman named Edmund Burke. Burke was still at this time the stalwart friend of Leadenhall-street and resisted with all his might the attempt of Parliament to extend State control over it.

The result of all these debates, inquiries, maneuvers and ferments was the Regulating Act of 1773. It was accompanied by another Act, better known in America, which gave the East India Company the right to export its tea to the American Colonies free of excise duty, resulting in the famous Boston Tea Party.

The importance of the Regulating Act in Hastings's life can hardly be overestimated. It marked a milestone in his career, for the whole of the rest of his administration was to be spent under the sway of this Act, he being the only Governor-General of India to suffer that unhappy fate. Its consequences to India in general were to be serious, but to him personally they were to be nothing less than catastrophic. For if ever a man has had his life ruined for him by Act of Parliament, that man was Warren Hastings. The story of his life during the next twenty years may be simply stated in two sentences, thus: Parliament by passing this Act was the prime cause of the troubles and difficulties in which he immediately became involved; and Parliament by impeaching him for the way he extricated himself from these difficulties shifted on to his shoulders the responsibility for its own negligence and folly.... Perhaps, if anybody deserved impeaching, it was Lord North, the author and executor of the Act.... Clearly, therefore, the Regulating Act demands careful examination.

The Act made the subjection of the Company to the Crown and Parliament definite, if yet far from complete. Henceforth, for instance, the Company had to submit half-yearly accounts to the Treasury and transmit to Ministers, within fourteen days of receipt, copies of all material correspondence concerning its affairs. The Crown, too, was to have a share in the making of appointments; nor could any one of the men composing the new Supreme Government of Bengal be recalled without its consent.

This new Government was to consist of a Governor-General and four members of Council. They were named in the Act, appointed for five years, and vested with the whole civil and military government of the Presidency of Fort William and its dependent territory. Liberal salaries were attached to their posts: £25,000 a year for the Governor-General, and £10,000 for each councilor; and they were strictly forbidden to engage in trade, receive presents, or otherwise add to their income by irregular means. The prohibition against the receipt of presents was extended to all the Company's servants, with penalties provided for its breach. All participation in the inland trade was also forbidden. The Act further empowered the Crown to establish by charter a Supreme Court of Judicature at Calcutta to consist of four English barristers as judges, the senior of whom was to be known as the Chief Justice. Where the Act failed, and failed lamentably, was in the way it defined the powers of the various branches of the new Government, the Governor-General, the Supreme Council, the Supreme Court, and the Governors-in-Council of the Presidencies of Madras and Bombay, now made subordinate to Calcutta.

In the first place, the Governor-General was not given any of the superior power for which Hastings was at that moment so earnestly and cogently pleading. Not only was he not granted the discretionary right to override his Council, but the only superior power he had in virtue of his position was still to be the casting-vote. All actions of the Supreme Government were to be determined by vote of the majority. Secondly, the authority exercisable by the Supreme Government over the subordinate presidencies was very loosely and inadequately defined, being limited vaguely to questions of war and peace and the negotiation of treaties. In such matters the subordinate governments could not proceed without the previous consent of the Governor-General and Council. But there were two exceptions to this rule that might in practice—and actually did—lead to confusion and trouble: when the case seemed to the local government of such great urgency as would render delay dangerous, and when the local government had received special orders from the Company. And thirdly, the precise relationship between the Supreme Government and the Supreme Court was obscure, and the jurisdiction of the Court ill-defined.

According to its charter, the jurisdiction of the Court, both criminal and civil, was to extend to all British subjects residing in the provinces of Bengal, Bihar and Orissa (excluding the Governor-General and Council), and to all servants and employees of the Company and of British subjects, but no attempt was made to define the term "British subject" or to specify what persons were to be classified as servants or employees. It was so ambiguous that it might be interpreted to include virtually all inhabitants of the provinces, both European and Indian—or, again, it could be interpreted strictly to include very few. Again, nobody could tell what law was to be administered by the Court. The Act said nothing on this point. Was it to be "the unregenerate English law, insular, technical, formless, tempered in its application to English circumstances by the quibbles of judges and the obstinacy of juries, capable of being an instrument of the most monstrous injustice when administered in an atmosphere different from that in which it had been administered?" [7]—which is how Sir Courtenay Ilbert describes it. Apparently it was to be that very thing, which meant that Hastings's worst forebodings were about to be realized. The only law that the four selected barristers knew was this English law, and all of them were equally ignorant of Indian conditions. The way was thus clearly prepared for a conflict between the executive and the judicial branches of the new Government.

The Act named the following gentlemen to fill the new offices: Governor-General, Warren Hastings, Esq.; senior member of Council, with the right of succession to the first post, Major-General John Clavering; other members of Council, in the order of their seniority, Colonel the Hon. George Monson, Richard Barwell, Esq., and Philip Francis, Esq. General Clavering, in addition, was given the Command-in-Chief of all the forces in India, which alone meant a serious diminution of Hastings's authority because the Governor of Bengal had hitherto held the chief military command in his presidency. Chief Justice of the Supreme Court, Sir Elijah Impey; "puisne" judges, Sir Robert Chambers, John Hyde and Stephen Lemaistre.

Contemporary opinion on the merits of the Act was very varied. It naturally accorded with George the Third's ideas, and he expressed pleasure at its smooth passage to the statute book. Equally naturally, it was bitterly resented and condemned by the Company and its friends. Burke denounced it as "an infringement of national right, national faith, and natural justice." [8] Others of them described it as "a medley of inconsistencies, dictated by tyranny, yet bearing throughout each line the mark of ignorance." [9]

The mark of ignorance was, indeed, but too plainly visible, nor need it excite surprise. The framers of the Act were utterly ignorant of India and had not, it would seem, seen fit to consult those, with the possible exception of Lord Clive, who could have given them good advice. Lord North might have paid heed to Hastings's views, but the Act was passed before he had time to deliver them. The suspicion rests upon Ministers of thinking more about obtaining for the Crown a share in the extensive patronage rights of India than of providing its government with a sound, workable constitution. In the eyes of both the supporters and the opponents of the Act the chief point at issue was the rights of the East India Company.

A recent verdict on the Act is that it was "probably on the whole an honest attempt to deal with a difficult problem." [10] Yet, even if conceivably this be so, the fact remains that by passing it Lord North very nearly achieved a double title to fame as the minister who lost Great Britain her Eastern as well as her Western Empire. The man who was to save him from this ignominy was Warren Hastings. America was to be lost for lack of a leader. (How different the outcome there might have been if Robert Clive, only forty-eight at the time, had been well enough to accept the proffered command of the British forces!) India assuredly would also have been lost if there had been the same lack there. Therefore, the appointment of Hastings as the first Governor-General was an event of the greatest importance in determining the course of modern history.

The interesting question arises, how did Hastings come to be appointed? On the face of it the answer seems clear enough: he was obviously the right man for the post, if length of service in India, reputation and proved ability were regarded as the essential qualifications. On these grounds only the claims of Lord Clive could have been considered stronger, and Clive might well have been the logical candidate (he had long wanted to be Governor-General of India) but for the poor state of his health and the violent assault that was at that moment being made upon his honor and reputation in the House of Commons and from which he was to emerge only partially victorious. Without doubt Hastings's credit stood for the moment very high both with the Company and with the public generally, and Lord North would seem to have proved beyond question that the obvious answer is the correct one by the eulogy he passed upon him in the House. He stated that as first Governor-General

"he should propose a person who, though flesh and blood, had resisted the greatest temptations—that though filling great offices in Bengal during the various revolutions that had been felt in that country, never received a single rupee at any one of them, and whose abilities and intense application would be apparent to any gentleman who would consider what he had done during the first six months of his administration."

Warren Hastings, therefore, was "a person to whom nobody would object." [11]

Even if we recall the fact that George the Third and his favorite minister seldom if ever made appointments on the sole ground of merit, it seems only to strengthen the case that for once the King had departed from his rule of making appointments that would aid his schemes for personal government and been inspired only by a genuine desire to place the government of India in the best possible hands. For Hastings had no parliamentary connections, he could control no votes, he had neither wealth nor family influence, and he could lay no claim to the favor of government. Yet doubts immediately begin to assail us when we look at the men who had been nominated to share the government with Hastings, for the cloven hoof of royal ambition is only too clearly discernible in the selection of at least two of them.

John Clavering was a soldier of mediocre talents and little experience. He had no particular intellectual or administrative abilities, certainly none sufficient to qualify him for such a responsible and difficult position. He was strikingly deficient in tact, extremely contentious and quarrelsome, and possessed a hot and ungovernable temper. While he was a man of strict honor and integrity, he had not sufficient strength of mind or will to maintain independence of judgement or to overcome his violent prejudices. That is to say, he was anything but the right kind of man to send at the age of fifty-two to manage the affairs of an empire under a new form of government.

Much the same can be said of George Monson. He was a brave soldier, but absolutely lacking in political capacity. He had seen service in Southern India, but, like Clavering, had never set foot in Bengal. He was not without sense, but, again like Clavering, he was prejudiced, ignorant and weak. A man of low intellectual caliber, he was unfit for more than a purely military command. Impey described him as "a proud, rash, self-willed man, though easily misled, and very greedy for patronage and power."

The only possible reason why these two men were selected was that they each had powerful parliamentary connections. They were the personal choices of the King, and Clavering, in particular, had the King's special favor. By appointing them George the Third was strengthening his new-found position as ruler in fact as well as in name, and stretching out toward the patronage of India.

In selecting the third member of Council the King, it would seem, reverted to his other aim and chose a man on the same principle as he chose Hastings. He wrote to Lord North: "If any of the Council at Bengal have acted in conjunction with Mr. Hastings, the naming of one of them will be right; but if otherwise, I can see no reason for putting he who has done his duty, and those who have not, on a foot." And Lord North replied: "Lord North has been advised to nominate one of the present Council in Bengal that, if any accident should happen to Mr. Hastings, there may be some person in the Council already acquainted with the country. It is thought also to be right not to discourage the Gentlemen at present there too much, by totally excluding any of them from the Council. The Senior Councilor whose abilities are spoken of as considerable is one Mr. Richard Barwell. His name, therefore, will be proposed." [12] Lord North's adviser was probably Clive, but it is somewhat surprising that the reward for loyal support of his chief should have been given to Barwell—of all people!

Experience, merit and local knowledge were now evenly balanced, two and two, with royal favoritism and political usefulness. The fifth Councilor, whoever he was, would decide which way the scales would fall. The momentous choice had fallen on Philip Francis.

III

"Who is Philip Francis?" Men asked themselves this question when his name was announced. The other four gentlemen they knew, but not Mr. Francis. On inquiry they discovered that he had until lately been the chief clerk in the War Office, that previous to that he had held other minor government appointments, and that his patron was Lord Barrington, the Secretary for War. But it was with difficulty that they found out much more about this man who had been promoted in so extraordinary a manner.

The story of his life up to this point is, indeed, very brief. Though he was thirty-three, he had advanced but little from his early obscurity. His father had been a Dublin clergyman who had emigrated to England in search of his fortune while Philip was a boy. After unsuccessfully trying his hand at school-mastering, translating the classics, and play-writing, he had joined the ranks of place-hunters and attached himself to Henry Fox, the Whig politician. Hack-writing in his patron's interest then became Philip Francis senior's means of livelihood. Pensions and preferments had followed as a matter of course, as the reward for his services, until a quarrel occurred because of Fox's refusal to obtain his employee a bishopric. Philip, junior, received a good education, and then was given his start in life by his father's patron, who obtained for him his first appointment as a junior clerk in the Department of State. After serving on a diplomatic mission to Portugal, he became chief clerk in the War Office, and so he remained until his resignation in March 1773.

During all these years of active manhood he had been eating out his heart in bitterness of soul because of his poverty and humble station in life. As a youth he had been precocious; a brilliant scholar at school, he had pursued his studies with undiminished zeal while performing the routine duties of his post. To his intimate knowledge of the classics he added a thorough mastery of French and of the works of modern political philosophers like Bacon, Locke and Montesquieu. He studied law, especially the Law of the Constitution, economics and the science of government. While still a very young man he began to write, and writing soon became his chief passion and occupation. An increasing number of letters and pamphlets on political topics flowed from his pen and appeared in the public press under various pen-names.

Great ambitions seethed within him. Having a wife and six children to support, he wanted fortune. He also wanted fame and power. And the doors to all three seemed tightly closed against him. He had exceptional abilities, yet no scope for their exercise in public. The four walls of a government office, thick, sound-proof and dark, shut him in. Over thirty, he had barely stepped on the first rung of the ladder. Lacking aristocratic birth, he lacked the chief passport to the higher realms of Parliament and public office. But he was in touch with those realms; from his seat, conveniently concealed from the public gaze, he could see what was going on, he could watch the chief actors as they moved about the stage, he could hear their words and follow their antics, catch the whispers in the wings, and even peer behind and watch the backstage intrigue and listen to its gossip. He had friends, more prominent than himself, and what his eyes and ears could not tell him, they did. The result was—Junius.

In 1768 letters had begun to appear in the Press bearing this name. They consisted of extremely able and bitter attacks on leading men of the day from the King downwards, including the Duke of Grafton, the Duke of Bedford, Lord North and Lord Mansfield. The anonymous writer showed himself to be a master of the art of political polemics, choosing his victims without regard to rank or reputation, sparing neither their vices nor their misfortunes, and barbing each shaft with the utmost possible venom. The excellence of his style—highly polished, lucid, epigrammatic, biting, vigorous—was only equaled by the malignancy of his fury. Since scurrilous personal abuse was the chief weapon he used, it is clear that only a man greatly wanting in a sense of delicacy and decency could have written these letters. From keen interest, not unmixed with malicious delight, the public feeling gradually changed to intense disgust, as the attacks became more virulent, culminating in a disgraceful "Letter to the King." It is little wonder, therefore, that their author took the utmost care to preserve the secret of his identity. He was so successful in this that even now the truth is not known beyond any shadow of doubt. Innumerable names were advanced, but at length, by dint of much careful investigation, close analysis of the evidence, and the elimination of practically all other possible candidates, it has come to be generally believed that Junius was none other than Philip Francis.[1]

Junius was a product of Francis's thwarted ambition and repressed desires. Since his great abilities were denied their proper outlet in legitimate channels, he took his revenge on Society—Kings, Lords and Commons—in this anonymous way. His bitter and malignant hate was such that he spared not even his patron, Lord Barrington. If Francis had suffered unmerited neglect, had not it been largely his patron's fault? In 1772 the letters ceased, and in January of the following year Junius took final leave of his publisher.

Francis was now out of employment, with no means of support, and with no immediate prospect of obtaining a new job. He had gained his humble pickings in the political arena by steady adherence to the Whig interest—he had hoped for more through Chatham, whose cause he had championed (whom, also, as Junius he had attacked)—but now his party was out of office, and he could think of nothing to do except to go to America, where he had purchased a thousand-acre estate in Pennsylvania, where a collateral branch of his family had settled. Suddenly he heard that there was an appointment to the new Bengal Council apparently going begging. In haste he wrote to Lord Barrington to ask for his recommendation. Lord Barrington gave it, and the appointment followed.

---

[1] This is no place to discuss this still debated question. I am well aware that the identification of Francis with Junius is disputed by some scholars and that the name of Lord Temple is frequently put forward as a more likely candidate. The handwriting test seems to point conclusively to Francis but it is entirely possible, perhaps even probable, that he acted only as amanuensis for Temple or some one else of high social rank. The subject would well bear a thorough fresh examination, would indeed make a fascinating problem in detective work for some of our contemporary enthusiasts.

Well might one of his friends ask him, *"But how did you get the appointment?* It is miraculous to me that a man should resign his office in 1772, and in 1773 without any change in the ministry, be advanced in so very extraordinary a manner." [13] We can repeat the question. Why, indeed, in the name of reason, should the government have chosen an ex-civil service clerk—and a Whig, to boot—to fill a post of so much importance and profit? (£10,000 a year was a princely salary.) It is still very much of a mystery, and the plausible suspicion has arisen that the appointment was a bribe—hush-money—to induce Francis to discontinue his activities as Junius. Attractive as the theory is, unfortunately there is no evidence to support it, nor is there any real reason to believe that either the King or Lord North knew Junius's identity. Francis himself asserted that he was a last-minute choice owing to the resignation of the man originally selected, and after Edmund Burke and others had declined. He was, however, scarcely known in high official circles, and the manner in which Lord North put forward his name to the King strongly suggests that he had no personal knowledge of him. George, replying, allowed him to be "a man of talents." To the Directors of the East India Company he was a total stranger. One possible explanation, though there is no positive evidence to support it, is that he was Clive's nominee. They were both connected with George Grenville, they had a mutual friend in Christopher D'Oyly, who had been Francis's colleague at the War Office, and Clive had considerable influence with Lord North. Clive's ambition undoubtedly was to be the power behind the throne in Indian affairs and he may well have wanted some one in the new Council who would represent his ideas and policy, especially now that he saw how far Hastings was diverging from them. It is certainly true that immediately after his appointment Francis became an intimate friend of Clive and very readily absorbed his views. [14]

IV

SUCH was the body chosen to be the Supreme Government of Great Britain's Indian Empire. Warren Hastings, generally recognized today to be the greatest man Britain has sent to India, had to share authority with two royal favorites of no political capacity, an experienced but not particularly distinguished member of his former administration, and an ambitious minor Whig politician. Truly, a strange and ill-assorted team! Even the dullest mind must have realized that there was not the slightest prospect of it acting together in harmony. George the Third and Lord North certainly were no fools. Therefore, one is bound to suppose that they must have had some ulterior motive for committing such a criminal act, nor is it difficult to see what it was. They recognized, it is true, Hastings's merits and abilities and the advisability of having a man of his great local knowledge and experience to inaugurate the new system, but their real aim was to prepare the way for the transfer of the government from the hands of the Company's servants to those of their own representatives. The fact that the Crown was waging a steady war against the Company must never be forgotten. It was being waged both openly and secretly, by direct and indirect means. The Company was too powerful to be overthrown at one stroke.

The intention was that Hastings should act as a stop-gap until such time as Clavering was ready to take his place. Moreover, his selection was useful as a sop to the Company to help assuage the bitter feelings of resentment caused by the clipping of its independent privileges. George and his minister were shrewd enough not to reveal their whole hand this early in the game. They wished to propitiate the powerful faction in the Company led by Laurence Sulivan, which was most friendly to Hastings as well as most hostile to the ministry. The Regulating Act had been direct action, but now they were to pursue more subtle methods in order to gain the control they wanted.

Sulivan was not deceived. He laid bare the whole plot to Hastings and told him that he was now rendered "a splendid cypher," as the Crown had carefully preserved a majority of three against the Company's two, as well as doubly secured the succession to the Governor-General's office, since Monson followed Clavering in line. [15]

There was only one crumb of comfort that Hastings's friends could find in the whole sorry business. It must surely have been an oversight on the part of ministers that they had actually increased the security of the new Governor-General's tenure of office. Under the old régime, as the servant only of the Company and wholly dependent for employment on its continued favor, a Governor had been liable to instant dismissal at any time, a liability that had been increased by the acute party divisions in the Company's Courts. The Direction was a fluctuating body and every election to it saw a bitter struggle for places. A party of reform, which was the group that supported Hastings, was balanced by a party of reaction, and the big posts in India were as often as not made the spoils of victory. But now, under the new Act, the power of removal was divided and both Crown and Company had to agree. How this would affect Hastings was shrewdly foreseen by Francis Sykes, who was strongly supporting his interests as a member of the Court of Proprietors. Sykes wrote to him:

"I think you bid fair to enjoy the Government of Bengal much longer than any of your predecessors, by the power being divided. Had it as usual rested solely with the Directors, they would in a short time have endeavored to have removed you, had you been God Almighty, and with Government they might have wished you away to make room for Clavering or for some of the younger branches of some needy family about Court, of which there are many." [16]

Added to this important change was the further fact that, even if Ministers and Directors combined, the Court of Proprietors still had the final say.

V

Two men held aloof from the general satisfaction that was felt at the appointment of Warren Hastings. One was Edmund Burke and the other was Philip Francis. The first conjuction of two names so full of ill-omen for him. The first small beginnings of a tragic story of misplaced passion and personal ambition.

The beginning of Burke's hostility to Hastings has generally been placed at a later date, after, not before, the institution of the new government. But Dr. Murray in his recent biography of Burke draws attention to the opinion expressed by Burke when he heard that Warren Hastings was to be Governor-General. "Mr. Hastings," he wrote, "is to have the casting-vote. Mr. Hastings is the individual nominated by this Parliament. If all that has been said is true, if the insinuations of the Committee of Secrecy and the speeches of today are true, this man is guilty of everything charged against the Company. Yet this man is to be the first President, and to him is given a controlling power in the Council." [17] Here is revealed an already full-grown belief in Hastings's guilt as the chief delinquent in India, the same belief that he was to hold to the end of his days. How had he obtained it? Apparently none can say. The only explanation Dr. Murray can give is that "the dislike of Hastings seems to have been intuitive." What adds to the perplexity of the problem is that Burke at this moment was stoutly defending, not only the rights of the East India Company but the character of Lord Clive, the man who had cheated Omichund the banker, forged a colleague's signature to a treaty, conspired to depose the ruling prince of Bengal, and enormously enriched himself in so doing—offenses that, as Dr. Murray points out, differed in degree, not in kind, from those afterwards charged against Hastings; and Burke was using arguments to defend Clive's conduct that were to be equally applicable to Hastings's case. Yet he acquitted the one and condemned the other.

Intuition it may have been, but even intuition requires a cause and an origin. It usually proceeds from personal acquaintance. Besides, the word implies perception of the truth not of the false—and what could be more false than Burke's idea? Can it be, therefore, that the two men had met? It is not possible, on the available evidence, to say that they had. On the other hand, it is difficult to believe that two such men could have been in London at the same time and not come in contact either in the political or literary circles of the metropolis, in one or other of which the chief actors of the day were wont to foregather. Hastings sat for his portrait to Sir Joshua Reynolds and was on friendly terms with Dr. Johnson, both of whom were members of the famous Club of which Burke was a leading light. Burke was more than ordinarily interested in Indian affairs. Surely, therefore, they must have met.

Why was it, one wonders, that Burke took such a violent dislike to Hastings? It is difficult to conjecture a reason. At that date one would imagine that their ideas on India would have been in comparative harmony—as indeed for the most part they virtually remained to the end, such was the irony of their conflict. Only one thing is clear, and that is that even in the short time that Hastings had been Governor of Bengal, before he had done anything to arouse violent criticism, and when almost all men from the King downwards were speaking well of him, Burke had his ear tuned to catch whatever slanders lying tongues were already spreading about "this man," and his mind set to believe them.

In the same letter that he condemns Hastings's appointment Burke refers briefly to the other members of the Council and, most significantly of all, to Philip Francis, whom he had met for the first time in October:

"Mr. Francis I know. He has some personal character. If appointed legally and constitutionally, I know no person better fitted for his post. But I cannot be wiser than the law. I shall always think, whatever talents any one has about him, that the man who is legally appointed to his office is the fittest."

He could not be wiser than the law, yet a few lines before he showed that he *was* wiser than the law, where it concerned Warren Hastings! Was not Hastings's appointment as legal as Francis's? Alas! It is clear that Burke's superlative mind was already going astray on the subject of India. Henceforth Burke and Francis were to be increasingly close personal friends and political allies.

If no drama is complete without a villain as well as a hero, the entrance of Philip Francis upon the stage of India will now more than adequately supply the deficiency in the drama of Hastings's career. The clash of these two antagonists forms one of the most spectacular, though at the same time one of the most melancholy, stories in all history, comparable to the tragic contest between Alexander Hamilton and Aaron Burr. It lasted for over twenty years, and ended without victory for either. The lives of both men were to be marred and blighted, their characters warped, their hopes ruined. Nor did the conflict fail to leave its mark on the future development of India. Principles, as well as personalities, were at issue, for in the persons of these two men were opposed the two chief schools of English thought of the day on the aims and objects of British policy in India. The tragedy is that such a man as Francis should have devoted his great talents and efforts to ends that were almost wholly harmful and ignoble, and thereby prevented Hastings from completing the great work that he had begun.

It was a wonderful prospect that had been opened up to Philip Francis at the age of thirty-four, almost too wonderful to be true. One day contemplating emigration, the next seeing himself the possible future ruler of India. Other men might have accepted the post reluctantly—Lord North declared that he had found difficulty in getting any one to accept it at all—and dreamed of wealth quickly made and carried home. Francis dreamed of power, fame and fortune, all three—and chief of the three was power. The fact that the post exceeded his highest expectations did not mean that it satisfied his ambitions. Anything but that. The junior of a group of five, he yet aspired to be the first. He would sweep aside the other four inferior men, purge British India of its evils, convict the arch-offenders, establish the Empire on firmer foundations, and return home a national hero with independent means and an established reputation. Nothing less would satisfy the vaulting ambition of Philip Francis.

At once he began to fit himself for the great enterprise. As ten months intervened between his appointment and his departure he had time to overcome the handicap of complete ignorance of Indian affairs. With an industry equal to that of the man whom he was to oppose, he threw himself into the work of accumulating information, and in a very short time appeared fully armed and equipped with a complete set of ideas regarding the nature of the task in hand, the purpose of his appointment and the objects to be pursued. He assumed that the purpose of ministers in establishing a new government for India was to censure and abolish the administration of which Warren Hastings had been head. Had not he heard on every hand of the enormities that were being committed in India? If it should appear—and Francis had no doubt that it would—that the Governor-General himself was the chief miscreant, so much the better, as it would facilitate his early removal, and that would bring Francis himself one step nearer his goal. Little by little he built up in his mind before leaving England a complete picture of what he should find when he reached Bengal—a foul swamp of corruption, wickedness, depravity and rapacity. And if that picture bore little or no resemblance to reality, was it altogether Francis's fault? He had painted it with the aid of the most prominent men in England, including Lord Clive. He had listened to the indiscriminate abuse that had been poured upon the Company's servants. All that he did was to draw his own conclusions in a way that best suited himself. Careless and unscrupulous politicians had sown the dragon's teeth: they were now to produce an abundant crop of trouble for all concerned.

The three gentlemen of the new royal dispensation to Bengal left England on April 1, 1774. Sailing on another ship went also the four Judges of the new Supreme Court. Their six and a half months' voyage afforded Clavering, Monson and Francis an excellent opportunity of getting better acquainted. Francis was a clever man. He saw at once the right strategy. By combining with Clavering and Monson he could at once assume command of the situation, for he took it for granted that Hastings and Barwell would quite naturally be in alliance. It was to be three against two, with the two soldiers acting as cat's-paws to pull his chestnuts out of the fire. He immediately took their measure, and it was not long before, by dint of a little judicious flattery and sycophancy, he had both of them eating out of his hand. Plans were prepared. Resolves were taken. And by the time their ship reached Calcutta the mine was laid, ready to be touched off.

Chapter X

GOVERNOR-GENERAL

I

ON October 19, 1774, a salute of seventeen guns roared out from the walls of Fort William, heralding the arrival from England of the three Members of Council. They were met by the senior member of the outgoing government, who attended them up the river to the city. From the landing-place they were conducted to the Governor's House, where the Governor and the whole Council were assembled to give them welcome.

It was with some trepidation that Hastings had awaited this day. All the advices he had received from his friends at home had been filled with gloomy forebodings of the trouble there might be in store for him. But he could hardly have imagined that things would begin to go wrong even before he had shaken hands with his new colleagues. Yet so it was. They reached Bengal in a very ill humor. After a long and dreary seven months' voyage, their ship had been nearly wrecked in a storm just as they were nearing the mouth of the Hugli, and when they arrived they found Calcutta still in the grip of the hot season. But the climax of everything was the manner of their reception. General Clavering, an arrogant, pompous man, was intensely annoyed, first because he and his party had not been given a twenty-one gun salute, the same as was given to colonial governors, and then because there had been so little ceremony: the garrison of the fort had not been called out on parade, there had not even been a guard of honor; they had, indeed, been received as though they were no more important than ordinary Members of Council. And so angry did this make the General that he filled his first dispatch home with vehement complaints.

So much fuss over what seemed to him trifles took Hastings completely by surprise. Averse to parade himself and little concerned with punctilio, he regarded Clavering's complaints as frivolous. But he was mistaken, for in this seemingly trivial matter lay a world of significance. Clavering's arrogance was part of his personality, but the extravagant way in which it displayed itself immediately he arrived in India was

OLD COUNCIL HOUSE, CALCUTTA, 1788

(From an aquatint by Thomas Daniell, R.A., in the possession of the India Office)

due to the fundamental difference between his and Hastings's inter-pretation of the meaning and object of the new constitution. Clavering thought that it implied the complete repudiation of the old system; in his eyes Hastings was merely a left-over from it, whose retention in office was a matter of temporary expedience. He, the senior member of the Supreme Council, was the virtual, soon to be the actual, head of the new government. Hastings, on the other hand, while recognizing that before long he would be expected to give way to Clavering, assumed that he would not have been appointed to his high office, if it had not been the intention of the Crown that he should exercise its powers and prerogatives. He knew that Clavering with his two allies held the majority and could outvote him if they pleased at any time, but it did not enter his head that they might entirely disregard his superior rank and title. He, the Governor-General of Bengal by Act of Parliament, was the head of the new administration, as he had been of the old.

It was futile to expect harmony in the new Council under these circumstances. The new arrivals were determined that no one should remain under a misapprehension of the meaning of their appointment. They were intended to be new brooms, and they were determined to sweep clean. According to their interpretation of the purpose of their appointment it was necessary for them to damn all the acts of the previous administration, this being the only way they could justify their intended line of conduct. "We do not understand," they said, "that we were sent into this country to pay compliments to an administration which we presume would not have been dispossessed of their power, if their use of it had been approved." [1] In fact, Mr. Hastings could not give a stronger presumptive proof of the weakness, impropriety or depravity of any political principle or public measure whatever than by telling them that it was adopted by the late administration. To his question, "if the purpose of the Legislature was to condemn the previous administration, why did it place me at the head of the new one?" they disdained to reply. When he went further and suggested that some superior authority or power might reasonably be thought to adhere to the office of Governor-General, and, therefore, to him, they did not hesitate to affirm their opinion that "the name of the Governor-General is, with all due deference, nothing; a mere empty sound." [2] Their conception of their prerogatives was such that there was no room for a competing, let alone a superior, authority.

The very first meeting of Council revealed to Hastings the situ-ation confronting him. The newcomers faced him with cold, insolent hostility. For three days he debated with himself whether to accept the commission or resign. He suspected that they had come out with a fixed determination to force him out of the government, and he had the most gloomy forebodings of what was in store for him if he stayed. He was also chagrined that he had been given less rather than more power. But he felt that it was his duty to abide the issue. What right, he argued, had he to allow his personal feelings of resentment to frustrate the purpose of Parliament in appointing him? Resignation would mean leaving the government in the inexperienced hands of the new Councilors. The letters that he received from his friends at home gave him reason to hope, too, that he would not be lacking influential support; such a letter, for instance, as the one he received from Lord Shelburne, his former school-fellow and now leader of an important wing of the Whig Party:

"India is a present source of regret to every honest man, and in the opinion of the wisest and best men, it depends upon Mr. Hastings to prevent that quarter, which was our chief place of strength, and where our happiest resources presented themselves, from changing to danger, weakness, distraction and vulnerability.—I wish you, dear sir, all success in your honorable though I believe painful station, and that you may retain sufficient health to enjoy the thanks of every good citizen on your return." [3]

Likewise, Frederick Stuart, son of Lord Bute, wrote him:

"For God's sake stay. . . . In short, your character and your support is so superior that nothing will be listened to that can any way impeach the former part." [4]

So he decided to stay and see things through. Naturally inclined towards optimism, he hoped for the best.

Five days later the Council met again to hear the Governor-General's review of affairs. He gave them a masterly résumé of all that he had accomplished in two and a half years of unfettered power. They listened—but their minds were already made up. What they wanted was not to acquire information, but to find a suitable ground upon which to open their attack. They did not find this in Hastings's account of his legal, economic and administrative measures. Land revenue was so much Greek to them, and since he was very plainly a master of the subject, they wisely refrained, for the present, from crossing swords with him on it. But when Hastings came to the Treaty of Benares and the Rohilla War, they knew that they had what they wanted. Both these measures lent themselves to sensational treatment which would catch the public ear in England. They afforded also a chance to deliver a resounding and crippling blow against the Governor-General's prestige and authority in India. Foreign affairs had always been the Governor-General's special and jealously guarded province. To attack him in it would be to attack him in a vital spot, and to dispossess him of it would be equivalent to dispossessing him of the government. The Indians would be quick to grasp the significance.

Clavering, Monson and Francis had already mapped out their plan of campaign and had come prepared with a resolution to reprobate the whole system of foreign policy and to take the speediest measures to negative the effects of the Rohilla War. The fact that they had only been in Calcutta a week was immaterial to them. They scoffed when they heard Hastings earnestly plead for a continuation of his policy. Continue his policy? Give their sanction to his impolitic and unjust war? What absurdity! They condemned it, the treaty that was its root and the war that was its fruit, in no uncertain terms.

So the battle was joined between the rival factions. Barwell fulfilled expectations by allying himself with the Governor-General. Under the pressure of his friends at home he had gradually been veering in this direction. Now he declared himself openly, "I am with the Governor-General, whose ideas are certainly right, whatever light they may be represented in, and whatever may be thought of them in Europe." [5] He was delighted at Hastings's resolve to stand his ground, and soon reported the establishment of perfect harmony with him. The utter lack of deference shown by the majority to Hastings cemented their alliance, and Barwell now found himself able to admit that "with all his peculiarities and extreme jealousy in honorary competitions, Mr. Hastings has many great and valuable qualities." Accordingly, "we are now one...." [6]

The first move of the triumvirate was clever. They asked to see the whole of the Governor's correspondence with Middleton, his representative at the Vizier's court. Hastings had to refuse. The correspondence was not only private but Hastings had encouraged Middleton to express himself freely, promising that none but himself would see his letters. Also, it had hitherto been the Governor's privilege to conduct the correspondence with the native princes and the Company's diplomatic agents independently of the Council.

The Majority were not satisfied and persisted in their demand, claiming as their sanction the latest instructions of the Court of Directors to the effect that all correspondence with the Company's agents had to be submitted to the Council. Hastings then offered to supply them with everything in the correspondence that might help them in their inquiry. When they still demanded the whole, he made the cogent rejoinder that, though they claimed to be seeking more information about the war, they had not even taken the trouble to read the sources of information that he had placed at their disposal. And there the matter rested. To justify himself, Hastings wrote to the Prime Minister offering to place the whole correspondence in his hands so that he could convince himself that it contained nothing improper. [7]

The Majority naturally insinuated that his refusal had been due to fear: he *dared* not produce the correspondence because it contained evidence of his own corrupt dealings. They, or at least Francis—and he conveyed his belief to the other two—were convinced that Hastings had struck a corrupt bargain with the Vizier and had enriched himself by the war to the extent of £100,000. Why else should he have left Calcutta to confer with the Vizier, when the treaty could perfectly well have been negotiated through the ordinary channels of correspondence? [8] When a man is under suspicion of being a criminal, it is dangerous for him to appear to be withholding information. Into such a position had they already forced him.

The Majority wasted no time in further argument but promptly ordered the recall of Middleton. Worse was to follow. The English brigade was still stationed in Rohilkhand while the Vizier was completing the pacification and settlement of the country. Hastings had been in no hurry to recall it, as it served as protection against possible Maratha activity and as security for the Vizier's payment of the forty lakhs. Besides, so long as it remained in Rohilkhand, the Vizier paid its expenses, and there was nothing to be gained by withdrawing it. Nevertheless, on Clavering's motion, the Majority ordered Colonel Champion to make demand on the Vizier for immediate payment and to march his men back to Bengal. Then, to complete the transference of authority into their own hands, they appointed their own agent to the Vizier's court in the person of Bristow, a protégé of Francis, giving him instructions to correspond privately with them. They justified these arbitrary measures to the Court of Directors by a story of imaginary dangers that were threatening Bengal, accusing Hastings of having imperiled the safety of the province by leaving the brigade in Rohilkhand. [9]

Hastings's and Barwell's vehement protests went for naught. They could denounce the orders to Champion as impolitic to the last degree. They could declare that the Rohilla War was an act of the previous administration, and as such was on the point of being concluded. They could deny that it had been attended with dangers and inconveniences and show that there was no cause for precipitate action. They could even show how the Majority's action might easily jeopardize the success of the whole transaction by giving the Vizier a pretext for withholding the forty lakhs. It was all to no avail. The triumvirate had taken the bit in their teeth and were not to be deterred by mere arguments.

From these preliminaries the Majority advanced to a sweeping condemnation of the Rohilla War and every other part of Hastings's foreign policy. In December they held a special inquiry into the manner in which the war had been conducted. [10] Their cross-examination of the officers of the brigade was directed at one object, and one object only, namely, to fix upon Hastings and the Vizier the stigma of having employed methods of barbarous cruelty. Here Colonel Champion's evidence naturally was very useful. Relying almost entirely upon it, they were able to concoct a very telling story of an atrocious crime. Now it was that Francis came into his own. No one knew better than he how to describe to the English public this sale of the national honor, this despoliation of a small, innocent and helpless people, this outrage to every principle of justice and humanity, and to embroider his account with impressive phrase and lofty sentiment. The mails to England became filled with lengthy charges, pleas, rejoinders and surrejoinders, emanating from both sides.

In order to account for conduct that could only appear to their employers as astounding, the Majority gave an interesting account of how their ideas about India and Hastings had changed from the time they left England. They told how they had arrived in India with every prepossession working in Hastings's favor. They had heard excellent reports of him, of his ability, statesmanship, probity and virtue. But as soon as they landed at Calcutta they began to entertain doubts. The first whiff they received of Bengal air as their ship moved up the muddy channel had, both literally and metaphorically, stunk of corruption and vileness. They were at first incredulous, then suspicion grew upon them —how quickly it grew!—and fast upon its heels followed conviction. "The first glance of the measures of the preceding administration," declared Francis, "convinced me that the root of the tree and every branch of it was rotten." [11] Not the second or third glance, but the first, was sufficient for Francis. He only had to shake hands with the Governor-General to perceive the utter depravity of his character. The first greeting told him to beware of this wolf in sheep's clothing. The Governor's pleasant smile, his friendly gestures, his candid manner, what were these but the Devil's wiles? "Oh that deceit should steal such gentle shapes. So smooth, he daubed his vice with show of virtue." Francis at least was not deceived. He at least could not be bought. Rather, he would tear away the mask of virtue and reveal to the world the despoiler of Bengal.

With his love of dramatic effect he told a story of how Hastings, knowing that his new colleagues had been strongly prejudiced in his favor on their arrival, had asked him in one of their earliest conversations, what had occasioned so sudden and complete a change in their opinion of him. "Sir," the virtuous Francis replied, "everything we expected to find white, we found black." ... "Mr. Hastings," he wrote Clive, "wholly and solely has sold and ruined Bengal. He is the most corrupt of villains. Mr. Barwell is an ignorant, false, presumptuous blockhead." And to another correspondent: "There is not one sound particle in this Constitution. ... Putrefaction is purity compared to the state of this settlement. ..." [12]

The tone of Hastings's letters home was a complete contrast. No bitterness, no recriminations, no rage against his enemies, but profound disappointment and grief, and a calm and dignified restraint. He had made great plans to be executed under the extensive new powers conferred on his government and had set on foot preparatory measures, so sanguine had been his hopes. "But," he wrote to Palk, "I find that we must hazard the fate of a *res consilii expers,* instead of aiming at flights of ambition." He had no hard words to say about his colleagues.

"General Clavering is, I verily believe, a man of strict honor, but he brought strong prejudices with him, and he receives all his intelligence from men whose aim or interest it is to increase those prejudices; and he has acted a foolish part, for which I could punish him, if I chose, by leaving him in the chair which he has taken much pains to strip of all its consequence, and to which neither his abilities nor his experience enable him to give a consequence of any other kind. Colonel Monson is a sensible man, but received his first impressions from Major Grant, and acts in all things from them. He no doubt thinks the second place better than the first. As to Francis, I shall say nothing of him. I shall stay out the issue of the troubles which their ill-humor, or whatever secret motive they have, has introduced." [13]

He added that he had tried to be conciliatory, but had not been met by the same spirit.

His mind went back to the similar conflict in Vansittart's administration. He expressed to Sulivan the hope that

"by the benefit of Vansittart's example and my own experience, and by a temper, which, in spite of nature, I have brought under proper subjection, I shall be able to prevent the same dreadful extremities which attended the former. . . . Without friends, without any kind of personal interest, I have but a discouraging prospect; but I am prepared for the worst, and shall return quietly and even contentedly to England the moment I hear of my recall, for there is no room for palliatives. I hope that my reputation will be spared, but, if it is to be blackened for the sake of giving a fair color to the severity which may be exercised towards me, I will most certainly defend myself, and I am sure that I shall be able to do it to the shame of my Calumniators. My actions are not to be condemned by maxims which are only applicable to the wild schemes of ambition." [14]

One source of real satisfaction he had, and that was in the person of the man who had come out as Chief Justice of the Supreme Court. He owned to Sir Elijah Impey, his old school friend of Westminster days, that nothing else but his appointment could have reconciled him to the constitution of the Court. He counted on his friendship to help remove the difficulties that must unavoidably arise. "The Court of Justice is a dreadful clog on the government," he told Sulivan, "but I thank God the head of it is a man of sense and moderation. In all England a choice could not have been made of a man more disposed to do good and avoid mischief; which, however, is not wholly in his power, and I am sorry for it."

It had by now become painfully obvious to Hastings that there was a premeditated design to drive him from the government. Every act of the Majority, every word they had spoken and written, seemed to have but one object, that of creating as wide a breach as possible between him and them and overwhelming him with calumny. He felt that he had to do something to counteract their design, so early in January 1775 he dispatched Colonel Lachlan Macleane as his agent to watch over his interests at home. Macleane was an officer in the Bengal army, who since 1772 had acted as Commissary-General. With him sailed John Graham and Frederick Stuart, two members of Hastings's old Council, both friendly to their former chief.

The Majority condemned Hastings's political measures mainly on the ground of their rapacity and bad faith. The withholding of the tribute, the sale of the Emperor's provinces to Oude, and the Rohilla War

—all three acts they considered part of a damnable policy of spoliation and treachery, their only motive being sordid financial gain. There was still time, however, to repair the wrong. If the forty lakhs due from the Vizier was blood-money, the acceptance of which would stain the hands of the receiver, it could be refused, without much likelihood of giving offense to the Vizier. If the withholding of the tribute was a gross act of bad faith, payment of it could be resumed. But the Majority did neither. Rather, they took unto themselves the entire credit for compelling the Vizier to perform his obligation. It was infamous for Hastings to perform the service, but for them to collect the reward was meritorious.

Not long afterwards there arose a still better opportunity for the Majority to prove the sincerity of their professions. On January 26 the Nawab-Vizier of Oude died, having first recommended his son and heir to the protection of Hastings. But it was the Majority, not Hastings, that decided on what terms recognition should be given to the new ruler, and instead of seizing the opportunity to correct what they considered unjust in the existing treaty, they did precisely the opposite. They declared the Treaty of Benares null and void and informed the new Vizier, Asaf-ud-Daula, that if he wished to have his succession confirmed and the alliance continued, he would have to make a fresh agreement. Since the support of the Company was vital to him he had no option but to agree. They then gave him the following terms: In return for the Company's military guarantee as hitherto given, he had to cede in perpetuity the province of Benares and Ghazipore, with all its revenues amounting annually to twenty-two lakhs, and to increase the monthly subsidy for the brigade by fifty thousand rupees!

The Majority, in reporting to the Directors, were careful to explain that in return for these large acquisitions and other substantial advantages besides, "hardly anything is granted on our part, but a personal guarantee of the same countries to the son which we were before bound to guarantee to the father. The frontier country of Ghazipore must, at any rate, have been defended by our arms in case of an invasion, whether the revenues of it had been ceded to the Company or not. These revenues are in effect a clear gain to the Company, and a seasonable relief to the declining circulation of Bengal." And in order that there should be no mistake about where the credit should go for this display of superior virtue, they added: "The measure is strictly and exclusively ours. The original plan was opposed in every step by the Governor-General and Mr. Barwell." [15]

It was indeed true that Hastings and Barwell had denounced the entire arrangement. In their opinion it was nothing less than highway robbery. "I cannot deem it honorable," declared Hastings, "to have extorted from the Nawab concessions inconsistent with our former treaties to which the necessity of his situation alone obliged him, however unwillingly, to submit." [16]

And Francis—how did he regard this transaction? It was his proud boast that he was the only member of the Council to insist on the acquisition of Benares and Ghazipore. He declared it to be "a preliminary and fundamental condition" in the treaty, which was "in the highest degree advantageous and honorable to the Company." [17] There were many, including Francis, who believed that the more the Vizier was stripped of wealth and power the better it was for the Company. An impoverished, debt-ridden ally seemed to them less dangerous than a rich one.

Judged by this theory, the Treaty of Fyzabad was a master-stroke of policy. It did far more than weaken Oude; it bankrupted and ruined her. For the Vizier's government, crippled by the rape of one of its richest provinces and saddled with an increased military subsidy, was to prove quite unable to meet its obligations, and it was not long before Oude sank into a state of collapse and anarchy from which it was never to rise again. The shadows of annexation had begun inexorably to close around the wretched country.

It is worth noting in passing—for the benefit of those who think of Hastings as the prototype of British imperialists of the nineteenth century with their strong annexationist tendencies—that the only addition made to British India in Northern India during his administration was made for him by the Majority against his will—Benares.

II

HASTINGS had lost his power and his enemies were making ready to secure a complete triumph over him. In a very short time the full extent of the revolution had become known through the length and breadth of the provinces. Word had gone forth, with the speed at which such news always does travel in India, that the once powerful governor was powerful no longer, and that the new wielders of authority sought his ruin and removal. In order to deepen the popular impression of their power the three new governors of Bengal had set up their own durbar for the holding of princely levees, where they conducted themselves with all the airs of vice-regal power.

All those who had an ax to grind or wished to curry favor with the new government flocked to Calcutta to pay court. All who had grievances seized the opportunity to present them. Europeans whom the previous administration had removed from office or denied employment, Indian officials whom it had set aside for mismanagement, nobles whose ambitions it had thwarted, all whose plans for private gain and personal advancement had been balked by its reforming zeal—they came, eager to make themselves heard, for the sake of revenge or in the hope of meeting with greater kindness.

The result was that the three already prejudiced gentlemen, knowing nothing of the Bengali character or recent Bengal history, drew their all-important first impressions of men and measures from these highly tainted sources; and, as a consequence, their prejudices became suspicions and their suspicions convictions. Being convinced by this horde of complainants at their audience chambers that the previous administration had been wicked and corrupt, the three believed that it was their duty to uncover the facts. They did not turn a deaf ear to the voices of accusation. Even if the slimy trail should lead to the Governor-General himself, it was still their duty to follow it.

They were in no mood to tarry. Time was slipping by, and already the situation was beginning to tell on their nerves, as was the climate on their health. Clavering became more irritable and overbearing every day. Though he was honest enough to doubt his own fitness for the post of Governor-General, he could not bear—such was his arrogance and vanity—to have it withheld from him. He threatened to resign rather than continue in such a humiliating position. Monson had better control of himself and could work and conspire to greater purpose. But the one who was complete master of himself and inspired all their moves was Francis. He led Clavering and Monson by making them believe that he was led by them. And Francis, while confident of success, was impatient, as he saw how ill-equipped his colleagues were to stand the strain of a long conflict.

The time had clearly come for the Majority to launch a decisive attack. They realized that getting rid of Hastings might not prove as easy as they had supposed. There was no sign of retreat on his part, nor were they sure that their condemnation of his policy would cause his dismissal. He had a fine reputation with the people at home, which it needed more than mere words, more than unsupported allegations of misconduct, to destroy. If he was corrupt, concrete and convincing evidence of the fact was needed if the truth was to be brought home. And this, very conveniently, was now forthcoming.

Well to the fore among their eager courtiers was old Nuncomar, now in his seventieth year. Though his reputation had grown no sweeter with the passage of years, Clavering, Monson and Francis did not allow this to deter them from making a close connection with him. He must have thought that at last his turn had come and that he would bask in the favor of government and at the same time revenge himself on the man who had used him so badly.

On March 11 Francis informed the Council that he had received a visit from Nuncomar, who had delivered to him a letter and asked him to lay it before the Board. He said that he had no knowledge of its contents, but felt that he could not deny the request in view of Nuncomar's rank. The letter was read and proved to be a subtle attack on the Governor-General. After making certain insinuations of corrupt practices it accused him of having accepted bribes from the writer and Munny Begum for having secured the appointment of the Begum and Rajah Goordass, Nuncomar's son, to the Nawab's household, amounting in all to three and a half lakhs (£35,000). [18]

Hastings asked Francis whether he knew of Nuncomar's intention of bringing such charges against him before the Council. Francis replied vaguely that he knew in general that the paper contained some accusations against him, but not the specific character of the charge.

Two days later another letter from Nuncomar was received in which he said he had further "incontestable evidence" to submit, and asked to be allowed to appear in person before the Board. Monson proposed that he be called, and Clavering and Francis both agreed. Then followed the first of many extraordinary scenes. Hastings considered the proposal a gross insult to him and a most flagrant and unpardonable attack on his prestige and authority in the eyes of the natives. He replied with burning words of indignation:

"I know what belongs to the dignity and character of the first member of this Administration. I will not sit at this Board in the character of a criminal, nor do I acknowledge the members of the Board to be my judges. I am induced on this occasion to make the declaration that I look upon General Clavering, Colonel Monson and Mr. Francis as my accusers."

He declared that Nuncomar was only a tool in the hands of the Majority, that he had been guilty of an act of great disrespect and insolence, that Francis had exceeded his duties as Councilor, and that he himself had long been aware of Nuncomar's intention to attack him.

"The chief of this Administration, your superior, gentlemen, appointed by the Legislature itself, shall I sit at this Board to be arraigned in the presence of a wretch whom you all know to be one of the basest of mankind? I believe I need not mention his name, but it is Nuncomar! Shall I sit to hear men collected from the dregs of the people give evidence at his dictating against my character and conduct? I will not. You may, if you please, form yourselves into a Committee for the investigation of these matters, in any manner you may think proper, but I will repeat that I will not meet Nuncomar at the Board nor suffer Nuncomar to be examined at the Board; nor have you a right to it, nor can it answer any other purpose than that of vilifying and insulting me to insist upon it."

The Majority continued nevertheless to insist upon it. Thereupon Hastings declared the Council dissolved and any acts of it as a Council during his absence illegal and unwarranted. He then withdrew, Barwell followed him, and Clavering forthwith took the chair, declaring that the Governor-General had no right to dissolve the Council.

Nuncomar produced a letter from Munny Begum accusing Hastings of accepting a bribe from her. The three Councilors "examined" him, but gently, in order not to hurt the old man's feelings. Though there were various grave discrepancies in his statements, they made no attempt to probe into them. And when it was discovered that the impression of the seal on the letter was undoubtedly the Begum's, they were satisfied that the document was genuine, and without further ado came to the conclusion that the Governor-General was guilty of accepting the sums in question and ordered him to make restitution to the Company.

Next day the proceedings followed the same course. The Council met. The Majority wanted to introduce further matter attacking Hastings's personal character. Hastings again declared the Council dissolved and withdrew with Barwell. The Majority continued in session. Three days later the same thing happened a third time.

On this occasion the Majority summoned Cantoo Babu, the Governor-General's private banyan. When he failed to attend, having been forbidden to do so by Hastings, they declared him guilty of contempt and proposed to sentence him to the common stocks, the same punishment as was meted out to the meanest inhabitants of Calcutta for committing a nuisance in the streets of the city. The dispute then became extremely warm, and Hastings and Clavering nearly came to blows. Hastings vehemently declared that if the General attempted anything in his own person and by his own authority, he would oppose it with his person, at the peril of his life, and if he made use of the law, he would oppose him by the law. A duel was in prospect, but the General thought better of it and dropped the proposal.

This direct attack on his personal character came nearer to throwing Hastings off his balance than any other episode in his life. The first attack on his public policy had been staggering. Indeed, the entire conduct of the Majority from the first day had horrified him. Now horror was swallowed up in indignation. To the world at large, and to his enemies in particular, he had maintained a bold front, showing a firm and patient resolve to hold his ground until the issue was settled, though actually he was in a state bordering on frenzy. But when they launched Nuncomar and others of the same stamp in a frontal assault on his personal honor, they brought him to such a depth of despair and misery that, there and then, they nearly gained their object of driving him from the government. He still kept a brave face to his accusers, but for once his defiance was more assumed than real.

His right to dissolve the meetings of Council was denied by his enemies, and questioned subsequently by unbiased critics. His action was certainly unprecedented, as was also that of the Majority. But the Company's legal advisers finally came to the conclusion that he was within his rights, though exercise of them was dangerous and inadvisable. At the time, however, he was beyond caring whether his action was legal or not:

"Right or wrong I had no alternative but to do that or throw up the service. Indeed I consider this as a case which supersedes all forms. Their violence had already carried them to lengths which no rules of the service would allow or justify, nor could I yield without inverting the order of it, and submitting to a degradation to which no power or consideration on earth could have impelled me. I beg you"—he was writing to Graham and Macleane—"not to pass unnoticed the disadvantages to which I am exposed in being obliged to repel their concerted attacks by unpremeditated resolutions extorted from me in the midst of provocations, the most likely to warp and disorder both my judgement and understanding. I thank God I have hitherto possessed both undisturbed, at least I think so.

"I shall continue the practice which I have begun of dissolving the meetings of the Council, that is, of leaving them to themselves, as often as they propose new indignities for me. Indeed, I expect to be able to do very little with them, and how the public business is to be conducted I cannot devise.

"The trumpet has been sounded, and the whole host of informers will soon crowd to Calcutta with their complaints and ready depositions. Nuncomar holds his durbar in complete state, sends for zemindars and their vackeels, coaxing and threatening them for complaints, which no doubt he will get in abundance, besides what he forges himself. The system which they have laid down for conducting their affairs is, as I am told, after this manner. The General rummages the Consultations for disputable matter with the aid of old Fowke. Colonel Monson receives, and I have been assured descends even to solicit, accusations. Francis writes. Goring is employed as their agent with Mohamed Reza Khan, and Fowke with Nuncomar....

"Was it for this that the Legislature of Great Britain formed the new system of Government for Bengal, and armed it with powers extending to every part of the British Empire in India?

"Colonel Monson, with a more guarded temper, and a more regular conduct, now appears to be the most determined of the three. The rudeness of General Clavering, and the petulance of Francis, are more provoking, but it is from the former only that I apprehend any effectual injury. I therefore retract the exception which I before made with respect to him. I cannot temporize; and after two years of anguish, I will either retain my seat in comfort, or I will not keep it. I never can be on terms of ease with these men." [19]

In the same mail he sent an earnest appeal to the Prime Minister for justice, ending it with:

"I now most earnestly entreat that your Lordship—for on you, I presume, it finally rests—will free me from the state I am in, either by my immediate recall, or by the confirmation of the trust and authority of which you have hitherto thought me deserving, on such a footing as shall enable me to fulfill your expectations, and to discharge the debt which I owe to your Lordship, to my country, and my Sovereign. The meanest drudge, who owes his daily subsistence to daily labor, enjoys a condition of happiness compared to mine, while I am doomed to share the responsibility of measures which I disapprove, and to be an idle spectator of the ruin which I cannot avert." [20]

At the same time he wrote to Graham and Macleane (March 27), informing them of his resolve to leave Bengal and return to England on the first ship of the next season, if the first advices from England contained a disapprobation of the Treaty of Benares or of the Rohilla War, and showed an evident disinclination towards him. "In that case I have nothing to hope, and shall consider myself at liberty to quit this hateful scene before my enemies gain their complete triumph over me."

If, on the contrary, his conduct was commended, and he saw clear signs of a proper disposition towards him, he would wait the issue of his appeals. He left it to their discretion to make such use of his resolution as they thought proper.

The Council Board had degenerated from a Government to a tribunal of inquisition. When the Governor-General would not submit, they asked him, "Are you not bound, sir, by the votes of the Majority?" "Do you presume to oppose the sense of the Parliament of Great Britain?" [21] The picture that Hastings drew of the active conspiracy to ruin him was true. The three grand inquisitors were trying, with Nuncomar's able assistance, to obtain information of presents having been received by Hastings, and they did not shrink from suborning witnesses. If any of the nobles and princesses of Bengal applied to the Council for relief, they were given to understand that their petitions would be refused unless they charged the Governor-General with malversation. The price of justice was perjury. Native officials who would not, or could not, make the necessary complaints were removed from office and displaced by those who responded to the demand, that is to say, by Nuncomar's creatures. Honors and rewards followed acquiescence, disgrace and imprisonment refusal. [22] "In short," as one prominent official of the Company wrote to another, "old Nuncomar has met with employers, who allow full scope to his genius." The employers paid attention also to Mohamed Reza Khan, but in vain. He only admitted having made the Governor one present, that of a persian cat. All his other offers of money, his town house, pieces of cloth, had been refused.

As if to impress upon the whole world the special esteem in which they held Nuncomar, the three gentlemen of the Council did him the honor of paying him a formal visit, driving to his house in two coaches, attended by a procession of vehicles containing their dependents and retainers. "In all the time of Nuncomar's prosperity, in the zenith of his power," wrote Barwell, "never did he see so formal and ostentatious a cavalcade, nor never had such extraordinary honors been paid to him." [23]

On April 11 the Majority made the following minute: "Whatever might have been Nuncomar's motives, his discoveries have thrown a clear light upon the Honorable Governor-General's conduct, and the means he had taken of making the very large fortune which he is said to possess, of upwards of forty lakhs of rupees, which he must have amassed in two and a half years." Forty lakhs equaled over £400,000, though Hastings's whole fortune then could not have exceeded £40,000.

Was there any truth in the charges? There is no doubt at all that the letter Nuncomar produced from Munny Begum was a gross and palpable forgery. Not only did the lady herself deny all knowledge of it, but there was subsequently discovered among Nuncomar's possessions an interesting collection of the seals of many eminent personages in the province, including that of the Begum. And once before, to Hastings's certain knowledge, Nuncomar had forged a letter from the Begum.

When the Council, on the advice of the Company's Attorney-General, referred the matter to the Company, the Directors, though not well-disposed to Hastings at the time, accepted the opinion of their legal advisers and declared the charges to be ridiculous, since they could not possibly be true. But the affair was not to end there; it came up again in the Impeachment. Lord Thurlow then once more disposed of it: "A more extraordinary or more insolent production never appeared, undoubtedly, nor one which carried falsehood upon the face of it more strongly." Despite the Lord Chancellor's marked predisposition in the accused's favor, his verdict must be accepted as correct. [24]

Hastings made no attempt at the time to refute the charges. Refusing to recognize the right of the Council to arraign him, he said that he would reserve his defense until a suit at law was brought against him. Writing to the Prime Minister he confined himself to reprobating the methods and objects of the Majority, condemning "these accusations, true or false," because they bore no relation to the public measures of his government and could have no other purpose but to destroy his private character in the eyes of the world. [25] To the Court of Directors he offered to submit all transactions to their judgement. When they dismissed the charges as unworthy of their attention, he regarded the matter as finally closed.

There was, however, another reason than contempt for his studied refusal at once to meet the charges with a flat denial. Nuncomar had with his usual craftiness included a small measure of truth in his lying deposition. One and a half lakhs of rupees (£15,000) had actually been received by Hastings from the Begum, not as a bribe, but as a sumptuary allowance to cover the cost of entertainment during his lengthy visit to Murshidebad in 1772. The sum has reasonably been condemned as excessive and without sufficient justification, but it cannot be said that its receipt by Hastings was illegal, or strictly improper. Not only had it been paid to every governor before him, so that he was justified by precedent, but it would have been manifestly unfair if he had to defray out of his own pocket the heavy expenses incurred while absent from Calcutta. They should have been paid by the Company, not by the Nawab, and therefore the fault lay with it rather than with the governor.

Hastings made a tactical error in not at once admitting the receipt of this sum. When later he did admit it, his enemies were able to claim that the admission had been extorted from him and to interpret his long silence as a clear sign of guilt. When he finally had to meet the charges at his trial he prepared a brief for his counsel in which he emphatically denied having accepted any money directly or indirectly from Nuncomar or, except for these one and a half-lakhs, from Munny Begum. [26]

This was, however, only the beginning of the attack on his moral character. New charges were flung at him. Charges of disloyalty to his employers, of virtual treason to the State, of malfeasance and misfeasance, and, invariably, of corruption. [27] And always it was a baiting process, designed to wear down his resistance, to drive him into a corner, to tempt him into some violent action that would lead to his own destruction. How severe an ordeal it was can scarcely be realized without reading the minutes of the Council's meetings. There are few men who could have emerged from it totally unscathed.

Hastings was especially handicapped because of his sensitive pride. Again and again his tormentors were able to provoke him to angry and bitter outbursts, which might appear unwarranted to those who did not appreciate the circumstances. An attitude of lofty, impregnable disdain would have spared him much suffering, besides giving his enemies less encouragement. Or he might, too, with greater wisdom, have swallowed his wounded pride and calmly met each attack with a straightforward defense. By allowing his sense of outrage at his colleagues daring to appear as his accusers and pose as his judges to govern his behavior, he made himself vulnerable. They were able to accuse him of trying to hide his guilt under the pose of wounded innocence, for there were many charges that he did not attempt to meet in any other way. Yet it must be remembered that his position was extraordinarily difficult. Every advantage lay with his accusers: the element of surprise, the choice of ground and weapons, the opportunity for careful preparation of each thrust, but, above all, the ease with which his measures could be presented in a suspicious light. He must often have felt the utter futility of trying to demonstrate to these men the propriety of his actions, especially when, as often was the case, they did not lend themselves to conclusive proof. If as he believed his only rightful judges were in England, how could he convince those judges that the appointment of a certain man to a certain office was proper and justifiable, when they did not know the exact nature of the office, nor the characters of the candidates, nor any of the other factors that necessarily entered into the decision? But Hastings would first have asked, why should he have to explain and defend all his actions, when the general tenor of his conduct was plain to all? It was, indeed, often easier for his enemies to accuse him of evil and corrupt motives than for him to disprove the accusation. But since the onus of proof lay on them, and since they could not, or did not, produce it, fairness and justice demand that their charges be dismissed as false and malicious.

III

THE attack reached its dramatic climax at the height of the hot season. As if to cap the charges of corruption the Majority informed the Court of Directors and Ministers that the whole country joined in their condemnation of the Governor-General's conduct and regarded him as a monster of iniquity. When Hastings read their letter he was filled with helpless rage. To Graham and Macleane he wrote:

"There are many gentlemen in England who have been eyewitnesses of my conduct. For God's sake, call upon them to draw my true portrait, for the devil is not so black as these fellows have painted me. There are thousands in England who have correspondents in Bengal. I wish it were possible to collect testimonies from these. If I am not deceived, there is not a man in Calcutta, scarce in Bengal, unconnected with Clavering and his associates, who does not execrate their conduct, and unite in wishes for my success against them." [28]

Suddenly despair vanished and a grim back-to-the-wall defense gave place to a vigorous and well-directed counter-thrust. His enemies had overreached themselves. One night an Indian who had been one of his accusers came to him privately and told him an extraordinary story of how he had been intimidated by Nuncomar and Fowke to bring a false charge. Hastings examined him with the utmost care, and when convinced of the truth of his story made up his mind to prosecute. He sent his informant to the Chief Justice. Thus it came about on April 20, while Calcutta still buzzed with the excitement caused by Nuncomar's charges and while the old gentleman was gayly riding his high horse of renewed power, that he was held to bail by the Supreme Court on a charge of conspiracy and bound over to take his trial at the next assizes. Before that time came, however, he was caught still more closely in the toils of the law.

The day of retribution had indeed arrived! Within a fortnight Nuncomar was committed to the common jail of the city on an entirely different and distinct charge. Some years before a civil suit had been instituted against him in the Mayor's Court for fraud, but failing to gain satisfaction, the plaintiff, Mohun Persaud, had at length transformed the case into a criminal prosecution for forgery, which brought it within the jurisdiction of the Supreme Court. It was this that had now led to Nuncomar's arrest. While he lay in jail he received fresh proofs of the high regard in which he was held by the Majority. They tried every means, short of violence, to obtain his release, besides visiting him with their families and daily inquiring after his health.

The trial for forgery opened on June 8. It was unbearably hot. The temperature of the court-room was for much of the time in the nineties. The Court sat from eight in the morning till late at night, and the trial lasted for eight days. All four judges sat on the bench, the jury was composed entirely of Europeans, and the prisoner was defended by the ablest advocate at the Calcutta Bar. After a fair trial—acknowledged as such by the prisoner's counsel—conducted according to the strict rules of English law, Nuncomar was found guilty. The judges were in doubt about the law to be applied, English or Indian. Under the former forgery was a capital offense, whereas Indian law and opinion viewed the crime indulgently. The judges finally decided to apply English law, and accordingly sentenced Nuncomar to death.

He might still have escaped the gallows if the Council had intervened in his behalf. A request could have been made to the Court for a stay of sentence pending a reference to England, and, according to Impey's testimony before the House of Commons, the Court would certainly have granted it. Now was the opportunity for the Majority, wielding the whole power of the government, to intervene to save their friend and ally from a shameful death. Considering that this was India, not England, the sentence was unjust. Nuncomar clearly looked to them for aid, as he sent them a petition beseeching their protection. But they ignored it. Not one of them moved a finger to save him! Not a word was heard in the Council chamber in his behalf! The law was allowed to take its course, and on August 5 Nuncomar was hanged.

"Poor old Nuncomar is at last fallen by his own villainies." [29] In commenting thus, Barwell expressed Hastings's attitude as well as his own. The change in the situation produced by his enemy's downfall had, indeed, given Hastings fresh hope. He wrote to Graham and Macleane to tell them with evident satisfaction that "the old gentleman was in jail and in a fair way to be hanged," and at the same time retracted the discretionary authority he had given them to offer his resignation. "Whatever advices the first packet may bring, I am now resolved to see the issue of my appeal, believing it impossible that men, whose actions are so frantic, can be permitted to remain in charge of so important a trust." [30]

In Hastings's nature, mild and benevolent though it was, there was nevertheless a streak of relentlessness. Malicious tongues in Calcutta said of him that he never lost a friend and never forgave an enemy. The truth was that while Hastings may have forgiven his other enemies he never forgave Nuncomar. At the time of his impeachment Hastings admitted that he was never the personal enemy of any man but him, "whom from my soul I detested, even when I was compelled to countenance him." Not unnaturally, he regarded his arrest, trial and conviction in the light of a piece of unexpected good luck. He must have realized that the sentence was unjust, because he had himself previously expressed the truth about it when discussing the applicability of the English criminal law to Bengal. "There may be a greater degree of injustice in making men liable at once to punishments with which they have been unacquainted, and which their customs and manners have not taught them to associate with their idea of offense." But he did not feel it incumbent upon him to stretch out a hand to save a man who had so grossly wronged him, who was his bitterest enemy, and who was meeting a fate that he had for so long richly deserved.

Philip Francis, for his part, not only assented to the execution but defended the judges against Nuncomar's charge of a miscarriage of justice, testifying to the high reputation the Court had acquired in the country. Yet it was not long before he was turning the circumstances of the trial to good account, as Impey anticipated he would. On August 8, three days after the execution, the Chief Justice had written to Alexander Elliot, telling him that he was "apprehensive the Majority of the Council will endeavor to assign undue motives for the late execution.... I would by no means have my attachment to Mr. Hastings be denied or extenuated. It was founded on friendship for a schoolfellow and has been confirmed by opinion of the man." [31]

None can say that Francis was not ingenious. Little by little, with hints carefully dropped in this quarter and in that, he popularized a new version of the facts, as follows:

"Nuncomar might have been a notorious rascal, but by ——, he spoke the truth, or why were they in such a hurry to hang him?" [32] "As things are now circumstanced the world may perhaps conclude that this man was too formidable a witness to be suffered to appear, and that any degree of odium or suspicion, which the violent measures taken to destroy him might throw on the Governor's character, was not to be weighed against the danger of his proving the truth of his accusations." [33] "The Governor is well assured that no man who regards his own safety will venture to stand forth as his accuser."

What may have given him the idea, or at least encouraged him to spread it, was the fact that the natives, awed by the fate of the great Brahmin, quite naturally attributed it to his having dared to accuse the Governor-General, especially as one event followed the other so swiftly, and that thereafter no more charges were forthcoming against him. Of course, Francis was careful not to state definitely his belief that Hastings had himself trumped up the prosecution and conspired with his friend Impey to put Nuncomar to death. He was too astute for that. He counted on the common weakness of human nature to believe such stories to turn his insinuations into positive assertions. And his confidence was justified. Before he had finished he had started another hare that was to prove as excellent sport as the story of the Rohilla crime. Nuncomar dead was to prove more useful to him than Nuncomar living.

Fate was kind to Francis! She could not have presented him with a better opportunity to employ his peculiar talents. He only had to take the series of unusual events that preceded the trial and execution, apply a little imagination to link them together in a chain, gloss over a few inconvenient facts—such as that the forgery prosecution was commenced six weeks before Nuncomar produced his charges against Hastings, that the trial was conducted fairly and regularly, and that no less than four judges and a jury of twelve were involved in the conviction and sentence—disregard the fact that there would have been no execution at all if Francis himself and his two colleagues had willed otherwise, enlarge instead upon the convenience to Hastings of what had happened—and behold! the execution of Nuncomar was transformed from an ordinary act of justice by due process of law into a startling judicial murder, committed by Sir Elijah Impey at the instigation of his friend the Governor-General.

Not only was this a plausible interpretation, but it was a triumph of imagination. It gave to a drama-loving world a situation and plot that could hardly be excelled. The idea of Hastings, desperate because his career and reputation were about to be ruined, trying to destroy his enemy and accuser before he was destroyed by him, framing the prosecution on a capital charge, and persuading his old school friend to save him by sending Nuncomar to the gallows—what is this but the very stuff of great drama?[1] How alluring it is! How irresistible to lovers of the stage! How artistically satisfying! Is there an imaginative artist—a playwright, say, or a novelist—who would not prefer to have such an arrangement of facts to work upon instead of the much more prosaic and flat truth of coincidence? That is why when Macaulay put this figment of Francis's and Burke's imagination into his essay on Warren Hastings, together with other similar flights of fancy, the result was a literary masterpiece that far transcends in interest and dramatic appeal everything else that has been written about him. Hastings emerges from his magnificent pages as a splendid, awe-inspiring, fearless, somewhat sinister figure of romance, instead of as the quiet, conscientious, patient, steadfast, loyal servant of the State that the sober facts reveal. The one is great fiction, the other is merely history. If we prefer the fiction let us at least do it with our eyes open, for artistic and æsthetic reasons, and not because of Macaulay's warning that only "idiots and biographers" think differently.[2]

IV

THE war in the Council now entered a new stage. Systematic defamation of Hastings's character was accompanied by systematic destruction of his work. Nuncomar had served his purpose. The three reformers, having conclusively shown what manner of man the Governor was, could proceed with a free conscience to overthrow his system of administration. When the hot season ended they got actively to work. As a preparatory measure Munny Begum was falsely charged with misconduct and removed from her post as guardian of the Nawab, Rajah Goordass was then appointed in her place (it would have been Nuncomar's but for his misadventure), and the young prince induced to write a letter to the Council expressing his gratitude for the change. The British Resident at the Court was imprudent enough to defend the Begum, and in consequence found himself charged with embezzlement. Hitherto the Majority had carefully avoided any public connection with Mohamed Reza Khan, but secretly, they had been in touch with him. Now with the removal of his bitter enemy, the Moslem became the object of their attentions and the chief beneficiary of their plans.

For a time the Majority lacked an excuse to carry out more sweeping changes. Hastings's reorganization of the administrative system had been warmly approved by the Directors, and they had made no suggestions for any revision of it. In October, however, the Council received

---

[1] Feuchtwanger bases his play *Warren Hastings* on this idea.
[2] It is worthy of note that three of the most eminent jurists of the day, Sir William Blackstone, Lord Mansfield and John Dunning (Lord Ashburton), found nothing wrong in the Court's proceedings and wrote Impey to tell him so. [34]

a letter from them which supplied the deficiency. One of the effects and accompaniments of the recent crisis in the Company's affairs had been a serious decline in the efficiency of the Court of Directors. The decline had begun when the Company became involved in financial difficulties and the Directors spent most of their time stock-jobbing and lobbying in the House of Commons to the neglect of the business of their Indian governments. The decline continued after the passage of the Regulating Act when most of the old experienced Directors lost their places, being replaced by new men without knowledge of Indian affairs. Ignorance as well as neglect then marked their dealings with the Company's servants. This particular dispatch displayed both defects. It related to the acquittal of Mohamed Reza Khan which had occurred two and a half years before. The Directors endorsed this act of Hastings's previous administration and expressed their desire that some reparation be made to the Moslem nobleman for the injustice that had been done to him. They proposed that he be restored to a moderate measure of power in the Nawab's household, suggesting that he might be appointed to the office held by Rajah Goordass under the regulations established by Hastings's government, but unfortunately they confused the names and functions of the several offices connected with the Nawab. They expressly stated that they did not mean that Mohamed Reza Khan should be restored to "any improper degree of power." Yet the Majority deliberately misinterpreted the dispatch and made the Directors' mistake a pretext for declaring that their evident intention was to restore the system in existence prior to Hastings's reorganization of it and to reinstate Mohamed Reza Khan in his old office.

Accordingly, against the vehement protests of Hastings and Barwell, the work of 1772 was undone, and the old Dual System of government was reëstablished. The whole sphere of criminal jurisdiction of the province was handed back to Mohamed Reza Khan as the Nawab's deputy. [35]

Six months later when Hastings surveyed the state of his government it was a truly melancholy picture that he had to draw. Paralysis had begun to seize the administrative machine, so lately established, as soon as the guiding hand was removed from the helm. Hastings, as we have seen, had placed a heavy load of labor and responsibility on the Council, which was essential to the proper functioning of his reforms. But when the conflict began the Board had no time to give to routine matters of administration; its members were too busy with their disputes. "Every page of our public records," wrote Barwell, "teems with matter of private and personal discussion which neither directly nor remotely bear relation to the interests of the country." The Majority spent all their time condemning the measures of their predecessors, and Hastings and Barwell had perforce, to spend nearly as much time defending them. What was equally serious, the spirit of discord spread from the top downwards until it infected the whole of the service, dividing the Bengal Civil Service into two bitterly hostile camps.

Faction generated feud, and duels became common. Under such circumstances it is not surprising that the Provincial Councils largely suspended operation. The machinery of government slowed down almost to a standstill.

Especially serious was the collapse of the forces of law and order, which was well-nigh complete. Hastings's court of appeal automatically went by the board with the rest of the Council's administrative duties. The local civil courts survived, but only in a state of suspended animation. The criminal courts, no longer under English control, ceased almost entirely to operate. As an inevitable result, all the old evils that Hastings had striven so hard to exterminate began to reappear. Crime and disorder rapidly increased, without any measures being taken to suppress them. The dacoit scourge received a new lease of life, and life and property threatened to become as insecure as in the evil days of irresponsible power. It was fortunate for Bengal that peace still reigned, for nothing was done to preserve it.

"I have seen," wrote the Governor-General to his employers, "all the labors of my former Administration rendered abortive and all my measures repealed for the sake of condemning the principles on which they were formed. Letters from all quarters lie for months unanswered" (Barwell stated that letters of the Provincial Councils were regularly not answered for six or eight months) "because the time of the Board is occupied in collecting proofs of my demerit and of the virtue of my adversaries in detecting it. The business of every department stands still, though the Board meets four days at least in every week, and I sit in them all a passive spectator without the power of giving motion to your affairs or for any other purpose that I know but to be the butt of everlasting contumely." [36]

His description of himself as "a passive spectator" was not quite accurate, for passivity was foreign to his nature. He submitted to the rule of the Majority because he had no choice, but he never missed an opportunity to make his presence in the Council serve a useful purpose. He had too great a sense of responsibility ever to adopt an attitude of indifference to the proceedings of the government of which he was the nominal head, particularly as he realized only too well how incapable his opponents were. He even at times took pity on their blundering incompetence by helping them to put the views they wished to express into an intelligible form, though they might be diametrically opposed to his own. And much of what routine business was transacted was left in his and Barwell's hands, as the Majority had no time for it. While powerless to do much good he was able in this way to act as a check upon some evil. But the check was very slight.

One quarrel did not satisfy the Majority, so they began a second. The constitution of the Supreme Court made some degree of friction between it and the Supreme Council inevitable. Both factions in the Council were of one mind in deploring the ill-defined limits that had been placed to the Court's jurisdiction and the temptation they gave to the

Court to interfere in the sphere of government. For once, indeed, Francis spoke the strict truth when he stated that Hastings was at first more averse than any of them to the institution of the Court and to the intro- duction of British laws in any shape whatever. But it was Clavering, not Hastings, who made this sentiment the ground for a furious quarrel. And once again Francis's comment was just and luminous: "The dif- ference between Clavering and Hastings is that the former lays the fault on the judges, the latter on the law." [37] Hastings did not blame men for performing what they considered to be their duty, merely because he deplored the Act of Parliament that had appointed them, especially when one of them was an intimate and dear friend. But Clavering and his two colleagues were incapable of conducting any controversy in a decent manner; opposition on public grounds invariably degenerated with them into personal rancor. Francis was no doubt the *agent provocateur*. "I wish you would inquire and tell me in what dirty corner of Westminster Hall these cursed judges were picked up," was what he wrote to one of his friends at home. [38]

Many hard things were said about the four judges, then and sub- sequently, but far from all of them were deserved. They were as mixed a body as the Council itself. Only two of them had any claim to dis- tinction, Sir Elijah Impey and Robert Chambers. Impey was a bril- liant scholar, a Fellow of Trinity College, Cambridge, and a worthy judge, energetic, courageous, public-spirited and fair-minded, with abili- ties above the average, and no noticeable vices. Doomed to share much of the abuse that was hurled at Hastings, and never since vindicated to the same extent as he in the popular estimation, he has been a much maligned figure. His loyalty to his friend was the chief cause of his undoing. Chambers was even more distinguished, having been Vinerian professor of law at Oxford, and a friend of Dr. Johnson (who had furnished him with a letter of introduction to Hastings). Lemaistre and Hyde, on the other hand, had neither reputation nor ability to help counterbalance their grave defects of character and disposition. They were narrow-minded, bigoted, arrogant, and vain. There was as a result the same lack of harmony in the Court as there was in the Council.

A remarkable change had come over the popular attitude towards the Court. Greeted at first with general hostility and suspicion, it was now being welcomed as the only body in Bengal able to afford relief and protection against the violence and malevolence of the Majority: a true blessing in disguise. The humor of the situation appealed to Barwell. Here, he said, were the Company's servants, generally regarded at home as foes of the law, fleeing to the law for protection against the men sent to India to give the country a civilized, just and lawful government! [39]

While the Majority were waging open war against the Court, Hastings, with the cordial coöperation of the Chief Justice, was busy devising a comprehensive plan for a new judicial system. The objects he had in mind were, to reconcile the conflicting jurisdictions of the Supreme Court and the civil and criminal courts of the Company, which he himself had established, but which had no legal standing because the Regulating Act had entirely ignored them; and to put an end to the confusion and injustice caused by the ill-defined limits of the former. He proposed, first, that the limitations should be removed from the Court, so that its jurisdiction would extend to all parts of the provinces and to all the inhabitants, both Europeans and Natives; and secondly, in order to confirm and strengthen the Company's courts, that the judges of the Supreme Court should be united with the members of the Council in their control and supervision, and that their existence should be recognized by law. "The truth is," he said in justification of these proposals, "that a thing done by halves is worse done than if it were not done at all. The powers of the Court must be universal, or it would be better to repeal them altogether." [40]

This shows the sagacity and magnanimity of a great statesman, revealing a man big enough to put the interests of the State so far above his own personal views and wishes as to absorb them entirely. Hastings had disliked the idea of the Court from the day it was first mooted, and had deplored its institution; yet now he not only did not plead for its abolition but proposed that its power be trebled, be made complete and universal, even proposed that it share with the Council the control of his own carefully fostered courts. Nothing, indeed, in his whole career gives us a clearer insight into the way in which his mind worked—its flexibility, its freedom from prejudice, its adaptability, its objectiveness, its absorption in the pursuit of the highest good of his trust. The defectiveness of the constitution of the Supreme Court was to him a challenge, not to cheap political warfare, as it was to his three colleagues, but to his resourcefulness. It was a problem of statesmanship that demanded a practical solution. So he and Impey put their heads together and devised this plan to transform the Court from a serious clog on the government to an instrument of maximum benefit to the province. The Court was established by Act of Parliament; therefore, only Parliament could change its constitution. So Hastings, besides sending the plan to the Court of Directors and the Prime Minister with the suggestion that it be made the basis of new legislation, got the Chief Justice to put it in the form of an Act of Parliament. Unfortunately the self-evident wisdom of the scheme did not help to gain consideration for it at this unfavorable time....

If in Bengal the proceedings of the Majority were producing anarchy and discord, beyond the borders of the province in Oude the results were still more serious. Hastings had not ceased to prophesy the woe that would follow from the Treaty of Fyzabad. And every month confirmed the accuracy of his judgement. When Shuja-ud-Daula died the country had been in a flourishing state, but he left as legacies to his son an army twelve months in arrears of pay and a considerable debt owing to the Company. The state treasures were in possession of his widow, who refused to surrender them. Asaf-ud-Daula, therefore, came to the throne surrounded with difficulties, which the Majority seemed more anxious to increase than to lighten. They initiated, indeed, a policy of interference in his affairs that could not fail to have the most pernicious results. The Vizier was at odds with his relations, his ministers and his nobles, and his army was mutinous for want of pay. If he had been left to himself, a revolution would shortly have disposed of him. Instead, the country was kept in subjection by the presence of a British army.

In December 1775, the Vizier applied to the Bengal Government for a number of British officers to command his mutinous troops. They were sent, and added to his distresses, as their presence only increased the disaffection. His zemindars became increasingly rebellious. The collection of revenue declined. The debt to the Company grew. The terms imposed by the Treaty of Fyzabad were not met. Bristow, the British Resident, tyrannized over the Vizier to compel payment, but his interference, unaccompanied by any intelligent attempt on the part of him or his government to deal constructively with the problem, made matters worse rather than better. Nor did the presence of many Englishmen, attracted thither by the prospect of lucrative employment, help matters. By the spring of 1776 Oude was well on the road to ruin, and already the prosperity of the country had greatly declined.

The year 1775 had closed with Hastings able to say, "a dead calm has prevailed here for some time past," affording him more ease and tranquillity. The calm, if a calm it was, continued into the next year and found him still resolved to stay until the struggle was decided. "If I live, I will see the end of it." The first indications of the attitude of the Company towards their disputes satisfied neither party. The Rohilla War was not condemned, but its necessity was deplored. This did not give the Majority much ground for exultation, but they made the most of it.

The first six months of 1776 passed without any startling developments. The deadlock in the Council continued unbroken, but the Majority party showed signs of weakening. Monson was a sick man. Francis was disgusted with both of his allies. Both he and Clavering were secretly trying to get rid of the other; with his usual propensity for blunt language, Francis was declaring to his friends at home, "You might as well hang me as make him Governor." At the same time his opposition to Hastings seemed to be moderating; he even said that he would oppose him no longer. As a result the Governor-General felt more and more confident that it was only a matter of time before his restoration to power. How, he asked, could the Directors with any regard to consistency and to their own interests do other than support him? The contrast between his own mode of conduct and that of his opponents seemed to him so great—for he avowed his pride in the fact that at no time had he ever disparaged the work of his predecessors, cast aspersions at his opponents or shown personal bias in his treatment of subordinates—that he was not afraid of the closest scrutiny of his record.

It must, therefore, have come as quite a shock to him to receive at the end of June a dispatch from the Directors that indicated very clearly that they were ranging themselves on the side of his enemies. Its arrival had been eagerly awaited; a feeling of suspense and excitement had been in the air; each party felt that their fate was about to be settled.

They were disappointed. The dispatch actually settled nothing. But it condemned the Rohilla War, applauded the Majority for their zeal in investigating and condemning abuses, and damned the Governor-General with faint praise.

Hastings was indignant. Not for a moment had he acted any other part but that of strict fidelity to his employers, and what was his reward? Unmerited censure upon himself, and the grossest adulation upon his opponents. But he would not be moved from his resolution. He would await the event, and if he had to fall he would not be the instrument of his own defeat by anticipating it, unless all his friends at home advised it and he himself was convinced of its expediency. He would not acquiesce in the censures but would defend himself. And so he told Macleane not to be surprised if he found his next defense shifted from his opponents in the Council to the Court of Directors' general letter. But he was infinitely weary of the disputes and could scarcely bear with patience the thought that another year must pass without hope of relief. A decision, one way or the other, must be reached quickly; not that he wanted fortitude to persevere, but he saw so many evils gathering round him from every quarter that he feared that if the Government of Bengal were left another year to anarchy, it would not be worth possessing, and, if possessed, would lead only to misfortune and dishonor, in which event he would gain less by victory than his enemies would by their defeat.

"A reconciliation never can take place. Fire and water may more easily be united. I think I possess as placable and as pliant a spirit as most men, but I feel that it is impossible for me to be ever on confidential terms with these men. At present I am the link which holds them together, for I am morally certain that if I were to quit them, they would break and begin a scene of continual warfare with each other in less than a month after." [41]

The dispatch exhorted the Council to unanimity. And the absurdity of it so struck the fancy of the Board when it was read that every member of it at once burst out into a loud and hearty laugh, "the only symptom of unanimity," remarked Hastings caustically, "that I have seen in that assembly these two years."

The reign of the Majority was more nearly over than any of them knew. Monson was sick, and it soon appeared that his sickness was mortal. He sent in his resignation, but before it could take effect he was dead. This was at the end of September. And the effect of his death was to restore to the Governor-General the use of the casting-vote. He was once more a power in his government.

Another chapter in his stormy life was concluded. And it was one that had a profound effect on his character. "Hope buoys up his mind," wrote Barwell to his sister in November 1775; "and I see not the least decline of vigor or ability. His temper has been so severely taxed on occasions which have arisen daily to vex and ruffle it that from a very impatient man, he is become as much collected and possessed of himself as any one I ever knew." [42] This was generous praise coming from Barwell, who was not given to paying compliments to Hastings, even though he had linked his fortune with his, and there can be no question but that it was well deserved. The eager, ardent man that we knew in 1772, so full of youthful ambition and confidence, so desirous cf praise and appreciation, so keen to achieve greatly, has given place to a much more mature man, still hopeful though his early dreams had been shattered upon the hard rock of circumstance.

Each strenuous, exacting year of office left its mark upon him. The sensitive, almost petulant, mouth became set in firm, determined lines; the brow became pensive; the kindly, honest eyes assumed a quiet and serene look, but piercing in its directness and intensity; the hair receded from his high Shakespearean forehead, accentuating the intellectuality of his appearance. Great composure, dignity and equanimity settled upon his face and demeanor. Always a gallant figure, he had now become the heroic figure that has been the object of unstinted admiration by countless writers. Enduring patience and fortitude, born of faith, hope and a clear conscience, indomitable courage, inflexible determination, all directed by a great purpose, guided by a clear vision, and controlled by a disciplined will—these were the dominating characteristics of Warren Hastings when he emerged from the fiery ordeal of two years of unending strife, humiliation and abuse; a man strong enough to endure eight more years of distracted burdensome government, and, on top of that, seven years of disgrace and obloquy.

This tenacity of purpose was well displayed by his ability to sit down calmly, when the fury of the Majority was at its height, and pen a long letter to the Prime Minister, in which he stated with his usual lucidity and skill his carefully considered views on such matters as the reorganization of the civil service, the best method of remuneration— by salary or by commissions—the management of the revenues, the reform of the department of commerce and its complete separation from the political department, the relations between the executive and the judiciary, and the powers of the Governor-General. [43] Nothing that his colleagues could do was able to draw him away from active thought on the practical problems of the Empire.

Chapter XI

PHILIP FRANCIS

I

THE coming of Philip Francis and his two colleagues had opened a new phase in the British connection with India. Hitherto the control of affairs had been in the hands of servants of the East India Company. Over them were now to be placed men chosen directly from the highest walks of English public life without prior connection with the Company or Indian experience. Increasingly henceforth this practice was to be followed, until it became a fixed rule of the Crown that no member of the Indian Civil Service was eligible for the highest office, the Governor-Generalship.

The success of the new policy depended upon the selection of the right type of man. In its favor was the fact that the Governor or member of Council so chosen would be free from the jealousies of the service, he would not be hardened to the low standards of conduct existing in eighteenth-century India, he would be largely exempt from the temptations that assailed the Company's servants, he would be better placed, given adequate powers, to introduce sweeping and much needed reforms, and he could look at things with a fresh eye. On the other hand, his knowledge about India was apt to be inadequate, he might have prejudices, and he might lack sympathetic understanding of the problems of the toiling millions of India and of the men engaged in the practical work of administration.

Francis's appointment was an instance of the wrong application of a sound principle. He was, whatever else we may think of him, decidedly not the type of man that should have been sent to initiate a new experiment of this kind.

He hated India from the day of his arrival to the day of his departure. He hated its climate and its people, its heat and its filth, its villainy and its corruption. "This cursed country!" "this infernal region," as he so often called Bengal in his letters. And nothing reconciled him to his exile but his fierce personal ambition. Nor need we suppose that he was merely indulging his love of bombast. He was probably sincerely shocked by the conditions he found. The characteristic English vices of this age of brutality and blunted sensibility were not only duplicated in Calcutta, they were combined with the vices of India, and the composite result was such as might well have disgusted any newcomer of refinement and enlightened views. Slavery was still an established institution. The pillory was in daily use. The criminal law was cruel and its punishments brutal. And coexistent with these relics of barbarism were all the elegancies of polite society, together with the frequent scandals, the bitter personal jealousies and feuds, the backstairs intrigues, and the everlasting gossip of a small and bored community.

To some extent Francis was at home in this atmosphere. It was typical of the eighteenth century, and Francis was very much a man of his age. He was a hardened cynic and took enormous delight in scandal and intrigue, as his letters and journal abundantly prove. In particular, he was very much of a ladies' man, being able to ingratiate himself even with the wives of his political opponents, like Mrs. Hastings and Lady Impey. But there was much that he resented intensely, particularly the physical discomforts of life in a hot, damp climate, the excessively high cost of living and the general rascality, as it seemed to him, of the people, both light and dark.

Alexander Macrabie, Francis's brother-in-law, secretary and member of his personal household, gives us through the entries in his journal a clear idea of what Francis and his *entourage* thought of the life of Calcutta. He was particularly distressed by the ungodliness of the place and its lack of religious observance. There was no church. Divine Service was held in the Fort, in a building that was used for the storing of goods and collecting of customs on the other six days, and he says that the European Colony were amazed when the new Councilors went there in a body the first Sunday after their arrival. He was strongly of the opinion, too, that a thorough reformation of manners, both public and private, was much needed. Almost at once he found that his temper was being ruined by the myriads of native servants, by the endless entertainments, all marked by a senseless extravagance and ostentation, and by a thousand other annoyances.

"Even the recreations of this country are little riots. Thirty people at breakfast, fifty at dinner. Suppers at midnight, dances till daylight. But we are now reforming apace. We now only toast healths and sentiments in gills and half-pints of claret. Formerly, instead of drinking a glass of wine with a gentleman it was usual to throw a chicken at his head—while the ladies pelted with sweetmeats and pastry. This was thought refinement in wit and breeding." [1]

The expensive living was too much for the thrifty Scotsman. He was horrified that Mr. Francis had to pay a rental of £500 for a house, "or rather a barn," with bare walls and not a single glass window; and ironically lamented that his establishment of servants was pitifully

PHILIP FRANCIS
(From a contemporary pastel; reproduced by kind permission of E. P. Dutton & Co.)

small. No more than sixty! Macrabie himself had fifteen, "and yet am forced sometimes to clean my own shoes. My greatest comfort is to turn them all out and lock the doors." He had, indeed, no words strong enough to describe the thieving brutes. "In short, I grow a perfect cynic—and have not laughed three times since we landed." So jaded was he with parade and pompous entertainment that more than once he feigned sickness to avoid them. In order to avoid confusion he classified their cares under several heads: "public cares, domestic cares, cares general and particular cares." He calculated that there were a hundred and ten servants to take care of the four persons in Francis's family, and the absurdity of it all struck him with tremendous force. It was always for him "this cursed country"—and how it had been ruined!

There is no doubt that the old evils of rapacity and corruption, dating from the lax days of the Company's rule, were still prevalent among the European community. But nobody was quite so conscious of their existence as Francis, or adopted a loftier tone of disdain, or expressed himself with greater moral indignation. His opinion both of the Indians and of his fellow-countrymen in India could hardly have been lower. How thoroughly he depised them is shown by the fact that he expressed the belief that Englishmen, by long residence in India, contracted the character of the country, "and without the insignia of black faces and white turbans are as completely Banyans as the people who serve them," and the banyans, let it be said again, were execrated by all from Hastings downwards as the world's most consummate rascals.

This contempt for the weaknesses and depravity of other men naturally made him proud and haughty, but it must be laid to his credit that he was himself free from the prevailing vice of avarice. It is true that one of his objects in coming to India was to seek an independent fortune, but there was nothing dishonorable in that ambition: it was the goal of everybody before the days of liberal pensions, and the Crown had recognized the fact by attaching princely salaries to the Council posts. Even so, the cost of living was so fantastically high that a man could not save enough out of his salary to gain an independence in less than six or seven years. Francis found another means of hastening the day. He was not corrupt, but he had one vice in common with the men of his age, and that was gambling at cards. He devoted himself to whist with the zeal and skill of the professional gambler, and the stakes in Calcutta in those days were high. In one night he admitted winning, chiefly from Barwell, no less a sum than £20,000, £8000 of which he promptly lost—and thereafter he played but little and for small stakes. His fortune was made and he took no chances of losing it. It is, perhaps, not to be wondered at that the people at home were astonished when they heard about this incident. It did not seem to them quite in character with the rôle of "the Reformer of India."

That Francis should have looked upon the problems of India with very different eyes from those of the men in the Indian service is not surprising. To them India meant primarily two things, first a career and a means of livelihood, secondly, a problem in practical government. The line of their duty lay stretched out plain before them; they were servants of the East India Company and as such felt an obligation to obey its orders and serve its interest. Many of them had been in Bengal for a long time and were intimately acquainted with the whole history of the British connection with the country, and knowing how the many extraordinary events of recent years had come to pass, they were disposed to accept them without much question and to turn their attention to the particular tasks in hand—the consolidation of British power, the improvement of the revenues, the reorganization of the administrative system, the rehabilitation of the Company's trade. The existence of the Empire was to them an established fact, and the only fruitful field of discussion that remained was how best to manage it. Francis, on the other hand, represented a large section of the English public that had no connection whatever with India or with the Company, no particular knowledge of the history of either, and no personal interest in the success of this extraordinary British enterprise; and yet at the same time held pronounced views about politics and government, which they were prepared to apply universally. His coming to share in the government of India meant inevitably that there would be a clash of ideas, principles and points of view, which would pierce much deeper than surface points of policy.

Francis belonged, as we have seen, to the Whig party. That meant a definite attitude of mind to such a problem as that presented by India. The English Whig was a traditionalist, and in particular a constitutionalist. He had a natural reverence for the past, for established institutions, rights and privileges; to disregard which was to stamp oneself in his eyes as a danger to society and an enemy of real freedom. He believed in political and social development, but only so far as it did not involve violent change that broke with the principles and forms of the past. For this reason he loved to appeal to the Revolution, "the glorious Revolution," of 1688, which was in his eyes the perfect, and only right kind of, revolution, because legality was its essence and correction of abuses and restoration of the old its principal object. This was the political philosophy of Edmund Burke, as the chief spokesman of the Whig party, and it was also the philosophy of Philip Francis.

Where Francis differed from Burke was the way in which he applied the conservative principle to the Indian question. Hitherto the Whigs had seen only one way in which it should be applied, and that was in defending the chartered rights and privileges of the East India Company against violent usurpation by the Crown. Francis saw that this was a very narrow view that looked at the question from a purely English standpoint and ignored India entirely. When he reached India and had gained some knowledge of the recent course of events in

Bengal, a great light dawned on him. He realized that the Crown's usurpation had been as nothing compared to the rights and powers that the Company had usurped in India.

British rule in Bengal had sprung from violence and had been built up by violence. It was the result of a revolution that in Francis's eyes violated every Whig principle. The old Mogul system, the indefeasible and natural heritage of the Indian people, had been overturned. The authority of the Emperor had been annulled (the British Governor had not shrunk from describing him as "a king of shreds and patches"), while his Viceroy the Nawab had been reduced to the status of a helpless pensioner, and the great nobles, the natural rulers and protectors of the peoples, had been stripped of their hereditary rights and privileges. And all for what purpose? That a body of alien traders might set up a species of rule that was arbitrary, irregular, despotic and inherently unjust. A great and terrible crime, Francis proclaimed to the world, had been committed in India, a crime that cut at the roots of morality and the principles of civilized government and ran counter to the best thought of the day. For Francis was more than a conservative Whig; he was, as a student of Locke, Montesquieu, Voltaire and the French philosophers, under the influence of the liberal forces of his day, a product (how curiously diverse those products were! Hastings and Francis!) of the humanitarian spirit of the age. Conservatism and Liberalism combined, as they also combined in Edmund Burke, to make Francis hate tyrants, and as tyrants he regarded the English both in Bengal and in their quarrel with the American Colonies.

The Whigs, secure in their aristocratic aloofness from the mean pursuits of ordinary men, despised trade. So did Francis, their proud and haughty camp-follower. Hatred of tyrants and contempt for trade found for him their common mark in the East India Company, the merchant rulers of Bengal. There was no lack, as we have seen, of strong feeling in England against the Company; all that Francis tried to do was to fan the smoldering flame of resentment and prejudice into a fierce blaze of indignation that would utterly destroy its sovereign power. He set out with a ruthless determination to strip it of every shred of honor and reputation, so that there should be no doubt left in anybody's mind that it was totally unqualified to exercise political power. He declared that its detestable rule was based on violated treaties, shameless rapacity and the most sordid self-interest. It knew not the meaning of the words truth, honor, honesty and justice, and its government of Bengal was nothing better than an organized system of spoliation. And why? For the simple reason that the Company was a commercial organization whose only *raison d'être* was gain. That fact alone rendered it absolutely unable to apply principles of civilized government to its conquered dominions, as nothing could reconcile the requirements of sovereignty with the aims of merchants. The idea that reforms and regulations could remove the disqualification was by the very nature of the case absurd, as the irredeemable could not be redeemed.

These pronounced views, held almost from the day he stepped ashore at Calcutta, quickly crystallized into a clear-cut policy. With resounding words and his customary vehemence, Francis declared that the Crown must at once assume the Company's political power as the essential preliminary to the righting of a great wrong. What the East India Company had destroyed the Crown must restore: it must restore the *ancien régime* of India, the Nawab to his authority and the great nobles and zemindars to their rightful place in the government. Direct British administration of the provinces must be abolished. The dispensing of justice, the control of the police, the supervision of the criminal courts, the collection of the revenues, these were not fit matters for alien management. The representatives of the sovereign power should restrict themselves to preserving the country from foreign invasion and internal strife and the control of relations with the outside world.

These were not new proposals originating from the mind of Francis. It is easy to recognize in them Clive's Dual System dressed up in a new way. Francis had absorbed Clive's views with especial readiness because he wished for the support of Clive's still powerful influence, but at the same time he gave them a new value. Clive's purpose had primarily been to use the Nawab as a screen to hide the real source of power in order to protect his employers from embarrassing complications with European powers; his system had been an expedient of national self-interest. Francis's was based on principle and aimed at restoring to Bengal a measure of autonomy. Clive had wished to facilitate the exploitation of Bengal by the Company, by saving it expensive and dangerous political and administrative responsibilities. Francis wished to relieve the province of its subjection to foreign rule and to limit its exploitation. The difference in object represents Francis's chief contribution to the discussion of the Indian problem.

It cannot be denied that much of his reasoning was based on false premises and analogies, and that it involved a grave distortion of history. Bengal before the English conquest had borne little resemblance to Francis's idealized conception. When he talked of the old régime, he was actually thinking of the Mogul system of government as it had been in the heyday of the Empire, not of the degenerate remains that still did duty for it in 1757. And when he saw the distressed state of the country in 1774 he did not compare it with what it had been but three short years before or stop to ask himself whether or not it was improving. The ruin of a country that had once been prosperous and the misery of a people that had once been happy blinded him to every other consideration, and made him jump to the conclusion that every evil he saw was the direct result of British rule, and that so long as that continued, so long would conditions get worse and the work of destruction proceed. Yet neither false premises nor false conclusions can altogether cancel that which was of real worth in Francis's thought: his championship of Indian autonomy. It can hardly be denied that the division of powers which he demanded, placing the legal sovereignty, with political and military supremacy, in the hands of the Crown, and leaving the native ruler free to manage his domestic affairs and to minister to the legal, social and economic needs of the people, is essentially the basis of the relations today between the Crown as suzerain and the native Princes of India. Its success would have depended, as it depends today, on the justice, firmness and wisdom of the vice-regal government, and the good will and efficiency of the prince. Without these essential conditions the restoration of the Nawab's government, if it had been carried out as Francis planned, would almost certainly have been a retrogressive move, attended by a return to the conditions existing prior to Hastings's assumption of the Governorship.

What spoiled Francis's scheme of thought was not that he wished to place the people of Bengal under their old rulers, but that he did not relinquish the idea that Great Britain should take tribute from her conquered provinces in the shape of the surplus revenues. How firmly he believed in this right of the sovereign power is shown by his defense of the Treaty of Fyzabad, ceding Benares to the Company:

"The permanent advantages, which this acquisition secures to the Company, require no illustration. Conforming to the policy we profess the spirit of the treaty is to acquire revenue without territory, that is without any direct interference of the Company, or influence of their servants in the internal government of the tributary dominion. If the same policy had been pursued in former times, I have no doubt that a considerable portion of the revenue of Bengal, on the footing of a fixed tribute, might have been enjoyed by the Company for a longer period, without distress to the country and without embarrassment to themselves either here or at home." [2]

Here Francis was, of course, deliberately pandering to the Company's desire for bigger profits and trying to prove that he and his two allies knew better how to obtain them than did Hastings, its much lauded servant. It is doubtful, therefore, whether this cold-blooded attitude represented Francis's genuine views. Moreover, severely as we may reprobate the idea of tribute, we must note in justice to Francis that it was still, in the minds of the vast majority of his fellow-countrymen, the natural right of Empire.

Francis's ideas look better in the abstract than in the concrete. We need not quarrel seriously with his desire to reverse the trend of British policy, so long as we do not follow him off the safe high ground of general principle. If we are so minded, we can even applaud him. But when we descend with him from the mountain tops of thought to the fields of practical work, to see the use that he made of his prophetic vision, we soon find ourselves being taken beyond the fields, beyond the sunshine of honesty and sincerity, down into the shadows, places scarcely penetrable by the ordinary eye, inhabited by the evil spirits of personal antipathies and selfish ambitions—and before long we begin to wonder whether it was out of this dank and fetid atmosphere, and not the pure air of the mountains, that Philip Francis drew his inspiration.

II

WHATEVER view Francis expressed on Indian affairs he invariably tried to make it appear that Hastings stood for something diametrically opposite. When he condemned the East India Company as the custodian of empire, he coupled with it the name of the Governor-General. When he denounced the rapacity and corruption of the Company's servants, he was careful to stress the fact that their executive chief was the worst offender. He could not rest satisfied with censuring the measures of the late administration on public grounds, but chose to attribute them to self-interested motives on the part of its chief. He could not lament the overthrow of the native government without attributing to the man who had abolished it the intention of substituting a wholly alien, arbitrary and despotic system. He was so obsessed with the idea that Hastings was "an abandoned villain," who was rapidly plunging Bengal to ruin and destruction, that there was nothing that he had done or could do that he did not condemn, upon one ground or another. And one is accordingly driven to the conclusion that, divorced from their connection with Hastings, Francis's views lose much of their virtue and meaning.

There was, of course, a whole world of difference between the two men, a difference of mind, spirit, temperament and outlook. One was a practical statesman, the other a political theorist. The mind of the one was open and supple, that of the other was closed and inflexible. One thought in terms of India, its peculiar needs, distinctive problems, complex history, and promising future; the other in terms of principles derived from European thought and prejudices developed in England. One based his actions on past experience and the dictates of natural intelligence, the other on a preconceived system of ideas. One inclined to confidence and optimism, the other to despondency and pessimism. One wished to make Bengal a strong, flourishing and well-governed state, the other to save it from impending ruin and to give it "freedom." Hastings, the benevolent despot, looked forward; Francis, the doctrinaire liberal, looked backward: he preferred that the despotism should be Moslem rather than British.

Not that there was the absolute, irreconcilable antithesis between all their views that Francis believed, or pretended there was. It would be a mistake, for instance, to suppose that Hastings was blind to the wisdom of ultimate control of the Empire by the Crown instead of the Company; he regarded the latter as the "temporary trustee" of the rights of the British nation in Bengal, and urged upon the Prime Minister very strongly the advisability of the Crown at once taking unto itself the sphere of relations with the Indian states. [3] He also realized as clearly as did Francis that "the details of commerce are not fit objects of attention to the supreme administration of a state," and wanted the line of distinction between the functions of governor and merchant drawn as sharply as possible. Then again, Francis was only displaying his own ignorance of Hastings's aims, when he accused him of over-turning the Moslem government in order to establish a bastard British system of his own concoction, of having "rashly forced the accumulated wisdom and experience of ages to yield to the crude ideas of a few foreigners." [4] When it came to a matter of argument, Francis was indeed at a grave disadvantage, because so much of what he preached could not stand the test of being brought up against the immense knowledge and experience of a man who had spent over fifteen years in the country and who had been there before a British Empire was even dreamed of.

This was not, however, of much consequence. The voting in the Council was not affected by points scored in debate, and there were few persons who paid any attention to such fine distinctions. The roots of Francis's antagonism to the Governor-General went much deeper than the superficial trivialities of fact. He could not deny that Hastings was an able controversialist; indeed, he once admitted that there was no contending against his pen. But this only acted as a spur, goading him on in his efforts to reveal the true nature of Hastings's policy and to bring about its reversal.

Francis knew only one way to express opposition—the way of Junius. He was as much the slave of his passions as of his principles. He could have opposed Hastings on public grounds, and emerged with credit from the conflict, but because the Governor-General was not only identified with the system that Francis condemned but was the chief obstacle in the path of his ambition, he hated him with one of the most terrible hates that history records. Hatred was the one domi-nating emotion of his Indian career: hatred of India, hatred of the Company, hatred of Warren Hastings, hatred of all who supported Warren Hastings. And in its expression it carried him to such ex-traordinary lengths as to make one wonder whether he was the tragic victim of a self-created delusion, or whether it was sheer malignity alone that made him invent lies and slanders of the most monstrous description. He alone could return a definite reply to this question, but a psychopathist would, perhaps, decide that both elements were present. He was a man to whom the whole of the meanest side of human nature was an open book: the envies and jealousies, the greeds, the selfish ambitions and unworthy desires, the frauds, the deceits, the lies—and, equally, all the nobler qualities of mankind were hidden. He was like a scared child who in every corner of a dark room sees bogeys and gob-lins. India was his dark room, and the bogeys and goblins he saw everywhere were bribery, fraud, corruption, jobbery, venality, the whole catalogue of misdoings possible to public officials. Even when Hastings's actions were committed in the full light of day, he refused entirely to accept them as those of a disinterested, honest, public-spirited statesman, but, whenever possible, attributed them to dishonorable motives and objects, falling back on insinuations when direct accusation was impracticable or unwise.

Not long after his arrival in Bengal he gave to his friends at home an elaborate character-sketch of the man he hated:

"Hastings has resided so long in Bengal, that in many respects he may be considered as a native. He assumes the arms as well as the name of the Huntingdon family, but no man knows with what right or by what authority. I understand him to be the natural son of a steward of the late Lord Darlington (so I have been repeatedly assured by Lady Anne Monson[1] who was a daughter of that family. She told me her father sent him with his own sons to Westminster School, where he was called the 'Classical Boy'). His birth, however, could never be the subject of a question but for his own folly in pretending to deduce it from the noblest blood in England. He has all the craft of a Bengalee, united however with a degree of vanity and impatience of contradiction which sometimes throws him off his guard. When these passions are under command, he can put on a smile and assume an air of innocence and candor enough to melt or seduce a generous mind, and to deceive any man unacquainted with his arts, or less proficient in hypocrisy than himself. His reserve, whether natural or acquired, is so excessive, that I firmly believe he never reposed an entire confidence in any man. This policy or temper suited the sordid objects he had in view, and the crooked ways by which he was obliged to compass them. . . .

"Mr. Hastings's first object is money, though I do not dispute that he would be well pleased to have honor into the bargain. Yet he is not strictly avaricious; for no man by all accounts takes less care of his money, or can occasionally bestow it more handsomely."

Rather, he used his money, Francis went on to state, to bribe every man returning home in order to secure his support, which accounted for the extravagant praises lavished on him by such gentlemen. He possessed sagacity, experience and industry, but as they were all applied to wrong ends and based on wrong principles they only served to make him a still more dangerous man. Finally, Francis noted the same weakness that Barwell had emphasized: his jealousy of all competition, which disposed him to monopolize the work of government and assume too much responsibility. [5]

A little later on, after he had been two and a half years in India, he delivered his "deliberate judgement" of Hastings, declaring "that he is a busy, projecting, intricate politician of the lowest order, and that it is not in his nature to walk straight." [6]

Francis wanted his friends to be in no doubt of Hastings's thorough incompetence for his position. His reputation was that of a very able, practical statesman. It was entirely false, Francis told them; indeed,

[1] Colonel Monson's wife.

the opposite was true. Hastings conceived impractical plans and neglected the means for carrying them out; he was very resourceful but, for no intelligent reason, preferred always the difficult resource to the easy. And in order to prove his point Francis told an anecdote about him:

"I happened to sup with him not long ago, when the conversation turned upon *Robinson Crusoe*. Everybody present gave their opinion of the book, of course without reflection. While the rest of the company were talking, Mr. Hastings seemed lost in a reverie, in which I little suspected that *Robinson Crusoe* could be concerned. At last he gravely declared, that he had often read the book with singular satisfaction; but that no passage in it had ever struck him so much, as where the hero is said to have built a monstrous boat at a distance from the sea, without knowing by what means he was to convey it to the water. 'And by Jove,' says Hastings, 'the same thing has happened to myself an hundred times in my life. I have built the boat without any farther consideration, and when difficulties and consequences have been urged against it, have been too ready to answer them by saying to myself: "Let me finish the boat first, and then I'll warrant, I shall find some method to launch it." ' This is the man's own political picture drawn by himself." [7]

And apparently Francis thought it the picture of a dangerous, unscrupulous and unprincipled opportunist.

Some gleams of what appear to be truth shine through these passages, not enough to enable us to identify the subject of the portrait if the name were not attached, but enough to give it some slight appearance of having been painted from life. Undoubtedly Hastings's long residence in Bengal, if not making him a native, had led him to see things from an Indian point of view. It was characteristic of Francis's attitude of mind that, though in principle he believed in Indian autonomy, in practice he heartily despised the people and despised Hastings for having absorbed so much of their mode of thought.

When we examine the strategy and tactics of his warfare against Hastings, we find that we are dealing with a man who was quite capable of appearing in several different guises according to circumstances. The Francis who occupied the fifth place at the Council Board at Calcutta was not the same as the Francis whom his friends at home saw through the medium of his letters. To the latter he appeared a veritable Saint George, setting forth to fight the dragon of human wickedness and depravity, fully armed, strong, courageous and determined. All that he needed, he told them on his departure, was some of Clive's fortitude. "Cabals, I hear are forming against us in India. But I fancy they are not half so determined to resist, as we are to overcome." [8] When the great fight began, he became the personification of virtue, battling against the entrenched forces of Evil, the one man who could save Bengal from ruin. Speaking with the voice of one of the old Hebrew prophets, he let his moral indignation pour forth in a stream of burning words. Honor, integrity, virtue, duty, truth, zeal—these were the ideals that inspired him and for which he was ready to sacrifice the pleasant things of life. The path of stern duty was unpleasant, even dangerous—"My heart is almost broken when I consider the woeful task I have undertaken"—but with entire self-abnegation he would follow it, trusting that in the end Right would triumph over Might. And the manner of his writing was impressive—vivid phrases, emphatic assertions, sweeping condemnations, a magnificent refusal to compromise with evil, a complete and most effective cynicism.

His colleagues in Council saw a very different man. A man who was not at all conspicuous in their conflicts, who seemed disposed to be much more moderate than his two allies and who was careful not to be in the forefront of the battle. Nor was this appearance of prudence and caution due to a sudden loss of confidence on his part, compelling him to change his whole line of conduct. It was the result of deliberate intention. Among his papers there is a remarkable document entitled "Hints for my own Conduct," written immediately upon his arrival in Calcutta. In it he carefully mapped out the line of action that he proposed to take, as follows:

Exercise care when speaking in public. Deliver no opinion without careful preparation. Be always alert and on the watch. Do not take the lead in business. Be affable and kind to all. Seem to be backward in all unpleasant business, such as prosecutions: "to seem to be forced into them." To keep his ears open for current gossip and opinions. To speak with the utmost respect of the Company and the Directors. In Council, not to dispute about trifles and never to protest except upon great occasions. Take great care not to give offense. If outvoted, "let it be supposed that I would do more good, if it were in my power." Avoid the odium of violent or offensive measures, "concurring only, not seeming to promote." Unite all Clive's friends to him. Be very cautious about committing himself to support of measures of Hastings's administration. [9]

That was the Francis that Calcutta knew. It is true that he often departed from this line of conduct, especially as time wore on and the bitterness of hope deferred grew and grew. But while Clavering and Monson were there to lead the attack in public—honest, misguided men who made no attempt to conceal their violent animus against Hastings—Francis preferred to act with stealth and caution, privately directing and inspiring their operations but in public claiming for himself the virtue of moderation and posing as the one man in the whole Council who was not actuated by the spirit of faction and violence.

This was the Francis that Hastings knew, though he did not accept him quite at his own valuation. He had expressed his opinion freely of Clavering and Monson, but of Francis he had written, "I shall say nothing of him." Why? Because he did not consider him of sufficient importance? Certainly it was not because he had any respect for him. In November 1776 he wrote to Alexander Elliot: "The movements of this man of levity are difficult to foresee or comprehend. His interest is the only steady principle in his composition, and operates in him as powerfully as in any man I ever knew, yet even this cannot always concentrate him, but by fits he flies off from it." He went on to state that Francis acquiesced in matters of routine business and either mildly opposed or disclaimed responsibility for measures of importance (this was after the reign of the Majority was over). "This temporizing conduct he calls moderation, and makes a merit of it. Yet, such as it is, I would avail myself of it if I could, having too much at stake to hazard by contending with a man whose character I despise, and whose friendship and enmity I should view with equal indifference, under any other circumstances." [10] "Man of levity!" Good heavens, we are moved to cry, how could any one think of Philip Francis as a man of levity? Yet that Hastings apparently did only proves the extraordinary cleverness of this man with a double face, whose nature had so much in common with a snake's.

Barwell was less easily deceived. "A deeper policy regulates his conduct than I immediately perceived": he was so artful that it was easy to be duped by him. "No small degree of caution is necessary to penetrate the veil his actions wear." [11]

Since Francis was anything but a fool, he knew very well where his weakness lay, and where his strength. He was ignorant of India, but ignorance could to a large extent be overcome, given such ceaseless, untiring industry as he possessed, the equal of Hastings's; and given, also, his skill at picking other men's brains. It was a common jest in Calcutta that Francis produced excellent minutes on the land revenue question when John Shore and David Anderson, experts on the subject, were in Calcutta. When they were not at hand to help him, he usually kept a discreet silence. He must have realized still more clearly that his *métier* was not that of an administrator, for he consistently refused to take an active part in the business of government and, as often as he could, shirked the responsibility of measures.

Francis's natural rôle was, indeed, that of an external critic. Not only did it suit his temperament but he possessed the ability to play it with maximum effect. Junius had been the most powerful and the most feared critic in English politics of his day, and the hand of the master had not lost its cunning by the change of scene, nor had it lost the itch to ply the pen. While Clavering and Monson were engaging Hastings and Barwell in open combat, Francis wrote. He wrote elaborate minutes that would appear in the Council's Consultations, recorded for the information of the Directors. He wrote the long dispatches that went home by every ship under the joint signatures of him and his two confederates. He wrote letters to the Prime Minister, to the Prime Minister's private secretary, to Cabinet Ministers, to Clive and Clive's secretary, to Directors, Proprietors, Members of Parliament, friends, and, not least of all, he wrote to Edmund Burke. Nor did he write only his own letters. As General Clavering was no writer, Francis composed his letters to the Prime Minister for him.

Never has a bolder effort been made to attain the summit of power by means of the pen alone than that made by Francis. He had wits, and he used them to practice upon the general credulity of mankind, varying his style according to his correspondent. First in importance was his bid for Clive's support. To this end he employed tactics of alarm, mixed with judicious flattery. Bengal was hopelessly ruined, and Mr. Hastings had wholly and solely ruined it. "When your Lordship came here in 1765, this country was in a state of Innocence and Purity! It was paradise before the fall, compared to the condition in which we found it." [12] The revenues were rapidly declining and his Lordship's *jaghire* [1] was in danger. If it was to be saved, Clive must see to it that Francis was not recalled; otherwise his Lordship might as well take his leave of Bengal forever. "I have no interest to serve personally." The most confidential parts of his letters to Clive and to Strachey, Clive's secretary, he put into a numerical code: 77, 6, 29, 52, 60, 12, 3, 73, 20, 102, 100, meant "Bengal is ruined."

To Lord North Francis declared that he had never personally attacked the Governor-General. Hastings had gone out of his way to attack him, as his aim was to divide the Majority and misrepresent them at home. To the Directors he posed as the faithful servant of the Company, zealously attentive to its interest—though at the same time he was inveighing against both the Directors and the Company in his confidential communications to Ministers. Finally, in his desperate pursuit of the Governor-Generalship, he did not hesitate to intrigue against his two allies, in the hope that they, as well as Hastings and Barwell, would be recalled, leaving him the senior, instead of the junior, member of the government. While Clavering and Monson served a useful purpose for a time, he made no secret to his intimate friends of his unmitigated contempt for them.

Thus far he had confined himself to destructive criticism of his associates. But he was shrewd enough to realize that destructive criticism was not sufficient of itself to qualify him for the chief position. He had to try to prove to Ministers and Directors that he had sounder ideas on public policy than the man whom he so uncompromisingly condemned. And so there followed a series of extremely able letters in which he expanded his views with a great show of plausibility and zeal for the public interests. Then, having left no stone unturned in pursuit of the object of his ambition, he sat back in confidence to await the result.... But he waited in vain. Ministers intended that Clavering should have Hastings's place, they had no idea of giving it to Francis. He was doomed to disappointment, deep, bitter and lasting. And Francis disappointed was as vindictive and dangerous a man as ever lived.

One power he had, and none could take it away from him. That was the power to influence public opinion at home on the subject of India. Whatever he or his colleagues said was bound to have great

---

[1] This was the grant of land that the Mogul Emperor had made to Clive after the battle of Plassey.

weight: it was the chief, and practically the only, source of information available to the people of England on Indian affairs before the coming of newspaper correspondents and Royal Commissions. And he had at least an equal chance with Hastings to make his views prevail.

It was as though a monopoly of Bengal news was held by two rival broadcasting stations, one situated in Government House, the other in the Council chambers; from one was heard the voice of Warren Hastings, from the other that of Philip Francis; and listeners-in in England could take their choice of stations. Prejudice, interest, or common sense decided them upon which one to bestow their trust and confidence. Each man recognized the vital importance of getting his views before the public, and of getting them accepted. In England, not in India, lay the decision of the issue. The war in the Council chamber was fiercely fought. Every question was fully debated as it arose. But so long as the result was a foregone conclusion, with three always voting against two, debate for the purpose of gaining a point or influencing an opponent was futile. The wordiness of the warfare arose from the desire of each party to justify its conduct before its constituents at home. Thus an endless debate was carried on through the mails to an invisible audience sixteen thousand miles away, from which no response could be obtained for twelve months. But they expected that the response when it came would decide which of them was to remain in the government.

Francis expected that the Company would listen to Hastings. His own hope lay in the Crown, the ignorance of the general public, and the violent prejudices that already dominated the minds of so many Englishmen. His reliance on the Crown seemed justified. Did not Welbore Ellis, M.P., an influential follower of Lord North, regard him as "the confidential friend of Government" in the Council, and use language that clearly implied that the Crown and the Company were irreconcilable enemies, each fighting for its own hand? [13] But if the Crown failed him at the end, ignorance and prejudice did not. If they had not it in their power to satisfy his ambition, they were at least able as time wore on to satisfy his desire for revenge on the man who defied him. For Francis cast his net wide. While appealing to Ministers of the Crown, he did not neglect the Opposition, the members of his own Whig party. Here was fertile soil, receptive to ideas that could be used to attack the author of the Regulating Act. Here too was Edmund Burke, wavering between his support of the Company and his hostility to its chief servant. By bombarding Burke with lurid reports of the Company's misrule and of the appalling state of affairs in Bengal, by describing to him how kings had been dethroned, nobles expropriated and the common people reduced to a state of starving misery, and especially how the whole innocent nation of Rohillas had been deliberately destroyed, Francis hoped to appeal to his well-known hatred of oppression and injustice and to wean him from his irrational championing of the Company.

In this he was entirely successful. For seven years after the passage of the Regulating Act, while the American War was absorbing the attention of Ministers, Indian affairs did not come before Parliament. The term of that Act was only five years; when it expired in 1778 it had to be provisionally renewed from year to year until the Government was ready to proceed with fresh legislation. This was done without debate. But when Parliament at length renewed its inquiries into the Company's affairs, Burke and most of his party took a position directly opposite to that which they had held before. This was Francis's great achievement, this was his life's work. Into his camp then came the forces of political faction and noble passion to join those of ignorance, prejudice and personal enmity. Together they formed an army of immense strength with which to attack Hastings and the Company he was loyally serving.

Such was Philip Francis, and such were his principles, views, aims and methods. It is unnecessary to condemn him or them: his worst enemy would not need to add a word to his letters or any adornment to his actions. Many men have convicted themselves out of their own mouths, but few so damningly as he.

Chapter XII

LORD NORTH

J. F. McCarthy
Crandwood, Wisconsin

T HE many mistakes of the Regulating Act began to recoil upon
its author in the summer of 1775, when reports of the first two
months' proceedings of the Supreme Council reached England.
They could not have arrived at a worse juncture. The disputes with
the American Colonies having passed into the stage of open rebellion,
the last thing Lord North wanted to hear was that Bengal as well had
become a scene of violent strife. The American situation was quite
enough for any government to handle: for Lord North it was more
than enough.

Lord North was everything that George the Third wanted in his
chief minister. It was a great relief to the King, after the intolerable
domineering manners of the Whig leaders, to find a minister who
really was a servant and not a would-be master. Lord North was loyal,
tactful, courteous, deferential, and at the same time so pleasant and
genial. After ten years spent enduring such men as George Grenville,
Lord Chatham and the Marquis of Rockingham, the King had attained
the peace and satisfaction that comes to any man with the possession of
the perfect valet. No better agent to take care of his business could he
have found. North's most important duty was to manage the House of
Commons, and this he did admirably. So placid and easy-tempered was
he that the bitterest shafts of his political opponents could not ruffle
his composure or provoke his resentment; so ready of wit, quick of
understanding and facile in speech that he could hold his own in any
debate. Versatile, intelligent, scholarly, always polite, he commanded the
good-humored respect of all and the affection of many. Honest and
disinterested himself, he was pleasantly tolerant of the foibles of his
fellows, and especially proficient in the gentle art of managing them.
Government in the eyes of his royal master meant primarily the holding
together of a majority, and this he knew well how to do, not, as was the
way of the Pitts, by means of personal leadership and superior ability,
resulting in moral and intellectual ascendancy, but by skillful use of the

material resources of the Crown to satisfy the cupidity of his followers. As the King's political manager and as leader of the House of Commons Lord North unquestionably was a great success. No one who is Prime Minister of his country for twelve consecutive years can be lightly regarded, and it was no small achievement for him to hold his post despite the constant failure of his measures. His failure was, indeed, the measure of his success. A good politician, he was a bad statesman. He could manage Parliament, but he could not manage an empire. And it was his misfortune to be minister at a time when it was the Empire rather than Parliament that most needed managing, if the nation's and not just the King's personal interests were to be served. His attempts to regulate the two branches of the Empire were disastrous; one rebelled, the other was flung into chaos. And all his blunders returned again and again to plague him, until at length they overcame his adroitness and ended his long reign of power.

If the American problem bothered him, the Indian problem only bored and annoyed him. He thought he had disposed of it two years before. What could be more vexing than to find the one apparently as refractory as the other? Why did these men have to inaugurate the new system by quarreling? And why, above all, did they have to solemnly appeal to him to decide between them? They had been strongly exhorted to maintain harmony. Surely, then, they should act like sensible men and compose their differences.

Very clear is it that at first Lord North did not want to take sides. The views he expressed to the King on the merits of the first disputes show a real attempt to reach a fair and balanced judgement. Clavering, Monson and Francis, he said, seemed to be in the right with respect to the Rohilla War, in which transaction the Governor-General's conduct was not quite free from suspicion, but in other matters he appeared to have been a very able and useful servant to the Company, and in particular to have put the finances of Bengal into a much better condition than they had been in before his time. The worst part of the business was, he sadly admitted, that the two parties in the Council appeared too much irritated against one another to act together with any cordiality for the future. [1]

Whichever way he looked at the situation it was full of difficulty. Clavering and Monson were the King's men and their friends were important cogs in the wheel of his own Majority. On the other hand, he felt that the time had not yet come when Hastings's able services should be dispensed with. He had reason, too, to be afraid of the strength of the Governor-General's following in the Company. There seemed only one thing for him to do and that was to follow his natural bent and temporize by appearing as the friend of both parties, and hope for the best. It soon became generally known that Lord North's desire was to cast no more blame upon the Governor-General than it was supposed he could bear, as his resignation would be considered a public misfortune, to treat the triumvirate tenderly that their friends in England might not be disgusted, and to exhort the five gentlemen again to harmony. [2] But, alas! his Lordship was soon to find the strain of sitting on the fence too great.

The first reports of the disputes threw public opinion into confusion. Whatever wickedness had been attributed to the Company's servants in general, an honorable exception had hitherto been made of Warren Hastings. He had many friends who were fervently devoted to him, and they never missed an opportunity of extolling his merits and silencing the slanders of his enemies. Hitherto they had held the fort for him with ease. Now their difficulties began. The ably written dispatches of Francis had their intended effect, especially at the west end of town, and as ship after ship reached port from Calcutta with even more startling news, the disturbance of opinion grew, and with it the anxiety of Hastings's friends. They urgently wrote him to hold his post. Have patience, said Sulivan. Be firm and resolute, said Sykes. Sykes and Sulivan were not friends: Sykes disliked and distrusted Sulivan and regretted that Hastings had entrusted his interests to Macleane, a close connection of Sulivan; but they, and all the rest of Hastings's supporters, made common cause in his behalf.

By some mischance the Majority's dispatches on the Nuncomar charges arrived ahead of the Governor-General's report. And such, now was the instability of opinion that the charges found almost universal credence and aroused intense feeling against Hastings. He was spoken of as the most corrupt governor Bengal had yet had. Even his most faithful champions knew a moment of sick fear lest the charges might be true. "I would have ventured my life nothing of this kind could have ever been laid to your charge," wrote Sykes in dismay. Then Hastings's own account arrived, and at once opinion swung back in his favor. The greatest excitement came with the news of Nuncomar's trial and execution.

By this time General Clavering's powerful friends were bringing all their influence to bear on Ministers to compel the recall of the Governor-General. It was the kind of pressure that politicians can least withstand, and very reluctantly Lord North prepared to climb down the fence on their side, being greatly helped in this decision by his secretary, John Robinson.

If Lord North was the perfect minister for an ambitious king, John Robinson was the perfect secretary for an indolent minister. He was a practical man of affairs and had a thorough grasp of the practical side of politics. He knew how parliamentary majorities were made and how they were kept, and how the business of the king's minister should be conducted. If there were delicate negotiations to be handled or some intrigue to be managed, Robinson was the man for the job. But he could make himself still more useful by relieving his chief of a great deal of tedious departmental work. That connected with India, for instance. All the letters and dispatches from the Government of Bengal came to him, and were by him carefully epitomized; for if there was one thing that Lord North disliked more than another, it was reading dispatches, whether they came from America or India. Robinson saved him this trouble, and he also saved him from continuing long in his present state of doubt and uncertainty. As a practical politician it was natural that Robinson should support Clavering against Hastings, and he made it much easier for his chief to come round to the same sensible view by suppressing most of Hastings's dispatches and coloring his summaries of Indian views by a strong proClavering bias. Clavering's friends were much too strong politically to be antagonized. If they demanded Hastings's head, Robinson for one wanted them to have it, and it was not long before he convinced Lord North that the gift would be both expedient and proper. The Court of Directors must be prevailed upon to petition the King for the Governor-General's recall, which meant that Mr. Robinson's abundant talents for intrigue were to find plenty of scope.

The way had been prepared for this maneuver the previous spring, when another round in the conflict between the Crown and the Company had been fought, ending wholly in the favor of the former. A new Court of Directors had been elected, and ministers had used the resources of the Crown to such good effect that the Court was now a packed body, with a majority of its members taking their orders from Downing street. Lucrative contracts had been given to six of them, and two others had been promised the next vacant seats in the Bengal Council. Among those that had lost their places was Laurence Sulivan. Lord North made no secret of his intention of gaining complete control. The work begun by the Regulating Act would then reach its logical conclusion.

The first-fruits of the election was the Court's dispatch of December 15, 1775, a curious *mélange* of censure, approbation, and applause. The last was reserved for the Majority, and if it had not been for the counteracting influence of Hastings's supporters in the Court of Proprietors, the dispatch would not have contained one word of approval for him. Four months later ministers issued their orders for the Court to proceed to extreme measures.

The Directors were not eager to recall Hastings. They had accepted ministerial gold, but they could not entirely overlook the fact that they owed a duty to the Company, and that that duty was hardly consistent with the dismissal of the man who had, beyond any question, rendered it magnificent services and with whom no real fault could be found. They could scarcely help but be troubled by the thought that what they were told to do was not only an act of the basest ingratitude to a loyal servant, but an act of the basest treachery to the body they had been elected to serve. Somehow they had to find a way to salve their consciences. As it happened, this was not so difficult as it might seem. The public interests demanded that an end should be put to the disputes in the Bengal Government. Both parties insisted on a decision, but as ministers would not surrender their own men, the subservient Directors could reasonably claim that the Company had no option but to recall its own servants on grounds not of justice but of expediency.

In the first week of May the removal motion was brought forward in the Court, suddenly, in order not to give Hastings's supporters time to rally to his defense. It was passed by a vote of eleven to ten, though subsequently *eleven* Directors claimed that they had voted for Hastings. The Hastings party then played their last card. Before the Court had time to draw up the formal petition to the Crown they called for a General Court of the Company to pass upon the matter. If the Proprietors failed them, all was over for their friend, and all was over for the Company, for Hastings's cause had now become the Company's. They stood or fell together. If the Crown won this fight, then the Company as an independent body was doomed.

The General Court was held on May 16, 1776. From near and far Hastings's friends came hurrying, fully realizing the importance of the meeting. Robinson was equally busy collecting votes. Macleane told Hastings that "forty-nine Privy Councilors, peers and men high in office attended on the part of the Administration; treasury letters were sent to almost all the Proprietors, and Lord Sandwich conducted the operations." [3] The proceedings were dramatic, and debate was warm and long sustained. The decisive ballot did not come until the 18th. When the result was announced, it was found that the Hastings party had carried the day against every effort of the Administration by the overwhelming majority of one hundred and six, or about two to one.

The victory was dazzling, though it was only to a very limited extent a victory for Hastings personally. It is true that the small group of men whom he could call his friends supplied the motive power of resistance, and without their activity and zeal the Opposition would never have been organized in time; but no more than about twelve names can be included in this group: Lachlan Macleane, Laurence Sulivan, Francis Sykes, John Graham, John Stewart, Josias Dupré, Samuel Pechell, Robert Palk, George Vansittart, Frederick Stuart (Lord Bute's son), General Caillaud, Sir Gilbert Elliot and his son Alexander; and not all of these were entirely disinterested. The rest of the two hundred odd votes came from a coalition of various groups: men who were supporting Hastings from motives of self-interest, independent stockholders (all of whom, according to Macleane, voted for him), friends of men whom the Majority had turned out of office (the powerful Bute family came under this head), and political opponents of the Administration. The question was, indeed, as much a party issue as if it had been fought out on the floor of the House of Commons, and Lord Rockingham had brought up the forces of the Opposition to help defeat the Government.

Yet the episode did show one thing very clearly. If not a vindication of Hastings's conduct or a recognition of his merits, it was a remarkable demonstration of the important position that he had come to assume in the British political scene. That he had become a storm center was no doubt partly due to his own commanding qualities. Both the staunchness of his friends and the enmity of his opponents were tributes to his character and personality. Without connection with any political group and with his mind centered on his work, he yet had succeeded in attaching to himself a party that made up for its weakness in numbers and influence by its enthusiasm and activity. He had become more than a mere servant of the Company, more even than Governor-General of India. Though he regarded himself as the servant of the Crown as well as of the Company, by the friends of the latter he was regarded as their most valuable possession in maintaining their unequal fight against the former. So long as he remained at the head of affairs in India, they could make out a strong case for the continuance of the Company's rule. Upon him rested the hopes, fears and ambitions of countless men. Some recognized his genuine greatness as a statesman, some only his ability to serve the Company; some merely hoped that by supporting him he in turn would patronize them and their friends and relatives. But the combined result was seen in this extraordinary fight to prevent his recall. Scarcely a voice would have been heard in protest if the motion had been for the removal of any ordinary governor. That would have been routine business, whereas this was a great emergency.

Ministers were naturally furious at this severe rebuff. "I have never known them so sore on any defeat," wrote Macleane. "So great a majority has stunned them. Lord North cannot bear the least mention of the India House, Directors or Proprietors." [4] They had a particular reason for being annoyed: after the pains they had taken to buy the Company, this was all the benefit they had reaped! It was the most mortifying blow that Lord North had experienced. For once his easy *bonhomie* was upset, and he went around fuming and uttering threats of dire vengeance. Parliament must meet before Christmas, so that the matter could be brought before it at once. The Company must be stripped of its power to thwart the King's Ministers. Its charter must be taken away. Hastings would be removed by Act of Parliament.

It was a clever move on North's part to threaten parliamentary action. Actually it was the last thing he wanted to do, as several of Hastings's friends realized. Caillaud told Hastings that Lord North dreaded the Indian business coming into Parliament "more than, perhaps, Nuncomar did his hanging." [5] His Lordship was having quite enough trouble as it was with the Opposition over America. But the ruse worked nevertheless. Macleane failed to grasp the situation and became filled with alarm at the prospect of Hastings being recalled in disgrace.

The poor man did not know what to do. Had he saved his chief only that worse should befall him? He knew that Hastings cared more for his reputation than he did for his office, and that he would sooner retire voluntarily, if he could do so with honor, than wait to be dismissed. He still held, too, the letter in which Hastings had instructed him to hand in his resignation if certain conditions were not fulfilled. These conditions had *not* been fulfilled. It is true that Hastings had since changed his mind and resolved to await the outcome and that Macleane had received his letter retracting his resignation, but Macleane felt that he would be acting in his best interests if he used his own discretion, should a favorable opportunity present itself to extricate Hastings without loss of reputation.

He did not have long to wait. With threats of what he would do in Parliament if forced to it, Lord North in August made indirect advances for a peaceful settlement on the basis of Hastings's retirement, and Macleane lost no time in entering into negotiations, which were kept a deep secret. After many delays and much distrust of the Ministers' good faith on the part of the Hastings party, with both sides threatening at times to renew hostilities, an agreement was reached in October. Drafted with Robinson's assistance, it provided for the restoration to office of such servants of the Company as had been displaced for reason of their attachment to Hastings, the conferring of some mark of favor from the Government on "such black servants as have been dismissed for the same cause that they may not appear disgraced in the eyes of the natives," equal treatment of Hastings's friends in the matter of promotions and favor, a pledge of no retrospective inquisitions and prosecutions, and the cordial reception of Hastings on his return, with the promotion of a vote of thanks and the displacement of nobody. [6] Knowing the magnanimous and disinterested spirit that actuated their leader, Macleane and his associates felt that they were observing his wishes by making no stipulations for him but all for his friends. So, deliberately ignoring his chief's latest instructions, on October 9, Macleane handed in a letter to the Court of Directors signifying Hastings's desire to resign and his request for the appointment of a successor. The Court called upon him to produce his credentials. He did so, handing in the letter of instructions that Hastings had given him when he appointed him his agent in England, but he could produce no document giving him legal power of attorney to sign his resignation. Hastings, he said, had not considered such a formality necessary. It might be expected that in a matter of such grave importance the Directors would have insisted that Macleane produce valid powers before they took definite action. But they were not, as it happened, looking for difficulties, and so without demur they declared themselves satisfied, and proceeded at once to nominate Edward Wheler, a former chairman of their body and one of the Directors whom the Crown had bought, to fill the forthcoming vacancy in the Council.

Macleane's action met with the approval of most of Hastings's friends. Knowing that it had extricated Lord North from an awkward dilemma, they were confident that Hastings would be kindly treated on his return home. Their surprise and indignation may then be imagined when, in the same gazette that published the news of Wheler's appointment, it was announced that the King had been graciously pleased to award the Order of the Bath to General Clavering. There was only one construction to put upon this act: they had been deliberately duped; for the essence of the agreement had been that Hastings should be treated with as much favor as his opponents. Macleane wrote hurriedly to him imploring him on no account to resign, until he heard that an adequate honor had been conferred upon himself. Macleane had indeed discovered, when it was almost too late, that Mr. Robinson was a gentleman who could always be depended upon to be double-faced as circumstances demanded.

Peace now descended for a time on the troubled waters of Indian politics. Lord North had done his best to satisfy the exacting demands of his followers. He had given the Governor-Generalship of India to Clavering. All that worried him now was what the consequences of this gift would be in India. The times were critical, and an able man like Hastings was needed there. Even Lord North felt that, little as he allowed the thought to influence him. Deep down below his easy-going serenity, which cares of empire seldom disturbed, there was an irritating feeling of apprehensiveness that he could not overcome. Nor was he quite easy in his mind that he had acted fairly by Hastings. He could not confess it in public, but he still retained a secret regard for this man who had so seriously deranged his plans and upset his followers. Perhaps even now it was not too late to undo what he had done. Very soon the news arrived of Colonel Monson's death. Wheler, who was at Portsmouth ready to sail, posted back to London to obtain a fresh commission. He thought it wiser to have his appointment made out to fill this new and quite certain vacancy—*just in case Mr. Hastings should not resign.* Whether Mr. Hastings would or not was something that none could tell. It was worrying Hastings's friends as well as Lord North. Would he feel obliged to honor Macleane's unauthorized action? Or would he disavow it? The Minister at least was prepared for the latter eventuality, and very readily gave Wheler the new commission; which meant that no successor had been appointed to fill Hastings's place in the Council. And Lord North consoled himself with the thought that, with no successor arriving, there was a chance that the Governor-General would not feel called upon to resign. He hoped that in this way he had solved the perplexing problem of how to retain Hastings's services without incurring the wrath of Clavering's friends. Perhaps, after all, he had squared the circle!

Yet neither he nor Robinson, nor any one else in England, could have anticipated what actually *would* happen when the fateful dispatches from the Court of Directors reached Calcutta.

Chapter XIII

"THE CONVULSION OF FOUR DAYS"

I

THE climate of Calcutta was Warren Hastings's best ally. New-comers had to beware; the first few years in the country were the most critical; whereas old campaigners like himself had learned by long experience the secret of overcoming its perils. And certainly this valuable ally was now taking a heavy toll of Hastings's opponents. First, Lady Anne Monson in February 1776, then her husband in September, then Alexander Macrabie in November. In Francis's diary is a melancholy list of the deaths among his party, and he himself fre-quently expressed surprise that he had survived so long. Clavering was already a sick man with the finger of doom pointing menacingly at him. But Hastings and Barwell! It was positively distressing to Francis to see what little apparent chance there was of them dying. Barwell was indeed worn to a shadow and there seemed to Francis no particular reason why he should still be alive except that death had not thought it worth while to kill him. As for Hastings, he was the toughest of them all and would surely never die a natural death! [1]

Those terrible summers! What chance had middle-aged men like Clavering and Monson to survive under the conditions of those days? One had to be young and of sound constitution and live the life of an athlete in training. It was a cruel thing to have sent them out, and both men tried in vain to escape their doom. They had sent in their resigna-tions when they heard of the defeat of the Government's attempt to remove Hastings. They had drunk their cup of bitterness and they had had enough. Their whole experience had been nothing but a ghastly failure. Unprepared physically, unsuited temperamentally, ill-equipped mentally, they should never have come.

How different was Hastings's situation! Despite all that had hap-pened nothing could quench his spirit. Gayety could still come bub-bling up to break the calm surface of cold determination. In many of his letters to intimate friends wit and humor dance lightly across the pages. Writing to John Stewart in January 1776 he said:

"I rely on your holding daily councils with Macleane and Elliot. Macleane left me too soon to know me through the reserve which it is not in my nature to throw off but by a long and familiar intercourse, but no man living ever won so much of my confidence in so short an acquaintance, and I love Elliot as much as his father can love him. As for you, my friend, after the many bitter arguments and peevish squabbles which have passed between us (and in which you must be sensible you were always in the wrong) you can have no doubt of my affection. I yet hope to see you the partner of my better days, and to rejoice with you in the reflection of our past and common sufferings. I shall then be content to return after my appointed time, and shall be happier to have you for my neighbor and bottle companion than almost any man I know. Lord, how our other neighbors will wonder when we talk over old stories together! But I am not yet ripe for retirement, nor hope for one social hour hereafter if my present hopes are blasted...." [2]

The death of Monson placed power again in his hands and it became a question of much concern to everybody what use he would make of it. Francis, being a hardened politician, naturally expected that he and his party would have to pay the usual penalty for the loss of their majority. He expected to receive no quarter. [3] In this he was mistaken. Hastings was full of resentment but he was not a man to allow resentment to govern his conduct. He considered the new situation carefully from all angles, without leaving out of account the public interests, and he decided that he had no particular cause for elation. He had been restored to power by an act of God, not by the will of his employers; indeed, he knew by what slight margin he had just escaped an opposite fate at their hands. No man in such a position is entitled to use power in the way that he normally would if it had been properly confirmed to him. The restoration, too, would in all probability be very fleeting as Colonel Monson's place was almost certain to be filled by a member of the ministerialist party. So far indeed was Hastings from feeling elated by Monson's death that he told the Prime Minister that he could have wished to avoid such a situation. "It has restored to me the constitutional authority of my station; but without absolute necessity, I shall not think it proper to use it with that effect which I should give it were I sure of support from home." [4]

The wheels of government could not, however, entirely cease to revolve while they were waiting to hear the decision on their disputes. Pressing matters were demanding their attention. The five year land settlement of the previous administration expired in April of the coming year, and no steps had as yet been taken to prepare for a new one. Hastings had, it is true, put forward a plan but the Majority had rejected it without discussion. As it was clear to them that the only object of his policy was to drain Bengal of wealth, they dismissed his claim of a desire to correct the evident faults of his first settlement as a piece of sheer hypocrisy. [5] But an attitude of negation and non-coöperation, useful as it was for destroying the Governor-General's reputation, would not, as Francis realized, suffice in a matter of so much importance as revenue. Here was his chance to demonstrate his abilities as a statesman and his superiority to his rival. He himself would produce a plan. And so with characteristic energy and thoroughness he had set to work, calling to his aid some of the best brains in the revenue department of the Bengal service.

Francis produced a plan cleverly designed so as to contrast sharply with that of Hastings. It was exactly the kind of plan that one would expect from a man whose ideas of land and land tenures were taken from eighteenth-century England, providing generously for a class of great landowners and reducing the humble cultivators to their proper status as tenants. No country in his opinion could be happy or prosperous without a land-owning class such as England fortunately possessed; its existence was ordained by a natural law; and he identified the zemindars with such a class. If they did not already possess the rights and privileges proper to their position, it was not because they had never in fact possessed them but because Hastings had foully usurped them. All that Hastings, on the other hand, sought to do, was what he had consistently done from the beginning: to fashion his new system as nearly as he could on the model of the old. And that meant remembering that both the State and the cultivators (ryots), as well as the zemindars, had an interest in the soil and rights that needed safeguarding. He knew that there was no analogy between Indian zemindar and English landed proprietor, and he was determined not to enrich or aggrandize the zemindar at the expense of either the State or the ryot. The Mogul government had protected the ryot against the oppressions of the zemindar, and he wished the Company's government to retain the same power. [6]

Francis sent his plan to England with a grand flourish. It was his only piece of constructive statesmanship during his six years in India and it made a big impression upon the people at home, as it was well calculated to do. Fifteen years later when the Bengal Government proceeded to make a permanent land settlement, it was his ideas that were adopted. Francis himself expected that he would be rewarded for his plan with the Governor-Generalship. "Perhaps the appointment may come of itself. I have a hold on this country which none of them can shake. Hereafter it may possibly be a question not for what reasons I should be recalled but by what arguments or solicitations I may be prevailed on to remain." [7]

It was while they were waiting for a decision on the rival plans that Hastings found himself compelled to take more severe action against his opponents than he had intended. He and Francis were at loggerheads over a proposal to prepare for the new settlement by setting up a temporary office to survey and value the land and collect all necessary facts. The proposal came from Hastings and Francis strenuously opposed it on the ground that it meant tampering with the sacred rights of the zemindars and revealed a clear intention to enslave the people of Bengal and destroy the country. He informed all his friends in England that the Governor-General was aiming to squeeze the last rupee out of the country for the enrichment of himself and his cronies: "I am weary of contending with ignorance, presumption, avarice and injustice. This wretched country now has no defense against the arbitrary power accidentally devolved to the Governor, and which he seems determined to use without reserve." Hastings was not to be diverted by those frivolous charges, so, using his casting-vote to give himself a majority, he forced the proposal through the Council. He soon found, however, that the work of the new office was being rendered abortive by the obstruction of Clavering's and Francis's friends and dependents, whom one by one they had been placing in key positions, having first ousted their former occupants who had been loyal to the old Administration. John Bristow, a protégé of Francis, was at Lucknow, Francis Fowke, a friend of Clavering, was at Benares, and Charles Goring, who had been one of the principals in the Nuncomar conspiracy, was among those who had been made members of the Provincial Councils. The service was no longer Hastings's to command, and since that was a situation that no one in his position could tolerate, he removed the chief offenders and substituted his own men, sending Middleton back to Lucknow and appointing Thomas Graham as Resident at Benares. The conduct of Bristow and Fowke had been such that their dismissal could be amply justified on other than personal grounds. [8] The only unfortunate aspect of the business was that it enabled his enemies to accuse him of unjustly and cruelly venting his spleen on his defenseless political opponents, turning public offices into the spoils of party warfare, and filling them all with his own partisans.

II

TIME dragged slowly on. "The old gentleman," as Barwell called General Clavering, did nothing but find fault with every single thing that Hastings and Barwell did, even with the most unexceptionable matters of routine. His unremitting perseverance was worthy of a better cause. Francis, true to character, was more guarded and circumspect. To his friends at home he was declaring his intention to change his line of conduct. The ways of Ministers and Directors were incomprehensible to him. They had condemned, and they had approved, both without stint, but they had not followed up their words with the next logical step, the removal of the man they had condemned. Francis's friends in the Administration were still encouraging him to continue his opposition policy, but he was impatient for the reward that was due to him, and wondered whether a pose of neutrality would not pay him better. He continued full of hope, ambition and energy. India attracted him no more than at first, he had no interest in its people, cared nothing about seeing anything of the country, scarcely stirred from Calcutta —all that he wanted was to be Governor-General. And all that Barwell wanted was to withdraw from the field as soon as he decently could and take his large fortune and what little remained of his health back to England before any ill could happen to either.

At the close of the year (1776) Hastings wrote to John Stewart:

"The General has been for some time ill—I don't know how he is now, for I never inquire—I have fancied a case which is not impossible, and would work wonders. Suppose the next attempt to remove Mr. Barwell and us should succeed. One member is gone. If the General should follow, Francis from a simple decimal will be the integer—aye, every inch a king—and possess the undivided and uncontrolled sovereignty of Bengal. If it should happen I verily believe he will run mad, and half the people with him.

"Have you read Lord P.'s pamphlet? [1] It begins, 'Upon my arrival in India, I found a general *reform* was necessary in the settlement to preserve the Company from *ruin*.' What a striking likeness there is in the language and characters of all Reformers! Remember that though I made a number of chops and changes, I never called myself a Reformer, nor lamented that all men were not as virtuous and disinterested as myself, nor thanked God that I am not like this or that publican whose place I wanted to occupy myself, a thief, oppressor, etc. . . ." [9]

For the first five months of 1777 the four men waited thus in unabated suspense for the news of the outcome of the battle that had been going on at home to decide their fate. Clavering's strength was nearly exhausted. His was a losing battle and there were times when he was completely incapacitated, lying on his bed with his body covered with boils. If the anticipated news of Hastings's recall did not come soon, it might be too late.

At last there came the day when both sides knew that their many months of intolerable waiting were ended. On June 14 Hastings received his first intimation in the shape of Macleane's letter telling him on no account to resign. It arrived ahead of the official dispatches and Macleane's earlier letter, having been sent express from the Cape, and Hastings was naturally at a loss to know what it meant. There were no letters for Clavering and Francis, but Francis, through private channels of his own, somehow got wind of this extraordinary message from Macleane and sensed that important news might be expected any day from England. The General was out of town, but an urgent note from Francis brought him hurrying back to Calcutta. The two of them met secretly to discuss the mystery.

Four days later a ship arrived from England. As soon as it became known that she bore a packet of dispatches from the Court of Directors, both sides became tense with excitement. On the 19th the Council met. The dispatches were opened and read and then was learned the acceptance of the Governor-General's resignation by the Court and the Crown's appointment of Edward Wheler to fill the vacancy. The Council adjourned. Next day Hastings as usual summoned his colleagues to

[1] Lord Pigot, Governor of Madras.

attend at the Revenue Board. But only Barwell obeyed. At ten o'clock that morning Clavering had issued a summons in his own name to his two fellow-members of Council, Barwell and Francis, to meet him in the general Council chamber.

The old soldier, violent, reckless and impulsive as ever, had lost his head completely. With the prize at last so nearly within his grasp, he threw all restraint and decency to the winds. He was not satisfied to wait for Hastings to hand over the government: he had decided that the government now belonged by right to him. In vain did the more cautious Francis try to restrain him. The obstinate man refused to be diverted from the course of action he had planned.

Francis obeyed the summons. Barwell did not. Clavering promptly took the oath as Governor-General, assumed the chair, and, with Francis's concurrence, passed a resolution proclaiming the change of government. He then sent a note to Hastings requiring him instantly to deliver up the keys of the fort and the treasury. Though this had always hitherto been the last official duty of a retiring governor, Clavering in this case wished to make it the first! Meanwhile Hastings was in an adjoining chamber wondering what had happened to his Councilors. Barwell solved the mystery by bringing to him the summons he had received from the new would-be governor. And before he had recovered from his astonishment Clavering's note arrived.

With indignation burning within him Hastings returned a point-blank refusal to abdicate. In a letter signed jointly with Barwell he stated bluntly that he knew of no act by which his position had been vacated, and declared his resolve to assert and maintain his authority. He then took immediate steps to frustrate the threatened usurpation, sending orders to the commanding officer of the garrison at Fort William and to other officers of the Company's forces, forbidding them to obey any orders not coming from himself, and writing letters to the Provincial Councils and Collectors, reminding them that their obedience was due to him alone as Governor-General. This done, he suggested to General Clavering that the matter should be laid before the Judges of the Supreme Court, offering for his own part to abide by their decision. Clavering and Francis after some demur consented. Only by so doing could they have prevented the outbreak of civil war in Bengal. As it was, the edifying spectacle had been presented to the Indian world of two parties, each formed of an equal number of the members of the Supreme Council, each claiming the government of India, and each sitting separately and separately issuing orders!

Hastings's action was as well-judged as Clavering's had been foolish. After deliberating all night the Judges announced at four o'clock in the morning that they were unanimously of the opinion that Clavering had illegally usurped the government, inasmuch as the Governor-General had not actually resigned or vacated his seat. Clavering and Francis contested their argument, but at noon agreed to acquiesce. Hastings had triumphed.

OLD FORT WILLIAM, CALCUTTA, FROM THE RIVER HUGLI, 1788

(From an aquatint by Thomas Daniell, R.A., in the possession of the India Office)

But the matter did not rest there. Two days later, without summoning their opponents Hastings and Barwell again met in Council and passed a resolution declaring that the General, by taking the oath as Governor-General and by his several other acts as such, had actually vacated his seat of senior councilor and his post of Commander-in-Chief. It was now the turn of Clavering and Francis to appeal to the Judges, and of Hastings and Barwell to acquiesce, and this time the Judges, showing a commendable desire to be impartial, decided for Clavering and advised a compromise.

Next day all four gentlemen met in Council as usual and were soon able to agree to refer their several claims for decision in England, and in the meantime to leave everything *in statu quo ante*. And thus ended what Hastings described as "the convulsion of four days, which might have shaken the very foundation of the national power and interest in India." [10]

Hastings's conduct gave great satisfaction to his many friends and admirers in Bengal, and most heartily did they congratulate him. Barwell voiced their feelings when he wrote to his sister, with rare enthusiasm:

"Few men could have stood so severe a trial or could have been so collected under a provocation of such great magnitude. Firm, decided and just in every measure he may challenge the severest test to which his enemies shall subject his conduct throughout the whole of this extraordinary attempt to turn him out of his office and debase him in the eyes of the people of the country." [11]

Outwardly Hastings seldom failed to appear resolute, but inwardly he was often sorely troubled by doubts and misgivings. Many of his most daring actions must have cost him hours of anguish and hesitation. Francis's picture of him as a "timid, desperate, distracted being" possessed as much truth as that more common view of him which sees him as a ruthless, fearless man of blood and iron, who broke his pledged word as readily as he trampled the people of India under foot. This particular episode was a case in point. If he had been the latter type of man, he would have laughed with scorn at the idea of resigning just when the ball was at his feet once more. Instead, he was greatly perturbed by the possibility that his conduct might be thought deceitful and dishonorable, and hastened to render a full explanation of it.

Clavering's mad action had been a great stroke of luck for him, as it absolved him from the necessity of abiding by Macleane's commitment. It was now out of the question for him to resign in the General's favor. For one thing, despite the Judges' ruling Hastings and Barwell were absolutely convinced that Clavering had no longer any legal right to be a member of the Council, having by his own act vacated his seat to thrust himself into Hastings's; in which case Barwell became the legal successor to the chair. Hastings had every right to be angry with Macleane as he had ignored Hastings's withdrawal of his resignation. Nevertheless, so he solemnly declared to Lord North and to his friends, he had actually decided to resign, and would have done so but for Clavering's monstrous behavior; and Barwell, who was with him almost every minute of those four hectic days, was convinced that he spoke the truth. It had been a condition of the engagement that the time of his resignation should be his to decide. So, after painful searchings of heart, he came to the conclusion that he was bound by every tie of duty to retain his post until he heard from home. But he knew the danger of this course. "I shall expect to be recalled, and with disgrace, and I expect that my recall will be followed by prosecutions and they may prove what they will against me, even rape and murder, if they are disposed to it when I am gone and Clavering in possession, yet I care not. What a reward, my friend,"—he was writing to Sykes—"is this to the services of a man who has devoted the labors of twenty-seven years of his life in the support of the Company, and the National interests in this country!" [12] He was not very far wrong in this prediction, for upon his conduct on this occasion was to be grounded one of the charges of his impeachment.

He defended himself to the Prime Minister and addressed an eloquent appeal to him for justice and fair play, which if his Lordship read it—which is not at all certain, since we know that many of Hastings's letters were never even opened—must surely have made him feel ashamed of the part he had acted:

"When your Lordship and the Court of Directors found it expedient to remove me from their service, not, I will presume, for any misconduct or incapacity, but because it suited better with the interests of the State that I should make way for another, it was your intention that I should be allowed an honorable retreat, and every circumstance of delicacy and tenderness which might alleviate it. I assert this from an internal conviction. It was impossible that your Lordship could have made an accommodation of peace the lure to drag me into the power of my most rancorous enemy, and to make me a sacrifice to the most brutal outrage and indignity; nor is it possible that your Lordship should expect from me a tame submission to such treatment.

"Exalted as your Lordship's station is, and though the world gives you the credit of having filled it with abilities equal to those of the most able of your predecessors, yet if I am rightfully informed, neither the integrity of your character nor the wisdom of your measures have exempted you from the malignity which is the inseparable attendant on eminence; and it has been your greatest praise, that your constancy, firmness, and moderation of temper have not only repelled all the shafts which have been aimed at your reputation, but have converted them to the means of increasing its luster. Do not, my Lord, condemn in me the qualities which do yourself so much honor, nor deny me your approbation for a conduct which you yourself would have pursued under circumstances like those which have been the guide of mine.

"I do not expect to be confirmed in this Government. I have long since given over all hopes of it. Let me be removed from it, but suffer me not, my Lord, to be dragged from it like a felon, after the labor of seven and twenty years dedicated to the service of the Company and the aggrandizement of the British dominion.

"And now forgive me, my Lord, if I may appear to have expressed myself with a warmth either unbecoming an address to your Lordship, or inconsistent with the temperance of my own character. What I have written, I have written from my heart, not heated by resentment, but warmed with the conscious sense of my own integrity, and with a respect for your Lordship which I shall ever retain, because I am assured that if I must suffer injustice from the hands of others I shall yet obtain every relief from you, which it shall be in your power to afford me.

"I have the honor to be, with the greatest respect, my Lord, your most obedient and humble servant.

"WARREN HASTINGS." [13]

Hastings was not a hardened politician, used to taking the "downs" of public life with as much *sang-froid* as the "ups." He was not a politician at all. If there was one thing that he never understood, it was the workings of the English party system. In this respect he was seriously handicapped, as it was impossible for his great post to be entirely unaffected by the exigencies of parliamentary government. He was unsophisticated enough to think that men in whom the King had reposed such confidence as to make them his ministers must be actuated only by patriotism and a high sense of justice and honor. His profound reverence and respect for the august twin institutions of his country, Crown and Parliament, imbued him with a spirit of complete loyalty to their service. When he found that they had feet of clay, that no amount of faithful, obedient and successful service on his part could gain him the deserved reward, he was painfully shocked and gave vent to his wounded feelings by this characteristic letter. He still expected too much of human nature and found it difficult to reconcile himself to the fact that life was full of injustice. A healthy measure of Francis's cynicism and of Lord North's amiable imperturbability and stolid imperviousness to abuse, perhaps also a stronger sense of humor, would have made his situation a good deal more bearable and made him less prone to indulge in self-pity. This was, however, when he was forty-five, and long before his troubles ended. The next ten years were to toughen him immeasurably, until at length he was able to accept with philosophic resignation the fact that to suffer injustice was his apparent lot in life. He was then able to adopt with truth the proud motto, *mens aequa in arduis*.

Irony attends the fact that the day before Hastings wrote this flattering appeal to the Minister, Clavering received a letter from Mr. Robinson, the keeper of his Lordship's mind on Indian affairs, expressing thanks to God for Hastings's resignation, from which nothing but the best possible results could be anticipated, "enabling you to establish a permanent system of government founded in rectitude and strength, for the happiness, prosperity, and welfare of Bengal," and assuring him of Wheler's firm intention to act in all things with him. [14] When the General read this he regretted that he had capitulated so quietly to the Judges' ruling.

On June 20 Clavering invested himself with the red ribbon of the Bath that raised him to the dignity of a knight. Exactly two months later, worn out by the prolonged disputes, the bitterness of frustrated hopes and ambitions, and the long painful struggle with sickness, he died. The devouring climate of Bengal had added another to its long list of victims taken from amongst these intruders from the West. Deprived by his own violence of the object of his ambition, he carried his bitter enmity and disappointment with him into the grave. As he lay dying, not bearing the thought that his rival might come in triumph to his funeral, he gave instructions that the Governor-General was not to be informed of his death until after he was buried.

Barwell noted that the superstitious people of Bengal believed Saturday to be Warren Hastings's lucky day. Nuncomar had been committed to prison, condemned to death, and hanged, Monson had died, and now Sir John Clavering had died—all on a Saturday, and all three had met their fate in the month of Bhadras (August 15 to September 15).

Chapter XIV

MARRIAGE AND PRIVATE LIFE

WARREN HASTINGS was a deservedly popular Governor. The charm of his personality, the kindliness of his nature, the lavish hospitality that he dispensed, and the thoughtful consideration he showed to all who approached him, endeared him to Europeans and natives alike. He was reserved, but he could on occasions be gay. Every year he gave a dinner to Old Westminsters, former pupils at his old school, and it is recorded that at these functions he was wont to throw off his natural shyness, becoming as "playful as a boy, entering with great spirit into all the laugh and nonsense of the hour, himself reciting a number of ridiculous circumstances that occurred in his time." [1] When he left India he established a pension fund in charge of friends from which were to be paid allowances to old servants and needy dependents. He gave freely of wise counsel and needed help to all who came to him with their problems and difficulties, and numerous were the domestic troubles that he helped to set right. He was very accessible and took a keen personal interest in the welfare of even the humblest member of the Service, regarding each one as part of one big family of which he was the head. [2]

Simplicity characterized his general mode of living. Though he was careful to maintain the dignity of his office, proudly thinking of it as the greatest within the reach of a subject of King George, it was the office, not his own person, that he sought to glorify. When he appeared in public it was always with an escort of aides-de-camp and mounted body-guards and a considerable retinue of native servants, but his own dress was of the plainest description, his demeanor modest and retiring, and his dislike of pomp and ceremony well known. The Governor's House had as yet none of the appearance of a Vice-regal Court, the Governor himself had not been exalted into "His Excellency," nor were the rules of etiquette as rigid and formal as they were soon to become. The European community in Calcutta, not having as yet grown to any great size, still retained many of the features of a pioneering society.

When the Governor-General gave his public entertainments, at such times as the New Year and the King's Birthday, all were invited and generously entertained.

He carried the same simplicity into his own private habits. Not for him were the excesses of eating and drinking. He seldom touched wine and, on official occasions when there were toasts to be drunk, he confined himself to a weak mixture of wine and water. He kept most regular hours; instead of indulging in carousals into the small hours of the morning, as was the custom with many of his colleagues, he retired to bed at eleven o'clock at the latest. His daily routine when he rose in the morning was "to ride for an hour with the first twilight of morning, with speed enough to perspire freely, then dismount and strip and throw cold water over my body, then dress, all very rapidly." [3] There were many Englishmen who could not survive five years in Bengal, but Hastings not only spent thirty years there but lived to the good age of eighty-five, and this was an achievement that he owed, not to an exceptionally strong constitution, but to his sound common sense and strength of character, which made him observe strict canons of health in entire disregard of the fast-living habits of the age. He had consecrated himself to the service of the State, and he neglected no means of keeping his mind and energies at their maximum efficiency.

So far he had lived a bachelor's life, but the time had now come when he could once again marry and so obtain for himself the intimate companionship and loving care that he needed, as well as a hostess to take charge of the social obligations of his office. Early in July 1777 he received news that must have been more welcome by far than the most flattering and convincing assurances of support that Lord North or the Directors could have given him, for he heard that he could at last after four years of waiting marry the woman he loved. Now he could seek the happiness in his private life that was being denied him in his public.

When Mr. and Mrs. Imhoff reached Madras in his company, Hastings had followed the custom of the day in extending hospitality. They became guests at his house, and Hastings befriended Imhoff and helped him to obtain commissions for portraits, even commissioning him on his own behalf to paint a portrait of Mrs. Imhoff. Imhoff, like many others, had only obtained a cadetship in the Company's service as a pretext to enable him to go to India, and in September 1770 he resigned from the Service and, having exhausted the portrait field in Madras, proceeded to Calcutta, leaving his wife in Hastings's care. Hastings wrote to a friend of his in Calcutta asking him to aid Imhoff to find lodgings, and he also corresponded with Imhoff in a manner that shows that their relations were cordial. [4] In October of the following year Mrs. Imhoff followed her husband to Calcutta; he had no doubt waited, before sending for her, until he could afford to maintain an establishment. Shortly afterwards Hastings was transferred to Bengal, and so the three came together again. The close and intimate friendship that had begun on shipboard continued, and Mrs. Imhoff was soon being spoken of as the

Governor's "principal favorite among the ladies." "They (she and her husband) do not make a part of Mr. Hastings's family"—so wrote Dr. Hancock, a medical friend of Hastings, to his wife—"but are often of his private parties. The husband is truly a German. I should not have mentioned Mrs. Imhoff to you, but I know everything relating to Mr. Hastings is greatly interesting to you." [5] There was apparently no scandal nor any knowledge that the Governor entertained warmer feelings for Mrs. Imhoff than those of friendship. In the autumn of the year 1772, however, fate intervened to break up the somewhat odd relationship between the three. Imhoff received peremptory orders from the Directors, who had heard that he had resigned the Service, to leave India at once: he was to be deported if necessary.

It was now that Mr. and Mrs. Imhoff decided to part company. She wanted her freedom so that she might marry Hastings, and her husband was willing to give it to her. So it was arranged that Imhoff would return to Germany and obtain a divorce in the liberal courts of that country, and his wife would remain on at Calcutta. Hastings for his part in the arrangement behaved with his usual generosity. He relieved the husband of the expense of his wife's maintenance, undertook to adopt and provide for their two sons, one of whom they had brought out with them, and no doubt furnished Imhoff with sufficient funds for the expenses of the legal process. There is no evidence, or reason to suppose, that he did more than that, nor that Imhoff was any richer when he left India than when he arrived. After sending his boy ahead of him to England, Imhoff sailed for Europe in March 1773. [6] In order to stop gossip Calcutta was allowed to think that he would be returning as soon as he had been reinstated in the Service. Within two years of his reaching Germany the divorce was complete, and Imhoff himself at once remarried. That there was no ill feeling on any one's part over the transaction is shown by the fact that his former wife and her sons kept in friendly contact with him and his family by his second wife, and that she even became godmother to one of his daughters by his second marriage. [7]

Mrs. Imhoff's position in Calcutta during the years while the divorce was pending naturally aroused some talk and speculation, especially as she continued to receive marked attention from the Governor, but there was still no active scandal. Was she his mistress? Possibly. Who knows? Calcutta did not know, nor did London—at least that is what Joseph Farrington said, [8] and strait-laced Queen Charlotte would *never* have received Mrs. Hastings at Court if she had thought there had been any impropriety. Francis pretended he knew, but Francis being —Francis, his opinion is worth precisely nothing. Actually he liked Mrs. Imhoff very much, describing her as "an agreeable woman and has been very pretty." [9] He had been on excellent terms with her, and after her marriage he admitted that she was really an accomplished woman who behaved with perfect propriety in her new station and deserved every mark of respect. [10]

The divorce granted, Hastings lost no time in arranging the marriage. The ceremony was performed quietly on August 8 by special license of the Chief Justice, the bride being married under her maiden name, Anna Maria Appolonia Chapusettin.[1]

There are many descriptions of Mrs. Hastings, but it is doubtful whether there is a single portrait that can be considered a fair likeness. It is not a little disconcerting to find virtually no resemblance between three of the best-known attempts that were made at different times to portray her, those of R. E. Pine, Zoffany, and Ozias Humphrey. The famous Zoffany portrait was painted in 1783. Mrs. Hastings did not like it, but Thompson, her husband's secretary, thought it "a very sublime performance," and Hastings himself liked it sufficiently well to hang it opposite his bed after her departure. One suspects that the painter was trying too hard to imitate Reynolds (the pose is similar to that of Mrs. Siddons) to do full justice to his subject. Ozias Humphrey painted a very pretty and charming woman with a singularly sweet expression, and the representation, we are told, is that of Mrs. Hastings in later life.

She was taller than her husband, and her figure was fine and queenly. Men admired her enormously, women not so much nor so uncritically. Men thought she had perfect taste, women that it was a little loud and unrefined. Men thought she dressed with elegant simplicity, women that she did it with ostentatious extravagance. Men found her sweet, gracious and affable, whereas women were more struck by the airs which she gave herself and by her no slight vanity. Allowing for these natural sexual differences of opinion, we can still happily obtain from the consensus a clear picture of this lady who had the honor of becoming Warren Hastings's second wife. Undoubtedly the admiration of men was pleasant to her and she derived enormous enjoyment from her elevated station in life and the gay society of Calcutta. Essentially *la grande dame,* she was at times abashingly regal in her behavior, at other times, gay, entertaining and kind, but always exacting respect and deference from her social inferiors. She was highly individualistic in her appearance and mode of dress, letting her beautiful auburn hair hang down in natural ringlets, unpowdered, and seldom following the current fashions; and she delighted in ornament, particularly diamonds. In other words, she was quite a personage, and it is not surprising that after a brief passage of arms with the Chief Justice's lady she should have made good her claim to first place in Calcutta society as a matter of course. "The Governor's dress gives you his character at once, unostentatious and sensible. His lady, however, is the great ornament of places of polite resort, for her figure, her manners lively and engaging, and her whole appearance a model of taste and magnificence." So wrote one observer in Calcutta. [12] And later, in England,

[1] She came of the family of Chapuset, which had been forced to leave France after the revocation of the Edict of Nantes in 1685 and take refuge in Germany. Her grandfather was Charles Chapuset de St. Valentin, whose circumstances became much reduced after he emigrated. [11]

MRS. HASTINGS
(From a portrait by Zoffany)

Fanny Burney described her as, "a pleasing, lively, and well-bred woman." But Miss Burney regretted that she should have aimed always at being the most conspicuous figure wherever she appeared, even to the point of dressing like an Indian princess. [13]

None of this criticism mattered, however, to her adoring husband. That she was perfection itself in his eyes was plain to all beholders. It was as Fanny Burney said: "In her sight and conversation he seems to find recompense adequate to all his wishes, for the whole of his toils, and long disturbances and labors." [14] Her every look and word were as balm of heaven to his tortured spirit. Like many another doting husband, he loved to think of her as weak and helpless, and was inordinately surprised and delighted when, as happened not infrequently, she showed courage and capacity both to do and to think. For actually she was a very competent person, particularly as housewife and business manager, though somewhat inclined to be too economical both for his tastes and for the requirements of their official position. With her very good sense of the value of money she managed to accumulate a considerable fortune in India, and it was whispered—with some considerable degree of truth, one fears—that she was not above receiving handsome presents, especially in the form of diamonds for which she had a positive passion. And there is no doubt that in this way she did hurt to her husband's reputation. Nevertheless, she unquestionably rendered him a service by curbing his extravagant liberality, which bade fair to send him back to England with nothing like the fortune needed to support his retirement.

It was as successful a marriage as history records. For the forty years they spent together they were all in all to each other. Hers was undoubtedly the colder nature, but she was able to inspire in him a love that was at once passionate and tender, constant and lasting. The letters that he wrote his intimate friends show that his beloved Marian— for he never used her baptismal name Maria—held first place in his thoughts; whatever tribulations he had to undergo, all was well so long as she was well; he suffered if she suffered, he was happy if she was happy; if he was in danger, she must be shielded from anxiety. And so it was until the day of his death. Whatever else life denied him, it did not deny him one of its greatest sources of happiness. Another— children of his own—he was not to enjoy.

Even in Calcutta's uncongenial air he and his wife succeeded in living the kind of life that he especially wanted to live, the life of a country gentleman. He had this love in common with so many other great figures in English and American public life at this period. Some time before his marriage he and three Bengal civilians had built a country house and plantation at Sooksaugur, a pleasant spot on the banks of the Hugli some forty miles above Calcutta. Here they established an experimental farm for the cultivation of coffee and other products. Many rare exotic plants and shrubs were collected and grown successfully, but unfortunately what should have been a valuable nucleus for a permanent botanical collection was dispersed after their owners' departure. Sooksaugur was a favorite resort of Mrs. Hastings, and many were the visits that she and her husband paid to that green and pleasant retreat.

In order further to enjoy peace and quiet and recreation away from the scene of his incessant labors Hastings built a mansion at Alipore, just outside Calcutta, which stands today, still bearing his name, as a silent but impressive witness to the cultivation of his taste, significant as an indication of his character as Mount Vernon is of Washington's and Monticello of Jefferson's. He was not born to the possession of noble mansions and broad and fruitful acres, but he was certainly born with the desire for both. The product of generations of Lords of the Manor of Daylesford and heir to a fast-decaying family tradition, his own great wish for himself was to be able to restore the past, Daylesford to Hastings, Hastings to the land.

Small but stately, built in the European style of the period, Hastings House displays in every detail of its architecture, decoration and landscaping, that meticulous regard for neatness, order, comfort and simple dignity so characteristic of the English manner at its best. He surrounded it with lawns, gardens, shrubberies, an orchard and a paddock, provided it with stabling for thirty horses, and then snatched every moment he could from his official duties to enjoy its delights. Most week-ends at least saw him there. He tried farming along English lines, and, as at Sooksaugur, made experiments in horticulture. For the rest, he devoted himself to the four things that afforded him the greatest happiness: the companionship of his wife, the society of his intimate friends, his horses, and his books. Riding and driving were his, as they were also his wife's, favorite outdoor recreations, and their mutual pride in their Arab horses, whose beauty was famous, repeatedly showed itself in their letters. An omnivorous reader, Hastings had arranged for every new publication, both books and magazines, to be sent to him from England. Nor did he lose his taste for the classics. A good Latin scholar at school, his colleagues in India considered him easily the best among them.

No account of his interests and pastimes would be complete without a mention of his fondness for verse-making, though he had but little time in India to indulge such a taste. The full flowering of his poetic genius had to wait until his retirement. Opinions may differ regarding the quality of his productions, but it can scarcely be gainsaid that they possess some fair amount of merit. That he rather fancied himself as a poet may be inferred from the way in which he allowed his family and friends to share the pleasure of reading his compositions, or, if they happened to be under his roof at the time, of hearing them read aloud. A fair-sized volume could be made of verses that have been preserved either among his or their papers, and several of them have become well known as a result of frequent publication.

One priceless possession he had, and that was the mind of a

philosopher. Nature gave him many choice gifts, but surely, when it gave him the power to appreciate and grasp philosophic truth and to weave it into the texture of his own deepest thoughts and responses to life, it gave him something so essential to his success that without it he could not have maintained that invincible front against his enemies and against adversity which was in the end to bring him complete victory over both. A man who can withstand all that he withstood and emerge from the ordeal not embittered or soured but contented, cheerful, and at peace with the world, must have something to cling to stronger than the urge of personal ambition, stronger even than the consciousness of personal rectitude and the satisfaction of a clear conscience. The knowledge that to be thwarted and reviled is merely the price of having done one's duty is consolation, but it is scarcely of itself enough to sustain a man in his hours of greatest trial. If there were no evidence at all that Warren Hastings derived strength and refreshment from sources outside himself, we should be justified in assuming the fact. But there is no need to assume anything. His letters are redolent of a philosophic spirit that permeated his whole attitude to life. Nor need we seek far for the springs of thought from which he drank. To the religious influences of his childhood had been added the enriching experience of a classical education that left more than a passing impression upon him. And then in India had come the opportunity to glean still more wisdom from the accumulated store of Oriental philosophy. He could not himself go to where the richest treasure lay buried, but he could encourage others to go and could profit from their labors.

Thus it was with immense delight that he received from his friend Charles Wilkins the first translation of the *Bhagavad-Gītā,* a philosophical and didactic poem forming part of the Sanskrit epic the *Mahābhārata,* and he took from it the eighth and ninth chapters to turn into verse as *The History of Rooroo and Promod-Bora.* [15] The work made a profound impression upon him, and he derived particular joy from the fact that the very rule of conduct that he employed to guide his own life had been recommended by the ancient sages who wrote it.

"My friend Wilkins," he wrote his wife, "has lately made me a present of a most wonderful work of antiquity, and I am going to present it to the public. Among many precepts of fine morality I am particularly delighted with the following, because it has been the invariable rule of my latter life, and often applied to the earlier state of it, before I had myself reduced it to the form of a maxim in writing. It is this: *'Let the motive be in the deed, and not in the event.* Be not one whose motive for action is the hope of reward. Let not thy life be spent in inaction. Depend upon application'—that is, as is afterwards explained, the application of the rule of moral right to its consonant practice, without care for the event as it may respect ourselves. 'Perform thy duty, abandon all thought of the consequence, and make the event equal whether it terminate in good or evil; for such an equality is called application.' To this good rule, I will adhere, careless of every event but *one,* and that shall console me though the voices of all mankind shall cry out against me. And what is that one?—O God! Grant me the blessing of a satisfied conscience, and my Marian to reward it!" [16]

Those lines contain the essence of his philosophy of life. "Do thy duty without regard to the consequence." And he was delighted when his wife put the maxim into her own words and applied it to him: "Besides, you have that self-satisfaction, and it has always been your characteristic, that you on all occasions have acted as a man of virtue and honor ought to do, whatever consequences may ensue." In reply he quoted again from the *Gītā:* "Wise men, who have abandoned all thought of the fruit which is produced from their actions, are freed from the chains of birth, and *go to the regions of eternal happiness."* [17] That was a happy thought, indeed, for him!

"O God! Grant me the blessing of a satisfied conscience." It was the kind of prayer that oftenest found utterance on his lips. Religion with him was a deep inner experience, and essentially simple in its content. He made no parade of it, nor is there any evidence that he was ever gripped by religious fervor. It is unlikely that he was ever particularly interested in theological controversy or attracted by popular ferments like the Methodist revival of his day. He was, indeed, essentially conservative in his thought; striving for the good, but not seeking new foundations for it or adventuring forth along freshly discovered and untried paths. There is no evidence that he was markedly touched by the new ideas that were setting men's minds and passions on fire in France and America; so he was able to accept with more calmness than many of his contemporaries the order of life and society as it existed in his day, with its inequalities, injustices and anomalies. In his private life, as in his public life, he adhered to a few simple, fundamental standards of thought and conduct. Reverence was one—reverence for God, King and Church, for the established institutions of his country, and for all that they represented. Loyalty was another—loyalty to his country, his employers, his trust, his wife, his family, his friends. The virtues that he cultivated and displayed were the basic Christian virtues —faith, hope, charity, pureness in heart, endurance, fidelity. His church was the orthodox English church of his fathers, his faith a simple trust in God, his guide conscience. The living of the higher life, as it was conceived by thinkers of a less complex and sophisticated age than our own, required character above all else, and of the sterling quality of Hastings's character no further proof is needed.

Chapter XV

THE OUTBREAK OF WAR

I

IT cannot be said that John Clavering was deeply mourned in Bengal. Though it may have been unchristian of him Warren Hastings was almost glad! The dead man was the one whose rancor he dreaded most and he now felt at some ease about the future because it would be impossible, he thought, to find his equal. ("Do not think I speak from an impulse of resentment. May God forgive him all the injuries which he has heaped upon me, and me, as I forgive him." [1]) He had not yet realized the much greater malignity of which Philip Francis was capable.

There was little danger now of his being removed from his post. The Crown had wished to promote Clavering but, for the time being, had nobody else in mind. Lord North was now, indeed, so completely involved in the miserable business of the American War as to be rid of all desire to burn his fingers a second time in the hazardous affairs of the East India Company. Even the King could not prevail upon him to take any action when the news of the events of June 18 to 22 reached England. George the Third, in his characteristic way, told him that the dignity of Parliament would be annihilated if Messrs. Hastings and Barwell were not instantly removed. It is significant that he gained his impression of what had taken place from two letters that Lord North had received from Francis. Nothing is said of those that Hastings had written. [2]

Francis had been cautious when there was a chance that Clavering might become Governor, but now that both of his former allies were out of the way, he was free to make his own bid for the post. Entirely oblivious to the motives that governed Lord North's policy, he tried to convince the minister that the time had come for his own promotion. After placing Hastings's conduct in the worst possible light, he concluded with a modest reference to his own fitness. "In short, my Lord, the plain question is, 'Shall the country be left at the mercy of these two men or do you mean to save it?' Three years' incessant application have made me tolerable master of affairs. In a much shorter time I do not think it possible for any man with whatever abilities, to qualify for the conduct of them." [3] But the minister who thought chiefly in terms of his parliamentary majority saw no reason why he should oblige this former government clerk who controlled no votes and lacked political influence, nor did he feel convinced that Francis's estimate of his own ability and superior merit was entirely accurate. So long as the choice lay between Clavering and Hastings, he might for political reasons prefer the former, but when it came to choosing between Hastings and Francis—well, that was a very different matter.

Francis never ceased his efforts to corrupt Edmund Burke's mind. He employed a mixture of flattery and conceit, playing on Burke's well-known devotion to the cause of honest and high-principled government. "Whatever your ideas may be of political characters in England," he wrote to him in November, "you have men to contend with at the worst, and many of them honorable—but these are devils. . . . You and I, Sir, seem to be traveling up opposite sides of a steep hill—but I hope we shall meet near the top of it. It is reserved for us, I trust, to look back from stations not too widely separated, to the weary steps we have taken—to compare the difficulties we have surmounted, and to descend into the Vale of Life together." [4] It is painful to reflect that fustian of this sort was apparently not displeasing to the great man to whom it was addressed.

At the beginning of December (1777) Wheler arrived, and immediately found himself ardently wooed for his support by both Hastings and Francis. Francis was, indeed, so anxious to gain him that he took the precaution of sending him a note that he would find when he called at Madras on his way up the coast, in which he warned him to have nothing to do with Hastings until he had been put in possession of all the facts. Hastings and Barwell, he said, were so desperate that they would promise anything. [5]

The Governor-General made Wheler's arrival the occasion for attempting to reach an accommodation with Francis. He wanted a truce. But Francis declined his advances, except on impossible terms involving first Hastings's and then Barwell's resignation. Hastings then turned to Wheler, seeking not his alliance but his neutrality, and proposed that he should assume the rôle of mediator. Caring only for the restoration of harmony in the government, he offered to surrender everything that personally interested Francis—in the matter, for instance, of appointments—in return for his concurrence in measures of public policy. There was a short delay while Wheler, who had expected to find Clavering alive and in the chair, considered his line of action. He was in a dilemma and vacillated for several days. But Francis's influence proved too strong. Within a fortnight of his arrival he indicated very plainly to the Governor-General that he had decided to combine with Francis. There was to be no change of policy. Persistent opposition and obstruction were to remain the only contributions that Francis and his new ally cared to make to the task of governing India. "So war is declared," cried Francis gleefully, when Hastings publicly taxed them with having concerted a plan of deliberate opposition. [6] And so once more the Governor had to rely on his casting-vote. This time he felt no hesitation about using it, as the new faction had not received, and was not likely to receive, the blessing of the home authorities. He put aside all his old doubts and scruples and again became resolute in his conduct of the government. From now on he was Governor-General of India, in name, in fact, in action.

That winter saw the last important change in the internal administration of the province before the menacing threat of war against a multitude of powerful enemies absorbed Hastings's attention. On discovering that Mohamed Reza Khan was intriguing with Francis in open hostility to his authority, he decided that the time had come to restore his own system. The Nawab had attained his majority and no longer needed the Moslem to manage his private affairs. So for a second time he divested Mohamed Reza Khan of his office, reinstated Munny Begum in the charge of the Nawab's household, and restored the criminal courts. The much debated question of the land settlement was temporarily settled by continuing the existing leases on an annual basis, which was all that could be done until the Directors came to a decision about the proposed permanent settlement. But even this obviously necessary measure was opposed by Francis and Wheler.

II

STORM-CLOUDS of war had been gathering on the Indian horizon for some time previous to the spring of the year 1778. They appeared in the west and in the south, and in both quarters they were as much caused by the blundering folly of the local representatives of the Company as by the restless ambition of native rulers. The governments at Madras and Bombay seemed to be possessed of an infinite capacity for folly. [7] Composed of small men whose chief concern was their own narrow and too often corrupt interests, oblivious of the existence of wider issues, innocent of statesmanship, jealous of authority, heedless of danger, and unmindful of their responsibilities, they were heading straight for disaster. At Madras the disgrace attending the mismanaged war of 1767 with Mysore had been followed by conduct towards the redoubtable Haidar Ali that could only be described as weak, mean and foolhardy, and deservedly earned his hatred and contempt. Members of Council intrigued with the local ruler, the Nawab of Arcot, in scandalous disregard of the orders and interests of their employers. When Lord Pigot was sent as governor to restore order and discipline, he was seized by a mutinous council and held under arrest until he died. Haidar Ali had desired to be friends with the English, but soon he was wanting nothing so much as the opportunity to sweep them entirely off the face of India.

On the west coast the Bombay government was also heading for trouble by sticking its fingers into a veritable hornets' nest. For some time the gentlemen there had smarted under the feeling that their con- frères at Calcutta and Madras had left them far behind in the race for power and wealth. They were still confined to the little island on which their city was built. Their ambition was to secure possession of the neighboring island of Salsette with the port of Bassein, but as it belonged to the Marathas, they had to proceed to their object either by war or intrigue. Three years earlier they had taken the first step, adopting the method that had proved so successful in Bengal and the Carnatic. There was always at least one pretender to the throne of every Indian state, and the Maratha state at Poona was no exception. In Raghunath Rao, commonly known as Ragoba, the English found a strong claimant, who was anxious for their support and willing to give them in return the island they coveted. It needed little persuasion to make them decide that this was their opportunity, and they hastened, without waiting to obtain the permission of the Supreme Government, to make a treaty with Ragoba, the uncle and murderer of the deceased Peshwa, promising to restore him to his former seat of power at Poona. Nor did they wait until they had fulfilled their part of the bargain before taking possession of Salsette. Only one result could follow these reckless proceedings— war with the Poona Regency government.[1]

When on May 31, 1775, the Council at Calcutta learned of what was afoot, it had intervened decisively to put a stop to it. There had been no difference of opinion between Hastings and his opponents: the treaty was "unseasonable, impolitic, unjust and unauthorized." [8] Where they had disagreed had been in the orders that should be issued to the presumptuous subordinate government. The Governor-General had wished to leave it with some discretionary power, as he realized the impolicy of a distant authority ordering an abrupt withdrawal from a positive engagement, when such action might be attended with greater danger than pursuance of the original design. The Majority, on the other hand, insisted that Bombay should have no option in the matter but should be ordered forthwith to withdraw its troops and call off the war. The Majority's views, as usual, had prevailed, and hostilities were abruptly halted. An agent from the Supreme Government then nego- tiated a hollow and disadvantageous truce with the Poona Ministers, the terms of which were never acted on. There was an interlude of no fighting, but no real peace. What came to be known as the First Maratha War is generally considered as having actually begun with the ill- advised and unauthorized intervention of the Bombay Government in Maratha politics in 1775. Lasting as it was to do for seven years, this

[1] The actual titular head of the Maratha Confederacy, the Rajah of Satara, was a mere figure-head, his authority having been usurped by his hereditary minister, the Peshwa. The Peshwa in turn had been shorn of most of his power, and the various great chieftains, like Sindhia, Holkar and the Rajah of Berar, had become almost completely independent. In 1775 the reigning Peshwa was an infant, and the power was in the hands of a Council of Ministers.

war was the first of many grave complications that occurred to upset Hastings's plans and plunge him into his worst troubles.

All might still have been well if the Court of Directors had not, with a puckish spirit of mischief-making and a total disregard for consistency, given its approval to Bombay's alliance with Ragoba. What had been criminal conduct in Hastings, when he waged "offensive" war on the Rohillas, was now made to appear meritorious conduct in the rest of the Company's servants. Two years later the Directors made matters worse by actually encouraging Bombay to renew the alliance, in defiance of the positive orders of the Supreme Government. They virtually gave the subordinate presidency permission to make war on the Marathas whensoever it pleased, and naturally it was not long before the Council at Bombay took advantage of the permission.

When the year 1778 opened the mine was well and truly laid for the explosion. The prestige of each of the three presidencies could hardly have been at a lower ebb. Bengal was still in the throes of faction, the progress of which had been watched with interest by the court of every native state in India. Nor did they have to rely only on hearsay and espionage to obtain their information. Many times Hastings had occasion to remark on the leakage that made the most secret consultations of his government common knowledge to every foreign agent in Calcutta, and he had grounds for believing that the source of the leak was a member of the Council—none other than Mr. Francis. Madras, similarly riven with divisions and burdened with an exhausted treasury, was like a leaf that the first strong wind would blow from its branch. Nor, as Hastings surveyed the scene outside the borders of the Company's possessions, could he have derived greater comfort from what he saw there. Oude, the sole ally, was dissolving into anarchy. With a vicious and incompetent ruler, an exhausted treasury, a huge burden of debt to the Company, a mutinous army, and an incipiently rebellious zemindari, it was as an ally more of a liability than an asset.

From the west came ominous signs that the Marathas were composing the divisions that for lengthy periods rendered them powerless to intervene effectively in the political arena. As proof of this they had recently sent an expedition against Haidar Ali. Given union of all the Maratha states and leaders, immediately there was created a most formidable military rival to the English, made more formidable by its possession of drilled and disciplined troops under the command of French officers. The same was true of Haidar Ali. In league with the French and expectantly awaiting from them strong reinforcements of troops, officers and money, he lay perched above the mountains of the Eastern Ghats, commanding every pass into the defenseless plains of the Carnatic, like an eagle ready to swoop. In his head had already been hatched the bold scheme of driving the English into the sea. And what was still more disturbing, every packet from England brought news of reverses and failures in the war that was raging beyond the Atlantic.

While Hastings gazed over the scene he must have thought of the well-known rule of Oriental politics that made weakness a sure invitation to attack and caused the impression of declining strength to precipitate a coalition of rivals to complete the declension. Amidst the confusion and anarchy of the eighteenth century, with a score of warlike states and leaders competing for supremacy and existence, the law of nature held sway: woe to the weak, for they shall be destroyed. It was already certain in January 1778 that the military powers of India had read what they took to be the writing on the wall for the Company and were engaged in composing their own bitter enmities for a joint attack upon it.

Nobody in the governing Council of Bengal was blind to the danger. Least of all, Philip Francis. Francis, indeed, took a strange delight in it. He seemed to revel in the idea that the doom of the Empire might be imminent, and did his best to hasten the day by spreading alarmist reports, more often false than true; undermining the Governor-General's authority among his officers, destroying his credit with the people of Bengal, and dispelling a spirit of sheer defeatism. Nothing now, he declared, could save Bengal from irretrievable ruin—probably not even he himself. He reported to Lord North that, with war looming ahead, the province was utterly defenseless: with a French invasion imminent it lacked both an army and a general. Nothing but mischief and corruption existed around him. [9]

There was plenty of cause for anxiety. It was scarcely possible for any one to believe that the material resources of the Company's governments in man-power and wealth were adequate to the task of waging a general war against a combination of powerful enemies. The army, though well disciplined and well led, was small in numbers. Money was entirely lacking, except at Calcutta, and even there, while the possession of the wealthiest province in India gave the Company an undoubted advantage, it had only been within the last two or three years that order had been introduced into the finances and the treasury relieved of the burden of debt that had made it nearly bankrupt in 1772. In August 1778 there were £1,200,000 in *specie* in the Calcutta treasury, but this was not a sufficient reserve to support a lengthy and expensive war. No financial aid could be looked for from home. The Company naturally expected its Indian agencies to be sources of profit, not sources of expense, and the national government limited its responsibility to sending military and naval reënforcements.

Once more the problem of security had become acute, and once more the man upon whom the burden chiefly lay of providing for it was not found lacking. From the time he became Governor-General, Hastings had been impressed by the need of the Company to establish a comprehensive political system for the protection of its scattered territories in place of the hand-to-mouth, isolationist policy—or rather, lack of policy —that it had hitherto pursued, which compelled it to rely entirely on its own meager military strength to resist attack. He believed that, so far as Bengal alone was concerned, its army *would* prove equal to the task of repelling any invasion that an Indian power, aided by the French, might attempt, not so much because of the superiority of the Company's troops over all possible enemies, as because of the natural strength of the combined Bengal and Oude frontiers. But he saw the wisdom of striving for a more ample security if it could be obtained, and he thought in terms of British India as a whole and not merely of the part of it for which he was primarily responsible.

He had early begun to formulate a plan to this end, but the arrival of the triumvirate had compelled him to postpone all thought of its application. When their reign ended and he was once more able to give it serious thought, he was still at a loss to know how to give it effect. Its essence was to extend the system of subsidiary alliances to include other neighboring native states besides Oude, such as Berar (which was part of the Maratha Confederacy), and to make them allies, not only of the East India Company, but of the King of England. [10]

The scheme was practicable, and in the hands of his successors it was to become the chief means of extending and consolidating British power and influence. The Company possessed a commodity that most Indian states were only too anxious to buy—a military power superior for purposes of defense to any other. With the fear of attack from their neighbors resting heavily on them at all times, it was a tempting idea for them to exchange perpetual insecurity for the assurance of protection that alliance with the Company would give. For the Company, the scheme was equally advantageous. Without any additional expense it would be provided with increased military strength, as the subsidies paid by each ally would be used to enlarge the army and to cover the increased cost of its maintenance. Each new alliance, too, could be counted upon to enhance the Company's power and prestige, at the same time as it lessened the numbers of states that might otherwise be drawn into the orbit of French designs, be absorbed by the Marathas, or for any other reason become hostile.

Though the scheme was undoubtedly soundly conceived, Hastings had cause to be afraid of the reception it would meet with in England. Nothing shows more clearly the weakness and isolation of his position than his fear to adopt the usual course and lay his ideas confidently before his superiors. After recent events he felt that he hardly dared do so. All official channels to the sources of his authority seemed closed to him. What was the use of his writing to Lord North? What was the use of his writing to the Court of Directors? The former did not read his letters, the latter had sunk to a depth of inefficiency and ignominy beyond all belief. Composed of a set of time-serving politicians, it had lost any claim it once had had to respect and obedience and become the worst imaginable body for guiding the affairs of an empire. Every dispatch that now came from these gentlemen filled Hastings with impotent rage at their imbecility and childish malice. He dared not write confidentially to the chairman or deputy-chairman of the Company, because, as a result of John Robinson's electioneering efforts, they were both his professed enemies and would be certain to use whatever he said to his prejudice.

All there was left for him to do was to put some personal friend in possession of his ideas and allow him to make such use of them as he thought prudent. And this is what he had done in February of the previous year when he had entrusted his scheme to his young and dearly loved friend, Alexander Elliot. Thus was this man left a lonely figure at a far-distant outpost of empire, denied counsel, confidence and support, at one of the most critical moments in that empire's history.

One fact about his plan needs emphasizing. He did not aim at an expansion of British territory, but only at an expansion of influence. He wrote to Elliot:

"You are already well acquainted with the general system which I wish to be empowered to establish in India, namely to extend the influence of the British nation to every part of India, not too remote from their possessions, without enlarging the circle of their defense or involving them in hazardous or indefinite engagements, and to accept of the allegiance of such of our neighbors as shall sue to be enlisted among the friends and allies of the King of Great Britain." [11]

The policy that Francis advocated was diametrically opposite. He was the isolationist, vehemently opposed to entangling alliances, to intervention in Indian affairs, and to the expansion of British influence beyond the confines of Bengal. He saw no need for an active foreign policy. Bengal, of course, had to be defended, but he maintained that the best way to do that was by concentrating its military forces within its borders and acting strictly on the defensive. Nor did he feel any sense of responsibility for the defense of the other presidencies: they should be left to work out their own salvation. Philip Francis was emphatically no builder of empire.

III

OTHER signs that a big storm was brewing in India were not absent. During the late summer an agent of the French government, the Chevalier de St. Lubin, had arrived at Poona to negotiate a French alliance with the Marathas. His specific object was to secure a seaport near Bombay and a factory, supported by military force, at Poona. The chief Maratha minister, Nana Farnavese, gave him a hearty welcome and treated him with honor and attention, in marked contrast to the studied discourtesy he showed to the British envoy.

This disquieting development caused Hastings to change his policy of strict non-intervention in Maratha affairs. Renewed divisions had broken out in the Poona government. Two factions were striving for supremacy. One was headed by Nana Farnavese. The other made believe they were opposed to a French alliance and looking to the British for assistance. Negotiations were opened with Bombay, and the old project of restoring Ragoba was revived. Nothing loath, and knowing that it had the approval of the Company, the Bombay Council agreed, and appealed to Calcutta for the approbation and support of the Supreme Government.

Francis remained firm in his strong disapproval of the whole plan, stressing its impolicy and denouncing it as a violation of treaty. With good reason he pointed out the danger of the Company being involved in a war that could only be supported by men and money from Bengal, Bombay's own resources being inadequate for the undertaking. In view also of the American War and the growing likelihood of war with France and Spain, he emphasized the importance of preserving peace in India. Hastings, on the other hand, now favored the project. Fear of France overrode all other considerations in his mind. If war was coming, and he believed it was, then it was most advisable that Great Britain establish "a firm interest in the most powerful state of India, and check in its first growth the seeds which the French have sown of an alliance with it, and which, if suffered to grow to maturity, may prove fatal to the British possessions in India." [12] Scenting the approaching struggle he wished to strike the first blow. He maintained that no violation of treaty was involved, and clenched his argument by pointing out that the Company had given its approval.

With Barwell's support and the aid of his casting-vote Hastings carried his policy against the united opposition of Francis and Wheler. The project was adopted and the decision was taken to supply Bombay with both men and money.

Hastings's adoption of the policy of armed intervention was open to serious criticism. It was the kind of undertaking that only success could justify. It is true, as he foresaw, that if successful it would have tremendously far-reaching results. If British influence could be made supreme in the councils of the Maratha Empire, then the chief military danger to British India would be removed. Britain would instantly attain the position of paramount power, and be secure from the menace of French intrigue. But was there any reasonable ground for hoping that this result could be obtained?

Hastings certainly underrated the difficulties. He made light of Bombay's military weakness and underestimated the fighting qualities of the Marathas. He used the surprising argument that the Bombay government possessed more troops than were necessary to win the battles of Plassey and Buxar. Considering how fearful he had been of Maratha military prowess a few years earlier when Oude was menaced, he could scarcely have been unaware of the vast superiority of Maratha troops over the Nawab's rabble. "I have no doubt of their being in a state to enter upon the measures which they have proposed. The distance of Bombay from Poona is but a march of four days." [13] Shortness of distance, however, as all students of military science know, is no sufficient criterion for judging the feasibility of a military enterprise. He made no allowance for possible blunders by those responsible for the expedition or for the consequences of failure. Then again, it was distinctly unwise to place any reliance on the pledges of Maratha leaders.

Maratha politics were notoriously intricate and fluctuating. A promise made today was apt to be withdrawn tomorrow.

Hastings's embarking on this hazardous enterprise reveals a prominent feature in his character that was both a virtue and a defect. Barwell saw it very clearly: "Hastings's only foible, if it is a foible, is excess of confidence, the happy enthusiasm of genius, but which from too weak or defective means may be a fault in his character, though it is one of his merits." [14] Francis also placed his finger upon it in his anecdote of Hastings's opinion of *Robinson Crusoe*. Over-sanguine, always preferring action to inaction and the bold course to the cautious, he generally visualized the end more clearly than the means, his eagerness to reach the goal causing him to underestimate the difficulties and dangers in the way.

Even if his Maratha policy had succeeded to the extent of occupying Poona and installing Ragoba as Peshwa, one wonders whether his real difficulties would not then have begun. Would he have succeeded in reconciling the Marathas to the change without involving the Company in war with the Confederacy? Lord Wellesley's experiences in pursuing the same policy suggest the probability that Hastings would have failed.

No time was lost in launching the expedition. Ten lakhs of rupees were sent, and a force of six thousand sepoys with Colonel Leslie in command was assembled at Kalpi on the banks of the Jumna under orders to march straight to Bombay.

This aroused Francis and Wheler to furious protest. Not without cause they considered it an insanely rash undertaking. It was the first time that any one had thought of sending an army beyond the borders of Bengal and Oude. Clive alone had possessed the spirit of audacious enterprise that wins empires, and Clive, a soldier, had led his armies in person. Hastings, a civilian, was now planning to march an army where even Clive had not dreamed of—from one side of India to the other, and by a route that took it through the heart of the Maratha empire. Little wonder, therefore, that timid men should stand aghast and prophesy nothing but disaster. But Hastings, positive that the enterprise was practicable, was deaf to all protests, declaring his inflexible determination to prosecute the expedition to its conclusion: "I am willing to stake my reputation on the event of it."

The first stage of the expedition did not augur well for its success. Colonel Leslie was an inefficient officer who had received the command through seniority, not through merit. Instead of obeying his orders to march as rapidly as possible, he dawdled. His route took him by the rich diamond mines of Bundelkhand, and Calcutta was soon full of gossip that he was more interested in the mines than in his mission, a belief that Francis did his best to foster. At the outset he met with resistance from local Maratha chiefs, which was almost enough to unnerve him from proceeding further. Francis magnified the encounter into a defeat, redoubled his predictions of disaster, and did his best generally to turn the public uneasiness into panic.

The Maratha enterprise soon came to a sudden pause. At the last minute the Bombay Council lost its nerve and decided to call off the expedition. Leslie received orders countermanding his advance. The expected revolution then took place in Poona, but as Ragoba and his British allies had not participated in it, it was without benefit to them, and in no way changed Maratha policy. Chevalier St. Lubin remained in high favor with the new faction.

Despairing of effecting anything through the irresolution of Bombay, Hastings forthwith dropped the project and reverted to the earlier plan of his own for an alliance with the Bhonsla Rajah of Berar. As early as 1773 the Rajah had made tentative overtures to him, which he had encouraged, but nothing had come of them. Berar had attained a virtual independence of the Poona government, and its ruler had pretensions of his own to the titular sovereignty of the Maratha Confederacy. It was this fact of which the Governor-General now tried to take advantage. While the Bombay plan in favor of Ragoba remained in effect, he only sought passage for Leslie's army through the Rajah's territories, which was readily granted, but as soon as that plan was given up he encouraged Mudaji Bhonsla to press his own claims at Poona and offered him British assistance. Leslie was now in Bundelkhand and could with equal ease continue his march to Bombay or turn aside to cooperate with Mudaji. Francis and Wheler were daily demanding that his army be recalled, but Hastings, weaving these ambitious plans in his head, flatly refused. He was determined, one way or another, to make British influence dominant at Poona. If not Ragoba, then Mudaji could equally well be the instrument of his policy.

It was now June, and momentous news from Europe was being rapidly carried across the thousands of miles of intervening sea to Britain's representatives in the East. On the 8th, Francis recorded in his diary: "Bitter news from America; Burgoyne taken, etc. Hastings and almost everybody here in high triumph. They seem to consider their own security as united with the ruin of the Empire." [15]

Francis used the news of Saratoga to press his demand for Leslie's recall. In his opinion it was a time for defensive action only. The news, indeed, conveyed a general feeling of impending disaster. But to Hastings it signified only the need for still greater enterprise and vigor. He stood firm as a rock, maintaining that there was no need for alarm. Not only would it be dangerous to stop abruptly an operation to which the government was committed, with the eyes of all India turned upon it, but, "on the contrary, if it be really true that the British arms and influence have suffered so severe a check in the Western world, it is the more incumbent on those who are charged with the interest of Great Britain in the East to exert themselves for the retrieval of the national loss." [16] It would be foolish, he urged, to recall Leslie when he occupied a position of such great strategic importance. Hastings held to his belief that Bengal was safe from invasion by sea and had nothing to fear on land except from the Marathas. Poona and Berar between them held the key to the situation. Why act then only on the defensive? Why not rather carry the war into the enemy's country and break up this Franco-Maratha alliance before it became effective?

On July 7 reliable word reached Hastings that war had been declared between England and France. He was the first in India to learn of it as the news had been sent him from the British Embassy in Paris by overland express via the new fast route to India through Suez, a route that Hastings himself had been instrumental in opening up.[1] A fortnight later news was received of the sailing from Toulon of fifteen sail of the line, with transports carrying five thousand troops, destined presumably for the East.

At once all of the Governor-General's fine powers of decision and vigorous action were brought into play. He was superb in a crisis, a model of cool self-possession and determined courage. It was no longer a time to temporize, he cried, but for speedy and decided measures. But if he hoped that his opponents would realize the need for a united front to meet the emergency, he was to be disappointed. There was to be no closing up of the ranks. Francis and Wheler compelled him to take every measure on his own responsibility. He had to make his casting-vote the means of saving the British Empire in India.

Even more serious still was the fact that every dispatch that arrived from the Court of Directors continued to heap reproaches and censures on Hastings for everything that he had done since power had been restored to him. If knowledge of their contents had been confined to the Council, no great harm would have been done, but such secrecy did not suit Francis's purposes. On August 18 Hastings wrote to Sulivan:

"It is a fact, nor will he dare deny it, that he sent copies of the letter written by the Court of Directors to General Clavering, in circular letters to the provincial stations, and translations of it to the Rannies of Burdwan and Rajeshahee, Mahomed Reza Khan, Rajah Chait Singh, and even to Nujif Khan, and to the Court of Shah Alum. I have copies of both in my possession. What was this but an invitation to the world to place no confidence in the present Government, and to its subjects to disobey its authority? In all our distant military quarters, and civil stations, I find it currently believed that a French armament is actually on its way to Bengal, and I suspect that this persuasion owes its birth to the same fruitful brain." [17]

If later some of these persons were suspected of treachery, part of the reason is plain to see.

Orders were immediately sent to the Governor of Fort St. George at Madras to attack Pondicherry. Three days later Chandernagore, the French settlement on the Hugli, was quietly seized before its governor was even aware of the declaration of war. Measures were also taken to prepare the province to resist invasion. Three months' supplies were stored in Fort William. Extensive fortifications were begun at the mouth

[1] See p. 350.

of the river. Nine new battalions were added to the sepoy army. A militia of one thousand Europeans was formed for garrison duty. Two vessels of forty guns each were manned and armed to reënforce Sir Edward Vernon's little squadron of His Majesty's navy. Seven other smaller ships of the Company were fitted out to form a marine defense force for Calcutta. The army was distributed, two brigades with the artillery corps at the presidency, three sepoy battalions on the southern frontier, one brigade for the defense of Oude, and a new temporary brigade, subsidized by the Vizier, for the defense of Rohilkhand. Chait Singh, the tributary Rajah of Benares, was required to contribute, as his share of the burden of the war, five lakhs of rupees—a measure at which Francis demurred, but upon which Hastings insisted, claiming that it was the right of the suzerain power. Finally, it was resolved, with the usual division of votes, to open immediate negotiations with Berar for an offensive and defensive alliance. The Governor-General confidently asserted that if these measures were insufficient for the protecton of Bengal against any enemy, or combination of enemies, none could protect it. Francis, on the other hand, openly declared them to be inadequate. Nothing, in his opinion, could save the province from defeat and conquest when the French armada arrived, and he accused the Governor-General of supine neglect.

Alexander Elliot was appointed to conduct the negotiations with Berar, and on July 20 he departed on his mission, upon which Hastings set great store. It was expected that he would reach Nagpore, the capital of Berar, by the middle of September. Leslie, who was approaching the River Nerbudda, was ordered to halt within the boundaries of Berar until Elliot had concluded his negotiations.

We have here reached another turning point in Hastings's career. Until now, it had been one of splendid achievement and truly amazing success, considering the overwhelming difficulties which he had had to face. He had made a stable, prosperous and well-governed state out of a ruined, distracted and famine-stricken province. He had preserved it from collapse during the mad reign of the Majority. He had triumphed over his enemies, surviving them in the battle with the deadly climate, and he had defeated the contemptible intrigues of corrupt and pettifogging politicians. Fortune had been kind to him. One happy chance after another had extricated him from his difficulties. His optimism had been almost miraculously justified. Now the crisis of foreign war, not of his making, had come. He was ready for it. He had made his plans, and these plans only needed to be carried out to ensure the complete safety of the empire entrusted to his charge. The French armada would have arrived, and finding the Marathas and Haidar Ali bound by friendly ties to Great Britain, for there was still a chance of securing Haidar's neutrality, would have been unable to effect anything and have had to turn around and sail home. There would have been no long and expensive war to exhaust the funds and credit of the Bengal treasury, no devastation of the Carnatic, no Benares insurrection, no necessity to seize the treasures of Oude princesses. And there would have been no impeachment of Warren Hastings. Bounteous honors, a peerage, an ample fortune, an unclouded reputation—these would have been his reward from a grateful country. If—what a burden of tragedy and frustrated hopes is sometimes contained in that little word!—if misfortune and the blunders, to use no harsher word, of his colleagues and subordinates had not upset his plans and precipitated one disaster upon another. Events could not move fast, distances were too great and means of communication too slow. Months elapsed between them where now there would only be weeks or even days. But as month followed month during the next three years, one by one the blocks that Hastings had built up in his mind into a massive pyramid of security came tumbling down. First went the alliance with Berar, then the establishment of British influence at Poona, finally the peace with Haidar Ali. And their collapse brought still worse calamities in their train, until at the end it was only to be by the most desperate efforts that Hastings could save the Empire from destruction.

IV

THE first blow fell in October. Alexander Elliot had died on the road to Nagpore. The loss was irreparable, to the Governor-General personally as he was one of the few men under him that he could really trust, and he not only trusted him but loved him; and to his plans, as the consequent delay ruined them. In the meantime, Colonel Leslie's dilatory and highly culpable conduct had further wrecked the scheme. He had loitered away four months in Bundelkhand, contrary to his express instructions. The Council had unanimously resolved to recall him and appoint in his place his second in command, Lieutenant-Colonel Goddard, when the news arrived of Leslie's death. The change of command was one stroke of good fortune, as Goddard was an excellent officer—one of the best, as Hastings said, in the service, "remarkably lively and enterprising, sensible, and the very reverse of the sordid disposition and morose and disgusting manners of his predecessor." "He immediately quitted the detested land of Bundelkhand, and without experiencing or expecting any of the many impediments which his predecessor had so long complained of, continued his march in peace, with ease and plenty." [18]

The next blow was delivered by the Bombay Council. As the year closed word came from Goddard that this vacillating body had once more changed its mind. The seductive whispers of discontented Maratha politicians had again been heard in Bombay, and had again found ready listeners. Without waiting to consult Calcutta, they got together their small army to escort Ragoba to Poona.

The day of reckoning had arrived, for it was now to be shown

how entirely the whole project centering round the miserable person
of Ragoba had been misconceived. History has repeatedly shown the
futility, nine times out of ten, of foreign intervention to effect a revolution or to impose a ruler on a country whose people are proud and
warlike; for the paths of such enterprises are profusely strewn with
empty promises, mutual suspicions, intrigues, treacheries, feuds, and
bloody scenes of strife and disaster. The Marathas as a people, given
though they were to internecine feuds like the Corsicans, were also like
the Corsicans jealous of their independence and hostile to foreign interference. A Maratha chieftain, involved in one of his perennial conspiracies, might invite outside aid to gain his ends, but woe was apt to
betide the meddler if he was ingenuous enough to place reliance on the
promises and pledges made to him. His only sure course was to rely
entirely on his own strength, after making sure that it was adequate to
the undertaking.

Hastings had sanctioned the project twelve months before, but
only on two fundamental conditions: first, that it was undertaken at
the express invitation of a responsible and dominant party in the Maratha state, and second, that Bombay should act in conjunction with Calcutta and the army that Calcutta was sending. If these two conditions had
been observed the expedition would have had some prospect of success.
But he had not allowed for the insane jealousy of the subordinate for
the superior government. Bombay thirsted to show what it could do by
its own unaided strength. So now, although the favorable moment for
intervention had passed and comparative harmony reigned in the regency government, it sent forth its diminutive army of five hundred
Europeans and two thousand native infantry to essay "the march of
four days" to Poona, without giving time to Goddard to lend his
assistance.

From the first the operation was woefully mismanaged. [19] The
Bombay Council adopted the imbecile policy of attaching civilian field
deputies to control the military commander, who was himself anything
but a competent officer. The result was disastrous. No sooner had they
penetrated Maratha territory than they found that all Ragoba's wide
promises of support were sheer delusions. Not a single important chieftain joined their camp. Instead, clouds of fierce horsemen, the same
famous raiders that had spread terror from one end of India to the
other, descended on their flanks and rear, harassing their march and
laying waste the country on which they were dependent for supplies.
And when the small force reached a point sixteen miles from Poona,
they found an army of fifty thousand prepared to dispute their further
advance. The prospect was too much for the civilians. They lost their
heads and their courage, ordered a precipitate retreat, and by so doing
gave the signal to the exultant Marathas to attack. The troops fought
well and doggedly, but not all the bravery in the world could over-

come such double odds, and the end was—surrender. The Marathas, showing greater magnanimity than might have been expected of them under the circumstances, signed the convention of Wargaum (January 17, 1779), permitting the British commanders to march their army back the way it had come. Salsette and Bassein had to be restored, Ragoba surrendered to his enemies, Goddard's army ordered to return, and English officers handed over as hostages.

The disaster and the disgrace attaching to it resounded throughout the length and breadth of India. Friends of the English groaned. Their enemies rejoiced. Francis—was he friend or enemy?—gloated. His prophecies of disaster were being verified to the very letter. Had not he predicted with wearisome reiteration the inevitable consequences of distant expeditions? A stunning blow had, indeed, been administered to British prestige, the most precious of all attributes of an imperial power: the kind of blow that acts as a signal for every dormant element of trouble to come to life and raise its head, for pretended friends to become secret enemies, and for open enemies to make active war.

Ominous rumors began to flow in from the South that the Nizam of Hyderabad and Haidar Ali were conspiring with the Maratha leaders for a joint confederacy, and it soon became apparent that only the arrival of a French armada was needed to set the match to the charge. The Marathas themselves, elated by their victory, became at once insolent and warlike. The smell of rich plunder was in their nostrils. All felt that the war for supremacy in India was about to begin. This of itself was enough to daunt the most fearless spirit. But for Hastings it meant even more. He was standing on the brink of a precipice. For he well knew how closely retention of his post was bound up with his success. The Regulating Act was about to expire, and none knew what would take its place. Any set-back at this moment was likely to spell his downfall.

He stood firm. Indeed, the news of the disaster only spurred him on to still greater exertions. "The terms of the treaty almost made me sink with shame while I read them," he declared. [20] He did not hesitate to disavow it. His one aim was to wipe out the disgrace.

Happily, Colonel Goddard was the right man in the right place. He knew how to respond to an emergency. When the news reached him on its way across India, he did not wait for orders but immediately set out on a swift rush to the scene of disaster. He covered the distance of three hundred miles to Surat on the coast in twenty days, which ranks as one of the finest performances in British military history. "The hour of danger is the opportunity of heroes." His timely arrival disconcerted the Marathas, saved Bombay, and restored the reputation of British arms.

All hope, however, of an alliance with Berar was at an end. How promising the prospects had been was shown by the fact that on learning of Elliot's death, Mudaji had written earnestly asking Hastings to commit the negotiations to some one else without loss of time. (Both the Poona government and the Nizam had learned of what was afoot and were threatening him with hostilities.) But the moment he learned of the rival plan for making Ragoba Peshwa instead of himself, he abruptly terminated all negotiations, having naturally concluded that he was being tricked. [21] The disaster of Wargaum completed his change of attitude. Hostile, rather than friendly, thoughts began to occupy his mind.

Chapter XVI

THE DUEL

I

AS the year 1778 closed Hastings again faced the prospect of loss of power. Barwell, his only support, announced his intention of resigning. For some time his thoughts had been turning homewards. Money had ceased to be an object with him, and if he had once entertained the hope of becoming Governor-General, he had come to realize that the post was beyond his reach. He had taken his disappointment philosophically, without resenting Hastings's refusal to retire: public office did not hold for him any irresistible charms, nor was he actuated by any high ambitions. For some time his relatives and friends had been pressing him to come home, and he was now ready to meet their wishes.

The announcement naturally filled Hastings with dismay. He knew it was as certain as night follows day that his departure would be the signal to Francis and Wheler to take control of the government, and the very thought made him shudder. First privately, then publicly in Council, he begged Barwell to retract his decision, or at least postpone his departure a little while. Francis scoffed and jeered, but the appeal was successful. Barwell, whatever his shortcomings, was not the man to desert the Governor-General in this hour of his greatest need. Putting what he considered to be his duty before his personal wishes, he consented to stay until the situation changed and his presence ceased to be essential. If there was one man to whom Warren Hastings was deeply indebted, it was Richard Barwell who alone made possible his record of achievement during these years. Nor did Hastings fail to acknowledge the debt, paying generous tribute to his unswerving loyalty, his sound judgement, his resourcefulness (greater, he said, than his own), and his affability ("which I am sometimes inclined to consider as the first accomplishment of a man of business"). [1]

Whether or not Barwell stayed, there was still danger of a hostile Council. The Council was one short of its full number, as General Clavering's place had not yet been filled. In a few weeks' time this deficiency would be made good, as Lieutenant-General Sir Eyre Coote was on his way out. Would he in a double sense take Clavering's place? Would the old majority of three against two reappear? Francis was full of hope. As soon as he heard of Coote's appointment he had written to his wife, "I look for him with longing eyes as Hotspur in the play does for his father's army." [2] "I have been trained in the school of disappointment" was his entry in his diary for December 11, but Coote might still put everything right for him. And Hastings was equally afraid lest Francis's hopes might prove justified. He had known Coote in his early days when Clive had arrived with his army to rescue the refugees at Fulta, and he had met him again at Madras, and his memory of him was not such as to make him confident that Coote would prove a congenial colleague. Seven years before, when he heard that Coote was leaving India, he had written to Sulivan, "May success and honor attend him in any other part of the world, but God forbid that he should ever return to any part of India again." [3] And now he was returning, and upon his behavior would depend the fate of Hastings's government!

Sir Eyre Coote was an excellent soldier, brave, vigorous, enterprising, though at the same time prudent, a real master of the art of war, and the idol of his troops. During his earlier service in India he had completed the ruin of the French power in the Carnatic by his smashing victory at Wandewash in 1760. Nobody therefore questioned his military genius. And if the post of Commander-in-Chief had only involved leading the army in war and fighting battles, none would have been more welcome in India at this critical juncture than Sir Eyre Coote. But the post involved far more than that: a seat in the Council, a share in the initiation and execution of policy, administrative responsibility, the exercise of tact, diplomacy and sound political judgement; in fact, the governing of an empire and not merely the commanding of an army. And unfortunately it was in his personal relationships that Coote's defects of character became marked, not to say glaring. It was an old story. Clive had had some harsh things to say about him when Coote was serving under him in Bengal, and Governor Dupré had been just as candid as Hastings when the three had been together at Madras. For the General was a man who did not take kindly to dictation or even to the sharing of authority. He was quarrelsome, wayward, vain and irascible, so much so that it was the unanimous opinion of those who had tried to work with him that he was temperamentally unable to maintain harmonious relations with any but the officers and men under his actual command. He was inordinately jealous of his prerogatives, had an inveterate dislike and suspicion of civilian control, saw slights where none was intended, and was liable to give vent to peevish explosions of wrath on the flimsiest excuse. Lion-hearted warrior and gallant gentleman as he was, his colleagues had to treat him more like a willful, irrational child than a mature man in order to obtain any coöperation from him.

Hastings was determined not to give him any excuse to take sides against him. He knew the man he was dealing with, and this in Coote's case was an important advantage. He was aware of the General's susceptibility to flattery, his love of attention and his fondness for money, and he had decided in advance to make good use of this knowledge. "Coote shall have all he wants," he wrote to Sulivan, "and more than he probably expects."

Coote arrived in March and was received with full military honors and showered with attentions. Hastings's encounters with Barker and Clavering had taught him that generals of His Majesty's army could be counted upon to possess greatly inflated egos, with which it was dangerous for a mere civilian to tamper. He further gratified Coote by telling him that he would be given a free hand in military matters. And he completed his happiness by granting him exceptionally liberal allowances for his expenses in the field. If this was bribery, Hastings was content to let his enemies make the most of it. He *had* to have the General's support at whatever cost to himself. And for the moment it looked as though he would have it abundantly. For the General promptly gave his approval to the plan of operations against the Marathas, and on other test questions voted with the Governor-General and Barwell.

Francis did not disguise his mortification at this unexpected turn of events. "Francis is miserable," wrote Hastings, with evident satisfaction, "and is weak enough to declare it in a manner much resembling the impatience of a passionate woman, whose hands are held to prevent her from doing mischief." [4] But he spoke too soon. Francis's hands were not tied, nor was he the man to give up without a struggle. He had, as even Hastings had come to realize, a diabolical talent for setting men, even intimate friends, at variance, and he at once began to employ it on Coote. While Hastings was trying to arrange things so that the General need have no part in the controversies of the Council, and would not therefore have to take sides, Francis was busily at work poisoning his mind, insinuating among other things that he had fallen an easy prey to the Governor-General's wiles. Nor were his efforts without avail. It had been Coote's honorable intention to take an independent part and confine himself to military matters, but he soon found this to be impossible, and the knowledge made him acutely uncomfortable. At first he tried to evade the issue by absenting himself from meetings of Council. Before the summer was out he sought refuge in flight, departing up country to join the army: the atmosphere of the camp was far more congenial to him than the faction-charged air of Calcutta. This was not, however, what Francis wanted, and he confided his disappointment to his journal with a typical outburst against the man who had slipped out of his grasp: "I will never content myself with saying I never knew, but upon my soul I never heard of so abandoned a scoundrel. It is a character to which your English ideas of dirt and meanness do not reach. Nor is it to be met with even in Bengal; even here it excites execration and contempt." [5]

Absence from Calcutta only served to bring out the capriciousness of Coote's temper. Although he and the Governor-General had parted with mutual professions of confidence and friendship, almost at once he began to condemn the measures he had previously approved and to complain of having been treated with indignity. "Sir E. Coote quarreled with me," wrote Hastings. "I made no return. He became when we met my fast friend, and has broke out into violent invectives against me since, and upon my honor I know not for what cause. . . . This I know that it is absolutely impossible for him to be upon terms of peace with any man living who possesses a power either superior or equal to his own, unless the latter is forever at his elbow, and coaxing him into good humor. If you doubt this, try him, and you will be convinced." [6] Nevertheless Hastings bore with him patiently. Sheer necessity, if nothing else, compelled him to do so.

Things were quiet for the moment on the foreign front. Goddard was negotiating with the Marathas with a view to making peace with them on the terms of the Treaty of Purandhar. The attention of Calcutta was centered once more on the dispatches from home. The Regulating Act expired on October 19, 1779, and that date arrived without any word of what was to take its place. The Governor-General did not know one day whether he would still be in office the next. Every fresh packet from England might contain orders for a change of government. It was even seriously debated in Council whether they could still consider themselves a legal government. The only dispatches that arrived continued to heap reproaches on the Governor-General. The Directors cared nothing any longer for consistency, and Hastings had come to the conclusion that it was quite useless for him to go on trying to meet their wishes; whatever he did was bound to be condemned, even though it might be entirely consistent with their latest orders. Even his Maratha policy and Goddard's expedition were certain to be disapproved, notwithstanding the fact that both were largely based on the Directors' own instructions to Bombay. He made his protest to them: "You hurt yourselves and your own affairs by treating with indignities the man whom you leave in charge of your interests and of the national credit in India." Now they had ordered him to reinstate Bristow, Fowke and Mohamed Reza Khan. This he flatly and indignantly refused to do: "When they abandon the line of their duty, leave me uninstructed upon every point of business, and fill all their letters, which are volumes, with gross invectives against me, and with orders which have no object but to gratify partial favor and personal rancor, they forfeit their title to my obedience." They might prosecute him, and he would defend himself as best he could. They might dismiss him, and he would rejoice at his deliverance. They had prostituted the national honor and the trust of their constituents, and, said he, "I will make my appeal to those very constituents and to the nation." [7] Thus East as well as West was issuing its declaration of independence from a corrupt and incompetent government!

At length in November they heard that the Regulating Act was to be continued in force for another year, without any change in the personnel of the government. For a short time at least one worry had been removed from Hastings's mind, but he was nevertheless bitterly disappointed that no change had been made. Were ministers so willfully blind that they could not see the monstrous defects of the Act? It was most discouraging to think that ministers were so distracted by the activities of domestic Whigs, American rebels and foreign foes that they had no time to give any attention to problems of Indian government. "In short, we are in a damned bad way," was how one of Francis's correspondents described the situation at home.

II

AFTER Sir Eyre Coote had departed up country, Philip Francis began to give indications of a possible change of attitude. Disappointed in all his expectations, he may have thought that he had nothing more to gain by an opposition policy. It was noticed that he and the Governor began to dine more frequently at each other's houses. Their social relations while strained had never been entirely broken off, as the smallness of Calcutta society made it impossible to carry political differences into its social life. Hastings had always been ready to welcome a conciliatory attitude on the part of his opponent, and he was prepared now to meet him more than half-way because of the Barwell situation.

Matters were brought to a head in the new year when Barwell announced that he would not defer his departure any longer. Since this occurred simultaneously with the renewal of war with the Marathas, who had refused to make peace on the terms offered, Hastings at once resolved to make terms with Francis. In February 1780 an agreement between them was reached through the mediation of Sir John Day, the Attorney-General, and Barwell at once took ship for England.

What the Governor-General wanted was a free hand in directing war operations and the initiative in conducting public business. By the terms of the agreement Francis promised him both. In return, Hastings submitted to the orders of the Court of Directors for the restoration of Fowke to the Residency at Benares and Mohamed Reza Khan to his offices in the Nawab's household. In addition, he offered Francis a share in the distribution of offices and emoluments; but this Francis refused, as he did not want to appear to have any self-interested motives.

This agreement, with all that followed from it, was the final proof of how completely these two men had misjudged each other's character. Francis could not comprehend Hastings's curious mixture of mildness and firmness. He misconstrued the one and underestimated the other. He mistook his conciliatoriness for weakness, the weakness of despair; failing to see that, while Hastings might do his utmost to placate an adversary in minor matters, he would never surrender on essential points of policy. The very benevolence of Hastings's expression helped to mislead him: he did not perceive that it cloaked a will of steel. On the other hand, all concessions were wasted on a man of Francis's type. Indeed, the more Hastings yielded the greater was likely to be Francis's contempt for him. If he did not see this himself, it was largely because he was capable of much self-deception. Not so long before he had been speaking of Francis as "this dangerous man," who was "without one generous or manly principle in his whole composition." [8] Now, because the wish with him was too often father to the thought, he deluded himself into believing that he was a man of strict honor, telling his friends that Francis had behaved so openly and candidly and shown so little reserve that he was sure that he would not regret Barwell's departure. Francis would remain true to his engagement and be ready and willing to lend him his support and assistance. "I am not the least fearful of the reverse." How far his trust was well grounded may be judged from the fact that at the same moment Francis was writing to his friends: "When I speak of a pacification with Mr. Hastings I mean literally what I say. It is *not* union. It is *not* alliance. . . . In short, it is more like an armed truce than like anything else; for it is to endure no longer than to October next" (at which date the term of their government again expired). [9] And to Lord North he promised: "I will make peace with the Marathas, the moment it is in my power." [10]

It should have been obvious to Hastings that he and Francis were likely to attach very different interpretations to any kind of agreement between them. He himself would naturally give it a wide interpretation, regarding it as a positive commitment of support; Francis, equally naturally, the narrowest possible. There was an unbridgeable gulf between them that only a man of more than usual credulity and trustfulness would have ignored. Furthermore, any chance of reality that the agreement might have had was lost by Hastings's failure to incorporate it in a formal written compact. "I regarded it as a deed of faith and honor not of law, and I required none," was his explanation. It was to prove a most unfortunate omission.

Three months were sufficient to end the pretense of an accommodation. From the start of the Maratha War there had been complete disagreement between the two men regarding the manner in which it should be conducted. On the renewal of the war this disagreement continued regardless of any compact. Hastings, as always, was for vigorous measures. While Goddard was operating in Gujarat, he wished to aid him by making a diversion on the enemy's eastern flank. He had already sent Major Popham with a small force into Gohud, a minor state on the western boundary of Oude with which an alliance had recently been made, and Popham had succeeded in expelling the Marathas. Thus encouraged, Hastings now planned a more ambitious operation. On June 12 he proposed sending Major Camac with a much larger force to invade the country of the chief Maratha leader, Mahdaji Sindhia, and attack his capital. This, he hoped, would have the effect of relieving the pressure on Goddard, who might then be able to take Poona.

Instantly Francis and Wheler opposed the motion, raising against it all their stock objections to offensive operations of any kind—the expense, the bad season, the danger, the necessity of peace. They had nightmare visions of British armies being annihilated by Maratha horsemen or wiped out by fever and disease in the unknown wastes of Central India, whilst the scanty funds in the Bengal treasury were being lavished to pay the expense. The Governor-General brushed all these arguments aside. How, he asked, could the war be ended by a policy of doing nothing? A speedy conclusion could only be obtained by a vigorous prosecution; feeble measures and advances for peace would but encourage the enemy and discourage the Company's friends.

"Acts that proclaim confidence and a determined spirit in the hour of adversity are the surest means of retrieving it. Self-distrust will never fail to create a distrust in others, and make them become your enemies; for in no part of the world is the principle of supporting a rising interest and depressing a falling one more prevalent than in India."

To obviate the objection on the ground of expense he offered to meet the expenses of the expedition out of his own pocket.[1] All to no purpose. He then reminded Francis of his pledge; and all he received in reply was derision. Where were the fine friends who might be discouraged? Francis asked. He wished that their names had been stated. He did not know that the Bengal Government had any friends. Before the war had begun he had foreseen and foretold its consequences, and he now judged of it by its effects. Further prolongation would mean utter ruin. [11]

The taunt of failure and the belief that Francis was breaking the terms of his agreement were more than the Governor-General could tolerate. He made one last effort to bring Francis to reason. Since the responsibility for the conduct of the war was his, he claimed the right to be allowed to carry out his own policy without obstruction, especially as it was utterly impossible to reconcile his views with those of his opponents. Francis's only reply to this was a refusal to sanction any measure until an outline of the whole campaign had been submitted to him. Hastings's patience being now completely exhausted, he determined to bring matters to a head by publicly exposing Francis's dishonorable conduct. He prepared a formal statement, deliberately charging him with committing a gross breach of good faith, which he intended to present at the next Council meeting on July 3. But Sir John Day prevailed upon him to withhold it, knowing that it would certainly lead to a complete rupture, while he tried to induce Francis to change his attitude.

For six weeks negotiations continued. Francis, who had gone up country for the sake of his health, at first agreed to withdraw the offensive minutes. Thereupon the Council in his absence repealed them

---

[1] For the story of this curious offer (the money was not his own, though he pretended it was) see p. 243.

and agreed to let Major Camac begin his march. Four days later a letter was received from Francis stating that he had been misunderstood: he had only consented to withdraw the minutes on condition that Camac's detachment should not be employed offensively until advices arrived from England informing them whether or not Hastings remained in the government. (As the Regulating Act had only been extended for one year, there was once more uncertainty about the future, of which Francis made full use.) Hastings peremptorily rejected this proposal, and the minutes were replaced. Sir John Day declared that he knew nothing of any such condition, and as Francis had disavowed his acts, he washed his hands of the affair but said he would be ready to give his testimony of what had passed when required. Hastings thereupon notified the Council that he intended to enter his own minute. Before actually doing so he awaited Francis's return.

On the evening of August 14 the fateful minute was put in Francis's hands, prior to being placed on record the following day. It ran as follows:

"I did hope that the intimation conveyed in my last minute would have awakened in Mr. Francis's breast, if it were susceptible of such sensations, a consciousness of the faithless part which he was acting towards me. I have been disappointed, and must now assume a plainer style, and a louder tone. In a word, my objections do not lie in the special matter of his minutes, to which I shall separately reply, but to the spirit of opposition which dictated them. I have lately offered various plans for the operations of the war. These have been successively rejected as I have successively amended and endeavored to accommodate them to Mr. Francis's objections. I had a right to his implicit acquiescence. I have lately proposed a service requiring immediate execution, and I have freed it from the only objection formally made to it. In truth, I do not trust to his promise of candor, convinced that he is incapable of it, and that his sole purpose and wish are to embarrass and defeat every measure which I may undertake, or which may tend even to promote the public interests, if my credit is connected with them. Such has been the tendency and such the manifest spirit of all his actions from the beginning. Every fabricated tale of armies devoted to famine or to massacre have found their first and ready way to his office, where it was known they would meet the most welcome reception. To the same design may be attributed the annual computations of declining finances and an exhausted treasury, computations, which, though made in the time of abundance, must verge to truth at last, from the effect of a discordant government, not a constitutional decay.

"I judge of his public conduct by my experience of his private, which I have found to be void of truth and honor. This is a severe charge, but temperately and deliberately made from the firm persuasion that I owe this justice to the public and to myself, as the only redress to both, for artifices of which I have been a victim, and which threaten to involve their interests, with disgrace and ruin. The only redress for a fraud for which the law had made no provisions is the exposure of it."

He then quoted the terms of the agreement, and concluded the indictment as follows:

"By the sanction of this engagement and the liberal professions which accompanied it, I was seduced to part with a friend to whose generous and honorable support steadfastly yielded in a course of six years I am indebted for the existence of the little power which I have ever possessed in that long and disgraceful period, to throw myself on the mercy of Mr. Francis, and on the desperate hazard of his integrity. It was impossible to afford a stronger demonstration of the good faith with which I entered into this accommodation, nor of my confidence in his, than thus consenting to deprive myself of the means of breaking the engagement on my part, and of preventing the break of it on his; and surely this difference in our relative situations ought to have impressed him with a sense of what he owed to the delicacy attending it, and have made him dread even an approach towards the precise line of his obligations by the slightest advantage taken of my inability to repel it; and how much more ought it to have restrained him from direct transgression of it." [12]

Hastings knew well what the consequences would be when he penned this, one of the most scathing indictments ever made by one statesman of another. He was desperate, and his desperation made him ready and anxious to bring matters to a crisis. The fate of India seemed to him to be laid in the balance. We are told that when Markham, his private secretary, who was writing it out at his dictation, pointed out that his words left Mr. Francis no choice between regarding them as a personal insult and accepting public disgrace if he passed them over, Hastings, with some sarcasm, praised his extraordinary discernment and remarked that that was precisely his intention. [13] The two men had come to the parting of the ways. With Francis, disappointment had brought him to such a depth of bitterness that he also had ceased to care what the consequences of his conduct would be, either to himself or to his country.

After the meeting of Council next day Francis asked to speak with Hastings in private. They withdrew to a private room, where Francis formally demanded satisfaction for the injury done to his honor. Hastings accepted the challenge, and the date and place were set for two days later, Thursday, August 17, at Belvidere, on the outskirts of the city, between five and six in the morning. The intervening day was spent by the Governor-General in putting his private affairs in order and writing a new will and a long memorandum for his secretary. He asked his friend Colonel Pearse of the Bengal army to be his second.

The day came that might decide the fate of India. Colonel Pearse called for Hastings soon after four. It was still early, and Hastings lay down again for half an hour; then he arose, dressed, and went with him in his carriage. They arrived at Belvidere at five-thirty, and found Francis and his second, Colonel Watson, awaiting them. They had some difficulty in finding a solitary spot, and could not escape the

Calcutta 16 Aug.t 1780.

My beloved Marian

My Heart bleeds to think what your Sufferings and Feelings must be, if ever this Letter shall be delivered into your Hands. You will too soon learn the Occasion of it. On my Part it has been unavoidable. — I shall leave nothing which I regret to lose but you, nor in my last Moments shall I feel any other Affliction. Let it be a Consolation to you to know that at this Moment I have the most grateful Sense of all your past kindness, and of the unremitted proofs which you have daily and hourly afforded me of your Affection. For these may God reward you! I know not how. — How much I have loved you, how much beyond all that Life can yield, I still love you, God only knows. — Do not, my Marian, forget me; but cherish my Remembrance.

to the latest Hour of your Life, as I should
vow, were it, my Lot, & to my Misery, to
survive you. — I cannot write all
that I feel & that my Heart is full of.

Adieu my best Wife, and most
beloved of Women. May the God of Heaven
bless & support you! — My last Thoughts
will be employed on you. — Remember &
love me. Once more farewell!

(Your

P. I shall enclose
with this the Key of my
Bureau. In the Upper Part you will find my
Will, which is so marked in large Letters.

Warren Hastings.

embarrassing attention of a small audience of natives, including an old woman whose eager curiosity especially disturbed Hastings. A distance of fourteen paces was measured, and the two took station. It was arranged that each should take his own time to fire. According to Colonel Pearse, Hastings was "in a state of such perfect tranquillity that a spectator would not have supposed that he was about an action out of the common course of things." [14] He evidently meant business, as he observed that fourteen paces was a great distance for pistols. Francis was equally determined. Neither of them knew anything about duelling or the use of pistols. Hastings said he had only fired one once or twice.

Francis at once took aim and snapped, but his pistol missed fire and had to be recharged. Hastings had resolved to defer his shot, but after Francis had twice aimed and withdrawn, he waited no longer. Taking careful aim he fired and hit his opponent, who fired simultaneously but missed. Francis staggered and fell, crying out, "I am dead."

"Good God, I hope not," muttered Hastings in a shocked voice, as he and the seconds ran to his assistance.

They found that he had been struck on the right side, but he was able to sit up and shake hands with the victor, who expressed his regret at what had happened. A stretcher was brought, and the wounded man was carried to Belvidere House, while Hastings hurried back to the city to send medical assistance. The wound on examination proved not to be dangerous; the ball had entered a little below the shoulder and lodged on the other side, without touching either the heart or the backbone. But before this was known the Governor-General had sent his secretary to the Chief Justice to inform him of what had passed. If the wound proved fatal, he said he would immediately surrender himself and let the law take its course against him. [15]

Hastings felt much more shame than pride in having taken part in "this silly affair." Like most intelligent men he regarded dueling as an odious institution. But if ever there was an occasion that justified recourse to it, he believed that this was it. Knowing what the consequences of his minute would be, he had debated long and earnestly with himself whether he, with his heavy public responsibilities, had a right to risk his life in a private quarrel. As his mood at the time was one of profound dejection, he had come to the conclusion that his death would be immaterial. What was he but "a mere name," whose removal would make room for a less obnoxious person whom his employers might judge worthy to possess their confidence and the rightful powers of his office? Why should he think his life more valuable than they evidently thought it? Far better a united and harmonious government in the hands of another than a continuance of the state of affairs of the last six years. [16] So, if he lost, nothing would be lost; and if he won, much would be gained. The chance of eliminating —by wounding, not, of course, by killing—the man who was the chief source of his troubles was a stake worth playing for, especially when the alternative meant conceding to him a complete triumph and becoming a helpless prey to his mocking gibes and malicious spite. His hand was therefore firm and his aim accurate. "I combat a phantom in the dark," he had written, but now that phantom had been exorcised by a bullet, because, though happily it did not kill, it nevertheless put an effective end to the Indian career of Philip Francis.

III

FIVE days after the duel thrilling news was received from the war front. Popham, by one of the most brilliant feats in Indian military annals, had captured the great fortress of Gwalior hitherto deemed impregnable, and without the loss of a man. "Its effect is not to be described," cried Hastings exultantly. "Other congratulations which I have received on the many important successes of our arms were but coldly offered, but scarcely a man mentions this without enthusiasm." [17] It was the key of Hindustan, and he hoped that its capture would prove decisive. Simultaneously, Goddard had been meeting with spectacular success in the west. The disgrace of Wargaum had been amply wiped out by the conquest of Gujarat and the defeat of a large Maratha army.

From other quarters the news was far less encouraging. A grand confederacy had been formed against the British by the Nizam of Hyderabad, comprising himself, the Marathas under their leaders Sindhia and Holkar, the Rajah of Berar, and Haidar Ali; and already a Berar army was posted at Cuttack threatening an invasion of Bengal; while from the south came disquieting rumors of impending catastrophe in the Carnatic. Only in the nick of time had Hastings rescued his government from the paralyzing grip of his opponent.

The result of the duel, painful as it was, had its compensations for Francis. It enabled him to join the ranks of the noble army of martyrs. It made him, at least in his own estimation, a hero. Martyrs and heroes rise above petty animosities; they are noble, generous, magnanimous; they forgive their enemies. So Francis from his bed of pain wrote to his friends in England:

"I consider this event as a quietus to all personal hostility between Mr. H. and me and I desire that you and all my friends *will speak and act accordingly.* This injunction goes to everything. It would be irregular and unbecoming in me *now,* as well as useless in every respect to suffer the public quarrel to lead me into anything that could bear the appearance of personal animosity to him. Let him be condemned or acquitted by the evidence that exists of his whole conduct. As I lay bleeding on the ground and when I thought the wound was mortal, I gave him my hand in token of forgiveness. From that moment to the end of my life, I am neither his friend nor his foe." [18]

The Duel

Hastings offered to visit him, but he declined the offer and every kind of intercourse with him except at the Council table, "from the consideration of what he owed to his own character." By September 11 he was sufficiently recovered to take his seat in Council and make his reply to the Governor-General's charge. In it he solemnly declared that he never was a party to the engagement stated by the Governor-General nor had he a thought of being bound by it, and he tried to show that the agreement had only covered operations of the war already under way and did not, therefore, apply to Camac's expedition which had not then been proposed. The Governor-General answered by saying: "What can I say to such a declaration but to declare on my part in as solemn a manner that Mr. Francis *was* a party to the engagement which I have stated? This I now do most solemnly declare, and may God be the judge between us." There were further recriminations, in which Hastings very definitely had the better of the argument. He was able to prove that the Camac plan had not only been suggested and discussed but all but accepted at the time of the agreement, and he had equally little difficulty in disposing of other of Francis's quibbles and prevarications. [19] And there the matter rested, and still rests. In the absence of a written contract the precise nature of the agreement cannot be determined.

All this, however, was merely the prelude to Francis's withdrawal from the scene. With an actor's eye on stage effect he had decided that the right moment had come for him to make his exit and ring down the curtain. The play had reached a fine climax; to prolong it would entail the risk of bathos. For six years he had bestrode the stage as a hero, laboring, fighting, suffering for a great cause. If in the end he had failed, it was because the odds against him had been too great. He could not single-handed prevail over the powers of darkness. His one hope had lain in the authorities at home, and they had failed him. Ministers and Directors alike had "deceived, deserted, sacrificed and betrayed" him. And now in the same noble cause he had risked his life and nearly lost it; he had fallen grievously wounded on the field of honor. A hero and a martyr, it was time that he went home to reap a hero's and a martyr's rewards. His period of usefulness in India was over. Nothing could now save the Empire from annihilation; its condition was "beyond the reach of human prudence." On every hand nothing could be seen but wars, imminent new wars, impending invasion, an empty treasury, vacillation, dismay, helplessness, corruption, chaos. Despite his efforts India was ruined. He had accumulated a moderate fortune and he had preserved his honor, so he would go home, before the waters finally closed over the sinking ship. *Après moi le déluge:* "The moment I shall have made my exit, enter desolation." [20]

But he was not going back to forget India or the cause for which he had labored. He was going back to continue the fight on terrain which he hoped would prove more suited to his tactics. So the last three months of his stay were employed in accumulating material. He had managed to collect a considerable amount in six years: the Treaty of Benares, the Rohilla War, the acceptance of bribes from Nuncomar, Munny Begum and others, the judicial murder of Nuncomar, the Governor-General's refusal to resign, his land revenue policy, the Maratha War. All these transactions could be turned to good account in England. And good fortune now placed in his way yet another, which, as he immediately perceived, was also full of dynamite—not only for use against Hastings, his chief quarry, but against Sir Elijah Impey also, for whom he entertained a hatred second only to his hatred of the Governor-General.

There were various reasons why he hated Impey. One was that Impey was Hastings's friend and loyal supporter. Another was that he detested the Supreme Court and therefore its presiding officer. A third reason was purely personal. In February of the previous year a suit had been brought against Francis in the Supreme Court, arising out of his unfortunate affair with the beautiful seventeen-year-old Mrs. Grand. He had been caught one night climbing down the balcony from the lady's bedroom, and the irate husband had not only divorced his wife but sued her venturesome lover for heavy damages. The result was an award of 50,000 rupees. And for his part in this Francis never forgave the Chief Justice.[1]

Simultaneously with Hastings's quarrel with Francis the long-smoldering conflict between the Council and the Court had broken out in a violent explosion. Hyde and Lemaistre had put pressure on their more moderate colleagues to give the widest interpretation to the powers granted to the Court by its charter, and to exercise them without regard to discretion or moderation. They began to act as though no class of persons in Bengal was exempt from their jurisdiction, not even zemindars of the highest rank. This immediately brought them into open conflict with the Government, which claimed that zemindars were neither British subjects nor the servants of British subjects and therefore were beyond the Court's jurisdiction. The dispute also extended to English and native officers of the Company employed in the collection of the revenues and the administration of justice in the Company's courts. Could they be held accountable to the Supreme Court for acts done in their official capacity? According to the Judges, they could.

Hastings, as we have seen, was ready to admit the need for a Superior Court to curb the excesses of the Company's officers and to give greater protection and relief to the poorer classes of the population. It was only when the Court began to exercise an independent coercive power of its own, issuing writs, sending its officers to arrest zemindars and officers of the Company, imprisoning all and sundry indiscriminately, without reference to the Council or regard for its authority, even

---

[1] The lady had an interesting subsequent history: after a short period as Francis's mistress, she made her way to France, where she had still further amorous adventures, which ended by her becoming the wife of Talleyrand, Princesse de Benevento.

treating with insolent contempt its remonstrances, that he felt compelled to take a strong stand against it, even to the extent of using military force to resist its high-handed proceedings.

For a time virtual civil war existed between the rival bodies. The administrative machine slowed down nearly to a standstill. How could the Company's courts and officials continue to function if they were liable, even for acts done in the course of their official duty, to the jurisdiction of a court administering a totally different and wholly alien system of law? Such a state of affairs could lead to only one result—anarchy. Hastings believed that the very existence of the executive government was at stake.

This dispute brought him more pain than any other he had engaged in because it placed him and his intimate friend Impey in opposite and bitterly divided camps. Neither was responsible for the unnecessary violence of the contest, but each by virtue of his position was directly and inextricably involved. "I suffer beyond measure by the present contest," Hastings wrote, "and my spirits are at times so depressed as to affect my health." [21] He could not escape a sense of injury done him by a man to whom he had borne a sincere and steady friendship for over thirty years. Happily, their friendship survived the strain without hurt. Hastings conducted the quarrel with as much moderation as he could, but there was no question of his not being in deadly earnest. At its height he even seriously suggested to the Council that they might have to abandon Calcutta and carry the seat of government to some other place, "which we could circumscribe by a line of our own, and keep the devil of the law without it"—and the idea met with unanimous approval. [22] He held no stronger conviction than that in such a state as Bengal the judicial power must be held in proper subordination to the executive. The Supreme Court was running wild and threatening to establish a species of legal despotism that had not even the merit of being based on Indian law and institutions.

Somehow the conflict had to be stopped. Statesmanship must come to the rescue with a compromise. In September Hastings proposed inviting the Chief Justice to combine his office with that of the Chief Judge of the Company's Court of Civil Appeal, which had hitherto been composed of the Governor-General and the members of the Council. The proposal was thoroughly logical and sound and could only have had beneficial results. Hastings's improvised courts of law would have been strengthened and their prestige increased; they would have received the legal instruction and expert supervision that they so badly needed, and the work of purifying the administration would have gone forward more rapidly. The overburdened Council would have been relieved of much heavy work, which it was ill-equipped to perform, and enabled to concentrate on the pressing cares of purely executive government. Above all, the gulf between the Council and the Supreme Court would have been partially bridged, and their contact made closer, with the chances of a clash of jurisdictions correspondingly diminished. The Court could hardly have continued to disregard the legal existence of the Company's courts when its own Chief Justice was also Chief Judge of the latter. All this Hastings pointed out. [23]

The motion came up for debate on October 3. Francis and Wheler opposed it, but the Governor-General had the support of Sir Eyre Coote, who had by this time returned to Calcutta, and by using his casting-vote he was able to carry it. Impey accepted the post, which was made revocable at the will of the Council.

This was the transaction that fortune put in Francis's way before he sailed for home. It was exactly suited to his purpose and admirably adapted to his methods. The two weak spots in it were that its legality under the Regulating Act was more than doubtful, and a salary had been attached to Impey's new post. It was easy for Francis to impugn the motives that had inspired the arrangement and to assert, with a fair appearance of plausibility, that the appointment was a corrupt job, a bribe to Impey to make him desist from upholding the rights of the Supreme Court.

For the short space of time that it lasted, the arrangement proved eminently satisfactory, more than fulfilling Hastings's hopes for it. But appreciation of its wisdom was to come from his successors, not from his contemporaries. Sir Elijah Impey—who did not, as it happened, draw the salary but referred the question of its propriety to the authorities at home—labored for eight months to prepare a legal code for the Company's courts, and then received his recall. For Francis's attack in his direction met with immediate success. Francis later planned to have him impeached, but the attempt failed at the same time as that against Hastings was succeeding. It is only necessary to add that there is no reason to believe that Hastings and Impey were actuated by other than the most creditable motives in devising and adopting what seemed to them the only practicable solution to an intolerable and dangerous situation.

Before Francis sailed he had the satisfaction of hearing that Haidar Ali had made his swoop into the Carnatic, dealt another staggering blow to British power and prestige, and with fire and sword was rapidly reducing the entire province to a desert, up to the very walls of Madras. At the last meetings of Council he attended, consistent to the bitter end, he vehemently opposed Hastings's plans to retrieve the situation. Just before taking ship he almost changed his mind about going. Breathing out fire and fury against his hated rival, he threatened to stay and "throw away the scabbard and neither give nor take quarter." But it was too late. He found now that he could no longer count on the support even of his former ally Wheler. A baffled and defeated man, he sailed for England on December 3, 1780, taking with him a fortune variously estimated as between £80,000 and £150,000, a heart burning with rage and disappointment, and a terrible resolve to wreak his revenge on the man who had thwarted and beaten him—and leaving behind him a rejoicing Service, and no more than one or two friends.

Chapter XVII

A CALL FOR HELP FROM MADRAS

I

IN July 1780 the savage warrior king of Mysore made good his threats. Like a thunderbolt of Mars he struck and blasted the country of the English. Though they had been fully warned for a year past of Haidar Ali's hostility, the gentlemen of Madras had continued their heedless, perverse ways, doing nothing to check the faction and corruption that had for so long played havoc with their affairs. As one observer remarked, they resembled the Greeks when Constantinople was threatened by the Barbarians: they forgot that they had any enemies but each other. They also resembled Nero fiddling while Rome was burning, for they were giving a grand masquerade ball for a bevy of beautiful girls who had just arrived from England on the very night when Haidar launched his attack.

Haidar's army, a hundred thousand strong, poured through the undefended passes of the Ghats and spread like a torrent over the plains of the Carnatic. And the Madras Council were not aroused to action until his advance guard had appeared at the very gates of their city. Then their state of unpreparedness aided by the incompetence of their generals brought disaster. The veteran commander-in-chief, Sir Hector Munro, the victor of Buxar, ruined his reputation as a soldier by allowing a large detachment under Colonel Baillie to be completely cut to pieces and annihilated within a few miles of his own army and then, panic-stricken, making a hurried retreat to Madras, after destroying his guns and ammunition, triumphantly pursued by Haidar's cavalry. Within a few days, except for one or two posts, the whole of the Carnatic, upon which Madras depended for its provisions and the wherewithal of its trade, was in the savage hands of one of the most ruthless rulers that has ever appeared in India. The inhabitants of Madras wrung their hands and hooted Munro in the streets while Haidar was drawing a ring of desolation around their city. All who could made hurried preparations to leave, and the Council dispatched frantic appeals to Bengal for help.

The news reached Calcutta on September 22, and entirely upset all Hastings's carefully worked out plans for securing the safety of the British dominions. What hope had he now of a speedy peace with the Marathas? Indeed, an offensive alliance against the British between the Marathas, the Nizam and Haidar had already been formed. Thirty thousand Maratha horse were even now threatening the frontiers of Bengal, and any day an invasion of Bihar might be expected. Nujiff Khan, a Rohilla chief, threatened Oude. The forces of Sindhia also threatened Oude. General Goddard had his hands fully occupied on the other side of India with the armies of the Poona government. News had come from Sir Edward Hughes, the admiral in command of the Indian station, that a French armament of seven ships of the line and seven thousand troops would shortly reach the coast. The Bengal treasury was all but empty. And now, with all these dangers accumulating, Hastings was called upon to rescue the Madras Presidency, attacked by a vast army led by the most redoubtable warrior in all India. If there was an occasion for even the most courageous and intrepid spirit to be daunted, it was surely this. But not Hastings! For him a crisis of this magnitude was a moment of opportunity, not a cause for despair: it was a call to action, demanding an exultant, magnificent response, and it brought out the best that was in him, making him calm, resolute, inspiring, resourceful.

He took two days to decide on a course of action and then called his Council together to put forward his proposals. As preliminary steps he had an immediate embargo laid on all the shipping in the river and gave orders to every sea-captain to be ready to sail in five days for Madras. He also ordered that the fifteen lakhs of rupees stored in Fort William for use in case of emergency be packed ready for transport. On the 25th, he met the Council and stated his views with the utmost emphasis. The time for lengthy deliberation and patient negotiations was past. Exertion and action, vigorous, bold and herculean, could alone save the situation. He proposed that Sir Eyre Coote should be sent to take command of the army in the Carnatic, carrying with him the fifteen lakhs and a body of troops and, further, that an immediate peace and alliance be offered to the Marathas. His opponents at once voiced their disapproval, declaring that "neither soldier, nor rupee should be sent to the Carnatic, for that country was irrevocably lost, and that every soldier and every rupee sent there would be uselessly expended." Bengal itself, they said, was in too great danger and all available forces should be concentrated to withstand a siege in Fort William itself until help could arrive from England. "Never," Hastings indignantly cried. "Never. While I have a soldier, or a rupee, I will never abandon the Carnatic; for if we do not fight Haidar Ali in that country, we shall have to fight him here." Coote supported him and Hastings's casting-vote carried the measure that was to save the day for the British Empire in India. [1]

The sailing of the expedition was delayed for three weeks as the transports were not ready for sea. Coote left the capital on October 13.

Though in poor health, he had gallantly yielded to Hastings's entreaties and agreed to accept the onerous command. The troops, to the number of six hundred, all Europeans, embarked the following day, but contrary winds held them in the river for several more days. Hastings went down the river to inspect them and bid them farewell, and on the 23rd the ships set sail. They arrived at Madras on November 5. Twenty-four years before the situation had been reversed: a rescuing expedition had sailed from Madras to Bengal. The two men who were now to share the honor of saving the empire, the one as war minister, the other as soldier, had in common their memories of that previous crisis in which each had played an honorable part.

Coote's first step on arrival was to carry out the orders of his government, unanimously agreed upon before he left, for the suspension of Whitehill, the incompetent and corrupt Governor, for willful disobedience to orders and contempt of its authority. That done, he proceeded to take over the entire management of the war in accordance with the powers that the Governor-General in Council had vested in him. But his first glance at the situation told him that the task that he had undertaken was likely to prove utterly thankless as well as exceptionally arduous.

The enemy possessed a vast superiority in numbers, but that fact alone would not have made it formidable, as all the British victories in India had in the past been won over armies much stronger numerically than their own. Clive at Plassey had three thousand men against fifty thousand. But Haidar Ali was no effeminate, debauched and incompetent prince like those whom Clive and his officers had overthrown with such consummate ease in Bengal and Oude. He was a warrior lusting for blood and spoil, a soldier by profession who had used his sword to win his throne, and the troops whom he now led against the hated English were well armed and well disciplined. They were an *army*, not a rabble of half-armed, mutinous levies that fled or deserted at the first shot.

But lack of numbers was almost the least of Coote's handicaps. His Madras troops were demoralized. He had virtually no cavalry. His field artillery was not ready for service, and if it had been, the few draft oxen that he could find were inadequate for the guns. The terrain over which he had to campaign had been swept from end to end by Haidar's cavalry and lay bare and devastated. There were no provisions five miles beyond Madras, and he was so lacking in transport that he could carry with him provisions for not more than two days.

It was the first of January before he could take the field, and then followed a long campaign, marked chiefly by tedious and laborious marches, hardships of every kind, and the inroads of disease and fever among his tired and often half-famished and dispirited troops, interspersed with all too infrequent battles when he was able to bring his wary and elusive foe to action. There was little comfort to be gained from the fact that he never suffered a defeat in any battle in which he commanded, because his occasional successes were no better than

Pyrrhic victories. "Our arms have been repeatedly successful," reported Hastings. "No decisive advantages have been gained, and we lose men by every victory." In each encounter Coote gained the initial advantage, but lack of cavalry, transport, provisions and men prevented him from driving it home. During the greater part of the campaigns Haidar, who soon learned to entertain the greatest respect for Coote's ability as a soldier and realized from bitter experience that he was invincible on the field of battle, shrewdly avoided open combat and concentrated on wearing his enemy down by a process of attrition and starvation. He knew that the English merchants drew their life-blood from the hinterland of the Carnatic, and that, deprived of it, their possession of Madras would be valueless and his great object would be gained.

The details of the military operations do not concern us, but one episode will show Coote's extremely perilous situation and the kind of difficulties with which he constantly had to contend. The French fleet had hove in sight off the coast and Haidar was trying to form immediate contact with it. Coote marched to Cuddalore, a few miles south of Pondicherry, in order to forestall him. When he reached it, he found enough provisions for only one day's subsistence for his army. "The alarming prospect," he wrote to his government, "which this presented me with produced feelings which are much easier to be imagined than described. I saw in the fall of this handful of men the destruction of the English interest in India. What to determine in a situation so critical, so difficult, and in its consequences so important, I confess, was a question which I dreaded the decision of." [2] Seaward the French fleet, landward Haidar's army—and only a few days' provisions! The old soldier's fighting spirit was aroused. He marched out and offered Haidar battle. But in vain! Haidar was too crafty to give him such a chance. So he was compelled to return to camp after four precious days had been wasted. His plight was now such that surrender seemed to be the only prospect in sight.

Surrender! During this same year another English army surrendered under similar circumstances on the North American coast and with its surrender an empire was lost. Coote at Cuddalore, Cornwallis at Yorktown. Two empires lost! Madras would have been doomed, the British hold on Southern India destroyed with command of the sea passing to the French and communications with home broken —could Bengal then have been saved?

But the peril passed at the very moment when the noose was tightening. In the afternoon the French unwittingly committed the greatest blunder of the war. Unable to communicate with Haidar and all unaware of the desperate straits to which the British were reduced, their ships weighed anchor and sailed out of the bay. Thus the way was cleared for help to come from Madras. But when at last the rice ships entered the harbor, the inhabitants of the town were starving, many had actually died of want, and two days more would have completed the dismal story as the troops also would then have consumed their last grain of rice. As a last desperate expedient Coote had collected a small quantity of grain to be used when this extremity was reached and had decided to break out with it and make a bold dash southwards into the Tanjore country in the hope of finding provisions there.

For four months following this narrow escape he was unable to move, owing to lack of numbers and the invariable want of provisions, transport and equipment. And it was June before he was able to resume operations.

II

ALL this time, Hastings (compelled to be a war minister against his inclination and deepest desires, with the same irony of fate that was also to be William Pitt's portion) had been putting forth herculean efforts, raising money, directing military operations on several fronts, recruiting fresh regiments of sepoys, organizing defense measures, sending a constant stream of reinforcements, supplies and funds to the Carnatic, sending also food-ships to the starving people of Madras, who were dying by the hundreds (some of the ships arrived and achieved their object but many fell into the hands of the French cruisers), and, last but most important of all, wielding the weapon of diplomacy to break up the hostile coalition of native powers. This, and much more, was to be the scope of his activities for the next four years. How great was the war effort made by his government may be indicated by the fact that before the end of hostilities it was supporting in the field no fewer than seventy thousand men, an unheard-of figure for the Company.

The task of smashing the coalition called into play all of Hastings's considerable talents as a diplomat, but the way was partly smoothed for him in advance. On paper it was an overwhelming military combination, including virtually the whole of India. Seen through the perversely distorted eyes of some modern propagandist writers, it might seem like the last despairing effort of a doomed but still militant nation to hurl back the alien flood that threatened to engulf it. In reality, it was composed of predatory and mutually distrustful states, each with distinct grievances against the British, against whom they had chosen to join forces for the moment instead of preying on each other as was their custom. A combination of that kind was clearly anything but proof against the counter-operations of a skillful statesman.

Hastings realized that the hostility of the Nizam and the Rajah of Berar was more apparent than real and that by deft diplomacy they might both be changed into neutrals, perhaps even into allies. The Madras government had provoked the Nizam by annexing some territory over which he claimed sovereignty, and they had done this in direct contravention of the orders of the Supreme Government. The Nizam's grievance was legitimate and Hastings saw the importance of redressing it, but in order to do so he had to strain his constitutional powers. He sent his own orders to the local agent of the Company, contradicting those of Madras, and when the latter dismissed him for paying heed to them, Hastings at once reappointed him as his own agent and took the negotiations entirely out of the hands of the subordinate government. He then surrendered the disputed territory, and in this way secured the Nizam's neutrality.

The Rajah of Berar was equally lukewarm in his attachment to the coalition; fear of his confederates rather than hostility to the British compelled him to make threatening gestures to attack Bengal and to post an army on its borders. The idea of an alliance with the Company still held attractions for him despite his abrupt termination of the previous negotiations. Yet however sincere his professions of amity might be, that army near Cuttack was a grave menace to Bengal, for there was no telling when it might get out of control and take matters into its own hands. The Maratha could with difficulty resist the impulse to plunder. As part of his plans to retrieve the situation in the south, Hastings had formed a detachment of sepoys under Colonel Pearse to march down the coast to join Sir Eyre Coote. To do this it would have to go through Berar territory and pass by the Maratha army. Would its passage be unopposed? Hastings did not know but he was prepared to take the risk. He ordered Pearse to march. If the Marathas tried to bar his path, he was to force his way through them. If they cut his communications, he was to march on. He was not to fight unless forced to, but nothing must hinder his reaching the Carnatic at the earliest possible moment. [3] "March on!" The order was that of a man who was letting nothing stand in the way of victory.

Shortly afterwards the commander of the Maratha army informed the Governor-General that he had exhausted the means of paying his troops and warned him that unless his Government would help the army would mutiny and supply their own wants by invading Bengal. There were no funds in the Bengal treasury to meet a contingency of this kind, but the danger was so real that Hastings knew that somehow it must be met. The money would have to be borrowed. It was true that paying it to the Marathas under such circumstances was scarcely distinguishable from submitting to their old demand for *chauth,* but even this did not deter him. What were a few lakhs and the appearance of purchasing immunity compared to the safety of Bengal and the saving of British India? He bargained over the amount in true Oriental style and with great success. In return for a comparatively small sum, professedly paid in gratitude for past favors and manifestations of present friendship, he obtained the unopposed passage of Pearse's force, the assistance of two thousand Maratha cavalry to accompany Pearse, the retirement of the Berar army from its threatening position, and the promise of an active alliance.

Hastings had gained a real diplomatic victory. The coalition was crumbling even before its strength had been brought to bear against the Company, and, what was even more important, British prestige had been restored. "We shall no longer be considered as sinking under the united weight of every state in Hindustan: the scale of power has evidently turned in our favor"; long experience had taught Hastings how vital the psychological factor was in Indian politics. The desire to be on the winning side was so strong that it governed the policy of most native states. [4]

Sindhia, the Maratha chief in Malwa, was the next to show signs of weakening. The war had gone ill for him; Goddard's, Popham's and Camac's successes had destroyed his confidence and abated his warlike ardor. As soon as Hastings learned of the Carnatic disaster he dispatched an envoy to him with offers of peace and alliance. The envoy found him disposed to listen, but some months were to elapse before he persuaded him to agree to Hastings's terms.

The tide had turned in favor of the British, even though the situation in the Carnatic remained as desperate as ever. It was there, Hastings knew, that the real fight had to be waged. The enemy to be fought to the bitter end and conquered was Haidar Ali, for there could be no peace in India so long as his restless, insatiate ambition remained uncurbed. To this end Hastings concentrated all his efforts. Men, money, supplies—these were the crying needs; and above all, money, for it could produce the other two. If ordinary resources were inadequate, extraordinary ones must be found. And the finding of them was now to be Hastings's chief problem.

Chapter XVIII

THE BENARES INSURRECTION

I

FRANCIS'S departure may be considered, as Hastings himself said at the time, to mark the close of one complete period in his career and the beginning of a new one. He had triumphed; congratulations poured in upon him from his friends; and for one brief moment he permitted himself the luxury of exultation. He would no longer have a rival to oppose his plans, to encourage disobedience to his authority, to write circular letters with copies of instruments from the Court of Directors, proclaiming their distrust of him, to thwart and embarrass him. "In a word, I have power!" *Power!* The power he had been wanting so long! That certainly was cause for profound satisfaction. Yet what a hollow victory it really was!

"An exhausted treasury, an accumulating debt; a system charged with expensive establishments, and precluded by the multitude of dependents and the curse of patronage, from reformation; a government debilitated by the various habits of inveterate licentiousness. A country oppressed by private rapacity, and deprived of its vital resources by the enormous quantities of current specie annually exported in the remittance of private fortunes, in supplies sent to China, Fort St. George, to Bombay, and lately to the army at Surat, and by an impoverished commerce; the support of Bombay with all its new conquests, the charge of preserving Fort St. George, and recovering the Carnatic from the hands of a victorious enemy; the entire maintenance of both presidencies; and lastly, a war either actual or depending in every quarter, and with every power of Hindustan: these, and many more evils which I could enumerate, are the appendages of that authority, which is devolving to me, and the fruits of that spirit of discord which has been permitted—how unaccountably!"

And it might all have been prevented, he added, if Ministers and Parliament had had the wisdom to appoint in his place some one in whom they and the Company had confidence, so long as he had possessed moderate intelligence, ability and integrity. [1]

If evil-doing had been Philip Francis's sole object, he could hardly have done more harm. And unfortunately some of the worst consequences had still to make themselves felt. The man whom he had been trying for six years to ruin had not emerged unscathed, nor had his victory been gained without heavy cost. When Francis took his departure on the *Fox,* he left behind him a Governor-General driven to desperation by the multiplicity of problems and dangers with which he was faced, weakened in mind and body from the strain of the several conflicts in which he had been engaged, and unable any longer to express pride, as he had when death removed Clavering three years before, in the fact that he had not experienced an hour of sickness. "Yet," Hastings then declared, "my constitution is rather infirm, and my temper naturally quick and irritable. Is it a virtue, or must I admit it to be the effect of an accident, that the first has never failed me nor the last forsaken me, in my severest trials?" [2] But now both health and temper were showing signs of weakening. No man, even with herculean powers of mind and body, can come through nine such years as he had spent as Governor —the most arduous without a doubt that any Governor-General of India has experienced—without some impairment of his physical strength and mental poise.

In August 1780, just before his duel, he was ill and had to suspend meetings of Council. His ailment was not serious and he soon recovered. But from then on he was seldom to be free from anxiety about his health. The Carnatic disaster coming on top of everything else doubled his burden. Yet, as other public men have found out, it was the little things that taxed him the most—the importunities of private individuals, and especially the constant pestering of people clamoring for positions of profit—nineteen, he tells us, on an average for each post. More and more frequently he complained of feeling neither well nor in good spirits. On October 5, he wrote to his wife: "I have a thousand things to do, and I am sadly out of spirits, having been all day tormented with a headache." [3] His one really serious illness came later, in August 1782, when he narrowly escaped a complete breakdown of health (even so, "many hours were still devoted to my duty and I dictated from my bed what I could not write at my desk").[4] It was only by his strict regimen that he was able to survive.

To what extent strain, anxiety and ill health affected his conduct during the still more troublous times that followed Francis's departure it is difficult to say, but undoubtedly their effect must have been considerable. Hastings was like a man in a race who has stumbled over a hurdle and is hurrying to make up the distance he has lost. Those words "I have power!" were as much a cry of last desperate resolve as of joyous exultation. The power had come too late for him to realize the hopes and aspirations he had been expressing to his friends a few years before. He had then hoped to give Bengal the blessings of peace, happiness, and prosperity. All he could hope to do now was to save it from the horrors of invasion. He could not even concentrate his efforts and resources on its defense and protection alone as he had to use them without stint for the saving of British India. His dream of being able to devise by slow and careful experiment a perfect system of administration for the great province had vanished before the malignity of Philip Francis and the maelstrom of a general war. He was not embittered. Somehow he never seemed to lose his astonishingly youthful spirit, full of hope and confidence, which always reasserted itself after his periods of despondency. But he did tend to become hasty in judgement and arbitrary in action, as one who feels the weight of intolerable responsibility and the sense of an intolerable lack of means with which to bear it. If, as he says, his temper was naturally quick and irritable, his grip on it now certainly weakened, plunging him into fresh disputes and troubles.

The Hastings we have seen hitherto, dutiful and obedient, anxious to earn the good opinion of his employers and to carry out their orders to the best of his ability, had vanished, and in his place was a man full of contempt and scorn for the way they exercised their authority, who had grown accustomed to the frequent necessity for disobedience of orders and for reliance on his own independent judgement. His impatience with opposition and criticism had increased with the passage of years, increased naturally as proof after proof had been given him of how factitious and baneful were the opposition and criticism which he had been receiving steadily from his superiors and colleagues. He had reached a state of mind where he felt that he alone could save the Empire and all who did not agree with him or who put obstacles in his way were enemies to the State and deserving of no consideration or forbearance. In this extreme state of mind, he had fought a duel of his own provoking with Francis. He had suspended the disobedient Governor of Madras. He was now about to arrest, with the intention of punishing, a powerful but recalcitrant vassal, dispossess the royal family of a neighboring allied state on a charge of rebellious conspiracy, and plunge headlong into a fierce contest with the new Governor of Madras. Nowhere in these actions can be seen the mildness and benevolence that marked his earlier behavior. He was more like a ruthless despot hewing his way to victory.

His was a dangerous state of mind, especially for a man directing the affairs of a government. No one, however wise and conscientious, can prudently place such excessive reliance on his own judgement. However justified by circumstances his egotism may be—and surely if anybody's egotism was justified it was Hastings's—those same circumstances are only too apt to warp the finest judgement. And the greater the danger and perplexity of the moment, the greater is the chance of that judgement going astray. If a man has an admirable dislike of half measures, he is likely, in a moment of special stress, to mistake brutal ruthlessness for common-sense thoroughness. Or if his virtue is decision, it may become the vice of rashness. Statesmanlike appreciation of the need for firmness and vigor may deteriorate into excessive use of arbitrary methods. He may exaggerate dangers, misinterpret facts, entertain unjustified suspicions, allow the nervous strain to get the better of his critical faculty.

All these dangers confronted Warren Hastings during this crisis when the fate of India rested on his shoulders, and never has a man stood in greater need of wise counsel, of sympathetic guidance and support from his superiors in England, intelligent advice and assistance from his Council, a tactful, coöperative, restraining hand that could help him frame the right measures. But all these aids were absent. His Council was reduced to one man, Edward Wheler—and Wheler was unfitted for the part. Hastings had complete freedom of action, he had absolute power, and he had made up his mind to use that power "to retrieve past misfortune, to remove present dangers and to reëstablish the power of the Company and the safety of its possessions." He saw in one quarter what he considered to be dangerous incipient rebellion; he went to crush it. He saw in another rising anarchy and a vast unliquidated debt; he devised his own means to end the one and collect the other. He acted with complete self-assurance. What he did may seem arbitrary, mistaken, high-handed, even reckless, yet his firm belief in the absolute rightness of his conduct was never for a moment shaken, either now or later. He did what he did because he was convinced it was the only thing he could do under the circumstances. Did he later acknowledge having made mistakes? Surely. He knew that where there is action, there must be mistakes. But it was the action, its motives, its objects, its consequences, that he claimed should count, not the incidental error, and there was not a major action in his life that he did not proudly and insistently defend. And when he decided that a measure was politic and just, he showed an inflexible resolution to carry it through to the bitter end, regardless of consequences.

In the following year (1782) he was to give John Macpherson some axioms upon which to regulate his conduct as a member of the Bengal Council. The advice is interesting. "Deliberate well; resolve with decision, and completely, not by halves: but when your resolution is once formed, and in execution, never admit even a thought of withdrawing it; but persist in it, even though in itself it should be wrong, if not ruinously wrong." [5] There is a rare pungency to this that smacks of his own applied philosophy. It is as though he has here put into words the concentrated fruit of his own experience. Was he perhaps admitting by implication that he knew that he had himself erred on occasion while refusing to let that knowledge deter him from persisting? Was he, perhaps, thinking of things he had done the previous year? Whether this be so or not, his greatest triumphs and his greatest tribulations sprang alike from the inflexibility of his will.

Hastings in 1781 had only one end in view—to save Britain's Empire at any cost. And for that end he did not hesitate to exercise despotic power or to jeopardize his reputation for just dealing. The need for doing his duty as he saw it transcended all other considerations and, above all, transcended the fear of incurring odium. Whatever else he may have lacked—discretion, circumspection, scruple—he never lacked courage.

II

AMONG the legacies left behind by Francis was the Treaty of Fyzabad. He had departed just when the evil effects of it were making themselves felt. By the spring of 1781, like a two-edged sword, it was hitting British interests in two very sensitive spots. By compelling the Vizier to cede the province of Benares to the Company, Francis had saddled it with an unnecessary responsibility and at the same time he had reduced the Vizier's revenues by the extent of the tribute he had been receiving from Benares, without reducing, rather indeed, increasing, his financial liabilities. And the result—an Oude that was virtually bankrupt, with its debt to the Company steadily growing and the country being given over to anarchy; while Benares itself had become a serious thorn in the side of the Bengal Government, despite the revenue derived from it.

Until 1775 Benares had formed part of Oude, the status of its Rajah resembling that of a feudal vassal. In return for recognition of his hereditary rights, which included the collection of the revenues, complete civil and criminal jurisdiction and the maintenance of order, he paid his suzerain the Vizier a fixed annual tribute, and, in addition, acknowledged his right to exact fines on inheritance and to demand additional contributions of men and money in times of special need. The relationship had evolved from the system of government established by the Emperor Akbar in the sixteenth century, the inevitable trend of Indian institutions towards hereditary right giving it its close resemblance to the great military tenures of feudalism. The rights of each party were stated in a lease, but the basis of the system was arbitrary power and nothing else. There was no court to which the zemindar could appeal against unjust treatment by his overlord; he either had to submit or risk forcible eviction.

It was just such an amorphous child as this that Francis had fathered on the Company. The rights that he obtained for his employers with the cession of Benares were exactly the same as those that had been enjoyed by the Vizier. No change was made in Chait Singh's status as zemindar, except that his power and independence were slightly increased. Unlike other zemindars, he was given not only the customary civil and criminal jurisdiction of his fief but the exceptional privilege of coining money. He maintained a considerable army, lived in semi-regal state, and waxed rich and powerful. And his only fixed and clearly defined obligation was to pay to his new sovereign the annual sum of twenty-three lakhs (about a quarter of a million pounds), which was less than half his annual revenue.

The Company had graciously accepted the present, and the Directors had noted "with particular pleasure" the solid and permanent advantages that it seemed to promise them. Characteristically they then proceeded to forget everything about it except the nice fat sum that would automatically drop into their Calcutta treasury every twelve months.

For four years it did so drop and all was well. Then came the Maratha War, which raised in acute form the question of the special emergency rights of the sovereign power. In addition to the long-established custom that a vassal should afford extra aid in money and troops at such times—a custom that Shuja-ud-Daula the Vizier had frequently enforced—there was a clause in Chait Singh's contract that read, "it shall be my duty to do everything that may be needful and usual for the interest of the country." What could be more open to diverse interpretation by sovereign and vassal than those few innocent-sounding words? But it had never been necessary, or indeed expedient, for the Moguls to frame a clearer definition of their vassals' obligations: they used to state merely what the "everything" was to be in a particular instance and then see to it that it was done!

Now that Chait Singh had by curious circumstance come under the ægis of British power it might be expected that something would have been done to bring his status into harmony with British law and practice. But nothing of the sort happened. The egregious anomaly was not only allowed to continue: it was ignored. No word came from England to the Governor-General-in-Council to indicate how he was expected to act towards this important vassal, and a glance at the contents of the Regulating Act shows that Parliament had made no provision for a contingency of this kind. The Act merely invested the Company with the government and administration of the kingdoms of Bengal, Bihar and Orissa. Parliament had carefully avoided making any attempt to define the relations of the Company either with the Delhi emperor or with such semi-independent vassals as the Rajah of Benares. Even the nature and extent of the authority exercised by the Governor-General-in-Council were not fixed.

The Company was of no assistance. Parliament was of no assistance. There was nothing in British law applicable to the case. All of which meant that Hastings and his colleagues were left to decide for themselves what course they should follow. Could anything have been more natural than for them to follow Mogul custom and claim a sovereign's rights?

Hastings probably knew Mogul law better than he knew the law of his own country. He had spent the greater part of his adult life in India and had come to regard problems such as this in a different light from that in which a governor fresh from England and the atmosphere of Westminster would have regarded them. Perhaps he had been in India too long and adopted too many Indian ways of thought and action. It is certainly true that he would only partially have subscribed to Burke's dictum that "it was the duty of a British Governor to enforce British laws; to correct the opinions and practices of the people, not to conform his opinion to their practice."

He was to make his attitude abundantly clear in the defense he prepared against the subsequent charge of illegal conduct. He first emphasized the fact that he had been opposed from the start to the acquisition of Benares and that his wishes had been overruled by the Majority.

"I considered Chait Singh precisely *what they had made him,* a tributary landholder, not what *I* would have made him (but was overruled), an independent prince and a powerful ally, placed as a barrier between the Vizier and the Government of Bengal.... *I* would have renounced the sovereignty of his country. *They* assumed it. *The sovereignty* which they *assumed,* it fell to my lot, very unexpectedly, to *exert.*"

He admitted that he was not enough of a lawyer to tell whether powers of that nature were delegated to him by any Act of Parliament; and yet by act of the Council that sovereignty had been assumed by the Company. So, he argued,

"if the sovereignty of Benares, as ceded to us by the Vizier, have any rights whatever annexed to it (and be not a mere empty word without meaning) those rights must be such as are held, countenanced, and established by the law, custom and usage of the Mogul Empire, and not by the provisions of any British Act of Parliament hitherto enacted."

Should Parliament abolish those rights, and the exertion of them, then the much vaunted sovereignty of Benares would become a burden instead of a benefit—unless, that is, Parliament substituted a comprehensive constitutional system for the present confusion of laws, customs, rights and tenures that existed in India.

He explained why it was that he did not wish to see his government saddled with the sovereignty of Benares and forced to exercise it according to Indian practice. The strong hand of power had been the basis of the Indian system ever since the Moslem conquests.

"Sovereignty in India implies nothing else; for I know not how we can form an estimate of its powers but from its visible effects—and those are everywhere the same, from Kabul to Assam. The whole history of Asia is nothing more than precedents to prove the invariable exercise of arbitrary power."

He had wished to make Chait Singh independent in 1775 because in India dependence caused a thousand evils.

"I knew the powers with which an Indian sovereignty is armed, and the dangers to which tributaries are exposed. I knew that from the history of Asia, and from the very nature of mankind, the subjects of a despotic empire are always vigilant for the moment to rebel, and the sovereign is ever jealous of rebellious intentions." [6]

Whether Hastings realized quite so clearly all the factors involved at the time when he decided on his course of action is doubtful. Probably he acted more by instinct than by logic, and did not attempt to rationalize his conduct until after his critics had stated their objections. But he never acted blindly, and there is no reason for thinking that his elaborately rea-soned defense does not fairly represent his consistent attitude towards the problems of Indian government. He was expressing one of the deep-est convictions of his life when he said in the same part of his defense: "It will, no doubt, be most happy for the inhabitants of Asia when the despotic institutes of Jengheez Khan or Tamerlane shall give place to the liberal spirit of a British legislature; and," he added, "I shall be amply satisfied in my present prosecution, if it shall tend to hasten the approach of an event so beneficial to the great interests of mankind...."

When war came the Bengal Government demanded from Chait Singh a special war contribution of five lakhs and renewed the demand for each of the next two years. "It is a right inherent in every govern-ment," Hastings declared, "to impose such assessments as it judges expedient for the common service and protection of all its subjects, and we are not precluded from it by any agreement subsisting between the Rajah and this government." [7] In 1780 a fresh demand was made on the Rajah. In September when a Maratha invasion of Bihar was threat-ening, Sir Eyre Coote proposed in Council that he should be required to furnish a body of cavalry for the Company's use. He pressed the matter again with greater urgency in November, and Hastings then agreed. The number was fixed at two thousand, to be raised and maintained at Chait Singh's expense.

Chait Singh attempted to evade both demands. When he paid the subsidy it was under protest and generally only after considerable delay. He made excuses and feigned poverty, all in true Oriental fashion. To the demand for cavalry he at first made no reply. The requisition was then reduced to one thousand horsemen. At last he made the response that he had mustered five hundred horse and five hundred foot, but not another man could he spare from the forces required for the collection of the revenues and enforcement of order. Actually not one man was ever sent. When the third demand for the extra subsidy came, he offered Hastings a bribe of two lakhs to obtain a remission of the subsidy. The Governor-General refused the bribe but not the money. Instead he ac-cepted it as though it had been intended as a free-will offering to the Company, and applied it to defray the expenses of Camac's expedition. And even after taking the money he did not withdraw or soften his demand for the five lakhs. Rather, he threatened to apply military force when the delay overtaxed his patience.

Such was the position in June 1781. Hastings was then about to set out on a journey up-country to visit Oude in order to use his personal influence with the Vizier to straighten out the confusion in his govern-ment and find means to liquidate the debt, and with the object, too, of keeping in closer touch with his agents who were conducting negotiations with the Marathas. As he would have to pass through Benares to reach his destination, he naturally included a meeting with Chait Singh in his plans.

If Hastings's nature had been subtly orientalized during the course of his thirty years' contact with the East, it was now that the process became apparent. For his own mind was not free from those same suspicions that he declared could never be absent from the mind of an Indian sovereign. Rumors and reports reached him that Chait Singh was in secret communication with the Marathas. Using his knowledge of Indian history, its centuries-long record of intrigue, conspiracy and rebellion, he jumped to the conclusion that he was confronted at Benares with exactly the same situation that had confronted Indian rulers a thousand times in the past. He saw British India attacked at all points both on land and sea and hard pressed to maintain its existence. And now, to cap it all, he saw a new peril rising at Bengal's very doorstep, threatening to take the province in the rear, sever its communications with Oude, complete the collapse of that distressed ally and open up the country to the raids of the Maratha horsemen. Everything for which he was striving tooth and nail was imperiled by what his imagination—or was it his intuition?—told him was preparing in Benares—the security of Bengal, the saving of an empire. And no one can definitely say today whether his belief was well or ill founded.

His distrust of Chait Singh was increased by other things that had happened. Originally Chait Singh was a protégé of his. He had intervened with the Vizier in 1773 to secure to him the succession to his father's rights when difficulty had arisen owing to the fact that he was an illegitimate son. And Chait Singh had repaid him four years later by deputing an agent to General Clavering to compliment him on his supposed accession to the government at the time of Hastings's "resignation." This, in Hastings's opinion, was "indecent with respect to my office, unjustifiable with regard to his situation, and a proof of his rooted disaffection to the English administration." It is true he insisted that this incident had no influence on his subsequent treatment of the Rajah. "I never sought to punish him but on public ground. And had he faithfully discharged his duty to the Company he would never have heard a syllable of my resentment. Implacability to my inferiors is no part of my character."[8] But his mind was seething with pent-up irritation at the whole spirit of faction and disloyalty that Francis had stirred up against him on every hand. He suspected that that spirit had infected Chait Singh, causing him to offer insult and derision to the Governor-General's authority and to harbor rebellious designs. [9]

Whatever his reasons and suspicions were, Hastings determined before he left Calcutta to "make him pay largely for his pardon, or to exact a severe vengeance for his past delinquency." [10] He considered his independent power, his wealth, his forts, his crowds of armed retainers, and he decided that Chait Singh was an overpowerful vassal grown insolent and consequently a source of danger to the State. He even threatened to seize his treasures and forts and sell his land to Oude, not, however, with any intention—so he said—of carrying his vengeance thus far, the threat being meant only *in terrorem*.

Forewarned, the perturbed Rajah now made him a last minute offer of twenty lakhs as a peace offering, but Hastings sternly rejected it as insufficient. It had, he grimly said, come "too late." Before he left Calcutta he confided to Wheler his intention to exact a fine of "40 or 50 lakhs." [11] Fifty lakhs (£500,000) was equal to Chait Singh's annual revenue from his zemindary. The precise amount, however, was to be decided by circumstances and more exact particulars of Chait Singh's amassed wealth. As his officers had reported to him that the Rajah had accumulated between one and two million pounds sterling, Hastings was convinced of his ability to pay a large sum. In his defense Hastings was to say in justification of this intention: "I who was vested, by my situation, with exactly the same powers as were exercised by Shuja-ud-Daula, never thought of a greater fine, as a punishment for the most flagrant offenses"—referring to the fact that Shuja-ud-Daula had fined Chait Singh £200,000 plus £30,000 per annum on his investiture with his father's rights. "The inference, therefore, is," he added, "that the right of fining was general—perhaps arbitrary; but for that I am not responsible: it is a defect woven into the texture of the Mogul system."

Hastings left Calcutta on his Mogul-like mission on July 7. But he did not travel in imperial style. Considering that he was going, as he believed, to stamp out a rebellious conspiracy, the escort he took with him was ridiculously small. No more than five hundred men. Nor was his personal retinue any more imposing—his private secretary, a few officers and aides-de-camp, William Hodges, the Royal Academician, who wanted the opportunity to paint the scenic beauty and historic spots of the country, and Mrs. Hastings, who accompanied the party as far as Monghyr. But the Governor-General traveled with an easy mind. He had been able during the interval following Francis's departure to reach an excellent understanding with his weak and easily influenced colleague Wheler, who had been materially helped to an amiable frame of mind by being given the lion's share of the patronage rights that usually fell as a matter of course to the Governor-General. Hastings cared little about such trifles and was quite ready to exchange them for an implicit support of his policy. He was thus able to write: "I am easy, and my colleague satisfied, and the public will reap the fruits of the good understanding which subsists between us." Coote being away, Wheler was the only remaining member of the Council left at Calcutta, and accordingly, he and Hastings vested each other with supreme powers of government for their respective temporary spheres—Wheler for Bengal, Hastings for beyond its confines. [12] The arrangement suited both men admirably.

The party journeyed by easy stages up the river, stopping at Murshidebad for a few days while Hastings gave the young Nawab some paternal advice regarding the management of his finances and *ménage*. The journey so far had worn more of the aspect of a pleasure trip than of a stern political mission. Everywhere along the banks of the Ganges the natives crowded to watch the passage of the famous Governor-General, perching themselves on the roofs and walls to catch a glimpse of his revered countenance. If they expected to see a magnificent presence bearing the hauteur of a conqueror, with "pride in his port, defiance in his eye, and a duke's ransom on his back," they were no doubt disappointed; for all they saw was a slight, dignified figure, simply dressed, simply attended, and manifesting nothing but a benign benevolence and a general friendliness.

At length on August 12 they reached Buxar on the borders of Chait Singh's zemindary. Here they were met by the Rajah in person and the serious business of the mission commenced. The very meeting was inauspicious, for the Rajah, disregarding the rules of etiquette, had the insolence to appear with a large retinue of two thousand men. The Governor-General received him coldly and refused to accept his turban, which he tried to place in his lap as the customary token of submission. After a brief formal exchange of compliments they parted, each proceeding separately on his way to Benares. On reaching there, Hastings refused the Rajah's request for another interview and sent him instead a detailed statement of his offenses, in which he reminded him that his failure to make prompt payment of the subsidy of 1780 in accordance with his promise had seriously endangered Colonel Camac's detachment which had been dependent upon it, and accused him of violating one of the conditions of his contract by permitting all manner of disorders to exist in his zemindary, even daily murders and robberies in the streets of Benares itself. His secret agents had endeavored to excite disaffection and infidelity to his sovereign, occurring at a time when it was his duty most especially to exert himself in its support. An immediate answer was demanded.

Chait Singh's reply, while couched orientally in humble, submissive terms, was evasive and unsatisfactory. It contained recriminations instead of the expected promises of atonement, and it is not at all surprising that the Governor-General should have considered it "not only unsatisfactory in substance, but offensive in style," and so filled with "shuffling excuses and palpable falsehoods" as to force him to the conclusion that Chait Singh would never come to terms until he had felt the hand of authority. [13] He felt the times to be too critical to permit such behavior to go unchecked, and without further parley he ordered the Rajah to be put under arrest and sent two companies of sepoys to mount guard over his palace.

This was almost certainly a blunder. Such a measure inflicted a most serious blow to the Rajah's prestige and dignity, and it was hardly to be expected that he would take it lightly. It was probably an unnecessary action, and as things were it was foolhardy in the extreme. If Hastings had come with a sufficient show of force to support such severity, everything would probably have passed off peacefully, the fine would have been demanded and, after a little more pressure had been brought to bear upon the prisoner, duly paid, and Hastings could have gone on his way satisfied that he had left Chait Singh a chastened and wiser man. But as it was he was tempting fate and had to pay for his rashness.

By a shocking piece of carelessness the sepoys sent to guard the palace were without ammunition. And, to make matters worse, their commanding officer was foolish enough to allow the Rajah's officers to be admitted to him. The result was calamitous. Before the English were aware of what was happening, scores of Chait Singh's guards had collected around the palace, blocking all the entrances. Hastings must have scented possible trouble because he sent Chait Singh a verbal message: "Every sepoy is as an European, and every European is as the Company. If a drop of their blood is shed yours shall answer for it." [14]

He was too late. Reinforcements, fully armed, were on their way to the palace when the tumult at the gates broke out into a murderous attack on the helpless sepoys. A horrible massacre ensued. Before the rescuers could reach the spot the ghastly work was finished and scarcely a man was left alive.

In the confusion Chait Singh used a rope of turbans to escape over the wall of his palace and down the bank to the river. He crossed to Ramnagar on the opposite bank where he was quickly joined by large bodies of his troops. From there he fled with his family and treasure to his fortress at Latifpur, leaving Benares and all the surrounding district in a state of wild excitement and full of his armed men thirsting for more blood. Next day, a second disaster befell the English. A rash English officer, acting without orders, led a small detachment of the Company's sepoys into the narrow streets of Ramnagar where they were fired upon from every house and completely wiped out.

The news of these events spread like wildfire, and instantly the whole province of Benares broke out in open insurrection that swept from one end to the other.

What was the precise cause of the outbreak has never been determined; it may have been due, as Hastings believed, to Chait Singh, with his secret rebellious intentions, deciding that the right moment had come to strike—"it was a mine sprung before its time" was how he expressed it—or, as is equally likely, it may have been a case of spontaneous combustion, arising from the anger of the Rajah's followers at the indignity offered to their prince and the paucity of the Governor-General's escort. Fear of Hastings's intentions may, also, have been a contributing cause, impelling Chait Singh to take this desperate course to escape punishment. It seems certain that Chait Singh was in communication with the Marathas and with every disaffected element in Bengal and Oude, and he may well have thought that he had more to gain by lighting the fires of general revolt than by tame submission, especially as his own army numbered no less than ten thousand men, well-armed and well-equipped, not counting the many thousands more who leapt to arms at the first outbreak.

Hastings was now in the utmost danger. He had only four hundred men left, all but thirty of whom were sepoys who had been demoralized by the fate of their comrades, and the nearest British troops were at Chunar, twenty miles away. He at once sent orders to the commanding officer of this garrison to hurry to the rescue, but as all communications had been cut with the outside world there was no way of knowing whether the messages would reach their destination. To make matters worse, his position at Benares was indefensible, as he had taken up his quarters on an estate in the suburbs shut in on every side by houses and trees.

Several days passed while he waited anxiously for the relieving force. The Rajah's levies were collecting, large bodies of men had been seen crossing the river from the opposite bank, water was lacking, food was running short, and there was still no sign of the Chunar battalion.

He detested the very thought of retreat. What would be the effect in Oude, in Bengal, in all India, when it was known that the Governor-General had had to flee for his life? But his officers were emphatic: they could not possibly hold the place against an attack. At last he bowed to the inevitable. As night fell, the little body filed silently out and took the road to Chunar. They marched all night unmolested and in the morning met the relieving battalion on the way. Together they reached Chunar in safety, but the baggage and its escort, which had taken a different road, fell into the hands of the enemy.

Safe behind the walls of the fort at Chunar, Hastings's anxiety was but little diminished. The insurrection was spreading far and wide, even to Oude and Nepal. But his courage never faltered for a moment, nor did his coolness and swift resource fail him. Somehow he had to get word to his officers, and he hit upon the plan of sending his messages rolled up in a quill which the messenger carried in his ear. He sent several copies by different bearers in the hope that one at least would reach its destination.

While he was shut up in Chunar rumors of catastrophe were spreading to Bengal. The natives universally believed that the Governor-General had been killed. They produced eye-witnesses who reported having seen his head and right hand suspended over the gateway of Chait Singh's fortress. Here and there mutiny and desertion broke out among the sepoys and every discontented element began to rear its head. The Rajah became the center of a rapidly widening web of conspiracy. Calcutta buzzed with reports. Everybody knew that something had happened but nobody knew what. Anxiety was intense as all realized what it would mean if the great Governor-General had lost his life. Well might Sir Eyre Coote write to Wheler, "Had an accident happened to Mr. Hastings, what in the name of God could you or I have done with the Government?" [15] Panic spread to the European inhabitants of even a great city like Patna, and they would have taken to the boats and fled had it not been for the firmness and address of Mrs. Hastings who reached the city from Monghyr in time to recall them to a sense of their duty.

Nobody knew less of what was happening than Hastings himself while he was waiting for reinforcements to reach him. He was tortured with anxiety but for the moment he was powerless to move. Not the least of his worries was a lack of money. His credit locally was gone and he was without funds to pay his sepoys. When the Rajah of Berar's envoy, who had met him by arrangement at Benares and stayed by him throughout the crisis, refusing to remain with his family in Benares, offered him a loan of a lakh, Hastings gratefully accepted it with public acknowledgements of this unexpected mark of confidence in his government.

The insurrection began on the 16th of August, and a fortnight elapsed before sufficient forces could be collected for Hastings to take the offensive. Then progress was rapid. The tide turned when a small detachment sent out from Chunar to Pateeta, seven miles away, routed four thousand of the enemy, with heavy loss. By September 13, Major Popham with a considerable force was on the scene and the shortage of funds had been relieved. Hastings then made the bold decision to attack all of Chait Singh's fortresses at once. The story is told that when Major Popham came out of the conference at which the Governor-General delivered to his officers the plan of operations with his instructions, his only remark was, "He should have been a general," expressed in a tone of fervent admiration; [16] which is perhaps the finest compliment a soldier can pay a civilian.

Within two months all of Chait Singh's fortresses had been taken, the wretched Rajah himself had fled the country, taking with him a considerable part of his fortune, and the last remnants of the insurrection had been stamped out.

III

HASTINGS remained at Chunar until September 25, when he returned to Benares. But before that day came he had already attended to the other important matters that had brought him up country. Through his agent, Colonel Muir, he had continued the negotiations with Mahadaji Sindhia, and with so much success that terms of peace were being arranged at the very time when Hastings himself was surrounded by the rebels; nor did his plight impede the progress of his negotiations with the Berar Government by which he eventually hoped to make peace with the central Maratha state at Poona. Most important of all, he had been able to have his interview with the Vizier of Oude.

As soon as the news of the Benares insurrection reached him the Vizier had hurried towards the scene of action, professing the utmost fidelity towards the Company and offering Hastings his assistance against Chait Singh. Hastings, anxious not to lower the dignity and prestige of his Government by accepting outside aid for the suppression of an internal disturbance, thanked him for the assurance but refused the assistance. He allowed him, however, to come as far as Chunar to discuss his affairs.

The Vizier owed the Company £1,500,000, but to the Governor-General's demand for payment he made the unwelcome reply that not only were his funds exhausted, so that he could not meet the expenses even of his own government, but in addition he could not continue to maintain the brigade employed in defending his dominions, let alone pay his debts. The news opened up to Hastings an alarming prospect. Not only was he in sore need of money himself, but the successful outcome of the war, the security of Bengal, everything in fact for which he was striving, hinged on maintaining Oude as a stable barrier against invasion. The Vizier, utterly incompetent to solve his own difficulties, looked to Hastings to solve them for him. And Hastings knew how imperative it was that he should succeed. Resourceful when he rescued Bengal from imminent collapse, he had to be equally resourceful now under circumstances of even greater difficulty. No ordinary expedients would suffice. He had to take his courage in both hands, devise the measures best calculated to serve his purpose, and be inflexible in enforcing them. It was a situation that justified arbitrary action, made it, in fact, not only excusable but imperative.

The main problem was that of finding a big enough sum of money to enable the Vizier to pay his debts, and to this there was one solution and, so far as Hastings could see, only one. The question he had to decide was whether it could be adopted without a breach of faith on the part of his Government. It would involve some hardship, even, perhaps, some measure of injustice, to the individuals concerned, but, if it did not involve anything worse, would not he be justified in adopting it for the common good of both Oude and the Company?

The late Vizier, Shuja-ud-Daula, had accumulated in his lifetime a hoard of treasure amounting to £2,000,000 which he concealed in his palace at Fyzabad. When he died his widow, who had been a devoted consort,[1] exercised right of possession and refused to surrender the treasure to her son, state property though it was, claiming it all on the strength of a will that was never produced, though according to Moslem law a widow was only entitled to one-eighth of an inheritance after payment of debts. The late Vizier's debts, principally owed to the Company, were large but went unpaid, and thenceforth the government of Oude had to labor under the double handicap of an incompetent ruler and crippled finances; for Asaf-ud-Daula was a worthless prince, a profligate who wasted on himself and his favorites money sorely needed to pay his army, a spineless weakling whose fear of his strong-willed and hot-tempered mother was so great that he was unable to pluck up enough courage to take by force what was plainly his by right. No wonder that she heartily despised him, defied his authority and withheld

---

[1] When her husband had needed money to pay the war indemnity to the English of fifty lakhs in 1765, she had despoiled herself and her ladies to furnish it, which she did completely. [17]

from him the savings of his thrifty father. Twice in his desperate need of money he besought her to give him some of the treasure, appealing as a suppliant to her bounty. The first time, when she was kind enough to grant him a loan of £250,000, he showed his gratitude by giving her in exchange a grant of land worth four times as much! The second time, not desiring to go himself to Fyzabad, he appealed for aid to the British Resident, and Bristow very inadvisedly allowed himself to be drawn in as arbiter of the dispute. He went to Fyzabad in person and bargained with the two Begums, the mother and the grandmother of the reigning prince. The result did little credit to his judgement. In return for a full acquittal as to the rest of the treasure and a guarantee of their lands for life, the Begums surrendered half a million pounds. And so for an immediate sum in ready cash, the Vizier signed away over half of his inheritance and the revenue of no small part of his dominions. And not only did Bristow guarantee the arrangement on behalf of the Company but the Triumvirate in the Council gave it their sanction. [18]

It is more than probable that Hastings would have honored the agreement, scandalous and grossly detrimental to the interests of the Company though it was, if other circumstances had not arisen to invalidate it, according to his judgement of the facts. Those circumstances were the part that the Begums were alleged to have played in the Benares insurrection. They were accused of aiding and abetting Chait Singh.

It must be admitted at once that the ground we are here treading is very doubtful and uncertain. No incontrovertible, or even reliable, evidence exists of the Begums' complicity. The truth is largely a matter of conjecture. The times were troublous. The Vizier's dominions seethed with discontent, provoked by his own abominable misgovernment. His army, tired of waiting to be paid, was mutinous. His chief vassals and zemindars were in open revolt. Only the presence of the British troops prevented a revolution and civil war, and there is little doubt that the Begums were deeply involved in the turmoil, though how far sedition could be interpreted as hostility to the British is another matter. They had been a thorn in Asaf-ud-Daula's side ever since his accession, scorning his authority, intriguing with his officers, going so far even as to implore the Bengal Government to dismiss his ministers and choose others of their own selection. They were ladies with a strength of character seldom found in the zenana and it had gone hard with them to have to acquiesce in the passing of authority to hands weaker than their own, of their own flesh and blood though they were, and to witness the ruin of their country which Shuja-ud-Daula had done so much to enlarge and enrich. They had appealed to Hastings for protection against their son, and he with his chivalrous nature must have wanted to extend to them all the protection that he could reasonably give. But no amount of sentiment could alter the fact that these ladies with their obstinate defiance of the lawful authority of the state presented a serious obstacle to a settlement of the Vizier's affairs. Perhaps they themselves were only partly to blame as their affairs were in the hands of two eunuchs, crafty and ambitious men, who not improbably were using their mistresses' wealth and position in ways unknown to them and contrary to their wishes. General report had it that the eunuchs were at the bottom of the mischief.

The belief that the Begums and their servants were in league with Chait Singh was widely current in the British camp, and Hastings, foreseeing the need of evidence to justify the course that he proposed to take, decided to collect affidavits from officers and men having knowledge of the facts. He sent an urgent request to Sir Elijah Impey, who happened at the time to be up-country on a tour of inspection of the local courts, to join him at once and lend his assistance so that the affidavits might be vested with the additional weight of his high judicial position. Impey, acting with the spontaneous generosity and public spirit-edness that distinguished him, came at once. In his desire to help his friend and render a service to the State at a time of such crisis he did not care whether, in taking the affidavits, he was overstepping the bounds of his official duty. Even if he had known how fiercely his and Hastings's enemies would exploit his action to the common hurt of them both, he probably would have done no differently.

Hastings attached altogether too much importance to the value of this evidence. Impey being a lawyer could, if he had read them, which he claimed he did not, have told him that they were worthless in the eyes of the law, as they were made by persons who could not escape the suspicion of being interested parties, since, being employed in the Vizier's service, they may have fabricated or exaggerated the Begums' complicity in order to screen their own share in stirring up the disorders in Oude. Also they were based wholly on hearsay—not one of them contained a clear, authenticated, trustworthy account of an actual instance of hostility to the British, and the Begums themselves were vehement in their protestations of innocence. These were not, however, Hastings's sole source of information. His chief officers on the spot, both military and civil, corroborated the story. Colonel Hannay, the commander of the Oude corps, stated explicitly that the Begums were assisting Chait Singh with troops and money and inciting rebellion in Oude, and that the scattered detachments of British troops were in danger owing to their activities. He laid the blame squarely on the shoulders of the eunuchs. The report of Middleton, the British Resident, was to precisely the same effect. He was particularly severe on the younger Begum, stating that, "by her own conduct, and that of all her agents and dependents during the Benares trouble, it may with truth and justice be affirmed she forfeited every claim she had to the protection of the English Government, as she evidently, and it is confidently said, avowedly espoused the cause of Rajah Chait Singh, and united in the idea and plan of a general extirpation of their race and power in Hindustan." [19]

Hearsay again! And the idea that the Begums were aiming at the overthrow of the British Empire has since been generally scouted. [20] Perhaps—and the suggestion has been made—Middleton and Hannay were lying. If so, the conspiracy of deceit must have been general, for, said Hastings at his trial, "most assuredly no unprejudiced man in the country, whether native or European, ever entertained a doubt" of the Begums' guilt. But even supposing that his officers were mistaken— that they even deliberately deceived him—and admitting that he may have been at fault—as Mr. P. E. Roberts asserts [21]—in not investigating the facts more carefully before proceeding to judgement (Mr. Roberts makes very little allowance for the circumstances of the moment, the acute danger, the need for haste, the folly of embarking on a formal process of trial at such a time), there is still no ground for questioning Hastings's integrity. And why, after all, should some weight not be attached to the emphatic statements of the men on the spot? "Let this," wrote Hastings to Scott, after relating the reports that had reached him from his officers, "let this be an answer to the men of virtue who may exclaim against our breach of faith and the inhumanity of declaring war against widows, princesses of high rank, and defenseless old women. These old women had very nigh effected our destruction." [22] How accurately he foretold the kind of attack that his enemies, "the men of virtue," would make against him!

"It remains, therefore, for justice to decide whether in so doing they did or did not forfeit their claim to the protection of the Company, by which alone they had hitherto maintained whatever they possessed." Hastings himself had no doubt what the answer was, nor did he shrink from translating it into action. The Vizier must be allowed to recover both the treasure and the revenue that he had squandered by his gifts of land.

Another cause of the disorders was the presence of a swarm of English adventurers who had taken advantage of the British alliance to enter the Vizier's service. Lucknow was full of them—some as officers in the army, others in the civil administration—and the result was demoralizing alike to the employer and the employed in a way that was strongly reminiscent of the old unhappy days in Bengal following the revolution of 1757. Removed from all proper surveillance, occupying privileged positions under a vicious and corrupt government and at a time of internal disorder, it is hardly surprising that many of them made the most of their opportunities for self-enrichment.

Hastings was quick to perceive the shame attaching to the situation. He wrote to John Macpherson, who had just arrived in Calcutta as a new member of Council:

"Lucknow was a sink of iniquity. It was the school of rapacity. What will you say of beardless boys rejecting with indignation the offer of monthly gratuities of 3000 and 5000 rupees? What will you think of clerks in office clamoring for principalities, threatening those who hesitated to gratify their wants with the vengeance of patronage, and in the confidence of exhaustless resources, gambling away two lakhs of rupees at a sitting, and grumbling that their wants are not attended to? What will you think of men receiving the wages of service from the Nabob, and disclaiming his right to command; and what of a city filled with as many independent and absolute sovereignties as there are Englishmen in it?" [23]

Clearly an end had somehow to be put to the scandal, and in the treaty that Hastings signed with the Vizier on September 19, the removal of these adventurers was agreed upon.

The treaty was primarily an attempt to introduce order in the Vizier's chaotic finances. His military establishment was so greatly reduced that the Company virtually became wholly responsible for defense. Permission was granted him to resume the jaghires—grants of land with their revenues—that he had lavished on his nobles, and an attempt was made to introduce some measure of control over his expenditures. But the clause of the treaty that overshadowed all others was that relating to the Begums. As a matter of form the proposal for the recovery of the treasure came from the Vizier; actually the decision was Hastings's, and he soon made it clear that his consent was equivalent to a command. As it was only with that money that the Vizier's accumulated debt to the Company could be liquidated, he was determined that it should be done, regardless of the Vizier's personal wishes. As it happened, it was only by his insistence that it *was* done, for Asaf-ud-Daula repented of his resolution almost before the ink had dried on the treaty. A natural reluctance springing from a Moslem's sense of piety, allied with his habitual cowardice, made him most disinclined to undertake the task, and the money was still in possession of the Begums when Hastings returned to Benares.

IV

In his journey from Calcutta up the sacred Ganges, Hastings had passed from Bengal into Hindustan, the part of India which is the heart of the Hindu race. It stretches from Monghyr, its eastern gate with its great rocky promontory bounded on two sides by the broad stately river, as far as Delhi. Every mile of the way had carried him past innumerable relics and monuments of a civilization that began in the dim recesses of history. And when he came to Benares, with its fourteen hundred temples, its innumerable palaces and bathing ghats, its teeming human life, intricate streets and winding ways, he had reached the most sacred spot of all, the Hindu Rome, the goal of pilgrims from all parts of the Continent.

This was the city which he now had to provide with a government. It was at his disposal. And to Hastings, with his keen historical sense, wide sympathies and imperial breadth of vision, the task was no mere matter of official routine but a great opportunity. No city in all India, except possibly Delhi, could have held for him a greater fascination or appealed more strongly to his lively imagination. It was the metropolis of the land where the imperial destiny of his country was set. When and where could there be a better opportunity to display the beneficent aims of British policy? The eyes of all India would be watching to see how their new conquerors would treat their holy city.

The opportunity was especially favorable because of the conditions prevailing there under Chait Singh. From the time that the Bengal Council had entrusted him with the superintendence of the police, "the appearance of public justice," reported Hastings, "was gradually effaced, till at last without any system of police, any courts of judicature, or any awe of the sovereign power, the inhabitants of Benares were guilty of enormities and crimes which reflected the greatest disgrace on the Government to which they were subject. The relations and dependents of the Rajah, or the merchants whose credit was useful in the payment of his revenue, might violate the rights of their fellow-citizens with impunity, and the sacred character of a Brahman or the high rank of the offender were considerations which stamped a pardon on the most flagitious crimes." [24]

Hastings's first step was to issue a proclamation offering pardon to all inhabitants of the province except Chait Singh and his brother. From the moment of the massacre at the palace the Rajah had become an outlaw in his eyes.

"I rejected every advance from Chait Singh for peace, even when he had 40,000 men in arms and I had not 2000 to oppose them; and even when I was at his mercy at Benares, if the wretch had known his advantage; because I thought it dishonorable to treat on equal terms with a vassal and a murderer; and because I thought that the future existence and permanence of our state depended on the issue of this first instance of open defection in its own subjects." [25]

Hastings conferred Chait Singh's rights on his nephew, increased the tribute to the Company from twenty-three to forty lakhs, and transferred the departments of police and justice to the charge of a native magistrate directly responsible to the Governor-General-in-Council. "The Police which I have established for the town of Benares," he wrote to Scott, "is all after my own heart. The men of business in England will not know what to make of it; and my enemies will sneer at it. But the people are pleased, and if it answers my expectations, its influence will extend my reputation to the remotest parts of India." [26]

Hastings was highly gratified by the compliments which these measures drew from his Council, now increased to two by the arrival of John Macpherson: "Your guarded attention to the security and convenience of the pilgrims, and your abolition of those taxes and embarrassments which have grown up against them from the rapacity of a corrupt government are peculiarly to your credit." They wished to have the news of what he had done noised abroad throughout the

length and breadth of Hindustan, so that all Hindus might know of the
benefits which the British Government had conferred upon their sacred
city, and so form a more favorable opinion of its liberality, justice and
regard for their interests. [27]

Unfortunately, Hastings's hopes were not immediately realized. He
was apt to overrate the capacity of Indians for efficient government, not
realizing, perhaps, how thoroughly debased the whole ruling class of
India was at that time. Three years later when he paid another visit to
Benares he found little improvement in conditions and had to make
further changes.

The tragic melodrama of Chait Singh's fall ended in sordid anti-
climax. Major Popham's brief but brilliant campaign closed on November 10, with the capture of the fortress of Bidjeygur, together with
the Rajah's family, much spoil and all the treasure left behind him in
his flight from the country, amounting to a quarter of a million pounds.
The moment the place was taken there was a scramble for the gold,
and the clamor and vehemence of his officers were so great that Popham weakly gave way to their demands. Before Hastings knew anything
about it the entire sum had been distributed as prize-money. The only
excuse Major Popham gave for permitting this unpardonable act of
military rapacity was a private letter Hastings had written him some
time before, which, though carelessly worded, obviously referred to
ordinary booty, not to treasure, which belonged to the State alone.
Hastings was mortified in the extreme, for it meant that his last hope
of salvaging some substantial benefit for his treasury out of the convulsion had disappeared. He had gone to Benares to exact a heavy
fine; he now had come back with empty hands, knowing that his visit
had led to further expenditure of life and money, and all to so little
purpose. The increase in the tribute was the only tangible gain. It is
scarcely to be wondered at that when the officers sent "a very elegant
sword as a present to me, and a set of dressing boxes for Mrs. Hastings, all beautifully inlaid with jewels," he promptly returned them,
and then began legal action for the recovery of the money. [28]

He remained at Benares, where his wife joined him, until the
New Year and then traveled leisurely back to Calcutta, which he reached
on February 4. During all this time the agreement he had made with
the Vizier was a source of continuous trouble and vexation. He had
trodden on many toes by recalling the gentlemen enjoying lucrative
commands at Oude. "This has excited a world of clamor against me."
Also, three months had passed and not only had the Vizier made no
move to carry out his part of the bargain but Middleton seemed equally
disinclined to take any action. Hastings was in no mood for any dilly-
dallying, and his orders to Middleton became increasingly peremptory:
"You must not allow any negotiations or forbearance, but must prosecute both services until the Begums are at the entire mercy of the
Nawab." [29] This was in December. When January 1 came and still
nothing had been done he threatened to go to Lucknow himself and

warned the Vizier that unless he took immediate action he would exact from him assets for the discharge of his debt to the Company, withdraw the British troops, and leave him to his own devices.

These threats were sufficient. Acting under the joint orders of the Vizier and the Resident, a detachment of sepoys forthwith marched to Fyzabad, occupied the palace, seized the two eunuchs, and put the whole household under open arrest, with the women confined to their quarters pending delivery of the treasure. The Vizier took charge of the eunuchs but it was some time before he was able to make them disclose the secret hiding-place of the money. By the time Hastings returned to Calcutta fifty-five lakhs (close to £600,000) had been disgorged and paid over to the Company's account. But this was not enough to satisfy the Vizier or to extinguish his debts. Now that he had the eunuchs in his power, he wanted to extract from them the uttermost farthing. They were imprisoned, lightly fettered, placed on short commons, and possibly beaten—mild treatment compared to what was usually meted out by Indian rulers under the same circumstances. (When the Resident reported to Hastings that "all that force could do has been done," he was certainly guilty of gross exaggeration.) The relative lightness of the treatment was proved by the fact that it took nearly a year to finally break down the eunuchs' stubborn resistance, nor did they apparently suffer any ill effects from it. But in these later proceedings Hastings was only indirectly concerned, though undoubtedly the responsibility for the measures remained primarily his. After giving his orders to the Resident, he left him to devise with the Vizier the practical means of carrying them out.

Twenty years later one of the eunuchs was seen in Lucknow, still hale and hearty despite his eighty years, still very wealthy, and still an influence in the affairs of his country. The Begums, for their part, seemed to be quite unaware that they had suffered any outrage, nor did they bear any apparent malice for their rough treatment. Not long afterwards a reconciliation took place between them and the Vizier and their lands were returned to them. To the end they remained warmly attached to Hastings and never ceased to regard him as their benefactor and friend. Among the numerous testimonials that his Indian friends and admirers sent him during his impeachment was one from these ladies commiserating him on his hard and undeserved fate.

There was a different story to tell in England. When the enemies of the Governor-General heard about the business they were quick to perceive its value to them. Not even the Rohilla War lent itself quite so admirably to their purpose. By omitting a number of inconvenient facts, inserting their own conjectures regarding motives, and adding a few deft strokes to the picture here and there, they were able to produce a masterpiece of distortion, which they presented to the public as the true account of one of the greatest crimes in all time.

Looked at in the sober light of history and apart from its effect on the personal fortunes of Hastings himself, the story has an interest that has nothing to do with the ravings of his persecutors. As an object lesson in the intricacies and pitfalls of statecraft, particularly of Indian statecraft, it has real significance.

Hastings's troubles with Oude in 1781 were not just accidental; that is to say, they were not due wholly to the follies and blunders of the various individuals concerned. When critics in England blamed the troubles on Hastings himself, they only revealed their own misunderstanding both of conditions in India in general and of his policy in particular; and when Hastings, for his part, laid the blame on the individuals chiefly concerned, he was right only up to a point. The actions of these individuals had, indeed, been contributing factors, but they had only aggravated what was in reality a chronic condition. The root cause of the trouble, which escaped Hastings's notice, lay deeper and must be traced to the evils inherent in the system of subsidiary alliances.

When the Vizier of Oude accepted the Company's proffered alliance, it meant that he was permanently relieving himself of a ruler's primary duty to his people, the duty of defending them from foreign attack. It also meant that he was relieving himself of a ruler's primary inducement towards efficient government, the fear of deposition. He had exchanged a vital duty for a sense of irresponsible security, and thereby made inevitable a general degeneration in the State. For the prince, by the sacrifice of an essential part of his country's independence, lost both prestige and stimulus to self-discipline, and all too often degenerated into a sensualist, a miser, or a mere creature of caprice. The same demoralization, attended by loss of self-respect and of loyalty to the State, spread to all ranks of society.

This was what happened to Oude immediately upon the death of Shuja-ud-Daula, and the evil grew steadily worse with every year of his successor's reign. Nor was it to end either with Hastings's departure—as one would expect after reading Burke's speeches—or with Asaf-ud-Daula's death in 1797. The misgovernment of Oude was to continue down to the very day of its annexation in 1856, and there was not to be a single Governor-General during that period who did not have to lecture its ruler on his shortcomings, very much as Hastings had done, and always to as little purpose. Thus Hastings's failure was to be the failure also of all his successors.[1] The same holds true of other states—the Carnatic, for instance—as the system of alliances was extended.

The debts, which were only another aspect of the same problem, also continued. It was an inveterate habit of Indian rulers to be lax in money payments and to let arrears accumulate. Hastings's successors experienced the same difficulties as he—though, happily for them, they were never driven to adopt his 1781 expedient—until Lord Wellesley

---

[1] It is impossible to agree with Messrs. Thompson and Garrett when they speak of the Nawab of Oude as one "whose country, *as a result of Hastings's energetic intervention in his affairs* and his own imbecility, was in the deepest misery." [30]

(Governor-General, 1798-1806) decided to put a final stop to the abuse by appropriating territory in lieu of subsidy. In enforcing this policy in Oude—and it had much to recommend it, though probably in the long run it was unwise—he was guilty of more high-handed conduct than any that can be charged to Hastings. Hastings did his best to maintain the fiction of the Vizier's independence, treated him with courtesy and respect, and strove hard to avoid interfering in his affairs more than was absolutely necessary. Wellesley's policy was precisely the opposite. He felt himself at liberty to do whatever he thought fit, regardless of the Vizier's "independence," treated him with scant courtesy, and forced on him a treaty ceding half of his dominions to the Company, regarding his consent as a mere matter of form. But Wellesley, being a great nobleman, a friend of Pitt and a political power in England, could do such things with impunity. Circumstances were different, and—Edmund Burke was dead!...

Happily for India, when the evils inherent in the subsidiary alliance system were realized, its place was taken by a better and more enlightened system which made away with the mockery of independence and substituted the present treaty relationship of loyalty and confidence between the British Crown and the native princes that is today in process of being adapted as the basis of a Federation of all India— only by the time that was done most of the native states had passed out of existence.

Chapter XIX

MORE MATERIAL FOR THE PROSECUTION

1

IF THE theory that the terrific strain and anxiety of these two
years, 1780 and 1781, upset Hastings's mental equilibrium, disturbed
his judgement, and drove him into wild, reckless and unjust courses
is at all tenable, it has as its strongest foundation his treatment of
Faizulla Khan.

Faizulla Khan of Rampur was the only Rohilla chieftain who
escaped expulsion from Rohilkhand after the war of 1774. He fought
with Hafiz Rahmat Khan, and after the battle in which the latter was
killed he rallied his followers in the northern part of the country and
prepared to make a stout resistance to the allied forces. But the Vizier
stayed his hand and made peace with him. By the terms of the treaty
between them, Faizulla Khan had his lands guaranteed to him in return
for an acknowledgement of the Vizier's sovereignty, an agreement not
to take more than five thousand Rohillas into his service, and an undertaking to supply "two thousand or three thousand men according to
his ability" when the Vizier was at war. Colonel Champion attested the
treaty, and thereby made the Company virtually responsible for its
due observance by both parties. Faizulla Khan, not content with this,
pressed the Bengal Government for a formal guarantee of his rights,
and at length obtained it. He was an able and vigorous ruler and
warmly attached, it would seem, to the British connection.

The war came and Faizulla Khan of his own free will offered
to lend the Bengal Government two thousand horse, for which mark
of goodwill he received its grateful thanks. He did not, however, send
that number but only five hundred. In October 1780, before sailing for
the Carnatic, Sir Eyre Coote presented to the Council his recommenda-
tions of measures to be taken for the defense of Bengal and Oude,
and among them was one advising that Faizulla Khan should be called
upon to supply as many troops as possible for the defense of Rohilkhand.
The Council adopted the suggestion and unanimously agreed to ask
the Vizier to demand from him five thousand horse. The Vizier did

so, but Faizulla Khan in his reply pointed out that a mistake had been made about his obligations and offered to discharge his liability by sending two thousand horse and one thousand foot. Hastings seems then to have realized the mistake, which both Francis and Wheler as well as he himself had made, as he declared in his defense before the House of Commons that they had been led into it by the commanding officer in Rohilkhand, whose statement regarding the exact terms of the treaty they had failed to verify owing to pressure of business. Instead, however, of accepting Faizulla Khan's offer, Hastings recorded in a minute that he had evaded the performance of the treaty, and in the following March sent an officer to him to demand three thousand horse on pain of being denounced for disloyalty. The officer, Mr. Johnson, reported various infractions of the treaty by Faizulla Khan, in particular that there were many more than five thousand Rohillas in his service, and conveyed back the Khan's firm refusal to meet the demand. This caused Hastings formally to declare that he had broken the treaty, though at the same time he admitted that the demand exceeded the letter of the treaty.

He might easily have foreseen the consequences of taking this extraordinary position. When the Vizier met him at Chunar and asked to be allowed to resume the jaghires of his nobles and favorites, he very naturally included that of Faizulla Khan. There was no reason why he should not. The Rohilla had been declared by the British Government guilty of a breach of treaty. Why should *he* retain his lands and not, for instance, the Begums? Hastings, realizing perhaps that a blunt refusal was impossible, gave a vague consent. "We shall do it when time shall suit." [1] This, Hastings was to acknowledge at his trial, was "formally wrong, and yet more than formally, as it might become a precedent for worse purposes"; he confessed his fault and excused himself by emphasizing his distraught state of mind at the time. [2] The manner in which he tried to explain and justify what he had done to the Council Board certainly suggests mental confusion. After stating that he had assented to the Vizier's proposal because it was essential to the interests of the Company, and then, almost in the same breath, that his actual intent was to refuse it for the same reason, he said in his minute:

"The conduct of Faizulla Khan, in refusing the aid demanded, though not an absolute breach of treaty, was evasive and uncandid.... So scrupulous an attention to literal expression, when a more liberal interpretation would have been highly useful and acceptable to us, strongly marks his unfriendly disposition, though it may not impeach his fidelity, and leaves him little claim to any exertions from us for the continuance of his jaghires." [3]

Faizulla Khan retained his lands. He remained for some time longer under suspicion of disloyalty, and the Vizier and the British Resident both made repeated complaints against him, but Hastings refused to be moved. Eventually he negotiated a fresh arrangement with him which obviated all further grounds of distrust by eliminating the vague undertaking to supply "two thousand or three thousand men according to his ability." Faizulla Khan agreed to pay a lump sum of fifteen lakhs as commutation of the engagement to furnish military aid. And the story ends with the Governor-General acquitting him entirely of hostility or infidelity to the Company.

Hastings's extraordinary minute has caused a recent writer on the subject, Mr. P. E. Roberts, to declare: "Even at this distance of time the thought that a British administrator could have written such words arouses a flush of shame and it may safely be surmised that such a justification for charging a ruler with disaffection has never been offered before or since." [1][4] This may be perfectly true, but it would nevertheless be unfair to Hastings to let it be the last word. Though he undoubtedly behaved unjustly and ungenerously, his honor is not necessarily involved. In this minute he was obviously making an attempt—and a pitiful one it truly was—to save his face, to explain a course of action that could not be satisfactorily explained without the admission that he had blundered. The very fact that his explanation does not make sense is the most significant point about it, for Hastings was not given to writing nonsense. It was, indeed, too bad to be true, too factitious to be treated altogether seriously; and the blaze of indignation it evokes from Mr. Roberts is for that reason a little excessive.

When Hastings relinquished his trust he made the proud declaration, "the faith of treaties I have ever held inviolate." [5] It was his boast that he had sought to cultivate good relations with the native princes and had studied constantly how to gain their trust and respect and attach them as friends to the Company; he even claimed for himself a virtue superior in this respect to that of his predecessors. Hitherto, he said, the English had not had a friend in India: they had tricked and betrayed their allies: they had been despised, hated, envied, feared, never trusted. But *he* had set himself to change all that; *he* had seen the need of substituting the highest for the lowest standard of good faith and just dealing. And if a native prince was disaffected, *he* had first made sure that his own countrymen were not to blame and, if they were, he had sought to remove the cause of complaint—which is what he claimed to have done when he found that the bad faith of the Madras government had caused the Nizam of Hyderabad's hostility.

Those were his professions, and that they were not mere idle words is proved by the stand he had taken on the question of the retention of Gwalior. Under the treaty of alliance with the Rana of Gohud, the Bengal Government had agreed to deliver up the great for-

[1] Mr. Roberts's account of the episode omits several facts that help to place Hastings's conduct in a less unfavorable light, *e.g.* that Faizulla Khan had offered 2000 horse but only supplied 500, and that, according to the reports of the Company's officers, he had not adhered strictly to the terms of the treaty. He also ignores Hastings's emphatic statement that he never had any intentions of letting the Vizier evict Faizulla Khan.

tress to the Rana immediately upon its capture from the Marathas. But when Hastings proposed carrying out this pledge, he met with opposition on all sides. Francis and Wheler were against him, and Coote was vehemently so. In fact, said Hastings, all the English world were so proud of the conquest that they justified its retention with all manner of reasons. When the Rana became dissatisfied Hastings tried to conciliate him by assuring him that the English were only holding the fortress for his use and that he should have it in due course. But his soothing words produced no effect. And as the Rana's exasperation increased, so had the feeling against him grown at Calcutta. Hastings, however, had stood firm. "What title have we to his attachment?" he asked. "We have conquered for ourselves. We treat him with contempt. We withhold from him the rights which we ourselves had given him, and yet resent every symptom which he betrays, or which we choose to impute to him, of indisposition towards us. I never looked for so disinterested a character in the chief of any state or province, nor would it have excited my indignation so much as my compunction had he declared himself openly our enemy." Fearing for the damage that might be done to his government's reputation, he made it generally known that it was his firm determination to deliver Gwalior to the Rana, and eventually his influence prevailed over his colleagues. "I heartily wish," he said when closing his account of the episode, "that the law would declare it a felony to break treaties. Nothing would contribute more to the permanency of our influence." [6] Strong, convincing words like these would hardly have come from the mouth of a man who made it a practice himself to break treaties.

It would seem, then, that Warren Hastings's treatment of Faizulla Khan was not in keeping with the general tenor of his policy. Rather it would be fair to regard it as an aberration resulting from particular circumstance and a peculiarity in his own mental processes. He was—to repeat a statement already made—essentially a realist in politics. Not that he was not also an idealist, or that he ignored the sanctions of the moral law, but his idealism was so rooted in his realism that it had no separate existence; while nothing was more moral to him than his own purposes, disinterested and high-minded as they were. It was not that he claimed, or even thought of claiming, that the end justified the means, but that, knowing his ends to be right and in his eagerness to attain them, he adopted the means best suited to gaining them without always stopping long enough to gain a complete and objective view of the whole matter. Faizulla Khan had a good case—in law an unassailable case, but Hastings failed to see this because what possessed his mind at the time was not the precise terms of a contractual obligation but the pressing needs of the political situation. What he saw was that Faizulla Khan, like Chait Singh and the Vizier, had an equal interest with the Bengal Government in resisting invasion. They were mutually dependent; one weak link in the chain of defense might mean disaster to all. Therefore, if the war entailed for its success the putting forth of the greatest exertions, each ally should contribute to the utmost of his capacity to the common effort. He felt that he had a right to expect it and, if necessary, to demand it. Strict fulfillment of contractual obligations was not enough—under the circumstances it might even be deemed unfriendly. Was not each one of these princes enjoying the full benefit of the Company's protection? Why then, when the Company needed aid and the danger was common to all, should Faizulla Khan begrudge supplying three thousand cavalry (cavalry being the only arm that could be of use to the Company) when he had at least five thousand men—and it was commonly reported that he had considerably more—in his service? Could he refuse and still be considered loyal?

Francis once described Hastings's statecraft as "intricate," but it was not intricate to any one who took the trouble to study and understand the cut of his mind and the aims that prompted his actions. In this time of great crisis the safety of the state intrusted to his care obviously transcended in his mind other considerations, and if he had been free to do so, he would probably have acted still more vigorously on that conviction and paid even less heed to the obstructions of inferior law. The trammels of legality and the constant necessity of having to account for his every act to his colleagues in Council and to his employers always irked him, but he could not escape them. When he did follow the dictates of his own mind, he still had to justify what he did upon grounds which *they* would understand and improve. Thus it was in the case of Faizulla Khan. It was a pity that he did not frankly avow his reasons for charging the Rohilla with disloyalty instead of attempting the impossible dialectical feat of making his case against him square with the terms of the treaty, for that course led straight into a pit lined with sophistry and deceit; but why he did not do so is plain, assuming that the analysis of his mind here given is correct. He was caught on the horns of a dilemma: the measures that he considered essential to the existence of the empire conflicted in this instance with the precise terms of a treaty. He had to make a choice, and he naturally chose to safeguard the empire, but he dared not admit, perhaps not even to himself, that in so doing he had overstepped the bounds between legality and purely arbitrary action. Perhaps he did not realize the full significance of what he did; he may have been unaware of the existence of the dilemma. It would hardly be surprising if amidst the press of more important affairs and the weariness of mind and body that constantly assailed him he should have failed to understand the nature of the problem and the illogicality of his reasoning. The task of carrying on his shoulders the entire burden of government of an empire in travail was almost more than ordinary flesh and blood could bear.

II

THE same curious heedlessness to certain legal and moral aspects of his acts is revealed again in some of his financial transactions at this time, and particularly in his readiness to accept presents. The taking of presents from Indian princes and nobles had been one of the practices of the Company's servants during the early days of the Company's rule that had been most condemned at home. Clive had set the example when he accepted from Mir Jafar a princely reward for his king-making services, and it had been followed with alacrity by the gentlemen who succeeded him, despite the efforts of the Company to stop the practice. A big step towards its suppression had been taken by Parliament when in the Regulating Act it prohibited the whole service from the Governor-General downwards from accepting "directly or indirectly from any person on any account whatsoever any present or reward pecuniary or otherwise." But it weakened the force of this injunction by providing for forfeiture of all presents accepted and adding "that every such present or reward ... shall be deemed and construed to have been received ... for the sole use of the Company"; which clearly opened a loop-hole for diverse interpretation. Hastings seems not to have doubted that the Act left him at liberty to receive presents so long as he did so "for the sole use of the Company," and he did not hesitate during this period of grave financial difficulty to adopt this as one of his methods of raising money.

His acceptance of two lakhs from Chait Singh in 1780 is a glaring instance. They were unquestionably offered as a bribe, but Hastings disregarded that fact and took the money as though it were intended as a free gift to the Company, and had it paid into the treasury. Under similar circumstances, when he was without funds to pay the troops employed in suppressing the Benares insurrection, he accepted ten lakhs (£100,000) from the Vizier, again on the Company's behalf. He never attempted to justify either transaction except on the ground of the most pressing necessity, and it is difficult to see how they could have been justified on any other. Chait Singh certainly obtained no special favor from Hastings for his free-will offering, and the Vizier was already so overburdened with debt to the Company that the least that the Governor-General might in fairness have done would have been to accept the ten lakhs as a payment on account instead of as a present.

In the following February (1782) the Vizier offered Hastings another present of the same amount. This he at first refused, but then changed his mind, as he had done with Chait Singh's offer, telling the Resident at Lucknow that he would accept it on the Company's behalf "with a thankfulness equal to that which I should have felt and expressed for the gift had it been made to myself, the wants of the Company being at this time of equal concern to me as my own." [7] But when he learned that the Vizier still owed a big balance of debt to the Company, he did what he should have done the first time and withdrew his acceptance, declaring that he wanted nothing from the Vizier's bounty, when he was claiming so much as a right.

Hastings took considerable sums, also, from leading citizens of

Calcutta, sometimes as donations, sometimes as loans. When money was needed to protect Bengal from invasion by buying off the Berar army, and the treasury was empty, Hastings used his own private credit to borrow £30,000. In fact, as he said, wherever he could find allowable means of relieving the exigencies of his government he eagerly seized them, and he believed this to be an allowable means because Calcutta was full of wealthy Indian merchants whose pockets could not be reached by means of taxation. The motive might be goodwill, gratitude, hope for favors from government, but whatever it was Hastings felt no compunction about accepting the sums proffered. Most of the transactions were private, because Hastings knew that an Indian would give privately to him as his ruler where he would not give publicly to an impersonal government. As he had always been accustomed to personal rule this was natural, and proved nothing except that East and West had different conceptions of government: to the Indian, Warren Hastings, not the Company, was the ruler of Bengal, and the Company, if it meant anything at all to him, meant a strange, distant, shadowy body that in some incomprehensible way exercised authority. Hastings knew, too, that, if appealed to in the right way, no people could be more generous in their giving or more loyal in their attachment, as was to be proved again and conclusively in 1914 on the outbreak of the Great War. To suggest, as has sometimes been done, that these donations or loans could not have been made disinterestedly and could not properly be accepted by Hastings casts an unwarranted slur on the Indian character and implies that it is incapable of magnanimity in its dealings with its rulers. A more likely supposition is that many of the donors were moved by a genuine esteem for the Governor-General and welcomed the opportunity to help him in his hour of need. Some of them, too, may well have felt a desire to contribute towards the defense of their country.

That Hastings was in dire need of money is not open to question. He had been an able and resourceful financier from the moment that he became Governor and found that his first task was to disburden his government of a huge load of debt. Whatever else may be said of such measures as the withholding of the Mogul's tribute, the sale of the provinces of Kora and Allahabad, and the Rohilla expedition, they were of immense benefit to Bengal, serving to place it on a sound financial basis for the first time since the establishment of the Company's rule. In addition, he had made large retrenchments in the cost of government, increased the land revenue by progressive improvements in the system of administration, and found new sources of revenue by converting the salt and opium manufactures into valuable government monopolies. In 1781, for instance, besides extracting money from reluctant Begums and Rajahs, he reorganized the land revenue collection system, abolishing the Provincial Councils and District Collectors, as he had long wished to do, and appointing in their place a central committee of four at Calcutta, at an annual saving in expense of over

£500,000. Altogether he increased the revenue of Bengal from £2,000,-
000 to £5,000,000.[1]

And yet all this was not enough to carry his government through
the war, the reason being that it not only had to pay its own expenses
but those of Madras and Bombay as well. The two subordinate presidencies were not completely self-supporting even under normal conditions and had to be subsidized by Bengal. Bombay began to draw
heavily on Calcutta from the beginning of the Maratha War, and
Madras became a complete charge upon it as soon as Haidar Ali deprived it of its only source of revenue by conquering and laying waste
the Carnatic. Not only had Hastings's Government to maintain all the
armies that were fighting the Company's battles in every part of India,
but it had to provide supplies to keep the civil population of Madras
from starving. More than two and a half million pounds sterling were
drained out of the Calcutta treasury over a space of four years to meet
these demands. And all the time he had to go on providing rich cargoes
of Indian goods for his mercantile employers at home. To suspend
the investment altogether was something that he dared not do, however great his extremity, though once he was on the verge of doing
so. As a result, the civil service and the army were often in heavy
arrears of pay, and the public debt once more began to pile up. It was
a severe blow to Hastings's pride when he had to appeal for loans,
"the most mortifying act to me of my government, after having been
instrumental in discharging a former debt of one crore and a half
rupees (£1,500,000) and filling their treasuries with near double that
amount." [8] But the reservoir of wealth that could be tapped by
borrowing was small and chiefly confined to the European community.
The credit of his government was limited, and before long no more
could be borrowed and the value of the treasury notes declined, but he
refused to admit that this denoted a lack of confidence in his government; rather, he declared that it was due to a lack of means in the
small investing public.

When he came to survey his administration in retrospect he felt
he could be justly proud of his financial achievements. Not for a moment had the vital stream of gold—vital for supplying the sinews of
war—from Calcutta to the Company's governments and armies in other
parts of India been interrupted, despite the drain of the currency. Nor
was the stability of Bengal impaired. In February 1783 he confidently
declared that, given the necessary support, he could restore the province
to its former affluence and pay all its debts in two years of peace. [9]
When he left office the debts of every denomination amounted to little
more than £3,000,000, or slightly more than half the annual revenue,
which was, as he said, an inconsiderable charge upon the province's

---

[1] The actual figures were:

	Revenue	Expenditure
1772	£2,373,650	£4,705,279
1785	£5,315,197	£4,312,519

fixed resources. The attempts made by his enemies to fix the stigma of insolvency on the Calcutta treasury were, therefore, "too contemptible for argument." During the same period the British National Debt had been increased by £114,500,000 to nearly double what it was before.

"Were Lord Clive or Mr. Vansittart to awake from the dead, great as was the mind of the former and extensive as was the knowledge and ready the resources of the latter, and be told what great exertions had been made by Bengal during the past six years, and what was its actual state afterwards, neither of them would believe it possible." [10]

The note of self-gratulation was, perhaps, pardonable under the circumstances.

Hastings's enemies concentrated their efforts on trying to prove that in accepting the presents his intention was to pocket the money, that he did not divulge the transactions to his employers until forced to by fear of discovery, and that most of the money never reached the Company's treasury but remained in his pocket. They failed in their attempt, but what they did succeed in proving is no less interesting as a revelation of the man's character. They produced a multitude of facts regarding the way in which he treated these transactions, which were easily susceptible of the worst interpretation. He was extremely secretive about them, so much so that not even his best friends, let alone his colleagues in Council, knew what he was doing. He was reluctant to give full information to the Court of Directors, and tried to pass the transactions off as matters of no importance. Five months elapsed before he officially informed the Court of Chait Singh's present, and then he did not reveal its origin; he merely said that the money was not his own, but had been accepted by him for the public use. It should, however, not be forgotten that he did at once send Laurence Sulivan, who had just been reëlected Chairman of the Company, a full statement, adding:

"I believe I shall communicate this fact to the Court of Directors; but if I do not, I give you permission to make what use of the above relation of it you think proper, declaring upon my honor that I never will reclaim the money, and that I disclaim any title to it, as I should not have taken it but for and on the occasion which induced me to receive it, or one similar to it." [11]

When the Court demanded a complete statement of receipts he delayed making one until after he returned home and then declared that he could not recall all the details. His accounts were confusing and showed a complete lack of care in their keeping. He had difficulty in proving that every rupee that he had accepted had actually been paid over to the Company. Indeed, an extraordinary casualness marked every part of his conduct, and his enemies naturally inferred that he was trying to cover up his dishonesty.

Hastings was a man to whom money personally meant little,

especially when weighed in the balance against the really important ends of life. While a man was in mid-career it was not something that he should struggle and sweat to get and to keep. Unlike so many of the men who went to India in his day he was not just a fortune-hunter. We see his colleagues Barwell and Francis counting their rapidly growing piles of gold, counting also the days when the pile would reach the desired size, and exulting in the fact that service in India meant a comfortable independency for life. We see many of their successors doing the same—even Thomas Babington Macaulay; there was nothing necessarily dishonorable about it; they could give good and honest service and still return home with a useful saving. But we do not see Hastings doing it, though his inducement was fully as strong; even Francis admitted he was not avaricious and was careless with his money. Before he became Governor he by necessity followed the usual practice and made his livelihood by legitimate private trading, but whereas most of his fellows were inclined to give more of their attention to their private interests than to the interests of the Company, he very definitely reversed the order, and the result was that he did not grow rich. A year after he became Governor he wrote to his friend Sykes:

"If I was to lose my government today, I should leave it a poorer man than when I assumed it. Some addition I made to my fortune at Madras, if I recover all I left behind me there. There I had some leisure to attend to my own affairs, and you will stare when I tell you that my books were balanced to the month preceding my departure, and my cash account closed to the very day of it." [12]

From this time on any pretension he may have had to being a good economist in his own interest vanished, and for many years he probably neither knew nor cared greatly how his own finances stood. As Governor-General in receipt of a huge salary, he must have felt with a sense of relief that he no longer needed to give a thought to money.

Lord Wellesley, when he held the same office saved half his salary, despite his taste for magnificence and ostentation. Hastings, paradoxically, saved little, though his personal tastes were simple. And the reason is that what he saved on himself he spent doubly in other ways. An indulgent husband, he must have spent a small fortune in decking his wife with the diamonds she so notoriously loved. As a host, his hospitality was boundless; he kept open house for all who came to Calcutta on business or on pleasure. As an alms-giver, it was said of him that he never kept a half-crown in his pocket if a poor man wanted it. As the possessor of many needy relatives he was spending hundreds of pounds a year providing for them and their wants. When a young cousin died penniless, leaving him as a legacy his debts, his native wife and his two children, Hastings paid the debts, provided for the wife and daughter and sent the boy to be educated in England at his expense. Among his pensioners were the two daughters of his first wife, his sister, Mrs. Woodman, an aunt, Mrs. Elizabeth Hastings, an aged uncle, Mr. Warren, and that uncle's sister, Mrs. Turner, and the daughter of another uncle, Mrs. Hammond. Indeed, according to Miss Hilda Gregg ("Sydney C. Grier"), who made herself particularly familiar with this side of Hastings's life,

"if Hastings spent little upon himself, his letters leave us in no doubt that he was surrounded by as eager a throng of harpies as ever preyed upon any public man. The majority of his relatives were in poor circumstances, and fully appreciated their good fortune in possessing, as it were, a private gold mine in him." [13]

Nor was he preyed upon only by members of his own family. In his character of a supposedly wealthy and kindly philanthropist his help was besought by all and sundry; sometimes the demands were made only on his time and sympathy, but frequently they were made on his pocket, and in each instance they were seldom denied. Hastings was regarded, and no doubt liked to regard himself, as a kind of foster-father or "big brother" to the whole English community in Bengal. Generous to a fault, he paid little heed to the worldly-wise counsels of his friends, who constantly advised him to attend to his fortune and not to come home poor. [14]

He found yet other ways of spending his £25,000 salary. A man's money is apt to follow his heart. Hastings's heart was in his work, and he thought nothing of using his salary to further some pet project that he had initiated outside the scope of his official duties. Instances of this were the financing of the pundits that compiled the digest of Hindu law and the founding of the Madrassi College.[1] He identified himself so completely with the interests of the Company and of Bengal that it did not occur to him to draw a clear dividing line between the money that was his personal property and that which belonged to the Company. He used both alike as the public interest demanded. What did it matter, therefore, whether the presents that he received were paid into his account or into the Company's? What did it matter whether he made an exact accounting of them to his employers? Was it not sufficient that he did not take the money for his own personal use?

His intense concentration on the great task of saving British India was nearly his undoing, because it caused him to pay less attention to appearances than is usual, and desirable, for a man in his position. The wise man in public life takes the utmost pains to keep his financial affairs, both public and private, in such perfect order that they may, at a moment's notice, pass the closest scrutiny; he avoids the slightest appearance of evil. Alexander Hamilton by putting that sound maxim into practice was able instantly to confound his enemies. Hastings was singularly deficient in that kind of wisdom. His friends agreed that he was "uncommonly regardless of money and uniformly negligent and inattentive to all monetary transactions." Entirely honest and incorruptible, as no one who has studied his character denies, he experienced the

[1] See Chapter XXV.

greatest difficulty when put on trial in actually *proving* his innocence to hostile or doubting minds. That he was not altogether blind to appearances is shown by his evident desire to avoid publicity for his transactions, and especially his efforts to keep them secret from those who would be likely to place the worst construction upon them. That is why he privately gave his friend Sulivan the facts about Chait Singh's present, but withheld them from the Council and from the Court of Directors. But the inevitable result was that when the facts did come out his accusers were able to use his secretiveness as a strong point against him. *Prima facie,* their case was strong, and the cynics no doubt greeted with derision Hastings's naïve and priggish reply: "Attentive only to provide for the pressing exigencies of the State, I did not reflect on an interpretation which might be put on my actions so totally foreign to the purity of their motives." [15] *O sancta simplicitas!* Yet those who knew him knew that it was true. In his whole-hearted devotion to the service of the State, he acted with a kind of childlike simplicity that reckoned not with the opinions of a cold and skeptical world, long accustomed to the spectacle of corruption and dishonesty in high places, and, most of all, in the Company's service.

The day came when Hastings suddenly awoke to the unpleasant realization that his retirement was in sight without his having accumulated any kind of fortune to meet it. He reacted to the knowledge in a way that made his friends regret that he had previously been so improvident and gave his enemies a chance to blaspheme. In 1783 he was, according to his own statement, unable to draw his salary for a space of several months and, finding himself as a result in need of money, he borrowed £30,000 from one of the leading native merchants of Calcutta, a certain Nobkissen. Nobkissen desired him to accept the money as a gift, but he declined and gave him bonds for the amount. The money, however, was never paid back. Hastings first decided to accept it as a gift to the Company, and then, shortly before his retirement, wrote to the Directors asking their permission to appropriate the sum to his own use to cover certain public expenses that he had incurred out of his own pocket, not intending at the time to charge them to their account, but which he now found himself unable to bear. (He had in mind those special enterprises of his, the missions to Tibet, the financing of the pundits and the founding of the Madrassi College.) The Company assented to his request.

Even his staunchest friends could not approve this transaction; not even Lord Thurlow, who admitted, when the matter was debated by the House of Lords, that it reflected discredit on him, as a man with his position and salary should never need to borrow money. "I think it is the weak part of his character." [16]

Another similar request of Hastings is equally difficult to justify. He asked the Court of Directors to give back to him as a token of its approval the £100,000 that the Vizier had given him at Chunar, and he never seemed to entertain the slightest doubt of the justice of his claim and the unfairness of having it rejected. Apparently his idea was that as the Company was a commercial body and he by his efforts at Chunar had improved its finances so greatly he was entitled to a special reward or bonus. He admitted that the request might be thought "extraordinary: indiscreet by my friends and presumptuous by my enemies—at least they will affect to think so. But," he said, "I am neither a prude nor a hypocrite." [17] After its rejection he made a virtue of the fact that he had not taken this, and other similar gifts, for his own use. He said that he had altogether provided the Company by private means with twenty-eight lakhs: "The whole of this sum might have been mine; and what a lesson have the Directors preached to others, by telling me that I had no right to do otherwise than I have done!" He was so disgusted by what he considered the ingratitude of his employers that he said he would refuse to accept any offer of an annuity that they might make instead, no matter how poor he might be. [18] No doubt his sense of grievance was aroused because he knew that scores of men occupying positions in the Company's service much inferior to his had enriched themselves beyond the dreams of avarice by various dubious means and without asking their employers' leave, whereas he, who had served them faithfully for thirty years and from whose services they had benefited the most, was about to return home a comparatively poor man, having kept his hands clean. He overlooked the fact that a man drawing a salary like his has scarcely a right to claim more, no matter what the circumstances may be.

Upon his return to England Hastings made to the Court of Directors a statement of his financial position. He said that at no period of his life had he possessed more than £100,000. When it was that he possessed this amount, he did not state. His fortune but slightly exceeded £80,000 when he retired. The smallness of this sum, by comparison with the money-making efforts of his colleagues, is eloquent testimony both to his integrity and his thriftlessness. His friends were quite shocked that he had allowed so much money to slip through his fingers. Lord Thurlow declared that he ought to have left Bengal fairly and honorably possessed of £400,000 from the known and allowed emoluments of his office and the accumulating interest upon his fortune.[1] [19] His enemies first refused to believe him and then tried to comfort themselves with the theory —first stated by Francis—that he must have spent his fabulous millions in bribes to obtain support for his abominable policy. The one thing they could not give him credit for was that of being different from themselves and different from the Nabobs who were flaunting their wealth in every county in England.

---

[1] Comparative scale of Indian fortunes: Clive's, probably well over £1,000,000, with a known income of £45,000; Barwell's, estimated at £800,000 after twenty-four years' service; Francis's, at least £80,000 after six years; Macaulay's, £25,000 (estimate) after three and a half years. If Hastings had saved half his salary, as Wellesley without any difficulty did, his fortune would easily have amounted to £200,000. Francis's and Macaulay's salaries were only two-fifths of Hastings's.

Chapter XX

SUPPORT FROM HOME

I

AFTER six months' absence Hastings was back in Calcutta again. Disappointing as his trip had been, it had yielded one solid achievement which had gone far to compensate him for the Benares fiasco. He had succeeded in detaching Sindhia from the hostile coalition and making peace with him. Bengal was now safe from invasion. The fight still raged in the Carnatic and a state of war still existed with the Poona Regency Government, but one more milestone on the road leading to a general peace had now been passed.

He had especial cause for satisfaction because of the effect the news would have on his own uncertain fortunes. Though peace was the object of his whole policy, he was being depicted at home as a thorough-going imperialist who had brought about the present war for the sake of conquest. The accusation cut him to the quick. "Let me conjure you to believe," he wrote to Macpherson, the new member of Council, "and I call God to witness my truth, that I seek for nothing but peace as the end and design of all my pursuits." And, again:

"As to myself, I can lay my hand to my heart, and can declare, as I would at the altar of God, that in all my dealings with public states and provinces I have observed the principles of truth and good faith as sacredly as I would, and as I have ever observed them with individuals.

"The war with the Marathas was not my war; but begun without my knowledge, and with a design adverse to my government; I have only supported it, and in the most vigorous prosecution of it have aimed at peace, and contributed more effectually to the attainment of it than I could possibly have done either by the most unbounded or the most guarded submissions.

"I am determined to bring about a peace; but I must use for this end the weapons which I can trust, which I can manage, and which I have hitherto practiced. I will throw away the sword before those who appear unarmed before us: I will keep it sheathed in the presence of those who are yet undecided; and I will hold it with the alternative of peace or destruction to those who are armed against us with threats of the latter, and rejection of the former. This is not a time to temporize. If my superiors, and the whole people of England in a body join in proscribing this system of policy, and in exclaiming 'Peace, peace, peace!', with a host of enemies assailing us, I must either persist in my own line, and you and Mr. Wheler must unite with me in it; or I must yield up my place, and trust to that providence or fortune which has hitherto wrought miracles for our deliverance, for our future salvation." [1]

The next step was to obtain, through Sindhia's mediation, an extension of the peace so as to include the Poona government and the rest of the Maratha Confederacy, with the additional object of an alliance against Haidar Ali. The proposed basis of negotiation was to be a mutual restoration of conquests, for, in order to end the war, Hastings was willing to sacrifice every inch of ground won, not excepting Bassein (the port adjoining Bombay that had been coveted so long by that government). "Reserve Bassein if you can," he instructed his envoy, Anderson. "But do not insist on the reservation of Bassein to the hindrance of peace." And, he added, "You may consent to yield what is ours, and what we can in honor grant, but we will never suffer our treaties to be infringed, nor our faith to be violated." [2]

Meanwhile, the war in the Carnatic was pursuing its slow, heartbreaking course. Sir Eyre Coote had been able to resume operations in June, and on July 1 he had won an important, but indecisive, victory at Porto Novo. The difficulties with which he was contending remained still the same, and formed the subject of a constant stream of complaints to the Bengal Government—lack of transport and provisions, weakness in cavalry, big arrears of pay for the troops, frequent desertions among the sepoys, lowered prestige, inferiority of numbers. "A day's rice, more or less," he said in one of his reports, "may decide the fate of the British Empire in India." But he gallantly grappled with them all and refused to admit defeat or failure. He formed a junction with Pearse's Bengal force (greatly reduced in numbers after being visited by the first outbreak of cholera known in India) after a forced march of one hundred and fifty miles with an army daily diminishing in strength owing to sickness, but even when thus reinforced he still could do little more than act on the defensive, for more men meant more mouths to feed. A second, and then a third, battle was fought, each ending the same way—in tactical victories merely.

At length, the breaking of the monsoon ended the campaign and Coote retired into cantonments near Madras, leaving his antagonist still master of the Carnatic. The veteran soldier's health was completely shattered. After being compelled to retire to his bed for a long spell, he announced his intention of resigning his command and returning to Bengal, as therein he felt lay his only hope of recovery. But before he could do so, Haidar suddenly resumed the offensive, attacked the British garrisons and compelled Coote to leave his sick-bed and place himself once more at the head of his army. Three days later the General was found sense-

less in his tent, seized with a stroke of apoplexy. For hours no hope was
entertained of his life and the utmost dismay prevailed on the English
side. The government urged his immediate return, "for the preservation
of a life so valuable to the State." Yet a day later, having come to his
senses, he had himself placed in a palanquin, and so led on the army again;
the besieged garrison whose relief was the object of his march was
reached and relieved on the very day that its commander had fixed for
the absolute end of his resistance.

II

A NEW figure of importance had recently appeared on the Indian scene.
The home authorities had given Madras a new governor. To Warren
Hastings all events of this sort were matters of great concern. Was
the new arrival to prove a friend or a foe? Clavering, Monson, Francis,
Wheler—all enemies—and now Lord Macartney. Judging from what his
friends told him he had this time no cause for alarm, because the intention of Lord Macartney's appointment was to support him and bring
harmony into the relations between their respective governments. And
that was Macartney's avowed intention when he left England. Clearly
something must have happened at home to make this possible. For it was
the first time since the passing of the Regulating Act that Ministers of
the Crown had given their representative in India any support at all.
What had caused the change of policy?

It would have been a little strange if ministers had acted from a
pure sense of duty and patriotism, for they—that is, these particular
ministers—had scarcely been known to act from such motives. Lord
North required a more potent reason. And it is not difficult to see what
it was. The game was going against him; his majority in Parliament
was steadily dwindling. More votes in the House of Commons—that
was his reason.

Things at home were really in a very bad way. The nation was
shocked by its military failures in America, discouraged by the appearance of half of Europe in hostile array against it, appalled by the pros-
pective loss of command of the sea after a hundred years of maritime
supremacy, and disgusted by the ineptitude and venality of its leaders.
No reassurance could be found by looking to the national government,
for the Ministry, tottering towards its inglorious end, possessed a head
who, instead of being the natural prop of popular confidence, was vainly
imploring his sovereign to grant him release from his insupportable
responsibilities. Even the kind of majority that eighteenth-century ministers were accustomed to obtain for their governments was not proof
against the tide of events. There comes a time, in moments of national
disaster, when such properties as offices, pensions, commissions, contracts, titles, lose their hold on men's votes and what was thought to be
solid mortar dissolves into sand.

Lord North himself, though heartily tired of office, was loyal yet to his royal master, whose fortunes as a would-be personal monarch were dependent on his minister's success, and he was frantically clutching at straws to maintain himself in power. Wistfully now he looked towards the East. No longer bored by the mere mention of India, he perceived that the dreary record of failure in the West, which was responsible for his Ministry's undoing, might conceivably even yet be redeemed by success in that other quarter, and he was bound to admit that no one was more likely to obtain that success than the man whose removal he had tried so hard to effect. If this proved to be so, he would be glad to share the glory if the resulting political profit could be his. Warren Hastings had become in fact one of his straws. There were other good reasons, besides, for his decision to show Hastings some countenance. The Governor-General was no longer without powerful supporters in the House of Commons. Without any management on his part he had become the beneficiary of the kind of votes that the Minister was willing to sell his political soul to win.

The history of this particular group in the House of Commons and its strange and incongruous connection with Warren Hastings is one of the curiosities of that time. The most corrupt influence of the day in English politics, the evil in its most dangerous form against which Chatham, Burke and other custodians of English liberties had been inveighing, the worst of the many bad fruits of British Imperialism in India —were all represented in this group. The men who formed it were corruption's and rapacity's finest flower, the most successful of the scoundrels that were wringing their wealth out of a people's sufferings and a country's ruin. The source of their wealth was the Carnatic, where the system of "double government," with all the abuses that it involved, had outlasted its counterpart in Bengal which Hastings had swept away. By working in collusion with the native ruler, the vicious and despicable Nawab Mohamed Ali, from their posts in the Company's service at Madras, aiding and abetting his nefarious schemes for personal aggrandizement, making him large loans of money at usurious rates of interest on the security of the mortgaged revenues of his lands, and rack-renting the helpless tenants to obtain payment, they had amassed enormous fortunes. If in the process the Company's interests had been outrageously betrayed, the British name dishonored, the terrible wrath of "the Lion of Mysore" aroused, and the miserable people of the Carnatic subjected to the foulest oppression, it was no more than could be expected. Having built up by these means a most profitable investment, they were naturally interested in protecting it, so they had turned their attention homewards. Their partner in crime, the Nawab, had for some time maintained a powerful "lobby" at Westminster, whose efforts to influence British policy had not been unavailing. Now his creditors joined forces with him. Their leader, Paul Benfield, whose own profits are said to have amounted to £500,000, bought his way into Parliament in 1780, and eight of his fellows similarly found seats within a few years. It was a simple matter for them also to buy sufficient India stock

to give them an influential voice in the affairs of the Company, and
Benfield's right-hand man soon obtained election as a Director. At once
their influence became considerable. Edmund Burke might declaim
against them and everything that they stood for with all the power of
his magnificent invective—as witness his speech on "the Nabob of
Arcot's Debts"—but he could not prevent their obtaining in the end
what they had entered Parliament to get. A few years later Henry
Dundas, the President of the Board of Control for India in Pitt's cabinet, obligingly put through Parliament a resolution charging Mohamed
Ali's debts, amounting to £5,000,000, to the depleted revenues of a ruined
country, without any inconvenient examination into their history.[1] ...
How was it that such men as these became connected in any shape or
manner with Warren Hastings? What was the unlikely link between
them? The question clamors for an answer.

The link was a man whom Hastings had lately made his agent in
England. It has often been remarked how unfortunate Hastings was in
the men whom he chose to represent him at home. There was Macleane,
honest but seemingly not too intelligent; there was later to be Major
John Scott, a tactless, over-zealous busybody. And now there was John
Macpherson, energetic, able, amiable—but scarcely honest and not in
the least loyal. His record was decidedly against him. He had entered
the Company's service by back-stairs' influence and at Madras had
attached himself to Mohamed Ali's interest. For his conduct there he
had been dismissed by the Governor, Lord Pigot, and had returned to
London as the agent of the infamous Nawab, in close alliance with
Benfield and his gang of creditors. Hastings's friendship with him had
sprung from their association together at Madras when Hastings was
second in Council. The Governor-General cannot be suspected of any
part in the financial operations of Macpherson's friends or concern in
their political intrigues, but he was not ill-disposed to Mohamed Ali and
gladly availed himself of Macpherson's offer to represent him at home
at the same time as he was representing the Nawab.

The Benfield group supplied Lord North with valuable votes. In
exchange Macpherson obtained for Hastings a little, and quite shortlived, ministerial support, which was made evident in several ways. The
Regulating Act was kept in force—and Warren Hastings retained as
Governor-General. The Court of Directors, quick to respond to the hand
at the helm, changed its course. Laurence Sulivan was reinstated as
Director and Deputy Chairman. And when selections were made to fill
vacancies in the governing Councils of the Presidencies, the appointments were given to men thought likely to support the Governor-General.
Macpherson had himself nominated to fill Barwell's place; John Stables
was later appointed to Francis's; and Lord Macartney was made Governor of Madras.

---

[1] Paul Benfield, "Count Rupee," as the caricaturists dubbed him, came, one is
not sorry to find, to an evil end. He lost his ill-gotten fortune in unlucky speculation and died, a pauper, in Paris.

III

IT is at this point that Edmund Burke steps to the front of our stage. But with what a change of face does he come! We have hitherto been dimly aware of him as a fervent champion of the East India Company's rights, spending his eloquence in demonstrating that the Company was independent of the control of Parliament. Now he has changed his uniform and his flag. Now he is the enemy of the Company and the reviler of all its works.

Burke was the supreme luminary of his age, shedding a sublime light on its great political questions, a source of wisdom, uplift and new life to a country acutely in need of all three. But there were spots on the face of this sun that dim the radiance of its beams. The splendor of his advocacy of the American Cause is diminished by the fact that he was the paid agent of New York. His change of face on the Indian question invites the query, was he sincere in either attitude? Or, if only in one, which one? No man can be really convincing when he has been guilty of such a glaring and unexplained inconsistency.

There were other spots, too, visible but not even now fully understood. Edmund had a brother named Richard and a kinsman named William, and the three lived together in the closest intimacy and were generally known as "the Burkes." William was Edmund's "dearest, oldest, best friend" since boyhood, and he was the first of the trio to "make good." Their common friend and patron was Lord Verney, who is chiefly known to fame as a gambler and a wastrel. Another intimate friend was "Secretary" Lachlan Macleane, second cousin to Hastings's agent. A land speculator, interested in Grenada and the West Indies, and a big gambler, he also was a thoroughly disreputable character and a strange bedfellow for the noble Edmund.[1] Until the year 1768 Edmund Burke was financially worth nothing, but in the spring of that year he bought a large country estate at Beaconsfield and paid over £20,000 for it, and thenceforth, though always in financial difficulties, out of which his wealthy, aristocratic friends had frequently to help him, he lived the life of a country gentleman and dispensed wide and lavish hospitality. "The Burkes" at this time were adventurers of poor repute among their contemporaries. They gambled in Indian stocks and made a small fortune and it was a matter of common report that they were

---

[1] It is quite time that the mistake of identifying the Lachlan Macleane who was Hastings's agent with the Lachlan Macleane who was a well-known member of the political underworld of London and Lord Shelburne's secretary, should be corrected. Miss Stuart Sutherland (*op. cit. English Historical Review,* July 1934, p. 482) follows Mr. Namier in making the error (L. B. Namier, *England in the Age of the American Revolution,* 1930, p. 316). My authority for making the correction is Major V. C. P. Hodson, the compiler of *The List of the Officers of the Bengal Army,* 1758-1834, publication of which is in progress. At the time, 1759, when Macleane "the secretary" was, according to Mr. Namier, a doctor in America, Macleane "the agent" was, according to Major Hodson, a captain in the Bengal Army, and when the former was appointed governor of the West Indian island of St. Martin, the latter was a major and still in India. The two second cousins seem to have been afterwards in England at the same time, but in 1772 "the agent" was

engaged in stock jobbing. By some they were even referred to as "knaves" and their methods as "chicanery." The year following Edmund's purchase of Beaconsfield—and at a time when he was a proprietor of the East India Company—there came the big collapse of Indian stock, and "the Burkes" met with disaster. Lord Verney and Macleane were ruined, Richard and William never recovered from their losses, and Edmund and Richard between them owed Verney £25,000. William had indeed to flee the country to escape the many heavy judgements recorded against him in the courts. In 1777 he suddenly sailed for Madras bearing a letter from Edmund recommending him to Philip Francis: "Let Bengal protect a spirit and a rectitude which are no longer tolerated in England," was Edmund's euphemistic way of explaining matters. In other words, worthy William was in search of "present and certain advantage." While in India he became agent for the Rajah of Tanjore, the bitter enemy of the Nawab of Arcot. (It is not a little significant, as possibly explaining to some extent Edmund Burke's animosity to Hastings, that whereas his dearest friend was agent for Tanjore both Hastings's agents, Macleane and Macpherson, acted in a similar capacity for Mohamed Ali, so that inevitably Hastings was involved in the enmity against the Nawab.) William and Richard Burke, Lord Verney and Macleane were all declared defaulters to an enormous amount on their Indian stock, and subsequently Lord Verney filed a bill in Chancery against Edmund, alleging that he had refused to defray his share of their joint losses—but Edmund remained for the rest of his life the master of his costly establishment at Beaconsfield for which he had paid over £6000 in cash—the rest came from mortgages—though at the time he is not known to have possessed more than a few pounds of his own. The implication, of course, is that he borrowed money from Verney for speculative purposes, won, and invested his winnings in his estate, then lost—and found himself unable to repay the original loan. Among the other friends from whom he borrowed large sums of money from time to time, running into thousands of pounds, were Lord Rockingham, Lord Holland, David Garrick and Sir Joshua Reynolds. And as a somewhat natural consequence to all this, we are told that throughout his life he was an object of deep suspicion both to his friends and his enemies and the victim of much calumny.[3]

These are the seamier facts of his life, whatever light they may be thought to shed upon his motives. It is disturbing—to say the least—to

reappointed to the Company's service as Lieutenant Colonel and Commissary General of Bengal.

Apparently the first, and altogether the most complete and surprising confusion of them was that made in 1783 by Capt. J. Price in his *Some Observations and Remarks on a late Publication entitled "Travels in Europe, Asia and Africa"* (a work written by William Mackintosh and generally attributed, at least in inspiration, to Philip Francis) where the author claims to have been "an intimate friend of the famous Col. Macleane not unknown in the ministry of Lord Shelburne and so much exposed by his newspaper correspondence with John Wilkes, Esq.," and yet speaks of his "most shameful betrayal" of Hastings! Captain Price was also, it would seem, in error in stating that Colonel Macleane was drowned at sea on board H.M.S. *Swallow* on returning again from India.

find one pot of gold at the foot of his numerous rainbows, even though no connection can be shown to exist between the two. And it would certainly be better for his reputation if he were not known by his friends. Any man who could be on terms of intimate friendship with two such unpleasing characters as William Burke and Philip Francis lays himself open to serious doubts regarding his fitness to judge men and measures—even, possibly, the absolute integrity of his character.

Burke's deplorable friendship with Francis particularly stands in need of explanation. It can scarcely be defended; can it be extenuated? Perhaps it can, if we remember that Francis looked out upon the world with two faces—the one that he turned to his enemies and political opponents, and the one that he turned to his friends. To the latter he was a man of strong but generous passions and rigid principles, an enemy of tyranny, meanness and corruption and a friend of justice and liberty, a kind and generous man, full of fine public spirit and not lacking in personal charm—all in all, a very fine and likable fellow, not at all unlike Burke himself. Above all, Francis was a Whig, and Burke, a strong party man, loved men of his own party. Unquestionably, too, Francis's antecedents stood him in very good stead with Burke. They were both Irish adventurers who had started out in life without fortune or what the world considered family. This fact alone was enough to recommend him to the sympathetic and warm-hearted Burke, whose own problem of winning recognition for himself from the *haut monde* of London had been the same as Francis's. Thus there was a solid basis for friendship between them. But it was Burke's great weakness that he could not put the proper bounds to his friendships. Lacking discrimination in his choice of friends he lacked also the power to retain independence of thought and judgement. So the way was prepared in advance for the great tragedy of his utter surrender to Philip Francis in all that appertained to the affairs of India.

One further fact needs to be noted. It is disturbing not being able to feel that we know the full facts about Burke's close connection with Indian affairs. Too much is buried in obscurity for one to have an entirely easy mind. All that is known for certain is that in 1768 he was a shareholder of the Company, in 1769 he suffered heavy losses, in 1772 he was offered an important place in the Bengal Government, which he declined, in 1773 he defended Clive and revealed his strange dislike of Hastings, between that date and 1780 he developed his equally strange friendship with Francis, whose views and ideas he absorbed bodily, and through his kinsman William and his questionable financial interests in Tanjore was led into taking an active part against Mohamed Ali and all who were in any way allied with him.

If the causes of Burke's Indian apostasy are obscure, its consequences to Warren Hastings are glaringly evident. He had gained some support for his policies but only at a fearful price. For whereas the friendship of Lord North was to last only for a day, the enmity of Edmund Burke was to last a lifetime.

IV

LORD MACARTNEY arrived at Madras in June 1781. He was a nobleman of rank, reputation and ability who had rendered distinguished service to his country both as a diplomat and as a colonial administrator, and he was happy in possessing the favor of the King and the support of influential members of both political parties. The intention of his appointment was that he should coöperate closely with the Governor-General and support his policies. But it was a lamentable and stupid blunder to select for this purpose a man drawn from outside the ranks of the Company's indentured servants and possessing advantages of rank and influence that the man under whom he was to serve lacked. If it was a step forward towards a decent standard of government in India to break with precedent and appoint to the highest posts men of public rank and of absolute integrity, common sense demanded that the new policy should be begun at the top. The stigma attaching to Warren Hastings that he was merely a servant of the Company, undistinguished by any mark of honor from the Crown, could have been, and surely should have been, removed. The least that a wise government could have done would have been to raise him to the peerage, giving him a rank equal to—or better, superior to—that of the man they had chosen to serve in a subordinate capacity. But political prejudice and blindness prevented this. So Warren Hastings was given a colleague who was full of pride, obstinate, opinionated, and resentful of dictation, and, if it be remembered how intent Hastings was upon extending his control over the subordinate presidencies until the authority of the superior government became supreme, it will be obvious that the ground was well prepared for a conflict, despite the excellent intentions with which Macartney set out for India. If additional provocation were needed it was provided by the failure of the Regulating Act to define the jurisdictions of the respective governments and to determine the exact amount of control vested in the Governor-General-in-Council.

Macartney experienced an initial shock immediately upon arrival. For between the retribution for past misconduct that was being exacted by Haidar Ali, on the one hand, and the measures taken by Hastings to save it, on the other, the government over which he was about to preside had ceased almost entirely to function. Not only had the Governor-General suspended the acting Governor and divested the Council of the conduct of the war, but he had also assumed the direction of British relations with Nawab Mohamed Ali. It had long been his wish to exercise the authority of his government to straighten out the Nawab's tangled relations with Madras and to regulate them by a formal treaty; [4] but no opportunity for his interference had presented itself until Haidar Ali's onslaught laid bare the utter helplessness and incompetence of the Madras authorities and the appalling state of the Nawab's finances. When the Nawab declared himself insolvent and unable to contribute anything to the cost of a war that was as much his affair as it was the Company's, he automatically, in Hastings's opinion, relinquished his claim to be considered the sole proprietor of a country whose fate depended entirely on the British arms and whose greater part lay in the enemy's hands, and rendered it indispensably necessary and just for the Company to obtain from him the transfer of all his revenues in exclusive assignment for the expenses of the war. So Hastings had entered into direct negotiations with the Nawab and, two months before Macartney's arrival, succeeded in arranging a provisional treaty with him, subject to the Company's approval, by which the revenues were assigned to the Company for the duration of the war, with an acknowledgement of the Nawab's sovereign rights. [5]

For a short time comparative harmony reigned between the two Governors, notwithstanding the fact that Macartney carried Hastings's policy far beyond anything that Hastings had contemplated or desired by negotiating a transfer to himself of the Nawab's sovereign rights in their entirety. He assured the Governor-General of his desire for confidence and friendship and promised his coöperation, and Hastings in turn was conciliatory. It soon, however, became clear that his idea of coöperation differed materially from Hastings's in that it did not imply unquestioning obedience. In fact he at once began to lecture Hastings in a very pompous and tactless manner on the defects of his policy, as tending to diminish the authority of the Madras Government. [6]

At first Hastings was disposed to approve Macartney's plans, agreeing with him that Madras should assume and exercise the entire and undivided administration of the revenues. But the arch-intriguer, Mohamed Ali, soon began to make trouble. His aim was to evade carrying out the assignment agreement, and his method was one that he had employed successfully before: the playing off of the Supreme Government against the subordinate in such a way as was bound to provoke discord between them. With his usual shrewdness he chose as his tool Sir Eyre Coote, the vain, irascible, troublesome meddler in politics, making a flattering offer to vest him with all the powers of his government. Coote, foolishly dazzled by the prospect of greater power and importance, succumbed to the bait. Instead of flatly rejecting the suggestion, he dallied with it. The result was that when news of the intrigue reached Macartney, his suspicions were aroused and a violent quarrel between him and the General followed. When Coote reported the offer to the Bengal Government, Hastings saw at once that the grant would conflict with the Nawab's agreement with Macartney and forbade him to accept it.

Other forces of intrigue were also at work in Mohamed Ali's behalf: Paul Benfield (who was back in India again bearing letters of introduction from North and Robinson) and his friends, and John Macpherson, the new member of the Bengal Council and late agent for His Highness. A good understanding between the two Governors would have rendered their efforts fruitless, but this did not exist. Hastings and Macartney were already drifting apart. Hastings accused Macartney of betraying his confidence to his enemies at home, and although Macartney wrote to him protesting his innocence, he could not undo the mischief, as Hastings had given credence to rumors that the Governor of Madras was grooming himself to be his successor at Calcutta. And the result was an immediate end to all pretensions of friendship between them. In the production of this unfortunate misunderstanding John Macpherson had played his own dishonorable part as the faithless friend to both men. In pursuit of his own selfish ambition he deliberately betrayed each in turn, holding back from Hastings Macartney's letters protesting his innocence, and allying himself with Coote to bring pressure to bear on Hastings against Macartney. [7] This combination of the two most influential members of his Council could not help but weigh strongly with the Governor-General.

The quarrel thus engendered soon found fresh fuel to feed on. When Hastings dispatched Sir Eyre Coote to Madras, he had entrusted him with the supreme command of the army, the direction of the military operations, and the spending of the public funds remitted from Bengal. In other words, he had virtually suspended the discredited Madras Government, following the precedent established by Clive and Watson in 1756 when they went from Madras to rescue their confrères of Calcutta. The arrival of a new governor at Madras did not alter his attitude. He told Macartney plainly that, as the whole financial burden of the war rested on Bengal and as it was urgently necessary to terminate it quickly, he had to regard it "as our own." [8] In other words, he not too politely told Macartney to keep his hands off all war matters. Macartney had other ideas and refused, claiming that Coote should be under the orders of his government. By all sound rules of government Hastings was entirely right. There was clearly no room for conflicting authorities at such a critical juncture. Yet according to a strict interpretation of the limited powers of control that the Regulating Act gave the superior government over the subordinate presidencies, Macartney was right and Hastings wrong.[1]

An open rupture between the two governments might still have been averted, if it had not been for the bitter personal quarrel between Macartney and the Commander-in-Chief, marked as it was by exhibitions of extremely bad temper on both sides. The General's temper, which had never been other than irascible at any time, had grown more violent and unrestrained with the passage of time, the increasing burden of his labors and the breakdown of his health, until now his childish petulance reached the proportions of mental derangement. His relations with Madras became one long wrangle, which set both parties writing furiously to Calcutta with abusive complaints and denunciations of each other.

[1] The power of control that the Act gave to the Governor-General-in-Council was confined to: (a) the declaring or making of war against any Indian powers, and (b) the negotiating and concluding of any treaty with an Indian power; and only in these instances was obedience to his orders declared obligatory. In all other respects, Madras and Bombay were left on an equal footing with Bengal.

Hastings did his best to reconcile them, though his sympathies were on the side of Coote. Not that the hot-tempered General had shown himself much better disposed to him; for he had always found it difficult to be polite to his superiors. He had been full of bitter complaints throughout the campaign: complaints of affronts to his dignity, of how he had been shown "gross and unmerited neglect," of things that had been done without his knowledge or consent; for all of which he held the Governor-General personally responsible. But Hastings, knowing his man, bore with him patiently. He once said that Coote was the only man living from whom he would take personal insults, and not only forgive them but requite them with praise and esteem for his public virtues. He knew that he was the only general in India capable of coping with Haidar Ali, for with all his failings Sir Eyre Coote was nevertheless a grand lion-hearted soldier.

When Coote set sail two years later on his last fatal voyage to Madras, Hastings wrote a letter to a friendly member of Council at Madras which deserves to be remembered as a fine instance of his tact, kindness and magnanimity. He asked the Councilor to use his influence to prevent any more incendiary letters being sent to the General.

"His temper which is naturally too subject to irritation, has acquired an increased sensibility from the distempers which oppress him; and if, under the weight of these, he will again adventure on so arduous and fatiguing a service, he merits at least the return of personal attention and tenderness. He cannot bear the provocations of official letters written in the spirit of reproach and hostility. I have studied him, and find him capable of the most connected and perfect exercise of his understanding when his spirits are composed. But if they are agitated, and a slight cause will agitate them, it weakens his recollection, and sometimes throws him into sudden and dangerous fits of sickness." [9]

It was on the Madras authorities, not on Coote, that the Governor-General's anger fell, for having dared to revile the Commander-in-Chief. And on occasion none could be more scathing and outspoken in his use of language, as witness the following, written on March 24, 1783:

"No artifice of reasoning, no perversion of distorted quotations, no insinuations of delinquency, no stings covered with compliments, no mechanism of the arts of coloring or sophistry can strip Vice-Admiral Sir Edward Hughes nor Lieutenant-General Sir Eyre Coote of the credit of having in repeated and well-fought days defeated the powerful invaders of the Carnatic on the ocean and in the field.... When you venture to impeach with undistinguished indecency these great officers of the public to whose efforts Great Britain is indebted for the safety of India, and in the continuance of whose services the best hopes of the public are placed, you act criminally towards your country, and in the present crisis of affairs no crime can be greater, for none can have a more dangerous tendency than a conduct of which the effects may be to sever from the State the services of her best commanders by sea and land." [10]

One thing can be said of Hastings with absolute certainty. His incessant pleas for the confidence and support of his superiors were merely symptomatic of his whole attitude to the public service. What he sought was not for himself alone; it was a matter of principle, the first principle in his opinion of all sound government, and especially valid for the ruling of a distant empire. And what he asked for himself he gave abundantly to his subordinates; nor was he disappointed with the results, declaring in after life that he had "never been so faithfully and zealously—I may add affectionately—served, as by those in whom I reposed the most unreserved credit." [11] The indignation that he felt at the attitude of the Madras Council towards Hughes and Coote was of like nature, and arose from the same spring, as the indignation that he felt because of his own treatment at the hands of Ministers and Directors.

The making of peace, not the conduct of the war, was the matter that chiefly engrossed Lord Macartney's attention. Being fresh from England, he and Macpherson knew the trend of public opinion at home. "Give us peace" was the general cry in loud crescendo—peace with America, peace with France, peace with India; nor was it mingled with any talk of conquest, or glory, or advantageous terms, or even of peace with honor. The East India Company, above all, was bemoaning the ruin to its revenues and profits. And Hastings was the suspect. The imperialistic designs of conquest that were attributed to him led to his being regarded as the chief stumbling-block to an immediate pacification.

With the same arrogance and egotism that the triumvirate had brought with them, Macartney believed, if there was to be peace, he must be the maker of it. And, like them, he had wasted no time in setting to work. Without troubling to consult the Supreme Government, and without the slightest regard for legality, propriety or common sense, he and Macpherson—who did not even wait until he reached Calcutta and assumed his place in the government—had addressed from Madras a formal letter to the Maratha ministers at Poona declaring that not only the Company but the King had ordered the suspension of hostilities and the conclusion of peace, and pledging the Governor-General-in-Council to support their pacific views. The enormity of the offense was such that Hastings might then and there have justifiably suspended Macartney in accordance with his powers under the Regulating Act. Nor were Macartney and Macpherson alone in their blundering interference. For some years Ministers of the Crown had pursued the baneful practice of sending their own officers to negotiate directly with the native states independently of the Company's governments, a practice which had helped to produce the imbecility that had marked all the Madras proceedings throughout the period. Following evil precedent Sir Edward Hughes, Admiral of the King's Navy, had been sending secret letters on his own account to Poona, demanding peace in the name of his sovereign.

There is little wonder that the Governor-General found some diffi-

culty in inducing the astute Maratha ministers at Poona to accede to the
treaty he had negotiated with Sindhia. And he was naturally indignant.
As soon as he heard what Macartney and Hughes had done, he sent a
letter post-haste to Anderson, warning him of what was afoot and
informing him that he would receive a similar communication from the
same gentlemen, authorizing him to conclude peace on any terms. He
told him he was to disregard such orders entirely and not to let them
influence him to make one single advance to obtain his object. "Answer
it respectfully, but go on your own way. These men will ruin their own
affairs by proclaiming that they are desperate." [12] To Macpherson, as
soon as he reached Calcutta, Hastings merely wrote the letter quoted at
the beginning of this chapter solemnly affirming his desire for peace.
He still regarded him as his friend and put the kindest construction
possible on his strange conduct.

It is plain that Hastings had more than one legitimate grievance
against Lord Macartney. Considering that he was sparing no effort to
save from extinction the government of which his lordship was the head,
and involving himself in endless difficulties in so doing—for there would
have been no occasion for his much criticized financial measures if it
had not been for the bankruptcy of Madras—it is not surprising that
he should have lost all patience with Macartney's calm and insolent
assumption of equal, even at times superior, powers, and, in writing to
him, have adopted a tone of unusual asperity.

V

ILL as the war had gone in 1781, the next year was to tell an even
gloomier tale, and for a time during the spring the fortunes of Britain
in Southern India reached a lower depth than at any period since
Dupleix had captured Madras. The crisis was reached with the arrival
off the Coromandel Coast of Admiral Suffren, one of France's most
brilliant commanders, with twelve ships of the line, against which Sir
Edward Hughes could only muster nine. Could the vital command of the
sea be held with this disparity in force? Accompanying Suffren were
transports crowded with French troops. Would these disciplined white
reinforcements for Haidar's army suffice to turn the balance against
Coote? The General had hitherto more than held his own on the field
of battle. Would the war of tactical success and strategic failure now
end in complete defeat? Also accompanying Suffren were numerous
frigates and cruisers. Would they succeed in severing Bengal's communications with Madras and the communications of both with England?
Would they intercept urgent dispatches, sweep the East India merchantmen off the seas and capture the food ships designed for the relief of
the starving inhabitants of Madras and the provisioning of the British
army?

These were dire possibilities. Yet there was scarcely a grain of
compensating comfort to be derived from the reports that continued

month by month to reach Hastings of the progress of the war on land. It did not need the arrival of a French armada to make the situation seem desperate. Despite everything the recriminations and quarrels in the Madras government continued unabated. Coote was at loggerheads not only with Macartney but with every one with whom he had to share authority. An officer of the King's army, he shared the prevailing jealousy of that service for the Company's military officers and lost no opportunity to show his contempt for them. When Colonel Pearse, a most able Company officer, joined him after his record-breaking march from Bengal, Coote, with inexcusable harshness and injustice, removed him from his command and broke up his detachment—much to Hastings's disgust.

In February a column under Colonel Braithwaite was surrounded in Tanjore by Tipu, Haidar's son, who had been joined by a body of French troops, and destroyed. The general demoralization at this time was acute. Sick, half-starved, exhausted, and unpaid, the sepoys were dying or deserting by hundreds. And still the hosts of Mysore moved freely up and down the Carnatic, burning and ravaging, capturing weakly held fortress towns, and threatening constantly to coop up the British within the walls of Fort St. George at Madras.

At length Coote, sick and worn out as he was, gathered together his failing strength once more and sallied forth in a last desperate endeavor to drive the enemy out. Back and forth he went after his elusive foe for two months, successful in his efforts to relieve beleaguered garrisons, but able only once to bring him to action—and then it was the same story as before: another "victory" without material result.

It should have been plain to the British commander by this time that the war was being fought along wrong lines. In the Carnatic he could do no more than act on the defensive, but more than that was needed if Haidar was ever to be expelled and brought to terms. The right strategy was clearly to carry the war into the enemy's territory by attacking him on his exposed western side. Hastings was among the first to realize this, and in June urged Bombay to undertake this operation. But Coote stupidly opposed the idea on the ground that every available man was still needed in the Carnatic—despite the lack of means to feed and move them. [13] In subsequent wars with Mysore the right strategy was employed with complete success. Again Hastings had shown his consummate ability to grasp a situation.

Only from Sir Edward Hughes was encouraging news received. Months of torturing suspense passed while Hastings was awaiting from the Admiral tidings that would decide the fate of India. What was going to be the outcome of the first clash between the two fleets? Word arrived on the first of April. A drawn battle with both fleets severely damaged. Hughes had escaped defeat! And this under the circumstances was tantamount to a victory. The Governor-General showed his appreciation of the fact by ordering a triumphant salute to be fired from the guns of the fort. The crisis, he felt, was past; the Carnatic could still be saved. Hope later passed into certainty when Hughes reported two more hard-fought actions, in which neither side had lost a ship, although each had suffered great damage; bringing discouragement to the French and renewed confidence to the British.

Meanwhile, Hastings had been pressing on the negotiations with the Maratha Government of Poona. He was in a hurry, afraid lest some unforeseen setback in the war in the South would put fresh hope into his enemies and change their inclination towards peace. "It is not peace with conditions of advantage that we want," he repeatedly told Anderson, "but a speedy peace; and we would rather purchase it with the sacrifice of every foot of ground that we have acquired from the Marathas, excepting Salzette and the little islands adjacent to Bombay, than hazard the loss of the present opportunity by contending for more. I am afraid of nothing but delay." [14] The negotiations were long and intricate, the disappointments many, but at length, on May 17, 1782, the Treaty of Salbai was signed: all territories conquered from the Peshwa were to be restored, Haidar Ali was to restore the territories he had taken and all Europeans, except English and Portuguese, were to be excluded from the Maratha dominions. Sindhia stood as guarantor for the due fulfillment of the treaty by the contracting parties, and the Marathas agreed to bring pressure to bear on Haidar to compel his acquiescence in its terms.

It was an important achievement; yet its immediate results were but small. Hostilities with the Marathas ceased, but the Poona Government endlessly delayed the ratification; and when Coote drew Haidar's attention to the treaty the old warrior replied sarcastically, thanking him for the information and expressing surprise at the inclusion of his name, as he had received no notice of it. The *pourparlers* that followed proved equally fruitless. Haidar told Coote's envoy that he had entered the war with the intention of "destroying and laying waste your country till never a lamp is left to burn there," regardless of the expense to himself. "And I have since kept my word. I have come, and for these two years have desolated your whole country and burnt all to ashes. In future, too, you will know what I can do, for what care I if it cost ten crores of rupees more than I have spent already? You, indeed, will suffer, but to me it is a trifle, or nothing." He scoffed at the idea that the Marathas would join the Company to bring him to terms:

"You will march four coss in a day, more you cannot for your lives, and so keep trotting after me all round the country; my business in the meantime I shall take care to dispatch. I shall lay waste all around you; this will be my employment, and then *you* do your best. Bring the Nizam and the Marathas to help you, and see what you can do. You were all three united for a time once before, and what did it end in? And what think you will it come to in future? Why, each will go back the same way he came."

And the final words of the old lion to the cowed envoy were: "Sindhia has written to ask me what is my real intention with regard to the

Poona treaty. My answer to him is that, let that measure take place when it may, I am bent upon war." [15]

Haidar Ali had spoken, and none could mistake his meaning. If peace with him was to be obtained it would have to be imposed at the point of the sword. Yet, as it happened, this was the lion's last roar. A few weeks later, word reached Madras of his sudden death.

Without any question Haidar Ali was the most formidable foe that the British had hitherto encountered in India. He had also been the most relentless. Two wars he had fought with them and in neither had he been defeated; he had succeeded in everything but what he had set out to do; which was to drive them out. Unable to read or write, he had nevertheless been absolute ruler of his state. The throne that he had gained by the blackest treachery he had held by his exceptional vigor and ability and his natural shrewdness, aided by the most ruthless cruelty. Bold and brave as a lion, he had feared neither God nor man. Yet, worn out by disappointment and exertion, even he had at the last grown weary of fighting. Defiant though he was to Coote's envoy, he still had sufficient intelligence to realize the hopelessness of the struggle in which he was engaged, and before dying he had hidden in the folds of his turban, where Tipu found it on his hurried return from repelling a British attempt to invade Mysore from the west, a scrap of paper on which were written these words to his son:

"I have gained nothing by the war with the English, but am now, alas! no longer alive. If you, through fear of disturbances in your own kingdom, repair thither, without having previously concluded peace with the English, they will certainly follow you and carry the war into your country. On this account, therefore, it is better first to make peace on whatever terms you can procure, and then go to your own country." [16]

It was sound counsel, but Tipu was not yet minded to follow it. He inherited his father's pugnacity as well as his hatred of the English, and was far from disposed to sue for peace.

A few days before the news of Haidar's death reached Madras, the man whom he had been vainly trying to vanquish had also left the scene of war. Having closed the fruitless negotiations for peace and brought back his army to Madras, the campaign being temporarily ended, Sir Eyre Coote had at last yielded to the insistence of his doctors, who informed him that only a complete rest and change of air could save his life, and sailed for Calcutta. It was then December, and the year closed with the struggle still undecided.

Chapter XXI

THE GATHERING STORM

I

THE spell of fair weather that had attended Hastings's political fortunes at home in 1780 was as short in duration as it was barren of results. Almost at once the storm-clouds began to pile up again on the horizon and to move slowly but inexorably across the sky towards him. Lord North was a reed that had only to be shaken by a small gust of wind to break.

The opening of the year 1781 found England's isolation complete. Holland had joined America, France and Spain in open hostility, and Prussia, Russia and Sweden were baring their teeth in a league of armed neutrality. But her worst enemies were her own statesmen and politicians. Though gleams of success attended the efforts of her soldiers and sailors, they were largely stultified by the mismanagement of a corrupt government, while the members of the Opposition gayly continued to play football with the fate of her empire as they had been doing from the beginning of the crisis. The Fox, Shelburne and Rockingham groups were pulling in opposite ways, and there was no salvation to be hoped for from them. America was lost and there was now no Chatham to fight the French. Thus the process of humiliating a proud nation was going triumphantly forward both on land and sea, and Horace Walpole hit the mark when he wrote:

> Oh England, no wonder your troubles begin,
> When blockaded without, and blockheaded within.

Britain was, in fact, fighting two wars. While the King and his government were fighting foreign enemies, they in turn were being fought by the embattled forces of the Opposition in Parliament. On the outcome of the second war depended very largely the outcome of the first. And on it, too, chiefly depended the fate of Hastings himself. For the Whigs, dominated by Edmund Burke, were now his bitter enemies. Their victory in Parliament would mean not only that George the Third had lost his fight for personal government, but that the gathering storm would at once break on the head of the man in charge of Britain's interests in the East.

Victory had almost come within their grasp during the session of 1780, and during the autumn recess the King played his last card. He dissolved Parliament and in the ensuing general election threw every ounce of royal influence into the voting scales. But though he spent twice as much money as in any previous election, he did not obtain commensurate results. He was fighting a losing battle against the combined forces of democracy, reform and party politics. The Whigs were not routed; they merely suffered a very temporary check.

The stage was now being set for the opening of a great attack on the Governor-General. Already the chief performers were taking their places. When Parliament assembled, Fox and Burke were there under the banner of the Marquis of Rockingham, and Henry Dundas, also, as a member of the Government. And with them came two new recruits to the Opposition. A young man of twenty-one named William Pitt, the worthy son of a great father, and Richard Brinsley Sheridan, the playwright-manager of the Drury Lane Theater and the friend of Fox. The cast would be complete as soon as two leading actors, already on their way, arrived from India: Philip Francis, and the man whom Hastings had deputed to uphold his cause at home, Major John Scott, successor in that rôle to Macleane and Macpherson. And when in April the House of Commons appointed a Secret Committee to investigate the causes of the war in the Carnatic and a Select Committee to inquire into the administration of justice in Bengal, the first steps were taken in the long process of arraignment that was not to end until the final verdict was pronounced in Westminster Hall twelve years later.

Francis was on his way home, but he had already thrown his shadow before him, and as his ship moved steadily westwards that shadow increasingly darkened the political scene. While still at Calcutta, he had begun his campaign to give the country "the facts" about the Indian situation. Anonymous pamphlets began to pour from the presses, depicting the Governor-General as a bloody tyrant, the oppressor of India, a rebel to authority, a man so greedy for power and wealth that only by plunging India into general war could he satisfy his lust. [1] However, as Hastings's friends still held the upper hand, the campaign at first bore little fruit. Only as a portent was it significant.

Francis reached England on October 19, 1781, after an unusually prolonged voyage. Much to his chagrin he was not received like a conquering hero. He was cold-shouldered at India House and ignored by the public at large. Only at Court was any cordiality displayed and for that he could thank Lord North, who showed his loyalty to Hastings by reminding the King of the support Francis had given to Clavering. [2] It was never Lord North's way needlessly to antagonize any one who, like Francis, might be useful politically. Francis was disappointed but not discouraged. The frigidness of the air acted as a spur rather than as a deterrent, and he at once began his work of revenge. First he captured (though, indeed, they were already of one mind with him) the hostile party in the Direction; Burke was already in his pocket and, with his aid, he had little difficulty in capturing the bulk of the Opposition in Parliament and the Committees of Inquiry, both of which Burke dominated.

The fight was on, and it soon waxed fast and furious. November brought news of Yorktown, the last bitter pill that the Ministry had to swallow before its fall. Lord North, still clutching at straws, and anxious to find compensation in the East for his failure in the West, regarded Francis's jeremiads with displeasure. It suited him now to salute Hastings as the savior of British India. Hurrying to the Governor-General's defense and singing his praises came also the Archbishop of York and Lords Mansfield, Stormont, Sandwich, and Thurlow; and Lord Shelburne admitted again, as he had done before, his partiality for him. [3] But Francis steadily gained ground. He assumed personal direction of the anonymous press, in the manipulation of which he had as Junius (if Junius he really was) been a past master. He also collaborated closely with Burke in directing the onslaught in Parliament. Nothing was left undone, no charge was too base to be dragged into service. Old Nuncomar's hanged corpse was disinterred to cry "murder!" "Nuncomar is returned," proclaimed Francis, gleefully, "and, like Cæsar's ghost with Até by his side, is now raging for revenge"—meaning he had succeeded in persuading the Select Committee to take up the Nuncomar case. [4] Another notable victory was scored when Dundas, the President of the Secret Committee, was induced to join the valiant cause. Meanwhile, the presses were being kept busy turning out pamphlet after pamphlet, some written by Francis himself, some by his friends, but all dealing with the same subject in the same way. [5] Lies were dressed up to look like cold facts, and cold facts were made to burn and sizzle with the fire of a righteous indignation. Junius, though dead, yet lived. Francis was rampant.

In December Major Scott arrived to take up the cudgels in his principal's defense. But his feeble, though ardent and loyal, efforts to stem the tide through the press with plain, unvarnished statements of plain, unvarnished fact were in vain. What hope was there, indeed, for them? He was trying to beat Francis with Francis's chosen weapon. Francis produced floods of "facts," admirably sensational and apparently well authenticated, and there could be no question which set of "facts"—Francis's or Scott's—was most likely to find favor in the minds of a public that had been fed for a score of years on stories —true stories, too, many of them—of the shocking misconduct of the Company's servants in India. Scott's activities were those of a pigmy contending with a giant and they merely impelled Francis to redouble his efforts.

In February 1782 the First Report of the Select Committee was issued. Its nature was such as to make it abundantly clear that the

Committee had gone over in a body to Francis's side. All pretense of fairness and impartiality, of hearing all sides to the questions in dispute, had been flung to the winds; witnesses had been dragooned and bullied; and only evidence—like that of Charles Goring—unfavorable to Hastings had been accepted. It was with some reason described as "the greatest farce ever perpetrated by a public body." [6]

On March 20 the Ministry fell. But before that day arrived conclusive proof had been given of the precise value to the Governor-General of Lord North's support. While Burke and Francis were triumphantly greeting the First Report of the Select Committee, a party of Hastings's partisans waited upon the Prime Minister to seek his intervention in their friend's behalf. His Lordship met them as usual with fair words, admitting the justice of their pleas but, true to his nature, failed to come forward publicly in Hastings's defense. [7] He had noticed the direction of the strengthening breeze, and held back.

Rockingham and Shelburne succeeded to office. Both these Whig noblemen had previously supported Hastings, and his friends took fresh hope. But they might have saved themselves their subsequent disappointment. Although Ministers might privately think well of the Governor-General, they always found it politically inexpedient to support him in public. And there is no need to search far for the reason. In the absence of clear lines of party division, the chief power in the House of Commons was wielded by Burke, Fox, Dundas and their friends. North had not dared to move a finger to prevent the Committees of Inquiry being packed by them. His successor, the Marquis of Rockingham, was in the hands of Burke, and Burke at once threatened to resign his office as Paymaster of the Forces if his chief did not do his bidding in Indian affairs. "What can we do?" lamented Ministers. "We entertain the highest personal respect and regard for Mr. Hastings, but we cannot imperil the interests of the nation. We cannot, to save an individual, however worthy, ruin our party and break up the Government." [8] Hastings had no lack of loyal friends. Even the King now showed signs, at times, of a friendly disposition; and the Proprietors of the Company were whole-heartedly for him. But of the representatives of the nation there were few, except those whose positions raised them above fear or favor, like members of the House of Lords—Lord Mansfield, the eminent Lord Chief Justice, and Lord Thurlow, the Lord Chancellor, were both staunch adherents— who dared openly to confess themselves his friends. It was group politics rather than party politics that lost England America, and nearly lost her India as well.

The tide now began to flow strongly against the Governor-General. A new election in the Court of Directors saw the influence of Ministers flung bodily against him, with the result that the Court became more bitterly hostile than ever before. Dundas, Burke and Fox in the Commons were demanding a new system of government for India;

Burke demanded it in the name of justice and humanity; Dundas and Fox, with their eyes on Indian patronage, sought a means of bringing fresh strength to a weak Ministry. [9] Francis, with these powerful men as his allies, was triumphant. The Reports of the Committees were substantially his work. Some of them were composed by Burke, and then corrected by Francis, but Francis claimed the whole credit for their contents. Regarding the Ninth Report, which was one of Burke's contributions, he wrote some years later: "I think I can say with truth that there is not one material principle or deduction in it which may not be fairly and honestly traced back to some antecedent opinions of my own, dilated on and expanded by a superior power. In some respects, I am the acorn...." [10]

When the Reports came to be presented to the House on April 15, 1782, the climax was reached. Dundas led the way, Burke followed. Every act of Hastings's government was passed in review and condemned. He was described as a man of boundless ambition, arbitrary, extravagant, bloodthirsty, without mercy or compassion, the most heartless and mercenary monster of the age, whose private fortune already exceeded £1,000,000, too exalted and powerful for his employers either to remove or to restrain. [11] The Ministers admitted that they could find no fault in him, but the rage of the high priests of Parliament was too great to be resisted. Nor did the House of Commons as a whole have any real appetite for their proceedings: a month later when Burke rose to move Forty-four Resolutions, ending with "that it was the duty of the Court of Directors to address the Crown for the recall of all those whom the House of Commons had censured," only twenty-six members made their appearance; but the resolutions were carried nevertheless. [12]

The first report of the Benares insurrection reached England shortly afterwards. It was entirely inaccurate, being based only on rumor, and for that reason it suited Francis's purpose admirably. In advance of authentic information from Hastings himself, the House listened to Dundas's account of what had taken place and registered its opinion. It is scarcely surprising, therefore, that when immediately afterwards Dundas proposed a resolution calling upon the Directors to take immediate steps to remove Warren Hastings "for having in sundry instances acted in a manner repugnant to the honor and policy of this nation," the resolution should have been carried. [13]

Apparently all was over. Hastings was at last to be recalled in disgrace. But was he? The Court of Proprietors had again been forgotten; and when the Court met on June 19, it first defeated the motion of recall and then resolved by an overwhelming majority (428 votes against 75) that "the Court of Directors were not bound to attend to any suggestions which might emanate from any one branch of the legislature." Twice the shareholders of the Company had intervened to save Warren Hastings from dismissal, and who can doubt that in so doing they had also saved India for the nation? The rage of Burke

WARREN HASTINGS
(From a portrait by an unknown artist; reproduced by kind permission of
M. G. Dashwood, Esq.)

and his allies knew no bounds; they cried out that the House of Commons had been insulted and must avenge itself, and they vowed their intention to put an end to this intolerable state of affairs by making a new arrangement for the government of India. Parliament then adjourned for six months.

The death of Rockingham a few days later once more revived the drooping spirits of Hastings's friends. They told themselves that Shelburne, Rockingham's successor as Prime Minister, had always shown himself well disposed. Again, however, they were doomed to have their hopes dashed. The entire Rockingham group, including Burke and Fox, seceded from the government with the death of their chief, leaving the Ministry too weak to take an independent stand, and the situation continued unchanged. Shelburne, who as a politician was neither high-minded nor particularly scrupulous, even went so far as to intrigue with the Directors in an attempt to get rid of Hastings before Parliament re-convened, and failing in this encouraged the Court in its renewed attitude of bitter hostility. [14] The result was that Hastings was ordered to reinstate Fowke at Benares and Bristow at Lucknow, and received a severe reprimand for his conduct to Chait Singh. Not content with this, the Directors adopted the Commons' Resolutions of May and caused them to be transmitted to India and published. The Proprietors rose up in arms at such malicious and insane proceedings, but their indignant protest could not undo the damage that was caused to the Governor-General's prestige in India. For it was now to be publicly proclaimed throughout India that Britain's representative there had been disowned by his country, all his measures condemned, and his recall sought.

II

IT was November (1782) when the first news of these proceedings reached Calcutta, and the moment chosen by the home government to proclaim its lack of confidence in its representative could scarcely have been better timed for the attainment of the purpose in view. For the issue of the war still hung in the balance. The Marathas naturally wanted to be sure that the English were really going to win before they ratified Sindhia's treaty. Haidar Ali still maintained his grip on the Carnatic, relentless as ever in his resolve to maintain the struggle until he had driven the English into the sea. The French, whose efforts hitherto had been quite ineffective, were for the moment masters of the sea as the British squadron had retired to refit, and they were about to fling several thousand fresh troops of their own into the fray. Madras was in a sorry plight with refugees from the wasted plains dying from starvation at the rate of fifteen hundred a week. If the home government wished to prize the Governor-General loose from his office, it was obviously a wise course to encourage the enemy in every way possible. For if he could be denied his repeated victories, or if peace could be endlessly delayed, why then, it was clear, Warren Hastings would be a doomed and discredited man. If he could not be ejected, it was equally right and proper that he and all India should know that his own people wished him ill.

Hastings could hardly be expected to see things in quite the same light. If his dismissal had to come he was prepared to submit with a good grace, but he thought it would have been better, considering the state of affairs, if his dismissal and the appointment of his successor had accompanied his condemnation. He was seldom, however, given to irony or sarcasm, and the matter was, in any case, far too serious for a display of wit. "Think, my Lord," he wrote hurriedly to Lord Shelburne, "of the English newspapers and Leyden gazettes circulating through every state in Europe, and every European colony in Asia, the suspension of the power of the first British Government in India, at a period such as the present, in the express words of the resolution of the House of Commons; and a French emissary at Poona in possession of such an instrument to work on the procrastinating spirit of the Marathas!" [15] Feeling no doubt that the gesture was expected of him, he offered his resignation, begging only that his Lordship would not allow his character to be blackened in advance by criminal charges nor his credit destroyed by public censures.

He was well aware that his enemies' strategy might prove successful. Already his failure to complete his negotiations with the Marathas was telling against him, and the report was being freely circulated that he had been duped by Sindhia. It was lamentable to what a low ebb the morale of the nation at home had fallen, and none lamented the fact more than he. He noted sadly how every reverse of fortune sent men in England, both high and low, into utter despondency, while every small success made them expect immediate victory. Whereas *he* knew that neither games nor wars were won without many ups and downs of fortune: "I wish that our rulers would play at chess, and learn that even with the best play many both pawns and capital pieces must be given and taken before the game can be won. All my friends tell me that unless I make a Maratha peace, I am a lost man." [16] The Company complained endlessly of their loss of trade and diminishing dividends; muttered, grumbled, and swore, their one idea being to utter the magic words, "let there be peace," with the expectation that immediately there *would* be peace. Hastings knew better. For people who spoke as though a dignified, honorable and lasting peace could be obtained merely for the asking he had nothing but contempt. Whatever might be true of the West, he knew that it was worse than futile to clamor for peace in Asia. "Let new negotiators come and avow peace to be their determination and sole object, and they will revive every claim that the composed insolence of Maratha presumption can devise." [17] And he was right, as the experience of others before and after his time abundantly prove. His enemies might rave and rant as they pleased; he could do none other but steadily pursue the course he had marked out.

It would be a mistake to suppose that he did not complain of his hard usage. He complained loud and bitterly to his friends, though his tone was one of pride in his achievements and a grim determination to see things through. Though he had offered his resignation, he nevertheless wrote:

"No considerations of family, life or fortune shall tempt me to desert, and I hope I know myself when I declare that no sense of personal injury or disgrace shall abate the zeal with which I have hitherto discharged the duties of it. For this assurance, let my past conduct be the pledge. I have now held the first nominal place in this Government almost twelve years. In all this long period I have almost unremittedly wanted the support which all my predecessors have enjoyed from their constituents. From mine I have received nothing but reproach, hard epithets, and indignities, instead of rewards and encouragement; and instead of being allowed to exercise the powers of my own Government for the benefit and improvement of their service; these, during a series of six years, were not only denied me, but converted even, with their connivance and incitement, into instruments of hostility, of which I myself personally and all my measures were the objects. Yet under all the difficulties which I have described, such have been the exertions of this Government since I was first placed at the head of it, that in no part of the Company's annals has it known an equal state, either of wealth, strength, or prosperity, nor, let it not be imputed to me as a crime if I add, of splendid reputation." [18]

The following month he heard of the death of Rockingham and the resignation of Burke. Having been assured by his friends that these were changes for the better, he wrote again to Shelburne, this time to tell him that he did not wish to hold his post "longer than the duration of the present scene of multiplied warfare," unless he had the confidence and support of ministers and the Company. He would stay until the cessation of hostilities, unless this would involve him in "public ruin and private ignominy." But he stoutly defended every part of his foreign policy and disclaimed all responsibility for having caused the war. [19]

In February the Directors' Resolutions condemning his conduct in the Benares affair and justifying Chait Singh reached Calcutta. The time was again singularly well chosen—from their point of view—for at that very moment Chait Singh was soliciting the protection of Sindhia and there was a distinct possibility of the Maratha leader supporting his cause. This was too much even for Hastings to tolerate. "Are these men," he cried, "the rulers of India?" "Are they aware," he asked Scott, "that in their eagerness to vilify me, they sow the seeds of distrust and rebellion among their own subjects, and that a declaration so authentic in favor of a rebel, now residing under the protection of the Chief of the Maratha State at the crisis of our negotiations with him, might tempt the former to resume his pretensions and the latter to espouse him?" [20] He was compelled to regard the Resolution not only in the light of a personal insult, but as a direct incentive to the princes of India to throw off the authority of the Company and assassinate their servants. The black ingratitude revealed by it was also more than he could bear. In his efforts to do his duty, he had shirked no responsibility and allowed no fear of odium to deter him from the line of his duty, and all that they repaid him with was censure, still more censure, and nothing but censure. To others of his friends at home he also poured out his feelings, making no attempt to conceal his pain. How bitterly he contrasted his actual conduct with what it might have been if he had thought only of himself and not moved an inch beyond the precise line of his orders, as Francis would have had him do, but how proudly he claimed that by acting on his own responsibility he had saved Bombay, saved Madras, and saved the Company itself! [21]

In his reply to the Court of Directors he carefully reviewed his whole policy, defending it eloquently but apologizing for whatever might appear offensive. He declared that he would have submitted in silence to the severest expressions of censure had they been no more than expressions and applied to real facts. "But when the censures are not applied to real facts and are such as substantially affect my moral character, I should myself be an accomplice in the injury if I suffered the slightest imputation to remain which it was in my power to efface." He then presented his ultimatum: if the Court ordered Chait Singh's reinstatement at Benares, he would immediately resign. And he concluded with a request that the Court proceed to the early appointment of his successor, as it was his intention to resign their service as soon as he could do so without prejudice to their affairs. [22] When Hastings wrote this letter, he had decided to leave India the beginning of the following year.

Chapter XXII

"THE READIEST ROAD TO PEACE"

I

THE rivalry of the two governors reached its climax when Hastings tried to coerce his colleague at Madras into submitting to his direction in matters of war policy. At first the dispute centered around the question of what was "the readiest and the easiest road to peace" in India. Later it shifted to another ground where the clash of views was equally acute if less vital to the national interests.

The Governor-General entertained no doubts regarding the right road to peace.

"That policy consists in a vigorous prosecution of the war; moderation amidst success; firmness in every adverse change of fortune, but a guarded avoidance of that submission which in eagerly soliciting and courting pacific arrangements adds to the insolence, encourages the obstinacy, and justifies the perseverance of the enemy in war, and in every case gives him the plea of dictating his conditions." [1]

He wanted no such peace as that which Madras had made with Haidar in 1769. He refused even to talk about peace while the enemy still occupied the Carnatic. But what was the use of his holding such convictions? What was the use of his pleading for a vigorous prosecution of the war? He no longer possessed the means of enforcing his orders. Sir Eyre Coote had been his strong right arm for the execution of his policy, and there was no one to take his place. The time had not yet come when a Governor-General could go himself to Madras and take matters into his own hands.

With Coote away the war languished. His successor, General Stuart, true to the traditions of the Service, quarreled with the civilian authorities but—unlike Coote—did not supplement this display of military temperament with an equal display of military genius. He might well have ended the war at a single stroke, if he had had the intelligence to take advantage of the momentary confusion in the affairs of the Mysore State consequent upon the death of Haidar. Instead he allowed Tipu to consolidate his position as his father's heir without let or hindrance.

The wastage of such a grand opportunity naturally moved Hastings to anger. And when it was followed by Lord Macartney making overtures for peace to Tipu on terms equivalent to admitting defeat, his no longer calm and even temper burst out in wrathful indignation. It was not enough that his Lordship had neglected the formality of obtaining the Supreme Government's permission before opening negotiations: he had the effrontery to demand that he be given plenipotentiary powers. Hastings in his reply showed once more how capable he was of administering scathing rebukes when necessary. He expressed his amazement that his Lordship, despite the aforesaid lost golden opportunity, should now have the audacity to ask for power to acknowledge Tipu as his father's representative and "to yield to him whatever his father in all his power amidst all our distress was subjected to resign by the treaty which we had concluded with the Marathas." "Records of laborious altercation, stinging invective, and mutual complaint," he added, "are no satisfaction to the public in compensation for a neglect that may cost millions, and upon a field where immense sums had been expended to maintain our footing." [2]

Tipu was as little disposed as the Governor-General to listen to any peace talk. He was deriving no little encouragement from his opponent's inaction and he construed both it and Lord Macartney's evident lack of appetite for war as welcome signs of weakness. Victory seemed once more to be within his grasp and no partial triumph would satisfy him.

Clearly the end of the war was not in sight. Yet its whole course had made it so evident that all the British needed to win speedily and decisively were able generalship and a sufficiency of transport and supplies that Hastings may be excused if his temper threatened to get the better of him. Nothing could shake him from the conviction that one more vigorous effort would end it all, and it was exasperating in the extreme to know that this effort would never be made so long as Lord Macartney was in control.

The Governor-General had one last trump card that he could play. Coote! And certainly it was not a card that he would want to play except as a last resort, for Sir Eyre Coote's health was still so bad that to ask him to resume his command was almost tantamount to sending him to certain death—a hero's death, it is true, which was the kind of death that the lion-hearted veteran would have liked the most. And that is why when the call of duty did come to him from the man whose fighting spirit was akin to his own, he heard it and responded with a ready acceptance.

Nothing that Macartney did could possibly be right: this was now the state of mind that Hastings had reached. Not even his policy towards Nawab Mohamed Ali, which previously Hastings had approved. The assignment of the Nawab's revenues no longer seemed to him an act of obvious wisdom and policy, though he himself had negotiated it, but became instead a gross usurpation of the Nawab's sovereign rights. He credited the Governor with the ultimate intention of annexing the Carnatic outright and, as this would violate the pledge that had been given to the Nawab, he could plausibly declare that the national honor required the cancellation of the assignment.[3] Accordingly, he decided to utilize Coote's mission for the accomplishment of this further object, and with every confidence that his views would meet with the approval of his colleagues, he formally proposed the measure to his Council, annexing to it an additional resolution that if the Governor refused compliance he should forthwith be suspended from office.

Few of Hastings's actions are more open to question than this ill-timed championing of the Nawab's sovereign rights. As a matter of general principle and applied to any other Indian ruler not yet reduced to absolute dependence on the Company, there was everything to be said for it. Even when applied to the Vizier of Oude it had not yet lost all its virtue. But to champion the cause of the Nawab of Arcot was to advocate the prolongation of the foulest system of misgovernment that ever cursed a country. Moreover, it was to advocate the continuance in the Carnatic of that duality of authority that had been the bane of Bengal and that Hastings himself had abolished. Sooner or later it had to be abolished in the Carnatic too, and by the same means. It is strange, therefore, to find Hastings strenuously resisting any move in that direction. The explanation probably lies in the fact that he had allowed his distrust of Macartney to overcome his better judgement. Much, also, as he deplored the state of affairs in the Carnatic he had the same respectful regard for the Nawab as he sometimes showed for other unworthy princes (the Prince Regent, George the Fourth to be, is a noteworthy instance) and, perhaps too, he resented what he thought to be Macartney's intention of aggrandizing himself at the Nawab's expense. His sympathies were easily aroused and not infrequently ill-given, and misdirected chivalry was quite likely to have been at least partly responsible for his surprising action. Nor must the influence of Macpherson and Coote, the two members of his Council whose views carried the most weight, be overlooked. Macpherson, the erstwhile agent of His Highness the Nawab and friend of Benfield, had every reason for wanting to restore to the Nawab his rights. And Coote also, flattered and cajoled as he had been by the crafty prince. Vile intrigues were going on around Hastings at this time. [4] Finally, there was the very important fact, which must have carried considerable weight with Hastings, that the assignment treaty had not met with the approval of the authorities at home.

Hastings received one of the greatest shocks of his life when his colleagues delivered their opinions on his resolutions. He had counted on their support as he had every reason to do. Instead of receiving it he was voted down! Wheler, Stables and—of all men!—Macpherson voted against him and Coote was his only supporter.

The suddenness of the desertion staggered him. Only the previous October had he written to Macpherson:

"I was most pleasingly surprised with Mr. Stables' company the other day at breakfast. I promise myself great comfort from his becoming one of us. What a pity that such a group should be broken! For I do not think that a knot of more rational or better-tempered men (I speak for myself at least) could be selected from all England." [5]

Clearly Hastings had been nursing hopes that in the light of subsequent events were absurdly false. He had deluded himself into thinking that these men were really his friends. Macpherson a loyal friend!—the idea was almost ludicrous. John Macpherson was no man's friend—except his own. Yet Warren Hastings had for long treated him as such, giving him his confidence and showing him the greatest kindness. One of the saddest letters Hastings ever wrote was that in which he had to confess his mistake. Macpherson had come out at last in his true colors, and the man who thought him his friend sorrowfully wrote:

"A ray of inspiration very early flitted across my imagination more than once and showed me the naked character of Macpherson, with his borrowed robes lying about him; but I either treated the warning as an illusion, or it escaped me while some more pressing object called off my attention; or I chose rather to be deceived than to yield to doubtful suspicion." [6]

But now not even his habitual blindness to the faults of those he loved and trusted could any longer conceal the unpleasant truth.

Macpherson was false through and through—a crooked, timid, ambitious man. A born intriguer, he had been Hastings's evil genius throughout this whole wretched quarrel with Macartney, using his influence with Hastings to prejudice him against the Governor and trying at the same time to make him the unwitting agent for the furthering of Benfield's corrupt interests. That he should at the last moment have changed sides in the matter of the Carnatic Assignment was quite in keeping with his character. His contemporaries knew him for what he was and called him flatterer, liar, sycophant, placebo, a snake in the grass—and later writers have fully confirmed their estimate.[1]

The truth of the matter is that Macpherson and the two weak men who went over into opposition with him were trimmers first and last: they trimmed their sails to every wind that blew from England. They were political agents whose votes were controlled, not by their own independent judgement, but by the wills of those who nominated them, whose favor they courted, or whose enmity they feared. They were trimming their sails now: the wind had lately begun to blow from a fresh quarter. Somewhere in their pasts they must have remembered

---

[1] He is aptly described by Lord Curzon as "a combination of the political adventurer, the adept intriguer, and the society darling." [7]

hearing that excellent maxim for aspiring politicians: "Do not cling to the falling bough." When the Governor-General asked for their consent to the adoption of extreme measures against the Governor of Madras, he was inviting them to incur the bitter enmity of a man with powerful political connections who was being freely canvassed as the probable successor to their present chief. And who had made this difficult demand of them? A man whose recall had been voted by the House of Commons, who was anathematized by the most powerful politicians at home, whose every action exposed him to the slaps and censures of his—and their—employers. It was asking too much of them. "They see less danger in doing nothing than in acting," commented Hastings bitterly. How often he erred in his judgement of human nature! Even after long and bitter experience he still had little understanding of some of the baser springs of human conduct.

The rejection of the Governor-General's resolutions averted an open breach between the two governments. Lord Macartney was fully prepared to defy the authority of the Supreme Government, and his actual suspension from office would have been necessary. Instead, the whole matter was referred to London for decision. The decision was long in coming, but when it was announced some years later, though Hastings was no longer in India to receive it, he must have derived a little consolation from the knowledge that it upheld him. The Directors ordered the assignment to be cancelled and the administration of the province restored to the Nawab.

The end of the duel between the two governors came with startling suddenness. The now wholly tragic figure of Sir Eyre Coote moved once more across the stage of Indian history, only to be struck down by the hand of Death before even beginning the accomplishment of his mission. And in striking down Coote, Death thrust from Hastings's hands the last of his weapons and compelled him to leave affairs in the South to take Macartney's course.

Coote sailed from Calcutta on his final mission on the 20th of March, 1783, admitting before leaving that he had "one foot in the grave and the other at the edge of it." His voyage was rapid and uneventful until he neared Madras. Then as night fell four other ships were sighted astern steering the same course. When dawn broke it was discovered that they were French. At once the chase was on. By day the British ship had the advantage in speed, but in the night calms the French made up the lost distance. For four days and nights the pursuit continued with never more than five leagues separating them. But the strain and suspense proved too much for the General. "On the third day," so ran the report that came back to the Governor-General, "big with the fate of the service, wrapt up with his country's cause, and feeling, I believe, his own consequence and the benefit the enemy would reap if they captured him, his family also on board, and a thousand other points crowded on his shattered frame, the trial proved too great, and the General dropped on deck, struck with a paralytic stroke." [8]

It was his end. On the last day of the voyage the British managed at last to outdistance their pursuers and reach Madras in safety. The dying soldier was carried ashore and breathed his last two days later on the 27th of April.

Felix opportunitate mortis Eyre Coote. The Thirteenth Charge in the impeachment of Warren Hastings related to the additional, and allegedly illegal, allowances that the Governor-General had granted him —corruptly, so it was said—and it is possible that Coote would have been included in the impeachment proceedings. The thought occurred to Hastings, and he wrote in 1788: "What would poor Coote have suffered had he lived to have been placed where I have been? The first three days would have killed him." [9]

To Sir Eyre Coote dead his country paid the customary honors accorded to national heroes. His remains were carried back to England where they were awarded burial in Westminster Abbey. A magnificent monument over his tomb and a statue at India House completed the edifice of commemoration.

II

COOTE being dead, there was nothing now to stop Macartney from seeking peace, even if he had to pursue it on bended knee. Earlier in the year, the Poona Government had at last ratified the Treaty of Salbai and promised its coöperation to compel Tipu to enter the general pacification on the basis of a mutual restoration of conquests. But Tipu still remained unsubmissive. He had but lately repelled an invasion from the West, and driven the British force attempting it to an ignominious surrender. In April he was joined by the renowned Bussy with a large body of French troops that Admiral Suffren had at last succeeded in landing on the coast. These events served to keep alive Tipu's hopes of ultimate success, and they were not lessened by anything that General Stuart had so far done. The coming of Bussy's force had, indeed, greatly changed the military situation in Tipu's favor.

At the beginning of June, when Stuart, after many delays, at length came to grips with the French, disaster was actually staring the British army in the face. It had done so once or twice before when Coote was in command, but now there was no Coote to save it. Just however when Bussy by land and Suffren by sea appeared on the verge of inflicting an overwhelming defeat on Stuart, the news arrived from Europe on June 23 that peace had been concluded with France, and at once all hostilities between them were suspended. Bussy withdrew his troops from Tipu's service, and Stuart led his army back to Madras in inglorious safety.

Nearly a year was still to elapse before Tipu gave up the struggle. He did so then only because the ever-increasing success of the British arms, under more able leadership, convinced him of its hopelessness. But, though his complete overthrow was only a matter of time, the

Governor of Madras would not wait for it. Heedless of Hastings's emphatic orders he allowed his envoys to follow Tipu around the country begging for peace, allowed them to suffer his gibes, to accept his insults, and to endure all the hardships and indignities that he flung in their way. When at last Tipu did admit them into his presence, he intimidated them into making concessions that nothing in the military or political situation warranted; for *he* knew he was beaten, even though Lord Macartney did not.

And so at length, on March 11, 1784, a treaty of peace was signed with the last of the Company's enemies. It provided for a mutual restoration of conquests, rescued a thousand and more captive Englishmen— all that remained alive after the savage Haidar had done his worst— from a slow death of torture, left the power of Mysore unbroken and its ruler more arrogant, ambitious, and contemptuous of the British than even his father had been, and made no mention of the Marathas, the Nizam or the Nawab of the Carnatic, all of whose names should, according to Hastings's orders, have been included as parties to it. [10] But that was a matter of no importance to the Governor of Madras, whose friends could now proudly boast, "Mr. Hastings makes war, but Lord Macartney makes peace."

In June, when he was at Lucknow, Hastings received a copy of the treaty to sign. In his absence the Council had already ratified it in his name so that what was required of him was a mere formality. Yet he recoiled fiercely even from this obligation. The mere sight of the treaty made him boil with fresh indignation and, if he could have had his way, he would even at this late date have suspended Macartney for disobedience to orders. But calmer reflection showed him the uselessness of resistance. The treaty was a *fait accompli*, he had no power, and his colleagues turned a deaf ear to his suggestions. So he submitted to his humiliation and attached his signature. "What a man is this Lord Macartney! The wit of man could not devise such effectual instruments of a nation's ruin as this black eagle portends to every land and state over which he casts the shadow of his wings. I yet believe that, in spite of peace, he will effect the loss of the Carnatic." [11] Having relieved his mind to Scott to this extent, he turned to matters of more moment and profit.

Chapter XXIII

PUBLIC FAILURE AND PRIVATE LOSS

I

THOUGH peace reigned once more in Northern India and one by one the many dangers threatening the British hold on India were receding, there was as yet but little diminution in the Governor-General's load. At the same time as he was disputing with Macartney over the direction of policy he was still engaged in the Sisyphean task of trying to roll the rock of the Oude alliance up the mountain created by native misrule and the misconduct of English officials. He thought he had succeeded at Chunar. He was mistaken. That was only the beginning of his troubles. Oude was indeed to Warren Hastings what the Irish problem has been to so many British statesmen. It remained always with him defying solution; producing endless friction and controversy; causing repeated splits in his government; absorbing an immense amount of time and effort; making him many enemies and no friends; bringing him endless vexation without compensating glory; and, at the last, contributing very materially to his own impeachment.

No one has yet disentangled from the confusion of conflicting accounts the exact truth about what followed the Treaty of Chunar. Perhaps no one ever will as the story seems hopelessly embedded in intrigue and falsehood. Hastings had very definite views about what was going on and who was to blame and why, but we cannot be sure that he was always right. His sources of information were the partial reports of interested parties, the Vizier, the Vizier's minister, and the British Resident. However, it is hardly likely that he would have laid the blame quite so positively on the British agents without some cause. Wherever the truth may lie, a certain melancholy luster surrounds his unremitting efforts to cure this constant running sore. The task of debt-collecting is always odious; yet, while Hastings seldom shirked the task, he did not lose sight of the fact that there were other and higher ends of policy to be served, and his failure—for such it must be judged —was more honorable than the success of some of his successors when they tackled the same kind of problem.

One chief source of Hastings's difficulties was the inefficiency of the two men who alternated as Resident at Lucknow. Neither possessed the requisite integrity, tact or ability for such a delicate and difficult mission. Middleton, though he was Hastings's own selection, was singularly incompetent, if he was not actually dishonest, and cut a very poor figure throughout his second tenure of the post—how poor was shown when he appeared to give evidence at Hastings's trial. Bristow was still worse. A man of equally mean talents and of still less integrity. The fact that he was a creature of Francis and a party to his patron's worst schemes and intrigues was in itself sufficient disqualification for the post.

When Hastings returned to Calcutta in January 1782 he had left the task of liquidating the Vizier's debt in the joint hands of the Vizier's minister, Hyder Beg Khan, and Middleton. Both failed him. Hastings accused Middleton of misleading him by pretending that the debt was paid off, whereas he found that it was actually accumulating again rapidly. He suspected him of corrupt collusion with Hyder Beg Khan for the purpose of concealing the true state of the Vizier's finances. Not only was the debt unliquidated but the unlicensed Europeans still remained at Lucknow and the disorders continued.

At length, unable either to tolerate the evasions of the treaty or to go himself to Lucknow to straighten things out with the Vizier in person, he sent Major Palmer, his military secretary, as his deputy. But again failure resulted. Palmer either misunderstood his instructions or allowed himself to be deflected from them. It needed a man of great shrewdness and experience to avoid the pitfalls of intrigue and chicanery that beset his path at the Vizier's court. Within a few weeks Hastings was writing him, "Indeed, my dear Palmer, you cannot leave Lucknow too soon. You walk through snares, and every step that you tread, either entangles you in them or detects them." [1] Hastings knew what an Oriental court was like: he had not spent four years as Resident at Murshidebad for nothing. At the same time (June 1782) Middleton tried to evade his responsibilities by resigning. Hastings sternly ordered him to stay until the balance of debt had been paid, and he threatened Hyder Beg that, if this were not done by the close of the year, he would insist that the Vizier change his ministers. The only result of the Treaty of Chunar, he bitterly exclaimed, had been "an accumulation of distress, debasement and dissatisfaction to the Nawab, and of disappointment and disgrace to me." [2]

Orders, reprimands, reproaches, threats, none of them apparently produced any effect, and the tone in which Hastings referred to Oude affairs became increasingly despondent and fretful. He rebuked Palmer for making fresh demands of the Vizier when it was only with the utmost difficulty that he could be got to perform his present obligations. "I am disappointed," he wrote him, "and write with strong feelings of all the disorders which I see, and to which every remedy that I have applied to them has but served to increase. I am vexed and angry." He told him to inform the Vizier that he was ready to withdraw both the troops and the Residency the moment the debt to the Company was paid off—"I am weary of the reproach of being the instrument of a nation's ruin." All the time he was oscillating between a policy of interference and non-interference. The exigencies of debt-collecting seemed constantly to demand the former, but a deep-rooted principle of policy, respect for the sovereign rights of the native princes, held him back. Only the belief that his own reputation was intimately bound up with the success of his Oude policy made him persevere in his attempt to solve a baffling problem.

In October 1782, bitterly disappointed in Middleton, Hastings yielded to the insistent orders of the Directors and gave back the Resident's post to Bristow. Though he had previously declared this friend of Francis to be "an object too mean for public attention"—"his abilities are contemptible, his political principles mean and centered in himself and his presumption and insolence insupportable" [3]—he was yet apparently sanguine enough to expect that he would now justify the trust reposed in him, out of gratitude if for no other motive, though he must have known that Mr. Bristow was well aware to whom he was indebted for his appointment! What was to be expected followed. Hastings found his trust utterly misplaced. ("I never give great trust without confidence, nor confidence by halves," he wrote to Scott à propos of Bristow's appointment.) No improvement in the state of Oude was discernible. Things continued as before, and by the following year he was laying the whole blame on Bristow. He charged him with openly usurping the powers of the Vizier's government.

The charge brought on a fresh division of opinion in the Council. Hastings, in an able minute, exposed and denounced the whole trend of Bristow's policy, tracing its origin back to Clavering and Francis. He maintained that as its object was to make the Vizier a vassal of the Company it was contrary not only to his own positive instructions but to justice and policy, and he proceeded to give an impressive exposition of the fundamental principles that he believed should govern British policy both in Oude and in India as a whole:

"His titular rank of Vizier of the Empire rendered him a conspicuous object of view to all the States and Chiefs of India, and on the moderation and justice with which the British Government in Bengal exercised its influence over him, many points, most essential to its political strength, and to the honor of the British name depended. . . . By a sacred and undeviating observance of every principle of public faith, the British dominion might have by this time acquired the means of its extension, through a virtual submission to its authority, to every region of Hindustan and Deccan."

Little as he would have advised such an ambitious design, he now feared it had been made nearly impossible because of the unenviable reputation for perfidy and deceit that the Company's governments had acquired. Every native ruler that had trusted to their good faith and entered into alliance with them had suffered in power, prestige and wealth. Each one had been imposed upon, intimidated and humiliated. And in support of this severe assertion he pointed to the treatment that had been meted out to the Nawabs of Bengal, Arcot and Oude. These were "terrible precedents against us." "Every power in India must wish for the support of ours; but they all dread the connection." He maintained that rigid restrictions should be placed on the interference of a British Governor or Resident in the affairs of the Vizier or of any other prince in alliance with the Company. The limits should be advice and persuasion. Anything more was a usurpation of authority. He claimed that his own behavior towards the Vizier had invariably been marked by a studied respect, that he had addressed him in public as his acknowledged superior and in private used firm but decent language in making his demands and that he had always obtained his cheerful and willing consent. But now he was receiving from him vehement complaints of Bristow's behavior. Instead of showing him every ostensible and outward mark of respect, as his instructions had prescribed, Bristow was being insolent and dictatorial. Not content with interfering in every department of state, he was prescribing to him "the number of horses which he should be allowed to use and the dishes which should be cooked for his table." [4]

This courageous and wise minute was fearfully prophetic. Hastings had looked into the seeds of time and seen which grain would grow and which would not. Interference in the affairs of the native states, encroachment upon the rights of the native princes, nullification of rights solemnly granted by treaty, these were the grains, sown in the first days of empire, that were to grow and flourish for a century and more after Hastings's time, attended by shame and dishonor to the government that nurtured and tolerated them. Hastings's noble words should have been emblazoned in letters of gold where every succeeding Governor-General could see and ponder over them, for if they had been undeviatingly acted upon from that day to this it would not now be possible for any one to refer to the treaties between the British Crown and the protected native states as being in many instances no more than "scraps of paper." [5]

Hastings's colleagues, however, preferred to give their support to Bristow against him. Macpherson had by this time made his influence supreme among them. The scales had fallen completely from Hastings's eyes. Macpherson was now to him the man who "loves the crooked better than the straight path," without honor and apparently without shame; and Wheler and Stables were "the puppets of his direction." [6]

"You will wonder," he wrote to Scott on October 15, 1783, "that all my Council should oppose me. So do I. But the fact is this: Macpherson and Stables have intimidated Wheler, whom they hate, and he them most cordially. Macpherson, who is himself all sweetness, attaches himself everlastingly to Stables, blows him up into a continual tumor, which he takes care to prevent from subsiding; and Stables, from no other cause that I know, opposes me with a rancor so uncommon, that it extends even to his own friends, if my wishes chance to precede his own in any proposal to serve them. In Council he sits sulky and silent, waiting to declare his opinion or to contradict, in language not very guarded, and with a tone of insolence which I should ill bear from an equal, and which often throws me off the guard of my prudence; for, my dear Scott, I have not that collected firmness of mind which I once possessed, and which gave me such a superiority in my contests with Clavering and his associates. My last year's sickness has left a debility upon my constitution which I cannot remove, nor shall I till I try a colder climate...." [7]

A severe conflict had begun in his mind. Should he retire or should he stay? In October he was so hurt by the manner in which Lord North displayed his "kindness" to him, more hurt, he said, than if he had declared himself an open enemy, that he felt it was full time for him to quit. "I want not such friendship, nor shall I thank him for it. I thank those only who support me because they think me fit for my office. If I am not fit, let his Lordship give his friendship to a fitter; but that I see is not the merit for which my successor is to be elected." [8] At last he seems to have realized the bitter truth that nothing that he could do, no amount of ability he could display, no successes he could win or achievements he could record, would avail to continue him in his post when weighed in the balance against the demands of political expediency.

In December he took fresh hope from the knowledge that Lord Shelburne, whom he considered one of the best informed men in England on Indian affairs, was in power. "If no new changes not foreseen intervene," he told David Anderson, "I am sure of remaining as I am. I repeat, my friend, that I am not easy of removal; and spirits as determined as any that now seek it have experienced that I am not." [9] "I will resign this thankless office on the first favorable opportunity; but I will not be driven from it either by the folly of my subordinates or the injustice of my superiors—I have saved India in spite of them all, from foreign conquest, neither will I quit my post until the internal affairs of this great country shall have been restored to something like order." [10]

But another event was impending that, while still distant, filled his mind with anguish and made him think still more longingly of retirement. Mrs. Hastings's health was visibly declining. In October, with a heart torn with sorrow and anxiety, he decided to send her home at the time which he had fixed for his own departure with her. He felt that duty compelled him to stay a year longer.

"I stay most reluctantly on every account, for my hands are as effectually bound as they were in the year 1775, but with this difference, that there is no lead substituted to mine: and my constitution is, I fear, broken beyond the power of any aid in this climate to repair it. I have held a court of conscience in my own breast, which has determined the duration of my service, and beyond that no consideration upon earth shall induce or compel me to act longer with such associates.

> "These wicked creatures yet do look well-favored
> When others are more wicked: not being worse
> Stands in some rank of praise.

"I in my heart forgive General Clavering for all the injuries he did me. He was my avowed enemy. These are my dear friends, whom Mr. Sulivan pronounced incapable of being moved from me by any consideration on earth. I thought so too...." [11]

Fear of what Macpherson would do with the government was one of his principal reasons for remaining, but other grave matters occupied his mind. When he made his decision peace had not yet been concluded with Tipu, and famine threatened to invade Bengal. The rains had failed in all the western part of Hindustan and a serious shortage of grain was feared in the Company's territory. Hastings took immediate steps to deal with the situation by placing an embargo on grain export and appointing a commission of three food controllers. "I shall see their daily proceedings," he wrote Scott, "and you may swear in my name that the famine of India shall not invade the provinces of our dominion. I hope it will draw the emigrants of other countries into our own, and be the means of establishing a scheme which I have labored to bring to pass these eleven years, a chain of granaries on the banks of the two great rivers, built of solid masonry, to be filled in times of super-abundance, which always hurts our revenue, with a provision of three months, and closed." [12] He had already begun such a provision in Fort William in a building that he had erected for the purpose where the grain could be stored in air-tight compartments and kept in a sound state, according to his calculations, for fifty years.

Before the end of the year the dispute over Oude policy came to a head. The Vizier had vehemently complained of Bristow's arrogant conduct and the Governor-General had called upon Bristow to explain and answer the charges. When six weeks had passed without a reply being forthcoming Hastings moved to have him recalled. The Council refused. Bristow at length replied, alleging that he had acted strictly according to the Governor-General's orders. The statement infuriated Hastings, first because it was utterly untrue—"There is not a syllable of my instructions which will admit of a construction of a power to assume any authority whatever in the administration of the Nawab-Vizier"—and, secondly, because it amounted to a personal insult. He believed now that nothing less than the independence of Oude was at stake, and if the Council insisted on supporting the Resident's pretensions to irregular and unauthorized authority, it was necessary for them to go further and authorize him to avow the power which Bristow had assumed and to exercise it in the Company's name. [13] But this they hesitated to do.

The temerity of this subordinate and the equivocal attitude of his colleagues brought back some of his old imperious vigor and fighting spirit. He challenged them. Did they mean to support Bristow or to restore the Vizier's authority? To let things stay as they were meant anarchy, for which he would hold them solely responsible since they would neither enforce his instructions nor give the Resident others. The blunt question alarmed them. They had consistently tried to avoid taking a definite stand, especially when it involved supporting their chief in acts likely to provoke his enemies at home—as in the present instance. But now that the issue had been put squarely up to them, they dared not shirk it. Yet they still tried to wiggle out of the dilemma. After twelve days' discussion they agreed to recall the Resident if Hastings made himself personally answerable to the Company for obtaining the liquidation of the Vizier's debt within three months. Hastings naturally rejected such an absurd offer, and the Opposition then collapsed. It was agreed that as soon as the Vizier had given written guarantees on the security of good bankers for the discharge of the debt, amounting to over fifty lakhs, the Residency should be withdrawn, and for the propriety of this measure Hastings consented to be specially answerable because it was contrary to the advice and opinion of the Council. In other words, since the Council refused to take the charge and responsibility of Oude affairs into their own hands, they reluctantly agreed to wash their hands of the matter altogether and leave it to Hastings to handle as he saw fit on his own responsibility. On December 31 Bristow and the whole Residency staff were withdrawn and Hastings was once more left face to face with the most baffling of all his problems.

II

With the beginning of the new year the time had come that Hastings had fixed for the departure of his wife. It was to be the saddest and most tragic moment in his life. Into it was poured the concentrated essence of a love that was as intense as it was lasting.

During the hectic years that followed their marriage the story of their life together runs like a gentle melody that is unheard much of the time while the drums of war and the cymbals of politics are beating and clashing, and yet at rare moments comes clearly to the ear. It needed the absence of Mrs. Hastings from her husband's side to provide those moments, for then the expression of love was transferred to writing in letters that have been preserved. The result is a collection of some of the most beautiful love-letters in the English language. Though they give no more than occasional glimpses of eight years of married life they are too revealing to need further support.

The first glimpse occurs at the time of the duel with Francis. Mrs. Hastings had gone up-river to a health station to escape the ordeal of a Calcutta summer and the unhealthy rainy season that followed. Except for flying visits to her over week-ends her husband was tied to Calcutta by pressure of work and the impending crisis in his relations with Philip Francis. When the challenge was made to him and he was putting his affairs in order, he sent her no word of what was afoot but instead wrote her a letter that was to be given her in the event of the worst befalling him.

"CALCUTTA, 16 *Aug.* 1780.

"MY BELOVED MARIAN,

"My heart bleeds to think what your sufferings and feelings must be, if ever this letter shall be delivered into your hands. You will too soon learn the occasion of it. On my part it has been unavoidable.—I shall leave nothing which I regret to lose but you, nor in my last moments shall I feel any other affliction. Let it be a consolation to you to know that at this moment I have the most grateful sense of all your past kindness, and of the unremitted proofs which you have daily and hourly afforded me of your affection.—For these may God reward you! I know not how.—How much I have loved you, how much beyond all that Life can yield, I still love you, He only knows.—Do not, my Marian, forget me; but cherish my remembrance to the latest hour of your life, as I should yours were it my lot, and my misery, to survive you.—I cannot write all that I feel and that my heart is full of.

"Adieu, my best wife, and most beloved of women. May the God of Heaven bless and support you!—My last thoughts will be employed on you.—Remember and love me. Once more farewell!

"Your

"WARREN HASTINGS.

"P.S.—I shall enclose with this the key of my bureau. In the upper part you will find my will, which is so marked in large letters." [14]

(By what must be a later will, since it is dated September 6, 1782, he left all his property to her.)

After the duel he briefly assured her of his safety and welfare, excusing his inability to visit her until Francis was out of danger:

"My Marian, you have occupied all my thoughts for these two days past and unremittedly." [15] As the weather at Calcutta continued bad with a great deal of sickness prevalent, Mrs. Hastings remained some time longer up-river, her husband, as before, escaping from his work to pay her occasional visits. When on a Friday the news of the Carnatic disaster reached him, he characteristically forsook everything to spend the week-end with her at Hugli, where in the peace and quiet of her sympathetic company he was able calmly to decide his course of action, so that when he met the Council on the Monday he was ready with all his plans matured.

The next glimpse comes during the fateful visit to Benares in the following year. Mrs. Hastings accompanied the party in their pleasant journeying as far as Monghyr, where a curious presentiment of trouble caused her husband to leave her—"more," he said, "from a secret impulse than from any solid reason." When rumors of calamity began to penetrate through the country, Mrs. Hastings was at Patna. Communication with Benares had ceased, and the usual false reports were current. It was said in native quarters that the Governor-General had fled to Chunar before he had actually done so. But he was fortunately able to get a reassuring note through to her before the rumors became too terrifying. One side of his mind was occupied in the task of saving British India, the other in thought for his wife. Still her anxiety was naturally great and was increased as fresh reports of catastrophe, even of his death, flowed in. When mutiny and desertion broke out among the sepoys and panic fell upon the European inhabitants of Patna, to whom the Patna massacre of 1761 when two hundred of them had been slaughtered in cold blood was still a fresh and hideous memory, Maria Hastings rose to the occasion in a manner worthy of her husband. She stopped an evacuation of the city, when it was proposed, and in so doing prevented by her courage and decision what might have been a second catastrophe more serious than the first. Hastings in after years loved to relate how "she proved the personal means of guarding one province of the Company's Indian dominion from impending ruin by her own independent fortitude and presence of mind, varying with equal effect as every variation of event called upon her for fresh exertions of it...." [16] He wrote to her from Chunar: "Be confident, my Marian, I will return to you triumphant.... I never loved you, as I love you in the midst of my greatest troubles and have suffered more in my fears of you, than, I hope, I ever shall for myself."

Again we skip a year and reach the month of August 1782, when Hastings was undergoing his first serious illness. His wife was four hundred miles up-river, having as usual left Calcutta for the unhealthy season. When the news of his illness reached her, she set off at once in a small boat and reached him in three days—very quick time for such a journey—after having been very nearly wrecked and drowned in a stormy sea amid the dangerous currents of the big river. Hastings had not wished her to be informed of his illness for fear lest she would endanger her health by returning to nurse him in the wet season. But in doubly risking her own life she may have saved his.

When the unhealthy season came around again an anxious and devoted husband began to be concerned. Mrs. Hastings was suffering from no specific disease but she was plainly ailing. Her very freedom from actual illness gave him cause for fear. The fixed seasons for the winds in Indian waters made the winter and spring the time of departure for homeward bound ships. If she did not go then she would have to stay another year. Would she survive that length of time? He tortured himself with the question. Could he take the risk of answering it with a "yes"? He remembered the tragic fate that had overtaken those who had stayed too long. Their number was legion. Calcutta was a playhouse with death lurking constantly behind the scenes. Well one day, the actors might be dead the next.

There were no hill stations in those days, no system of short furlough home. To go home meant to resign the service. English men and women who went out to India went knowing that they might be dooming themselves to an exile as long as life itself. No relief from the climate could be gained except by short trips up-river to slightly higher-lying country, helpful but insufficient, or occasionally by sea-voyages, as far at times as the Cape of Good Hope, expensive and dangerous and not always efficacious. Women and children were the worst sufferers. A few went home, but most stayed with their husbands and fathers and lived or died as their fate might be. The life of Calcutta was gay, but it was the forced gayety of people to whom the presence of death and sickness was a constant reality. Husbands saw their wives, and wives their husbands, slowly wasting away before their eyes, and were helpless to save them.

Yet the alternative to staying was almost as terrifying. It involved a perilous voyage lasting anything from four to twelve months, unspeakable hardships due to being cooped up in squalid, stuffy and confined quarters, exposed to the risk of dysentery, scurvy and fever, without any proper medical care, in ships that were frequently ill-conditioned, with only a fair hope of ever being reunited with those left behind. Too many East India men were lost with all hands or driven ashore on a savage coast or captured by foreign enemies to make the voyage anything else but a terrifying ordeal, and it is not surprising that most wives preferred to risk death in company with their husbands than face these perils in the loneliness of separation.

After Hastings had made his decision, he had to fight hard to keep his resolution to the sticking point. He knew that when he parted from his wife he was parting with everything that made exile bearable. But, though torn with anguish and doubt, he valued his wife's health and life above his own comfort and happiness. There was also the consoling thought that he would be following her within the year. He chose the East Indiaman *Atlas* to bear this most precious of all cargoes and lavished his money in special arrangements for her comfort. At vast expense, he had the round-house, the choicest part of the ship, fitted out in a manner worthy of a queen and procured for her a congenial traveling companion to mitigate the hardships and loneliness of the voyage.

When the day came he accompanied her down the river to where the *Atlas* swung at anchor in the estuary. On the 10th of January, 1784, she sailed. The rest may be told in the letter that he wrote her the day after he had watched the ship slowly recede from view out into the Bay:

"I followed your ship with my eyes till I could no longer see it, and passed a most wretched day with a heart swollen with affliction, and a head raging with pain.... In the heavy interval which I have passed I have had but too much leisure to contemplate the wretchedness of my situation, and to regret (forgive me, my dearest Marian; I cannot help it) that I ever consented to your leaving me. It appears to me like a precipitate act of the grossest folly; for what have I to look for, but an age of separation, and if ever we are to meet again, to carry home to you a burthen of infirmities, and a mind soured perhaps with long, long, and unabated vexation.... Indeed, my Marian, I think we have ill-judged; the reflexion has often for an instant occurred to me that we were wrong; but I constantly repressed it; I urged everything that could fix the resolution beyond the power of recall, and felt a conscious pride in the sacrifice I was preparing to make.... Yesterday as I lay upon my bed, and but half asleep, I felt a sensation like the fingers of your hand gently moving over my face and neck, and could have sworn that I heard your voice. O that I could be sure of such an illusion as often as I lay down!—and the reality seem to me an illusion. Yesterday morning I held in my arms all that my heart holds dear, and now she is separated from me as if she had no longer existence. O my Marian, I am wretched; and I shall make you so when you read this. Yet, I know not why, I must let you go, nor can I add anything to alleviate what I have written; but that I love you more by far than life, for I would not live but in the hope of being once more united to you. O God grant it, and grant my deserving, my blessed Marian, fortitude to bear what I myself bear so ill, conduct her in health and safety to the termination of her voyage, and once more restore her to me with everything that can render our meeting completely happy! Amen! Amen! Amen!"

Chapter XXIV

THE LAST YEAR

I

EARLY in January, while the sorrow of his wife's departure lay fresh and heavy upon him, Hastings received a call for help that he could not refuse. The Vizier insistently urged him to go to Lucknow to aid him in restoring the country to order. Nothing less than the Governor-General's own presence there, he declared, would serve to quiet the minds of the people and instill confidence.

Only the strongest sense of duty made him undertake this mission. He felt that he was facing a thankless and nearly hopeless task. Every circumstance seemed to point to certain failure. On top of all the other ills that were distressing the Vizier's dominions there was now the famine, and it seemed to him probable that the country was ruined past hope of redemption. He wrote to his wife: "I go without a fixed idea of the instruments which I am to employ or the materials on which I am to act, with great expectations entertained by others, but very moderate of my own. . . . Add to all the foregoing a mind unequal to its former strength, and a constitution very much impaired." His chief hope lay in the proved strength of his personal influence with Asaf-ud-Daula. It was well known that the weak and spineless prince regarded him with great respect and admiration, aptly styling him, in the manner of the East, the Nawab Amaud-ud-Daula, "the Prop of the State." When "the Prop" was with him Asaf-aud-Daula made a show of moral strength that was altogether lacking at other times. He was the creature of those whose wills were the strongest, and when left to his own resources he became the victim of the worst influences in a corrupt court. The only personal consolation that Hastings could hope to derive from the arduous journey was, as he confessed to his wife, that he would be relieved from the tumults and importunities of Calcutta, for "no one had mercy on me, and my gates, though shut, let people through like a sieve."

Clearly, though only fifty-two, Hastings was a tired and worn-out man. There was a time, only ten or twelve years before, when it seemed that difficulties had existed for him only to be overcome, when he was the embodiment of the poet's dream of the Happy Warrior. He still could not shirk the call of duty nor turn his back on a difficult problem, but what before he would have taken in his stride now becomes "a desperate adventure," undertaken without zest or confidence. It is only too evident that he had reached the most painful stage in his career, the last, when he had to reconcile himself to the realization that his star was rapidly sinking, that he was regarded as a discredited man, that his views and proposals no longer carried weight in the government, that his authority was gone. Above all, that his colleagues were hourly expecting news of his downfall and were waiting with ill-concealed impatience for him to go. "And all this," as he said, "as well known to the Indian world as our own."

Yet it was hard for him to bow to the inevitable. For twelve years he had identified himself with India, and all the time he had been firmly buttressed by the knowledge, tacitly admitted by his superiors—for Parliament had three times extended the Act under which he held office—of his indispensability to the State. But now he was no longer indispensable. Though he could not bring himself to admit the fact, he had finished his work and India could do without him. Even if the government fell into the hands of a man like Macpherson, it would not now be fatal to the Empire.

It is not surprising that he was slow to realize the change, or that he could only see the darker side of the picture. He had so completely identified himself with the success of the Company's affairs that he now fell into the mistake of judging their situation in the light of his own personal fortunes. He was as gloomy now when Bengal was secure as he had been brimful with hope and confidence when things were at their worst. He tried to shut his eyes to the painful truth, because, like many another man who has grown gray in his life's work, he found it terribly hard to let go, to realize that his period of usefulness was over, his work done. Even the worst evil afflicting Bengal, the weakness of its government that arose from its chronic divisions, could be best and quickest cured by his own retirement. A bitter thought, indeed! Yet, though the habits of decision and command still held sway, a vital change had already come over him. He was no more now than a machine that continued to operate after the motive force had been cut off. Like a man who craves for food long after all real desire to eat has left him, Hastings still felt the craving for power and authority. When he spoke, the words were still the words of the Hastings that had vanquished Clavering, Monson and Francis—only the spirit, the vital generating force, was missing. It had died with the sailing of the *Atlas*.

Fifty-two is not old, and at that age a man is usually just reaching the pinnacle of his career—not just about to leave it. But a man is young or old according to whether he is going up or coming down. Hastings's career was over; he was coming down; he was old, even though more than a third of his life still lay ahead of him. And when his wife left him the sweets of office turned to dead ashes in his mouth. The greatest post within reach of a British subject became to him an empty mockery, without power, without future, without satisfaction, comfort or happiness. It was as well that it should have been so, because it made it easier for him to drop the reins when the time to do so came. No, fifty-two is not old, but at fifty-two Hastings was almost ready to think only of retirement and of the peace and quiet that he hoped to find back in his own country. Before another year was passed he was entirely ready.

The moment Mrs. Hastings had sailed he was gripped with terrible grief and loneliness. For days he bitterly reproached himself for having sent her away, torturing himself with the idea that perhaps, after all, it had been unnecessary. He was counting the cost of a decision that he had taken in a moment of supreme self-sacrifice. Forgetting the insistent advice of his doctors, or inclined now to attach little weight to their opinion—and why, after all, should he have attached much weight to them, when we remember the absurdly primitive state of medical science at this time?—he became a pitiable victim of alternate pity for himself and acute anxiety for her safety and welfare. The month following found him writing to her:

"I miss you in every instant and incident of my life, and everything seems to wear a dead stillness around me. I come home as to a solitude. I see a crowd in my house, and at my table, but not the looks of smiling welcome which used to make my home a delight to me, no Marian to infuse into my heart the fullness of content, and make me pleased with everybody and with everything about me. Even in my dreams I have lost you."

He had been able to cast away care and fatigue when she was with him. He had been able to endure disappointment, anxiety, trouble of every kind, without loss of spirits, so long as she was there. A few minutes of her gay and sprightly company had been perfect balm to his soul. And now when he felt that he needed her most she was gone. Not a day passed but he counted it gained towards the time of their reunion.

He was saved from the state of complete morbidity that threatened to settle upon him by the pressure of work and the necessity of arranging for his long journey. Nevertheless he closed his country residence at Alipore, unable to bear the thought of living in it after she was gone, and placed it and all his other estates upon the market preparatory to his own departure. His concern for his health, also, greatly increased and he began to take precautions that he had never thought of taking before. His diary at this time records a continuous struggle against physical weakness:

"Feb. 9th, 1784.—Woke with a severe cold and swellings in the glands of my throat. Much indisposed and go to bed at one.... 12th.—

Better.... 15th.—Awoke sick with a headache, remained ill all day. Slept well.... 16th.—Better but languid.... 17th.—Great languor all day.... 19th.—Much better...." [1]

Now, too, it was that he began at last to pay some heed to the state of his private fortune and to realize, when it was almost too late, the need for economy. Panic seized him lest the day of his leaving India would find him without the means of supporting his retirement, and he brought to mind all the public enterprises that he had financed out of his own pocket: the compilations of law made by the Pundits and the learned Moslem professors, the establishment of a Moslem seminary and the missions to Tibet. So now it was that he wrote to the Court of Directors to tell them that, although he had not originally intended to carry these expenses to the account of the Company, he felt at length constrained to do so on account of poverty:

"Improvident for myself, zealous for the honor of my country and the credit and interest of my employers, I seldom permitted any prospects of futurity to enter into the views of my private concerns. In the undisturbed exercise of the faculties which appertained to the active season of my life, I confined all my regards to my public character, and reckoned on a fund of years to come for its duration. The infirmities of life have since succeeded, and I have lately received more than one severe warning to retire from a scene to which my bodily strength is no longer equal, and am threatened with a corresponding decay in whatever powers of mind I once possessed to discharge the laborious duties and hard vicissitudes of my station. With this change in my condition, I am compelled to depart from that liberal plan which I originally adopted, and to claim from your justice—for you have forbid me to appeal to your generosity—the discharge of a debt which I can with the most scrupulous integrity aver to be justly my due, and which I cannot sustain." [2]

II

When he wrote this letter he was already on his way to Lucknow. He went by boat up the Ganges, which was the usual and most comfortable means of making the journey. As soon as he passed the borders of the Company's dominions he found the country in a wretched state. The famine had laid a heavy hand on a land that was already groaning under misgovernment. He reported that from the confines of Buxar to Benares he was fatigued by the clamors of the starving and discontented inhabitants. The new administration he had established in Chait Singh's former dominion had proved too inefficient to control the local government agents and tax collectors who were oppressing and robbing the peasants and ruining trade. Only the city itself seemed tolerably well governed.

Once more Hastings tried his hand at reformation. During a stay of five days in the city he drew up a new plan of government that had as its main aim giving to the Rajah a more direct interest in its efficient functioning. New officials were appointed, all of them, as before, natives. This last point was one upon which he laid special emphasis: "I hope," he wrote to the Council, "that neither the present nor any future administration will think of committing the inferior detail to the control of a British subject. We have already too many English Collectors now in our own dewanny districts. To establish them in this would be to subvert the rights of the family, to injure the revenues, and to loosen the attachment of the ryots which it will be ever good policy to conciliate." [3]

In this terse manner he made it clear what side he took on one of the most important questions of policy that the British rulers had to decide: whether to place the administration of all parts of British India in the hands of Englishmen, or whether to employ natives. There was much to be said on both sides. If good government were a sufficient end in itself, the best hope for its attainment lay in pursuing the first policy. The moral and intellectual degeneration of the ruling classes of India had in the course of a century of anarchy been so complete that it was useless to expect high standards of honesty and efficiency from them, and their retention meant of necessity that the government had to tolerate and accept as inevitable much maladministration. [4] If, however, efficiency were not the sole end of government, there was a great deal to be said in favor of *not* subjecting the country wholly to the rule of a foreign race. And no one has said it better than Sir Walter Lawrence when, in the course of an address before the Royal Institution in 1914, he said that he would like to see the whole of British India turned into Indian States because he was convinced that the inhabitants of the latter were happier and more contented than those of the former.

"They have a government more congenial, more in accordance with their own ideas, in short, a government that is Indian.... If I were an Indian I should most certainly elect to live in an Indian State. There is more chance, more scope for individuality. There is more freedom and less overt and ever-present government. There is a career there open to the talents, there is no one there to jar on their sensibilities, and to run counter to their religious and social prejudices, and, above all, there is no one to disturb their quiet." [5]

There can be no doubt that Hastings would have heartily endorsed these views, for they were in truth his own. And he tried to give them practical effect. He was, as it happened, under less temptation than his successors to depart from this policy. Under the conditions existing in his day, with a dearth of competent men whether in the ranks of the Company's servants or among the Indians, a high standard of administration was an impossibility. Later, when the Civil Service had been organized and recruited from among the finest of Britain's sons, every man highly trained for the work, it became an easily attainable goal. It then became increasingly difficult for British Governors to remain passive and acquiescent spectators of misconduct on the part of govern-

ment agents; and since it was futile to look for improvement by sub-
stitution of one incapable and dishonest native official for another, it was
scarcely surprising that they chose the alternative of displacing them
with Englishmen. The immediate success of this policy led finally to a
fixed belief in the immeasurable superiority of British over any native
government, and that in turn to the conviction that the greatest benefit
that Britain could confer on India was to extend the area of direct
British rule as widely as possible. The final result was that the existence
of native misrule in any part of the country was accepted as sufficient
justification for annexation or, at the very least, intervention by the
suzerain power. In this way the indigenous political life and activity
of the people wilted and died. The all-embracing and strongly organized
paternalism of a foreign bureaucratic government proved too much for
it, and Indians were excluded from every avenue to honorable service
in their own country.

Today we are inclined to think the contrary, or Hastings's, policy
the more liberal and the wiser. Certainly the whole course of Indian
development would have been very different if it had remained the
British policy and the annexationists had stayed their hand—it would
have been different and it might have been more fortunate. In Hastings's
own day, however, no credit was given him for any liberality of view.
In fact, in the eyes of Edmund Burke, his policy only increased the
weight of the offenses for which he was impeached. As sporadic excesses had been committed by some of the Indian officials whom
Hastings had appointed, Burke could not resist the temptation of laying
them together with everything else that was amiss in India—at his door,
after due exaggeration of their nature according to the Burke method.
These atrocious acts had been committed by scoundrels appointed by
Hastings himself, therefore he was responsible for them, therefore he
was a co-partner in villainy—so ran the Burke logic. In no other part
of his extraordinary performance was Burke's lack of knowledge and
real understanding of actual Indian conditions more glaringly revealed.
(The common idea that Burke was well informed on India is a myth.
He was astonishingly full of information, it is true, but it was largely
misinformation supplied by Philip Francis.) John Shore disposed of
the whole fallacious argument in one sentence when he declared in
his evidence before the House of Lords that it would have made no
difference what Indians Mr. Hastings had appointed since the abuses
complained of would have continued; which meant that, in order to
be logical, Burke would have had to assume what would have been for
him the paradoxical position of condemning Hastings for not having
placed the entire administration of the country in British hands. It is
futile, however, to attempt to explain in terms of logic the workings of
Burke's mind on the subject of his great hallucination....

At Lucknow, which he reached at the end of March, Hastings
settled down for a stay of five months. There was much to be done.
He first devoted himself to the intricate task of auditing the Vizier's

confused accounts with the Company and ironing out the disputed points. He then discussed ways and means for making retrenchments in expenditure and showed the Vizier and his ministers how by better handling of their finances they could liquidate all debts and still have ample funds for current expenses. Finally he elaborated a five-year plan for the revenue that would afford much-needed relief to the ryots and devised a sweeping reform of the Vizier's inefficient and expensive military establishment.

While engaged on this latter task, he discovered that the Vizier was paying the Company the full subsidy as agreed upon by treaty, though the subsidiary force itself had been reduced in numbers. He wrote at once to the Council:

"Neither the Vizier nor any of his ministers have ever mentioned to me this deficiency, but it is not the less our duty to take it into consideration. In all our adjustments of accounts with the Vizier for many years back, we have been regulated by the strictest regard to justice, and the Vizier on his part has on every occasion relied most implicitly on our justice as well as the accuracy of our Accountant-General. Let us then confirm that confidence which is so happily reposed in us by pointing out mistakes, even although we must be losers by correcting them." [6]

But the Council could not see the force of this reasoning and refused to take any action.[1]

Hastings extended his stay in order to help put the reforms into operation. And when he left he expressed satisfaction with what he had accomplished. "The Nawab," he wrote his wife, "solemnly promised that he would not break a single thread of my engagements, and these, if undisturbed" (it was a big "if!") "will discharge all his debts to the Company in the course of a year, and leave him a free and independent man. His uncle, his mother and grandmother, the most respected of his family, are all in my interest, and look upon me as the guardian of their house; nor do I believe that I have left an enemy in all the Nawab's dominions, except among the most worthless, whose influence I have been the means of repressing...." The mother and grandmother, it should be observed, were the Begums whom he had "robbed."...

[1] "Even in those days, before any bureaucrat in the Administration had thought of making 'policy' a reason for forgetting justice in the solution of difficulties with the Indian States, a Governor-General might find himself thwarted in his efforts at fair play by a system which was too strong for him." (*The British Crown and the Indian States.*) The history of the subsidiary alliance with Oude during this period followed a course that was to be duplicated on a large scale when Wellesley extended the system to include a large part of India. The particular infraction of the Vizier's treaty rights that Hastings here pointed out was to become an all too common feature of the system. It was repeated, for instance, in 1807 when the subsidiary force in Hyderabad was reduced without the saving in expense being credited to the Nizam, who had ceded revenue-bearing lands to pay the cost of a fixed number of troops. Later Governors-General were sometimes more disposed to turn a blind eye to the practice than was Hastings.

While Hastings was at Lucknow he found himself compelled to play host to no less a personage than the Shahzada, the Mogul Emperor's son and heir. The young man had fled from Delhi in fear of his life and had come to implore the Governor-General to rescue him and his father from the cruel and treacherous hands of the Marathas. He was an attractive youth, full of estimable qualities, and Hastings took an immediate liking to him. He listened sympathetically to his story and his pleas for help, and as he did so he was seized with one of his most ambitious ideas. This appeal for British aid was an opportunity that should not be missed. The empire of the Moguls might be dead, the king of Delhi might be no more than the puppet of whoever possessed his person, but—he was still the symbol of *imperium,* and that symbol, like its analogous symbol of the western empire of Rome, was still of value to any power aspiring to universal dominion. The heirs of the great Akbar still held in their palsied hands a "sovereignty universally acknowledged, though the substance of it no longer exists"— they were still in the minds of countless millions the legitimate rulers of India. So, Hastings reasoned, it would be a stroke of wise statesmanship for the British to relieve the Marathas of their possession of the capital and the person of the king; also, by rescuing him and his family from the cruel and murderous hands of the Marathas and raising them from the abject state of degradation into which they had fallen, they would be performing a humane and generous act that would redound to their credit in the eyes of the peoples of India. [7]

Without doubt the idea was finely conceived, but it is with some eye-rubbing in amazement that we contemplate it as a proposal for immediate execution. The fact that it would have meant a military expedition, and possibly renewed war with the Maratha confederacy, and the fact of his putting it forward seriously at this precise juncture in his life—these are hard facts to swallow. Under the circumstances it was a fantastic suggestion, but not without value for understanding the character of the man. It is additional evidence of his liking for *bravura,* noticeable in other of his political schemes—that love of his for brilliant political projects requiring nothing less than the hand of a master genius for their execution. (Francis's *Robinson Crusoe* anecdote comes again to mind.) The idea also, perhaps, bears upon it a trace of sentimentality. How different is this conception of the Delhi monarch from the hard practical one of 1772 embodied in the contemptuous phrase, "a king of shreds and patches"! It was a difference brought about by advancing years, softening the hard contours of his mind and inducing a more idealistic view of empire. Now that he was about to relinquish his post he could indulge his emotions more freely, give wing to his imagination and let it roam at will amidst conceptions of empire from which the stern realities had hitherto debarred it. He was still dreaming the old dream, which had haunted him from his first days as Governor, of the power that might have been his and the use to which he would have put it. Power to translate his schemes into action, power wide and unfettered to serve his country and India as both ought to be served! A dream of freedom from the control of petty minds, of men without vision and without intelligence, of freedom from the constraints of other men's weakness, timidity and inertia, of the ignoble cowardice that refuses to accept responsibility, of the supineness that paralyzes action, of the jealousy and rancor that obstruct effort and defeat initiative. And out of this dream had now come the most completely imperialistic of all his schemes, the kind of scheme that would be expected of a young vigorous man, fresh from England, just beginning his term of office, and full of high hopes and ambitions!

Hastings was a man ahead of his time. Or rather his time was both present and future. He wanted to compress a century of time into his own few years—to do in a year what his successors could only do in twenty. His mind spanned with ease the gap that lay between the Empire of 1784 and the finished structure of 1858, and he wanted to send his body after it, to bring to completion the work that he had begun; and if he had had the power, as he had the mind and ability, of Akbar the Great, who shall say that he might not have succeeded as Akbar succeeded? His successors were only to bridge the gap by slow and painful stages; it was characteristic of him that he visualized the completed structure more readily than the labor and risk involved in its building. Most of his plans and enterprises, even the grandest of them, were to come to fruition in the fullness of time, often when all memory of them had been forgotten. Tibet, Egypt [1]—and now Delhi, were instances. In 1805 the British, led by the man upon whom the mantle of Warren Hastings fell, the Marquess Wellesley, occupied Delhi and became the custodians of its king and the inheritors of its imperial grandeur and traditions exactly as Hastings had intended.... In 1784 the proposal was received with cold derision by his Council. It was declared contrary to the Company's orders and far too dangerous, and they very wisely and emphatically vetoed it.

He began his return journey on August 27. The first part of it, as far as Benares, proved quite exciting and full of danger. The rains began and continued for a fortnight without intermission. Rivers overflowed. Streams appeared where before there was dry land. Men of his escort were drowned. He crossed "one new-born river on a raft which sunk below the surface with my single weight, and a few hours after wrecked my buggy which is yet lying in the channel where it fell." Further mishaps occurred after he had reached the Ganges. His boat— "my beautiful *budgerow*"—was wrecked through the stupidity of the crew. He told his wife, however, that he left the Vizier "in great good humor, and I do verily believe that his feelings and sentiments do justice to the kindness which I have shown him." Yet he was still in the same vile hands of his unworthy favorites—and that being so there was no real hope for any lasting improvement. Hastings had done his best, but it had all been futile.

[1] See next Chapter.

III

ALL this time ships had been arriving at Calcutta bringing news of rapid and important changes in the political situation at home, accompanied by corresponding changes in Hastings's unstable fortunes. The anxious man awaited each successive packet of letters in a fever of impatience, for he was still debating with himself the question whether to stay or to go. He knew that the answer would depend on the contents of these dispatches. The state of politics at home had become a matter of supreme importance to him.

The first thing he learned was that in the spring of the previous year an unnatural, discreditable and most unpopular coalition between Lord North and Charles James Fox had displaced the weak Shelburne ministry and that Fox's friends had swarmed into ministerial posts and on to the Government benches. Burke and Sheridan held office, while Lord North, for his part, showed himself as ready to withdraw his support from the Governor-General as to ally himself with the man who had for twenty years been his own bitterest political opponent; for it was he who seconded a resolution of Burke's for an inquiry into Hastings's conduct in Benares and Oude. The moment, however, was not opportune for another frontal attack on the Governor-General's position. This was one time when the smoke-screen methods of Philip Francis could not obscure the brilliance of his rival's success. The news that an honorable peace had been concluded with the Marathas stirred the nation to real enthusiasm. Here was one part of the Empire where the late war had not ended in disaster. Here was one leader who had been victorious.

For a brief space Hastings was a national hero. His enemies could not prevent the Court of Proprietors, consistently loyal to its great servant, from meeting to pass a formal vote of thanks to him for his splendid services. They did succeed, however, in prevailing upon the friends of Macpherson and Stables to insist on their inclusion in the vote—presumably on the principle, as Lord Mansfield remarked, of "I and the doctor cured the fever." Many voices were now heard singing his praises. The Earl of Stair, with no particular interest either in him or in the Company, remarked on "the frequent, trifling, partial, peevish interferences of Parliament in the Company's affairs." "Above all," he added, "the late attempts in Parliament to dismiss from his government with disgrace the Company's great minister, the powerful Chatham of the East, were proceedings of a most absurd ingratitude, for which no reason can be assigned but a detestable one, viz. his possessing what many men covet to possess." [8] Lord Stair voiced the feelings of many high-minded and intelligent men of the time in thinking it strange that all the forces of reform should have been bent towards that quarter of the globe in which alone Britain's affairs had been conducted with success.

Yet if a frontal attack was for the moment impracticable, there was nothing to stop ministers from striking at Hastings's flank. Lord Macartney had by this time come into action and was making his influence powerfully felt. Letters of burning denunciation of the Governor-General poured in from him. The Court of Directors, subservient as usual to ministerial influence, maintained its consistently hostile attitude and continued to pursue him with endless and irrational censures. The news that he intended shortly to resign was received with general rejoicing; for even his friends felt that it was a wise decision under the circumstances.

Fox was encouraged to go to extremes, ignoring the King's growing partiality for the Governor-General and the general hostility towards the ministry. With Burke and Francis urging him on to the grand assault, on November 18, 1783, he introduced his—or rather, Burke's, because he it was who had drafted it—India Bill, and coupled it with a fierce attack on Hastings. In most essentials, especially in its treatment of problems of Indian administration, the Bill (or Bills, for there were two of them) incorporated Francis's ideas, providing for the restoration of the lands of Bengal to their hereditary holders as landed estates, enjoining non-intervention as the system of foreign policy, and prohibiting schemes of conquest. In addition, it provided for the complete annihilation of the Company's power, both political and commercial, and its transfer to the Crown. Burke supported the measure with his customary brilliant oratory, curdling the blood of his hearers with his description of Indian horrors and eulogizing the noble labors of the martyred Majority and, in particular, Mr. Philip Francis, who, with his majestic thought, large legislative conceptions, grand plans of policy, angelic patience and temper, and his disinterested and unrewarded services, had been the one bright star in the dark night of Indian government. [9]

The fate of the Bill is a familiar story. Passed by the House of Commons but defeated in the Lords by the combined efforts of the King's, Hastings's and the Company's friends, assisted by the treachery of North's *quondam* confidant Robinson, it served to bring about the downfall of the hated coalition and the succession of Pitt as Prime Minister. It was at this time that Lord Temple, Pitt's intimate friend, said to Major Scott: "I hope to God Mr. Hastings will not think of quitting Bengal. I have taken great pains to make myself acquainted with the transactions there during his administration, and I find the deeper I go the more reason I have to admire the conduct of Mr. Hastings." [10]

It was generally agreed that one main cause of the government's overthrow had been Warren Hastings. This, also, was the opinion of the defeated ministers, and consequently their rage against him rose to still greater heights. The new ministers came into office professing their sincere esteem and respect for their absent benefactor. Lord Gower termed the government "The Hastings Administration." [11] The Governor-General's friends were jubilant, confident that their troubles were at an end. Scott, appearing this year in Parliament with a seat for which Hastings had paid £4000, wrote to inform him that even Dundas, who, he said, was now his steady friend and supporter, was positive that when Pitt's own India Bill passed he would be appointed Governor-General under it, and had boasted that, sooner than allow the House of Commons to carry an address to the King to remove him, ministers would dissolve Parliament. "If we have strength enough," said this sudden convert to the cause, "to carry the bill, be assured we shall have strength enough, and more than enough, to preserve Mr. Hastings." [12]

Such was the language of ministers in January 1784. At last it appeared as if this man, who had been a storm center of English politics for ten uninterrupted years, had won the final victory over his enemies. It appeared even more likely when Parliament was dissolved in March and Pitt won a sweeping victory. The Opposition was reduced nearly to impotence and Fox almost lost his seat. With a powerful and friendly government behind him it was possible for Hastings either to continue in office with the comfortable assurance of steady support or to retire in triumph to the accompaniment of well-earned honors. His friends held out to him nothing but the most rosy prospects. Even the Court of Directors veered round again. Taking its cue from ministers as usual, it retracted its orders for the reinstatement of Chait Singh and supported Hastings in his quarrel with Lord Macartney. There was scarcely a member of the Government who did not admit his obligation to him.

Almost immediately, however, it began to appear that all was *not* well. Once more Hastings's friends had miscalculated, and this time they had misread the character of the young man of twenty-five who now held the Administration, the House of Commons, the East India Company, Warren Hastings, all of them, in the hollow of his hand. William Pitt was not a man to be impressed by the largely insincere tributes of gratitude lavished on the Governor by his followers, nor to surrender his views to theirs. And his regard for Hastings was probably at no time more than a lukewarm admiration.

A cold, proud, somewhat austere young man, Pitt inherited brilliant gifts and a positive genius, excelling his father's, for politics. Admirably equipped for the management of two great spheres of government, the national finances and the national Parliament, he at first lacked breadth of vision and depth of knowledge and understanding outside them. In particular, he shared with the great majority of his fellow-countrymen a lamentable ignorance of India and everything that pertained to the administration of British affairs there; with the almost inevitable result that he imbibed all too freely the distorted views so prevalent at the time. There were very few British statesmen at this time who escaped the malign influence of Philip Francis. He remained an oracle even when under suspicion of being biased. Pitt's cold, dispassionate, mathematical mind enabled him to avoid the unrestrained fury of Burke and the insane excesses to which it carried him—these he scorned and despised. But he had absorbed and accepted enough of the Franciscan legend to regard Hastings in the light of an aggressive and extravagant imperialist. Perhaps the powerful figure of the proconsul of India assumed in his eyes something of the sinister character of a Bonaparte. Pitt was not like his father, who had reveled in conducting great military enterprises and schemes of conquest, for whom Clive had been a man after his own heart, and who would have supported Hastings in his work of consolidation and preservation with all the resources at Britain's disposal. Pitt the Younger's genius "was of a different bent, his eloquence of a different class, his statecraft of a different school." He was cast in the modern mold that produces economists and financiers, rather than empire-builders and conquerors. His fastidiousness and dominating constitutionalism, his distaste of arbitrary power and of war and war's extravagance, sufficed to make him distrust the man who was popularly supposed to incarnate these evils. The dyed-in-the-wool Parliamentarian, the stickler for legal forms and the niceties of government by discussion and compromise, is not the man to approve the very different methods necessarily employed in the governance of an Oriental empire.

Pitt's critics, and even some of his friends, asserted that he was jealous of Hastings's prestige and importance, and that wounded pride made him anxious to prove that he was indebted to no man for his office. And there may well have been some truth in their belief. A young man in his early twenties is naturally apt to be hyper-sensitive where his own position is so intimately affected. Pitt had attained the supreme position in the State at an age when most men were just stepping on to the first rung of the ladder. Such success is a powerful incentive to youthful self-conceit. To a nature naturally haughty, proud, not a little ungenerous, it must surely have been mortifying to hear constantly such sentiments as these so tactlessly expressed by his Lord Chancellor:

"I do not know a man who cuts so great a figure upon the stage of the world as Hastings: to his other extraordinary actions must be added that of giving a ministry to Great Britain, for whether we may choose generally to confess it or not, the fact is that this is Hastings's Administration, and that he put an end to the late ministry as completely as if he had taken a pistol and shot them through the head one after another. It would therefore be base and dishonorable in ministers not to advise His Majesty to confer some mark of his royal favor upon a man who, to his other great and important services, can boast of performing this meritorious action also." [13]

But whatever the reasons were, Pitt certainly did not share Lord Thurlow's enthusiasm. When Hastings's friends pressed for a peerage for him, the Prime Minister objected and managed to find a specious excuse for withholding his consent. Hastings was a great man. Certainly! He had rendered splendid services to the State. Indubitably! He had a claim upon government for anything he could ask. Surely!

But there was a difficulty: the resolutions of censure were still standing on the records of the House of Commons. Of course, he knew that the charges were false and unjust, yet until the stigma of those resolutions had been removed by the passing of a vote of thanks, he did not see how he could with propriety advise His Majesty to confer an honor upon Mr. Hastings. An attitude which was all very right and proper, even though it might appear to those who were disposed to carp that an unusual weight was being attached to the resolutions of a House that had condemned other men at other times in like manner—including Mr. Pitt himself—without thereby disqualifying them from receiving honors and offices from the Crown. Yet, even admitting the point, there is still cause to doubt Pitt's sincerity. He had a large majority in Parliament ready to do his bidding and, if he had wished, he could have gone to the House of Commons the very next day and secured the vote of thanks. But he did not so wish: he preferred to shuffle. Lord Thurlow lamely excused him by saying that he was afraid to put the matter to the test.

A curious story is told of how the Lord Chancellor went to the Prime Minister to inquire his reasons for refusing to honor Hastings and to try to refute them. Pitt is said to have named four: first, because Hastings had attempted to extend the British dominions in India; second, because he had by his conduct forfeited the confidence of the native princes of India; third, because he had, in various instances, disobeyed the orders of the Court of Directors; and, last, because he had fixed enormous salaries to offices in Bengal and wasted the public money to gratify the servants of the Company who were attached to him. Thurlow challenged Pitt to produce specific instances of these offenses, and promised him that if he could not rebut each one satisfactorily he would not only consent to sacrifice Hastings but would insist upon his being sacrificed to national justice. He is alleged to have said, "Come, Mr. Pitt—I see you know as little of the matter as I do." Scott related this story to Hastings as having been given to him by Lord Thurlow himself. [14]

Pitt's patent indisposition to Hastings was not displayed only in a negative refusal to do him an act of common justice. Fresh legislation for the affairs of India and the East India Company being the most urgent need of the day, he lost no time in introducing his own bill. Drafted by Dundas—in collaboration with the ever-blooming and egregious Robinson, who had wisely transferred his allegiance and his services from North to Pitt—it incorporated in its essentials the same principles and prejudices as the late lamented bill of Mr. Fox: that is to say, it incorporated the ideas of Philip Francis, though that gentleman, being a Whig, refused to recognize or acknowledge his own child. The only essential difference between the two bills was that Pitt's left the commercial and some of the political power in the hands of the Company, the latter to be exercised, however, only under close supervision by a Board of Control composed of members of the Cabinet and the Privy Council; whereas Fox's had transferred practically all of both kinds to the Crown.

When the Bill was introduced, the process of hoodwinking Hastings's friends into believing that the Ministry was favorable to the cause of their chief was still going on, and they were foolish enough to allow themselves to be prevailed upon by flattery and empty promises to give their cordial support to it. They had not the sense to see that in its fundamentals it ran counter to many of Hastings's most cherished ideas, nor were they able apparently to read between the lines of Pitt's introductory speech, in which he carefully avoided any mention of the Governor-General's name or allusion to his conduct. By implication, at least, he admitted all the slanders of Burke and Fox, and his appearance of moderation and fairness made the attack the more subtly effective because coming from an apparently candid and judicial mind. He arraigned the administration of the Company for gross mismanagement and misconduct. He admitted the urgent need for the interference of the legislature. He assumed that the Bengal Government had been bent on ambitious schemes of conquest, which had involved the Company in expensive and bloody wars and been detrimental to British interests. He asserted that it had been extravagant and wasteful, and that there was need for regulation to prevent "the continuance of that rapacity, plunder and extortion, which is shocking to the feelings of humanity and disgraceful to the national character." He implied that crimes deserving of severe punishment had been committed and declared that unless restraint was imposed "offenses equally shocking to humanity, opposite to justice, and contrary to every principle of religion and humanity, will prevail unchecked, uncontrolled and unrestrained." [15]

No names were mentioned. It was not necessary when the accusations of Burke and his friends were still fresh in every one's mind. Burke would have been explicit in naming the chief culprit, but otherwise there was little discernible difference between his attitude towards Hastings and that of Pitt. The Bill encountered no effective opposition and soon reached the statute book.

IV

THE news of his triumph—if the expulsion of Fox and his friends from office can be regarded in that light—reached Hastings at a moment when he was in an unusually responsive mood. Compelled to break his journey while his wrecked boat was being repaired, he was spending a quiet week in the fort at Chunar. It was three years exactly since his last visit. How different were the circumstances now from then! Brief as his stay now was, it afforded him the first genuine interlude of rest and relaxation that he had enjoyed for no one knows how long, and he was feeling greatly refreshed, both in health and spirits. "My complaints, such as they are," he wrote to his wife, "evidently proceed from

the weather, and are languor, lassitude and inactivity. I eat sparingly:
I never sup, and am generally abed by ten. I breakfast at six. I bathe
with cold water daily, and while I was at Lucknow twice a day, using
sooreys [large pots of porous clay] cooled with ice." But, he added
sadly, "the best health that I gain or can hope to gain in India, is but
a palliative acquired with continual sacrifices and unmanly attentions.
I want a multitude of aids to cure me thoroughly, all which may be
included in two comprehensive but comfortable terms, a hard frost and
my own fireside."

The news worked an instantaneous, if shortlived, change in his
state of mind. He was like a man rejuvenated—gay, exuberant, optimistic. Despondency and gloom vanished. And for no other reason than
that he believed the downfall of the Coalition meant that his own
reputation was completely established! "My fortune is in its flood," he
cried. He read with admiration the accounts of Pitt's brilliant uphill
fight, of how he had maintained himself in power against the fury of
Fox and North and their superior numbers. "Would to God that I was
in England," he wrote in a burst of enthusiasm. "I could give to such
a man my labor with pleasure, without office or reward, or desire of
either."

Yet when he came to analyze the reports more closely, doubts
sprang up in his mind. The education of Warren Hastings in the ways
of the political world was progressing. He was now much wiser than
the friends in England who assured him that both his reputation and his
position were safe as a result of the change in government. Unlike gul-
lible Major Scott he was careful to take the perfervid protestations of
ministers with a very large pinch of salt.[1] When, for instance, he came
to examine the public statements and actions of Mr. Pitt, he noticed
at once that, while he had defended the Company against Fox, he
had not defended Warren Hastings. In fact, he saw that Pitt had very
carefully refrained from committing himself publicly to any definite
course.

His reasoning was shrewd. If he was expected to stay, why had he
not been told so by authority? Especially, why had he not been told so
by the only packet that could reach him before the date that he had
set for his departure? He had committed himself to going. What reason
could he now have for remaining, if not definitely asked to do so?
So, he wrote Mrs. Hastings, "I must either change my purpose, in
obedience to authority, or assume an air of contemptible self-importance
and say on my own authority that my services cannot be spared." It
seemed to him probable that all the Ministry wanted was that he should
remain as a cipher until they had time to appoint some one of their own
selection—which was, as it happened, the truth! Dundas was pressing
for the appointment of Lord Cornwallis, who had not long returned

[1] It is possible, as Mr. Holden Furber suggests, that Scott's reports to his chief
regarding the views and intentions of Dundas and other ministers are not to be
trusted. Mr. Furber says, "they were obviously written to please." [16]

from America and was not loath to blot out the memory of his humiliating experience at Yorktown. [17]

He was still willing to remain—but on his own terms only. If his employers gave him their support and entrusted him with adequate powers, if, that is to say, they ordered his colleagues to support him and allow him to take the lead in policy, with the responsibility when they disagreed, and *requested* him to stay, then he would deem himself bound to remain, against every consideration of domestic comfort and happiness, of life and fortune—"my income is not equal to all my present expenses" (not even an income of £25,000 a year!)—though it were to mean sacrificing them forever. Otherwise, never! Otherwise, he would return home in the hope of arriving in time to lend his assistance in framing a new constitution for the government of India. "It is hard to see the good that I could do, and am not permitted to do it."

One thing especially annoyed and embarrassed him, and that was the immoderate and indiscreet zeal of his friends in England acting in his behalf, and above all their mistaken pursuit of honors and pensions for him. He wanted none for himself. "If I have enough for a decent subsistence, I want no pensions and despise titles." A peerage would merely put him on a level with men whom he despised, like "that paltry fellow," Lord Macartney. So far as it concerned himself alone, he was satisfied to remain a commoner. If a peerage was freely and honorably offered him he would accept it, more for Mrs. Hastings's sake than his own, knowing as he did how much it would please her.

After explaining at great length and with evident candor his sentiments regarding the effect of the late news from England on his position, he closed his letter to his wife:

"I have now but one wish remaining—(yes, one more) viz., to be able to leave the stage of active life while my fortune is in the zenith of its prosperity, and while I have a constitution yet repairable.... Adieu, my beloved, my most deserving and lovely Marian. May the God whose goodness I have so wonderfully experienced, bless you with health, safety and comfort, and me with the possession of my sweet Marian! Amen! Amen! Amen! I never loved you so much as I do at this instant."

Hastings moved on from Chunar to Benares, where he stayed a while to see the result of his recent reorganization of the government, the Council having allowed him to put his proposals into effect on his own responsibility, though almost all his other suggestions had met with a flat rejection. He was still accompanied by the Mogul Crown Prince whom he was at a loss to know how to dispose of. Knowing that the young man's presence would be embarrassing as well as dangerous both at Calcutta and Benares, he finally supplied him with sufficient men and money to secure his safe return to Delhi. The only advice he could give him in parting was to look to Sindhia for protection from the dangers threatening the Emperor.

What Hastings saw in the province of Benares encouraged him. The recent plentiful rains gave promise of an abundant harvest. Some improvement was also discernible as a result of his measures. In the city itself a marked change for the better had taken place since Chait Singh's days. The news of Wheler's sudden death speeded his return. He left Benares on October 22 and reached Calcutta a fortnight later. Awaiting him was a letter from the Court of Directors, "as unpleasing as any that I ever received from that body in the time of General Clavering."

His state of suspense was now nearing its end, and as a preparatory step he reserved his passage on the *Barrington,* which would be ready to sail early in the New Year. By delaying until then he could get the latest word from England, just in case.... One by one all the ties that had held him to his post were snapping. He no longer felt indispensable: "I cannot go at a time of more quiet or public ease than the present." The constant struggle to retain what little was left to him of his health irked him greatly. And he was heartily tired of Calcutta and the endless round of official duties. "What care I for society?" he wrote to Marian. "My days pass in incessant writing, reading, hearing and talking, and ever close with weariness and little headaches, which sometimes grow to great ones. If I am doomed to remain another year, and survive it, I must carry witnesses of my identity, or return like Ulysses an old man and a beggar to my Penelope, and with only one scar, which cannot be seen, to convince you that I am your husband."

He was not, however, to be so doomed. On December 20 he received particulars of Pitt's India Bill, and that finally ended his hesitation. He had given his loyalty to the Company, to the Proprietors in particular, much of whose power was stripped from them by the new constitution. His disappointment with Pitt was profound. He felt that no act more injurious to the Company and its servants and his own character and authority could have been devised, "though fifty Burkes, Foxes and Francises had clubbed to invent one." Only a short time before he had written to its framer in terms of compliment and admiration, amounting, as he admitted, to adulation, under the impression "equal to the faith of religion, that I was writing to a man of strict honor and virtue." Faced by the grim reality of his speech, he now believed him to be wanting in both.

"Why, Scott," he cried, "what devil has Mr. Pitt dressed for his exemplar, and clothed with such damnable attributes of ambition, spirit of conquest, thirst of blood, propensity to expense and troubles, extravagance and improvidence in creating overcharged establishments, disobedience of orders, rapacity, plunder, extortion!!! It is a pity that the thirst of blood was out of its place. Had it closed the list, it would have made a complete climax, gradually heating the imagination to a degree of abhorrence due to the utmost perfection of human guilt. But lest this effect should be lost, Mr. Pitt winds up his description in a general display by which the great prototype of the mighty master's mind shines forth in the full blaze of complicated horror; armed with crimes shocking to the feelings of humanity, disgraceful to the national character, fatal in their tendency, opposite to justice, and contrary to every principle of religion and morality!!! And am I this character? Assuredly not: but most assuredly was it the declaimer's intention to fix it upon me; for much of this, and the whole in substance, but with less aggravation, had been before given to me by my avowed enemies, and no part of it to any individual but myself. I am therefore the sole proprietor of the whole aggregate allowance.

"Perhaps, if I were to reproach him with the gross injury which he has done me, he would deny the intention. But why should he? He is above my reach; and a mind capable of using such insidious means to taint an innocent character with such a mass of infamy may easily affect to glory in the consciousness of its own virtue, and lay claim to the public applause for such a manifestation of it...." [18]

The die was cast, and there were to be no more hesitations. On New Year's day he penned his resignation to the Company, proudly declaring—and who can deny it?—that "no man ever served them with a zeal superior to my own, nor perhaps with equal." [19] But he had one last obligatory duty to perform: to obtain from the Council a pledge that they would respect his arrangements with the Vizier. And when they had given it to him, he was able to write to his wife (December 26): "This point settled, it is determined absolutely—I will wait for no advices. They have given me my freedom and opened the road to my happiness." He had just heard of her safe arrival in England and of her cordial reception at Court: the fact that she was a divorcee had not, as might have been expected, prejudiced her in the eyes of Queen Charlotte. The Queen, indeed, had been graciously pleased to accept from her the gift of an ivory bed.

Then came the final preparations for transferring the government without loss of prestige and confidence. The Indians, accustomed always to hereditary personal rule, had scarcely grasped the idea of being governed by a company that never died, yet constantly changed its agents. In these thirteen years Hastings had so stamped his name and personality on the consciousness of India that his departure was regarded in the same light as the death of a king, and when rulers in India died there was always fear and uncertainty, because of the danger of a disputed succession, of civil war and revolution, of broken treaties and an abrupt change of policy. He was especially anxious to lull the fears of the native princes whose friendship and confidence he had gained and to whom he appeared as a veritable child of Victory. They could hardly be expected to understand that the day he left the shores of their country might be the day when he severed all connection with them and became of as little consequence as though he had never set foot in India. Although he knew the utter uncertainty of the future, he wrote reassuring them regarding the intentions of his successor and promising to use whatever influence he might possess at home to obtain the sanction of his employers for all existing treaties, alliances and other engagements.

Almost the last act of his administration was to carry out a plan of retrenchment affecting the entire civil and military establishment, a necessarily unpopular reform that he would not have undertaken if he had had regard only for his own interests.

Then he made his farewells to the men whom he had led for thirteen years and who had served him so loyally and devotedly. In his last message he paid a warm tribute to the Service, pronouncing it "to be eminently marked with a liberality of sentiment, a susceptibility and firmness of attachment, a disdain of sordid emolument, with a spirit of assiduity, and the consequent expertness in business, exceeding, I dare venture to affirm, the habits of any community under the British Empire." He expressed the hope that the time would come, and he would use what feeble influence he might have to help its coming, when the cloud of prejudice that obscured its true worth would disperse and it would be displayed in its full luster. He was, indeed, loyal to a Service that was not nearly so immaculate and disinterested as these encomiums upon it would suggest, immensely improved though it was from the time when he took office. Actually, if the truth must be told, this was one part of his task that he was definitely leaving unfinished. The system, full as it still was of graft, peculation and abuses of many kinds, had proved too strong for him. He had had to compromise to some extent with evil and to use his patronage rights in ways that would be severely frowned upon today, though quite customary at that time. If he had complacently allowed some members of the Bengal administration to continue to enjoy annual emoluments of £5000, £10,000, £15,000, even £18,000, it was because he, like nearly all public men of that tainted period, had come to accept such facts and figures as almost inseparable features of government as it was then practiced—nor, even if his reforming zeal had continued undiminished, had it been within his power to do all the purifying of the service that was necessary.

When all was in readiness for his departure, he took part in a touching scene. The gallant survivors of Colonel Pearse's corps of the Bengal Army, who had made history by their march to join Coote in the Carnatic, had just returned, reduced to less than half their original strength. Hastings could not leave without a word of congratulation and farewell to the men who had served him so well. So he met and reviewed them. There was as much sadness on both sides, perhaps, as there was on another similar occasion a little more than a year before when George Washington had bade farewell to his army; sadness on the side of the sepoys who were losing an admired and beloved leader as well as on that of the man who was making his last public appearance as Governor-General.

He left Calcutta on February 1, attended by a small group of sorrowing friends, and sailed on the 6th. The next day—Mrs. Hastings's birthday, as he carefully noted in his diary—they lost sight of land.

"If I am conscious," were his parting words, "of having maintained to the last act of my public life the integrity of conduct and the consistency of those principles which I had laid down for the regulation of it; neither my constituents, whose interests even in this instance were my leading object, nor my friends, who had withheld from me their belief in my professions, nor my enemies, if I yet have such, who have labored to effect by violence that act which I have performed upon myself, have any right to pass their censures upon me. I am accountable to myself alone; and in the approbation of my own mind, I feel a support which the world cannot move. Yet may I feel a regret to see that hope which I had too fondly indulged, and which I had sustained during thirteen labored years with a perseverance against a succession of difficulties which might have overcome the constancy of an abler mind, of being in some period of time, however remote, allowed to possess and exercise the full powers of my station, of which I had hitherto held little more than the name and responsibility; and to see with it the belief which I had as fondly indulged, that I should become the instrument of raising the British name, and the substantial worth of its possessions in India, to a degree of prosperity proportioned to such a trust; both vanish in an instant, like the illusions of a dream; with the poor and only consolation left me of the conscious knowledge of what I could have effected, had my destiny ordained that I should attain the situation to which I aspired, and that I have left no allowable means untried, by which I might have attained it." [20]

Chapter XXV

BROAD HORIZONS

I

IT is safe to say that none of the many men whom Britain has sent to India has been more splendidly equipped for rulership than Warren Hastings. When the essential element in a government is the personality of one man, its efficient functioning depends on the ability of that man to manage and direct every part of its varied activity. He cannot be an expert in just one department and leave the others to the care of his subordinates, without detriment to the whole. That was Hastings's great merit, that there was no department of government of which he was not master and which he did not actively supervise and control. Some of his successors may have been more versed in the highly complex matter of land administration. Others may have been better military strategists and organizers. But none of them possessed greater all-round capacity or stretched out a hand in more directions. And with Hastings it was not a matter of taking up different questions and enterprises in rotation; he had an amazing capacity for attending to everything at once.

The extent of his versatility, of his breadth of vision and manifold interests, is even better shown by what he did outside the scope of his ordinary duties than by what he did inside, remarkable as that was. He was, indeed, the ideal ruler, not content merely to administer and to govern but reaching out to the higher realms of the mind, working to extend the bounds of knowledge and improve the intangibles of civilization. To read his story is to be carried for a space at breakneck speed along a rushing torrent of events, past rocks and shoals, twists and turns, eddies and whirlpools of fate and circumstance, only to find oneself suddenly and at unexpected moments moving quietly and serenely along some placid backwater out of sound of war and politics and the clash of hostile minds. Such moments are precious and their unexpectedness is half their charm. It is not a little surprising, for instance, to learn that during the summer of the year 1783, amidst all its stress and strain, a peaceful mission of friendship and scientific exploration set out into the unknown Himalaya tableland, or that the month which saw the departure of Mrs. Hastings saw also the founding of a learned society in Calcutta, and that the Governor-General was responsible wholly or in part for both. The fact is that to think of Warren Hastings only as an able administrator and servant of the East India Company is to perceive only one side of his character. The other was that of a cultured man of intellectual pursuits, a lover of arts and letters. He belonged to the choice company of those lovers of the things of the mind and the spirit who brought science and philosophy into close contact with the busy world of affairs. A type not too common at any time, it was particularly rare in the Company's service during its pioneering period.

Reference has been made to the general character of the age in which he lived, the coarseness of manners, the prevailing inhumanity and callousness, the dearth of idealism, the low tone of moral, intellectual and spiritual life. It took England a hundred years to recover from the effects of the intense reaction against Puritanism that marked the Restoration period. But the turning-point had come before the end of the third quarter of the century. Reform movements of different kinds were slowly making headway. The seeds from which a rich harvest was to be reaped in the following century were then being sown. The tone of English life, low as it was, was already steadily improving. Manners were becoming more decent, thought more liberal, culture more widely diffused; intellectual activity, marked by a special taste for antiquity, was increasing; books were being published in greater number and being more widely read; the great romantic movement was beginning. John Wesley, Johnson, Hume, Gibbon, Burke—to name only five of the great liberating forces of the period—were exercising their profound influence on English thought. Cities, roads, art, religion, politics were each in their diverse way to bear increasingly the marks of a new-born passion for improvement. England was, in fact, in process of becoming more civilized.

The change was reflected in India. The same civilizing forces that were at work in England came into action there. The work was of many hands and no one man did more than advance it a little. But Hastings's title to being one of the first and most important of these forces is clear. We have already described the Calcutta of his day with its open cesspools, its unburied corpses, its filth and squalor; nor was there much done to clean it up until the end of the century. Nevertheless, the city made rapid strides during Hastings's administration, and the change was all towards greater refinement and amenity. A visitor in 1780 describes the banks of the river below the town as being "studded with elegant mansions called garden-houses. These houses are surrounded by groves and lawns, which descend to the water's edge, and present a constant succession of whatever can delight the eye, or bespeak wealth and elegance in the owners." The same observer speaks also of the beautiful appearance of the Esplanade, with its magnificent "palaces." [1] The city had begun to take on an appearance worthy of the capital of an empire, and for this improvement it was indebted, according to William Hodges, the Royal Academician, who arrived in Bengal in March 1781, "solely to the liberal and excellent taste of the late Governor-General." Mr. Hodges also gave Warren Hastings credit for having erected the first house deserving the name of a piece of architecture—that was his own residence at Alipore. [2] Among the public works he sponsored was the building of a new church adequate to the needs of the European community. He gave the land, presided over the executive committee and headed the subscription list, with the result that the foundation-stone of what is now St. John's Cathedral was laid in April 1784.

Both by example and active effort Hastings strove to promote culture, elevate thought and improve conduct. A man of highly cultivated taste himself, as many of his contemporaries, including Dr. Johnson and Boswell, bear witness, he took delight in being the friend and patron of painters. Zoffany and Devis, as well as Hodges, visited Bengal during his term of office, enjoying, like so many others, the free hospitality of Government House. Lord Curzon, in fact, has declared that "he was almost the only one in the long list of the British rulers of India who took a real interest in literature, scholarship, and the arts." [3] Some of the ways in which this interest revealed itself deserve a fuller exposition.

Perhaps the greatest service Hastings rendered India was in giving the first impetus to a new outlook on the part of the British rulers towards the country they governed. He did this, not by tightening the grip of Britain upon her, but by sublimating the early sordidness of that grip. No sooner had he become Governor than he set out, as we have seen, to educate his countrymen, to make them understand that India was not merely a source of profit, that she had more to give the world than lakhs of rupees and bales of silk, that she was a land where men had lived and thought and grown wise for thousands of years, and where many civilizations had flourished, and that, therefore, she was worthy of study from a human, and not only an economic and political, standpoint. A new era in human thought and conduct dawned when this truth was driven home.

In this attempt he was encouraged by Samuel Johnson, who in a letter introducing his friend, Mr. Justice Chambers, wrote:

"I can only wish for information and hope that a mind comprehensive like yours will find leisure amidst the cares of your important station to inquire into many subjects of which the European world either thinks not at all, or thinks with deficient intelligence and uncertain conjecture. I shall hope that he who once intended to increase the learning of his country by the introduction of the Persian language, will examine nicely the traditions and histories of the East, that he will survey the remains of its ancient edifices, and trace the vestiges of its ruined cities, and that at his return we shall know the acts and opinions of a race of men from whom very little has been hitherto derived...." [4]

Hastings had not the leisure to carry out this ambitious program, but the fact that Johnson considered him qualified to do so is in itself significant.

Sanskrit, the ancient literary language of India, was the focal point of the new movement that Hastings helped to initiate. Sanskrit was the key that would unlock the door to a marvelous treasure-house containing the accumulated wealth of Indian learning and wisdom, a door that had been closed to the world through all the centuries. Here were the Vedas, the sacred texts that laid bare the foundations of the Brahminical system of religious belief, over three thousand years old. Here were the great epic poems the *Mahabharata* and the *Ramayana,* comparable in many ways to the two great Greek epics of Homer, of untold interest and importance to the ethnologist, the historian, the lover of poetry and legend. Here also, like a great pile of precious stones, were poems, folk-tales, fables, lyrics, plays, a vast library of scientific and technical literature—on law, philosophy, rhetoric, music, medicine, astronomy and mathematics. All here—but all a closed book until some one from the Western world should learn the language and decipher the contents.

To five men goes the chief credit of giving these treasures to the world—Nathaniel Halhed, Sir Charles Wilkins, Sir William Jones, Henry Thomas Colebrooke, and Warren Hastings: Halhed and Wilkins as pioneers, Jones and Colebrooke as the master scholars, Hastings as the enthusiastic patron.

The start was made when Hastings removed the dislike of the Brahmins for foreign study of their sacred books and assembled the *pundits* at Calcutta, engaging them in the task of compiling a digest of the Gentoo law. As no European knew Sanskrit the work was written in Persian, and Hastings employed Halhed, a young civil servant just out from England, to translate it into English. His translation was published in England and justly became famous; it was the first of a great series. That was in 1776. Shortly afterwards Halhed established the first British printing-press in India, which he used to publish, in 1778, his grammar of the Bengal language. Halhed knew no Sanskrit, but he helped to start other men's minds and curiosity working. He and William Jones had been friends together at Oxford. [5]

Wilkins came next. Arriving in Bengal in 1770, he began the study of Sanskrit eight years later, the first Westerner ever to do so, and with Halhed's assistance, he set up a press especially for the printing of oriental languages. Within six years he had mastered Sanskrit sufficiently well to complete a translation of the *Bhagavad-gita,* the culminating episode of the *Mahabharata.* Then at the close of Hastings's administration Colebrooke and Jones arrived to crown the work so ably begun.

Sir William Jones was one of the most remarkable men that Britain has ever sent to India. Perhaps no greater linguist has ever lived. Born in 1746, he was educated at Harrow and passed from there to Oxford, where he became a Fellow of his college. Before he was twenty-six he was made a member of the most exclusive and famous literary circle of the day, Dr. Johnson's Club, and a Fellow of the Royal Society. By this time he was a thorough master of Arabic, Persian, Latin, Greek, French, Italian, German, Spanish and Portuguese, with a little Hebrew and Chinese thrown in. He must also in the course of his life have acquired other languages in addition to Sanskrit, because it was said of him that he knew thirteen thoroughly and twenty-eight partially. His first book, published when he was twenty-four, was a translation from Persian into French, and next year there appeared his *Grammar of the Persian Language,* a copy of which Johnson sent to Hastings. Tired of academic life, he took up law and soon became a profound jurist. Eager to pursue his researches in oriental languages at first hand, he obtained for himself appointment as Judge of the Bengal Supreme Court, and landed in Calcutta in December 1783. [6]

The day was a landmark in Indian history. It was also a day of rejoicing for the Governor-General and his small band of enthusiastic orientalists. Few official acts could have given Hastings greater satisfaction and pleasure than to welcome this man whose fame had reached India long before. They were close friends from the first day of meeting. Together they lost no time in celebrating the auspicious event by forming a permanent association for the pursuit of the studies they loved. Summoning Halhed and Wilkins, they founded in January 1784 the Asiatic Society of Bengal. Hastings was pressed to be its first president, but he modestly declined, recognizing that one greater than he had come. He proposed the name of Sir William Jones, which was accepted.

Evidence of the high esteem in which Sir William Jones held Hastings is contained in his papers, and it is especially remarkable because Jones was an intimate friend of Edmund Burke.[1] When the Governor-General declined the presidency of the Society, Jones paid him a graceful compliment: "As to myself, I could never have been satisfied if, in traversing the sea of knowledge, I had fallen in with a ship of your rate and station, without striking my flag." [8] When Hastings sailed for home, Jones wrote expressing his keen regret because it meant that he was losing a friend. [9] And in October 1791 he wrote him a warm and cordial letter, obviously that of an ardent admirer, expressing his hope for Hastings's complete triumph over his accusers. [10] The esteem of such men as William Jones and Samuel Johnson must have largely compensated Hastings for all his afflictions.

For ten years Jones labored in India, then he died at the tragically early age of forty-eight. During these years translations from Sanskrit literature flowed from his pen at an astounding rate. His ten presidential discourses to the Society were epoch-making in the history of Western knowledge of the East. He explored the recesses of language, literature,

---

[1] When he went to India Burke wrote him an outrageous letter, telling him that if he so much as *heard* that he had sided with Hastings he would do everything he could to get him recalled. Jones in his reply snubbed him vigorously and properly, reminding him that he was a *judge* and that a judge never took sides, and asserting that in any case he would form his own opinion! [7]

philosophy and science, and laid them open to scholars of the whole world. The pioneer of Sanskrit learning, he aspired to be even more— no less than the Justinian of India. With his knowledge of the sacred language he could do much more than Hastings and Halhed. He could, and did, go to the original texts, and his translation of the *Laws of Manu* was the result. But he died before completing the task.

His mantle fell upon Thomas Colebrooke. Receiving an appointment in the East India Company's service in 1782 at the age of seventeen, Colebrooke had preceded Jones to Bengal, but he did not master Sanskrit until later. When appointed Assistant-Collector at Tirhut in 1786, we read that he "was not sorry to leave Calcutta where the gambling and drinking of the representatives of English civilization disgusted him." [11] His subsequent labors were as prodigious and fruitful as Jones's, and he finished Jones's codification of the law.

What Hastings's encouragement meant to these men was demonstrated shortly before he sailed for home. Wilkins brought to him the translation of the *Bhagavad-gita* that he had just completed and was about to send home to be published. He asked the Governor-General to write an introduction offering the work to the East India Company, a request with which he gladly complied. His introduction appears in the published work under the date "Benares, October, 1784," Hastings being at the time on his way down from Lucknow. Wilkins, in his preface, repaid him with a fine tribute of "a pupil to his preceptor and patron," testifying to the constant encouragement that Hastings had given to the Company's servants to learn the languages of India and to study the laws, customs and literature enshrined in them. He laid the *Gita* publicly at his feet in token of profound gratitude.

Hastings's introduction gives us the final proof—if any further proof be needed—of the elevated cast of his mind and of the liberal and enlightened spirit which he brought to bear on the immense problem of Britain's relations with her great dependency. In extolling the moral and intellectual value of a study of Vedic literature he drops, quite casually, this most striking and pregnant sentence: "It is on the virtue, not the ability of their servants, that the Company must rely for the permanence of their dominions." The *Bhagavad-gita,* he declares, contains passages "elevated to a track of sublimity into which our habits of judgement will find it difficult to pursue them," and he describes it as "a performance of great originality, of a sublimity of conception, reasoning, and diction, almost unequaled, and a single exception among all the known religions of mankind, of a theology accurately corresponding with that of the Christian dispensation, and most powerfully illustrating its fundamental doctrines." And he compares the Wilkins translation to "the best French versions of the most admired passages of the *Iliad* or *Odyssey,* or of the First and Sixth Books of our own Milton, highly as I venerate the latter."

It was not, however, only for its moral value that he urged this study. He grasped, as no one had so far done, the great need for sympathy, appreciation and understanding between West and East. *That,* he felt, was the crux of the mighty problem that faced his country in acquiring an Indian empire.

"Every accumulation of knowledge, and especially such as is obtained by social communication with people over whom we exercise a dominion founded on the right of conquest, is useful to the state: it is the gain of humanity: in the specific instance which I have stated, it attracts and conciliates distant affections; it lessens the weight of the chain by which the natives are held in subjection; and it imprints on the heart of our own countrymen the sense and obligation of benevolence. Even in England, this effect of it is greatly wanting. It is not very long since the inhabitants of India were considered by many as creatures scarce elevated above the degree of savage life; nor, I fear, is that prejudice yet wholly eradicated, though surely abated. Every instance which brings their real character home to observation will impress us with a more generous sense of feeling for their natural rights, and teach us to estimate them by the measure of our own. But such instances can only be obtained in their writings: and these will survive when the British dominion in India shall have long ceased to exist, and when the sources which it once yielded of wealth and power are lost to remembrance."

What the world owes to the pioneering enthusiasm of Warren Hastings in this field has been eloquently stated by a modern writer, himself a well-known Sanskrit scholar. [12] After referring to Thoreau's tribute to that achievement in his log-book of his exploration of the Concord and Merrimac Rivers in 1839, Mr. Charles Johnston says:

"Its influence has been world-wide; the Valley of the Merrimac River is only one of innumerable regions to which the wave of intellectual and spiritual life set in motion at Benares a hundred and fifty years ago has spread. To the influence of the first Governor-General of British India, the scholars who worked with him and their successors, we owe our knowledge of Eastern scripture, the comparative study of religious thought."

And it is not only the Western world that is indebted to these men. By translating the Vedic scriptures into English, they preserved them for the whole world, and thereby for the Indians themselves, since, Brahminism being an esoteric religion, none but the priests hitherto had had access to its sacred books. Now every literate Indian can read and study them for himself. [13]

II

EDUCATION as a branch of government activity was a problem that did not rise to the surface until well into the next century. It was not until 1813 that Parliament imposed upon the Government of India the obligation of spending a minimum of one lakh of rupees for "the revival and improvement of literature and the encouragement of the learned natives of India." Yet Hastings, with his capacity for being in advance of his time, was fully alive to the importance of the matter and showed his interest in a concrete way. In 1781 he founded "an academy for the study of the different branches of the sciences taught in the Mahomedan schools." This was the famous Moslem college, the Calcutta Madrassi. The expense involved was unauthorized and he felt it needed justifying to his employers. He therefore wrote them:

"It is almost the only complete establishment of the kind now existing in India, although they were once in universal use, and the decayed remains of these schools are yet to be seen in every capital, town, and city of Hindustan and Deccan. It has contributed to extend the credit of the Company's name, and so soften the prejudices excited by the rapid growth of the British dominions; and it is a seminary of the most useful members of society." [14]

No doubt can exist in anybody's mind which side Hastings would have taken in the great controversy that raged fifty years later between the Anglicists and the Orientalists, between those who advocated that English should be the vehicle of instruction and those who supported the claims of Sanskrit and Arabic. Hastings would certainly have opposed Macaulay, the chief champion of the former party, with the same determination and cogency of argument that he displayed in so many of his own similar controversies. All his sympathies were passionately on the side of protecting and encouraging the Indians in the possession of their indigenous cultural inheritance, and it was that that made him so anxious to disseminate knowledge of it among his own countrymen. He believed that they only had to know to appreciate.[1]

III

HASTINGS's eager curiosity and restless energy carried him into other fields of activity that were equally off the beaten track of routine administration. He grasped, as few of his successors were able to do, the immense possibilities, responsibilities and requirements of the British position in the East, and he did this while the Empire was still in its infancy and before it had taken firm root and assumed a definite form. What it spelled to him was Opportunity, boundless in extent—opportunity for human enterprise, for the extension of human intercourse, the widening of human knowledge, the deepening of the channels of human life. And his vision, ever broad in its statesmanlike reach, extended far beyond the narrow confines of British territory.

Thus it was that science, as well as literature, felt the eager touch of his hand. He encouraged, particularly, the accumulation of the kind of scientific knowledge that was important to a government: such as

[1] Macaulay's views unluckily prevailed. He won his case by oracularly stating that "a single shelf of a good European library was worth the whole native literature of India and Arabia." It is generally agreed now that his policy was mistaken and that it had the effect of weakening the foundation of British rule in India by alienating the people from their rulers.

the geography and natural history of the country. He knew that to the
statesman geography is as vital as a land survey to the road-builder,
and that knowledge of flora and fauna is the first step to experiments
in breeding and horticulture that may lead to the introduction of
valuable new industries and sources of wealth. The shawl goat interested him because of the superior fine texture of its hair (might it not
be possible, he even wondered, to introduce it into England?), and
coffee, because experiment might, and actually did, show that it could
be successfully and profitably cultivated in Bengal.

He sent forth his officers to explore and survey. They went north,
east and west; to Tibet, to the Red Sea, to Cochin China; into the
interior of the continent, on friendly missions for the development of
trade and diplomatic relations, and along the coasts to sound the waters
and map the harbors and rivers. He put road-makers to work and
organized a regular service of posts along the main routes from Calcutta, northward to Patna and eastward to Dacca. Among the able men
who served under him was Major Rennell, who had been appointed
Surveyor-General of Bengal as early as 1764. His memorable *Bengal
Atlas,* which earned Rennell the distinction of being known as "the
father of Indian geography," bore the date 1781.

The most noteworthy of all the missions that Hastings sponsored
were the two he sent to Tibet, that land of mystery above the mighty
Himalayas, which was not only unknown to the West but had hitherto
been closed to all contact with the West. It was his ambition to break
down that wall of seclusion and open up for India her old trade routes
into the heart of Asia. He looked beyond Tibet to China, and in the
minute that he wrote expressing his hope to open up relations with
that country he said:

"Like the navigation of unknown seas, which are explored not for the
attainment of any certain and prescribed object but for the discovery of
what they may contain; in so new and remote a search, we can only
propose to adventure for possibilities. The attempt may be crowned with
the most splendid and substantial success; or it may terminate in the
mere satisfaction of useless curiosity. But the hazard is small, the design is worthy of the pursuit of a rising state." [15]

George Bogle was his chosen emissary. He sent him forth in 1774,
armed with instructions that bring irresistibly to mind the maritime
expeditions, sponsored by the Courts of Spain, Portugal and England,
to explore the unknown oceans of the world and bring back the products
of the new lands discovered. They illustrate so well his characteristic
blend of intellectual curiosity and practical objectiveness that no apology
is needed for quoting them in full:

"1. To send me one or more pairs of animals called *foos* which
produce the shawl wool. If by a *dooly,* cage, or any other contrivance,
they can be secured from the fatigue or hazard of the way, the expense
is to be no objection.

"2. To send one or more pairs of cattle which bear what are called cow tails.

"3. To send me, carefully packed, some fresh ripe walnuts for seed, or an entire plant, if it can be transported; and any other curious or valuable seeds or plants, the rhubarb and ginsing especially.

"4. Any curiosities, whether natural productions, manufactures, paintings, or what else may be acceptable to persons of taste in England. Animals only that may be useful.

"5. In your inquiries concerning the people, the form of their government and the mode of collecting their revenues are points principally meriting your attention.

"6. To keep a diary, inserting whatever passes before your observation which shall be characteristic of the people, their manners, customs, buildings, cookery, the country, the climate, or the road, carrying with you a pencil and a pocket book, for the purpose of minuting short notes of every fact or remark as it occurs, and putting them in order at your leisure, while they are fresh in your memory.

"7. To inquire what countries lie between Lhassa and Siberia, and what communication there is between them. The same with regard to China and Cashmere.

"8. To ascertain the value of their trade with Bengal by their gold and silver coins and to send me samples of both.

"9. Every nation excels others in some particular art or science. To find out this excellence of the Bootans (Tibetans).

"10. To inform yourself of the course and navigation of the Burramputra, and of the state of the countries through which it runs." [16]

A letter that Hastings sent Bogle while he was engaged on the mission is equally characteristic:

"I feel myself more interested in the success of your mission than in reason perhaps I ought to be; but there are thousands of men in England whose good-will is worth seeking, and who will listen to the story of such enterprises in search of knowledge with ten times more avidity than they would read accounts that brought crores to the national credit, or descriptions of victories that slaughtered thousands of the national enemies. Go on and prosper. Your journal has traveled as much as you, and is confessed to contain more matter than Hawkesworth's three volumes. Remember that everything you see is of importance. I have found out a better road to Lhassa, by the way of Deggerchen and Coolhee. If I can find it I will send it to you. Be not an economist if you can bring home splendid vouchers of the land which you have visited." [17]

Bogle was kindly received at Lhassa and established cordial relations with the Tashai Lama, who in turn used his influence with the Emperor of China to interest him in the idea of opening up trade and diplomatic relations with the Bengal Government.

Nine years later Hastings, freed at last from the worst of the difficulties that had been impeding him in the intervening years, sought to follow up this promising beginning by sending a second mission. He chose for the purpose a young kinsman of his named Samuel Turner,

It was, however, too late. When Turner reached Tibet he found that the Lama had died and the project with him. The chief fruit of his visit was an amusing report of his interview with the new Lama, who, though only an infant in arms, seems to have been so phenomenally precocious as to set Hastings wondering for a moment whether there might not after all be some truth in the Tibetan superstition that each successive Lama chosen by lot was a reincarnation of his predecessor. He decided to term it "a physical curiosity, since," he wrote Lord Mansfield, "it is perhaps the first example which was ever produced to the Western world of the effect of education on an infant mind." [18]

That was the end of Tibetan adventure, so far as the British rulers of India were concerned, for over a hundred years. None of his successors could see the wisdom of following his lead, and even the memory of his enterprise, fantastic as it must have seemed to most of his contemporaries, was all but forgotten. When Lord Moira became Governor-General Hastings urged him to maintain the connection, not for political reasons nor specially for trade but more out of curiosity, a desire for knowledge, "if that is a legitimate pursuit of Government"; [19] but Moira did not take the advice. For over a century Tibet was to be forgotten and ignored as completely as though the country did not exist, and when at last in 1903, during the administration of Lord Curzon, a fresh attempt was made to establish relations with its people the result was far different from the pleasant journeys made by Bogle and Turner. Where Hastings sent peaceful one-man missions Curzon had to send a military expedition, and the man who led it, Sir Francis Younghusband, is in no doubt about the reason why. "If Warren Hastings's policy," he says, "had been followed up, we would gradually have created a neighborly feeling with the Tibetans, drawing them bit by bit closer to us." Instead he found when he reached the frontier that his countrymen were held in no esteem whatever in those parts—even their power was not known—and instead of being welcomed as friends his mission was received as enemies and had to fight its way in. "And all this need never have been if we had followed Warren Hastings's example and continued to send agents into Tibet to keep the Tibetans in touch with us and accustomed to look on us as friends," and he quotes this as "the best example both of the folly of inertness and of the good that comes from running risks for an adequate object." [20]

IV

IF prescience is the hall-mark of great statesmanship then Hastings's claim to the title cannot be disputed. He foresaw new needs and dangers long before they became pressing. Who else, for instance, would have been able as early as 1784 to foresee the time when the Sikhs of the Punjab (which at that time lay far beyond the boundaries of British territory) would become a most serious menace to the expanding British power, given only a leader and favorable circumstances? "We are too apt," he wrote at that time, "to despise the danger which we have not experienced, and to conclude that what has not happened in the ordinary course of events never will happen. On such a presumption my conclusions may expose me to the ridicule of those who may deem them the mere effusions of a wild imagination. I am willing to submit to this consequence if the events which I have foreboded shall be prevented by reasonable means of opposition; but I trust to time, and that not distant, for verifying my prediction if this nation is permitted to grow into maturity without interruption." [21] His prediction was fulfilled to the letter sixty years later.

He was keenly alive to the higher strategic needs of the British position in the East. He knew the vital importance of Sea-Power. He recognized that the turning-point in the war in the Carnatic was Sir Edward Hughes's repulse of the French fleet, for, though he was not victorious, he was still able to maintain an equal share of the command of the sea. He recognized, also, the future importance of the Persian Gulf. In his later days he described it as "the most important position in Asia, one of the most important in the world." Above all, he appreciated the importance of Egypt and the Red Sea. (He told Lord Moira in 1812 that he wanted to see England become the absolute master of the Red Sea.)

He assumed the Governorship of Bengal at a time when the Directors of the East India Company and British statesmen generally were showing increasing concern, as was only natural, over the problem of safe and rapid communication between England and India. The period of his administration coincided with the beginning of a slow process of change in Britain's world outlook and imperial policy. Hitherto she had looked chiefly westwards towards her colonial empire in North America. She was now to lose the greater part of that empire at the same time as she fastened her grip on a new empire in the East, and this was naturally to change the orientation of her policy from West to East. Instead of centering her attention on disputing with France and Spain the possession of West Indian islands and the river ways into the interior of America, she began increasingly to concentrate on securing the strategic points on, first, the long and, then, the short route to India until, when the process was complete a century later, there was not a single one of these points outside her possession.

In 1772 the little island of St. Helena was the only port of call between Europe and India in British hands. The Cape of Good Hope and the island of Ceylon were Dutch, whilst the all-important Ile de France in the Indian Ocean belonged to France. The fact that two of the vital links in the chain were in the possession of the Dutch was at first of little moment as Holland was a close ally, but when Holland joined the coalition of France and Spain against Britain, the matter became serious, and British and French naval policy in the East largely turned on a struggle to secure them. Although the British promptly seized Trincomali in Ceylon, Sir Edward Hughes with his inferior fleet was unable to prevent Admiral Suffren from recapturing it, and Suffren had previously prevented an English squadron from seizing the Dutch colony at the Cape. Thus the three chief naval bases on the route to India were for the time being in the hands of the enemy.

This was too serious a situation to be tolerated for long and within twenty-five years the whole position was changed. Cape of Good Hope was to become British in 1795, Ceylon in the following year, and the Ile de France (renamed Mauritius) in 1810, and, in addition, various other islands and stations along the vital route were to find their way into British hands—Ascension, Tristan de Cunha, Seychelles, Maldives, Chagos; so that nothing but the island of Réunion was left to the French.

It needed no exceptional intelligence in 1772 to foresee this development. Anybody with ordinary sense could see that to a European state that nursed ambitions for an Indian empire sea-power for the control of communications was fully as essential as land-power for the protection of the territory itself, and sea-power depended on naval bases. But it was altogether different with Egypt and the Red Sea. The Suez Canal was a hundred years in the future, the British occupation of Egypt still further, and stretched right across this future route lay the dead weight of Turkish rule. Nearly thirty years were to elapse before Napoleon came on the scene to remind the world that Alexander had reached the East by way of Egypt, and cause his startled enemy to send their greatest admiral to bar the way for him and at the same time acquire for his country the first stepping-stone across the narrow seas that lay between. Malta first appeared as a red spot on the map in 1800. Egypt as a short cut for commerce and important dispatches, however, was thought of long before its military significance became clear. And Hastings was the man who took the first steps to utilize its strategic position. Behind what he did undoubtedly lay the realization that Egypt and the Red Sea held the key of the future to lock or unlock the gateway to India.

The first suggestion of a definite plan to open up this "new" route (really it was the oldest route of all) is contained in a dispatch from him to the Court of Directors, dated November 18, 1773. He followed it up, with the Court's approval, by sponsoring voyages to survey the Red Sea. The first venture was wrecked, but he persevered, considering the undertaking to be "of great public utility." In 1775 he sent agents to Cairo to negotiate for privileges of trade from India and for the right to establish a system of communication through Egypt. With the aid of liberal *backsheesh* the agents succeeded in obtaining from the Egyptian Beys, who ruled the country as viceroys of the Sultan, a "treaty of navigation and commerce between the most serene and Mahometan Bey of upper and lower Egypt, and the Honble. Warren Hastings, Esq., President and Governor for affairs of the British Nation in Bengal."

The terms, which were remarkably favorable, provided for "a reciprocal and entirely perfect liberty of navigation and commerce between the subjects on each part, through all and every the Dominions and Provinces under their Government in India and Egypt, concerning all and singular kinds of goods." A small fixed duty was to be paid on all goods after they were sold, and all restrictions on the sending of express messengers through Egypt with sealed packets were to be removed. It is a startling fact that it has only been within the last few years that the memory of this extraordinarily interesting treaty has been resurrected. For a hundred and fifty years it lay buried in the archives of the India Office, its very existence forgotten. [22]

The reason for this strange oblivion is not far to seek. Hastings was a pioneer, but a pioneer without immediate followers. His treaty was premature, shortlived, and largely abortive. The seed of so much promise fell on stony and unfruitful soil. For a short space it did indeed grow rapidly. British merchantmen began to appear in increasing numbers in the ports of Suez and Alexandria, and the practice of using the route for the conveyance of important dispatches grew more and more frequent; until within a year after the treaty had been signed the Directors found it necessary to appoint a resident agent at Cairo to take care of the Company's affairs. Much attention was given to removing the chief obstacle in the way of a rapid and efficient service, namely, the difficulty of coördinating the arrival and departure of ships at the two ports. The enterprise was rendered especially difficult by the serious hazards and expense of the voyage from India to Suez due to the baffling and storm-ridden winds of the monsoon that raged during the greater part of the year. Yet by the year 1777, despite every obstacle, a workable system had been evolved which enabled both the authorities at home and their respresentatives in India to depend on this route for their most urgent communications. Almost at once, however, other difficulties arose to hamper, and finally end, this promising venture. The decisive factor was the bitter and implacable hostility of the Ottoman Porte. First the trade dwindled and died, then the use of the route for purposes of communication also gradually diminished, until by 1780 it was said that "English vessels no longer come to Suez." A few dispatches continued to reach India by another alternative route overland through Mesopotamia by way of Aleppo and Bussora, but this also was very costly and unsafe owing to difficulties with the Arabs. A fresh start was to be made later in the century which was to meet with greater success, but the real fruition of the enterprise did not come until the opening of the Suez Canal in 1869. And meanwhile the first venture passed from mind, obliterated by its own abortiveness.

However, the smallness of the immediate results cannot detract from the merits of the design or the credit due to its originator. Hastings, as in so much else that he did or planned, was ahead of his time, and he lacked the means of turning the fruit of his enterprising spirit to the full advantage of his country. Yet the policy that he initiated with regard to Egypt did have one outcome that was of real immediate importance. When dangers were threatening the British Empire from every quarter and the crisis of its fate was approaching, Hastings in his lonely outpost received via Suez advance information of what was happening in Europe and America. Most important of all, he received advance news of the sailing of a French armament for the East and of the declaration of war with France. Armed with this knowledge he was able to seize the French settlements while they were still in ignorance of the hostilities, and to take prompt action to defend Bengal and forestall the French designs.

Chapter XXVI

FAREWELL TO INDIA

I

THE achievement of Warren Hastings in India is not to be estimated by the criteria usually applied to empire-builders—the
number of battles won and enemies vanquished, the number of
square miles of territory conquered and annexed, the plunder and the
glory amassed. His generals gained few battles; only the Rohillas and
Chait Singh were vanquished; there were no conquests or trophies of
victory; there was no plunder and little glory; all the superficial evi-
dences of success were strikingly lacking. To outward appearances he
had done no more than justify his retention of his post and the trust
reposed in him, by bringing the Company safely through a great crisis
with its territories intact and its resources unimpaired. Actually, however, he had achieved immeasurably more and to estimate what that
more was we have only to recall the extent of British power in India
at the beginning of his administration, and to compare it with what
it was at the end. On the one hand, two weak footholds on the coast
at Madras and Bombay, undisputed but undefined authority over the
vast, chaotic, famine-stricken province of Bengal, a weak alliance with
one native state, no friends, no security, bankrupt finances, demoralized
officers, incompetent leaders. And on the other, an empire in being
that had conclusively proved itself to be the most powerful state in
India, an empire that was built on secure foundations, buttressed with
treaties and alliances, doubly strong because it had gained the respect
and good will of no small part of the Indian world, and that only
required a continuance of the same able statesmanship to become the
paramount power. The contrast is a fair measure of Hastings's achievement.

Britain and India should equally recognize the debt they owe to
Hastings. Britain should recognize it because he effaced the disgrace
attaching in 1772 to her Indian enterprise by transforming what was a
curse to the people of India into a source of new life, new happiness
and new strength, and because he ended a serious menace to her national

life. If there had not been a quick change in English standards of conduct and aims in India, England would have been ruined, in the same manner as Rome and Spain were ruined when the acquisition of unlimited power over subject races weakened and finally destroyed the primitive simplicity of their national life and the integrity of their institutions. The wealth of India was poisoning the stream of English life; the unethical methods that were being employed to obtain it were weakening the moral fiber of the English people. The signs of degeneration were there and did not escape the notice of men like Chatham and Burke. Unchecked greed threatened to destroy both victim and oppressor. Britain was saved when Hastings attacked the evil at its source.

To India likewise he was a benefactor because he saved its civilization from a state of collapse. All the forces that were tending to destroy its political and economic life and plunge it into utter anarchy and misery were decisively checked when he assumed charge of Bengal. He turned back the Senassies and the Marathas, put down crime, restored order, brought back justice to a land that for a generation and more had known it not, prevented oppression to the peasant, reopened the channels of trade, and restored a sense of security and confidence that had long disappeared. All this he did, as the Indians of his day were quick to appreciate. If he was successful, it was because of their ready response, their immense relief at finding at last some one who could deliver them from their many oppressors. And if today there is a tendency, common the world over, to depreciate these and other benefits that India has derived from British rule and to emphasize instead the moral injustice of depriving a country of its independence, the reason lies in man's forgetfulness of the past and his weakness for undervaluing what he has and overvaluing what he has not. In the eighteenth century it can be asserted with confidence that the people of India were glad to exchange the terrors of so-called "independence" for the assured peace, order and protection that were given to them by their new "alien" rulers from across the seas.

When Hastings's administration ended, the lines of future growth and development had been so firmly described that it needed no great exercise of the imagination to picture it encompassing the whole subcontinent from the Himalayas to Cape Comorin. It was indeed already becoming apparent that that was England's manifest destiny. Hastings, who feared to see it realized, knew before he left India that it was attainable. All that the Empire's rulers needed to do was to observe consistently a few fundamental principles of policy, principles that he had discovered for them, and whose efficacy he had to the best of his ability demonstrated by practical application. In his final account of his stewardship, written during his voyage home, [1] he tried to make plain to his countrymen what were the ends he had sought, what he would have done if he had been given the means and the opportunity, and what were the rules that they should follow in directing the affairs of their Empire. His concern was not only for himself and his reputation—lest his enemies should succeed in their efforts to distort facts and misrepresent his policy—but for India and the future of his country's connection with it.

The first object to be sought was to make the interests of the Indian people paramount. To this end the Company should be divested of its commercial character and the British nation should recognize the complete change that had taken place in the character of their Indian enterprise. It was too late to inquire whether the nation had benefited by the change, since it was impossible to retrace "the perilous and wonderful paths" by which territorial dominion had been superimposed upon trade, "impossible to redescend to the humble and undreaded character of trading adventurers." "The seed of this wonderful production was sown by the hand of calamity. It was nourished by fortune, and cultivated, and shaped (if I may venture to change the figure) by necessity." Burke expressed the same pragmatical view when he said: "There we are: there we are placed by the Sovereign Dispenser, and we must do the best we can in our situation. The situation of man is the preceptor of his duty." Hastings wrote of the change: "Perhaps the term of the national existence in India may have become susceptible of a shorter duration by it; but it is that state which it must henceforth maintain, and it must therefore adopt those principles which are necessary to its preservation in that state."

A policy of peace followed naturally as a corollary to the first principle, "Seek peace, and pursue it." Aim not at Conquest but at the welfare and prosperity of the provinces already under British rule. That, he asserted with all the emphasis at his command, had been his chief concern. Peace had been the all-important need of Bengal when he assumed the government.

"All my acts were acts of peace. I was busied in raising a great and weighty fabric, of which all the parts were yet loose and destitute of their superior weight, and (if I may so express myself) their collateral strength. A tempest, or an earthquake could not be more fatal to a builder whose walls were uncovered, and his unfinished columns trembling in the breeze, than the ravages or terrors of war would have been to me and to all my hopes."

The desire for peace had to be accompanied by a definite policy to obtain it and to preserve the Empire's security. Such a policy, in Hastings's opinion, included as its two chief constituents the maintenance of superior military strength (in 1777 he had written: "If peace is to be our object, I cannot devise a more likely way to insure it than to command all the means of war."—A more efficacious maxim for the government of India than for a modern world composed of competing nations), and the development of his system of defensive alliances. He condemned a possible third expedient, extension of territory, as tending to dissipate the strength of the Empire. In other words, he would have sought for his country the same kind of position in India as the American Republic holds in the two American continents— strictly limited territorial expansion combined with absolute military and political supremacy.

It was equally important for the preservation of peace to maintain the sanctity of treaty rights and of the pledged word. This was a matter in which the British, who had in the past, he declared, so often and so glaringly disregarded the demands of good faith, must set the example. And despite the several instances when he seemed to overstep the bounds, if not of good faith, at least of fairness, he *had* set the example, and it was due to the confidence that the Indian rulers placed in him that he had been able to break up the coalition against the Company and to convert such princes as the Nizam, the Rajah of Berar and Mahadaji Sindhia into friends. The result was that for the first time since they had acquired political power the English were respected and trusted. It was not sufficient, however, Hastings urged, for them to be mindful of their promises and pledges; they must exact equal fidelity towards them from the Indians; they must be firm in their insistence on their rights and quick and vigorous to repel infringements.

"I have never yielded a substantial right which I could assert, or submitted to a wrong which I could repel, with a moral assurance of success proportioned to the magnitude of either. . . . I have ever deemed it even more unsafe than dishonorable to sue for peace; and more consistent with the love of peace to be the aggressor, in certain cases, than to see preparations of intended hostility, and wait for their maturity, and for their open effect to repel it. The faith of treaties I have ever held inviolate."

The application of the principle that the happiness and welfare of the people were the first care of government had produced Hastings's great work of social and economic reconstruction in Bengal, and it was the success of that work, undertaken just in the nick of time, that had enabled the Empire to survive its first great crisis. Moreover, in basing his administrative system on the interests of the ryots, who formed a vast majority of the population, he had made one of his chief contributions to the future strength and stability of the Empire. The policy that he had initiated was to become a cardinal rule of British administration.

He carried the principle still further by his earnest regard for native institutions and modes of thoughts. He had nothing of the spirit that regarded government as a glorified missionary enterprise, whose duty it was to "carry the white man's burden" by ministering to the spiritual welfare and uplift of the poor benighted natives; rather, he wished to make government accord with the fabric of Indian life and thought. His conception of the part that his countrymen should take was that of a controlling, unifying, stabilizing force, whose efforts should be directed towards harmonizing and arbitrating between conflicting elements and, by preserving law and order, eradicating war and governing justly and honestly, towards enabling the people of India to enjoy all the fruits of their own civilization. For that reason he prescribed as the duty of the magistrate "nothing but attention, protection and forbearance." He envisaged Bengal as a state distinguished above all others in India for the size of its population—increased by immigration from other, less fortunate parts of the country—the extent of its cultivation, and the contentment and prosperity of its people, freed, as they would be if his aims were realized, from the fear of famine, invasion and oppression. He believed that the materials to be used for the construction of such a state should be essentially Indian—Indian institutions, Indian law and law courts, Indian land system, and Indian culture and social and religious customs—and that Britain should confine itself to supplying the mortar and the design. Both the system and the methods of government should be suited to the character, the needs and the wishes of the people. That was why he was so impressed with the need for a strong executive, the importance of prompt and firm decisions—better in his opinion, wrong decision than no decision—and the value of personal rule and of direct relations between the ruler and his subjects. He wanted the mechanism of government to be kept simple, and the working of it to be left, so far as possible, in Indian hands, that no cumbersome bureaucracy might clog the natural current of Indian life.

Hastings's thought on India, like his conduct as Governor, was distinguished by its human quality, its broad tolerance, wide sympathy, and freedom from racial prejudice. It was impossible as yet for the British to regard the natives as a subject race and to give themselves the lordly airs of a ruling caste. Ideas of racial superiority, where they existed at all, were confined to a comparative few. Hastings himself declared that "the superiority which the English possess over the other powers of India is derived from two causes, the authority of their Government and their military discipline. It is by these advantages only that they can improve or maintain it." He never uttered a word suggesting that he considered the natives of India as an inferior breed of men or a backward race, nor did he make the common mistake of measuring them by Western standards. There was, therefore, in his day a better chance for mutual understanding and respect between the two races than there is today. There were Englishmen who regarded the Indians as incapable of loyalty or gratitude. Hastings was not of their number. He reposed trust in them and found it no more often misjudged than that which he placed in his own countrymen.[1] He did his utmost to win their confidence and to no small extent succeeded.

[1] His sanguine expectations of men was never better exemplified than when he wrote to Scott (February 1, 1783): "Mahdajee Sindhia is firm and consistent. *He will prove the best ally we ever had.* Remember this." [2]

In point of fact, Sindhia never became other than a very powerful rival, whose strength and prestige were greatly increased by the treaty that Hastings was compelled by necessity to make with him.

As Lord Curzon said, "He was regarded by the Indian community in
Bengal as their champion and friend." "The tenacious affections of the
Indian peoples," wrote Hastings in retirement, "may be illustrated by
the fact that, though I have left that country for twenty years, I
continued to be addressed by natives from all parts of the land who
believe themselves to have been treated with injustice, and who imagine
that I am still in a position to give them protection or redress."

Only one conclusion can be drawn from this summary of the
underlying ideas and principles of Hastings's policy and of the aims
that he recommended to his countrymen to follow, and in this conclusion lies the essence of whatever there was of good and of permanent value in his life's work. He wished to establish the Empire in
the hearts and in the interests of the peoples of India, and did not
wish it to maintain a precarious existence by virtue of its own independent resources. He knew that if it had to depend on the sword
alone its days were numbered. Such dependence has ever been the
resource of unimaginative and incompetent statesmen. Hastings was not
working for his own glory, or for the kind of national glory that
Napoleon sought for France, but for something that would be a splendid
common heritage of Britain and India alike. To this end he made a
special point of studying the views, interests and circumstances of the
native states, and laid it down as a rule that no treaty of alliance with
them should be deficient in conditions of mutual and equal dependence,
but should instead be firmly grounded on fairness and mutual advantage, so that by the example of alliances already existing the British
Government would become "an object of solicitation" to all the states
of India, and thus with the consent and by the desire of the people
themselves would it establish and maintain its sovereign authority.
Unlike any other empire in the world's history the Empire to whose
making he had devoted his life would serve the interests, exist by the
will, and depend upon the active coöperation, of its subjects.

II

A CENTURY and a half has elapsed since Warren Hastings handed
over the government of India to Sir John Macpherson, and during
that time his maxims have been tested in the crucible of experience.
Some have survived as axioms, some have been modified, while others,
wisely or unwisely, have been discarded. Time has brought about great
changes in India, and it stands to reason that principles and policies
suited to eighteenth-century conditions should to some extent become
obsolete. But the art of government in its essentials, like the other
arts, remains the same from one age to another, and what were sound
principles a hundred and fifty years ago are likely to be equally sound
today.

That Warren Hastings was a master of the art, or science, of
government—Indian government, that is—no one would now dispute.

In this respect he ranks with Akbar, the greatest of the Mogul Emperors. He knew always what had to be done and seldom erred in his choice of the best way to do it. Perhaps to no other Governor-General of India has as large a measure of all-round wisdom been vouchsafed. No better proof of the truth of this statement can be found than by tracing the path of empire through the years that followed and seeing how far his maxims and principles were acted upon or disregarded, and the results in each case. How did they stand the test of time and experience? What is the verdict of history?

His contemporaries, and many of his successors, answered this question differently from the way it is usually answered today. Even as late as 1858 we find a prominent English statesman giving vent to the opinion that British rule in India was until the close of Hastings's administration "the most corrupt, most perfidious and most capricious civilized government that ever existed on the face of the earth." [1] Pitt's Act of 1784, which in the opinion of this particular critic and of countless others at that time marked the end of this disgraceful period, was, both by intent and in effect, a repudiation of the Hastings system as that system was conceived to be by Parliament. It provided for a thorough reform of the administration and of the civil service, reprobated the pursuance of schemes of conquest and extension of territory, prohibited aggressive war and treaties of guarantee with Indian states, and called for redress of grievances of native landholders. The Marquis Cornwallis was chosen to be the executor of this new dispensation.

The choice was deliberate. Warren Hastings's origin, according to Edmund Burke, had been "low, obscure and vulgar": he had been "bred in vulgar and ignoble habits." And to these grave defects was attributable his "disgraceful" disregard of the rights of rank and privilege. By his "atrocious" treatment of the princes and nobles of India, his withholding of tribute from, and contempt for, the Mogul, his reduction of the Nawab of Bengal to the status of a pensioner, his dismissal of the great Moslem nobleman Mohamed Reza Khan and "murder" of the equally great Brahmin Nuncomar, his "tyranny" over the Vizier of Oude, deposition of Rajah Chait Singh and "robbery" of the princesses of Oude, and finally by his dispossession of some of Bengal's richest landowners, he had shocked the class-conscious rulers of England, and they showed their disapproval in the selection of his successor. Lord Cornwallis as a member of their own oligarchy could be depended upon to uphold the rights and interests of blue-blood. He was, indeed, so thoroughly imbued with the ideas of his class that he was honestly shocked when he found that Bengal did not possess such a class, and he hastened to make good the deficiency. Like Philip Francis, whose land settlement plans he inherited and put into effect,

[1] Sir George Cornwall Lewis, Chancellor of the Exchequer, in a speech in the House of Commons, February 12, 1858. And as recently as 1891 Gladstone agreed with Lord Morley that Warren Hastings was in the wrong and Burke in the right. [3] Is it any wonder, therefore, that the ordinary man still has wrong ideas on the subject?

he was quite sure that the country could not flourish without a body of wealthy landowners to form the mainstay of its social fabric. Who else was to secure the happiness and prosperity of the people? He found one-third of the country a jungle inhabited only by wild beasts. Who was to clear it and bring it back to cultivation? Who else but a landlord class?

Accordingly, Cornwallis introduced a British system of land tenure, giving to the zemindars a heritable, transferable right of property in the soil, ignoring the ancient rights of multitudes of under-proprietors and depriving the ryots of protection against oppression and extortion. Under the delusion that any benefits conferred on the landowners would be passed on to their tenants, he fixed their rents immutably, so that any further increase of value in the soil should belong wholly to them.

Here was one great departure from Hastings's policies, and the results of it were wholly disastrous. Evils of every kind sprang from what is known as the Permanent Settlement, with scarcely any compensating benefits. If there was a gradual extension of cultivation in the years that followed, it has not generally been attributed to Lord Cornwallis's Settlement. Government lost a huge amount of legitimate revenue, the ryots suffered, and by a curious stroke of irony the measure failed to produce even the effect most desired of it: far from creating a strong, prosperous and progressive landowning class, it ruined the whole body of zemindars and landholders by the means that were adopted to compel punctual payment of rents. Most of these unfortunate men sooner or later lost their estates and were reduced to utter destitution.[1] It was fortunate, therefore, that no attempt was made to copy the Permanent Settlement of Bengal in other parts of India, as province after province came under British rule. Thus one great principle that Hastings had laid down had been justified for all time: the ryots, not any zemindar or middleman class, were the basis of the Indian land system. Cornwallis's hasty and ignorant attempt to introduce English ideas into the Bengal system of government was a notable failure.

Cornwallis's best work in Bengal was done in the sphere of reform, especially of the civil service, and in this he followed closely in Hastings's footsteps. The provision of adequate salaries for all the Company's servants, the improvement of the system of criminal jurisdiction, the completion of the system of local courts, the purging of the civil service of the last traces of jobbery and corruption—what were these measures but the carrying to completion of schemes and aims that his predecessor had formed but had not been able to effect for lack of the powers and advantages that Cornwallis possessed, such as high rank, the whole-hearted support of his superiors, freedom from the envy and jealousy of his subordinates, ability to resist the influences

---

[1] "So far as the hoped for creation of a landed aristocracy of a progressive character ... was concerned the permanent settlement was a ghastly failure. The pecuniary benefit was reaped chiefly by rogues." [4]

of patronage, coming even from the highest quarters, and, above all, the power to override his Council, which Cornwallis had made a condition of his acceptance of the post?

On such points of policy as the employment of Indians in government, the introduction of British law and regulation into newly conquered territory, and the method of securing peace, stability and security for the Empire, there was for many years a wide divergence of view that led to sudden reversals of policy, following changes in the government. In matters of war and peace one Governor-General would pursue the Hastings policy, the next one would revert to the ministerial and Directorial policy of isolation, with results that repeatedly and conclusively proved the wisdom and soundness of the former. In all these matters, when we examine the judgements passed by historians upon the records of the several Governors-General that followed Warren Hastings during the succeeding fifty years, we find that they were favorable or unfavorable according as each Governor-General based his policy upon the principles enunciated and acted upon by his great predecessor.

The Act of 1784 set the seal of Parliamentary approval upon the Company's non-interventionist policy. Its prohibition of alliances and "aggressive" war meant in practice loss of influence and a "peace at any price" attitude of mind. Sir John Shore, Cornwallis's successor, carried non-intervention to its logical conclusion, by preferring to break faith with Indian princes rather than incur the risk of being involved in war. The result was a big decline in British political power and influence during the twelve years following Hastings's retirement. Shore's refusal to come to the Nizam's assistance when that prince was attacked by the Marathas led not only to the utter defeat of the Nizam and his alienation from the English, but to the aggrandizement of the Marathas and the revival of their hopes of universal dominion; in other words, the return of the Maratha menace to the Company's dominions. The confidence of the Company's allies was shaken and its enemies took fresh hope. Governor-General, Directors, Ministers, Parliament, alike, still made the mistake of regarding political power in India as a static condition that did not require positive action for its maintenance. They failed to see that the measures essential to preserve it tended of necessity to increase it, while a policy of passive inaction tended equally inevitably to weaken it; "that no ground of political advantage could be abandoned without being instantly occupied by an enemy; and that to resign influence, was not merely to resign power, but to allow that power to pass into hands hostile to the British government." [5] As Vincent Smith says, "The self-denying ordinance of the act of 1784 ... although honestly intended, was founded on a fundamental misunderstanding of the Indian situation. Instead of securing peace, it insured war." [6]

War was, indeed, the result—war bloodier, more expensive and hazardous, and more extensive in its effects by far than any that would have occurred from pursuing a contrary policy. By 1798 all that Hastings had accomplished towards making British influence supreme from one end of India to the other had been undone, and Lord Wellesley, on assuming the government, was confronted by a repetition of the situation of 1779: Tipu, the Maratha confederacy, and the French, were once more ready and eager to try conclusions with the English.

In his understanding and interpretation of Indian politics, Wellesley was Hastings's heir. He saw the necessity of India being brought under the ægis of one supreme power if she was ever to have peace and order, and he set out with the intention of making Britain, once and for all, that power. His methods also of dealing with the situation were the same: strong measures, forceful diplomacy and, if necessary, vigorous war. He realized, as had Hastings, that the power that the fanatical Haidar had transmitted to the equally fanatical Tipu must be destroyed, as experience had twice shown that leniency was ineffective. He resumed the policy of negotiating subsidiary alliances with the native states, and upon the refusal of the Marathas to relinquish their universal plundering habits and to recognize the existence of a Pax Britannica over their neighbors' lands, he made brilliantly successful war against them and overthrew the whole confederacy. When Wellesley left India, British influence was supreme at the five chief nerve centers of non-British political India, Mysore, Hyderabad, Nagpore, Poona and Delhi; which meant that Hastings's aims of 1779 had been entirely accomplished. Britain had become the paramount power in India. Wellesley himself defined his object as that of "establishing a comprehensive system of alliance and political relation over every region of Hindustan and the Deccan"—a declaration that differs from the one made by Hastings only in its suggestion of universal sovereignty. History has allotted to Wellesley a place second only to Hastings among the great Governors-General.

Where Wellesley differed from Hastings was in his belief in the superiority of British over any native Indian government and his readiness to make unlimited annexations, on the theory that each annexation was in the interest not only of England but of the native inhabitants. And once more the verdict of history is in Hastings's favor. Wellesley was a thorough-going imperialist, in the modern sense, and the present age has good reason to suspect, if not definitely to deny, the wisdom and justice of imperialism. Wellesley, however, refrained from introducing British rule into conquered Mysore, and, so reads the verdict, "the precedent might have been followed with advantage in other cases." [7] He took away its independence, but not its institutions. The administration remained in native hands under British supervision, with the happiest possible results, for Mysore still ranks as the best governed native state in India. This fact, with its corollary, that the introduction of British law, law-courts and regulations into other annexed provinces was much less successful, [8] is conclusive proof of Hastings's prescient wisdom, which has been confirmed since by increasingly numerous critics of British rule.

Wellesley has received praise for his statesmanlike appreciation of the need for a properly trained and educated civil service, for his realization that the English officials were no longer agents of a commercial company but ministers and representatives of a sovereign state—magistrates, judges, ambassadors, governors of provinces, statesmen. He emphasized the fact that they should have an intimate knowledge of the history, language, customs, and manners of the people of India. But there again he was only reiterating Hastings's views. The Directors listened to him, as they had not to his predecessor, and established a college at Haileybury for the training of the Company's servants.

With Wellesley's recall commercial considerations of the East India Company once more became paramount and "dividend" policy prevailed. Hastings's cardinal principle, that the faith of treaties must ever be held inviolate, was again disregarded, again with disastrous consequences. A policy of weakness was pursued, peace for its own sake was sought, regardless of whether it was a real peace or not, allies were abandoned, political influence was yielded in the name of non-interference, and honor and reputation were sacrificed. And again war on a large scale followed. Lord Hastings, the Governor-General who conducted the war, returned to the policy of Warren Hastings and Wellesley and, by finally subjugating the Marathas and eradicating the hideous system of rapine and terrorization that they nurtured and maintained, established a state of general peace, the Pax Britannica, with a minimum of interference in the autonomous native states. "As new territory was acquired the absurdity of introducing a complicated code of English law among communities wholly unprepared to receive it began to be recognized, and the necessity for a simpler, more elastic form of administration was acknowledged." [9] Lord Hastings crowned the work of his great namesake. Meanwhile, Lord Minto who had preceded him had made Britain supreme in the eastern seas by destroying the last fragments of French power. He had also sent missions to Persia and Afghanistan, similar to those that Warren Hastings had sent to Tibet and Egypt.

This virtual completion of Warren Hastings's work came in the year of his death, 1818, thirty-three years after his retirement from the government, and he must have felt the satisfaction of knowing that experience had time and again shown the wisdom and soundness of his political principles and the evil results that followed every departure from them. There was, however, a process of change already going on, much more profound in its nature than the expansion of territory and growth of political power. A process that was gradually to alter the whole character of the Empire. It was not merely that the Empire cast off its swaddling clothes of commerce and exploitation and in time took on the full garb of a well-managed modern state, with schools, colleges, roads, railways, telegraphs, and other accompaniments of Western civilization; the change transcended these external signs of progress and may be measured by the extent to which the Empire today in its essential nature differs from what it was when Hastings left India. At that time the Empire was nearly as Indian as the states that lay outside its borders. It was little more than a continuation of the Mogul system under British control, and to preserve it in that form after perfecting it was, as we have seen, the deliberate aim of Warren Hastings.

Since then the Empire has developed a character of its own, and that character is as much British as Indian. When it discarded its swaddling clothes, it assumed the sober raiment of Victorian England. It took on an air of much greater respectability, and the solid virtues of economy, honesty, fairness and devotion to duty, displaced the vices that disfigured the Company's rule in the old days. Fixed salaries were a swift and effective cure for the fortune-hunting, the lavish spending and gambling, the "easy come, easy go" spirit so characteristic of eighteenth-century Calcutta. The age of the Nabobs was soon as dead as the age of the Moguls. Discipline reigned in place of license. A general tightening up of the administrative machinery put an end to laxity and inertia, so natural in the East but so contrary to Anglo-Saxon ways. Corruption, another typical by-product of Indian government, vanished from the Anglo-Indian world. The virtues most stressed—incorruptibility, impartiality, efficiency—and the end chiefly sought by government—material prosperity—were of English origin. It was natural, therefore, for the Governors-General, drawn now by an almost invariable rule from the ranks of the English aristocracy, to place the work of government in the hands of Englishmen, and to believe, as Lord Cornwallis believed, that all administrative reform was useless while executive power was vested in "any native whatever." As a result "the administration of British India after the commencement of the nineteenth century was a British administration, conducted by British agents, in the main on British lines." [10] With a strong central government, aided by a powerful and well-organized bureaucracy, progress towards a new, reconstructed India was rapid. It became, indeed, too rapid. When rulers with superabundant energies like Dalhousie and Curzon embarked on a course of feverish reform, the effect was profoundly disturbing on the conservative Indian mind, and serious disruptive results followed. Progress and efficiency were the twin ideals that dominated the government, and neither was Indian. As a powerful aid to both, English was made the official language, and the Indian mind was directed away from its ancient indigenous cultural inheritance towards the literature, science and philosophy of the West. It began to drift further and further away from its moorings and to be carried into new uncharted and perilous waters.

To these two ideals was later to be added a third, that of democracy. English liberal thought came in the twentieth century to govern policy. In pursuit of the democratic ideal, a vast constitutional experiment was initiated with the object of giving to India popular representative institutions on a western model, a form of government radically different from any hitherto known in the country, unfitted to the character and the needs of the people, and ill-adapted to the peculiar conglomerate racial and political circumstances of the country. Whatever may be said about the future benefits that democracy will bring to India, it can hardly be denied that its hasty introduction, without adequate preparation, has helped in bringing about the present situation, the chief features of which are a new and growing racial antagonism, a militant nationalism, widespread political, social and agrarian discontent, revolutionary movements, outbreaks of crime, bitter discord between rival religious communities, and a general feeling of uncertainty about the future; all of which together threaten to destroy not only the Empire but the political unity of India, to plunge the country into anarchy and start it on the same road that China has taken. An increasing alienation of the people of India from their English rulers has succeeded the harmony of interests, aims and methods that was the central feature of Hastings's policy. . . .

Warren Hastings's place in history, therefore, is not that of a statesman, whose plans for a new state, like those of his contemporaries Washington and Hamilton, became a permanent part of a national policy, his writings the lasting heritage of a people. Rather, he pointed one way, and his countrymen have traveled another. He tried to see India with the eyes of an Indian, his successors saw it with the eyes of Englishmen. He sought to give India the things he knew it needed: they sought to give it the things they thought would benefit it. Each represented two opposing schools of thought, the conservative and the liberal, and the liberal has prevailed. Only the future can determine which road would have been the wisest for England to travel—wisest for India, for herself and for the world. Warren Hastings's exact place in history cannot be finally settled until the future has revealed its secrets and the Empire that he founded has become, if become it must, like that of Rome, a thing of the past. Another Gibbon will then no doubt arise to deliver the final judgement.

Chapter XXVII

HERO FOR AN HOUR

I

THE voyage of the homeward bound Governor-General was rapid and uneventful. Favorable winds and a friendly sea bore the *Barrington*—"a clean and tight ship"—on swift wings out of the Bay of Bengal down the Coromandel Coast, and into the lonely wastes of the Indian Ocean, then round the Cape of Good Hope, and on to England, calling only at St. Helena on the way. The tedium was relieved for her distinguished passenger by his good fortune in finding "a society that I loved." He had no complaints to make, except that his mind was "stupid" and he was visited every night by a slight fever. "Thompson," he wrote his faithful secretary, "never take the counsel of a physician that shall bid you go to sea for health." His mind, however, was not so stupid that he was not able to make it do good work. He utilized the four months of leisure to draft his final report, no doubt hoping that the lengthy vindication of himself which he included in it would be the last word that he would have to utter on that tiresome topic. He also amused himself by keeping a complete log of the voyage (latitude, longitude, barometer, thermometer, mileage, wind and sea. Total mileage, 14,231, [1]) and, as was his wont, with poetic composition. His well-known verses in imitation of Horace, composed while rounding the Cape of Good Hope and dedicated to his fellow-passenger John Shore reveal clearly the tenor of his thoughts as he faced the unknown fate that lay ahead of him when he reached his native land:

> He who enjoys, nor covets more,
> The lands his father own'd before,
> Is of true bliss possess'd:
> Let but his mind unfetter'd tread
> Far as the paths of knowledge lead
> And wise, as well as blest.

> No fears his peace of mind annoy,
> Lest printed lies his fame destroy,
> Which labor'd years have won;

Nor packed Committees break his rest,
Nor avarice sends him forth in quest
    Of climes beneath the sun.

For me, O Shore, I only claim,
To merit, not to seek for fame,
    The good and just to please;
A state above the fear of want,
Domestic love, Heav'n's choicest grant,
    Health, leisure, peace and ease. [2]

He also composed a few lines for the benefit of his friend David
Anderson:

Friend David, let this maxim be
Your Guide through life's unsteady Sea:
    Your course prescrib'd to mind;
If fair, prepar'd against a gale;
If foul, to yield a point, nor sail
    Too close upon the wind. [3]

In a letter to Thompson headed "Cheltenham, 21 July 1785,"
Hastings describes his arrival in England: "We landed at Plymouth on
the 13th of last month, and passed through a Lucknow heat to London,
where I passed two most uncomfortable days by Mrs. Hastings being at
Cheltenham. Having performed all the duties of loyalty, respect and
civility, I ran away to this place, where I have been since the 5th. We
have been drinking the waters ever since, but without any benefit hitherto, and rather the reverse, which people say is a sign that they will do
us good...." Maidenhead was the scene of this blissful reunion. Hastings had dispatched express messengers to let his wife know of his
arrival but, unable to curb his impatience long enough for her to reach
London, he set out to meet her on the road. [4]

His return home was quite an event in the lives of his countrymen.
It was only natural that he should have been an object of general attention and curiosity. For years his name had been upon every one's lips
and a vivid picture of him, either as a hero or a villain, implanted in
every one's mind. The whole political and social world wanted to see
him, and whether the gaze that was turned upon him was one of warm
admiration or of stern disapproval none could regard for the first time
a man who had cut such an impressive figure in the world without
feelings of awe and respect. His reception, indeed, left little to be desired—"as flattering," he himself said, "as pride could wish it." His
friends naturally gave him an enthusiastic welcome. The King and Queen
were also most gracious, while even that other court of semi-regal
power, the Court of Directors, tried its best to make amends for its
shabby treatment of him in the past by entertaining him to dinner at the
London Tavern and passing a unanimous vote of thanks to him for his
great services.

London society in particular tried to lionize him—a fact that in itself speaks volumes for the agreeableness of his personality, when it is remembered what barriers of prejudice and dislike were raised against all returning "Indians." The ladies especially—even the pious and worthy Hannah More, friend of Burke, Wilberforce and, in later life, of Thomas Macaulay—were charmed by him and could not hide their astonishment at finding him so little of a Nabob. They were particularly struck by his humility and modesty and the simplicity of his manners and dress. Fanny Burney remarked with enthusiasm on his gentleness and candor, and though she was a friend and admirer of Edmund Burke she violently disagreed with him on the subject of his pet aversion. Hastings seemed to her to be one of the greatest living men and one of the most pleasing. [5] Nor were the men far behind in their expressions of admiration. Sir Nathaniel Wraxall, M.P., described him as "thin but not tall, of a spare habit, very bald, with a countenance placid and thoughtful, but when animated, full of intelligence," and remarked particularly on his aloofness from pecuniary concerns: "Never perhaps did any man who passed the Cape of Good Hope display a mind more elevated above mercenary considerations." He was amazed, too, by his gayety and the buoyancy and elasticity of his mind, which permitted him to mix in society "like a youth upon whom care had never intruded." [6] John Nichols was impressed by the strength of his intellect and the dauntlessness of his courage. "In one word, he came nearer to the idea which I had formed of an able statesman, than any other man with whom I ever had intercourse.... I think of his memory with the highest veneration." [7]

Hastings's head was not turned by this acclaim. He knew that society would soon tire of him and pass on to some new sensation. He knew, too, that he still had plenty of enemies who might try to make trouble for him. But he had few fears on their account and he was quite sure that he would retain for many years "the esteem of those whom all esteem." [8] He still hoped to be of some use in the world, particularly in the world of public affairs, and of India most especially. He hoped, for instance, that he might assist in undoing "the mischiefs created by the last Indian Act." [9] He immediately entered into correspondence with Pitt and Dundas, the President of the new Board of Control for India, on various Indian matters, and his relations with them seemed to be sufficiently friendly to give him a sense of security and confidence. His own private affairs, however, were what concerned him most during the months following his return. He was sorely in need of rest and recreation and a chance to regain his lost health. It delighted him to find Marian better than she had been for years, even if his own health improved but slowly. They spent the whole of that first summer together in England visiting the fashionable health resorts, Bath, Cheltenham, Tunbridge Wells, and but seldom appearing in London.

The matter of a permanent residence was one that they were most impatient to settle, nor—needless to say—did he have to make any search for what he wanted. In all England there was only one such spot, the one that he had dreamed about all his life, his heart's desire—Daylesford.

The village of Daylesford is no distance at all from Cheltenham. What, then, was more natural than for him to take an early opportunity to pay it and his birth-place a visit? In fact, after reaching Cheltenham he allowed only seventeen days to pass before doing so. On July 22, a wet day though it was, he set out accompanied by Mr. Woodman his brother-in-law. On account of the rain they spent the night at Burford, returning to Daylesford next day when he "again viewed the grounds and paced the great meadow, 267 paces to the river." There, close by, were the well-remembered scenes, the house at Churchill where he was born and brought up, the stream he had loved as a boy, the little school that he had attended, the church where his grandfather had officiated and he himself had worshiped; above all, there was the big house— not, it is true, the same one as his ancestors had lived in, for it had been pulled down before his birth. But, no matter, the associations were there, the place was beautiful, and the possibilities of improvement infinite. He wanted it, ardently, urgently, and without loss of time he started negotiations with its owner.

On August 9 he received Mr. Knight's answer. It was to the effect that he had consulted with his family and that they were by no means willing to part with the estate. He continued the negotiations but on the 27th received a final letter from Mr. Knight dashing his hopes. Three days later he "rode over all the grounds of Dailsford before breakfast," and refusing to be put off, then tried approaching Knight's daughters directly. [10] He found them more open to persuasion. But the negotiations were to prove, as he afterwards put it, with wry humor, "longer than would have served for the acquisition of a province." For, although he offered John Knight, the son of the man who had purchased the estate in 1715, double its market value, the offer was still refused. And for the time being Hastings had sadly to look elsewhere for a home. He had already rented a furnished house in London in St. James's Place, moving from it later into another in Wimpole-street, but neither his means nor his inclination were suited to residence in town. What fortune he possessed he wished to spend on a country estate. He was still unsettled when the next spring came, but by July he was able to inform Thompson that he had bought "a very pleasant little estate of ninety-one acres in Old Windsor, called Beaumont Lodge, a *modus agri non ita magnus, hortus ubi, etc.*, exactly answering Horace's wish; and if I live in England, I may probably end my days upon it; for I see nothing in England that I like so much." [11]

Hastings adapted himself with the greatest ease and happiness to his new life of well-occupied leisure. He filled it full of many things, but they were the kind of things he had always loved, if seldom enjoyed. One of his earliest commissions to Thompson was for his favorite Arab horse, though the cost of sending it all the way from India must have been enormous. The horse arrived safely and in excellent condition and was "wonderfully admired." Its proud owner rode him "in spite of his beauty and long tail, though both valid objections; for this is a land of ostentation, and therefore everybody detests it in others." But he added—and truly, for he had neither the means nor the inclination to imitate his former colleague Barwell, the typical Nabob, now installed in a magnificent estate at Stanstead in Sussex—"I give them little cause." [12] Ordinary English horse-flesh, however, pleased him not, either for himself or for his wife, and before long he was asking Thompson to send over another Arab for her.

II

Few persons during this summer of 1785 could have entertained doubt that Warren Hastings could now at last ease his mind, bask in the sunshine of popular esteem, and seek, if he so wished, honorable retirement, fortified and consoled by the good opinion of his country. True that he was scarcely a national hero, for India as yet evoked very little patriotic sentiment, and what there was was reserved for warriors like Clive and Coote who had fought and vanquished the wicked French and covered themselves generally with military glory, which was far more to the popular taste. For that matter, what returning Governor-General of India has *ever* been a popular hero? With few exceptions the only place considered suitable for them has been the shelf. And even if all had gone well for him Hastings would probably have found himself there too, little as he would have wished for it...; A few members of Parliament may have remarked upon the somewhat cryptic announcement that Edmund Burke made to the House on June 20, only a week after Hastings's arrival, that he would at a future day "make a motion respecting the conduct of a gentleman just returned from India"; [13] but if so, they had quickly forgotten it when Parliament adjourned shortly afterwards. Yet, though the sky above Hastings's head seemed bright and clear, there was nevertheless a threatening heaviness in the air. The political atmosphere of England was murky, undependable, and charged with explosive forces; it brewed strange and unpredictable disturbances. A storm signal had been hoisted at Westminster. The storm it presaged might blow over, it might break without doing any damage—or then again, it might strike with devastating force.

There was something rotten in the state of England that such a storm should even have been a possibility. And the rottenness lay in its press and its politics. The English press was distinguished for nothing so much as for its shameful abuse of its freedom. Its sheets sprang from the political gutter. Men who earned their living by practicing the art of systematic detraction of their fellowmen under cover of the rule of anonymity—these were the leading journalists of the day. And Philip Francis was their chief. The return of the Governor-General had helped rather than hindered his and his friends' efforts, as it had brought them more readers. The spotlight of publicity was turned upon

Warren Hastings and Francis worked day and night to give it the color of his own choosing: a whole fresh series of anonymous pamphlets began to make its appearance shortly after Hastings's arrival.

The state of English politics was slowly improving; the nadir of public morality had at least been passed, and the era of the Whig oligarchy and of the King's Friends was disappearing. Public offices, votes and elections were not being quite so freely and openly bought and sold, for the shameful disasters of the late war had sounded the death-knell of organized corruption. But it was to take more years than three before the vital interests of the nation could be relieved of its vicious grip, or before members of Parliament could be brought to regard any subject coming before their attention in other than the most narrowly partisan light. The public services were still being managed in the private interests of those with power and influence, and public office was not yet regarded as a trust but mainly as a means of self-enrichment. How, then, could intelligent observers of the scene be other than cynical in their comments? Hastings was caustic on more than one occasion after having taken a good look at his country: "I fear that in the article of patronage even the most virtuous men of this kingdom lack virtue," [14] and again—though this was written to Macpherson while he was still in India—"there is not virtue in England for the punishment of wealthy villainy." [15] [1] Again and again that very practical man of the world's affairs Macpherson had urged him not to come home poor unless he sought disgrace and vexation: "If you do not take such effectual care of your private affairs as will enable you to have influence in the country, you will regret it the longest day you have to live." [16] And now he was to regret it, though even if he had had the wealth of Lord Clive it is much to be doubted whether he would have made the same kind of use of it. Clive had bought seats in Parliament for no fewer than eight of his relatives and friends, for Clive knew, as did Paul Benfield, the way to safeguard himself and his fortune from attack.

Hastings was, indeed, singularly ill-equipped to deal with conditions as he found them at home. It was beneath his dignity to reply to the scurrility of the anonymous publications; he disdained the use of his opponents' weapons, and even if he had tried he would not have known how to handle them. He was Olympian in his disdain alike for the Robinsons of politics and the Francises of journalism. He was not versed in the politician's ways, and neither by education, experience, inclination, nor in any other way was he suited for playing a politician's rôle. Indeed he would have been a mere child when it came to taking an active part in the hurly-burly of English politics. He could scarcely

---

[1] Cowper's well-known lines express the same sentiment:

> It is not seemly nor of good report
> That thieves at home must hang, but he that puts
> Into his overgorged and bloated purse
> The wealth of Indian provinces, escapes.

tell a Whig from a Tory, or Mr. Pitt from Mr. Fox. Nichols at once discerned this weakness in his mental equipment when he qualified his estimate of him by saying: "But he was a statesman only for the affairs of India. He knew nothing of the various parties in England, their interests, their designs, or how far they were likely to be influenced or restrained by moral considerations. These were subjects on which he seemed to me never to have formed an opinion." In fact he detested politics and politicians—the latter in his opinion were all tarred with the same brush—and would have nothing to do with either. He turned his back on the whole sordid scene and went on quietly, imperturbably and contentedly with his own life. All his subsequent troubles, therefore, may plausibly be attributed to his three principal failings: his independence in an age of political connections, his candor and honesty in an age of shams and insincerity, his moderate means in an age when wealth meant security. "Whether this man really means what he has threatened," he wrote to Thompson in December, referring to Burke, "I know not, having heard nothing about him for many months, nor have I ever made him the subject of my inquiries." [17]

Chapter XXVIII

THE GREAT ASSAULT

J. F. McCarthy
Oconomowoc, Wisconsin

I

SEVEN months had elapsed since Hastings's return. A kind providence had granted him that much respite. But now his period of quiet enjoyment of his retirement was to be abruptly ended. For on January 24, 1786, Parliament met again, and among its members was the one who had announced in the previous session that he had a motion to make respecting the conduct of the former Governor-General.

Edmund Burke had not been idle in the interval. With the aid of his instructor in Indian affairs, Philip Francis, he had been busy preparing himself for his self-appointed task—the bringing to justice of the great tyrant and criminal of the age. By meeting frequently at each other's houses and corresponding regularly when apart, they had succeeded in preparing a thorough plan of attack to be opened at the first opportunity. [1] They had at first little hope of success as they could not count on any support from the all-powerful ministerial following, nor were they even sure of the support of their own party, many of its members being definitely opposed to the undertaking. However, they managed before Parliament met to enroll Fox and Windham. [2] They had reason, too, to hope for at least one ally in the enemy's camp in the person of Henry Dundas, remembering the violent attack he had made on Hastings in 1782.

Burke was relieved of the necessity of having to make his own opening. No sooner had Parliament met than Major Scott made the unfortunate move of reminding "the member for India"—as Burke's admirers liked to describe him—of the notice he had given at the close of the previous session. The business, replied Burke promptly, would not be neglected—but a general did not consult the enemy as to the time or place of a battle. And within a month the attack on Warren Hastings was launched.

At first it seemed that Burke was merely banging his head against a stone wall. His each successive move was repulsed in short order. He asked for copies of Hastings's correspondence relative to certain of his actions. Permission was refused. He was told to state his case first and allow the House to judge of its merits. [3] The situation bore every appearance of being exactly as Francis described it: that of two individuals arrayed against the whole kingdom and every power and influence in it. [4] Popular interest in the debates was slight as the result was regarded as a foregone conclusion, assuming, as every one did, that ministers would support the late Governor-General. Politics, it was felt, not the rights and wrongs of the case, would nullify all of Burke's efforts; and Horace Walpole was only expressing the general opinion when he cynically remarked: "Most other debates roll on the affair of Mr. Hastings, who is black-washed by the opposition, and is to be white-washed by the House of Commons. I do not know who is guilty or innocent; but I have no doubt but India has been blood-washed by our countrymen." [5]

The cynicism is understandable, for while belief in the chronic misconduct of the Company's servants had long been so general as to have become a settled conviction of the general mass of the people, they had likewise grown accustomed to the spectacle of the miscreants being allowed to enjoy complete immunity from prosecution and punishment. The gentlemen of Parliament might orate, floods of sensational and informative pamphlets might pour from the press, the House of Commons might set up secret and select committees of investigation and pass condemnatory resolutions—it might even resolve to recall the chief offenders—but what had all this agitation effected up to now? Exactly nothing. The culprits could still return home at their own pleasure and without any fear of molestation. How then could Edmund Burke and Philip Francis hope for success when the man whom they were attacking was the most prominent of the whole Indian fraternity? The attack would surely end exactly as the attack on Lord Clive had ended—in fiasco.

Edmund Burke persevered, however, despite all rebuffs. On April 4 he brought forward eleven charges, on which it was proposed to ground the impeachment, and at intervals during the following month he added eleven more, making twenty-two in all.

The publication of the charges produced an immediate and profound effect. Indifference vanished, and in its place there rose a tide of indignation against the accused. The reason is not hard to discover. The wit of man could not have devised anything better calculated to impress an ignorant but already prejudiced nation than these charges. The length of them alone was staggering. They occupied four hundred and sixty pages of an octavo volume. And the sources from which the material was drawn were equally impressive: the consultations of the Bengal Council, the Court's "general letters," the evidence given before the Parliamentary Committees of Inquiry, private letters, minutes, and so forth. The detail was overwhelming in its mass and intricacy, but the conclusions were stated with so much forcefulness of reasoning and clarity of exposition, and supported by so much apparently irrefutable evidence, that even now the most reluctant mind can scarce resist accepting them as sound. Only the brain of a diabolically clever man could have produced such a colossal work, nor was it the production of a day or of a week. The better part of twelve years had been spent in accumulating the material and the hand of Philip Francis was plainly visible in every part of it. The whole of Hastings's record was brought under review, and there was scarcely any of it that was not made to appear highly culpable, if not actually criminal, and by means that are easily recognized as those consistently employed by Hastings's former colleague at the Council Board.

Long familiarity with this mode of attack enabled Hastings to catalogue, with very fair accuracy, the devices employed. "The charges," he informed his friends in India, "are made up of mutilated quotations; of facts which have no mutual relation but are forced by false arrangement into connections; of principles of pernicious policy and false morality; assertions of guilt without proof, or the attempt to prove them; interpretations of secret motives and designs which passed within my own breast, and which none but myself could know; actions of others imputed to me, in which I had no concern, or which passed in opposition to me; and epithets and invectives affixed to acts ascribed to me, equally to those which in the construction are bad, as to those which are indifferent, or even meritorious." [6] Every word of this description is true. The impeachment of Warren Hastings can scarcely, indeed, be regarded in any other light than as a continuation, under the kindly auspices of the mother of Parliaments, of Philip Francis's own personal feud. All that gave it an appearance of being actuated by worthier motives and directed towards higher ends, was the association in its conduct of men like Burke, Fox, Grey and Windham; they were to be the instruments of Francis's revenge.

Francis's contribution to the work having been, as Burke put it, "to make it what it ought to be," [7] Burke merely had to supply whatever was lacking to give it maximum effectiveness. "I am so much yours"—thus did he acknowledge his indebtedness to his instructor— "and have so much of yours, that your triumphs puff me up as with a sense of personal merit." [8] Burke advised Francis to leave nothing out. It was not enough, he said, to concentrate on three or four criminal acts, heinous as these might be, because the popular mind might not be sufficiently impressed, prone as it was to judge a man by the general tenor of his conduct. It was necessary to show "a general and habitual evil intention." [9] It had to be shown that Hastings was that rare —Burke evidently did not think it nonexistent—specimen of the human race, a wholly bad man. Every particle of dirt had to be carefully scraped together and flung in a mass, in the hope that enough of it would stick to extort an impeachment out of a reluctant assembly. The more there was of it the less chance the House of Commons would have to exercise its powers of judgement.

Francis scarcely needed the hint, and the success that attended its adoption proved the shrewdness of Burke's reasoning. When each charge had been filled to the brim with a great mass of heterogeneous matter, it was presented to the House with the demand that a vote be taken on the simple question, "Is Mr. Hastings guilty on this charge or not?" And if the answer happened to be "Yes," it was because, as Burke had hoped, there were sufficient members each of whom found in the grotesque medley of accusations some point which impressed them, and determined their vote on the whole accordingly, though if each of such points had been voted upon separately the result would almost certainly have been reversed.

Hastings may usually be relied upon for graphic descriptions of situations in which he was involved, and his burlesque of Burke's plan of attack is not only amusing but contains more than an ounce of truth:

"To ask a mob of giddy and uninformed men, is Mr. Hastings impeachable for having 'pared his nails, shaved his beard, put on two stockings not fellows, got drunk on the King's birthday, eat bad rice instead of wholesome, and entertained a treasonable design against Chait Singh, etc.,' including five hundred affirmations, some of which were true, but innocent; some blameworthy on a good principle; some wrong, but of no consequence; some right, but applied to wrong construction; and many strictly right and most meritorious, but contrary to a false, wicked or dangerous principle which Mr. Burke would establish in the stead of mine;—what is this but to punish me because the House of Commons cannot solve his enigmas?" [10]

"Let this business end as it will," he wrote, correctly divining the intention of his accuser, "a great portion of mankind will think they judge with candor, if, unable to comprehend any part of the accusations, they acquit me, at a guess, of some, and conclude that where so much is alleged against me, much of it must be necessarily true." [11] Nor did he have any illusions about the possible effect of this method of attack on his reputation, then and in the future: "Though the most complete acquittal should end the present trial, my reputation will still be blasted by writers yet unborn, and will continue to be so as long as the events which are connected with it are deemed to deserve their place in the history of this country." [12] It was an appalling prediction— could he have really meant it without losing his faith in God and man? —yet, as it happened, it was the truest prophecy he ever made, and even now, a hundred and fifty years later, it has not wholly lost its truth.

What can be said, then, of Edmund Burke, the noble humanitarian, the defender of the weak and oppressed? For does not Lord Morley claim that "Burke is entitled to our lasting reverence as the first apostle and great upholder of integrity, mercy, and honor in the relation between his countrymen and their humble dependents?" [13] Much could, of course, be said, but most of it might as well be left unsaid: Burke in the matter of Hastings is too easy a mark. Moreover, it behooves us to walk carefully in how we judge such a truly great man, and to be charitable. For truly great he was in his hatred of cruelty, injustice and oppression, and his championship of noble causes. Usually he was magnificently right in the causes that he espoused, and no doubt his detestation of Hastings sprang from his intense sympathy for the suffering masses of India. It was a thousand pities that he should have fallen into the grievous error of identifying him as one of their oppressors, because then the passion and vehemence of his nature became a curse instead of a blessing to the cause of Right and made him little more than a vulgar ranter. The hater of injustice then became the incarnation of injustice, and the man whose warm and generous heart was deeply moved by all forms of suffering and waxed indignant over cruelty and wrongdoing, himself inflicted untold suffering and cruelty on an innocent victim of his misdirected fury.

II

THE first eleven charges were presented to the House on April 4, 1786. Hastings watched eagerly to see their effect. At first he was confident. "The clouds of error are dispersing and truth must appear." But no— he soon saw that the reverse was happening: the clouds were actually thickening! Serene confidence turned to incredulous doubt, and doubt to bitter disillusionment. The people of England were actually making their decision after hearing only one side of the case! "The world knew the character of my accuser, and had seen nothing but his accusation. It knew that something could be said on the other side; yet decided on the accusation before it. Such is popular judgement!" [14]

He felt that there was only one thing for him to do, namely, to apply the acid test of appearing in person to answer his accusers. His friends, all but Lord Thurlow, advised against the step. And undoubtedly they were right. Not only was he no orator but he had, as he once acknowledged, a defect in his speech that made him anything but an effective public speaker. And, added to that, he misjudged the temper of the House. In naïve ignorance he thought that he had only to appear before it, with the dazzling light of innocence and benevolence shining from his countenance and demeanor, and state the plain facts of his record, and he would instantly scatter confusion among his enemies and rally all men to his side. He forgot that the temper of popular assemblies is seldom judicial, that the ruling deities in them are Politics, Prejudice and Rhetoric, and that when the dull facts of an unskilled intruder are pitted against the brilliant oratory of their own members, victory is apt to go to the latter. Was it likely that these legislators, utterly ignorant of the merits of the case and unable to distinguish truth from error, would prefer the word of an accused stranger to that of honored members of their own arrogantly august and select body? He was a rash man who dared to question the veracity of anything that was said in this House, or the justice of anything done by its order. He would surely be told that he had insulted the sovereign representatives of the people of England, than which there was no more heinous offense. The voice of the people is Law—which is sometimes confused with Justice.

Hastings was not alone in thinking the whole process of impeachment monstrously unjust. He was supported by one of the most eminent lawyers of that day. In a letter to a certain unnamed Peer, who was one of Hastings's friends, Thomas Erskine, the future Lord Chancellor and the intimate friend of Fox and Sheridan, expressed the following opinion:

"Although Mr. Hastings is prosecuted by a person whom I love and respect, and although his prosecution is likely to be supported by many of those whose principles are the most congenial to my own, yet I should have been happy in an opportunity of showing him, by my desire of being introduced to him, that an English lawyer does not conclude that a person is guilty of crimes because he is prosecuted for them, and that it is not the genius of this constitution to try men for their honors, liberties and properties in assemblies not competent in their very constitution to the administration of private justice....

"There is another principle now against Impeachment, which is that a man is, from the present state of society, subject to be ruined with the public and the very judges trying him *pendente lite,* which was not the case in former days. Now, the person who is the subject of a bill of Impeachment, which is or ought to be analogous to a bill of indictment, is treated with hourly calumny and invective before the Grand Jury who are to have the bill before them.

"Before the bill is found, the prosecutor, who is also one of the Grand Jury, prints the bill. It is sold in every shop, and is the conversation of the coffee houses. Parliament adjourns while things are in this shape, and if no new game is started it is the topic of the recess. Will any man, whose reason is not disordered, say that when Parliament reassembles it can try the object of all this proceeding upon any principle of English justice?

"Bound by no oaths, limited to no principles of judgement, confined to no rules of evidence, and every man's mind made up on the subject. I know nothing of Mr. Hastings's guilt or innocence, but these considerations lead me to feel for him; and if I were to be a member of the House of Commons while his Impeachment was before the House I would never make so free with my conscience as to venture to be one of his judges." [15]

All honor to Lord Erskine—the only man of his party whose eyes were not blinded, whether it was by malice or passion or just the ordinary weak follow-the-leader spirit of party politics.... [1]

[1] "Of all kinds of credulity, the most obstinate and wonderful is that of political zealots; of men who, being numbered, they know not how, or why, in any of the parties that divide a state, resign the use of their own eyes and ears, and resolve to believe nothing that does not favor those whom they profess to follow." Samuel Johnson, *The Idler.*

Lord Clive, when similarly attacked, had prudently intrusted his defense to a man who was well versed in the idiosyncrasies of the House. It was characteristic of Warren Hastings to choose to appear in person. When his petition was received, Edmund Burke opposed not only the granting of it but even the granting to the accused of a copy of the charges: it would be time enough, he said, for him to produce a defense after the Commons had ordered his impeachment. Burke, however, was voted down, and Hastings was ordered to appear five days later. [16] That is to say, he was given five days "to reply to a volume that could not be read in less than two," and that had taken untold months to prepare. But he was not wholly unprepared and with the help of several friends and colleagues who had been with him in India, including Anderson, Shore and Middleton, he was able to whip together a document which took him and two clerks, relieving each other by turns, two whole days to read.

The defense taken as a whole was not an adequate and completely satisfactory reply.[1] Lengthy as it was, it was still much briefer than the charges. It was, in fact, too brief to cover the ground thoroughly; it passed over lightly, and somewhat too disdainfully to be wise, many of the accusations; and it was not entirely free from inaccuracies. None of these defects can justly be laid to the door of the accused. They arose unavoidably from the circumstances under which the defense was put together: the haste, the lack of time to obtain verifying documents, the want of assistance, the complexity of the issues involved. He was replying, Hastings explained, to charges that had been composed from a labored scrutiny of his whole official life, "comprehending perhaps a greater variety of interesting events than have fallen to the lot of any man now living." In order to make a complete rebuttal it was necessary for him to make an equally thorough examination of the thousands of relevant documents preserved in India House. So obvious, indeed, is it that every advantage lay with his accusers that almost any other course than the one he actually took might have been better: he might have refused to make any defense at all at this juncture, or he might have confined himself to a short dignified statement that did not attempt to traverse the whole vast ground covered by the charges. It subsequently appeared that much of the defense as delivered had not even been read and approved by him, such had been the haste with which he and his collaborators had had to work.

The finest and most effective part by far is the introduction, [17] which Hastings wrote himself, and which is couched in simple, moving, dignified language, in the use of which he was a past master:

---

[1] What Burke thought of it is shown by the marginal notes he made in his copy of the published work, which now is in the Owen D. Young Library in New York. They reveal a complete disbelief even in Hastings's most positive statements of fact, and show Burke eagerly detecting apparent discrepancies and inaccuracies. His whole attitude is clearly indicated by one such comment: "This history may possibly be fabulous because taken from himself." No credence, in Burke's opinion, could be attached to any statement of the accused,

"I received the government of Bengal with incumbrances, which might have intimidated a firmer spirit than mine; and I felt the perilous situation in which it placed me. I found myself the titular head of a numerous, and not always accordant, council, appointed to manage the affairs of a great state, which yet wore the marks of recent acquisition; but had neither determinate form nor system, nor any orders or instructions which could enable them to give it either.

"I attempted, and with the aid of my colleagues, where I was allowed them, I gave it both form and system; for every office into which it was distributed, to the time of my departure, received its institution during the period of my administration, and all the transactions of it have, except the first two years of the general government, in some part of their progress, received their direction from my guidance.—Yet in every step I had difficulties to surmount, which are unknown to the rulers and ministers of other governments. Besides the conciliation of discordant opinions, and their more frequently confirmed opposition, I had my conduct circumscribed by orders which would apply to few of the cases which occurred, and those orders uncertain in their construction."

He went on to show that in a government so constituted and forced to undergo so many vicissitudes no perfectly consistent policy was possible. Events of every kind had conspired to divert it from its set course. It had been pulled hither and thither by conflicting forces that the man at the helm had been powerless to control. When he had yielded to the storm he was accused of inconsistency; when he had used a lull to regain the course he was accused of innovations. He had had no instruments to guide him but the compass of his own intelligence; he had been faced by situations for which he could find no rules or precedents to regulate his conduct; he had exercised an authority without known limits in any of its branches.

"Under such circumstances I humbly apprehend that since it is not, as I have said, the lot of human nature to be exempt from error, some notorious calamity, affecting the interests of which I had charge, or some well-ascertained ground of corruption, or other moral deviation from my duty, the loss of national reputation or of substantial property, ought to have appeared, before I become the subject of a parliamentary impeachment. But what losses has the nation sustained through my mismanagement? Have provinces been dismembered from it? Have its armies been defeated in operations of my formation? Or war or famine wasted the countries of my jurisdiction?—No; the reverse has been the attendant of my fortunes in every stage of it; and so little ground have I afforded, from the notoriety of my character, for such an inquisition into it, that I dare affirm that I stand, even at this hour (notwithstanding the prejudices excited against me) as high in the estimation of the world as any man of my own rank and pretensions in it."

All that he asked of the honorable House was a fair trial, and that he be not punished before conviction by the admission of hard epithets and dishonoring invectives. But this was a plea that his judges were hardly likely to take very seriously. Orators of the day were too well versed in the art of vituperation to let slip a heaven-sent opportunity like this. Vituperation was part of the stock-in-trade of every aspirant to parliamentary honors. What would today be called unparliamentary language was then the fine flower of public speech in general use to embellish the daily exchange of compliments between political opponents. Yet there was a difference between using it as the medium of parliamentary debate and using it when the House was sitting as a court of justice. Fox and North could denounce Pitt as a corrupt tyrant, a second Strafford—and Pitt could remain scornfully silent. The House of Commons could pass a resolution declaring Lord Temple guilty of "a high crime and misdemeanor, derogatory to the honor of the Crown, a breach of the fundamental privileges of Parliament, and subversive of the Constitution of this country"—guilty of high treason, in other words—and Lord Temple could pass it off with a laugh. Both alike were protected from their assailants by their positions, their control of great political forces, which made them invulnerable. But not so with Warren Hastings. He was more used to the barbaric ways of the East than to the refined customs of his own country, and what was mere child's play to North and Pitt was to his sensitive nature an ordeal of torture. Added to which was the fact that, not being a member of this highly privileged company of exalted legislators, he was without effective means of defense. He was like a man who had to fight with one arm strapped to his side.

He came away from Westminster well pleased with himself, and very confident that he had succeeded. He was under the impression that he had been heard with unusual attention. "My credit now stands higher by many degrees than it ever did." Immediately afterwards Burke brought forward another charge. Again Hastings petitioned to be heard in reply. He was this time given two days to prepare his defense. He complied, but did not appear in person. Though still confident, he pitied the fate of the next unhappy victim who might be subjected to the same iniquitous procedure, "for the purest integrity alone can stand it." [18]

After the examination of Burke's witnesses, which followed, the debate on the first charge opened on June 1. The subject of it was the Rohilla War. Dundas opposed the motion for impeachment, on the ground that since that event, condemnable as it was, the accused had been thrice appointed Governor-General, which amounted to a tacit pardon. The ministerial party led by Pitt followed suit, and the motion was lost. Everybody thought that this vote had decided the issue.

On the 13th, Fox opened the debate on the Benares charge, with a speech of great power, vehemence and malignity. Francis supported him. The House was crowded with ministerialists come to hear and vote with their leader, the opposition to hear and vote with Fox, and all to enjoy the oratorical fireworks.

Pitt rose. Great enthusiasm from his followers. He began to speak. Point by point he refuted every one of Fox's contentions, tearing his whole case to pieces. Fox had asserted that Chait Singh was an independent prince and not a vassal of the Company. Pitt—who had familiarized himself with Hastings's arguments—demonstrated that he was not the former and was the latter. (Continued enthusiasm: Pitt was scoring off Fox with every stroke!) It followed that Chait Singh was liable for special contributions to the defense of the Company's possessions, that he had been guilty of gross delinquency, and that Hastings was justified in seeking to punish him by the exaction of a fine. Then the Prime Minister paused, and, in a changed tone, went on: "But in proposing to inflict a fine of fifty lakhs, Hastings had set a penalty utterly disproportionate to the offense, and therefore disgracefully exorbitant, and he must in consequence find him deserving of censure upon this point." [19]

The House was thunderstruck at this totally unexpected turn of events, and utter confusion fell on the ranks of Pitt's followers. They knew not which way to vote, having come expecting to be told to vote, as before, against the motion. The result was that the docile majority behaved like sheep, following their leader into the opposition lobby. The motion was won; "the farce" was turned into a serious reality; Burke and Francis were victorious. Pitt's vote was the decisive factor in bringing about the impeachment of Warren Hastings.

The "mystery" of Pitt's vote has exercised the minds of every writer on the subject. It seems so inexplicable that he should, without any warning, have completely reversed his attitude, and on such inadequate ground. The explanation advanced by his biographers—that he was trying to act the part of an unbiased juryman, judging each charge on its merits, and finding, when the Benares charge was reached, that his conscience would not permit him longer to support Hastings—is probably the right one, and certainly the only one that seems to fit the facts, but it is only acceptable if to it is added the further postulate that he was under the same kind of delusion that had afflicted so many other members of the House. It was once thought that Pitt was influenced by Dundas, who saw in Hastings a dangerous rival to himself for the control of Indian affairs and sought to remove him from his path by the simple means of getting him impeached. But this theory, fondly held by many of Hastings's biographers—and by Hastings himself— has been shown to lack any foundation in fact or probability, [20] though Burke did indeed try to instill in Dundas's mind the idea that Hastings was about to become the leader of an Indian party which would be so strong as to overpower the government of which Dundas was a member. [21] It was Pitt's declared intention to hold the scales of justice even; at the outset of the debates he had stated: "I am neither a determined friend nor foe of Mr. Hastings, but I will support the principles of justice and equity. I recommend a calm dispassionate investigation, leaving every man to follow the impulse of his own mind." But in the poisoned atmosphere that Francis had created it was by no means easy for a man even of Pitt's intellect and honesty to disentangle the truth from the false. Pitt, like Dundas, had liberally imbibed the views and prejudices of Francis. Dundas had once been Hastings's bitter critic, and he never became more than lukewarm in his support—when he joined Pitt in office he urged the appointment of Cornwallis in Hastings's place. He was an expert politician, with few inconvenient principles, loyalties or convictions, and it must have been a matter of small concern to him whether Hastings deserved impeachment or not. If, then, he and Pitt—who had always in his cold fashion disapproved of Hastings—upon examination of the charges and the defense found it "impossible to refuse our concurrence to the impeachment," the credit for this achievement must surely go to Francis and Burke for the ability they had shown in preparing the charge and the strategic way in which they forced the attack. If Pitt had continued to defend Hastings the Opposition would have gleefully claimed that he was shielding a criminal from justice.

Thus it was that Hastings was condemned to impeachment because, as he himself said of Pitt's action, he had "been declared guilty of a high crime and misdemeanor in having *intended* to exact a fine too large for the offense, the offense being admitted to merit a fine from Chait Singh," and none but himself knowing of his intention, which was not even fixed when it was taken as he allowed for circumstances and more exact knowledge of the Rajah's wealth to modify it. Pitt had exonerated him on every other part of the charge: he condemned him on *this*. Verily, there was something strange in the working of Pitt's mind; he must have been a paragon of a statesman if he himself never harbored unjust intentions, and he certainly was an exacting judge if he believed that the mere harboring of such an intention without actual translation into action was a crime worthy of impeachment. . . .

Eighteen months were still to pass before the impeachment preliminaries were completed. Immediately after the vote on the Benares charge, Parliament adjourned. When it met again, the resumed debates on the other charges lasted until April 3, 1787. On that day Burke completed his victory by persuading the House to present articles of impeachment in Westminster Hall. The only notable event to enliven the dreary proceedings had been Sheridan's famous masterpiece of oratory on the subject of the Begums of Oude, which produced another vote by Pitt against the accused and a vote by the House of three to one to make it one of the charges. On May 21 Warren Hastings was arrested by the Sergeant-at-Arms and brought to the Bar of the House of Lords to hear the articles of impeachment read. He was then released on bail.

The time had come to appoint managers to conduct the prosecution. This was to be Philip Francis's great moment, his hour of triumph, when he was at last to be given his chance of revenging himself, in the sweetest possible way, on his hated enemy. He had waited seven long years for this hour to strike. Burke, as a matter of course, included his name in his proposed list of managers.

The hour struck, but instead of bringing triumph and fulfillment to the tortured, twisted soul of Philip Francis, it brought only the crowning disappointment to a life that was one long succession of blighted hopes. Pitt the arbiter opposed his nomination on the ground of his violent and notorious animus against the accused, and the House accepted his ruling. Burke nearly wept at the decision and entreated the House to reverse it. How hard and eloquently he pleaded! But it was in vain. When the list of managers was announced, it included Burke, Fox, Sheridan, Wyndham, Grey, Sir Gilbert Elliot—but not the prime mover of the whole affair. *He* had to console himself by working behind the scenes. [22]

Pitt and Dundas refused to take any share in the management of the prosecution, but promised Burke "to give that support to it which appears to us consistent with national justice and the credit of the House of Commons." [23] Thus by the end of the session of 1787 all was in readiness for the opening of the great drama.

III

DURING this time of uncertainty over his fate Hastings had been quietly enjoying his life of retirement partly in London and partly in the country. His tastes were unchanged and only the opportunity to pursue them undisturbed was lacking. We are given a glimpse of him by a German lady, Sophie V. la Roche, who came on a visit to England in the summer of 1786 and rapturously admired all the eminent personages she met. And none more so than Mr. and Mrs. Hastings. She dined with them one day at their house in St. James's Place, and wrote ecstatically of all that she saw and heard. Mr. Hastings, she noted in her diary, "has one of the noblest and most manly faces I have ever seen; large, fiery, blue eyes, keen and friendly; a mind peculiarly adapted to great things, for I have never yet met with thought so precise, expression so terse, and remarks so subtle or an intellect so keen, tempered with such infinite charm." [24] His collection of paintings and Indian curiosities caught her attention; she noticed pictures of ancient temples and remarked on the splendor and beauty of their architecture. "Yes," said Mr. Hastings, "you see how unjust is our European attitude when we take these people for ignorant barbarians; believe me, they are fine, splendid people." They talked about *suttee,* and he deplored the powerful hold the custom had on the people, telling how he had once tried in vain to dissuade a poor woman from it. Some one asked him whether he did not think England might one day lose India as she had lost America. "Yes," he replied, "and in precisely the same way—through the people in Parliament—in no other way." Sophie was much impressed by his magnanimity, even where his enemies were concerned—"all his remarks on Burke's 'The Sublime and Beautiful' were great, simple and noble." "He loves his wife intensely, as also his king, and respects his queen." There was nothing more that she could say in praise of him.

Some days later she spent a day at Beaumont Lodge where her host took evident pride and pleasure in showing her the special attractions of the estate—the fine trees, the animals that he had brought back with him from India and Tibet, the extensive gardens, the long, sweeping lawns, and the view which the park commanded of Westminster and Windsor. It was a splendid view, and it was a pity that all too soon it was to be associated in his mind with the threatened impeachment. After trying hard to persuade him to write his reminiscences but without success, his admirer went away filled with delight.

Though this picture of placid contentment caught by a casual foreign visitor was superficial, Hastings was not by any means unhappy. His love of the soil and keen delight in the life of the English countryside were too great for that. In the following summer he wrote, "We are much interested in the success of our haymaking, which has been prodigious, and never feel a tendency to be out of humor or spirits but when we look towards London." He had made it his hobby to obtain the seeds of Oriental trees and fruits and try to grow them in England, as well as Oriental animals for experimental breeding. He was most anxious for Nesbitt Thompson to send him seeds of the lichen, the cinnamon, the custard apple and the mango, while from Samuel Turner he wanted shawl goats, turnip seeds and other Bhutan animals and plants. Without interests of this sort to absorb his attention he could scarcely have endured the long drawn-out ordeal of the next few years. And, characteristically, he was more concerned about his wife than about himself. He could endure it all, but could she? It seemed to him that she was suffering far more than he—"I only from her sufferings." Now, as ever, she occupied the foremost place in his mind and affections, and he could not bear to see her suffer. Little by little, however, as the shadow of impeachment deepened so did his own spirits droop and his health suffer.

The disillusionment of his hopes for speedy vindication came as a fearfully hard blow to one whose spirit was as proud and sensitive as his. It made him want to shut himself away from the world. For several months he went nowhere and saw no one. As usual he sought refuge in the citadel of his own integrity and innocence, happy in the thought that his enemies could never penetrate there, however much havoc they might work on his material wealth and the outer defenses of his reputation. As for the members of the House of Commons, his opinion of them and their power to do him serious hurt was one of contempt and little more: "I shall never admit the effect of any vote that they can give as either conveying real credit or dishonor on my character." Only the fantastic injustice of the whole proceeding amazed him—especially its appalling slowness. That months should pass by while a criminal prosecution was hanging over his head, as though it were a chancery suit, and "in a land where the laws will not permit the jury to sleep over a trial for murder!"—this, he felt, was the most monstrous part of the whole business.

Nor was there much that was gratifying in the India news he received from Thompson. Macpherson's retrenchment measures had inflicted great hardship upon the Service, and many of his most valued and trusted officers now were out of employment. Piteous appeals for help began to reach him, to which he was powerless to respond. It pleased him greatly, however, to know that his Indian friends had not forgotten him.

"It has been much the fashion with Europeans to accuse the natives of insincerity. I have seen," wrote Thompson, "unanswerable proofs to the contrary in the conduct of many of your native friends, who to their honor continue their usual visits and respect to me merely from their remembrance of you. I have a large levy every Sunday morning at Alipore in which you are the constant subject of conversation. They all beg me to assure them that you will come back again, and though I tell them I cannot give such hopes on any valid grounds, they still conjure me to tell them so, for they say it would be impious, ominous and horrid to say otherwise. We may talk of the devil and his horns appear, but they really think that to mention evil will conduce to the production of it." [25]

Many were the letters that Hastings received from his Indian friends, and they were loud in indignation when they heard of the manner in which he was being treated by his own countrymen. Thompson voiced their feelings when he called the "persecution" a disgrace to humanity. His admiration for his old chief was boundless.

"The former part of your life furnishes an example of all that is disinterested, great and good in action; the present period of it displays an instance of all that is patient, firm and dignified in suffering—it exhibits you, though suffering for your virtues, still relying on them, and gives to God (for I will not talk like a heathen) that sight of which Cicero says he is most fond—a virtuous man struggling with misfortunes. I have never thought that your actions were such as to meet the applause of the day—they are calculated for posterity, and what is better for eternity—a lasting fame, and eternal happiness will be their reward. I am obliged to look beyond this world for considerations that can reconcile me to your present situation, and there alone I find them." [26]

If Hastings was able to attain something of the philosophic calm and indifference of a Stoic, he did not neglect the matter of his defense. He was prepared for the worst, but he was not going to give up without a stout fight. He was ready to face his accusers, as he had faced them in India, and combat their false charges with the truth as he knew it. So, as his counsel, he chose Mr. Thomas Plumer—who had defended Sir Thomas Rumbold, Governor of Madras, four years before—Mr. Edward Law, and Mr. Robert Dallas. All three members of Lincoln's Inn and able barristers; the first, as Sir Thomas Plumer subsequently became Master of the Rolls (he was also to defend successfully Henry Dundas in his impeachment), the second, as Lord Ellenborough, became Lord Chief Justice, and the third, as Sir Robert Dallas, a Privy Councilor and a High Court Judge.

Their client labored with them in the accumulation and arrangement of the materials for the defense and the mustering of witnesses. In particular, having noted that the chief indictment against him lay in the charge that he had oppressed the people of India, he wrote to John Shore, who had returned to India, and to Thompson, asking them to obtain the permission of the Governor-General, Lord Cornwallis, to solicit testimonials from all the chief communities and classes of people. This they did, though they were refused the government's coöperation and met with considerable obstruction from local officials; and the results were remarkable. It needed only a hint that they would be rendering a service to the great governor to elicit from the Indians a spontaneous flood of the most eulogistic testimonials imaginable. Printed by order of the House of Commons in 1789, they came from persons of every rank of society—Brahmin priests, Moslem lawyers, officers of government, zemindars, princesses, nobles, merchants, bankers, judges. Among them were the Vizier and his two Chief Ministers, and the two Begums of Oude, the Brahmins, principal inhabitants and merchants of Benares, the Nawab of Bengal, Munny Begum, the Rajah of Nuddea, the Rajah of Burdwan, the Zemindars of Bheerboom, Rajshay and Dinagepore.

One great nobleman of the province of Bihar wrote:

"I affirm, swearing by the Prophet and by the Holy Father . . . that without ever having seen Mr. Hastings I am thankful to him. In truth, that excellent Gentleman was without an equal. Even in former times, there were few rulers so just, and possessed of such liberality, that all mankind, from the high to the low, from the great to the small, should on all accounts be thankful to him; and not one of the whole human race should complain of him. God is witness, that the late Governor-General is one of those rulers who are of distinguished eminence. Wherever he is, may God keep him under His holy protection!"

Even the formerly wild and uncivilized inhabitants of Jungleterry, to whom Hastings had given settled government, wrote expressing their deep sense of gratitude to him: "We never experienced other than kindness, nor have any of us heard of any oppression from him."

To obtain the precise value of these glowing tributes something should no doubt be discounted because of the customary extravagance of oriental sentiment. But even so, they form the grandest testimonial that has ever, perhaps, been paid by a subject people to their ruler. The recipient of them really needed no other justification. The very victims of his "crimes" had themselves arisen to fling back the lie in the teeth of his accusers, saluting him as their friend and benefactor, and exalting him to the eminence reserved for only the best and most just of rulers. Burke, the advocate in his self-imposed cause, naturally did his best to destroy their value as evidence, but there was no way in which he could do so except by the grossest misrepresentation. He declared them to be the worthless work of "anonymous swearers," from whom they had been extorted by force. To such pitiful lengths was he driven in his desperate attempt to sustain his unworthy cause.

On August 2, 1787, Hastings informed Thompson that he was prepared for his trial. He hoped, whatever might be the result of it—"for
I should not be too sanguine, if the only crime laid to my charge was
that I was concerned in the revolt of America"—that it would be ended
before the end of the next session of Parliament. [27] But it was
February of the following year before the High Court of Parliament
was even ready to begin. Meanwhile, in September, Mr. and Mrs. Hastings made a tour of Scotland.

When the time approached, the whole nation was tense with excitement. "Puppet-shows are coming on," remarked Walpole, reflecting
the popular feeling; "the Birthday, the Parliament, and the trial of
Hastings and his imp, Elijah.[1] They will fill the town, I suppose." [28]
He was correct in his guess: the "puppet-show" that opened in Westminster Hall on February 13, 1788, filled the town. "How long the
trial will last, God knows," wrote the chief "puppet" five days before,
"but I believe it is not yet in the power of men to conjecture." And *he*
also was correct in his guess.

IV

How was it that Warren Hastings came to be put on trial for his life?
—for if he had been found guilty of such abominable crimes as he was
accused of, his life must surely have been forfeit. The reasons were
many and complex and the nature of most of them has already been
sufficiently indicated; but there was one in particular to which sufficient
weight has seldom been attached. That was Hastings's refusal to throw
into the scale of fairly equally balanced forces the power of his own
winning personality. That he gave comparatively few of his fellow-
countrymen a chance to make his acquaintance, and those few almost
all admirers, is proved by the fact that when he appeared at the Bar
of the House of Commons to read his defense there was a rush of
members to see him, for though he had been in England a year scarcely
any of them had even as much as laid eyes on him.

It was his misfortune to have so sensitive a pride that he held
himself utterly aloof from those whom he knew to be unfriendly. It
would have been merely common prudence for him to have tried to
correct the totally false ideas of him that many people had. But so
little inclined was he to that course that he actually gloried in his refusal
to employ even the most ordinary sort of diplomacy.

"I have not visited any of the ministers since the prosecution began. I
have not been at the levee nor drawing-room. I have not desired the
attendance of a single member. I have broken engagements which were
officiously, but kindly, made to bring me acquainted with members of
the House. I have disdained every species of management. I have acted
against all that the world calls discretion. Every artifice of a man who

---

[1] Sir Elijah Impey, whose impeachment was also planned but was rejected by
the House of Commons after Impey's brilliant and triumphant defense of himself.

has long thrown away the check of shame has been practiced against me. Yet, my friend, I promise you that he will be most foully discomfited, and my name shall shine the brighter for the means which have been taken to extinguish it." [29]

This may be magnificent—his faith in ultimate justice and vindication may be sublime—but it was flying in the face of plain common sense to adopt such an attitude. One can admire his refusal to seek through favor an immunity that should have been his by the operation of an impersonal and immutable sense of justice, yet the actual effect of his conduct was to prevent the operation of that sense by giving free range to the prejudice and ignorance that existed in men's minds on the all-important question—*What manner of man was Warren Hastings?*

It is worth while speculating what would have been the result if he had acted otherwise. A vivid picture has been left us of how two of the managers of the prosecution felt as they gazed upon the prisoner at the opening of the trial. One of them is William Windham, whose emotions are recorded by Fanny Burney in her well-known account of the trial. All eyes in the Hall were looking in a single direction: at the slight, frail figure of the prisoner at the bar, with his pale, emaciated and tortured countenance, his proud and dignified demeanor, the cynosure of hostile eyes, sympathetic eyes, callous eyes, curious eyes. Windham, gazing down on the scene from the Ladies' Gallery, was seeing him for the first time—"What a sight is that!" he cried. "To see that man, that small portion of human clay, that poor feeble machine of earth, enclosed now in that little space, brought to that Bar, a prisoner in a spot six foot square—and to reflect on his late power! Nations at his command! Princes prostrate at his feet!—What a change! How he must feel it!"—He continued for a short time in the same strain, forgetting everything for the moment but a common fellow-feeling of commiseration for the awfulness of the prisoner's ordeal. Then he collected himself, recalling to mind the grounds upon which he was impeaching this man. And his tone changed: "O could those—the thousands, the millions, who have groaned and languished under the iron rod of his oppressions—could they but—whatever region they inhabit—be permitted one dawn of light to look into this Hall, and see him *there!* There—where he stands—it might prove, perhaps, some recompense for their sufferings!" As William Windham could not believe it possible that anybody could honestly and sincerely think differently about Warren Hastings, he was frankly amazed to hear Miss Burney remark that she had found him "so mild, so gentle, so extremely pleasing in his manners." "What? Gentle!" he cried. "Yes, indeed; gentle, even to humility," she replied. "Humility? Mr. Hastings and *humility!*" Mr. Windham could scarce believe his ears. He felt sure she was being facetious. How could such a monster, such a man of blood, rapine and avarice, be humble? His expression now was proud and contemptuous. Could he ever look pleasant? But when Miss Burney assured him that she meant exactly what she said, William Windham, incredulous though he still was, looked intently at the prisoner again and sighed, as though he felt a faint stirring of regret at the part he was playing. Again he came to his senses and tried to shake off this dangerous feeling of doubt. But, as he made his departure, he was heard to mutter, "I must forget that *he* is there, for how else can I go on?" [30]

The other manager was Sir Gilbert Elliot, Bart. (afterwards Earl of Minto and Governor-General of India), whose father had been one of Hastings's most faithful adherents, standing by him in 1776 when the attempt had been made to remove him, and whose younger brother Alexander had been one of Hastings's dearest friends. Upon returning from Westminster Hall Sir Gilbert Elliot wrote to his wife:

"I never saw Hastings till today, and had not formed anything like a just idea of him. I never saw a more miserable-looking creature, but indeed he has so much the appearance of bad health that I do not suppose he resembles even himself. He looks as if he could not live a week. I always feel uncomfortable in the reflection of his connections with Alick, and I cannot say I was insensible to that idea on seeing him today. But the clearness of his guilt and the atrociousness of his crimes can leave no hesitation in anybody's mind, who thinks as I do about him, what one's duty is." [31]

Clearly neither man, seeing him for the first time in the flesh, could make their impressions quite agree with the preconceived notions they had formed about him, and the discrepancy made each one momentarily uncomfortable. But what if they had met and conversed with him as Fanny Burney, one of their own group, had done? It is a most significant, yet little noticed, fact that quite a number of Edmund Burke's intimate friends and admirers became, *upon personal acquaintance,* ardent friends and admirers of Hastings too. Seven names spring to mind: Sir William Jones, Sir Joshua Reynolds, Dr. Johnson, Fanny Burney, James Boswell, Mrs. Elizabeth Montagu and Hannah More. [32] If Burke's influence counted for anything—and it counted a very great deal with all of them (although Johnson and he were diametrically opposed on political questions)—it is most surprising that in a matter that lay nearest his heart they should all have held such a different opinion. It is fair to assume that other members of Burke's party would similarly have differed from him if they had had their own opportunity of knowing the man he was attacking. Windham was a chivalrous gentleman and the very soul of honor. And Charles James Fox—Fox the black prince of folly, the giddy, brilliant, lovable profligate, the greatest of debaters, the most finished of rakes, the despair of his friends, the terror of his opponents—he at least was a generous-hearted man, agreeably lacking in Burke's intense fanaticism. Elliot, too, was a man of integrity, strong intellect, moderate views, and a calm, dispassionate nature. All three were warmly, devotedly attached to Burke and, lacking personal views of their own, not unnaturally allowed him to dictate their course regarding Warren Hastings. "What a friend to kindness is party!" was Fanny Burney's sorrowing comment. She might with equal truth have added, "and what a friend to justice is ignorance!" Hastings asked too much of human nature by expecting ties like these to be severed merely by the assertion of his own innocence and the production of masses of tedious printed documents and intricate arguments in support of his plea. These men knew and loved Burke, they did not know or love Hastings, and they naturally preferred to accept Burke's presentation of the facts.

We are driven to the conclusion that Hastings brought his impeachment largely upon himself by his disdain of worldly discretion. In fact, if Mrs. Hastings can be believed, he actually *wanted* to be placed on trial in order to dispose once and for all of the calumnies of his enemies. [33] If this is true, it affords one good reason why he did nothing to ward off the attack. Not content to play for the low stake of immunity he played for the highest stake of complete vindication, and in this way he played right into Burke's hands, for otherwise it is almost certain that he and Francis would have been two lonely voices crying in the wilderness. If Burke was infuriated by Hastings's lofty attitude of complete innocence, other members of the House must also have been exasperated by it; whereas a more humble and submissive attitude might well have disarmed and propitiated them. It is not true, however, as has commonly been said, that Hastings's action of challenging Burke through the mouth of Scott was all that prevented the attack from being abandoned. It precipitated matters, but Burke had meant business from the beginning, as his correspondence with Francis clearly shows. [34] He was intent on getting Hastings impeached from the day he landed in England. Both men were playing for the highest stakes, and if both were to be disappointed in the issue of their great gamble neither can be held wholly free from blame.

APPENDIX TO CHAPTER XXVIII

(Translation from the Persian of one of the testimonials
to Warren Hastings.)

Sealed on the 5th of Rabi' II 1202 A.H. (= January 14, 1788)

WE, the residents of the town of Murshidabad in the Province of Bengal, represent to the Ministers of His Majesty the King of England—whom God preserve—and to the Directors of the East India Company that the ex-Governor Mr. Hastings during the period of his governorship in this country from his first coming to the time of his departure earned our satisfaction and gratitude by his good conduct and pleasant behavior. He devoted himself constantly to the comfort of the people and to the security and prosperity of the country, he protected the community from the harm of nocturnal marauders, highwaymen and assassins by establishing his system of administration and by inventing the plan of civil and criminal courts, and he caused justice to be administered to all in accordance with their own religions and customs. To such an extent did he provide for the defense of the realm that none of the factious and seditious could exercise violence and rebellion. Consequently we continued in complete tranquillity and security, and in spite of the lack of rain his organization was so good that we were not troubled by famine or scarcity of corn. The aforesaid Governor never cast envious eyes upon men's property, wealth or honor, nor did he ever take bribes. He always bore himself courteously toward the noble and learned of every community and treated them with due honor and respect. He founded colleges for the acquisition of learning and the education of students and established graduated stipends, which up to now have benefited many, who pray for the continuance of the rule of the King of England and the government of the East India Company. The power, might and majesty of the King, the Company and the English people in India have in the time of the aforesaid Governor become such that no one has raised his head in arrogance or rebellion. In short, during the governorship of Mr. Hastings we were in perfect peace and security, we suffered no trouble or injury of any kind and we are pleased and satisfied with his behavior and his merits.

On all four sides of the text, but mainly above and on the right, are impressions of seals, including those of Saiyid Ahmad Ali Khan, Chief Muhammadan Justice, and subordinate judges. [35]

Chapter XXIX

WESTMINSTER HALL

Burke's Speech

THE *First Year.*—Time was of little account in the leisurely days of George the Third. In the time-table of the trial of Warren Hastings years, not days nor weeks nor even months, must be used to mark the successive stages. A day was not nearly enough for a single speech, particularly if it happened to be a speech of Mr. Burke's. It is true that a tremendous amount of ground had to be covered, and it was out of the question for the Court to sit continuously until the case was finished. Parliament had other and more pressing business to attend to and could only give its spare time to the trial. It was accustomed to sit for no more than five, or at most six, months in the year, with frequent recesses, and as during a part of that time the judges were away on circuit and the Lords felt they needed their assistance, the number of days in the year available for the impeachment was still further reduced. In fact, the average number of days in each of the seven years that the trial lasted was only twenty.

It was the third day when Mr. Burke began his exhausting performance, and his first effort—the opening speech for the prosecution —lasted four days. [36] As a *tour de force* it was truly magnificent and filled his hearers with amazement at the prodigality of his genius. In the course of it he presented an astonishing and highly original version of Indian history that excited, even if it did not edify, his vast audience. The method he practiced was that of shock: he tried to stir the Court into a state of hysterical rage against the accused, pulling and fretting at their emotions until mental and nervous exhaustion should compel them to admit the justice of his case. He did not argue; he only declaimed. He did not let cold facts speak for themselves. He did not flatter the intelligences of his hearers by letting them form their own opinions and draw their own conclusions and do some of their own qualifying. He did everything for them—teaching them their history, instructing them in ethics, revealing to them the subtle differences between right and wrong—confident that, having profited by his tuition, they would bow to his superior intellect and adjudge the prisoner guilty. If it is true that violence defeats itself, since it usually implies a weak case, and the greater the violence the greater the weakness that it has to conceal, then Burke would have done better to remain silent, for every time he opened his mouth he did more harm than good to his cause.

Burke loved violent contrasts, painting pictures in which black and white were the only colors used, contrasting a Golden Age of Indian civilization that existed only in his fevered imagination with the hell that was let loose when Hastings and his fellow-bandits descended upon the country, panegyrizing the martyred Triumvirate and execrating their hated rival and all his works. He exhausted the catalogue of crime before he finished describing the iniquity of this man: he charged him with fraud, abuse, treachery, robbery, murder, "with cruelties unheard of and devastations almost without a name," "with having scarcely left in India what will prove satisfaction for his guilt"; he impeached him "in the name of the Commons' House of Parliament, whose trust he has betrayed; in the name of the English nation, whose ancient honor he has sullied; in the name of the people of India, whose rights he has trodden under foot, and whose country he has turned into a desert; in the name of human nature itself, in the name of both sexes, in the name of every rank"; he impeached "the common enemy and oppressor of all."

Such was the manner of Burke's oratory. And that of Mr. Fox was not very different—more restrained, perhaps, but scarcely less brilliant or less vehement. When he opened the first charge relating to Chait Singh he told their Lordships that the honor of the British nation rested in their hands, that the eyes of the world were fixed on these proceedings, and that the question to be decided was whether the name of Briton, proud and glorious as it had been, should be doomed to scorn. Burke had indeed set the keynote, and all who followed him adopted the same style of speech. Even the sober-minded Grey, whose name was to be honorably linked in history with the passing of the great Reform Bill, even he could not refrain from perorating in the grand Ciceronian manner about "enormities": "Outrage, exaction, devastation and death! the plunder of provinces! the distress of nations! all nature blasted by the withering malignity of man! the helpless and the unoffending—what is useful and what is honorable—the peasant, and the prince—all prematurely swept together to the grave!" Little wonder that the tender sensibilities of the feminine element in the audience should have been touched, that the strong should have wept and the weak fainted, and that even the prisoner Warren Hastings himself should have wondered whether the man accused of such dreadful crimes could possibly be innocent! The knowledge that these men displayed of India, its history, its customs, its opinions and its condition, amazed all who heard it; for they even knew more than those who had spent half a lifetime there!

The prosecution had wished to proceed article by article, intro-

THE TRIAL SCENE IN WESTMINSTER HALL, 178

(From an original engraving)

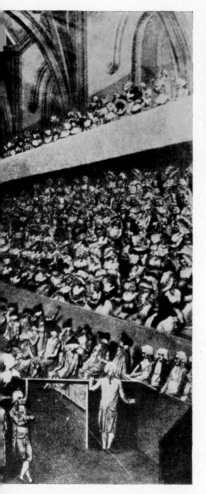

KEY TO THE TRIAL SCENE.

A	Throne.	W	Bishops.
B	Queen's Box.	X	Earls.
C	Prince of Wales, etc.	Y	Viscounts.
D	Foreign Ministers.	Z	Barons.
E	1st Row, Duke of York's;	*a*	Speaker of the House of Commons.
	2nd, Royal Household;	*b*	House of Commons.
	3rd, Lord Chancellor's tickets.	*c*	Managers and Committee for the Prosecution.
F	Attendants on the Royal Family.	*d*	Mr. Burke opening the charges.
G	Peers' tickets.	*e*	Shorthand Writer for the Commons.
H	Duke of Newcastle's gallery.	*f*	Repeater of the Evidence.
I	Board of Works.	*g*	Witness or Evidence Box.
J	Lord Chamberlain of the Household.	*h*	Mr. Hastings.
K	Deputy Great Chamberlain's tickets.	*i*	Prisoner's leading Counsel.
L	Peers tickets.	*j*	Counsellors for the Prisoner.
M	Peeresses and their daughters.	*k*	Prisoner's Shorthand Writer.
N	Marquises.	*l*	Counsellors' Clerks.
O	Dukes.	*m*	Counsellors for the Managers and their Clerks.
P	Prince of Wales and Duke of York.	*n*	Clerks of the India House.
Q	Sir Isaac Heard, Knight, Garter Principal	*o*	Shorthand Writer for the Lords.
	King of Arms on the right of the Throne	*p*	Usher of the Black Rod.
	and the Herald of Arms on the left.	*q*	Deputy Usher.
R	Peers Minor on each side of the Throne.	*r*	Serjeant of Arms and Deputy.
S	Judges seated on Woolsacks.	*s*	Mace Bearer to the Chancellor.
T	Lord Chancellor.		
U	Masters in Chancery.		
V	Archbishops of Canterbury and York.		

ducing evidence, hearing the defense and obtaining judgement on each one before passing on to the next, but the Court denied them this procedure. Each charge had to be completed before any part of the defense was heard. So the next stage reached was the hearing of testimony on the first charge. This was dull after the floods of oratory, and the public interest naturally waned.

The managers of the prosecution would have been wise to have dispensed altogether with oral evidence, as it had an unfortunate way of turning upon them when they least expected it. The printed word was more amenable to their wishes: it could be selected and winnowed and arranged in nice order, without any fear of it making the wrong reply or telling more than it should. Although the living witnesses were all witnesses called by the prosecution, sometimes, in unguarded moments, they proved themselves very capable witnesses for the defense. There was one of them, for instance, who denied that the province of Benares showed any sign of being oppressed during the years when, according to the prosecution, it had been transformed into a desert. There was another who, on cross-examination, gave the prisoner an excellent character. The managers had to give some kind of an explanation of this strange inconsistency, so they said: these men, having been the instruments of oppression, were influenced by favor, fear or gratitude to conceal or palliate the acts of their chief.

Once in a great while the prisoner opened his lips. "It's a lie!" he was heard to murmur when he was accused of falsifying his account of the transactions with the Begums of Oude. "What?" cried the indignant Mr. Adam, who was opening the second charge. "What? Shall I hear, my Lords, and bear that my assertion shall be contradicted? Shall I, who stand here as the delegated manager of the Commons, be told that I am advancing what is untrue? In the situation in which I stand—and from that degraded man at your bar, loaded with crimes, and groaning under his enormities" (how the prosecution loved that word!)—"I will not bear it. To your Lordships I appeal for protection." So, after a short speech of three and a half hours he abjured them as Judges, Fathers, Sons, Peers, Englishmen and men, to find the accused guilty.

More witnesses appeared, but, though these were examined for sixteen days, the dish of evidence that they presented for their Lordships' enlightenment was more than a little mixed. One of them under cross-examination turned out to be another character witness for the defendant. Mr. Middleton, examined, cross-examined and examined again for hours, was entirely unable to be coherent about anything.

Sir Elijah Impey was called. When he defended the assistance he had given Hastings at Chunar in the matter of the affidavits, Burke broke forth in a characteristic outburst: "O miserable state of the East India Company! O abandoned fortune of Mr. Hastings! O fallen lot of England! When no assistance could be found, but what was given by Sir Elijah Impey!"

Though evidence of every kind was presented, much of it damaging to individuals connected with the episode, the prosecution entirely failed to drive home their charge that the prisoner had treacherously planned to rob the Begums, had compelled the Vizier to act as his tool, and had afterwards fabricated the story of the Begums' rebellion to justify his actions.

On June 3, the thirty-second day of the trial, the stage was set for the next great scene. All London knew that it was Sheridan's turn to orate, and by six A.M. the avenues leading to the Hall through New and Old Palace yards were packed with ladies and gentlemen awaiting admission; many of them had spent the night at nearby coffee-houses. The social season was at its height and the trial was one of the principal attractions. Peeresses in the latest Paris creations stood in the street for an hour or more before the doors were opened. Tickets sold for as much as £50 apiece. And at eleven o'clock, an hour before the proceedings began, there was such a frantic rush for seats that some ladies went in hatless and shoeless.

Richard Brinsley Sheridan was the popular playwright of the day. He was also its most recent sensation as an orator. The fame of his prodigious effort in the House of Commons the year before had spread far and wide. He was now to speak on the same topic, the woes and wrongs of the Begums of Oude, and he therefore addressed an audience which was breathless with suspense, anticipating sensations, and seething with pent-up emotions in need of release, and which had come to hear him as it would to see David Garrick in *King Lear*. Nor was it to be disappointed. Though there were some who thought the speech in the House of Commons was the finer, this one also was a masterpiece of oratory. Step by step, during four stirring days, the drama of a stupendous crime was unrolled like a Shakespearean tragedy before the astonished eyes of an eager and delighted audience. He appealed especially to the tender susceptibilities of his feminine admirers in the gallery, when he described with matchless eloquence the frightful sufferings inflicted on the poor, helpless, innocent ladies by the cruel, merciless and unchivalrous Governor. His moralizing was superb. Even Shakespeare would not have been ashamed to admit authorship of some of his passages. Listen to his panegyric on filial piety, as he moved the groundlings to tears:

"Filial Piety! It is the primal bond of Society. It is that instinctive principle, which, panting for its proper good, soothes, unbidden, each sense and sensibility of man! It now quivers on every lip! It now beams from every eye! It is that gratitude, which, softening under the sense of recollected good, is eager to own the vast countless debt it ne'er, alas! can pay—for so many long years of unceasing solicitude, honorable self-denials, life-preserving cares! It is that part of our practice where duty drops its awe, where reverence refines into love! It asks no aid of memory! It needs not the deductions of reason! Preëxisting, paramount over all, whether law or human rule—few arguments can increase and

none can diminish it! It is the sacrament of our nature—not only the
duty, but the indulgence of man. It is his first great privilege. It is
amongst his last most enduring delights! When the bosom glows with
the idea of reverberated love—when to requite on the visitations of
nature, and return the blessings that have been received! When—what
was emotion fixed into vital principle—what was instinct habituated into
a master-passion—sways all the sweetest energies of man—hangs over
each vicissitude of all that must pass away, aids the melancholy virtues
in their last sad tasks of life, to cheer the languors of decrepitude and
age, explore the thought, explain the aching eye!"

No tyrant in history, no Nero or Caligula, was the equal of Warren Hastings. See him then as he sat with his fellow-conspirators and
the wretched Nawab and prepared his monstrous crime. But first—

"Oh! Faith! Oh! Justice! I conjure you by your sacred names to
depart for a moment from this place, though it be your peculiar residence; nor hear your names profaned by such a sacrilegious combination, as that which I am now compelled to repeat! Where all the fair
forms of nature and art, truth and peace, policy and honor, shrink back
aghast from the deleterious shade! Where all existences, nefarious and
vile, had sway—where amidst the black agents on one side and Middleton with Impey on the other, the toughest bend, the most unfeeling
shrink!—the great figure of the piece, characteristic in his place, aloof
and independent from the puny profligacy in his train! But far from
idle and inactive, turning a malignant eye on all mischief that awaits
him! the multiplied apparatus of temporizing expedients, and intimidat-
ing instruments! now cringing on his prey, and fawning on his vengeance! now quickening the limpid pace of Craft, and forcing every
stand that retiring nature can make in the heart! the attachments and
the decorums of life! each emotion of tenderness and honor! and all the
distinctions of national characteristics! with a long catalogue of crimes
and aggravations, beyond the reach of thought for human malignity to
perpetrate, or human vengeance to punish! Lower than perdition—
blacker than despair!" ...

Sheridan had finished at last, and with a final superb gesture he
sank back into the arms of Burke, who gleefully hugged him to his
breast in token of the admiration of one master for another.

The Second Year.—At the rate at which the trial had so far proceeded it was possible to calculate that it would last for twenty years.

Mr. Burke took charge of the proceedings once more. He dismissed a complaint of the accused's that he would soon be ruined by
the protracted trial, with the remark that the prisoner was worthy of
no compassion on that score because his expenses would be but a
trifling part of his immense fortune, swelled as it had been by bribes,
exactions and peculations. Would their Lordships think it a hardship
if wealth so acquired should be so diminished?

With that as an introduction, Burke launched his next massed
attack, which for sheer malignity and fury transcended all his previous
efforts. Though his subject, the acceptance of bribes, was one that

obviously called for accurate statement and close reasoning, he wallowed in the foam and froth of debased rhetoric, surrendering completely to his partiality for the language of the gutter and indulging in the grossest invective. "The crimes which are laid to the charge of Mr. Hastings are of the groveling kind, which do not usually grow upon a throne, but are hatched in dunghills." Mr. Hastings had reduced fourteen hundred nobles of Bengal to beggary: "He could not so much as dine without creating a famine. He was a vulture fattening upon carrion. He lay down in his sty of infamy wallowing in the filth of disgrace—and fattened upon the offals and excrements of dishonor."

It was passages of this sort that immediately inspired the famous epigram:

> Oft have I wondered that on Irish Ground
> No poisonous reptiles ever yet were found;
> Reveal'd the secret stands of nature's work,
> She sav'd her venom to create a Burke.

The author of these lines was for long thought to be Hastings, as they are preserved among his papers in his handwriting. But they have been claimed by his biographer for Robert Dallas, one of Hastings's counsel, who must have passed them over to his client as he sat in his place, who thereupon copied them out.

On one point Burke overstepped the almost limitless bounds of indulgence that his constituents allowed him. He introduced the affair of Nuncomar and denounced Hastings as a murderer, and this happened not to be a part of the articles of impeachment. Major Scott did not let the opportunity slip to present to the House of Commons a petition from the prisoner praying for redress. The House debated it heatedly, with the managers demanding for themselves complete license to conduct the case in any manner they saw fit. Pitt, however, was against them, and a vote of censure was passed on Burke. "No matter!" cried he, afterwards in Court, quite impenitent and incorrigible; "the charge is true, though I am forbidden to say so."

Just once did the prisoner break silence. That was when he learned that the Court was about to adjourn until the next session of Parliament. He then pleaded the intolerable hardship of his position, declared that he would have pleaded guilty if he had conceived that such protraction of the trial was possible, rather than sustain this ordeal, and offered to waive his defense and so permit their Lordships to proceed to judgement on the evidence already before them. The trial itself, he declared, had been a punishment a hundred times more severe than any punishment their Lordships could have inflicted upon him, had he pleaded guilty. But the Court decided that the case had to continue, no matter how long it might last.

A large part of the session had been consumed in attempts on the part of the prosecution to introduce evidence that the Court considered inadmissible. It was the claim of the managers that all ordinary rules of law should be disregarded in an impeachment.

Third Year.—The trial had now occupied a total of fifty-four days, and the prosecution was still on the subject of bribes. It told how the prisoner had accepted a bribe of £40,000 from one scoundrelly native, £34,000 from another, £15,000 from a third, £6000 from a fourth, all of whom had in return been armed with power to reduce the land to ruin and desolation. One witness called was David Anderson, late President of the Board of Revenue, but as he was known to be a close personal friend of the accused, the favorable evidence he gave was under suspicion. The same suspicion could hardly be attached to the testimony of John Shore, the greatest living authority on Bengal revenue matters, who was soon to be appointed Governor-General to succeed Lord Cornwallis, and he at once and in few words disposed of the whole case that the prosecution had built up against Hastings's management of the lands. On being asked whether he would continue on friendly terms with Mr. Hastings were he the corrupt and cruel man described in the charges, he replied, "I should hope not."

Much use was made by the managers of the accused's own papers and writings, though it must have seemed strange to some of their hearers that a man guilty of criminal conduct should have taken such pains to uncover facts which otherwise would have been concealed from view. But the managers were at no loss to explain the riddle. Long-continued indulgence in vice, they said, weakens the intelligence. *Quem Jupiter vult perdere dementat prius.* Occasionally they found contradictions in what he had written, and these were still easier to explain. "Memory," quoth Fox, "was not able to keep pace with the enormities which he had to extenuate." It was a case of "guilt entangling itself in its own toils."

Another oration by Fox followed the hearing of evidence. He was again at his dazzling best, superb in logic, perfect in the marshaling of his facts and the lucidity of his argument, remorseless in his application of cold reason, magnificent in his manipulation of the evidence, extraordinary in his intuition. He, like his friends Burke and Sheridan, revealed an amazing ability to read the hearts and minds of men as easily as he could the printed page. His omniscience concerning every single transaction of a thirteen-year administration was nothing less than astounding, surpassing the knowledge of even the chief actors themselves. When they were uncertain, Mr. Fox was emphatic. When they disagreed, Mr. Fox knew which one to believe. He did not need concrete evidence to tell him that the prisoner had never done an honest, disinterested act in his life, because he had a seventh sense that enabled him to detect hidden crime and the secret springs of action. He knew that where motives are, or can be made to appear, obscure they must needs be dishonorable, and that when a man in public office changes his mind and his policy, he must surely do so for corrupt ends. But one thing was lacking in Mr. Fox's equipment of talents, as it also was lacking in Mr. Burke's and Mr. Sheridan's. They were all three great orators, they possessed splendid imaginations, they know how to reason, how to declaim, how to draw plausible inferences, to argue, to plead, to impute guilt, to misrepresent, to garble, to misquote, to distort, to make part of the facts appear to be the whole, to make the innocent act seem the most guilty. But one thing they could not do—they could not *convince*.

For two days Mr. Fox held forth to uncover, step by step, the chain of corruption, vast and unceasing. The fact that no more accepted bribes had come to light since 1776 had no significance for him, as the prisoner had completely destroyed the means of detection. Fox finally announced the sum total of all bribes *known* to have been received by the prisoner to be £240,000. "If I do not clearly prove all these particulars, upon his head—may the arm of that God they have invoked fall heavily upon me, and make me living the scorn of man, the striking monument of his anger, whose attribute is Truth, and from whom the punishment of Falsehood is assured." Fox failed in his undertaking, but God remained merciful.

Fourth Year.—A new Parliament had come into being since last the Court sat, and a very knotty point of constitutional law had to be settled before the proceedings could continue. Did a dissolution of Parliament automatically terminate an impeachment? This was a question for the pundits to determine. Mr. Burke held one view and sympathizers of Mr. Hastings naturally held another, but Mr. Burke prevailed. Some thought that the trial had already lasted too long, but to these Mr. Burke retorted by asking whether the gentlemen who measured the trial by the length of time it consumed "are better able to ascertain what ought to be the length of an impeachment than a rabbit, which breeds six times in a year, is capable of judging the time of gestation of an elephant." But as a concession to those who preferred animals that gestated quickly, he agreed to drop all the charges beyond Article IV, which related to corrupt and wasteful contracts. It was May 16, 1791, before the House of Lords expressed its concurrence in the Commons' decision and declared its readiness to proceed.

Four days were consumed on this Fourth Charge. It was composed of six distinct items: (1) A corrupt contract for the sale of opium given in 1781 to Stephen Sulivan, son of Laurence Sulivan, Chairman of the Court of Directors. (2) An alleged attempt made by Hastings to smuggle opium into China. (3) A contract given for the supply of bullocks to the army. (4) The illegal and excessive allowances given to Sir Eyre Coote. (5) An agency given to Mr. Auriol for supplies of food for Madras. (6) An agency given to Mr. Belli for supplying Fort William with provisions.

These charges proved to be the weakest part of the indictment; for the most part they were demonstrably stupid and false. All that the managers could prove was that in effecting the contracts the Governor-General had not carried out the instructions of the Company, which had ordered that they be publicly advertised and let to the lowest bidder; but Hastings was able to show that in each instance he had been the best judge of what the Company's interests required, and to give excellent reasons for having departed from his instructions. The course that his employers had ordered was not advisable for the opium contract and was impracticable for the bullock contract, and Hastings only followed his own better judgement in letting them privately to officials of his own choosing on terms that insured efficient performance. A typical example of the absurdity of so much of the managers' case was their argument that because Coote had in 1779 declared 4074 bullocks sufficient for the army, should it have to take the field, Hastings was guilty of criminal extravagance in later letting a contract for 6700. Bitter experience in the ensuing war proved not only that Hastings's estimate was more correct than Coote's, but that he, too, had greatly underestimated the army's requirements. Three times that number of bullocks would not have been too many. Regarding Coote's allowances, Hastings grimly remarked that it had not been a time to cavil with the general; such had been his knowledge of the value of Coote's services and his indispensability to the task of saving Madras that there was hardly anything he could not have asked which he would not have given him, and if he had refused to grant him these allowances, Coote would probably have thrown up his post in disgust, or at least stayed inactive at Calcutta, as his predecessor Clavering had done. As regards the Auriol agency, it had been the means of saving Madras from starvation—as Pitt had handsomely admitted in the House of Commons, declaring at the same time that Mr. Auriol had well deserved every penny he had made out of it, having honorably discharged the commission. Some taint of jobbery may have surrounded these transactions, but the managers entirely failed to show that they had been corrupt, wasteful, or unwise. It was a cooked-up charge, unworthy of serious attention. The absurdity of the opium smuggling charge was so patent that not a single Peer was found to vote against Hastings upon it.

At last the managers declared their case closed. The time had arrived for the hearing of the defense.

It was the last day of the session, and the seventy-third of the trial when the prisoner rose. He thought it unlikely that his defense would take very long as most of his witnesses were no longer available; some were dead, some had returned to India, others, after waiting for three years to be called, had departed for distant homes. But he had long grown indifferent to the matter of his defense: he was quite willing to waive altogether his right to be heard in exchange for a speedy judgement.

He made an eloquent and telling speech, which was in every way a marked contrast to the speeches of his accusers. His best defense, he maintained, was contained in a few simple incontrovertible facts. Was he accused of having ruined and depopulated Bengal? Look, he said, at the Indian accounts lately laid before Parliament. Was he accused of having broken faith with the princes and rulers of India? Those same princes had asked his successor to treat them as he had done. Was he accused of having oppressed the natives? Those same natives had united in sending testimonials in his favor. (When these testimonials were received Burke had scornfully declared that he would offer them in evidence for the prosecution, since they had been extorted by torture—but unaccountably he had omitted to do so!) "It is very seldom that mankind are grateful enough to do even common justice to a fallen minister; and I believe that there never was an instance in the annals of human nature of an injured people rising up voluntarily to bear false testimony in favor of a distant and prosecuted oppressor." Was he accused of having squandered public money? Compare the expenditure of his government with that of his successor—the latter had been considerably greater. Was he accused of having disobeyed orders? True it was that on occasions he had done so, but if that was so reprehensible, why had he received a hearty vote of thanks from the Directors on his return? And why had he never lacked the support of the Court of Proprietors, his real constituents?

He had made mistakes. True! He acknowledged the fact. But the worst that could be said of his mistakes was that they were errors of judgement. There were many inaccuracies in his accounts. True! "I have been imprudent to a degree that merits some of the reflections so illiberally thrown out against me." But corrupt? Never! He was ready to swear solemnly before God that he never intended to apply any of the sums he had received to his own use. He had been too intent upon the means to be employed to preserve India to Great Britain to bestow a thought upon himself or his own private fortune. It was strange, too, he remarked, that so many of his actions had been repeatedly approved by the Company and by Ministers and only now, fifteen years after they had been known publicly, were they found to have been criminal! Could it be that they had not been thought of as criminal until his accusers thought they might be of use to load the scale of criminality? (Shrewd thrusts these!) Moreover, the whole system of government in Bengal —all its departments, institutions and regulations—had been of his formation, and remained to that day unchanged, or changed only—in Lord Cornwallis's own words—"to strengthen their principles and render them permanent." How could this be if, as his accusers stated, they were wholly and utterly iniquitous?

"I maintained the provinces of my immediate administration in a state of peace, plenty and fecundity, when every other member of the British Empire was involved in external wars or civil tumult. In a dreadful season of famine, which visited all the neighboring states of India, during three successive years, I repressed it in its approach to the countries of British India, and by timely and continued regulations, prevented its return; an act little known in England, because it wanted the positive effects which alone could give it a visible communication, but proved by the grateful acknowledgments of those who would have been the only sufferers by such a scourge ... have made their sense of the obligation which they owe to me for this blessing, a very principal subject of many of the testimonials transmitted by the inhabitants of Bengal, Bihar and Benares.

"And lastly, I raised the collective annual revenue of the Company's possessions under my administration from three to five millions sterling, not of temporary and forced exaction, but of an early continued, and still existing production, the surest evidence of a good government— improving agriculture and increased population.

"To the Commons of England, in whose name I am arraigned, for desolating the provinces of their dominion in India, I dare to reply, that they are, and their representatives persist in telling them so, the most flourishing of all the States of India. It was I who made them so.

"The valor of others acquired, I enlarged and gave shape and consistency to the dominion which you hold there; I preserved it; I sent forth its armies with an effectual but economical hand, through unknown and hostile regions, to the support of your other possessions; to the retrieval of one from degradation and dishonor; and to the other from utter loss and subjection. I maintained the wars which were of your formation, or that of others, not of mine. I won one member of the great Indian Confederacy from it by an act of seasonable restitution; with another I maintained a secret intercourse, and converted him into a friend; a third I drew off by diversion and negotiation, and employed him as the instrument of peace.

"When you cried out for peace, and your cries were heard by those who were the objects of it, I resisted this, and every other species of counteraction, by rising in my demands, and accomplished a peace, and I hope everlasting, with one great state; and I at least afforded the efficient means by which a peace, if not so durable, more seasonable at least, was accomplished with another.

"I gave you all, and you have rewarded me with confiscation, disgrace, and a life of impeachment."

Fifth Year.—Nothing, not even the prisoner's willingness to waive his defense, could prevent the trial from pursuing the insufferably tedious tenor of its way. The gentlemen of the law who represented him seemed nearly as inclined to spin it out to its furthest length as the prosecution, even though every day they labored for their client brought him nearer and nearer to beggary. Mr. Law opened and spoke for three days; Mr. Plumer followed and spoke for four. Many more days were spent in the examination of witnesses. And when the session closed, the Court having sat for twenty-two days, the defense had not progressed beyond the first charge.

The high point in the testimony had occurred when William Markham, the principal witness—the son of the Archbishop of York, who was sitting among the Peers judging the case, and the Company's Resident at Benares at the time of Chait Singh's insurrection—declared, with a voice scarcely audible through emotion and laying his hand upon his heart, "I am convinced, my Lords, Mr. Hastings is the most vir-

tuous man of the age in which he lives." The evident sincerity of the
words made a profound impression upon all who heard them, and even
Burke showed by his agitation that he realized the defense had scored
a telling point. He alone among the managers did not now relax his
efforts or lose hope. The case of the Commons had been torn in shreds
and its utter falsity exposed completely to view, and when Mr. Dallas
sat down after making the closing speech, no one but Mr. Burke could
have been in doubt about the verdict on this particular charge.

Sixth Year.—Weariness and boredom had by now become so universal among the Peers that often they attended in numbers scarcely
sufficient to form a court. Yet still the indefatigable Burke gave them
no rest. He cross-examined witnesses for hours at a time, in a way that
suggested that his only two objects were to prove them liars and rogues
and to prolong the trial to the limit of human endurance. On one occasion the Archbishop of York, exasperated beyond control, told him
bluntly that he examined witnesses as though they were not gentlemen
but pickpockets. But nothing aroused Burke's ire more than the accusation that he and his colleagues were responsible for the long duration
of the trial. Then it was that he hurled his bitterest shafts at his critics
for daring to cast such a slur on the honor of the Commons' representatives. And whenever the prisoner pleaded for speedy justice he retorted
by denying that there was any need for haste.

At length the defense was closed, and on the last day of the session
the prisoner addressed the Court once more:

"In the presence of that Being from whom no secrets are hid, I do,
upon a full review and scrutiny of my past life, unequivocally and con-
scientiously declare, that in the administration of that trust of Government, which was so many years confided in me, I did in no instance
intentionally sacrifice the interest of my country to any private views of
my own personal advantage; that, according to my best skill and judgement, I invariably promoted the essential interest of my employers, the
happiness and prosperity of the people committed to my charge and the
honor and welfare of my country, and at no time with more entire devotion of mind and purpose to these objects, than during that period in
which my accusers have endeavored to represent me as occupied and
engrossed by the base pursuits of low, sordid and interdicted emolument."

The Lords were anxious to proceed further, but as the managers
professed themselves unready with their reply, they were compelled
to make yet another adjournment.

Seventh Year.—The French Revolution had by this time been in
progress for four years and Great Britain was at war with the French
Republic. Yet whenever the trial appeared likely to die a natural death
Edmund Burke resuscitated it by appealing to the House of Commons
not to allow any paltry and unworthy feeling of sympathy for the
accused to get the better of their determination to see justice done.
Having once put their hand to the plow, they must not draw back,

for what were a few years as compared to the crimes of Warren Hastings? Even if the end of the world had come Edmund Burke would have continued to plead his cause before the High Court of Heaven.

Yet the end of the trial was actually in sight. All that now retarded it and prevented managers and counsel from proceeding at once with their closing speeches were the procrastinating tactics of Burke and the arrival from India of two gentlemen whose special knowledge of the facts under discussion made them extremely important witnesses. One of these gentlemen was the Marquis Cornwallis, who had returned home after serving his term as Governor-General, and the other was William Larkins, the Company's Accountant-General at Calcutta, who had full knowledge of Hastings's financial transactions. As a special indulgence to the accused the managers permitted Cornwallis to be called though the defense had been declared closed. But the noble Lord was taken sick and it was not until April 9, being the hundred and twenty-third day of the trial, that he was able to attend. The interval had been completely occupied by the attempts of Mr. Burke to introduce inadmissible evidence. Each time he had done so caused a prolonged delay because the Lords were compelled to retire to their own House to discuss the point, and when on their return they announced their decision, which in nine cases out of ten was against the managers, Mr. Burke and his colleagues consumed more hours arguing about it. March 1 had been reached in this way, and then the Court had adjourned until April 7 to permit the judges to go on circuit.

The appearance of Lord Cornwallis naturally revived popular interest. For the first time since Sheridan's speech there was a large attendance of Lords and Commons and there must have been a pretty general feeling of relief that at last a strong gust of the fresh air of truth was about to sweep away some of the fog of lies and unreality that had hung so thickly about the walls of the Hall for seven years; for was not Lord Cornwallis the man best qualified to express an authoritative opinion on the merits of Warren Hastings's administration, without possible suspicion of bias or prejudice?

Cornwallis's testimony, given briefly and with no superfluity of words, fully answered the hopes of the defense. He did not remember that any complaints had been received against Mr. Hastings. He believed that Mr. Hastings was much esteemed and respected by the native inhabitants. He did not think that the Begums of Oude had suffered any pecuniary distress or that the character of the British nation had suffered by Mr. Hastings's conduct towards them and Chait Singh. And he concluded by asserting that Mr. Hastings had undoubtedly rendered essential service to his country.

The few remaining hopes of the managers were now pinned on Mr. Larkins. Whether it was by craft or merely as they said from a desire to avoid further delay, the defense had not asked permission to call him. Mr. Burke was gleeful; the only reason that he could think of why the defense did not apparently want to call Mr. Larkins was that they were afraid of his testimony, for had not the accused repeatedly lamented his absence? That being so, the managers would call him as a witness for the prosecution. The defense, he cried, *dared* not call him because to do so would reveal "such a scene of fraud, deception, iniquity that the prisoner would wish for mountains to cover him."

Mr. Larkins's testimony corroborated Hastings on every point: every rupee that he had received in the form of presents had been expended in the public service. He was known to be absolutely careless of the state of his own fortune, and it had been with the greatest difficulty that he could be got to devote an hour to consideration of the state of his private affairs, "so very inattentive was he to everything that concerned himself." Mr. Larkins then stated that, while he had had the entire management of everything that bore a relation to the private fortune of Mr. Hastings during the whole of his administration, he verily believed that in no one instance—and he had had full opportunities of making the observation—had Mr. Hastings done any one act, either with an immediate or remote view to his own personal advantage; on the contrary, "his known and fixed character is the very opposite to that which has been imputed to him, namely a man venal, corrupt and oppressive, who, in all his acts, looked only to the accumulation of exorbitant wealth." Burke cross-examined Larkins for many weary hours but every additional answer served only to put Hastings's case in an ever more favorable light.

The only material point in Larkins's testimony that the prosecution could seize upon was that Hastings had mistaken the date at which he had endorsed over to the Company some bonds amounting to £35,000 which he had accepted in his own name on its behalf. They had been received in November 1780, at the crisis of the war, and Hastings had stated that he had endorsed them in July 1781, when he was on the point of leaving for Benares. He was so convinced of the truth of this assertion that he had written to Larkins asking him to transmit the bonds to the Company to verify it, thus furnishing the evidence to prove his own mistake, for when the bonds arrived it was found that the endorsement was dated May 1782. It is fair to assume that Hastings had intended to endorse the bonds in July 1781, to insure their delivery to the Company in the event of his death while on his dangerous mission, and had forgotten that he had not actually done so until after his return. Larkins stated in addition that Hastings had given him to understand that the bonds were not his property but the Company's. Nevertheless the managers used these facts to insinuate that it had been his original intention to retain the money for his own private use and that he had only endorsed the bonds when he found it impossible any longer to conceal the transaction.

The latest holder of the post of Governor-General—the noblest part of whose character was his honesty and integrity—and the Company's Accountant-General—whom this same Governor-General had described as "a man whose knowledge, abilities, and acknowledged integrity en-

titled everything that came from him to the fullest consideration"—
had both spoken and with their words the whole edifice of guilt that
Burke and Francis had labored so long to raise fell in utter ruins.

For a little time longer Burke persevered, charging first in one
direction, then in another, like a mad beast brought at last to bay.
Defeated on every one of the stated articles, he attempted to introduce
entirely fresh material with the object, he said, of proving the accused
guilty of fraud, robbery, swindling, cheating and forgery—he might as
well have added arson in order to make the list complete. Rebuffed by
an indignant court, he next tried to open up the question of the Maratha
War, with the idea of proving Hastings the author of it. Rebuffed a
second time, he spent the better part of a day proving that he could
not be held responsible for any delays in the proceedings. Finally, he
made a third vain attempt to introduce evidence respecting "atrocities"
committed by the accused's native agents, though each time permission
had been refused as the subject did not form part of the Articles of
Impeachment.

The time had come at length for the final speeches, and Grey,
Sheridan, Fox and Burke each harangued the Court in turn. The
speeches of the first three gentlemen were in themselves proof of the
complete collapse of their case. A few immaterial points were all that
were left to them to argue about. The mountain had labored and brought
forth a diminutive mouse. Not so Edmund Burke! His fanatical fury
was not a whit diminished. Rather, the passage of time and the increasing weight of his years had only served to increase it. Nothing could
cool the passion of his nature, and he held at the end of the trial precisely the same opinion of the accused as he held at the beginning.
He began his final onslaught on May 28, 1794, and continued it through
May 30, June 3, 5, 7, 11, 12, 14 and 16, but over what he said it is best
to draw a veil, so utterly deplorable and atrocious was his language.

Disgust is swallowed up in pity when the curtain is about to be
rung down on this tragedy of Edmund Burke. From the beginning he
had pleaded, with all the power at his command, that "it is not that
culprit who is on trial, it is the House of Commons that is upon its
trial, it is the House of Lords that is upon its trial, it is the British
nation that is upon its trial before all other nations, before the present
generation, and before a long, long posterity " [37]—and, not only that
but it was, also, he himself who was on trial. If, therefore, the culprit
was acquitted, all the others stood condemned! But the man who thus
laid on the altar of justice all that he held dearest was himself lonely
and grief-stricken and embittered. It was said of him two years before
that when he discussed politics his irritability was so great that "it
gives immediately to his face the expression of a man who is going
to defend himself from murderers." [38] One by one his dearest friends
had died, and the greatest friend of all, Charles James Fox, was
separated from him by a bitter political quarrel that nothing could
mend. This nine-day speech was his last important performance on the

parliamentary stage, and when it ended there was very little of life left in him. His dearest hopes and ambitions were centered on crowning his career, spent in the championship of many great and noble causes, with one last triumph in a cause that meant more to him than any other he had espoused. Is it surprising that, within little more than two years after the verdict was given, he was dead?

Chapter XXX

VINDICATION WITHOUT REPARATION

I

A LL things have an end; even impeachment trials by Parliament;
even the trial of Warren Hastings. On June 14, 1794, the
Lords withdrew to consider the case, and the Commons returned to their own House, where Pitt at once moved a vote of thanks
to the managers. A fruitless attempt was made to exclude Burke's name,
several members expressing their shame and indignation at his vile
language. The verdict was held over until the next session.

The political scene had changed so completely that the proceedings had become an anachronism, futile and meaningless. A new world
had come into being since that cold winter's day when the Lords of
Parliament first went in procession to the Hall of Westminster. There
had been a hundred and seventy peers in that procession. Sixty of them
had died in the interim. A hundred and twenty members of the lower
House who had been connected with the early proceedings had disappeared from the scene. A new Lord Chancellor sat on the wool-sack.
Pitt, it is true, was still Prime Minister, but his government had been
reconstituted. The old Whig Party of Fox and Burke had split asunder,
and the two leaders, once bosom friends, had become bitter opponents.
The French Revolution, followed by war with the French Republic, had
changed everything, blotting out from men's minds all thought of the
woes of India, as completely as the Great War obliterated the Ulster
question in English politics in 1914. If we can imagine Sir Edward
Carson being impeached in 1913 for seeking to stir up civil war in
Ireland and resistance to the authority of Parliament, and his trial still
being in progress in 1919, we can form a good idea of how the gen-
erality of people must have regarded Warren Hastings's trial in 1794.

At the beginning public opinion had been against the accused,
but it had long since changed. The violence of Burke had defeated its
purpose. At first people, enjoying a good show, had applauded, but
that did not mean that they were convinced. Very soon wonder spread
that where accusation was so loud proof should be so feeble. The

409

Hastings that had saved British India and the Hastings of Burke's imagining could not possibly be one and the same man. And as each year passed it became clear to all which was the real man. When those who were supposed to curse his name arose to bless it, the trial became in the popular estimation a farce, and all interest in it was lost. Hastings's innocence was a settled question long before his judges arrived at the point of debating it. [1]

The change in popular sentiment was reflected in the cartoons of the day. Gillray, the foremost cartoonist, rubbed salt into the wounds of the despairing managers by depicting "the Political Banditti assaulting the Savior of India"—Hastings protecting himself with a shield of honor, Burke discharging a blunderbuss at his chest, Fox attacking him with a dagger from behind, and Lord North making away with his money-bags. In other cartoons the Benares flea was magnified to the size of an elephant, and the Begums' tears to the size of hen's eggs. So much ridicule was indeed poured upon "the Managers' Farce" that it looked as though Hastings's confidence that the trial would prove a veritable boomerang to his accusers would be justified. Every manner of story had been circulated about him at the start. Not only was it said that the Nizam's diamond was a bribe to the king from Hastings himself, who had forged the letter of presentation from the Prince, but it was rumored—and the rumor given public credence by Burke— that he had arranged to convey his fortune to Europe and to follow it himself in flight to defeat the ends of justice. Burke also announced as a positive fact that the accused's fortune amounted to £300,000— which he was using to subsidize the press and bribe the court.

Undoubtedly the worst part of the ordeal for Hastings personally had been the preliminary proceedings, when hope, at first strong, had gradually died, giving way to a staggering and terrible certainty. Then had followed the ignominy of being taken into custody, held to bail, and brought as a prisoner accused of heinous crimes before the highest court of the realm, there to be compelled to kneel before it in token of submission. It was that last humiliation that had proved almost more than he could bear.[2] All observers on the opening day of the trial noticed his stricken appearance. "Pale looked his face—pale, ill and altered. I was much affected by the sight of that dreadful harass which was written on his countenance," was how Fanny Burney described it. [3] But when the first shock of his disgrace wore off, his immensely strong spiritual resources proved more than equal to the strain of sustaining a seven-year trial. And when Burke, Fox and Sheridan launched into their impassioned orations, it was almost as though the proceedings ceased to have a direct connection with himself and became for him, as for the rest of the audience, a spectacle that traversed all the stages from the sublime to the ridiculous. Once again, as when he had to face his accusers at the Council Board, this sense of innocence made him invulnerable to the ferocious invective that they poured out against him, and as he could not recognize himself in the man that was being flayed, the torrent of words ceased to have any but the remotest application to himself. He listened to the foul language, the impudent assertions of fact, the bombast, the fallacious arguments, the highly wrought and irrelevant oratory, the fine flights of imagination, the perfervid declamation, the assumed fury, the cant, the sallies of pleasantry and ill-timed jests, the abuse of witnesses and the distortion of evidence—and his chief feelings were those of amazement, indignation, and contempt—amazement that men with such honored names should make such an atrocious exhibition of themselves, indignation at such a travesty of justice, contempt for his own countrymen, "who not only bear to see the fundamental principles of the law and Constitution openly violated to gratify the vengeance or policy of two factions in the government with the prosecution of an unprotected individual, but make his sufferings the subject of their entertainment, and the argument of convivial discourse." [4]

On one occasion, while he had to listen to Grey indulging in a panegyric on Francis, he picked up his pencil and wrote off the following lines:

> It hurts me not that Grey as Burke's assessor
> Proclaims me tyrant, robber, and oppressor,
>   Though for abuse alone meant;
> For when he calls himself the bosom friend—
> The friend of Philip Francis: I contend
>   He made me full atonement. [5]

Yet, however much his sense of humor, allied with his clear conscience, *mens conscia recti,* helped to dull the pain of hearing his name and reputation dragged in the dirt day after day, he naturally continued to suffer acutely, and the only advice he had to offer to anybody so unfortunate as to find himself in the same situation was to plead guilty in order to avoid the same slow torture of the process of trial as the worst punishment he could receive would be less painful.

The further long wait of nearly a year for a verdict that was generally anticipated was characteristic of the proceedings, but that fact scarcely made it more tolerable to the accused man and his friends. "Impatiently do I expect the hour which in your acquittal is to restore to me the pride which I once felt in calling myself an Englishman," wrote Thompson. "The Lords may by bare possibility condemn themselves, but after what has passed they cannot condemn you." [6]

On April 23, 1795, the peers proceeded for the last time to Westminster Hall, where a crowded audience, reminiscent of the opening days, had assembled to witness the closing ceremony. The prisoner was called in; after once more kneeling at the Bar, he was ordered to rise, then asked to withdraw. The Lord Chancellor, Lord Loughborough, who happened to be an old enemy of Hastings, then put sixteen questions to each peer in turn and asked for a verdict of "Guilty or Not Guilty." Only those—twenty-nine of them in all—who had actually sat in judgement throughout the trial appeared in robes and voted, the others by common consent abstained.

By large majorities the vote was for acquittal on every charge. On the two most serious, those relating to Chait Singh and the Begums, the voting was twenty-three to six. On the charge of receiving bribes from Nuncomar, Munny Begum and others, he was unanimously voted "Not Guilty." On those relating to the receipt of presents and the granting of corrupt contracts the average majority in his favor was twenty, the number of votes against him never exceeding five. "That he was guilty of other high crimes and misdemeanors. Not Guilty, 25; Guilty, 2."

The peer who, more than any other, was responsible for this verdict was a big, beetle-browed man with a thunderous scowl, a biting tongue, a surly temper, and an overbearing manner, ex-Lord Chancellor Thurlow. A rather low-grade politician, who owed his prominence to his possession of the royal confidence in a peculiar degree, combined with considerable debating powers and a dynamic forcefulness that made him a dangerous opponent and gained him commanding influence in the House of Lords. As chief among the King's Friends, he had been an unwelcome member of three cabinets, too influential to be excluded, too ill-tempered and treacherous to be liked. A defender of the Slave Trade, an opponent of Parliamentary Reform, general factotum and intriguer for his royal master—with an unenviable reputation for duplicity and insincerity—this is the man, strange though it may seem, who for fifteen years had championed Hastings's cause, both in Parliament and in the Cabinet, and for whom the verdict of the peers was a real triumph. During the first four years of the trial he had presided over the Court, not as an impartial judge, but with unfailing regularity and diligence and with a vigilance that the tactics of the Managers of the Prosecution demanded. Then Pitt, who had only tolerated him as a disagreeable necessity, had dared the King's anger and dismissed him. No longer Chancellor, he had still maintained his interest in the proceedings, and when the Lords at length debated the charges he had assumed the rôle of advocate for the defense and argued the case with compelling force and ability. No one who has read those debates can help being impressed by his skillful handling of the intricate issues involved and his mastery of the facts. If his reputation rested on this one phase of his career alone, we could honor him as a noble-minded defender of a maligned and innocent man.

Strange paradox! And only explainable, one fears, by supposing that he was acting under orders from his royal master, unless it be— and let us give the Devil his due and believe it to be so—that he was to some extent moved by a feeling of genuine admiration for the man whose cause he espoused so zealously and ably. That the King must have wished Thurlow to adopt this course is quite certain, for his attitude towards Hastings had undergone a complete change since Clavering's death, as he showed by the marked favor with which he received him on his return from India. The Court was, indeed, strongly for Hastings, even though Pitt saw fit to take a contrary line, and it was this fact that in no small measure accounted for the fanatical hostility of the Whig leaders towards him.

Against Thurlow in the debates had been matched his successor in the Chancellorship, Lord Loughborough. And a truly well-matched pair they were, especially in the particular brand of politics they both favored! Loughborough, however, was undoubtedly the greater rogue of the two, his final betrayal of Pitt in 1801, which led to Pitt's resignation on the Catholic Emancipation question, surpassing in sheer infamy any of his rival's earlier similar maneuvers. (When he died, the King's only comment was, "Are you quite sure that he is really dead? Then he has not left a greater knave behind him in my dominions"; upon hearing which Thurlow is said to have remarked, "Then I presume that His Majesty is quite sane at present.") [7] The fact that Clive, when he was similarly attacked in 1772, was defended by Loughborough (then Alexander Wedderburn) and attacked by Thurlow —a complete reversal of their subsequent rôles—scarcely suggests that the attitude of either towards Hastings was a matter of strong conviction. Yet, whatever may have been Thurlow's motives, no admirer of Hastings can do other than feel grateful to him for the part that he played, nor blame Hastings's friends for bestowing on him the chief credit for the triumphant acquittal. . . .

When the voting was concluded Hastings was called in and informed of his acquittal. He bowed respectfully and retired. So ended a trial that, from beginning to end, extended over seven sessions of Parliament and occupied one hundred and forty-two sittings of the Court.

II

It has been the commonly held view that out of the trial of Warren Hastings arose a new order of things for India, that in 1788 the British Empire in India stood at the crossroads—was it to follow the Roman plan of exploitation of subject peoples without any regard for justice or the interests and welfare of the governed, or was it to follow a new road, the road marked out for it by Edmund Burke, of trusteeship, bringing India within the pale of right and duty? That as a result of the sufferings of one unjustly accused man, many, the whole people of India, were given justice never accorded to them before, and that the public conscience of England was at last awakened to the misdeeds committed by Englishmen in India, of which previously it had but barely heard. [8]

It is natural for apologists of Burke to hold this view, as from it they can deduce the comforting conclusion that, by committing a wrong to a single individual, he was enabled to do transcendent good to a whole people. But is it true? Was the public conscience awakened for the first time by this trial? And if it was awakened then, did the awakening have such far-reaching effects? Had the misdeeds in India only "been barely heard of before 1788"? Was it only after these proceedings that British officials in India began to think of Indian Government in terms of justice and duty? Did this trial transform a rule of fearful blackness into a thing of shining whiteness?

This book will have failed in its main purpose if an affirmative answer is given to these questions. It is obvious, of course, that while it lasted the trial *did* prevent the nation from forgetting India, *did* compel it to do some serious thinking on the subject, and *did* make it more keenly alive to its responsibilities. It is likely, too, that it inspired British officials with a healthy fear of having to account for their actions to Parliament. In other words, the trial undoubtedly had both an educational and a monitory value. But beyond that it is impossible to see that it served any useful purpose. It marked no turning-point in British Indian history. It ushered in no new day for India. Fully as many "crimes" were committed by British Governors after 1788 as were committed by Warren Hastings. The work of reformation of the Indian Civil Service, so ably carried on by Cornwallis and his successors, had been begun by Warren Hastings. If there was a definite turning-point in that history, it had already come—and the date was 1772. Burke only put into words—imperishable words, it is true— what Hastings had already put into practice—that government is a trust to be exercised primarily in the interests of the governed.

It was not Burke that "saved" the Empire: it was Warren Hastings. To regard him as "at heart a proconsul of the Roman Empire," imbued with the old ideas of exploitation, is to mistake completely his character and the principles and objects of his policy. In a way, judged from a modern standpoint, it can even be said that his views were more truly enlightened than those of Burke himself, because, unlike his great accuser, he did not regard the Indian people as "a backward race," to whom the British, being "a forward race," owed a special duty, that of importing for its benefit the superior system of Western morality. [9] He recognized that the Indian peoples had their own moral code, their own customs and traditions, and peculiar modes of thought, which were as much entitled to respect as those of the West, even though they included some practices that no civilized government could tolerate. And when Burke pleaded—and earned thereby the unstinted admiration of his subsequent apologists—that "the laws of morality are the same everywhere," [10] he was surely speaking more like a doctrinaire philosopher with the provincial mindedness of an Englishman who cannot accept the fact that other races may think and behave differently from his own, than as a great universal thinker, a man fit to decide with the infallibility of a god the right or wrong of great questions of Indian government.

If Burke was a conservative, so was Hastings: he sought to preserve what was best in the Indian institutions that he found and to

WARREN HASTINGS, 1791
(From a bust by Thomas Banks, R.A., in Westminster School)

discard only what was corrupt and effete. He laid the basis of an empire of which both Britain and India could be proud.

III

HASTINGS emerged from the trial a ruined man. Not only was his public career finished but the moderate fortune of £80,000 that he had brought back from India was gone. It must be admitted that he had spent it extravagantly, most of it being consumed in buying Daylesford at an exorbitant price, and then in rebuilding the house and laying out the grounds. In a report to the Court of Directors on his financial condition he stated:

"I possess the estate of Daylesford in Worcestershire, which cost me, including the original purchase, and what I have expended upon the house, gardens and lands, about £60,000. The estate is 650 acres, and may be valued at £500 clear yearly rent.... In 1789 I purchased the principal part of the estate, and about two years since the remainder. It was the spot in which I had passed much of my infancy, and I feel for it an affection of which an alien could not be susceptible, because I see in it attractions which that stage of my life imprinted on my mind, and my memory still retains. It had been the property of my family during many centuries, and had not been more than 75 years out of their possession." [11]

The purchase had been made possible by the death of John Knight in 1788 without issue. The estate had been entailed and the fact that the heir, a younger son of Jacob Knight, was an old man, who also had no children and took no personal interest in Daylesford, made it easy to arrange a sale. The purchase price was £10,780, with an annuity of £100 to Knight and his wife for their joint lives. The original estate had included the whole of the parish but pieces had been alienated before the sale of Daylesford to Jacob Knight, and Hastings was not satisfied until he had recovered it all. In 1792 he bought a farm of fifty acres at the price of £3150, and in 1808 he paid £1050 for a house with sixteen acres of land. [12] Besides buying Daylesford he had in the same year sold Beaumont Lodge and bought a town house, 40 Park Lane (the last house at the Oxford Street end, which has since been pulled down), where he lived during the trial, until he decided, soon after its conclusion, that he could no longer afford the luxury of two residences. He then sold it, and retired to Daylesford for the remainder of his life.

His legal expenses for the trial alone had mounted to £76,528, and other expenses incidental to the trial had absorbed another £22,000; so that his debts totaled £97,000. This meant that without outside assistance he was bankrupt. He had no money even for the regular expenses of his household. When a friend advised him to seek rest and quiet in the country, he confessed that he was not sure that he could pay the expense of posting down to Daylesford.

In his Defense he had asked, "What atonement"—in the event of his acquittal—"will this Honorable House in its justice ordain for the injury which I sustain by having been branded on its records, and under the sanction of its authority, with the vile and abhorred character of a Verres, an oppressor, a defrauder, a traitor, and even of a liar?" He was now to receive his answer. He drew up a petition to the House of Commons in which he set forth the heavy expenses to which he had been subjected and asked for compensation. He sent it to the Prime Minister, and asked him to lay the case before the King. In a few days it was returned with a short note to the effect that under all the circumstances Mr. Pitt did not conceive that he should be justified in submitting the petition of the late Governor-General of India to the consideration of the sovereign.

Hastings's friends urged him to lay his case before the Court of Directors and to demand of them, as a matter not of favor but of right, that the Company defray his expenses. But he refused, not because he did not feel the great injustice of being left to pay his own costs after having been acquitted on every charge, but because "My claim lies, not against the Company, but against the British Nation." If Parliament refused him reparation for the loss that it had inflicted upon him by an unmerited prosecution, he must submit. "I can have no claim whatever upon the Court of Directors." [13] But his friends were not to be deterred. They were sure that the services he had rendered the Company were so immense that the Proprietors would feel bound, at the very least, to make good his losses. Had he not been in reality the scapegoat for the sins of the whole body of the Company's servants? Had it not been the Company itself, as much as its chief officer, that had been on trial? It was tactfully suggested to him that he should allow his employers to reward him out of their bounty, and, inasmuch as it was about to make a similar grant to Lord Cornwallis in token of appreciation of his services, he agreed.

The Court of Proprietors met in May, and showed again, as it had shown so often in the past, how highly it esteemed him. It acknowledged his merits with a unanimous vote, and then passed by large majorities resolutions for paying the expenses of his trial and granting him an annuity of £5000. But the consent of the Government still had to be obtained. The recent India Act made the sanction of the Board of Control necessary for any extraordinary financial grants by the Company. And this meant that the matter of reparation rested again in the hands of William Pitt.

Both grants were refused. Apparently Pitt, the austere arbiter of justice, did not consider that the verdict of the highest court of the realm was sufficient to remove the stigma of guilt that his own House had placed upon Warren Hastings. It seems a pity that a great statesman like Pitt—England's greatest in the opinion of many—should have done nothing by his treatment of the man whom not a few regard as the greater one of the two, [14] to gain for himself a reputation for magnanimity and generosity. During his administration of sixteen years he created a hundred and forty-one peers—an altogether unprecedented number in those days—but Hastings was not one of them. And later in his life he allowed his own debts to be paid by a grateful country. No doubt in his own mind he was satisfied that the part he acted towards the former Governor-General was correct, but the suspicion rests upon him of allowing resentment at the refusal of the Lords to sustain the impeachment for which he had voted to govern his conduct. It is certainly true that the members of the House of Commons who had been responsible for the impeachment never forgot that in acquitting Warren Hastings the House of Lords had in effect condemned them, and never by word or act were they ready to admit that the condemnation was just. Hastings would have to outlive them before he could expect them, or the proud body to which they belonged, to treat him other than as a criminal who had escaped conviction by a miscarriage of justice.

Hastings's friends, however, refused to give up the struggle. For months they kept up a constant agitation, using their influence in both Courts of the Company to bring severe pressure to bear on the Board of Control. And at last, in March of the following year, they succeeded in squeezing something out of Mr. Dundas and his reluctant colleagues. The Board agreed to a compromise by which the Company was permitted to grant Hastings an annuity of £4000 for the term of twenty-eight and a half years dating from the date of his return from India (so that he received £42,000 in one accrued payment), and a loan of £50,000 without interest for the term of eighteen years. [15]

The concession extricated Hastings from the worst of his difficulties, but it was far from sufficient to meet his needs, and the Court itself deprived him of its full benefit by making it a condition that he repay the loan in annual installments of £2000 and taking an assignment on half of his annuity, which meant that the Company gained, and he lost, the interest upon it. He said nothing at the time, but three years later, when he found his debts increasing rather than diminishing, he drew the matter to the Directors' attention, suggesting that he should be credited with compound interest on the £2000 withheld annually from his annuity, and to this they at once agreed.

This cannot be considered ungenerous treatment on the part of the Company, though it loses some of its luster by the fact that the Company voted much larger sums to both Cornwallis and Wellesley, neither of whom needed the money as much. But the melancholy fact remains that for the rest of his life Hastings was never to be entirely free of financial embarrassments, and more than once he was compelled to appeal afresh to his former employers for more liberal help. He was not accustomed to the need for strict economy and his old carelessness about money continued. He hated keeping accounts and accurately balancing expenditure against income, nor did the lavish hospitality that he loved to show his friends diminish with the straitening of his means. The Court later made still more ample amends, first in 1804, by granting him the full amount of the annuity for the remainder of the term and remitting the unpaid balance of the loan, and then in 1813, when the term expired, by extending it for the rest of his natural life, though it refused his request to extend it to include his wife.

Chapter XXXI

DAYLESFORD

CONGRATULATIONS upon his acquittal poured in upon Hastings, not only from his own countrymen at home and in India, but from his numerous Indian friends, as well as foreign admirers, who had followed his checkered fortunes with the greatest interest and marveled at the way he had been treated—the French especially, who knew to their cost the immensity of the service that he had rendered to his country. Big celebrations, too, followed the verdict. His neighbors especially overwhelmed him with their expressions of joy. The bells rang throughout the countryside. A band welcomed him back to Daylesford, and the gentlemen of the district opened their houses and gave lavish entertainments to all their friends. The Bengal Club held a great banquet in London, "partaking more of the splendor of the East than anything that was ever seen in this country." Five hundred were present. Mrs. Hastings presided, and Lord Thurlow especially was fêted. In July Sir John and Lady D'Oyly, old friends of Hastings in India, gave a *fête-champêtre* at their country house in Hampshire, at which the bells again rang joyfully. In a large pavilion, garlanded with flowers, Hastings's portrait was hung, supported on each side by those of Thurlow and Mansfield, and the guests were presented with bouquets tied with white ribbons, inscribed in gold with the motto, "Virtue Triumphant." [1]

But the excitement of the acquittal was soon over, and then Hastings retired altogether from the public gaze, and, with a sense of unspeakable relief, settled down to the pleasant life of a country gentleman as lord of the Manor of Daylesford. He sternly put away all repining over his lot, his defeated hopes of being able to combine this life of rural ease with prolonged employment in the service of his country and of his beloved India—"I love India a little more than my own country" was the confession he once made—and gave himself whole-heartedly to the enjoyment of the good things in life that were still his to enjoy. The companionship of his wife and Charles Imhoff his step-son—whom he regarded with as much affection as though he were his own son—the welfare of his tenants, the society of his friends, the development of his estate, the management of his farm, his animals, his books, his pictures, and the beauties of nature.

> Be this enough for me:
> To bear contented my accomplished lot,
> Impeach'd, revil'd, acquitted, and forgot.[2]

The gray stone house that he built is a spacious and dignified mansion, similar in most respects to those built by the English aristocracy in the eighteenth century. About it there is the usual air of solid comfort and cultured refinement, of classic simplicity and sylvan calm, with an absence of anything flamboyant or out of harmony with its surroundings. Its setting is also typically English, surrounded as it is by extensive, well-wooded, undulating park-lands. He laid out the grounds with great care, having regard only for their charm and none at all for expense. Besides gardens, lawns, lily-ponds, and orchards, there was a large lake, made by damming the Evenlode stream, with an island upon it. The house itself he furnished richly with all the treasures that he had brought back from India. Marvelous sets of ivory furniture, intricately carved and gilded by the hands of master craftsmen, paintings, drawings, tapestries, illuminated parchments, chain-mail, weapons, old china, portraits by old masters and many by contemporary artists whom he had patronized in India, books in great quantity, documents, manuscripts, prints, and a remarkable collection of Persian drawings. [3]

He continued in retirement the temperate habits formed in India, including his love of early rising and his preference for simple living. His recreations remained the same, riding and driving, reading and writing (particularly indulging his fondness for verse), with an occasional game of cards with his wife, at which, he sadly confessed, she always beat him! His literary occupations took curious forms: "A fragment of a novel"—a parody of the Richardsonian type of epistolary novel; an essay on "The Means of Guarding Dwelling Houses by their Construction against Accidents by Fire," which the London firm of Carpenter & Son published in 1816; historical essays, including a history of England to the reign of William Rufus. [4] He continued, too, his boundless hospitality, which had been so famous in Calcutta, and his table seldom lacked guests. He was an excellent conversationalist, both entertaining and well informed, and liked nothing better than to have his neighbors drop in of an evening for a round of talk, which was sure to be lively and witty. He attended church regularly, and family prayers were said every night. Among his papers is a prayer that he composed for daily use. [5]

Nothing so impressed itself upon all who knew him as his kindness, his truly Christian spirit of friendliness, sympathy and helpfulness. To his old friends of Indian days he was always ready to extend a helping hand, even to the extent of lending—or more often giving—them money, when he himself was so hard pressed to make ends meet.

Nathaniel Halhed was one to whom he gave financial assistance, and Nesbitt Thompson was another. Thompson's was an especially hard case. He came home, married, bought himself a nice country estate, had six children in quick succession, and then found himself being ruined by his wife's extravagance and by heavy taxation. Two of his daughters died, and finally, when he was faced with bankruptcy, his wife left him. In complete poverty and dependent on charity, he appealed to his former chief for aid in getting employment. Hastings lent him money—in June 1813 he lent him a second £100—until at last he found a post and regained his independence. Many requests came to Hastings, also, for assistance in obtaining posts in the Company's service, but these were more embarrassing than any others, as he had sadly to admit—and galling indeed the admission must have been!—that so far was he from possessing any influence with the Directors of the Company that a recommendation from him might even be a handicap to a candidate. Every such request only served to revive the pain of his ostracism from the seat of power.

Perhaps what endeared him most to his friends was the lively and unflagging interest he took in all their affairs—their domestic happiness, their children, their business concerns, their activities large and small. He had the gift of making the joy and sorrows of others his own, and if, like himself, they were engaged in experimental agriculture and stock-breeding, his interest and curiosity became boyish in their intensity. He would send them presents, sometimes a pig or a cow, sometimes a packet of special seeds or a portion of some prize crop, sometimes only a useful recipe. And he was always ready with helpful tips based on his own experience. Since there was never a suggestion of condescension in his attitude and all his acts and words of kindness sprang straight from his warmly affectionate nature, it is not surprising that there could have been few men in England as dearly loved by his friends as he. And he was kind not only to his friends and social equals but to his tenants and the village-folk of Daylesford; he was kind to all without distinction.

He was very fond of young people and always a favorite with them. He and Mrs. Hastings were the god-parents of many of the children of his old friends, and not a few were named after him. Sir John D'Oyly left one of his boys under his care when he went back to India and Hastings performed his duties with rare and delightful thoroughness, selecting the lad's schools with the utmost care, watching over his progress with a shrewd eye, bringing him to Daylesford for the holidays, tutoring him, and advising him with a kindly wisdom and sympathy that must have won for him the lad's warmest affection, besides saving him on one occasion from being expelled from the Company's College at Haileybury. It always paid, he told him, to act the man and do the honorable thing even at the risk of severe punishment. D'Oyly had another son already in the Company's service in India, and in his progress too Hastings took the greatest interest. Remembering how he himself had lacked the benefit of wise counsel when embarking upon his own

career he gave freely of the fullness of his knowledge and experience to
these youngsters.

So far as the affairs of the outside world were concerned he was
merely an interested spectator of what was for him a very distant scene.
He was no better able to judge of what was happening than any of his
neighbors, and the improvement of his little parish and the success of
his harvests were matters of much greater interest. He frequently expressed admiration for Napoleon and could not join in the feelings of
contempt and loathing for him that most of his countrymen indulged in.
At times he could not help feeling rather acutely the utter neglect of
himself "even by those who proclaim their belief of my past services
and subsequent retention of what talents I formerly possessed. My
opinions upon matters that come more within the cognizance of my
experience than that of any man living have never been asked, but upon
personal occasions, in which it was hazardous to give them." But these
expressions of disappointment were rare and confined to his intimates.

His reading during these years of uninterrupted quiet was wide and
varied—Spence on Commerce, Malthus on Population ("Malthus' appears to me to be one of the most enlightened publications of this and
the last age"), Lord Selkirk on Emigration, Walter Scott—for whose
poems he had an unbounded admiration—these he particularly recommended to his friends. He hated the Edinburgh Reviewers, "because
they are sneerers, a character that from my heart I abhor, as a compound of the meanest self-admiration and the most malignant hatred
of others"—a comment to which added interest is given by the fact that
it was for this *Review* that Macaulay wrote his famous essay on Warren
Hastings, which so misrepresented the man and distorted the facts of his
career out of all resemblance to the truth.

Throughout the twenty-odd years of life that still remained to him
Hastings was a very faithful and prolific correspondent. A large number of his letters have been published; in particular, those to Nesbitt
Thompson (and Thompson's to him), Edward Baber, Sir John D'Oyly
and his son Charles, and General Sir Charles Hastings, [6] and they
afford a very clear and full picture of the man during his retirement
when little information can be gained from other sources.

The year after the acquittal he took one of his few trips of any
distance away from home. He made a mid-summer tour of the Cumberland Lake District. Hastings was no traveler at all in these later years
of life. Occasional visits to Bath, Cheltenham, Oxford, Brighton, and
other centers of the aristocratic world of his day, seemed to satisfy his
need for change, and travel for the sake of seeing new places and new
things did not apparently appeal to him. He might have been tempted
to make the Grand Tour of Europe like most men of his day, if it had
not been for the war, and he might have wintered frequently abroad, as
the English winters tried him severely after thirty years in India.

DAYLESFORD HOUSE, WORCESTERSHIRE

Daylesford in summertime was far too beautiful for him ever to want to be away from it for long at that season of the year.

In 1798 Bonaparte's ambitious designs began to awaken fears of invasion in England, and when in June he disappeared from Toulon with his expedition—none knew where—Hastings was busy with his hay, and wondering whether English or French horses would eat it. ("You were right," wrote Thompson, "when in allusion to Strafford's trial you thought your own the prelude to great calamities.") In September of this year, after Napoleon's occupation of Egypt, Hastings addressed the King, sending him a memorandum in which he emphasized the need of taking steps to forestall the French designs on India, stressing the strategic importance of Egypt and the Red Sea and strongly urging the immediate occupation and fortification of the island of Perim. [7]

Three years later found him again putting forward his proposal for establishing a chair for Persian at Oxford with a Moslem to act as assistant, but, despite the fact that Dr. White, Canon of Christ Church and Professor of Arabic and Hebrew, was interested in the proposal, nothing seems to have come of it. Hastings never ceased believing that some provision should be made in England for the study of Oriental languages, and when Wellesley produced his scheme for the education of Indian civil servants, he showed his keen interest by writing a detailed criticism, in which he developed his own views, stressing in particular the value of Sanskrit.[8]

It is fitting that this same year (1801) should have seen Hastings elected a Fellow of the Royal Society, "as a gentleman of great and extensive knowledge in various branches of science." He also received at this time a very kind letter from Admiral Nelson:

"Your kindness towards me on every occasion I can never forget, and I assure you that whatever and from whomsoever praises I may have received none can possibly be more grateful to my feelings than yours, you that have been the chief of an Empire nearly as large as Europe must be a fair judge of merit in whatever rank it may be placed and therefore I hope you have not been too partial on the present occasion." [9]

In April 1803, he wrote to Edward Baber, an old Bengal friend, on the anniversary of his own acquittal:

"I am not so humble minded as to disclaim the pretensions which you assign me, whether to the justice and simple honesty of my country (which ought to pay me what it owes me) or to the gratitude of my sovereign. But I am satisfied. I flatter myself that my reputation rather gains than loses by time, and that the day is not distant when it will be generally acknowledged. In the meantime I eat, drink, sometimes laugh, and amuse myself and possess some substantial blessings which do not fall to the lot of all men; and if I had all those which wealth could purchase, I am not sure that I should be happier."

During the summer of 1803 England was again in mortal fear of invasion. War had broken out afresh with France, after the short breathing-space afforded by the Peace of Amiens. The militia and yeomanry had been mobilized, and volunteers were called for to defend the nation. By August 300,000 had been enrolled. But a general feeling of panic prevailed as the dread shadow of Napoleon once more fell across the land, and out of it arose, among Hastings's admirers, a feeling of astonishment that at the moment of greatest emergency in the nation's history its ablest citizen, the man who had proved himself supremely qualified to take command in a crisis and direct war operations, should have been allowed to remain in complete seclusion, managing the affairs of his farm instead of those of an empire at war. "It is indeed to be lamented that whilst the vessel of our State is in so much danger, you should be confined to your cabin"; and had he as head of a military council been directing Britain's military operations, the apprehensions of Nesbitt Thompson, for one, respecting the safety of his wife and children would have been considerably lessened. Thompson well remembered Major Popham's words, "He should have been a general." The idea was, of course, fantastic, if only because Hastings was now an old man of seventy; but at least it shows how utterly his old friends and subordinates worshiped him as their hero. Thompson was reassured when he found that Hastings did not believe that Bonaparte would come; "for if *you* would find the attempt impracticable *he* probably will —you are, however, the only man in England of whom I can say so much."

Hastings responded to the national appeal for volunteers by calling out the youth of Daylesford and drilling them himself to give them an appearance of being soldiers, with the aid of Charles Imhoff, now a colonel in the British Army, and his old porter whom he brought from the Chelsea Veterans Home for the purpose. Perched upon his horse, with his white hair and tall hat surmounting a slight figure bowed down by length of years, he presented a picture that was long remembered in the neighborhood. But the rulers of Britain of those days were not prepared for the sight of the martial spirit gripping the common people as well as the gentry in a fervor of patriotism, and they were almost as terrified at the prospect of the whole nation appearing in arms as they were of a possible invasion. So Hastings's patriotic gesture was not welcomed by the authorities and he therefore disbanded his little force.

In 1804 Hastings for almost the first time in his life showed a gleam of interest in English politics, but it was purely personal in its nature and revealed how little understanding he had of the English system of government. Mr. Addington, Pitt's successor as Prime Minister, had treated him very kindly and considerately when Hastings had consulted him about his petition to the Company for further financial relief, and Hastings was so little used to kindness from any politician that he was very much touched and immediately believed that Addington was the man Britain needed. Upon hearing that Addington might yield to the united opposition of Pitt, Fox and Windham and resign, he made a personal call at 10 Downing Street to try to persuade him not to do so, but Addington had no difficulty in proving to him that he had no option in the matter.

There were few men in public life that he really trusted or admired. All his sympathies lay, as might be expected, with the soldiers and sailors who were fighting their country's battles. Politics, as usually practiced by his contemporaries, was something that he abhorred; it seemed to him, as it has seemed to many since, the absolute negation of truth and honor. In a letter to Sir Charles Hastings, written eight years later, occurs this passage:

"I have lived so small a portion of my life in England, and of that little so little in society, that for want of those habits of thinking on which many moral doctrines depend, I cannot (for one instance) conceive on what principle a man should be obliged to think as others do with whom he is thrown into political association, and to sin against truth and honor by saying that he does, when he does not."

The man in public life whom he seems most to have esteemed was —strange as it may seem—the Prince of Wales, who was shortly to become Regent and was finally to ascend the throne as George the Fourth. History has given the Prince a bad reputation, yet he had many good qualities—more, according to the Duke of Wellington, than he had bad—and not least among them were intelligence and affability. The former quality enabled him to appreciate Warren Hastings at something of his true worth, and the latter he used to gain for himself an easy popularity wherever he went. At a time when Hastings was being ostracized by the politicians—and not least by the politicians with whom His Royal Highness was closely associated, Fox and his friends—the Prince showed a kingly spirit by treating him with special marks of favor, and this was something that Hastings could never forget. In his letters he always spoke of the Prince with loyalty and affection, and he never missed an opportunity to pay his respects. He wrote to Sir Charles Hastings from Brighton in the New Year of 1805: "We met with a more than gracious reception from the Prince of Wales (God bless him!). We met him as we passed one of the streets, on horseback. He recognized and stopped our carriage, and we passed the evening at the Pavilion, and are to dine with him today."

In the spring of that year Hastings had the curious, and no doubt rather stimulating, experience of hearing that another man—none other than Henry Dundas, now Lord Melville, First Lord of the Admiralty —was about to undergo the same ordeal of impeachment as he had helped with his vote to inflict upon Hastings, the charge being that of misapplication of the public money. Many of Hastings's friends openly rejoiced at what they considered to be just retribution to the man who had played so dubious a part in their hero's affairs, and he himself was not disposed to condone the offender, especially when he saw him defended by Pitt—the very man who had given the decisive vote against himself nineteen years before. When Melville was acquitted in the following year, Hastings waited with much eagerness to see whether the House of Commons would reimburse him for his expenses. If it did, he had made up his mind to petition for an equal measure of justice to himself, though he felt sure that "let who will remunerate Lord Melville, my claim will be treated as an insult." In fact, he was so wrought up about the difference in treatment accorded himself and Melville upon acquittal that he wrote an elaborate memorandum on the subject. [10]

He never lost his interest in Indian affairs. He had a great respect for Lord Wellesley, who had just resigned as Governor-General, as he had had for Cornwallis—"a name which I can never remember but with veneration." At the same time he noted with concern "the dangerous extension of our territory and the lavish expenditure of our European soldiers and money." [11] Later, referring to Wellington, he remarked: "Say what you will of India, it is the best school the nation can boast of, both for statesmen and generals...." [12]

The year 1805 came—the year of Trafalgar—and the whole nation was stirred with excitement to know the outcome of Nelson's search for the elusive Villeneuve. Having searched for him in vain in the West Indies, Nelson was experiencing unfair treatment from the government, of the kind that Hastings had too often experienced himself, and the former Governor-General's indignation was aroused. But then came the great victory,

"more glorious than any that has ever yet been recorded, and which will stand for ever foremost in the annals of our kingdom by having purchased its victory by the death of Lord Nelson.... I do not rejoice for our victory. It brought tears to my eyes, and has struck a chill upon my heart. If I was not afraid of its being imputed to me as an affectation, I would put myself into mourning. I do mourn inwardly...."

Christmas that year was spent with Sir Elijah and Lady Impey at Newick Park in Sussex. James Boswell and the Halheds were there, and the party was very festive. It was to be almost the last time that Hastings was to see his old friend, upon whom decrepitude had fallen faster than upon himself. [13]

It was natural that, as Hastings saw honors being showered upon his successors in the Government of India—Cornwallis, Shore (who was raised to the peerage as Lord Teignmouth), Wellesley, and, later, upon Minto and Moira, and even upon Governors of Madras, Macartney, Hobart and Clive (son of the victor of Plassey)—one, or even two, steps in the peerage being the rule—he should have felt acutely conscious of the way he himself was being neglected. In March 1806 he made his one and only attempt to gain what he considered his due. Pitt being dead, he thought that his chance had come. So he approached the Prince Regent and made known to him his wishes: first, employment on the Board of Control; second, reparation from the House of Com-

mons ("Though acquitted, I yet stand branded on their records as a
traitor to my country, and false to my trust.") ; third, and chiefly on his
wife's account, a title. He was willing to waive the first two, as the least
practicable, but hoped for the third. [14]

The Prince sent him to Lord Moira, a member of the new cabinet,
and Lord Moira, despite his own friendly feelings for Hastings, was
compelled to raise difficulties. Some members of the Cabinet—which
included Charles James Fox, William Windham, and Charles Grey,
three managers of his prosecution—might, he said, refuse because it
would mean a reflection on their former conduct. If a peerage was
given, it would probably only come as a favor, granted at the Prince
Regent's request. And to this Hastings proudly, and with the utmost
dignity, replied:

"My Lord, I never will receive a favor without an acknowledgement,
much less will I accept a favor from men who have done me great
personal wrongs, though the act so construed should be the result of
their submission to a different consideration. I beg, my Lord, that the
affair may go no further. I am content to go down to the grave with
the plain name of Warren Hastings, and should be made miserable by a
title obtained by means which would sink me in my own estimation." [15]

The matter went no further. Six years later, when he was in his
eightieth year, he wrote to the Prince Regent again, offering his services
in the national emergency, but to no avail.

In 1808 there was "a great revolution in the state of Daylesford.
My dear Mrs. Hs. has assumed the management of our farm by my
abdication." Mrs. Hastings was no doubt right in her belief that she
was a better manager. Her husband was seldom happy or successful in
his business affairs. After his trial, when he was realizing some of his
effects to meet his expenses, he had allowed eleven fine paintings by
Hodges of Indian scenes (done during the eventful visit to Benares)
to be sold at auction for the miserable sum of £125—all because he had
forgotten to set a minimum price on them. [16] He had experienced
more difficulties that vexed him greatly when he sold his Park Lane
House to Lord Rosebery. At Daylesford he had tried horse breeding,
but again at more expense than profit. He too often allowed his enthusiasm to run away with his business sense.

And so, one by one, the years passed. Generally in good health,
but oftentimes in sickness, he was always occupied and always happy.
Though he felt that his race was nearly run, he was as cheerful as ever.
Every summer continued to see a constant succession of guests, many
of them with distinguished names: among them the Duke of Gloucester,
the King's nephew, with whom he was on intimate terms. The intervals
between guests found him paying occasional visits elsewhere, to London, Cheltenham, and the homes of his friends—Sir Charles Hastings
at Willesley Hall in Leicestershire, Lord Moira at Donnington Park,
and others not too distant. Once he visited an old Bengal friend, Major

John Osborne, at Melchet Park in Wiltshire. Like not a few others, Osborne worshiped his memory as that of a saint. In the grounds of his estate he had erected a Hindu temple dedicated "to the Genii of India, who from time to time assume material forms to protect its nations and its laws, particularly to the immortal HASTINGS, who in these our days has appeared the Saviour of those regions of the British Empire." [17]

The usual checkered fortunes of a farmer relieved his life from any danger of tedium. Rain and shine, tempest and drought, good luck and bad luck—but each alike he met with equanimity, as befitted a man whose whole life had followed the same pattern. 1809 was a wet year, but he managed nevertheless to harvest his crops. Next year was also wet, but his turnips were excellent and he could boast of five acres of the finest lucerne man ever saw.

"Such are my occupations and such have been the best that I have had to commemorate for the last 25 years of my probationary life, certainly not such as I had projected for myself for their commencement. Still they have passed in the unvaried and unremitted exercise of my best affections, and have left me no cause to repine at my lot, or to reproach myself with not having duly appreciated those best gifts of heaven. . . . Excluded as I am from the world, what else indeed have I to write upon?" [18]

He still entered with zest into all his friends' doings—as, for instance, Sir Charles Hastings's purchase of a country estate and embarking on the life of a country gentleman. He never wearied in his acts of kindness, and always he was ready with advice—sometimes serious, often humorous—in their agricultural, breeding or engineering enterprises. "Advice," he wrote to Sir Charles, "is always presuming, except when it is the fruit of well bought experience. On that foundation I offer mine, at no cost too; that in the construction of your lake of 18 acres, you provide that the water which you lead into it shall issue from it by no other outlet than one designed for that purpose. My pond has been leaking ever since it has been made, now twenty years past."

He made only a few trips to London, and they grew more infrequent as the years passed. One reason was that such trips were expensive: "I have a great variety of roads to ruin, but the road between Daylesford and London is not the least contributable of any to that termination." And his health was seldom the better for them. His chief object in going to London at all was to keep in touch with the outside world. But he found news hard to come by, and finally decided that the best way to get it was to retire to a distance from the source of it, "as the way to view a perspective is to go from it."

These were the dark days of the war. What passed for statesmanship in the government of Britain was mediocre and unimaginative. There was too much faction in politics and too little intelligence in action. The war record was inglorious, and the nation had sunk into a state of apathy and gloom, as the interminable struggle dragged on and on, with no early prospect of peace. All this was reflected in Hastings's letters, which now seldom touched on public affairs, and when they did, with more pessimism than confidence. In his occasional comments on India he more frequently than before harked back to his own experiences. Almost all his former contemporaries there were now dead, and the old order had changed too completely for him to be able to follow events with anything like the old keenness or intelligence. Once in a while he would sadly note that his successors, and particularly Wellesley, were able to do things, not only with impunity, but actually be praised for doing them—things for which he himself was impeached. As each year passed his friends never failed to remember the anniversary of his acquittal, April 23, and rejoice the old man's heart with a note of commemoration and congratulation.

As time slipped by his letters became longer—but less, rather than more, interesting; which was, perhaps, a natural result of his long isolation from public affairs and his lengthening years. He was not unconscious of the fact, and at times confessed that he had nothing to say worth the saying—and so had to use his frank on whatever thought happened to amuse him at the moment, absurdly trivial though it might be.

Thus did Hastings realize the dream of his childhood days, the dream that had never faded away.

"To lie beside the margin of that stream and muse was one of my favorite recreations. And there, one bright summer's day, when I was scarcely seven years old, I well remember that I first formed the determination to purchase back Daylesford. I was then literally dependent upon those whose condition scarcely raised them above the pressure of absolute want; yet somehow or other, the child's dream, as it did not appear unreasonable at the moment, so in after years it never faded away."

The end of that passage reads:

"God knows there were periods in my career, when to accomplish that or any other honorable ambition, seemed to be impossible, but I have lived to accomplish it and though, perhaps, few public men have had more right than I to complain of the world's usage, I can never express sufficient gratitude to the kind Providence which permits me, to pass the evening of a long and I trust not a useless life, amid scenes that are endeared to me by so many personal as well as traditional associations."

Chapter XXXII

SUNSET SPLENDOR

SIXTEEN years had passed—sixteen uneventful years spent in retirement that never once brought him into the spotlight of public attention. And each year had relegated Warren Hastings further and further into the limbo of the past, into that twilight zone where men who have played their part in life still linger before disappearing unnoticed into the night. Those few who knew him knew that, though old and growing feeble, he was still the same man, vigorous in mind and unbroken in spirit, who had for so long been the stormy petrel of Indian politics. But to the nation at large he had become a part of history, a relic of an age that had been swept away amidst the shouts of victorious revolutionaries in France and the din of seemingly endless war. A new generation of leaders had arisen, new heroes claimed the plaudits of the nation, new problems engrossed its attention. The eighteenth century was dead, but while the grim struggle with Napoleon went on there were few to give time or thought to the obsequies.

On December 6, 1812, he celebrated his eightieth birthday. He was beginning to be conscious of failing powers; his memory frequently failed him; and too often he found himself writing one word where he meant another. Each succeeding winter seemed longer and colder than the one before, and each one found him suffering a little more, and less inclined to desert the sheltering warmth of his own fireside. A gentle descent into the valley—that seemed to be all that now lay before Hastings, with the hope that when his day came his obituarists would think better of him than the men who put him on trial. The realization that he could not look for any honors coming to him in his lifetime had saddened him, but there is no sign that it disturbed in the least his cheerfulness and calm philosophic acceptance of his destiny.

If such were his thoughts as he entered his eighty-first year, a magnificent surprise was in store for him. Suddenly the clouds that had shadowed his life for so long rolled away and the setting sun shone forth in all its radiance, bathing him in dazzling glory and turning the grayness of obscurity into the burnished gold of popular acclaim.

It was Hastings's fortune to outlive most of his contemporaries, both friends and enemies. Burke, Fox, Pitt, North, Cornwallis, Minto, Windham, Impey, Dundas, Thurlow, Loughborough, Shelburne—all had gone. The first to go of those who had impeached him was Burke —within three years of the verdict that signalized the failure of the cause that lay nearest to his heart—carrying with him into the grave a belief in Hastings's guilt, which nothing had been able to change: Whether acquitted or not, Hastings remained in his eyes "the accused and accursed." And as he lay dying he solemnly declared, as he would before God's throne, that he had acted, not from mistaken enthusiasm —"being a sober and reflecting man"—nor from personal resentment and a sense of personal injury, "never having received any," nor from ignorance—"no man ever having taken more pains to be informed"— but from the most profound sense of duty and absolute belief in the rectitude of his conduct. [1] And none can doubt that he spoke the truth, melancholy and tragic though it was.

Pitt had been the next, dying in 1806, quickly followed by Fox. Windham had died four years later, but before doing so he had shown clearly that the pendulum was even then swinging back, by exclaiming in public, when the fear of invasion was at its height, "Oh that we had the spirit of a Hastings to contend against the ambition of Bonaparte!" Honorable, chivalrous, sagacious Windham had never been quite happy about that trial! Sheridan still lived, though he had retired from public life, and even he had experienced a slight twinge of what may have been genuine remorse, and made towards Hastings a belated gesture of penitence. Creevey tells a story of how Sheridan and Hastings had met in 1805 at Brighton. They were introduced to each other by the Prince of Wales, and Sheridan

"lost no time in attempting to cajole old Hastings, begging him to believe that any part he had ever taken against him was purely political, and that no one had a greater respect for him than himself, etc. etc., upon which old Hastings said, with great gravity, that 'it would be a great consolation to him in his declining days if Mr. Sheridan would make that sentence more publick': but Sheridan was obliged to mutter and get out of such an engagement as well as he could." [2]

To Philip Francis alone, of all the chief figures in the drama, was to be given the fate of surviving Hastings. Appropriately enough, he was to die the same year, four months afterwards. When he was invited to join in an attempt to get Lord Wellesley impeached, he had cried, out of the bitterness of his soul, "I will never be concerned in impeaching anybody. The impeachment of Mr. Hastings has cured me of that folly. *I* was tried and *he* was acquitted." [3] Yet he still pursued the object of his ambition, the Governor-Generalship of India. Once, as we have seen, it nearly came within his reach. But though his friends the Whigs, and his special friend Fox, were in power, it was impossible. As Lord

Brougham said, they could no more have obtained the Company's consent to the appointment of Francis than they could have transported the Himalaya Mountains to Leadenhall-street. [4] In high dudgeon he scornfully refused the consolation prize that was offered him, the Governorship of the Cape of Good Hope, though he accepted a knighthood, the Order of the Bath. Shortly afterwards, he closed his political career, a career that had been marked by bitter disappointment and almost constant failure.

Once, and once only, did the shadow of Francis cross Hastings's path during their last years. In 1816 a book was published, *Junius Identified,* by John Taylor, which awarded that dubious honor to Philip Francis. Francis was terribly upset. Wherever he went he was conscious of accusing glances, so he went nowhere, and when he could no longer endure the embarrassing questions of his friends in Brooks' Club, he withdrew his membership. [5] As he made no reply to the book, he presumably allowed judgement to go by default. Hastings's friends, being convinced by the argument, wrote to him telling him he must read it. He did so, and became so interested that he spent eight days making an elaborate criticism. The curious thing is the conclusion he reached! "I was convinced," he wrote to Baber, "that there was no foundation, nor even a plausibility for the belief; but I had drawn up my arguments so unskillfully (to say no more of it) that I prudently resolved not to let it go any further. So I must content myself with the simple conclusion, which I give you in terms, that the attribution of the book is false, and my refutation of it well-meant nonsense...."

Thus the men who had blocked the gateway to honors and kept alive the rankling memory of the humbling of an august assembly, had disappeared from the scene, and the way was cleared for a true expression of public opinion. The memories of peoples are commonly thought of as short, but somehow the British people had not allowed the long ordeal of the greatest war in their national history to make them forget the man who had helped them to weather a previous storm. And when the opportunity occurred, as it did in the spring of 1813, the floodgates of popular feeling were unloosed, and Warren Hastings received some at least—and the best—of those marks of honor for which he had waited a lifetime.

On April 30 he was summoned to give evidence before the Select Committee of the House of Commons, which was sitting to consider the renewal of the East India Company's charter. Thompson accompanied him to the House. While they were sitting in the Speaker's room with the other witnesses—so Thompson tells us—Sir Thomas Plumer (who had been Hastings's counsel in the trial) came to them, and congratulations were exchanged on the very different auspices under which they were now assembled from those which had formerly brought them there.

"Did you not hear just now the noise in the House?" asked Sir Thomas.

"No"—Hastings and Thompson had not heard it.

"I made sure you must, for when Mr. Hastings's name was mentioned and a motion made that he might be offered a chair, a louder acclamation followed than I ever remember to have heard within its walls."

Hastings was the first witness, and was examined for three and a half hours, being listened to with the greatest attention and respect. The examination turned mainly on two questions, the throwing open of the Indian trade to all British subjects, and the amount of liberty that should be allowed to Christian missionaries. On the first Hastings expressed views different from those in his *Review of the State of Bengal,* written during his voyage home. Then he had favored throwing open the trade, [6] whereas now he upheld the Company's monopoly, the reason being his conviction that if his countrymen were allowed to live and trade in India, as and where they pleased, the result would be grievous oppression of the natives. He expressed strong disapproval of any measure that would increase intercourse between Englishmen and Indians, believing that it would prove ruinous to the country and dangerous to the peace and stability of the Empire, since he did not trust his countrymen in general to treat the Indians fairly nor the courts to give the latter adequate redress. On the question of admitting missionaries without restriction and instituting a Church establishment for India he was non-committal, only insisting on the necessity of guarding against the danger of arousing apprehensions in the minds of the people that the Government intended to tamper with their religious beliefs. [7]

At the close of his evidence the members of the House with one accord sprang to their feet and stood with their hats off as he retired, while those remaining few who had been Managers in his prosecution remained seated and covered. [8] "You who know the warmth and generosity of his heart," wrote Thompson to Sir John D'Oyly, "will readily conceive how forcibly it was touched and how delightfully affected by so unequivocal, unlooked for, and rare a testimony of public esteem." It was, indeed, an unprecedented tribute, and worth infinitely more than any formal vote of thanks that the House might have passed. It meant that, without a word being uttered, the stigma which the House had placed on Hastings had been wholly removed. It was, perhaps, the happiest moment in Hastings's life, but Edmund Burke must surely have turned in his grave!

A few days later he appeared before the House of Lords. The Duke of Gloucester at his own request called for him, brought him to the House in his carriage, waited with him in the ante-chamber, accompanied him into the committee room, and after he had given his evidence, conducted him back to his carriage. His reception before the Peers was as flattering as that given him by the Commons. They gave him a seat, which in itself was a rare honor, and paid the most marked attention both to his person and his opinions. "The very officers of both houses, even to the printers of their proceedings as well as the persons employed by the East India Company seem to have vied with each other in manifesting their respect for him." [9]

Faithful Thompson's joy knew no bounds.

"I wish you"—Sir John D'Oyly—"were now in England for many reasons, but particularly that you might participate in the triumph which our great friend has obtained over all his enemies. He has not, I believe, one remaining. Those whom death has spared, remorse has converted into friends, and I am most perfectly convinced there is not at this moment a man in England the worth of whose private and public character is more universally and indisputably admitted than his is."

After Parliament, the Directors of the East India Company (the Directors had always been quick to follow the lead of ministers!). "I have had a handsomer letter from the Chairman," wrote Hastings to Baber, "and of more unreserved graciousness than was ever written by, or in the name of the Court of Directors. I have answered it, feebly. The colors of my setting sun are too vivid. . . ." And after the Directors, Oxford. At the end of June he attended the Encaenia to receive the honorary degree of Doctor of Civil Law, and the reception that he received was such as—according to a still surviving tradition—has never been accorded to any one else.

"But if it were possible for the feelings of admiration in an audience to be carried to a still higher elevation, such an expression was testified when Dr. Phillimore introduced the celebrated Warren Hastings; and sketched, in a manner unequaled for delicacy, pathos and glowing zeal, the leading features of his eventful life, from his first initiation at Westminster School, down to his late appearance at the Bar of the House of Commons, with his hoary honors full upon him, yet still in unimpaired possession of his intellectual strength. And, doubtless, the placable, unadorned and venerable aspect of this good old man, his cruelly protracted and most unmerited prosecution, the incalculable value of his services in India, his manners and conduct in private life adorned by the most transparent simplicity, and the chaste and unsophisticated devotion of these his later days to the embellishments of classical literature, all conspire to swell that universal note of congratulation, which, both upon his entrance and exit, was reverberated from every point of the Theater in frequent and fervid bursts of applause. It was obvious that Mr. Hastings was extremely interested by these hearty and unbought tributes of praise." [10]

It is impossible to exaggerate the intense happiness that all this brought to him. He experienced feelings such as he had never known in his life before. To Sir Charles Hastings he wrote:

"In the philosophical discourses which you and I have variously held together, I daresay we have transiently spoken of human life as a state of probation. Mine has afforded a most apt illustration of it: twenty or thirty years of it passed in the labored accumulation of materials sufficient to bespatter me with abuse through more than nine complete; and my closing years exposed to proofs of a nature the reverse of the former. With what spirit and magnanimity I bore my hard beating, you know, and the world has seen it. How ill I bear the undue honors which have since been heaped upon me, this exaggerated display—shame on it!—will too foully prove against me. I will therefore modestly put an end to the subject."

London was at this time ablaze in honor of Wellington's great victory at Vittoria, but Nesbitt Thompson declared he rejoiced more at Hastings's victory at Oxford!

The old man returned again to his beloved Daylesford—he admitted that he could scarce tear himself away from it—to his farming and his reading, though his interest in what was going on in the outside world was no less keen than before. He often recommended books to his friends, and he now earnestly recommended Sir Humphrey Davy's *Elements of Agricultural Chemistry*. "I daily lament the daily decline of my memory. . . ." He was far from well, and the next winter tried him severely, bringing on a severe attack of gout. "We are miserably cold, our sheep in danger of perishing for want of hay, and the foxes beginning to eat our young lambs." It was a late spring.

The following summer (1814) brought the defeat of Napoleon and the long looked for peace, and with it the visit to England of the Emperor of Russia, the King of Prussia and many of the German princes. On June 12, Hastings visited Oxford once more to attend the Encaenia in their Majesties' honor. He was the guest of Mr. Theophilus Leigh Cooke at Magdalen. On the 14th he dined at All Souls' by invitation of the Prince Regent, and next day at Christ Church. Returning to London, he was present at the Lord Mayor's Banquet, where the Prince introduced him to the imperial visitors, describing him as "the most deserving, and at the same time one of the worst used men in the Empire." Hastings had just been made a member of the Privy Council—the only honor from the Crown he ever received—and the Prince Regent now promised him much more than that—"he shall yet be honored as he deserves"—but did nothing. The "much more than, that" would have been peerage, and, perhaps, few will disagree with David Anderson's comment, "that plain *Mr. Hastings* in circumstances rather straitened is the noblest and most illustrious sequel to the character of the late Governor-General of India."

The following month Hastings presided over a dinner given by the Gentlemen of India to Wellington, whose health he proposed in a few well-chosen and fitting words. His own health was drunk, coupled with that of the Government of India. He also attended the Queen's garden party, where he was most graciously received by Her Majesty; made calls on the Duke of Wellington, Lord Hill and Sir Thomas Picton, the three chief heroes of the Peninsula campaigns; dined with the Court of Directors, when he again responded to the toast of "Mr. Hastings and the Government of India"; attended the Prince

Regent's court—from ten at night till six in the morning, after which he slept all day! and then left London to return home, visiting on the way his old friend George Vansittart at Bisham Abbey, [11] and arrived at Daylesford two days later, where he at once "gave a grand dinner to all the inhabitants of our little parish, and a few more, in honor of the peace; and yesterday evening tea and bread and butter to all the women and children; and I verily believe, we have infused more of the spirit of true loyalty into their hearts by it, than they had there before." [12] The person, he said, who had most enjoyed this excursion to London was Mrs. Hastings. The gay life suited her much better than it did him, and she always seemed to return home in better health.

Chapter XXXIII

LAST DAYS

THE Allied Sovereigns went back to Europe, the celebrations of a peace that was so soon to be interrupted came to an end, and Warren Hastings resumed his quiet life at Daylesford. His Indian Summer had come and gone, and winter lay just around the corner. He was attacked recurrently by brief spells of paralysis in his right side and hand, which deprived him of all power of articulation. But they passed, and for a short time longer his health remained good. Wit, cheerfulness, sympathy and good will continued to radiate from Daylesford House as abundantly as ever.

On October 6, 1815, he wrote to Baber:

"On the 8th of October, 1750, I first set my foot in the land of Bengal, unless my future biographer should detect a small error in the locality of the date and transfer it to the deck of the ship from which I first viewed it *sixty-five years ago!* What age is it permitted me to look back upon, with my bodily and mental faculties, though impaired, not destroyed; and as my memory presents to me the record of times past, to be able to say, 'quorum pars non parva fuit,' and like a grain of sand in the way of the ball of a billiard table, have given its eccentric direction to the rolling events of the world, which they would not have obtained, if I had never had existence."

There was no apparent diminution in his interest in the events of the great world of affairs, nor did his comments on them lose their vigor or sense. After Napoleon's final downfall and the Allied armies were in Paris, Hastings wrote to Sir Charles Hastings: "I should not think it necessary to dismember France for the purpose of weakening her. It seems probable that the restoration of their ancient dynasty will effect that purpose full as well." He regretted that the fallen Emperor had to end his life in a prison, and especially that St. Helena should be chosen for it. "It is too beautiful a spot to be made a state prison."

He was still reading Scott, and with undiminished admiration—

"Every inch that has fallen within the touch of Walter Scott is to me as consecrated ground." Many an evening was spent with Mrs. Hastings and Sir Charles and Lady Imhoff (his stepson had recently been knighted) reading the poet's works aloud. He was also keenly interested in Robert Owen's famous pioneering enterprise in factory management in Lanarkshire, and wrote to David Anderson, who lived in the north of England, for more information.

He got through the next winter with nothing worse than a severe cold and cough, and the following summer found him very happily engrossed in a new enterprise, the restoration of Daylesford parish church. It was a most ancient building, dating back a thousand years to Anglo-Saxon times, and long-continued neglect had brought it to a sad state of dilapidation; the roof even was falling in. He had it taken down and rebuilt, according to his own designs, taking particular care to retain the primitive simplicity of the old. "Two things will please you in the execution of this work"; he wrote to Baber, "one that the whole of the woodwork was composed of timbers, grown from twigs put into the ground (may I say, prophetically?) at the commencement of my Impeachment, and a second, that the rest of the building was made up of the same stones, hewn and unhewn, with a few exceptions, as lay in the original structure." The whole work of demolition and construction occupied no more than sixty days, and almost every day he inspected its progress, recording it in his diary. The labor was one of love, and helped to keep him in health, but the day came when he found that he had not the strength to walk the short distance from his house to the village, and that greatly saddened him.

On December 8 the church was reopened for service, and it was a proud and happy man who took his accustomed place in the congregation and listened to his nephew, Thomas Woodman, whom he had presented as Rector two years before, preach "a sermon as appropriate as I believe was ever delivered to a Christian congregation.... The congregation filled the church."

There are few enough memorials of Warren Hastings in England —only two, to be exact, a tablet erected by his widow in Westminster Abbey, and a statue in the India Office—but one would suppose that this church would be one of them. But no! It was pulled down in 1860, after a lifetime of only forty-four years—thereby making it, surely, the shortest-lived church in all England!—because it was "found to be too small"—a somewhat strange reason, considering that the population of the parish even today does not exceed a hundred.

March of the following year, 1817, found Hastings making his last visit to London, where he paid numerous calls on old friends. It ended with a serious attack of illness and a lengthy confinement to bed, which prevented his return home until May. In July he wrote to Baber:

"Mrs. Hastings is well and continues to possess her good looks. Boyle, speaking of some learned academician, who had said in a great book that he enumerated it among the blessings, for which he daily gave God thanks, that his wife still retained her beauty at a time of life in which women commonly lost theirs, that it was a mean thought, and unworthy of a philosopher. I am not of that opinion. On the contrary I am more pleased with Mrs. Hastings's good looks than with the restoration of Louis the 18th to his kingdom."

The zest for life still burned brightly, though the flame was slowly dying down. Flashes of humor lit up the pages of his letters with the same delightful spontaneity up to the end. In the last letter of the Sir Charles Hastings collection, dated September 28, 1817, occurs this characteristic passage: "The newspapers of India in the time of the old régime used to close many of their profound articles of intelligence with the monitory words, 'We shall see what comes of it'; and they always came to pass accordingly."

His thoughts were often with the man who held the great post that had once been his, and they were full of sympathy and concern, born of his own vivid memory of the trials that the post involved. The Marquis of Hastings (Lord Moira), a great Governor-General, was talking of resigning, but, said Hastings to their common kinsman Sir Charles: "If I was at his elbow, I would say to him: 'You have no right to quit your post from a sentiment of disgust, if you are satisfied that your continuance in it is necessary to the welfare of the great interests which have been committed to your charge: no, not though shame (present shame) and dishonor should attend your resolution.'" How well he remembered that feeling of disgust and his own refusal to yield to it! The spirit of the man who refused to surrender was still alive.

Spasms of intense cold afflicted him during his last winter, and early in the New Year the first signs of fatal disease appeared—an inflammation in the roof of his mouth that made it difficult for him to swallow. His entry in his diary for May 2 reads: "Heated, and my nerves shaken by walking. This is the third day that I have been affected with the confused sounds, as of distant multitudes." And for the following day: "I have been visited by confused and indistinct sensations, as of the sounds of distant multitudes—at times resembling slow music—but its effect!!!" [13]

He rallied for a few weeks, and was able to go out in his carriage and to attend service at his church. His last letters to his friends were written now, but they gave no sign of impending death. That to Baber, dated June 16, was a long chatty letter, filled with amusing stories and anecdotes.

The final illness began on July 13. Day after day and far into the night, he brooded away the hours seated in his big chair near the bed, waiting for the end and gradually growing weaker. The last entry in the diary that he had kept for many years was made on July 20. On August 3 he dictated a letter to the Court of Directors to make his dying request for a continuance of his pension to the beloved wife who had sustained him in moments of special crisis and difficulty. He offered his prayers for the Company's service, for his country, and for India, "for which I feel a sentiment in my departing hours not alien from that which is due from every subject to his own." [14]

At the last he was surrounded by those he loved best, his Marian, Sir Charles Imhoff and Charlotte, Lady Imhoff. To all three he was "our blessed saint." "Oh, such sweetness! such kindness! such patience! such affectionate thanks for little kindnesses and attentions, that our hearts ever prompted, was enough to break them before they had finished their duty." He wanted no medical care. "Surely at my age it is time to go. God only can do me good.... My dear, why wish me to live to suffer thus? None of you know what I suffer." For days he had swallowed nothing, and nothing gave him relief from the burning inflammation in his throat but a mouthful of the coldest water. "I am going at last, my Marian. I feel that I am going at last; and, oh! I am grateful...." Having blessed them he placed a handkerchief over his face, and when it was removed, it was found that his spirit had departed.

There was no apotheosis when he died. There was no tramp of marching feet, no lying in state, no booming of minute guns, no military bands playing slow and stately music, no burial in Westminster Abbey or St. Paul's Cathedral. There was no pomp and circumstance at all. *The Times* did remember to record his passing and even gave him an obituary notice:

"The late Warren Hastings, Esq., was educated at Westminster School. On his first return from India he was by no means in affluent circumstances; he gave up all idea of returning to the East, and resolved to open a school for the education of young gentlemen, but was advised to the contrary; and having received a new appointment from the Directors, he at length rose to the high station of Governor-General of India."

And that was all. He was buried quietly on September 9 behind the chancel of his church, his grave being marked by a simple stone urn inscribed "Warren Hastings, Died August 22, 1818"—nothing more. In death as in life—simplicity. And though the church was destroyed the grave was untouched and remains so to this day.

Appendix

I. SUPPLEMENTARY NOTE

WARREN HASTINGS's reputation has passed through many vicissitudes. During his lifetime the pendulum swung from one extreme of opprobrium to the other of acclaim, and it repeated the swing during the following hundred years. At times it has oscillated violently, and it still has not come to rest. James Mill's *History of British India,* which was so unfair in much of its treatment of Hastings, appeared in 1818, the year of Hastings's death. It was followed by the Rev. G. R. Gleig's *Memoirs of Warren Hastings,* published in 1841, an inadequate and mediocre work (though valuable for its publication of many of Hastings's letters), whose author made the egregious mistake of unadulterated adulation of his hero and was severely punished for it by Macaulay in his famous review of the book. Macaulay, however, grossly careless of his facts, leaned much too strongly in the other direction. Then came the serious investigators to correct the balance. When Sir John Strachey, Sir James Stephen and Sir George Forrest had published the results of their labors, the main outlines of the story were so firmly fixed as to make it impossible for all but frivolous and irresponsible writers to change its essentials. To complete the story there were many details that still had to be added, and this has been done in recent years by such writers as "Sydney C. Grier," Miss Monckton-Jones, Miss Weitzman, Professor Dodwell, Sir Evan Cotton and Sir William Foster.

One still, however, occasionally comes across some reluctance on the part of writers who have not made a thorough study of the subject to accept in full the revised estimate of the man. The latest biographer of Edmund Burke, for instance, Dr. R. H. Murray, prefers to regard him as belonging to the species of Roman proconsuls who made the exploitation of subject lands their chief aim, and in December 1932 on the occasion of the bicentenary of Hastings's birth, when countless voices were being raised to do honor to him, Dr. Murray in a letter to *The Times* reiterated this view. Presumably he was led to take it by a natural desire to make out the best possible case for Burke.

Two writers still more recent, Mr. Edward Thompson and Mr. G. T. Garrett, would have us believe that the balance has now been tilted too far in Hastings's favor and that present-day historians are possessed of an "idolatrous regard" for him. If this be so, it is a strange fate indeed to overtake the man who shares with Richard III, Mary Tudor and the Earl of Strafford (with a few others whom each reader can name for himself) the distinction of being during his lifetime the most abused figure in English history. Can it really be, as they claim, that there has been "an ignorant apotheosis" of him during the last quarter-century? It is difficult to see to what writers they are referring other than those mentioned above and a few others who have written on the subject, like Professor Ramsay Muir, Mr. P. E. Roberts, Mr. Vincent Smith and Sir John Marriott. Are we then to believe that the authors and editors of such works as the *Dictionary of National Biography,* the *Cambridge History of India,* and the *Oxford History of India*—to cite no others —are "ignorant"? If not, whom have the authors of *The Rise and Fulfillment of British Rule in India* in mind? It would be interesting to know because some of their own assertions regarding Warren Hastings are scarcely of a kind to win support to their claim of superior knowledge.

They state, for instance, that he was callous to the sufferings caused by war (p. 128), that he was "detested" by all his colleagues, was guilty of habitual dissimulation and "became incapable of giving a straightforward account of any transaction and wrapped all he did in maddening secrecy" (p. 132), that the Imhoffs were "living together amicably" in Calcutta while divorce proceedings were being put through in Germany (p. 115)—a palpable error, and that Chait Singh "was told to pay a fine of 50 lakhs" (p. 169). Most surprising of all, they have insinuated (p. 139) that Macaulay was right in believing that Nuncomar was legally murdered by Hastings and Impey. Do they, one cannot help wondering, include Sir James Stephen among the writers they contemptuously refer to as hooting this judgement out of court without troubling to study the evidence? As the sole support for their view they assert that "no one can successfully challenge that it was universally assumed that Hastings was the real prosecutor and that Nandakumar (Nuncomar) was put to death for venturing to attack him." On the contrary, apart from the fact that even if this were true it would not by any means be conclusive, or even presumptive, proof of guilt, actually nothing would be easier than to show that there was *no* such universal assumption; nay, more, that among Englishmen—whatever may be true of the natives of Bengal for whose opinions there is no real evidence—the assumption was confined to Philip Francis, who conveyed it inevitably to Burke, and was made by scarcely any one else! Several other similar assertions of these two eminent writers have already been noted in the text.

Is it, therefore, asking too much to suggest that we wait for more convincing proof of the alleged "ignorant apotheosis" before discarding the views of the recognized authorities on the subject?

II. NOTE ON THE PORTRAITS
OF WARREN HASTINGS

Contributed by Sir ARTHUR KNAPP, K.C.I.E.

THE commemoration, in 1932, of the bi-centenary of the birth of Hastings led to the tracing of a large number of his portraits which had not previously been recorded. These, almost without exception, are or have been treasured heirlooms in families whose ancestors served with Hastings in India; many were the gifts of Hastings himself; and their existence in such large numbers illustrates not only the open-handed generosity which, as the author of the *Life* has shown, was characteristic of Hastings but also his wonderful capacity for making and retaining friendships. "No man," it has been said of him, "ever had more devoted friends."

The thirty-five known portraits, enumerated in the list which follows, cover a period of fifty years of Hastings's life, from the time when as a young man of thirty-two, just returned from his first service in Bengal, he was painted by Sir Joshua Reynolds until his last portrait, at the age of eighty-two, painted at Daylesford by his friend Sir William Beechey. Apart from the artistic value of the work of the more famous artists who painted him—Reynolds, Hoppner, Zoffany, Stubbs, Romney, Lawrence and Beechey—a special interest attaches to the series of portraits by Lemuel Abbott. After many sittings Abbott produced a portrait [1] which Hastings, in presenting it to his old friend David Anderson, described as "bearing a stronger resemblance to me than any I have yet seen." Other sittings followed, for portraits to be given to Mrs. Hastings and to other friends, until finally there resulted the series of paintings (Nos. 16 to 21 in the list and probably also Nos. 22 and 23) each with slight but unmistakable differences in detail and expression to distinguish it from the others.

It was these portraits by Abbott which inspired the verses which Hastings wrote and sent to his friends to be inscribed on the picture:

VERSES TO BE INSCRIBED ON A PORTRAIT
PAINTED BY W. ABBOT

A mouth extending fierce from ear to ear,
With fangs like those which wolves and tigers wear;
Eyes, whose dark orbs announce, and sullen mood,
A lust of rapine, and a thirst of blood;
Such Hastings was, as by the Commons painted,
(—Men shudder'd as they look'd and women fainted—)
When they displayed him to the vacant throne,
And had the Peers the labor'd likeness own;
And such, in all his attributes array'd
Behold him here, on Abbot's canvas spread!
'Tis true to vulgar sense they lie conceal'd,
To Burke, and men like Burke, alone reveal'd.

[1] Reproduced as the frontispiece to this volume.

They, their own hearts consulting, see him here
In lines reflected from themselves appear;
With metaphysic eye the picture scan,
Pierce through the varnish, and detect the man.
To Burke it shews a soul with envy curst,
Malignant, mean, and cruel where he durst:
To Sheridan, a foe to shame, untrue
To ev'ry kindred tie, and social too:
To Fox, a shifting knave, with false pretence:
Michael alone described his want of sense.
And all in avarice agreed to find,
Or make, the ruling passion of his mind.
Yet he has friends! And they,—nay, (strange to tell!)
His very wife, who ought to know him well,
Whose daily sufferings from the worst of men
Should make her wish the wretch impeach'd again,—
Believe him gentle, meek, and true of heart.—
O Hastings, what a hypocrite thou art!

PORTRAITS OF WARREN HASTINGS [1]

I

Portraits in oil, extant in 1934

*a*1. By Sir Joshua Reynolds, 1764. Nearly full length, seated at a table. In the possession of Captain E. G. Spencer Churchill.
    Engraved by T. Watson, 1777; J. F. Bolt (head only), 1786; T. Knight, undated; and H. Davis, 1862.

2. By Tilly Kettle, *circa* 1780. Nearly full length, seated, left hand to cheek. In the possession of Mrs. Cortland MacGregor.
    Engraved (in reverse) by Angus, 1782. Head and shoulders only.

*b*3. A similar portrait by the same artist but half-length only. In the National Portrait Gallery.

4. Another portrait by the same artist and of about the same period. Full length, seated. Arms crossed. The property of the Asiatic Society of Bengal.
    A contemporary copy of this portrait, by Palmer, is in the East India United Service Club, London.

5. By J. T. Seton, 1784. Full length, seated at a table. In the Victoria Memorial Hall, Calcutta.
    Engraved by J. Jones, 1785.

*b*6. Another version of the same picture but three-quarters length. Now for sale in London.

7. By John Zoffany, 1783-4. Half-length in an oval. Life size. White waistcoat. In the possession of Mrs. Sanders.
    Engraved by Brittridge, Calcutta, 1784.

*b*8. A somewhat similar portrait by the same artist. In the possession of of Mr. C. F. Hastings.

9. Attributed to Zoffany, *circa* 1784. Half-length, with double-breasted sprigged waistcoat. In the possession of General Sir Francis Davies.

10. By A. W. Devis, *circa* 1785. Full length, seated at a table. The portrait, which was at one time in the Council Chamber at Calcutta, is now in the Viceroy's House at Delhi.
    Engraved by H. Hudson, 1794; and by C. J. Tomkins, 1887.

[1] The portraits marked *a* and *b* were exhibited at the British Museum and at Westminster School respectively during the bi-centenary celebrations in 1932.

Appendix 445

11. A replica of the above painted by Devis. In the possession of Rai Baijnath Das Shapuri of Benares.
b12. By George Stubbs, 1791. A portrait on china (37 in. by 28 in.) showing Hastings on his Arab horse. Now for sale in London.
13. A similar portrait also on china, but rather smaller, by the same artist. In the Victoria Memorial Hall, Calcutta.
14. Another similar portrait, on panel, by the same artist. In the possession of the Earl of Rosebery.

A stipple engraving, in colors, after this portrait but showing head and shoulders only was made by G. T. Stubbs, 1795.
a15. By George Romney, 1796. Full length figure, standing, with hands joined in front. At the India Office.
16. By Lemuel Abbott, 1796. Half-length, full face. Painted for Hastings and given by him to David Anderson. In the possession of Captain D. M. Anderson.[1]
17. A somewhat similar portrait by the same artist. Painted for Hastings in 1797 and presented to Mrs. Hastings. In the Victoria Memorial Hall, Calcutta.
b18. Another similar portrait, formerly the property of Sir Elijah Impey. In the possession of Lieut.-Colonel L. Impey.
19. A similar portrait by the same artist. In the possession of Mrs. F. R. Wansbrough, great-grand-niece of Hastings.
20. Another similar portrait by the same artist. In the possession of Miss Halhed.
21. Another similar portrait by the same artist, formerly in the Plumer family. Now at the Victoria Memorial Hall, Calcutta.
22. Attributed to Sir William Beechey, circa 1797. Resembles the portraits by Abbott (Nos. 16 to 21) and was probably painted by that artist. In the possession of Sir George Sutherland.
23. Attributed to John Simpson. Half-length, seated. In the possession of Sir Leicester Harmsworth. If the picture is by Simpson it must be a copy as it represents Hastings as he was about 1797 when Simpson was only fifteen years old. The portrait has also been attributed to Beechey but is probably by Abbott.
24. Attributed to Abbott and painted not later than 1797. Half-length, body turned slightly to the left. Red waistcoat. In the possession of Alice, Lady Teignmouth.

An engraving which presents this portrait, supported by two figures of Indians, was made by William Bromley in 1797.
25. A similar portrait. Sold at Stratton Park in 1929 when it was described as of the school of Hoppner. Its present whereabouts are unknown but a portrait resembling it is reported to be in the United States.
b26. Artist unknown. A half-length portrait with head turned to the left and the back of a chair showing slightly on the right. In the possession of the Auriol family, now represented by Mr. M. G. Dashwood.[2]
b27. By John Hoppner, circa 1800. Three-quarter length, seated at a table. In the possession of Admiral Sir Murray Anderson.
28. Attributed to Hoppner, circa 1800. A fine picture, half-length, inscribed on its frame as a portrait of Hastings, is in America, the property of Miss L. F. Emmet. Its history has not been definitely traced.
b29. Attributed to Sir Henry Raeburn, circa 1800. Small head, on wood. In the possession of Mr. Ulric Blyth.

[1] Reproduced as the frontispiece to this volume.
[2] Reproduced on p. 294.

30. Attributed to Simpson. A somewhat similar head. In the possession of Mr. Edward Impey.

b31. By J. J. Masquerier, 1806. Three-quarter length, seated. At the Oriental Club, London.
Engraved, half-length only, by S. Freeman, 1815.

32. By Sir William Beechey, 1806. Half-length with body turned to the right. Seated at a table with pen in hand. In the possession of Mrs. R. S. Balfour.

33. By Sir Thomas Lawrence, 1811. Half-length, full face. In the National Portrait Gallery.

34. By Sir William Beechey, 1814. Half-length, seated, with letter in hand. In the possession of Mr. A. W. Young at Daylesford House.
Engraved by W. Skelton, 1817.

35. By John Zoffany. A group picture of Hastings with Mrs. Hastings and her Indian maid. In the Victoria Memorial Hall, Calcutta.

II

Portraits of which the originals have not been traced but which are known from their engravings

1. Artist unknown. Engraving by J. Parsons, 1785. Copy in the Victoria Memorial Hall, Calcutta.
An engraving after the same picture (in reverse) was published by B. Crosby, 1795. Copy in the National Portrait Gallery.

2. By John Zoffany, *circa* 1784. An engraving appears in *Memoirs relative to the state of India,* by Hastings, published in 1787.

3. By C. A. C. von Imhoff (the first husband of Mrs. Hastings). Engraving by Klinger, 1788. Copy in the Art Collection at Coburg.

4. By R. Fulton. Engraving by W. Nutter, published by R. Cribb, 1801. Copy in the British Museum.

5. By Ozias Humphry. Large miniature. Three-quarter length, seated at a table. Engraving by E. Finden, published by John Murray, 1836. Copy in the British Museum.
An unfinished sketch by Humphry, corresponding to this picture, is in the Victoria and Albert Museum.

6. By Ozias Humphry. Large miniature. Half-length with arms folded. Engraving by Greatbach, published by Bentley, 1841. Reproduced in Gleig's *Life of Hastings.*
Note.—An engraving by H. Robinson, 1832, inscribed as being after Sir Joshua Reynolds, is clearly not from a painting by that artist: it is probably after Abbott.

III

Portraits which have passed out of view

1. A portrait of Hastings, believed to be by Mosnier, was included in the catalogue of paintings at Willesley Hall in 1848, and a portrait attributed to Morier, lent by the Earl of Loudoun, was shown at the Guelph Exhibition in London in 1891. These are presumably identical. The present whereabouts of the portrait are unknown. The description, as given in the catalogue of the Guelph Exhibition, namely, "Half-length, life size. Facing, in an oval," suggests a similarity to the Zoffany portrait, No. 7, Part I, *supra.*

2. A portrait of Hastings by C. A. C. von Imhoff was reported in 1925 to be in Calcutta in private ownership. Its present whereabouts are unknown.

3. A portrait by Abbott, differing apparently from those of the series described in Part I, was mentioned by Hastings in a letter dated May

6, 1797, as being in the possession of his friend Cowper of the Bengal Service. Neither this portrait nor a copy of it given by Hastings to his friend Edward Baber can now be traced.

IV

Miniatures

*b*1. By C. A. C. von Imhoff, *circa* 1769. Oval, 2½ in. by 2 in. In the possession of the Rev. E. W. M. O. de la Hey.

2. Attributed to Diana Hill, *circa* 1874. Oval, 1⅞6 in. Sold at Sotheby's on May 1, 1930.

*b*3. By Henry Bone, 1799. Oval, 4½ in. by 3¾ in. In the possession of Miss A. M. Woodman Hastings, great-grand-niece of Hastings.

4. A miniature of Hastings, by Cosway, set in diamonds, was bequeathed by Mrs. Hastings to her daughter-in-law Lady Imhoff. Its present whereabouts have not been traced.

AUTHORITIES

CHAPTER I

1. Rev. STEPHEN LIBERTY, *The Father of Warren Hastings—A Bicentenary Footnote*, 1932.
2. *Bengal Past and Present*, vol. XLVI, p. 48.
3. British Museum, Additional Manuscripts, 39, 903, f. 14.
4. HORACE WALPOLE, *Letters* (ed. Mrs. Toynbee, 1903), vol. XIII, p. 287.
5. Rev. G. R. GLEIG, *Memoirs of Warren Hastings*, 1841, vol. I, p. 8.
6. E. B. IMPEY, *Memoirs of Sir Elijah Impey*, 1847, p. 7.
7. *Bengal Past and Present*, vol. XLVI, p. 48.
8. Additional Manuscripts, 39, 903, f. 14.
9. Sir WILLIAM FOSTER, *John Company*, 1926, p. 218.
10. *Bengal Past and Present*, vol. XX, p. 19.

CHAPTER II

1. MARQUESS CURZON, *British Government in India*, 1925, vol. I, p. 2.
2. Sir JAMES MACKINTOSH's description, *vide* NEWMAN's *Handbook to Calcutta*.
3. H. E. BUSTEED, *Echoes from Old Calcutta* (2nd edition, 1888), p. 157.
4. *Ibid.*, p. 159.
5. SYDNEY C. GRIER, *The Letters of Warren Hastings to His Wife*, 1905, pp. 178, 414.
6. Mrs. ELIZA FAY, *Original Letters from India, 1778–1815* (ed. E. M. Forster, 1925), pp. 191, 199.
7. FRYER's *Travels*, 1696, p. 83.
8. LORD TEIGNMOUTH, *The Works of Sir William Jones*, 1807, vol. II, p. 19.
9. SIR GEORGE W. FORREST, *The Life of Lord Clive*, 1918, vol. II, p. 4.

CHAPTER III

1. House of Commons Reports, vol. III, p. 486.
2. Miss M. E. MONCKTON-JONES, *Warren Hastings in Bengal, 1772–1774*, 1918, p. 45.
3. Add. Mss. 29131.
4. GLEIG, *op. cit.*, vol. I, p. 61.
5. MONCKTON-JONES, *op. cit.*, p. 12.
6. *Ibid.*, p. 50.
7. Sir GEORGE W. FORREST, *op. cit.*, vol. II, p. 226.
8. *Bengal Past and Present*, vol. VIII, p. 214.
9. Add. Mss. 29206; MONCKTON-JONES, *op. cit.*, p. 68.
10. House of Commons Reports, vol. III, pp. 344, 486.
11. MONCKTON-JONES, *op. cit.*, p. 99.
12. *Ibid.*, p. 100.
13. GLEIG, *op. cit.*, vol. I, p. 124.
14. House of Commons Reports, vol. III, p. 359.

CHAPTER IV

1. Add. Mss. 29196, f. 4.
2. *Public Advertiser,* March 16, 1773.
3. *The National Mirror,* p. 78, cited by J. M. Holzman, *The Nabobs in England.*
4. *Speeches in the Trial of Warren Hastings* (ed. Bond), vol. I, p. 15.
5. *Autobiography of the Duke of Grafton,* ed. W. R. Anson, 1898, p. 112.
6. Miss STUART SUTHERLAND, "Lord Shelburne and East India Company Politics, 1766-9," *English Historical Review,* July 1934, p. 458.
7. *Memoirs of Warren Hastings,* by P. C., British Museum, 10803 e. 16.4; cited by Monckton-Jones, *op. cit.,* p. 102: "A pamphlet memoir of Hastings, written about 1820."

CHAPTER V

1. For these, and other, instances of his generosity, *vide* SYDNEY C. GRIER, *op. cit.,* pp. 18-20.
2. In a paper, written in 1801, giving his opinion of Lord Wellesley's scheme for the institution of a college in India for the training of the Civil Service, Hastings wrote: "About thirty-five years ago, I drew up a proposal for the establishment of a professorship of the Persian language in the University of Oxford, and presented printed copies of it to all the gentlemen who had at that time the direction of the Company's affairs. It had the approbation of the Noble Lord who was the Chancellor of the University, and the late Dr. Johnson promised, if it took place, to frame a code of regulations for the conduct of it. It met with no other encouragement, and therefore dropped." India Office Records, Home Miscellaneous Series, vol. 487, pp. 193-207; *English Historical Review,* vol. 44, p. 633.
3. Sir JOHN MALCOLM, *Life of Lord Clive,* vol. III.
4. Major-General Joseph Smith wrote to Robert Orme from Madras, June 26, 1769: "Hastings is coming, and bears a good character. The Lord send amongst us some men of spirit, for they were never more wanted than at this juncture." India Office, Orme Mss., vol. X, p. 168.
5. GLEIG, *op. cit.,* vol. I, p. 162.
6. MONCKTON-JONES, *op. cit.,* pp. 107-111.
7. *Ibid.,* p. 110.
8. EDWARD THOMPSON and G. T. GARRETT, *The Rise and Fulfilment of British Rule in India,* 1934, p. 128.
9. Sir GEORGE W. FORREST, *op. cit.,* vol. II, p. 377.
10. Add. Mss. 29132, ff. 434*b*-435.
11. Sir GEORGE W. FORREST, *op. cit.,* vol. II, p. 378.
12. GLEIG, *op. cit.,* vol. I, p. 173.
13. *Ibid.,* vol. I., p. 174.
14. *Ibid.,* p. 176.
15. *Ibid.,* p. 193.
16. *Ibid.,* p. 178.
17. MONCKTON-JONES, *op. cit.,* pp. 66, 120.

CHAPTER VI

1. MONCKTON-JONES, *op. cit.,* p. 142.
2. *Ibid.,* p. 143.
3. GLEIG, *op. cit.,* vol. I, p. 234.
4. MONCKTON-JONES, *op. cit.,* p. 146.
5. *Ibid.,* p. 150.
6. GLEIG, *op. cit.,* vol. I, p. 235.

7. *Ibid.*, p. 264.
8. Monckton-Jones, *op. cit.*, p. 149.
9. India Office Records, Home Miscellaneous Series, vol. 115, p. 143; Gleig, *op. cit.*, vol. I, p. 368.
10. *Ibid.*, vol. I, p. 225.
11. Monckton-Jones, *op. cit.*, p. 136.
12. Add. Mss. 29233, f. 17.
13. Gleig, *op. cit.*, vol. I, p. 316.
14. Monckton-Jones, *op. cit.*, p. 121.

CHAPTER VII

1. Sir Walter Lawrence, *The India We Served*, 1928, p. 230.
2. Gleig, *op. cit.*, vol. I, p. 269.
3. Monckton-Jones, *op. cit.*, p. 166.
4. Gleig, *op. cit.*, vol. I, p. 252; Monckton-Jones, *op. cit.*, p. 196.
5. *The Asiatic Review*, April, 1933.
6. Gleig, *op. cit.*, vol. I, p. 263.
7. *Ibid.*, p. 268.
8. *Ibid.*, p. 273.
9. *Ibid.*, p. 402.
10. A. V. Dicey, *Law and Opinion in England*, 1905, pp. 70-83.
11. R. H. Murray, *Edmund Burke*, 1931, pp. 244, 332, 346.
12. Gleig, *op. cit.*, vol. I, p. 403.
13. Add. Mss. 29233, f. 2.
14. Gleig, *op. cit.*, vol. I, p. 263.
15. *Ibid.*, p. 283.
16. Monckton-Jones, *op. cit.*, p. 224.
17. Gleig, *op. cit.*, vol. I, p. 301.
18. *Bengal Past and Present*, vol. XI, p. 51; XII, pp. 48, 71.
19. Add. Mss. 29127; Monckton-Jones, *op. cit.*, p. 201.
20. Gleig, *op. cit.*, vol. I, p. 255.
21. *Ibid.*, p. 286.
22. *Ibid.*, p. 375.

CHAPTER VIII

1. *Memoirs relative to the State of India;* G. W. Forrest, *Selections from the State Papers of the Governor-General of India,* vol. II, Warren Hastings, 1910, p. 64 (hereinafter referred to as Forrest, *Warren Hastings*).
2. Add. Mss. 29127, f. 8; Monckton-Jones, *op. cit.*, p. 182.
3. Gleig, *op. cit.*, vol. I, p. 279.
4. *Ibid.*, vol. I, p. 236.
5. Add. Mss. 29127; Sir John Strachey, *Hastings and the Rohilla War,* 1892, p. 60.
6. *Ibid.*
7. Letter to Sir George Colebrooke, Feb. 1, 1772; Gleig, *op. cit.*, vol. I, p. 178.
8. *Ibid.*, p. 355.
9. Strachey, *op. cit.*, p. 121.
10. *Bengal Past and Present*, vol. XII, p. 193.
11. Gleig, *op. cit.*, vol. I, p. 441.
12. Barwell's account, published in *Bengal Past and Present*, vol. XII, p. 193, fully supports this view. He took it from the lips of Major Hannay, second in command, and other officers. Barwell claimed to be unprejudiced because he had taken no part in the Council's decision, being chief at Dacca at the time, and declared that he would probably

have opposed the expedition as dangerous; also, he was not yet the supporter of all the Governor's measures indiscriminately that he subsequently became.

13. Defence to the Impeachment charges.

CHAPTER IX

1. Sophia Weitzman, *Warren Hastings and Philip Francis*, 1929, p. 207.
2. *Parliamentary History*, vol. XVII, pp. 454-459.
3. *Chatham Correspondence*, vol. IV, p. 276.
4. Horace Walpole, *Letters*, vol. VIII, pp. 149, 153, 157.
5. *Chatham Correspondence*, vol. IV, p. 271.
6. *Parliamentary History*, vol. XVII, p. 667.
7. Sir Courtenay Ilbert, *The Government of India: Historical Survey* (2nd edition, 1907), p. 53.
8. *Parliamentary History*, vol. XVII, p. 902.
9. *Ibid.*, p. 890.
10. *The Cambridge History of the British Empire*, 1929, vol. IV, p. 191.
11. *Parliamentary History*, vol. XVII, p. 896.
12. Sir John Fortescue, *The Correspondence of George III*, vol. II, p. 496.
13. Parkes and Merivale, *The Memoirs of Sir Philip Francis*, vol. I, p. 326.
14. *Vide*, S. Weitzman, *op. cit.*, pp. 18-20.
15. Add. Mss. 29134, f. 69*b*; Weitzman, *op. cit.*, p. 209.
16. *Ibid.*
17. R. H. Murray, *op. cit.*, p. 220.

CHAPTER X

1. *Selections from the letters, despatches, and other State papers preserved in the Foreign Department of the Government of India, 1772-1785;* edited by G. W. Forrest, 1890 (hereinafter referred to as Forrest, *Selections*), vol. II, p. 296.
2. *Ibid.*, p. 317.
3. Add. Mss. 29134, f. 367*b*.
4. *Ibid.*, 29135, f. 418. Sir Robert Palk, former Governor of Madras, wrote him in similar terms—Add. Mss. 29135, ff. 407-408.
5. Letters of Richard Barwell, *Bengal Past and Present*, vol. XII, p. 74.
6. *Ibid.*, p. 89.
7. Gleig, *op. cit.*, vol. I, pp. 471-476.
8. Parkes and Merivale, *op. cit.*, vol. II, p. 53.
9. Forrest, *Selections*, vol. I, p. 122.
10. *Ibid.*, pp. 162-176.
11. Parkes and Merivale, *op. cit.*, vol. II, p. 49.
12. Weitzman, *op. cit.*, pp. 221-233.
13. Gleig, *op. cit.*, vol. I, p. 477.
14. *Ibid.*, p. 470.
15. Forrest, *Selections*, vol. II, p. 462.
16. *Ibid.*, p. 494.
17. *Ibid.*, p. 266.
18. For the proceedings of Council relating to Nuncomar, see Forrest, *Selections*, vol. II, pp. 298-315.
19. Gleig, *op. cit.*, vol. I, p. 515.
20. *Ibid.*, p. 520.
21. *Bengal Past and Present*, vol. XII, p. 223.
22. Weitzman, *op. cit.*, pp. 248-252; Gleig, *op. cit.*, vol. I, p. 510.

23. Sir JAMES F. STEPHEN, *The Story of Nuncomar and Impey,* 1885, vol. II, p. 296.
24. *Ibid.;* FORREST, *Warren Hastings,* vol. I, pp. 89-94.
25. GLEIG, *op. cit.,* vol. I, p. 518.
26. Sir J. F. STEPHEN, *op. cit.,* vol. I, p. 73.
27. FORREST, *Selections.*
28. GLEIG, *op. cit.,* vol. I, p. 526.
29. Barwell's Letters, *Bengal Past and Present,* vol. XIII, p. 96.
30. GLEIG, *op. cit.,* vol. I, p. 533.
31. Add. Mss. 29136, f. 284.
32. FORREST, *Selections,* vol. II, pp. 475-481.
33. WEITZMAN, *op. cit.,* p. 292.
34. E. B. IMPEY, *Memoirs of Sir Elijah Impey,* p. 294.
35. FORREST, *Selections,* vol. II, pp. 431-436.
36. *Ibid.,* p. 417.
37. PARKES and MERIVALE, *op. cit.,* vol. II, p. 58.
38. B. FRANCIS and E. KEARY, *The Francis Letters,* p. 251.
39. Barwell's Letters, *Bengal Past and Present,* vol. XIII, p. 101.
40. GLEIG, *op. cit.,* vol. II, p. 37.
41. *Ibid.,* p. 48.
42. Barwell's Letters, *Bengal Past and Present,* vol. XIII, p. 112.
43. Letter to Lord North of April 2, 1775; GLEIG, *op. cit.,* vol. I, p. 534.

CHAPTER XI

1. FRANCIS and KEARY, *The Francis Letters,* pp. 218-220.
2. FORREST, *Selections,* vol. II, p. 462.
3. GLEIG, *op. cit.,* vol. I, p. 508.
4. FORREST, *Selections,* vol. II, p. 433.
5. PARKES and MERIVALE, *op. cit.,* vol. II, p. 58.
6. *Ibid.,* p. 82.
7. *Ibid.,* p. 81.
8. WEITZMAN, *op. cit.,* p. 218.
9. PARKES and MERIVALE, *op. cit.,* vol. II, p. 16.
10. GLEIG, *op. cit.,* vol. II, p. 114.
11. Letter of November 27, 1776, *Bengal Past and Present,* vol. XVI, p. 77.
12. WEITZMAN, *op. cit.,* p. 222.
13. PARKES and MERIVALE, *op. cit.,* vol. II, p. 101.

CHAPTER XII

1. FORTESCUE, *Correspondence of George III,* vol. III, p. 228.
2. WEITZMAN, *op. cit.,* pp. 256 ff.
3. GLEIG, *op. cit.,* vol. II, p. 64.
4. *Ibid.*
5. WEITZMAN, *op. cit.,* p. 265.
6. GLEIG, *op. cit.,* vol. II, p. 81.

CHAPTER XIII

1. WEITZMAN, *op. cit.,* p. 292.
2. *Bengal Past and Present,* vol. XXXVII, pp. 64-70; *The Times,* December 12, 1928.
3. WEITZMAN, *op. cit.,* p. 308.
4. GLEIG, *op. cit.,* vol. II, p. 112.
5. FORREST, *Selections,* vol. II, p. 363; WEITZMAN, *op. cit.,* p. 41.
6. *Vide,* WEITZMAN, *op. cit.,* Chap. III, section 3.
7. *Ibid.* p. 275.

8. *Ibid.*, pp. 97-99.
9. *Bengal Past and Present,* vol. XXXVII, pp. 64-70.
10. A. P. N. MUDDIMAN, "The Governor-General of a Day," *Bengal Past and Present,* vol. I, pp. 47-53; also vol. XII, pp. 1-31.
11. *Ibid.,* vol. XVII, p. 241.
12. Letter of June 30, 1777; Add. Mss. 29138, f. 492.
13. GLEIG, *op. cit.,* vol. II, p. 160.
14. WEITZMAN, *op. cit.,* p. 320.

CHAPTER XIV

1. *Memoirs of William Hickey,* vol. III (1782-90), p. 245.
2. SYDNEY C. GRIER, *Letters of Warren Hastings to His Wife,* pp. 20-23.
3. Add. Mss. 29234, f. 29.
4. H. H. DODWELL, *The Nabobs of Madras,* 1926, p. 172.
5. H. E. BUSTEED, *Echoes from Old Calcutta,* p. 133.
6. Decree of divorce of Mrs. Imhoff and Carl Christoph von Imhoff, Weimar, June 1, 1776, signed by Charles Augustus, Duke of Saxe-Weimar; Add. Mss. 39903, f. 65b.
7. Sir WILLIAM FOSTER, "A New Reading of the Hastings-Imhoff Romance," *Bengal Past and Present,* vol. XXXIII, p. 106.
8. *The Farrington Diary,* entry for June 4, 1795.
9. PARKES and MERIVALE, *op. cit.,* vol. II, p. 92.
10. FRANCIS and KEARY, *The Francis Letters,* p. 285.
11. *Bengal Past and Present,* vol. XXX, p. 9.
12. *Hartly House,* Dublin, 1789.
13. Madame D'ARBLAY, *Diary and Letters* (ed. W. C. Ward, 1892), vol. II, p. 451.
14. *Ibid.,* vol. I, p. 326.
15. Add. Mss. 29235, f. 51.
16. GRIER, *op. cit.,* p. 365.
17. *Ibid.,* p. 387.

CHAPTER XV

1. H. H. DODWELL, *Letters of Warren Hastings to Sir John Macpherson,* 1927, p. 55 (hereinafter referred to as Dodwell, *Letters*).
2. FORTESCUE, *Correspondence of George III,* vol. IV, p. 143; also, letter of May 11, 1779, *ibid.,* p. 339.
3. WEITZMAN, *op. cit.,* p. 332.
4. *Ibid.,* p. 335.
5. *Ibid.,* p. 334.
6. PARKES and MERIVALE, *op. cit.,* vol. II, p. 119.
7. *Vide, inter alia,* Sir JOHN W. FORTESCUE, *History of the British Army.* vol. III (1902).
8. FORREST, *Selections,* vol. II, p. 391.
9. WEITZMAN, *op. cit.,* p. 335.
10. GLEIG, *op. cit.,* vol. I, pp. 508-510; vol. II, pp. 136, 143, 198.
11. *Ibid.,* vol. II, p. 136.
12. FORREST, *Selections,* vol. II, p. 586.
13. *Ibid.,* pp. 568 ff.
14. *Bengal Past and Present,* vol. XVII, p. 300.
15. PARKES and MERIVALE, *op. cit.,* vol. II, p. 131.
16. India Office, Bengal Secret Consultations, vol. 48, p. 145; FORREST, *Selections,* vol. II, p. 632.
17. GLEIG, *op. cit.,* vol. II, p. 206.
18. *Ibid.,* p. 221.

19. FORREST, *Selections from the Bombay State Papers, Maratha Series,* pp. 369-374.
20. GLEIG, *op. cit.,* vol. II, p. 272.
21. FORREST, *Selections,* vol. II, p. 665.

CHAPTER XVI

1. GLEIG, *op. cit.,* vol. II, pp. 224, 243.
2. WEITZMAN, *op. cit.,* p. 113.
3. GLEIG, *op. cit.,* vol. I, p. 181.
4. *Ibid.,* vol. II, p. 263.
5. PARKES and MERIVALE, *op. cit.,* vol. II, p. 170.
6. DODWELL, *Letters,* p. 93.
7. GLEIG, *op. cit.,* vol. II, p. 239.
8. *Ibid.,* vol. II, pp. 186, 206.
9. WEITZMAN, *op. cit.,* p. 351.
10. *Ibid.,* p. 127.
11. FORREST, *Selections,* vol. II, pp. 693-702.
12. *Ibid.,* p. 711.
13. G. F. GRAND, *Reminiscences.*
14. BUSTEED, *Echoes from Old Calcutta,* p. 113.
15. This description is based on Hastings's own account as recorded in his diary. Add. Mss. 39878, supplemented from Colonel Pearse's account, published by the Calcutta Historical Society.
16. GLEIG, *op. cit.,* vol. II, p. 309.
17. *Ibid.,* vol. II, p. 311.
18. WEITZMAN, *op. cit.,* p. 355.
19. FORREST, *Selections,* vol. II, pp. 715, 735-738.
20. PARKES and MERIVALE, *op. cit.,* vol. II, p. 202; WEITZMAN, *op. cit.,* p. 359.
21. GLEIG, *op. cit.,* vol. II, p. 255.
22. DODWELL, *Letters,* p. 91.
23. Sir JAMES STEPHEN, *Nuncomar and Impey,* vol. II, Chaps. 13, 14 and 15.

CHAPTER XVII

1. FORREST, *Selections,* vol. II, p. 721.
2. *Ibid.,* vol. III, p. 764.
3. GLEIG, *op. cit.,* vol. II, p. 393.
4. The full story of these negotiations is contained in Hastings's dispatch, dated April 30, 1781; printed in FORREST, *Warren Hastings,* vol. II, pp. 199-262.

CHAPTER XVIII

1. GLEIG, *op. cit.,* vol. II, p. 329.
2. DODWELL, *Letters,* p. 55.
3. GRIER, *op. cit.,* p. 86.
4. GLEIG, *op. cit.,* vol. III, p. 173.
5. DODWELL, *Letters,* p. 179.
6. Warren Hastings's Defense at the Bar of the House of Commons.
7. Reports from Committees of the House of Commons, vol. V, p. 463.
8. Warren Hastings's Defense.
9. *A Narrative of the Insurrection which happened in the Zemeedary of Benares,* FORREST, *Warren Hastings,* vol. II, pp. 130-133.
10. *Ibid.,* p. 135.
11. *Ibid.,* p. 141.
12. FORREST, *Selections,* vol. III, p. 775.

13. *A Narrative of the Insurrection,* FORREST, *Warren Hastings,* vol. II, p. 148.
14. GRIER, *op. cit.,* p. 126.
15. *Ibid.,* p. 162.
16. *Ibid.,* p. 144.
17. *Bengal Past and Present,* vol. XXXIII, p. 45.
18. FORREST, *Selections,* vol. II, p. 439.
19. *Ibid.,* vol. III, p. 951.
20. *Vide, inter alia, The Cambridge History of the British Empire,* vol. IV, Chap. XVI.
21. *Ibid.,* p. 301.
22. GLEIG, *op. cit.,* vol. II, p. 456.
23. DODWELL, *Letters,* p. 106.
24. FORREST, *Selections,* vol. III, p. 815.
25. GLEIG, *op. cit.,* vol. II, p. 420.
26. *Ibid.,* p. 424.
27. FORREST, *Selections,* vol. III, p. 820.
28. GLEIG, *op. cit.,* vol. II, p. 429.
29. FORREST, *Selections,* vol. III, p. 950.
30. THOMPSON and GARRETT, *op. cit.,* p. 172.

CHAPTER XIX

1. FORREST, *Selections,* vol. III, p. 988.
2. Warren Hastings's Defense.
3. Reports from Committees of the House of Commons, vol. VI, p. 31.
4. *Cambridge History of the British Empire,* vol. IV, p. 304.
5. *Memoirs relative to the State of India,* FORREST, *Warren Hastings,* vol. II, p. 67.
6. GLEIG, *op. cit.,* vol. II, p. 301.
7. *Ibid.,* vol. II, p. 562.
8. *Ibid.,* p. 331.
9. *Ibid.,* vol. III, p. 34.
10. *Memoirs relative to the State of India,* FORREST, *Warren Hastings,* vol. II, p. 23.
11. GLEIG, *op. cit.,* vol. II, p. 326.
12. *Ibid.,* vol. I, p. 286.
13. GRIER, *op. cit.,* p. 18.
14. *Passim,* John Macpherson's letters to him, DODWELL, *Letters.*
15. Warren Hastings's Defense.
16. *Debates of the House of Lords on the Evidence Delivered in the Trial of Warren Hastings, Esq.,* Debrett, 1796.
17. GLEIG, *op. cit.,* vol. II, p. 459.
18. *Ibid.,* vol. III, p. 131.
19. *Debates of the House of Lords.*

CHAPTER XX

1. DODWELL, *op. cit.,* pp. 101, 103.
2. FORREST, *Selections,* vol. III, p. 823; GLEIG, *op. cit.,* vol. II, Chap. XII.
3. R. H. MURRAY, *Edmund Burke,* pp. 162, 290-291; CHARLES WENTWORTH DILKE, *The Papers of a Critic,* vol. II, pp. 309-384.
   For Burke's connection with Verney and the debt of £25,000, see *Verney Letters of the Eighteenth Century,* ed. Lady Verney, 1930, vol. II, p. 277. For "the Burkes" connection with Francis, see WEITZMAN, *op. cit.*
4. Letters to L. Sullivan, February 1770, Add. Mss. 29126.

5. H. H. Dodwell, "Hastings and the Assignment of the Carnatic," *English Historical Review,* vol. XL (1925), p. 378.
6. J. Barrow, *Memoir of Lord Macartney,* 1807, vol. I, pp. 475, 482.
7. Dodwell, *supra,* E. H. R., vol. XI, p. 391.
8. Forrest, *Selections,* vol. III, p. 847.
9. Gleig, *op. cit.,* vol. III, p. 66.
10. Forrest, *Selections,* vol. III, p. 937.
11. Add. Mss. 29233, f. 6.
12. Gleig, *op. cit.,* vol. II, p. 534.
13. *Cambridge History of the British Empire,* vol. IV, p. 285.
14. Gleig, *op. cit.,* vol. II, p. 531.
15. Forrest, *Selections,* vol. III, pp. 885-895.
16. *Ibid.,* p. 916.

CHAPTER XXI

1. *Vide,* Weitzman, *op. cit.,* p. 136.
2. Fortescue, *Correspondence of George III,* vol. V, No. 3431.
3. Gleig, *op. cit.,* vol. II, pp. 346-353.
4. Parkes and Merivale, *op. cit.,* vol. II, p. 212.
5. British Museum Collection of East India Tracts, 1781; Weitzman, *op. cit.,* p. 141.
6. *Ibid.,* p. 146.
7. *Ibid.,* Gleig, *op. cit.,* vol. II, p. 481, Scott to Hastings.
8. *Ibid.,* Scott to Hastings, June 26, 1782.
9. *Parliamentary History,* vol. XXII, pp. 1275-1283.
10. Parkes and Merivale, *op. cit.,* vol. II, p. 288.
11. *Parliamentary History,* vol. XXII, pp. 1291-1302.
12. *Ibid.,* p. 1302.
13. *Ibid.,* vol. XXIII, p. 75.
14. Gleig, *op. cit.,* vol. II, pp. 492-496, 503-506, Scott to Hastings, August 29, 1782, and January 1, 1783.
15. *Ibid.,* vol. III, p. 23.
16. Dodwell, *Letters,* p. 147.
17. Gleig, *op. cit.,* vol. III, p. 31.
18. Forrest, *Selections,* vol. III, p. 902.
19. Gleig, *op. cit.,* vol. III, p. 22.
20. *Ibid.,* pp. 36, 130.
21. *Ibid.,* p. 53, letter to L. Sulivan, March 27, 1783.
22. *Ibid.,* p. 78.

CHAPTER XXII

1. Forrest, *Selections,* vol. III, p. 1015.
2. *Ibid.,* p. 922.
3. Add. Mss. 29129, f. 48.
4. For a full account of them and of this whole episode, *vide* Dodwell, *op. cit.,* E. H. R., vol. XL.
5. Dodwell, *Letters,* p. 175.
6. Gleig, *op. cit.,* vol. III, p. 129.
7. Curzon, *British Government in India,* vol. II, p. 164.
8. Forrest, *Selections,* vol. III, p. 943.
9. S. Arthur Strong, *Critical Studies and Fragments,* pp. 220-225; *Harpers Magazine,* December 1904.
10. Forrest, *Selections,* vol. III, p. 1015.
11. Gleig, *op. cit.,* vol. III, p. 186.

Authorities

CHAPTER XXIII

1. GLEIG, *op. cit.*, vol. II, p. 577.
2. FORREST, *Selections*, vol. III, p. 884.
3. DODWELL, *Letters*, p. 93.
4. FORREST, *Selections*, vol. III, p. 1018.
5. *Vide* A. P. NICHOLSON, *Scraps of Paper*, which gives an account of the broken treaties in the nineteenth century, particularly of what happened in Hyderabad and Kashmir. Mr. Nicholson might well have included earlier instances and made Hastings's denunciation of the practice his point of departure. What happened in Hyderabad was only an aggravated and more successful repetition of what had previously taken place in Oude. *Vide,* also, *The British Crown and the Indian States,* an "outline sketch drawn up on behalf of the Standing Committee of the Chamber of Princes by the directorate of the Chamber's special organization," 1929, which deals fully with the whole subject, and, incidentally, confirms the view here given of Hastings's policy. It says (p. 14), "this incident is of importance because it shows clearly that Hastings was not misled by the military and political impotence of the Vizier into considering him a puppet ruler. In matters of external policy Hastings was not unduly scrupulous in securing the consent of the Vizier to his own plans. *But he never forgot that the Vizier was an independent ruler in whose internal affairs the Company had no right to intervene."*
6. GLEIG, *op. cit.*, vol. III, p. 130.
7. *Ibid.*, p. 121.
8. *Ibid.*, p. 130.
9. *Ibid.*, vol. II, p. 557.
10. *Ibid.*, vol. III, p. 113.
11. *Ibid.*, p. 129.
12. *Ibid.*, p. 132.
13. FORREST, *Selections*, vol. III, p. 1020.
14. Add. Mss. 41606.
15. All Hastings's letters to his wife, with the above one exception, are to be found in Add. Mss. 29197, and are printed *in extenso* in SYDNEY C. GRIER, *op. cit.*
16. GLEIG, *op. cit.*, vol. II, p. 452; III, p. 521.

CHAPTER XXIV

1. Add. Mss. 39879.
2. GLEIG, *op. cit.*, vol. III, p. 160.
3. FORREST, *Selections*, vol. III, p. 1099.
4. VINCENT A. SMITH, *The Oxford History of India,* 1923, p. 498: "It would be difficult to name an honest man among the prominent Indian notables of the time, whether in the north or in the south."
5. *Vide,* also, Sir WALTER LAWRENCE's reminiscences, *The India We Served,* pp. 175-185.
6. FORREST, *Selections,* vol. III, p. 1114; *The British Crown and the Indian States,* 1929, p. 15.
7. *Ibid.*, p. 1128.
8. GLEIG, *op. cit.*, vol. III, p. 97—letter of Scott to Hastings, November 10, 1783.
9. EDMUND BURKE, *Works* (ed. Bohn), vol. II, pp. 173-248; *Parliamentary History,* vol. XXIII, pp. 1312-1386.
10. GLEIG, *op. cit.*, vol. III, p. 101—letter of Scott to Hastings, December 20, 1783.
11. *Ibid.*, p. 102.

12. *Ibid.*, p. 108—letter of Scott to Hastings, January 11, 1784.
13. *Ibid.*, p. 171—letter of Scott to Hastings, August 15, 1784.
14. Add. Mss. 29167; GLEIG, *op. cit.*, vol. III, pp. 176-180—letter of Scott to Hastings, November 6, 1784.
15. *Parliamentary History*, vol. XXIV, pp. 1086-1099.
16. HOLDEN FURBER, *Henry Dundas, Viscount Melville*, 1931, p. 36.
17. *Ibid.*
18. GLEIG, *op. cit.*, vol. III, p. 226.
19. A draft of a letter of resignation that was never sent is preserved in Add. Mss. 29167, f. 322: "Believe not, hon'ble Sirs, that I can lightly part with a service which has assimilated itself with the modes, habits and affections of my life now that it is verging to the decline. If I at this time possessed the same bodily powers which I preserved unimpaired till a little more than two years past, the necessity now imposed upon me would have operated with the stroke of death upon my feelings, since it would have been the final and sudden disappointment of the labors of almost fourteen years in the unabated pursuit of an object which I sought only for the glory of being the instrument of your prosperity and of the increase of the national domain."

The actual letter sent is contained in I.O Bengal Letters Rec'd., vol. XX, pp. 496-497.
20. *Memoirs relative to the State of India*, FORREST, *Warren Hastings*, vol. II, p. 38.

CHAPTER XXV

1. Mrs. ELIZA FAY, *Original Letters from India* (ed. E. M. Forster, 1925), p. 181.
2. WILLIAM HODGES, R.A., *Travels in India during the years 1780-1783*, 1793.
3. *British Government in India*, vol. II, p. 155.
4. Add. Mss. 29196, ff. 1b-2.
5. *Dictionary of National Biography:* article on Sir William Jones.
6. *Ibid.*
7. E. B. IMPEY, *Memoirs of Sir Elijah Impey*, p. 231.
8. Sir WILLIAM JONES, *Works*, with *Life* by Lord Teignmouth, 1807, vol. II, p. 17.
9. *Ibid.*, p. 49.
10. *Ibid.*, p. 217.
11. *D. N. B.:* article on Colebrooke.
12. CHARLES JOHNSTON, "The Destiny of India," *Atlantic Monthly*, 1930, vol. 146, No. 6, p. 801.
13. H. H. GOWEN, *A History of Indian Literature*, 1931, Chap. I.
14. GLEIG, *op. cit.*, vol. III, p. 159.
15. *Bengal Past and Present*, vol. XLI (1931), p. 120; from the Home Department, Imperial Record Office, Calcutta.
16. GLEIG, *op. cit.*, vol. I, p. 413.
17. *Ibid.*, p. 415.
18. *Ibid.*, vol. III, p. 161.
19. Add. Mss. 29233.
20. Sir FRANCIS YOUNGHUSBAND, K.C.S.I., K.C.I.E., *The Light of Experience: A Review of some Men and Events of my Time*, 1927, p. 110.
21. FORREST, *Selections*, vol. III, p. 1124.
22. The full story is told by Professor H. L. HOSKINS, "The Overland Route to India in the Eighteenth Century," *History*, January 1925, and *British Routes to India*, 1928, Chap. I.

CHAPTER XXVI

1. *Memoirs relative to the State of India,* FORREST, *Warren Hastings,* vol. II.
2. GLEIG, *op. cit.,* vol. III, p. 34.
3. JOHN MORLEY, *Life of Gladstone,* vol. III, p. 469: "Table-talk with Mr. Gladstone at Biarritz.
   "Mr. G.—I consider Burke a tripartite man: America, France, Ireland—right as to two, wrong in one.
   "J. M.—Must you not add home affairs and India? ... Then he gave fourteen years of industry to Warren Hastings, and teaching England the rights of the natives, princes and people, and her own duties. So he was right in four out of five.
   "Mr. G.—Yes, yes—quite true. These ought to be added to my three."
4. VINCENT A. SMITH, *The Oxford History of India,* pp. 564-570.
5. Sir JOHN MALCOLM, *The Political History of India.*
6. *The Oxford History of India,* p. 580.
7. *Ibid.,* p. 587.
8. *Ibid.,* p. 592.
9. *Ibid.,* p. 643.
10. CURZON, *British Government in India,* vol. II, p. 130.

CHAPTER XXVII

1. Diary, Add. Mss. 39879.
2. *Ibid.* The complete poem of twelve stanzas is printed in Sir CHARLES LAWSON, *The Private Life of Warren Hastings,* 1895, and *Bengal Past and Present,* vol. XXVII, p. 79.
3. "Horace, 2d. Book, 10 ode—31st March." Add. Mss. 39879.
4. *Ibid.,* Nesbitt Thompson Papers, *Bengal Past and Present;* GLEIG, *op. cit.,* vol. III, p. 238; Sir CHARLES LAWSON, *op. cit.,* p. 45.
5. Madame D'ARBLAY, *Diary and Letters,* vol. I, p. 326.
6. WRAXALL, *Posthumous Memoirs,* 1836, vol. I, p. 329.
7. NICHOLS, *Recollections of the Reign of George III,* vol. I, p. 277.
8. GLEIG, *op. cit.,* vol. III, p. 238.
9. *Ibid.,* p. 241.
10. Diary, Add. Mss. 39879.
11. GLEIG, *op. cit.,* vol. III, p. 296.
12. *Ibid.,* p. 243.
13. *The Annual Register,* 1786, p. 147.
14. GLEIG, *op. cit.,* vol. III, p. 240.
15. DODWELL, *Letters,* p. 154.
16. *Ibid.,* p. xxiv.
17. Nesbitt Thompson Papers, *Bengal Past and Present,* vol. XVI, p. 209.

CHAPTERS XXVIII AND XXIX

1. PARKES and MERIVALE, *op. cit.,* vol. II, pp. 245-249; BURKE, *Correspondence,* vol. III, p. 44.
2. WINDHAM, *Diary,* p. 66.
3. *Parliamentary History,* vol. XXV, pp. 1060, 1182-1202.
4. *The Francis Letters,* vol. II, p. 363.
5. HORACE WALPOLE, *Letters,* vol. XIII, p. 368.
6. Nesbitt Thompson Papers, *Bengal Past and Present.*
7. BURKE, *Correspondence,* vol. II, pp. 38-44.
8. PARKES and MERIVALE, *op. cit.,* vol. II, p. 257.
9. BURKE, *Correspondence,* vol. III, p. 38.

10. Letters to David Anderson, September 13, 1786; GLEIG, *op. cit.*, vol. III, p. 300.
11. Letter to John Shore, February 19, 1787; *ibid.*, p. 325.
12. Letter to Thompson, July 17, 1788; S. ARTHUR STRONG, *Critical Studies and Fragments*, pp. 220-225.
13. JOHN MORLEY, *Burke*, p. 134.
14. Nesbitt Thompson Papers, *Bengal Past and Present*, vol. XVII, p. 79; GLEIG, *op. cit.*, vol. III, p. 287.
15. BUSTEED, *op. cit.*, Appendix D.
16. *Parliamentary History*, vol. XXV, p. 1413.
17. *The Minutes of what was offered by Warren Hastings at the Bar of the House of Commons...*, 1786.
18. Nesbitt Thompson Papers; GLEIG, *op. cit.*, vol. III, p. 288.
19. *Parliamentary History*, vol. XXVI, pp. 110-115.
20. HOLDEN FURBER, *Henry Dundas, Viscount Melville*, pp. 37-45.
21. *Bengal Past and Present*, vol. XXIX, p. 205; BURKE, *Correspondence*, vol. III, p. 44.
22. WEITZMAN, *op. cit.*, pp. 189-191.
23. Letter of Dundas to Burke, *Bengal Past and Present*, vol. XXIX, p. 204.
24. *Sophie in London, 1786*, 1933, pp. 254-258.
25. Nesbitt Thompson Papers, *Bengal Past and Present*, vol. XVI, p. 211.
26. *Ibid.*, vol. XVII, p. 99.
27. *Ibid.*, vol. XVIII, p. 104.
28. HORACE WALPOLE, *Letters*, vol. XIV, p. 43.
29. Nesbitt Thompson Papers, *Bengal Past and Present;* GLEIG, *op. cit.*, vol. III, p. 289.
30. Madame D'ARBLAY, *op. cit.*, vol. II, pp. 105-119.
31. Sir GILBERT ELLIOT, first Earl of Minto, *Life and Letters*, 1874, vol. I, p. 194.
32. CURZON, *op. cit.*, vol. II, p. 161; R. H. MURRAY, *op. cit.*, p. 128; BOSWELL, *Life of Samuel Johnson* (Everyman's Library), vol. II, p. 361.
33. Add. Mss. 41606.
34. WEITZMAN, *op. cit.*, pp. 172-176.
35. No. 10 in Persian Mss., India Office, 4223 (Testimonials in favor of Warren Hastings).
36. The account of the trial here given is based upon *The History of the Trial of Warren Hastings, Esq.*, published by Debrett in 1796, from which all quoted passages are taken.
37. BURKE, *Speeches* (ed. Bohn), vol. I, p. 456.
38. Madame D'ARBLAY, *Diary and Letters*, vol. II, p. 458.

CHAPTER XXX

1. *Vide, inter alia, The Hamwood Papers of the Ladies of Llangollen and Caroline Hamilton*, ed. Mrs. G. H. Bell, 1930, pp. 83, 128.
2. GLEIG, *op. cit.*, vol. III, p. 335.
3. Madame D'ARBLAY, *Diary and Letters*, vol. II, pp. 95-139.
4. Hastings's own account of his trial, S. ARTHUR STRONG, *Critical Studies and Fragments*, pp. 220-225.
5. Sir CHARLES LAWSON, *The Private Life of Warren Hastings*, p. 115.
6. Nesbitt Thompson Papers, *Bengal Past and Present*, vol. XIX, p. 11.
7. *Dictionary of National Biography*, article on Lord Loughborough.
8. A paraphrase of the latest presentation of this view by Dr. R. H. MURRAY, *Edmund Burke*, pp. 318-346; but it is the same as that held by practically all who have written from the English side of the fence. Dr. Holland Rose attributes "the comparative calm which set-

tled benignly on India for twelve years" largely to the impeachment, which brought "a renewal of confidence in the sense of justice of our people"—a deduction for which there is no evidence at all nor any likelihood of its correctness—*William Pitt and National Revival*, 1912, p. 240.

9. MURRAY, *op. cit.*, p. 332.
10. *Ibid.*, p. 337.
11. Letter of September 22, 1795, to the Court of Directors.
12. Mr. Justice ROCHE and E. G. HAWKE, article in *The Times*, December 6, 1932.
13. Add. Mss. 29205, f. 374; GLEIG, *op. cit.*, vol. III, p. 354.
14. Sir J. F. STEPHEN, *Nuncomar and Impey*, vol. I, p. 25: "If a man's ability is measured by comparison between his means of action and the results of his action, he (Hastings) must, I think, be regarded as the ablest Englishman of the eighteenth century."
    Professor Ramsay Muir, Introduction to WEITZMAN, *op. cit.*: "Warren Hastings was, in truth, one of the greatest of Englishmen, for my own part, I count him the greatest Englishman of the eighteenth century—an age prolific in great men."
15. Edmund Burke to Windham, March 6, 1796: "What I was given to understand but what I could not believe, nor could you, has happened—the House of Commons is condemned in costs and damages by the East India Company. We have charged Hastings with robbery of the people of India. Instead of punishing him we reward him with a second robbery."—Add. Mss. 37843, f. 99.

CHAPTER XXXI

1. Address from the British Inhabitants of Calcutta, Add. Mss. 29202, f. 265; M. STURGE GRETTON, *A Corner of the Cotswolds*, 1914, pp. 11-12.
2. Concluding lines of poem by Hastings on the Temple at Melchet Park, *Notes and Queries*, vol. 157, p. 57.
3. G. W. HASTINGS, *Vindication of Warren Hastings;* Sir CHARLES LAWSON, *op. cit.*
4. Add. Mss. 39891, f. 56; 29233, f. 222.
5. Add. Mss. 39893.
6. The letters to and from Thompson are to be found in *Bengal Past and Present*, vols. XIX and XX (and some of them in GLEIG, *op. cit.*, vol. III); those to Baber in *Notes and Queries*, vol. 154; those to the D'Oylys in GLEIG, *op. cit.*, vol. III; and those to Sir Charles Hastings in the Historical Manuscripts Commission's report on the Manuscripts of the late Reginald Rawdon Hastings, 1934, vol. III. Unless otherwise stated, all the following quotation of letters are taken from these sources.
7. Add. Mss. 29234, f. 32.
8. *English Historical Review*, vol. XLIV, p. 633; Add. Mss. 29234, f. 127.
9. Add. Mss. 39871, f. 78.
10. Add. Mss. 39903, f. 33.
11. Hist. Mss. Com., *op. cit.*, p. 315.
12. GRIER, *op. cit.*, p. 11.
13. E. B. IMPEY, *Memoirs of Sir Elijah Impey*, p. 409.
14. Diary, Add. Mss. 39885.
15. *Ibid.*
16. LAWSON, *op. cit.*, p. 140.
17. *Notes and Queries*, vol. 154, p. 190.
18. *Ibid.*, p. 111.

CHAPTERS XXXII AND XXXIII

1. *The Works of Edmund Burke* (Bohn's Standard Library), vol. VIII, p. 503.
2. *Creevey's Memoirs*, 3rd ed., vol. I, p. 59.
3. BUSTEED, *op. cit.*, p. 170; FORREST, *Warren Hastings*, vol. I, p. 197.
4. LORD BROUGHAM, *Statesmen of the Time of George III*—sketch of Francis.
5. PARKES and MERIVALE, *op. cit.; D.N.B.*—article on Francis.
6. FORREST, *Warren Hastings*, vol. II, pp. 85-89.
7. Minutes of Evidence taken before the House of Commons, 1813.
8. Diary, Add. Mss. 39887.
9. *Bengal Past and Present*, vol. XXIII, p. 46.
10. JACKSON's *Oxford Journal*, July 3, 1813.
11. Diary, Add. Mss. 39887.
12. Hist. Mss. Com., *op. cit.*, p. 375.
13. Add. Mss. 39888.
14. Add. Mss. 39871, f. 144.

Index

Adam, William, 395
Addington, Henry, 424, 425
Ahmed Shah, 42
Ain-i-Akbari, 71
Aliverdi Khan, 22, 25
Amyatt, Peter, 39, 41
Anderson, David, 167, 274, 286, 288, 310, 367, 379, 399, 435, 438
Asaf-ud-Daula, 135, 151, 152, 240, 243, 249 to 254, 256 to 259, 260 to 262, 265, 271, 306 to 309, 311, 312, 317, 323, 325, 335, 387
Asiatic Society of Bengal, 342
Auriol, J. P., 400, 401

Baber, Edward, 422, 423, 432, 434, 437, 438
Baillie, Colonel, 229
Barker, Sir Robert, 90 to 92, 98 to 101, 104 to 106, 108, 216
Barrington, Lord, 119, 121
Barwell, Richard, 90, 91, 106, 117, 119, 131 to 133, 135, 138, 139, 141, 145, 148, 150, 154, 157, 167, 182, 184 to 186, 198, 205, 214, 216, 218, 269, 272 *note,* 370
Batson, Stanlake, 39, 42
Beckford, Alderman, 111
Begums of Oude, 250 to 254, 256, 257, 323, 359, 383, 387, 395, 396, 405, 410, 412
Belli, John, 400
Benares; Acquisition of, by the Company, 135, 136, 240, 242; Administration of, 246, 255, 256, 320, 321, 333, 334, 395; Insurrection at, 246 to 249, 313, 314; Treaty of, 101, 130, 135, 226
Benfield, Paul, 276, 277, 282, 301, 371
Berar, *see* Mudaji Bhonsla
Bhagavad-Gita, 195, 341, 343
Bogle, George, 346, 347
Bombay, 199, 200, 201, 204, 205, 207, 210 to 212, 217, 267, 287, 288, 298
Bonaparte, Napoleon, 96, 422 to 424, 430, 435, 437
Boswell, James, 340, 390, 426
Braithwaite, Colonel, 287
Bristow, John, 132, 182, 217, 251, 295, 307 to 309, 311, 312
Buchanan, Captain John, 28
Buchanan, Mary, 28, 43
Burgoyne, General John, 111 to 113, 207

Burke, Edmund, 4, 48, 81 to 83, 108, 114, 115, 117, 122, 124, 125, 147, 158, 159, 167, 169, 170, 198, 241, 258, 259, 276 to 280, 290 to 295, 297, 322, 326, 327, 330, 339, 342 *note,* 354, 355, 359, 368 to 377, 379 *note,* 381 to 384, 390, 391, 393 *seq.,* 409, 410, 413, 414, 431
Burke, Richard, 278, 279
Burke, William, 278 to 280
Burney, Fanny, 193, 368, 389, 390, 391, 410
Bussy, Marquess de, 304
Buxar, Battle of, 42

Caillaud, General, 175, 176
Calcutta; Black Hole of, 26; Description of, 14 to 17, 156, 157, 339 to 340; Founding of, 13, 14; Made the seat of Government of Bengal, 78; Measures of Defence for, 1778, 208; 1780, 230; Recapture of, 29.
Camac, Major, 219, 221, 225, 235, 243, 246
Cantoo Babu, 139
Carnatic, The Assignment of, 281, 282, 300 to 303
Carson, Sir Edward, 409
Cartier, John, 61, 73
Chait Singh, 208, 209, 240 to 249, 251, 252, 255, 256, 263, 265, 297, 298, 328, 382, 383, 394, 405, 412
Chambers, Sir Robert, 117, 150, 340
Champion, Colonel, 105 to 108, 132, 260
Charlotte, Queen, 4, 335, 367, 435
Charnock, Job, 13, 14, 16, 78
Chesterfield, Lord, 49
Chunar, Treaty of, 254, 306, 307
Clavering, Major-General John, 117 to 119, 126, 128, *seq.,* 166, 167, 168, 172, 174, 178, 179, 182 to 188, 197, 216, 244, 275, 291, 308, 310, 311, 401
Clive, Robert, 18, 19, 23, 24, 28 to 37, 51, 52, 57, 58, 62, 69, 96, 110, 112, 115, 117, 118, 122, 124, 126, 160, 167, 168, 206, 215, 231, 265, 268, 272 *note,* 283, 329, 370, 371, 374, 379, 413
Cobbett's Parliamentary History, 109
Colebrooke, Sir George, 57, 60, 100
Colebrooke, Henry Thomas, 341, 343
Commentaries, Sir William Blackstone, 81 to 83

Index
465

Index

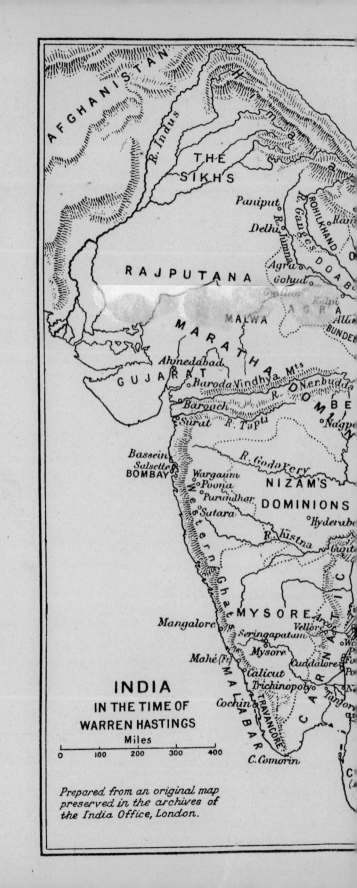

INDIA
IN THE TIME OF
WARREN HASTINGS

Miles

0   100   200   300   400

Prepared from an original map
preserved in the archives of
the India Office, London.